PUBLICATIONS OF THE
NATIONAL BUREAU OF ECONOMIC RESEARCH, INC.

NUMBER 26

INDUSTRIAL PROFITS IN THE
UNITED STATES

The National Bureau of Economic Research was organized in 1920 in response to a growing demand for scientific determination and impartial interpretation of facts bearing upon economic and social problems. Freedom from bias is sought by the constitution of its Board of Directors without whose approval no report may be published. Rigid provisions guard the National Bureau from becoming a source of profit to its members, directors or officers, or from becoming an agency for propaganda.

Officers

Oswald W. Knauth, *Chairman* George Soule, *Vice-President*
Joseph H. Willits, *President* Shepard Morgan, *Treasurer*
Charles A. Bliss, *Executive Secretary*

Research Staff

Wesley C. Mitchell, *Director of Research*
Arthur F. Burns Frederick R. Macaulay
Simon Kuznets Frederick C. Mills
Leo Wolman
Eugen Altschul, *Associate*

Directors at Large

Oswald W. Knauth Elwood Mead
H. W. Laidler Shepard Morgan
L. C. Marshall George Soule
George O. May N. I. Stone

Directors by University Appointment

Edwin F. Gay, *Harvard* Harry Alvin Millis, *Chicago*
Walton H. Hamilton, *Yale* Wesley C. Mitchell, *Columbia*
Harry Jerome, *Wisconsin* Joseph H. Willits, *Pennsylvania*

Directors appointed by other Organizations

David Friday M. C. Rorty
American Economic Association *American Statistical Association*
Lee Galloway Arch W. Shaw
American Management Association *National Publishers Association*
George E. Roberts Robert B. Wolf
American Bankers Association *American Engineering Council*

RELATION OF THE DIRECTORS TO THE WORK OF THE NATIONAL BUREAU OF ECONOMIC RESEARCH

1. The object of the National Bureau of Economic Research is to ascertain and to present to the public important economic facts and their interpretation in a scientific and impartial manner. The Board of Directors is charged with the responsibility of ensuring that the work of the Bureau is carried on in strict conformity with this object.

2. To this end the Board of Directors shall appoint one or more Directors of Research.

3. The Director or Directors of Research shall submit to the members of the Board, or to its Executive Committee, for their formal adoption, all specific proposals concerning researches to be instituted.

4. No study shall be published until the Director or Directors of Research shall have submitted to the Board a summary report drawing attention to the character of the data and their utilization in the study, the nature and treatment of the problems involved, the main conclusions and such other information as in their opinion will serve to determine the suitability of the study for publication in accordance with the principles of the Bureau.

5. A copy of any manuscript proposed for publication shall also be submitted to each member of the Board. If publication is approved each member is entitled to have published also a memorandum of any dissent or reservation he may express, together with a brief statement of his reasons. The publication of a volume does not, however, imply that each member of the Board of Directors has read the manuscript and passed upon its validity in every detail.

6. The results of an inquiry shall not be published except with the approval of at least a majority of the entire Board and a two-thirds majority of all those members of the Board who shall have voted on the proposal within the time fixed for the receipt of votes on the publication proposed. The limit shall be forty-five days from the date of the submission of the synopsis and manuscript of the proposed publication unless the Board extends the limit; upon the request of any member the limit may be extended for not more than thirty days.

7. A copy of this resolution shall, unless otherwise determined by the Board, be printed in each copy of every Bureau publication.

(Resolution of October 25, 1926, revised February 6, 1933)

INDUSTRIAL PROFITS
IN THE UNITED STATES

RALPH C. EPSTEIN
PROFESSOR OF ECONOMICS,
UNIVERSITY OF BUFFALO

ASSISTED BY
FLORENCE M. CLARK

A PUBLICATION OF THE
NATIONAL BUREAU OF ECONOMIC RESEARCH
IN COOPERATION WITH THE
COMMITTEE ON RECENT ECONOMIC CHANGES
NEW YORK · 1934

COPYRIGHT, 1934, BY NATIONAL BUREAU OF ECONOMIC RESEARCH, INC.,
1819 BROADWAY, NEW YORK, N. Y. ALL RIGHTS RESERVED

TYPOGRAPHY: ERNST REICHL
PRINTED AND BOUND IN THE UNITED STATES OF AMERICA
BY H. WOLFF, NEW YORK

AUTHOR'S PREFACE

THE data upon which this study mainly rests have been published by the Department of Commerce under the title *Source-Book for the Study of Industrial Profits,* by the author in collaboration with Florence M. Clark. As pointed out in the *Source-Book* and at various places in the present volume, the data are statistical samples and as such are subject to certain qualifications. These qualifications are discussed in Chapter 43, which should be consulted by critical readers who wish to examine the statistical bases for many of the conclusions presented in earlier chapters. Attention is called also to the Glossary.

It is not possible here to name all of the persons consulted in connection with the statistical, accounting and other problems encountered in the preparation of both this volume and the basic tables on which it rests. I do wish, however, to make mention of the generosity of Professor William L. Crum, Mr. George O. May, former Secretary of Commerce Robert P. Lamont, Dr. Julius Klein, Mr. Arch W. Shaw, Dr. Frank M. Surface and Professor Roy B. Kester in having given valuable aid on numerous occasions. Less directly, but also very kindly, the following persons have helped in either the collection or interpretation of the materials: Mr. W. T. Sherwood, Mr. Edward White, Mrs. S. B. Blandy, Professor J. Franklin Ebersole, Mr. George B. Roberts, Mr. Carl Snyder and Mr. Lawrence H. Sloan. I am indebted to Professors Frank H. Knight, Charles S. Tippetts, Shaw Livermore and Mrs. John D. Sumner for criticism of the manuscript (to Mrs. Sumner for valuable statistical assistance also), as well as to members of the staff and the Board of Directors of the National Bureau of Economic Research.

The faith of Edwin F. Gay and Wesley C. Mitchell in the ultimate outcome of what at even an early stage was seen to be a difficult and somewhat hazardous undertaking, and their constant support, are largely responsible for the study's completion.

Finally Mrs. Alice W. Herbst and Mrs. Lorna J. Marple are due thanks for their efficient services in helping to prepare the manuscript for press. The debt to Miss Clark throughout the entire course of the investigation is evident from the title page.

R. C. E.

CONTENTS

The Problem of Measuring Profits, *a Preliminary Note by Wesley C. Mitchell*   3

Book I

THE BROAD FINDINGS

1	An Introductory Summary	31
2	A General View of Industry	49
3	Earnings Rates in Different Industries	70
4	Return upon Sales in Different Industries	114
5	Size and Geographical Location of Corporations	128
6	Cyclical Fluctuations in Profits	144
7	Cyclical Fluctuations (*Continued*)	161

Book II

EARNINGS OF LARGE CORPORATIONS

8	Introduction	209
9	Manufacture and Its Major Groups	216
10	Foods and Food Products	246
11	Textiles and Textile Products	252
12	Leather and Leather Products	258
13	Rubber and Rubber Products	262
14	Lumber and Lumber Products	266
15	Paper and Paper Products	270
16	Printing and Publishing	274
17	Chemicals	278
18	Stone, Clay and Glass	283
19	Metals	287
20	Special Manufacturing Industries	295

21	Trade and Its Major Groups	300
22	Retail Trade	313
23	Wholesale Trade	318
24	Retail and Wholesale Trade	323
25	Mining and Its Minor Groups	327
26	Finance and Its Minor Groups	337

Book III

EARNINGS OF SMALL CORPORATIONS

27	Introduction	349
28	Manufacture and Its Major Groups	353
29	Foods and Food Products	371
30	Textiles and Textile Products	378
31	Leather and Leather Products	384
32	Rubber and Rubber Products	390
33	Lumber and Lumber Products	394
34	Paper and Paper Products	400
35	Printing and Publishing	406
36	Chemicals	412
37	Stone, Clay and Glass	418
38	Metals	424
39	Special Manufacturing Industries	430
40	Trade and Its Major Groups	436
41	Retail Trade	442
42	Wholesale Trade	447

Book IV

PROBLEMS OF ESTIMATION AND INTERPRETATION

43	Problems of Sampling and Weighting	455
44	Comparison of Minor Group Samples	496
45	The Valuation of Assets: Capitalization Problems	524
46	Problems of Classification	548
47	Profits and the Regulation of Production	577

CONTENTS [xi]

GLOSSARY 595

APPENDICES
  A Explanations of Methods Used in Preparing Certain Charts and Tables 601
  B Absolute Data Underlying Certain Charts and Tables 611
  C Supplementary Frequency Distributions 649
  D Block Diagrams of Earnings Rates 654

List of Tables 659
List of Charts 667
INDEX 671

INDUSTRIAL PROFITS IN THE
UNITED STATES

THE PROBLEM OF MEASURING PROFITS

A Preliminary Note by Wesley C. Mitchell[1]

THIS book is one of the series which has resulted from the cooperation of the Committee on Recent Economic Changes and the National Bureau of Economic Research. The publication of the two volumes on *Recent Economic Changes* carried the study of a major business cycle through its upward phase. This report provided a point of departure for the investigation of the complex and remarkable economic processes which the next phase, the ensuing depression, revealed. The opportunity thus afforded and the urgent need to interpret the phenomena of the depression decided the Committee to continue its explorations. It wished to examine, against the background of the research presented in *Recent Economic Changes*, the perplexing inter-acting factors of the depression itself, and to develop a rationale for the comprehension and appraisal of these factors. The comparative aspects of the situation, the contrast of post-War and pre-War changes, were illuminated by F. C. Mills in *Economic Tendencies in the United States*. In *Strategic Factors in Business Cycles* J. M. Clark provided an analysis of the broad relationships of the various causal factors. The present study is directed to the dynamic factor the varia-

---

[1] Three Directors of the National Bureau, Messrs. George O. May, George E. Roberts and Malcolm C. Rorty have given generous help to the writer of this note. He is heavily indebted also to Professors Ralph C. Epstein, Frederick C. Mills and Horace Secrist as well as to Mr. Solomon Fabricant.

tions of which dominate the direction and extent of business enterprise, viz., profits.

Like other studies in the series, this one was made possible through funds contributed by the Rockefeller Foundation, the Economic Club of Chicago, the Carnegie Corporation and a group of socially-minded citizens. To these and specifically to the members of the Committee on Recent Economic Changes: Arch W. Shaw, *Chairman;* Renick W. Dunlap; William Green; Julius Klein; John S. Lawrence; Dr. Max Mason; Honorable A. C. Miller; Lewis E. Pierson; John J. Raskob; Samuel W. Reyburn; Louis J. Taber; Daniel Willard; Clarence M. Woolley; Owen D. Young; E. E. Hunt, *Secretary;* grateful appreciation is expressed.

Business profits are one of the hardest kinds of income to measure. Any business enterprise should be able to state accurately the sums that it has paid out in the course of a year as wages, interest and rents; it should be able to state also what income it has paid out to its owners. But the profits of the enterprise itself are not definite sums fixed by past transactions. On the contrary, they are appraisals of net changes in the position and prospects of the business as a whole—appraisals that look forward to the uncertain future as well as back to the irrevocable past. Like all mixtures of past history and future anticipations, statements of profits are necessarily subject to variable margins of uncertainty.

Besides ascertaining the difference between actual receipts for whatever the business has sold and actual payments for whatever commodities and services the business has bought, the accountant who is estimating income must put values upon all the property belonging to the business. What will the raw materials, goods in process and finished products realize when sold? What part of the accounts receivable will prove uncollectable? What will the holdings of shares in other business enterprises be worth? If the enterprise owns franchises, patents or other income-bearing rights, what allowances should be made for their approaching termination? At what rate is the physical plant depreciating? Is it becoming obsolete faster than it is wearing out? Are there wasting assets for which a depletion charge should be made? Has the business other properties, such as lands or long-term contracts, that are growing more valuable or less valuable? What part of the profits flows from current operations such as will probably be continued and what part from 'capital gains and losses', such as the sales of securities owned by an enterprise, or the redemption of its own obligations at less than face value? Is the profits estimate to be made on the assumption that the enterprise will continue in business, or on the assumption that it will liquidate its affairs?

Questions like these call not only for technical skill but also for good judgment. Hence statements of profits are affected both by accounting methods and by the optimistic or pessimistic light in which the future is viewed at the time when the accounts are made up. So important a matter as making allowance for depreciation was often neglected by American corporations in the pre-War days and some inadequacy in this respect may still persist.[2] The

[2] In testifying before the Federal Trade Commission, March 22, 1918, Mr. George O. May, who had practiced accounting in this country a little over twenty years, said: ". . . in the early days of my experience here I lost a great deal of work because I refused to sign accounts as being correct unless they provided for depreciation." He thought the development of proper practice in this respect had been "more or less general . . . during the last ten or twelve years." This development he attributed to the influence of public accountants, to the Federal Trade Commission and even more to the Federal tax upon corporation profits adopted in 1909. See *Testimony before the Federal Trade Commission to Determine the Maximum Selling Price of Newsprint Paper*, Price, Waterhouse and Co., New York (no date), pp. 2, 25, 26.

influence exercised by business 'sentiment' upon profit statements is harder to gauge; but no one who compares the reports issued by corporations to their stockholders in January 1929 and January 1933 can doubt that this factor also affects the figures, though its influence may be hidden among the data used by the accountants in making valuations.

It follows that a statistician who is trying to measure profits must be critical of his basic data. It is risky to compare income statements from American companies in pre-War years with statements drawn up since public accountants and the Federal income tax have done their educational work. Even in dealing with recent statements, the statistician cannot take it for granted without inquiry that the figures are proper. The basis on which the valuations in the income statement (as contrasted with the records of actual transactions) have been made may be open to question. Another question concerns the line between profits and other types of income. Sometimes the partners in a firm or the executives of a corporation draw salaries less than they might command on a strictly commercial basis, and the 'profits' reported contain part of the 'wages of superintendence'. Sometimes the executives get compensation larger than they could obtain from corporations in which their stock holdings were relatively small, so that the 'profits' are understated. If an attempt is made to discriminate between pure profits and interest, the investigator must ask what amount of capital has been invested in the business and what is a proper rate of interest to allow. Even when no such line is drawn, the amount of the investment must be ascertained if rates of return are to be found. Finally since profits as figured in practice depend partly on accruals and deferred items, a competent income statement drawn up at the end of a year may turn out to be seriously in error.

Unforeseen changes in collections, in prices, in competitive conditions, in market demand, in replacement costs may raise or lower the values set upon the receivables, the inventory of stock on hand, the securities owned and even the physical plant. No doubt these changes will affect the next year's accounts, but new errors of forecast may vitiate this statement in its turn. A minutely accurate record of profits cannot be made up until the last transaction in the life of a business has been completed, and by that time the earlier records are likely to have disappeared!

How grave the inaccuracies of business income statements really are no one can say. Probably they are subject to a secular decline and to cyclical fluctuations; at a given time they must vary widely from enterprise to enterprise and may vary somewhat from industry to industry. The relative size of the items upon which an accounting valuation has to be placed and of the items that are matters of record is a crucial point. Often the valuation items are relatively few and susceptible of fairly accurate estimate, so that the margin of error in the profits reported for a given year can be kept narrow. Moreover, a statistician may claim that in a large sample of income statements there will be more or less offsetting of unduly liberal against unduly conservative figures.

It is pedantic, however, to treat profit statements as if their significance depended wholly upon their accuracy. To take that view would be to misconceive the role that profit statements play in modern life. They are made primarily as guides to future action. However difficult the task and uncertain the result, every business man who wishes to plan intelligently must make periodical attempts to ascertain whether his past policies have been successful, where they have left him at the moment, and what his prospects seem to be. Perfect accuracy is not attainable, but for working purposes it is not required—a fair approximation serves most practical needs. Anyone who wishes to get some insight into modern economic life must accept this situation as it is. The profits reported by business enterprises influence directly the policies of the enterprises themselves, of bankers and of investors; indirectly they influence the fortunes of the whole community. These influences are not diminished by the possibility that the reports of profits may turn out later to have been decidedly over-optimistic on the whole or over-pessimistic. Hence the uncertainties attendant upon all statements of profits do not lessen the practical importance or the theoretical interest of collecting and analyzing whatever sample statements can be had.

A second difficulty in the way of measuring business profits is that they are the most variable of the income streams. An individual's income from wages cannot fall more than 100 per cent; the profits of a business enterprise may, and often do, turn into losses. The National Bureau's latest estimates of national income paid to individuals show a fall of 40 per cent between 1929 and 1932; wage disbursements in the industries for which proper data are obtainable fell 60 per cent.[3] But according to another National Bureau study, based upon the figures of the Internal Revenue, the aggregate net income of all corporations in the United States, except tax-exempt and life insurance companies, suffered an even more catastrophic fall in the same period. Net profits of nearly eight billion dollars in 1929 were succeeded by net losses of over three billion in 1931 and of nearly five billion in 1932.[4]

[3] See Simon Kuznets, National Income, 1929–32; *Bulletin 49* (National Bureau of Economic Research, January 26, 1934), Table 2.
[4] See Solomon Fabricant, Recent Corporate Profits in the United States, *Bulletin 50* (National Bureau of Economic Research, March 1934), Table 1.

THE PROBLEM OF MEASURING PROFITS [9]

In dealing with certain problems—for example, business cycles—it is necessary to stress these violent fluctuations of profits from one year to the next. But in dealing with other problems it is necessary to work through the short-period oscillations to representative averages covering a longer run. That is clearly the case if one seeks to ascertain what return business enterprises realize over a period upon their investment, or if one asks what price society as a whole pays for the capital employed in supplying its needs.

Questions of the latter sort are so often asked that it is well to show in some detail why it is so difficult to answer them. An investigator who attempted to find out what is the average long-run return upon capital invested in American business would need a vast array of data. (1) His sample of profits should cover a considerable term of years, and this term should include average proportions of business-cycle expansions and business-cycle contractions, both of average intensity. (2) Even in the worst years some enterprises make good profits, and even in the best years some enterprises suffer heavy losses. To yield reliable results the sample should contain a fair representation of the successful and of the unsuccessful concerns. Furthermore, the losses which result when businesses conclude particular or final chapters of their life histories by liquidation, sale, or drastic reorganization, are only in small part borne by other going concerns and thus reflected in reduced averages of business profits. The major portion of these losses falls upon individuals and has its effect—substantial, but not readily determinable on the basis of available figures—in reducing the broad average of returns to investors.[5]

The net income referred to is that left after payment of income taxes, but before payment of dividends.

[5] Colonel M. C. Rorty adds this comment: The distinction between the average rate of return of going businesses on their capital investment and the corresponding average returns to investors on the money they supply is,

(3) If the business enterprises included in the sample change materially from year to year, the investigator cannot tell whether a given alteration in profits results from an alteration in the earnings of business at large or from the shifting character of his data. This ambiguity in the results is reduced if it is possible to secure returns from an unchanging list of enterprises. But the ambiguity cannot be wholly eliminated in this way; for business enterprises are most unstable units. Identity of name does not guarantee identity of products, management, or ownership. (4) As the present volume demonstrates more conclusively than any other investigation known to me, profits in certain industries may remain relatively high for years at a time, while profits in other industries remain relatively low. Hence the sample should cover a wide industrial range. Indeed, the sample should cover all important lines of investment if conclusions are to be drawn concerning average rates of profits in the country. (5) While statements of profit in millions of dollars have much importance, they do not show what rate of return a business enterprise gets, or what price society pays for capital, unless the amount of profits is related to the amount of the investment. Therefore, the sample should contain statements concerning the capital used by every enterprise every year, and these statements should separate the capital belonging to the enterprise from capital borrowed. The difficulties of getting reliable figures concerning actual investments need not be enlarged upon. (6) After

---

perhaps, necessary, owing to the almost insuperable difficulties in the way of determining the magnitude of unreported liquidation and reorganization losses. However, it is important to note that, with this distinction made, an adequate supply of capital for social needs can be assured only if the average of business profits of going concerns is substantially higher than the rate of net return, whatever that may be, which is required to maintain a continuing flow of new money from private investors. The social cost of private capital is determined by the necessary net return to such investors, rather than in terms of the current earnings of going concerns.

THE PROBLEM OF MEASURING PROFITS [11]

what was said above concerning the difficulty of estimating profits, it is scarcely necessary to add that the investigator would need to assure himself that the methods of accounting used in preparing his original data were sound at the outset of the period covered and that they did not change greatly in later years.

This formidable list of requirements for ascertaining 'the' average long-run rate of profits in all trades does not mean that it is impossible to learn anything valuable about business profits unless carefully audited income statements can be had for an unchanging sample including tens of thousands of successful and unsuccessful enterprises, fairly distributed among all of the industries of a country, continued for decades and supported by reliable records of capital invested. But what can be learned is obviously conditioned by the scope and character of the samples of profit statements that can be collected. The paucity and the indefiniteness of our knowledge of business profits is due to the narrow range or the defective quality of the data that have been available for analysis.

It has been hard enough to secure representative quotations of commodity prices at wholesale over considerable periods. Even today we have few price series for highly fabricated products. In view of the vastly greater difficulties of ascertaining what profits are realized, and the common reluctance to make income statements public, it is not surprising that the volume of properly authenticated data has not been sufficient to establish broad conclusions. But some samples have been available for years.

Governmental supervision led to the compilation and publication of statements concerning the profits of National Banks, later of interstate railroads, and later still of certain other public utilities. Dependence upon the general market for capital has led a growing list of corporations to publish condensed statements of income; but there has been little assurance that the accounting methods followed were sufficiently uniform to guarantee the comparability of these materials. Similar doubts have limited the usefulness of the data concerning profits in Great Britain that have been compiled for many years by the London *Economist*. A promising step was taken by Mr. J. E. Sterrett when he published carefully audited reports from 158 industrial companies, largely small manufacturing concerns, for the calendar years 1912 and 1913, or for the fiscal years covering substantially that period. "During this time," Mr. Sterrett held, "business conditions have been generally unfavorable . . . . It may, therefore, be assumed that the profits earned . . . have not been more than a fair average . . . ." The average annual net profits shown by this sample were 13.67 per cent upon the capital invested.[6] Unfortunately, the example set by Mr. Sterrett has not been widely imitated. It is true that numerous studies have been made of profits in particular industries; but the periods of time covered, the methods of stating profits, and the adequacy of the samples used have varied so much that it is impossible to make an adequate composite photograph by assembling these individual sketches.[7]

[6] The Comparative Yield on Trade and Public Service Investment, *American Economic Review*, March 1916. Compare the critique of the representative character of Mr. Sterrett's average by M. C. Rorty in *Some Problems in Current Economics* (Chicago, 1922), pp. 108–10. Many practical business men, says Colonel Rorty, refuse to accept such figures. "They claim that a study of 'going' concerns is meaningless and misleading, and that, if all the legitimate ventures in any competitive industry were followed through from birth to death, with full account taken of all gains and losses, the average earnings on the invested money would very slightly, if at all, exceed the going rate of interest."

[7] As examples of the literature, see the following books, reports and bulletins:

Horace Secrist, *The Triumph of Mediocrity in Business* (Northwestern University, 1933)

THE PROBLEM OF MEASURING PROFITS [13]

A far more comprehensive sample of American data was started when the Federal government incorporated an excise tax upon corporations having net incomes in excess of $5,000 per annum in the tariff act of August 5, 1909. The exemption of small incomes was dropped when the excise provision was superseded by the income tax law of 1913. The compilations of income statements required by these laws and by numerous amending statutes have grown into a formally continuous record of the net incomes of all business corporations in the United States during a quarter of a century.

Comprehensive as the income tax data are, they fall short of what is desirable in several important respects. (1) Those types of business which are carried on mainly by individuals or partnerships are under-represented, or even misrepresented by the inclusion of a few non-typical corporations; for example, farming, most of all, repair work, the professions and in considerable degree retail trade. (2) The returns are regularly divided into two groups—corporations reporting net incomes and corporations reporting no

Keith Powlison, *Profits of the National Banks* (Richard G. Badger, 1931)
Ralph C. Epstein, *The Automobile Industry* (A. W. Shaw, 1928)
Laurence H. Seltzer, *A Financial History of the American Automobile Industry* (Houghton Mifflin, 1928)
Melvin T. Copeland, *The Cotton Manufacturing Industry of the United States* (Harvard Economic Studies, Vol. viii, 1912)
Herbert Müller, *Kosten- und Rentabilitätsprobleme im deutschen und amerikanischen Buchdruckereibetrieb* (Betrieb und Unternehmung, Band 8, Leipzig, 1930)
Cecil E. Fraser and Georges F. Doriot, *Analyzing Our Industries* (McGraw-Hill, 1932)
Bureau of Business Research, University of Illinois, *The Earning Power Ratios of Public Utility Companies* (Bulletin No. 15, 1927)
Federal Trade Commission, *A Report on Prices, Profits, and Competition in the Petroleum Industry* (70th Cong., 1st Sess., Sen. Doc. No. 61, 1928)
Department of Finance and Accounting, United Typothetae of America, *1932 Ratios for Printing Management* (1933, annual)
Bureau of Business Research, Harvard University, *Operating Results of Department and Specialty Stores in 1930* (Bulletin No. 85, 1931)

net income. It is not possible to ascertain accurately the aggregate net income of all corporations by subtracting the deficits of the second group from the profits of the first group. For, as has been pointed out by George O. May, there is a certain duplication of losses in the income tax returns which is not offset by a similar duplication of income—this for the reason that the net income figures exclude dividends received from other corporations; but if one corporation loses money and fails, it will report its loss directly, and other corporations which are its creditors or stockholders will also report what they have lost by its failure.[8] Of course this duplication of losses in the returns varies from year to year, being a much more serious matter in 1921 and 1932, for example, than in 1919 and 1929. (3) Changes in the law and in administrative rulings have affected the amount of profits reported in successive years.

During the period of the excess-profits tax (1917–21) profits were affected by several unusual factors. For example, war contracts were let in many cases on highly profitable terms, with the thought in mind that a major fraction of the profits would be recouped through the tax. On the other hand, large sums were spent upon advertising or other plans for future expansion and charged as current expenses.

One of the chief reasons why the profits reported in 1917 were so much larger than in 1918 is that in the former year the tax was retroactive. Hence there was less opportunity in 1917 than in 1918 to enter into transactions which would reduce taxable income. In comparing 1917 with later years, it should be noted also that the law has been made more liberal to the taxpayer in important respects; for instance, by allowing discovery depletion and by increasing depletion

[8] See the footnote in *Recent Economic Changes in the United States* (National Bureau of Economic Research, 1929), II, 854–5.

allowance at large.[9] (4) The classification of the returns is inadequate. For example, the classification by size of net income has varied from year to year, it is not available for 1919 and 1924, and is not crossed upon the classification by industrial groups. The latter classification is not carried out in sufficient detail to answer many important questions. There is no classification by total assets (except in 1931), capital, gross income, net income (except in 1926), or any other criterion indicating the size of the corporations. (5) The taxable net income reported excludes certain items that an accountant or an economist would include in profits; particularly, dividends received from other corporations and interest upon tax-exempt bonds. In one of the following chapters, an attempt to ascertain the relative magnitude of these items is made. They appear to run on the average about one-ninth of the taxable net income reported to the government. (6) While the official reports show by 'major industrial divisions' the assets and liabilities of most corporations, a considerable number do not submit balance sheets, and no attempt is made in the reports preceding 1931 to relate the amount of the net incomes to the amount of capital invested. (7) The corporations included in the tables change from year to year. Corporations that have been wound up by bankruptcy or amalgamation disappear from the list; newly-formed corporations appear. A corporation that one year appears in the group reporting net income may shift next year to the group reporting deficits, and the year after may reappear in the first group. A student of the returns has no means of knowing what part of the fluctuations in profits is due to these changes in the corporations reporting and in the way they are classified.

[9] The same. Compare the official statement of 'Changes in the revenue acts affecting the comparability of statistical data from income tax returns of corporations'; *Statistics of Income for 1929*, pp. 404–7.

As part of its work upon national income, the National Bureau of Economic Research has had to estimate the profits withdrawn by individuals from business enterprises of which they are sole owners or partners, and the dividends received by stockholders. In some of its estimates it has ventured to include rough figures for corporate surpluses. To attempt a systematic study of business profits is a natural sequel of these earlier efforts. But the difficulty of securing adequate samples of data has delayed that undertaking.

Despite these difficulties, the National Bureau has been able to secure the use of two bodies of sample data upon profits, which, though they fall far short of what is desirable, merit study. One is a small collection of audited statements secured through public-spirited action by the American Institute of Accountants. Income statements and balance sheets covering the years 1927–29 were obtained from 714 corporations. Of these returns the greater part, but not all, were available in full detail for all of the corporations in the list for each of the three years covered. Though no very large corporations were included, the average book assets of the concerns in the sample were between three and four times the average net assets of all corporations submitting balance sheets to the Internal Revenue in the years covered ($2,244,000 as compared with $643,000). The average rate of earnings upon the equity of the stockholders during the three years was 9.2 per cent.[10]

The second sample, analyzed in this volume, consists of materials made public by the United States Department of Commerce in 1932, when it published in rotoprinted form a *Source-Book for the Study of Profits* by Ralph C. Epstein in collaboration with Florence M. Clark. While this official report made available to specialists a relatively large collec-

---

[10] This collection of profits data may be published at a later date.

tion of data concerning corporate earnings and investments in the fields of manufacturing, trading and finance, it contained no averages and no text aside from a brief preface and list of definitions. To work up these materials into a form useful to many people was a task requiring much additional thought and labor, which Professor Epstein undertook at the National Bureau's request.

The basic data underlying the first half of this report include statements for the ten years 1919–28 concerning the incomes and investments of 2,046 manufacturing corporations, 664 trading corporations, 88 mining corporations and 346 financial corporations. In all four groups, the same corporations are represented in each of the ten years covered. This use of strictly identical lists of corporations for a full decade gives the present body of materials a notable advantage over the official *Statistics of Income* and over the above-mentioned collection of audit reports. In addition, Professor Epstein has three sets of data concerning the profits of relatively small corporations which vary in identity and number from year to year. One of these sets covers a decade while the other two cover 1924–28. The annual number of corporations in the 'non-identical' lists varies from 1,421 to 1,665 in one case, from 406 to 1,118 in a second, and from 1,337 to 1,350 in a third.

All in all, this is the best authenticated and largest collection of data concerning the profits of American business enterprises in numerous non-regulated industries that has been made. Its scope and representativeness are impressive when subjected to detailed examination.

(1) In respect to the time covered, ten years is long enough to permit considerable shifts among investments—though of course, a longer series of records would be better. According to the National Bureau's chronology of business cycles, the decade 1919–28 contains 68 months of general

business expansion and 52 months of general business contraction. The durations of expansions and contractions work out 57 and 43 per cent. During the full period covered by our American chronology (1855–1933), the corresponding figures are 53 per cent for expansion and 47 per cent for contraction. Of the three contractions in 1919–28, that of 1920–21 was very severe, that of 1923–24 was of average intensity, and that of 1926–27 was decidedly mild. The expansion of 1919 was feverishly rapid; that of 1921–23 was of more than average vigor; that of 1924–26 was quieter, and that which began in 1928 did not run to grave extremes by the end of the year, except in stock-exchange and urban real-estate operations.[11] On the whole, I think the character of the period gives the sample a slight bias in the direction of over-average profits; but it might be difficult to select any other decade that is more representative of 'long-run' conditions.

(2) A second question concerning the character of the period concerns, not the volume of current earnings, but the ratio of profits to book capital. Doubtless some of the corporations in the sample were in existence before the War. If these corporations did not 'write up' the value of their fixed investments when prices rose in 1915–20, then profits in 1919–28, expressed as percentages of capital invested, would tend to run on high levels. On the other hand, the sample doubtless contains corporations that were established or reorganized with a changed capitalization at various times in 1916–18, when the general level of prices was high. It may contain other corporations that 'wrote up' their fixed investments in 1919–20 to match the advance of prices and earnings. If these corporations did not 'write down' their fixed investments after prices fell in 1920–21,

[11] These judgments are based upon the National Bureau's as yet unpublished studies of a large number of economic time series.

then profits in 1921–28 would form relatively low percentages of the capital invested. How important these two distortions of the percentages are we do not know. That they tend to offset each other is clear, but there may remain a net bias towards high profit ratios or towards low profit ratios.

(3) The lists of identical corporations contain both enterprises having net incomes and enterprises having deficits. But Professor Epstein points out that the proportion of corporations having deficits in most if not all of his lists is substantially lower than the proportion among the corporations reporting to the Internal Revenue. If the latter vastly larger body of returns is fairly representative of average experience, then the present sample tends to over-state profits.[12] Further, the supplemental lists of non-identical corporations contain only enterprises having net incomes and tend to over-state profits for that reason.

(4) The use of reports from the same corporations year after year reduces one grave doubt concerning the meaning of the variations in profits as reported in the official *Statistics of Income*. It is true, as said above, that the continuing life of an enterprise is not incompatible with very consider-

---

[12] See Professor Epstein's critique of his materials in Ch. 43. Colonel M. C. Rorty points out that the use of lists of identical corporations over a series of years has a bias towards exaggerating profits, because it excludes all corporations that go bankrupt within the period covered. When the period extends over a decade, this factor becomes of considerable moment, particularly in the field of trade where, as Professor Epstein remarks, the average life of corporations is relatively short. On the other hand, where fixed investments are large, corporations of considerable size are seldom abandoned, though often reorganized. It may be, however, that large corporations which suffer very heavy losses are more likely to be reorganized under new names and so not to appear in a list of 'identical' concerns.

Of course Professor Epstein's sample excludes concerns coming into existence during his period as well as concerns going out of existence. This exclusion may tend to depress the average profit rates. Compare the remarks of Frederick C. Mills concerning the probable bias in a smaller sample of identical corporations used in his *Economic Tendencies in the United States* (National Bureau of Economic Research, 1932), footnote pp. 144–5.

able shifts in the nature of the business carried on. But only those changes in industrial activities which go so far as to call for the shifting of corporations from one group in the classifications used to another group can affect seriously the conclusions drawn. In Chapter 46 Professor Epstein shows that there is no reason to fear grave distortion on this count.

(5) The industries covered include a wide variety of manufacturing; ten branches of retail and eight of wholesale trade; mining and quarrying of coal, oil, metals, stone, salt, clay, sand and gravel; banking of several types and other financial business, except life insurance. No data are presented for farming, construction work, transportation and other public utilities, the practice of professions, commercial amusements, hotels and restaurants. Considerable as is the range of the data, they cannot, of course, be made to reveal the average rate of return upon capital in the United States, except upon the assumption that this average is nearly the same whether the investment is made in one industry or in another. That is an assumption which Professor Epstein shows to be even more untenable than has been supposed.

(6) How high a standard of accounting prevailed among the corporations preparing the returns utilized by the Department of Commerce in its *Source-Book for the Study of Profits* there is no way of telling. Probably the larger concerns employed skilled auditors; many of the smaller ones may have relied upon their own rather simple bookkeeping. But the earliest of the returns included cover 1919. By that time the Federal income tax upon corporations had been in operation for several years and had brought the advantages of proper depreciation allowances home to all but the most careless of business men. As compared with the data contained in the *Statistics of Income*, Professor Epstein's results are better in that he includes

two substantial items of non-taxable income—dividends of other corporations and tax-exempt bonds. As said above, careful analysis of a portion of the sample indicates that these items increase net corporate incomes by about one-ninth.[13]

(7) Another feature of the sample that bears upon its representative character is pointed out by Professor Epstein. All four of his lists of 'identical' corporations show an average size larger than that of the corresponding groups shown by *Statistics of Income*. For example, the 2,046 corporations in his manufacturing list make up only 2 or 3 per cent of the manufacturing corporations reporting to the Internal Revenue in 1919–28, but they receive from 57 to 66 per cent of the total income. Similarly, the list for trade represents less than 1 per cent of the number of reporting corporations, but about 30 per cent of the income reported in the official income-tax document. The supplementary use of 'non-identical' lists of small corporations engaged in manufacturing and trading redresses the balance in a degree. But Professor Epstein makes clear that his sample represents the earnings of large-scale business more fully than it represents those of small-scale business.

[13] If the sample included all corporations much double counting of income would result from the inclusion of inter-corporate dividends, just as double counting in the opposite direction would result from the subtraction of the deficits of corporations that lost money in any year from the profits of corporations that made money. Since the whole sample includes only 3,114 corporations in the 'identical lists', plus at most three or four thousand a year in the 'non-identical' lists, and since 300,000 to 500,000 corporations have reported to the Internal Revenue in successive years from 1919–28, it may seem that double counting of income and losses cannot give rise to serious error. But the proportion of corporations that both receive and pay dividends is probably far higher among the 3,114 corporations of the 'identical lists' than among the three to five hundred thousand that report, and an appreciable sum of profits may appear twice in the sample. Whatever double counting there is does not affect profit rates; for the value of stocks owned by the corporations in the sample are included in the investments upon which the profit rates are figured.

(8) It may not be superfluous to add that data concerning the profits of business corporations as going concerns do not show what returns individuals receive upon their investments in corporate shares. To establish upon a statistical basis any conclusions concerning investors' profits would call for data different from those utilized here and a different method of analysis.[14]

[14] This distinction, mentioned in an earlier footnote, between the profits of investors in a business and the profits of the business itself seems to be overlooked so often that it requires elaboration.

In good years, the dividends paid to stockholders are likely to be smaller than the current profits of the business; in bad years dividends are likely to be larger than profits; sometimes a corporation pays dividends while it is incurring losses. Besides his dividends, a stockholder may receive 'rights' to subscribe to new issues of stock upon favorable terms—'rights' that he can exercise or sell as he thinks fit. On the other hand, the stockholder may be assessed upon the value of his shares, and so have a negative income from them. Further, the stockholder may make profits for himself, or suffer losses, from the purchase and sale of shares. He may have the value of his shares wiped out wholly or largely by the liquidation of the company or the sale of its assets; on the other hand he may have the value of his shares much enhanced by an amalgamation on favorable terms. Thus the sums received by the stockholders from their investments in a corporation's shares differ from the profits of the corporation and cannot be ascertained from the corporation's books. Likewise the amount invested by the stockholders in their shares differs from the amount invested by the corporation in its business, except perhaps when the corporation is launched or when there is no buying and selling of shares.

Since neither the investments nor the net gains of the stockholders equal the investments or the net profits of the corporation, it is only by accident that the rate of profits made by any investor equals the rate of profits made by the corporation. Suppose that a corporation starts with a cash capital of $100,000, makes profits of $20,000, distributes $10,000 in dividends, and that its shares rise from par to 200. If one of the original stockholders sells at that price, he receives 10 per cent upon his investment plus a capital gain of 100 per cent; but if conditions remain unchanged the new holder will get only 5 per cent upon *his* investment. Suppose instead that our corporation makes profits of 2 per cent, pays dividends of 1 per cent and that its shares fall from par to 20. Then the original stockholder who sells gets a meager dividend and suffers a heavy capital loss; but the new stockholder who buys at 20 may get 5 per cent upon his investment, like the man who pays 200 for shares in a highly profitable business. Of course the profits and losses of individual investors in business enterprises are related to the profits and losses of the business enterprises in question; but this relation is far from simple.

THE PROBLEM OF MEASURING PROFITS [23]

What, then, can be learned from this notable collection of data covering the profits of business enterprises?

Though the data do not suffice to show the average long-time earnings of capital in the United States, they throw some light upon that question which many ask and no one can answer with full confidence. Professor Epstein shows conclusively that, within the period and the industrial field covered, his sample is biased in the direction of over-stating

> Colonel Rorty offers the following observations:
> "The question of the average earnings from diversified investments in the common shares of legitimate business ventures is one that has been debated at great length by investment experts. The majority opinion among such experts is that, even with somewhat more than average skill in selection, a diversified list of investments at 'par' in new ventures will tend to earn less, rather than more, than an equal investment at average market prices in the shares of seasoned companies—or, in other words, that the premium usually paid, above book values, for seasoned shares is no more than an offset to the reduced risk. With respect to seasoned shares, there is also a similar majority opinion, supported by statistical studies, to the effect that the high rates of earnings on common share investments, so extensively advertised during the 'new era', were based on the fallacy of choosing the especially successful companies of a given date and calculating the results from prior investments in such shares. Selections made (as in practice they must be made) of the promising and popular issues of prior dates, when carried forward for a term of years, have shown radically lower rates of return. Long-term studies, covering periods of from 30 to 50 years prior to 1930, indicate that common shares in the United States could be bought, at normal average market levels, to *promise* returns in cash and stock dividends, rights, etc., averaging between 6 and 7 per cent, before allowance for losses through failures, reorganization and other major adverse developments. Opinions and experience as to the latter losses vary widely. Barring purely speculative profits, or profits due to extraordinary skill in selection, there are, however, few qualified observers who would count on a net return in excess of 6 per cent, and there are many who would set the net figure at 5, or even 4 per cent. These reduced figures correspond to estimates of from 1 to 3 per cent per annum for major losses which are generally unreported in income tax returns and current corporation accounts.
> So far as skilled estimates may be relied upon, the preceding figures seem to indicate the range within which the true long-term return on investments in corporation equities may lie, whether such investments be made at 'par' in new ventures, or at a normal average market in seasoned issues. And with very minor adjustments, if any, they would seem to represent, also, the true long-term earnings on the actual investment in corporation equities, after allowance has been made for all reported and unreported losses."

average profits. As said above, the years 1919–28 appear to have been on the whole slightly more favorable to profit making than an average decade drawn from the last eighty years of American experience. More important is the fact that corporations having deficits are not included in the supplemental lists of small 'non-identical' corporations and are under-represented in the lists of large 'identical' corporations; for corporations that survive for ten years or more represent successful, or at any rate large-scale, business rather than average business. Another factor that lifts Professor Epstein's figures for profits above the official returns is the inclusion of dividends from other corporations and interest on tax-exempt bonds. Of course this inclusion is a merit in the sample; but it may well be that large corporations receive a larger percentage of their gross income from such sources than do the under-represented small corporations. If so, that fact does not affect profit ratios; for security holdings make part of the base upon which these ratios are computed.

Unfortunately, we have no means of determining just how much the averages yielded by the sample over-state profit rates. Of course that could be told definitely only if we knew the average long-run rate of earnings upon capital for all enterprises. Comparisons with other samples do not settle the point, but they are interesting. The grand average rate of return which Professor Epstein gets for his 3,144 'identical' corporations in 1919–28 is 9.2 per cent after Federal taxes are deducted. This figure is substantially lower than the average derived by Mr. Sterrett from his small but interesting pre-War sample, namely 13.67 per cent. It happens to be just the same as the average derived from the National Bureau's collection of audit reports for about 700 corporations in 1927–29. It is substantially higher than the average which Professor Epstein himself gets from the official income tax data for all corporations engaged in manufacturing, trade, finance and mining in 1924–28, namely 6.2 per cent after the deduction of Federal taxes.[15] But even this comparison with the average earnings of over 300,000 corporations for five years does not show how far 9 per cent is above the 'true' average earnings of business enterprises. The five years 1924–28 were a relatively favorable period for profit making—slightly more favorable than the full ten years covered by Professor Epstein's study. The corporations engaged in manufacturing, trade, finance and mining that reported to the Internal Revenue are a changing list varying in number from 315,340 in 1924 to 359,992 in 1928. Of these changing corporations the vast majority are small concerns. In small corporations the accounting is often defective. On the one hand, allowances for depreciation may be inadequate; on the other hand, part of what should be reckoned as profits may be paid out in salaries. The capital on which the rate of earnings is reckoned excludes capital represented by funded debt. If funded debt be added to capital and interest payments to income, the average returns are reduced a trifle. This new figure for Epstein's 3,144 'identical' corporations after Federal taxes are paid comes out 9.0 per cent in 1924–28, while the corresponding figure for the changing list of corporations reporting to the Internal Revenue comes out 6.1 per cent. And there we must leave the problem.

However, too much stress can be laid upon the search for the 'true' average rate of business profits. If we knew that missing figure, we should have to say that it gives a most inadequate representation of the facts of greatest significance to business men and to the community as a whole.

[15] See Table 1 in Ch. 2. The corresponding figure for Professor Epstein's 3,144 'identical' corporations is 9.4 per cent.

More important than the precise arithmetic or geometric mean of earning rates over a long period of time are the facts that the profits earned by business enterprises as a whole fluctuate violently from year to year, that in every year the returns to different enterprises cover a range running from very high profits to very heavy losses, that certain industries remain relatively profitable and others relatively unprofitable for years at a stretch, and finally that business enterprises stabilize the disbursement of income to individuals in some degree by paying out dividends substantially greater than current profits in bad years.

In a vague and general way these facts have been surmised. But if we are to have the type of knowledge that is most useful to investors, to business executives, to bankers, to public commissions and courts concerned with regulating rates of different types, to accountants, to economists, to legislators and to government officials, we must replace our vague and general impressions as rapidly as may be by definite measurements. This volume makes a significant advance from the realm of personal opinion towards the realm of established fact. The materials here analyzed constitute the largest collection that has been published of well-authenticated data concerning the profits of the same business enterprises over a considerable period of years. Within their field, the figures show definitely the wide differences in the average profits made by numerous branches of business, the persistence of these differences over a period sufficiently long to admit of large shiftings of investments, the range covered by the profits of individual enterprises in numerous industries, the comparative profits of large, middle-size and small enterprises, the violent fluctuations of profits from phase to phase of business cycles, the differences between profits on the stockholders' equities and the returns upon this equity plus funded debt, and the differences in profits before and after the payment of Federal taxes.

The findings presented here can be put to many different uses and construed in various ways. One of their merits is that they raise as many questions as they answer and indicate what further work needs to be done in the field. The publication of Professor Epstein's inquiry should stimulate and guide the collection of larger samples of data concerning profits and the more thorough analysis of existing data.

Book I
THE BROAD FINDINGS

Chapter 1

AN INTRODUCTORY SUMMARY

1. Purpose of the Investigation

WHAT rates of profit do representative American corporations, large and small, earn upon their capital investments in various branches of manufacture, trade, finance and mining—that is, in fields of enterprise in which competition is relatively free and where there is little public regulation?

Over how wide a range are the profit rates of these going concerns scattered at a given time? In what part of the range is there dense concentration of profit rates?

How do these rates fluctuate from one year to the next?

Do the rates that prevail at a given time in one industry tend to equal the rates that prevail in other industries? Do such differences as appear in one year in the profitableness of various industries tend to disappear shortly, or to maintain themselves for considerable periods?

How do the earnings of individual corporations vary, from good years to bad, in different industries?

Do the larger enterprises in one or another industry earn profits at higher or lower rates than the smaller ones?

Such are the principal questions for which the present investigation seeks answers. The answers are not always complete or final. In some instances they seem to be of definite character; in others, they constitute merely what are believed to be good approximations. But the attentive reader will find that estimates and actual figures are clearly distinguished throughout the volume. Upon the whole, the data are more complete for manufacture and trade, and for their various subgroups, than for the two other divisions, finance and mining.

It should be noted that the questions dealt with concern *variations* in profit rates—variations from year to year, from industry to industry, from small to large concerns, from one corporation to another. To show what these variations are it is convenient to use average rates of profits for the groups treated. Though some of the averages cover over three thousand corporations and a period of ten years, no one should assume that any figure in this book shows the average long-time earnings of all business enterprises in the United States. To guard against such a misconception, as well as to indicate what the results do mean, a detailed examination of the representative value of the samples of data underlying the investigation is made in Book IV. There it appears that the samples yield average profit rates distinctly higher than those realized by all corporations that report to the Bureau of Internal Revenue. But it is no part of the present investigation to determine the grand average rate of profits earned by all business enterprises either in the short or in the long run.

The *raison d'être* of an investigation into the variations among profits of business corporations scarcely requires extended discussion. In all descriptions of the industrial system it is a commonplace that no set of agencies or individuals consciously controls our economic activities. Despite some degree of 'government in business', business men in the United States, indeed in most countries apart from the highly exceptional instance of Russia, are on the whole free to engage in the production, the market distribution or the financing of whatever commodities or services seem

AN INTRODUCTORY SUMMARY [33]

to promise an attractive return upon the capital invested. Not only are men free to choose what products they will make or sell, but also the amount of each commodity that is offered, per day, per month, per year, is left entirely to the decisions of the individual entrepreneurs responsible for its production. That is to say, neither the fixing of specific sales quotas nor the allocation of productive equipment is undertaken by the community itself. Rather is reliance placed upon the unconscious and spontaneous working of the twin forces of price and profit as the instrument of production control. If too much of one product is offered for sale—so runs the common explanation of the operation of this mechanism—its price will fall. Profits in that branch of manufacture or trade will therefore shrink, and production will be contracted until a happy balance is restored. Conversely, an undersupply of any one commodity is supposed to cause a rise of price and an enhancement of profit which lead to an expansion of output. The phrase employed may be 'a balancing of demand and supply', 'an equation', or 'an equilibrium'; but from Adam Smith to Alfred Marshall, this concept of prices and profits as the controlling mechanism that regulates production is fundamentally the same. Under a free economic system it is supposed that men unconsciously and automatically supply one another's wants by varying the relative output of this or that commodity or service in accordance with the comparative rates of net return to be made in the several fields of business enterprise.

To make this mechanism work rapidly and precisely, it would be necessary that (1) business men should have accurate information about the profits realized in all branches of enterprise; (2) capital which had been invested in trades that yield less than average returns could be withdrawn quickly; and (3) no obstacles should hinder the investment of additional capital in trades that yield profits above the average. Since these conditions have never existed, 'the tendency of profits to an equality' in different branches of industry has been a speculative tenet. How far that 'tendency' has been realized in practice has been a matter of opinion and opinions have varied. Some economists have written as if, over a wide field, business men can make fairly reliable estimates of the profits in different trades, as if sufficient capital can be withdrawn from unfortunate investments to restrict supply and raise prices to a profitable level rather promptly, and as if the hindrances to the investment of fresh capital in flourishing trades, either by those already engaged or by newcomers, are not sufficiently serious to prevent the reduction of prices and profits within a relatively short time. Other economists have hedged about their statement of the 'tendency' towards an equalizing of profits with such careful qualifications that it is difficult to determine what they think concerning actual conditions.[1]

To all who are concerned with the functioning of our economic organization, whether as men of affairs, government officials or investigators, the question of prime importance is the question of what happens in fact. Do the earnings of different industries really cluster closely about some central or average figure, over a period of time? Does competition so function in the industrial system that the differences in earnings rates during any one year are only temporary? That it does so function has often been challenged; but heretofore sufficient data to give a convincing

---

[1] It is interesting to compare the rather bold statements of Adam Smith (*Wealth of Nations,* Book I, Ch. X) with the more cautious exposition of John Stuart Mill (*Principles of Political Economy,* Book II, Ch. XV) and with the elaborately guarded discussion of Alfred Marshall (*Principles of Economics,* 8th ed., Book VI, Ch. VIII).

AN INTRODUCTORY SUMMARY [35]

answer have not been available.[2] A comprehensive body of materials that has been developed in the Department of Commerce,[3] however, affords a basis for more complete answers to the several questions involved, and the findings obtained through the analysis of those and other data are presented in this volume.[4]

2. CHARACTER OF THE INQUIRY

Book I gives the principal facts and conclusions, which Books II and III develop more fully. Doubtless the busi-

---

[2] William L. Crum, *Corporate Earning Power* (1929), presents data for the net return on gross revenues over a considerable period, while Lawrence H. Sloan, *Corporation Profits* (1929), analyzes the return upon investment for specific industrial companies and groups in 1926 and 1927. Other investigators—J. E. Sterrett, J. P. Müller, David Friday, J. H. Bliss and S. H. Nerlove—have discussed the return upon invested capital, but not for both a ten-year period and for the numerous subdivisions of industry designated in the present volume as 'specific industries' or 'minor groups'. Nerlove's *A Decade of Corporate Incomes* (1932) covers the period 1919–29. Raymond T. Bowman, *The Statistical Study of Profits* (1934), discusses the frequency distributions of earnings rates in a wide number of industries, utilizing data developed by the Federal Trade Commission, the Department of Commerce, and other agencies. Other writers, Lucille Bagwell, Horace Secrist, and most recently Leland Rex Robinson (Corporate Earnings on Share and Borrowed Capital in Ratios of Gross Income, *American Statistical Association Journal*, March 1934) have made illuminating contributions to the subject of earnings ratios, but have not had available comprehensive data for specific sub-branches of industry, or what in the present volume are termed 'minor groups'.

[3] Ralph C. Epstein, in collaboration with Florence M. Clark, *A Source-Book for the Study of Industrial Profits*, 1932. This is the source for all the basic data on which the analyses of the present investigation rest, unless otherwise indicated.

[4] Only the competitive fields of manufacture, trade, finance and mining are covered by the statistical data of the *Source-Book* cited, and only those four divisions will be discussed in the present study. They include the great bulk of what is ordinarily termed 'competitive' as distinguished from 'regulated' industry; construction and 'service' activities, such as restaurants, hotels and garages, are all that is omitted, save agriculture, in which the corporate form is somewhat anomalous. Earnings data upon railroads, public utilities and other regulated industries are available in the reports of the Interstate Commerce Commission and those of other Governmental rate-making and regulating bodies.

ness man, the investment banker and the general reader will find that Books I–III surpass in interest Book IV, which goes further into detail as to the significance of the data, methods of compilation and the like. But it must be borne in mind that most of the summary facts and estimates presented in Books I–III do not hold entirely without qualification, even though in many instances this qualification may be slight. The reader who wishes to utilize either the actual figures or certain of the estimates to obtain more than a 'sense of direction' or a notion of 'general drift' concerning a particular industry or group ought therefore to examine such qualifications as they are discussed in Book IV. This is also true for the more general purposes of either the economic theorist or the student of business cycles. Frequently the significance of the findings in one direction or another, even when the data are taken *en masse,* depends upon the importance attached to the several margins of error to which they may be subject.

There are, to be sure, scholars who would allow the inevitable obstacles to the attaining of precise results to deter them entirely from pursuing any investigations such as the present one. These persons can adduce many cogent reasons why this conclusion or that can never properly be regarded as possessing much validity, if it is in part predicated upon assumptions that cannot always quantitatively, within the closest of limits, be proved correct in all their implications. There being doubt concerning the absolute impeccability of some of its conclusions, such a study, they reason, ought not to have been made. This, however, is a defeatist attitude. Moreover, it does not entitle the holder to be regarded as 'scientific' simply because of his skepticism. The important thing is not the presence of ambiguity or errors; but, how *great* are the probable margins of error and to what extent can they affect the ultimate results? These are the sole questions of interest in appraising the validity, or the usefulness, of any piece of knowledge of the statistical, as contrasted to either the historical or the mechanical type.[5] An effort has thus been made to explain, either in the footnotes of Books I–III or in the text of Book IV, the underlying and contributory factors that may reasonably throw doubt upon, as well as support, the validity of the figures finally arrived at, for one purpose or another.

But in appraising the scientific utility of this or that summary figure—whether it be an amount or a ratio—the phrase, 'for one purpose or another' should be especially noted. Granted that the proper degree of care and conscience has been employed in the mechanics of its tabulation, a set of statistics such as this is rarely either entirely good or bad in an absolute or 'intrinsic' sense; its worth is purely functional or 'purposive'. To be sure, some collections of statistics are for almost no purposes useful. But the value of any compilation that has been honestly made and is reasonably free from mathematical error is variable. It may range all the way from *nil* to a very high point indeed, depending on the problems one seeks to solve.

3. RELATIVITY IN THE INTERPRETATION OF STATISTICAL DATA

Take, for example, the bearing which the valuation of assets has upon the validity of profit rates. Probably most corporations, by and large, no longer overvalue rather than undervalue their assets, relative to 'prudent investment' or to actual cost. But imagine that this is not so; and

---

[5] *Cf.* F. C. Mills, On Measurement in Economics, in *The Trend of Economics* (R. G. Tugwell, ed.); also Hans Vaihinger's concept of the 'as if' (*Die Philosophie des Als Ob*, cited by Havelock Ellis in *The Dance of Life*, Ch. III).

assume that the corporations included in manufacturing industry as a whole carry their assets at figures which average 50 per cent over actual (original) cost. Under these conditions, if net worth or invested capital amounts were drawn off the balance sheets, the aggregate capital investment would exceed by about one-half the figure at which it would otherwise be shown. This is of course an extreme assumption. If, however, it were so (and sufficient facts were not known to make possible any reliable correction or adjustment), the data would be valueless for purposes of, say, the social theorist whose primary interest lay in seeing just how much the return to entrepreneurial capital is, or of the socialist or other critic of the economic order who wished to see how 'high' a return was being made by 'capitalists' in general. But to the economic theorist whose interest lay in ascertaining whether an equality of return *among different industries* really is approximated, such inaccuracies in investment figures[6] would not much impair the usefulness of the data unless it appeared that the practice of one industry was, in general, very different in this respect from that of another. Or to the student of business cycles, whose interest lay in the fluctuations of profit rates from year to year, such inaccuracy in valuation might not constitute a vital defect unless the extent or direction of the error itself substantially changed during the period under review.

Questions such as these are treated in Book IV. It is not believed, however, that such extreme qualifications as the hypothetical one just suggested really attach to any of the data here presented, taken in their aggregate or average forms. Errors of 50 per cent or more may well be present in the individual figures for any one, two or three corpora-

[6] Inaccuracies, that is to say, from the point of view of valuation based upon original cost.

AN INTRODUCTORY SUMMARY [39]

tions in a group, but hardly for the entire series averaged together. Some reliance, in other words, may be placed upon the 'stability of large numbers' in assaying the probable validity of many of the data presented.

The reader who is willing to take on faith the underlying technique of compilation may accept without any great reservation the findings given in the present chapter, and also in the other chapters of Book I, as representing general summaries of fairly accurate approximations. Certainly this holds true of all 'major' group figures (for example, Food Products or Textiles). The 'minor' group figures (for example, Bakery Products or Railway Equipment), presented mainly in Books II and III, are sometimes to be used more carefully; but doubtless their representativeness as 'samples' will be appraised by the persons most interested in, and best acquainted with, the specific industries in question. Finally, the careful and patient reader who takes nothing on faith and who wishes to know the limits of error present, in so far as these can be estimated, can supplement his provisional acceptance of Books I–III with a close study of Book IV, which necessarily is addressed to the professional economist or accountant rather than to the lay analyst or general reader.

4. A CONCISE SUMMARY OF RESULTS

For the convenience of the reader who first desires a short summary of some of the outstanding results of the study, concise answers are here given to the questions raised at the beginning of this chapter. Qualifications are omitted, only the bare findings being outlined. Their economic and social implications are discussed elsewhere, particularly in Chapter 47.

(1) The average rate of return earned upon invested

capital by the large American manufacturing, trading, financial and mining corporations of our sample in 1928 was 10.7 per cent before the payment of Federal income taxes, and 9.6 per cent after such taxes,[7] as shown by the figures for 3,144 companies for which data were compiled over a ten-year period. The return in 1926 was 11.5 per cent before taxes and 10.2 per cent after taxes. In the depression year 1921 the figure was 4.4 per cent before taxes and 3.4 per cent after taxes. In all instances the income figures are the net amounts remaining after subtraction of the deficits of corporations which suffered losses.[8]

For the ten-year period 1919–28 as a whole, the aggregate net earnings of these 3,144 large corporations amounted to 10.5 per cent upon their combined investment before taxes, and to 9.2 per cent after taxes. In other words, an owner of the capital stocks of *all* these corporations would over this ten-year period have averaged approximately a 9 per cent return upon his equity, year in and year out, although in one year his return might have been four or five times as great as in another, the range being from 12.8 per cent after taxes in 1919 to 2.4 per cent [9] in 1921. Between 1922 and 1928, however,

[7] These averages are weighted, in accordance with the relative importance of manufacture, trade, finance and mining in the nation's economic structure. For details, see Appendix A, section that discusses Table 2, Ch. 2.

[8] The averages cited in this section, however, are for the earnings of large corporations that remained in business continuously during the period 1919–28; they do not reflect earnings rates for *all* corporate enterprise; see Ch. 43.

[9] These figures are not weighted as are those explained in a preceding note, since an hypothetical 'owner of the capital stocks' of the 3,144 corporations of the sample would receive simply the arithmetic average return. The difference between the weighted and unweighted figures, however, is slight. 'Equity' includes, of course, the book value of reinvested earnings (corporate surplus) as well as capital stock, and is shareholder's equity in the accounting and economic senses; the expression does not refer to the market prices that may be paid for such equities by other than original holders.

AN INTRODUCTORY SUMMARY [41]

the range of the return was only from 9.6 to 11.5 per cent before taxes, and from 8.6 to 10.2 per cent after taxes. Since the comparability of earnings rates from year to year is somewhat affected by changes in Federal income tax rates, the figures given in the remainder of this summary (and elsewhere in the volume unless otherwise noted) will be for earnings before the payment of such taxes.[10]

(2) The range between the earnings rates of different industries and trades is wide indeed, either in any given year or over a period. In 1928, of the 106 different manufacturing, trading, mining and financial groups in which our large corporations data can be separately tabulated, 8 industries show earnings of less than 5 per cent upon their invested capital, while 3 industries show rates of over 25 per cent. The extreme range of the 106 earnings rates is from 1.3 to 27.3 per cent. Summarizing the situation more completely, 42 of the industries earned under 10 per cent, 59 from 10 to 19.9 per cent, and 5 from 20 to 27.3 per cent.

The year 1928, however, was one of prosperity. What

[10] There are arguments for and against doing this. To be sure, the income that the owners of corporations actually realize is what remains after income tax payments. But when tax rates change markedly, or when they are themselves based upon the rate of profit upon capital (as with excess profits taxes), a better clue to comparative earning power—at different times and between different industries—is perhaps afforded by the figures before Federal income tax payment. (This is said with recognition of the possible inconsistency involved because local and state taxes are treated as deductions in both cases.) The figures for Federal income taxes are, however, given in Appendix B and may be utilized by the reader who wishes to compute any particular figures after subtracting all taxes.

It is further to be remarked that consideration of net income figures before the payment of income taxes is quite as permissible in analyzing corporate earning power as in surveying the incomes of persons. When we think of one individual's income being, say, twice that of another, or of "86 per cent of incomes being under $2,000 a year", we have in mind earnings before taxes (levied in some proportion to earnings) have reduced them.

do similar figures show for a year of depression? In 1928 none of the 106 industries showed deficits (some *companies* in each industry did, but not any industry as a whole). But in 1921 the range of earnings rates was from a net loss of 12.6 per cent upon investment to a net profit of 29.2 per cent. Fifteen of the 106 industries had deficits, the figures running from a fraction of 1 per cent of the amount of their capitals to the 12.6 per cent loss just indicated. Sixty-one industries showed earnings rates of from 1 to 9.9 per cent; 25 more earned from 10 to 19.9 per cent; and 5 earned over 20 per cent.

Taking the decade 1919–28 as a whole, and aggregating the annual earnings for all ten years in each of these 106 industries, we find that their earnings rates for the entire period range from 1.9 to 31.6 per cent. Twenty industries show earnings of from 1.9 to 9.9 per cent; 57 earned from 10 to 14.9 per cent; 22 earned from 15 to 19.9 per cent. The remaining seven industries earned from 20 to 31.6 per cent. The most common return is thus between 10 and 14.9 per cent; but as will appear shortly, this does not denote the existence of an average or central rate towards which all industries tend to 'gravitate'.

(3) Data for 71 large manufacturing corporations, available for the 13-year period 1919–31, show a 3.8 per cent return upon investment in 1921, a 10.4 per cent return in 1928 and a 3.6 per cent return in 1931. For all 13 years together the aggregate return is 10 per cent.

(4) For the ten years 1919–28 aggregated, 2,046 large manufacturing corporations show a net return of 10.8 per cent upon investment. The most profitable industry shows earnings of 31.6 per cent for the period, while the least profitable records earnings of only 1.9 per cent.

Of the 73 industries into which the entire manufacturing

AN INTRODUCTORY SUMMARY

field has been divided, the following ten are most profitable (aggregate results for the entire ten years in question):

	Per Cent
Toilet Preparations	31.6
Newspapers	25.6
Scientific Instruments	25.5
Miscellaneous Printing and Publishing	22.9
Proprietary Preparations	20.8
Motor Vehicles	19.7
Confectionery	17.8
Planing Mills	17.7
Road Machinery	17.5
Boots and Shoes	17.3

The following ten industries are least profitable:

	Per Cent
Meat Packing	1.9
Beverages	3.8
Castings and Forgings	5.8
Rubber Products	5.9
Miscellaneous Leather Products	6.8
Weaving Woolens	7.2
Stationery	7.4
Miscellaneous Food Products	7.9
Railway Equipment	8.1
Blank Paper	8.4

Half of the 73 industries show earnings, for the ten years, of over 13.6 per cent upon investment; the highest quarter earn over 15.8 per cent, while the lowest quarter earn under 10.6 per cent.

(5) When the industries that show the highest rates of profits in any given year are followed through successive years and their earnings rates checked, they show no substantial declines in earning power. In other words, not only do discrepancies exist among the earnings rates of different industries for a period, but the 'high' industries of any given year are also high industries in most succeeding years. While considerable shifting of position takes place, no general tendency towards an 'equality of profit rates' is

discernible. To illustrate, Toilet Preparations was the third most profitable of all 73 manufacturing industries in 1919. It was the most profitable in the depression year 1921, again the most profitable in 1922, and the third most profitable in 1928.

In some industries long-time increases or declines in relative earning power are to be observed, but secular influences of this sort in no way suffice to bring about any approximately uniform rate of long-run return; at least, competition brings no such result about over the ten-year period studied. It is to be observed in this connection that while some of the 'high' industries are those characterized by the possession of trade-marks, etc., on the part of the corporations that belong to them, few are industries commonly regarded as subject to monopoly control. Nor *are* they really 'monopolized' in any usual sense of the term; numerous independently-owned enterprises operate and 'compete' in each of the industries in question.

(6) In every industry wide variations exist between the average return on investment and the rates received by the individual corporations whose incomes and capitals contribute to that average figure. Taking first manufacturing as a whole, the average return on investment received by 2,046 large corporations in 1928 was 11 per cent. But one-quarter earned under 6.6 per cent; half earned from 6.6 to 18.4 per cent. The highest quarter earned over 18.4 per cent.

Generalizing upon the basis of the data of this and other samples for smaller corporations, our estimate is that in years other than those of depression, about a third of all manufacturing corporations in the country earn over 10 per cent upon their investments, and about a sixth earn over 18 per cent. But at the same time roughly half of the com-

AN INTRODUCTORY SUMMARY [45]

panies earn under 5 per cent, a number experiencing deficits.[11]

(7) But of the manufacturing corporations *that show net incomes,* approximately half earn over 10 per cent on their investments in years of prosperity, while one-fourth earn over 18 per cent. The earnings of the lowest quarter range from 1 to 5 per cent.

Of the trading corporations with net incomes of over $2,000, in years other than those of depression, one-half earn over 13 per cent upon their investments; one-fourth, over 20 per cent, and the lowest quarter, from 1 to 8 per cent.

(8) Shifting our emphasis from the *number of corporations* earning net returns upon their capitals to the *amount of capital* on which a profit is earned, we find that in prosperous years such as 1926 or 1928 about 95 per cent of the capital of our 2,046 large manufacturing companies earns a net income. In a poorer year such as 1927 about 90 per cent of the capital shows a net return, while in a year of severe depression such as 1921 net incomes are earned on 70 per cent of the total capital investment.

(9) The larger manufacturing enterprises, in the main, do not earn profits at higher rates than the smaller ones. In 1928, for example, 1,421 small companies, with invested

[11] No effort is made to estimate the exact proportion with deficits. The definition of a true deficit in the case of small corporations is difficult because many enterprises that report deficits are 'close' concerns in which the deficit appears after the payment of relatively large managerial salaries (large relative to the corporation's income before their deduction) to the corporation's owners (see Ch. 43). The common impression, based upon Bureau of Internal Revenue data for *taxable* net incomes (in the technical or legal sense of that term), that "about 50 per cent of the corporations in the country lose money" is misleading because of this difficulty of definition. To be sure, the figures for publicly-owned corporations are frequently subject to questionable accounting practices also, ordinarily of other sorts (see Ch. 45). Apart from exceptional instances, however, the latter are seldom so pronounced as to convert book profits into nominal losses.

capitals mostly under $250,000, earned an average net profit of 11.3 per cent, while 1,970 larger companies, with capitals of over $250,000, earned 10.6 per cent.

But the net incomes received by companies with capitals ranging from $250,000 to several hundred million dollars each indicate that by far the highest rates of profit are earned by the corporations with capitals of from $250,000 to $500,000. In both 1924 and 1928 the latter averaged earnings of 20 per cent upon their investment, while the very largest companies of all, those with capitals of over 50 million dollars each, earned less than 10 per cent in both years. The evidence seems fairly clear that, beyond a certain point, mere size is accompanied by no increased effectiveness in production, at least as reflected in terms of earning power. In spite of the successful income showings of some of our largest corporations, numerous smaller companies not only equal but excel them in earning capacity per dollar of capital invested in the business.

(10) Analysis of the data upon earnings rates, sales and investment for the broad upswing in general business that occurred between 1922 and 1929 shows that the peak of profits, in terms of the rates earned upon investment in many industries, was reached in 1926 rather than in 1928 or 1929. Contrary to popular belief, 1926 was a more prosperous year than 1928, and was just as good as 1929.

(11) The percentage of manufacturing industry's gross income, as measured by sales, that goes to 'capital' in the form of long-time interest and net income together shows no substantial change during the years 1926–28. Interest payments on funded debt plus net income on capital stock and surplus amounted to about 10 per cent of the gross product of industry in *each* of the years 1925, 1926, 1928.

(12) As has already been remarked, the major groups of manufacturing industries (such as Foods, Textiles,

Metals) and likewise specific industries in each group (such as Castings and Forgings, Motor Vehicles) varied greatly among themselves in respect of earnings rates in any one year. But more important, for purposes of cyclical study, the courses of their earnings over the period 1922–28 varied enormously. Only one-fifth of the 73 industries analyzed show increasing earnings rates over this period. Another two-fifths show marked declines. The remaining two-fifths either remain stable or show such fluctuations that no trends are detectable.

In over one-sixth of these 73 industries capital investment increased faster than the volume of sales, in spite of the fact that earnings rates were declining both absolutely and comparatively. This indicates either that the facts were unknown to entrepreneurs or that changes in profit rates fail to function in directing the flow of productive resources as efficiently as is ordinarily supposed. One reason for the failure of declining earnings rates to halt investment may be that the cost of new capital during the period in question was substantially less than even the declining return that was being obtained upon the capital already invested in these industries. But, in order to be permanently profitable, any additional fixed investment in plant and equipment must yield a return that exceeds its annual charge *over the period of its entire life,* and not just for a few years. Whether many of the investments made in these industries during the late years of the period 1921–29 will do this remains to be seen. But there can be no doubt that unwise expansion in several industries contributed to the crisis of 1929–30.

(13) Consumers' goods industries in general enjoy both higher and steadier earnings than those which manufacture producers' goods. When consumers' goods industries are divided into those making highly durable goods, those making goods of intermediate durability and those making

quickly consumable goods, the sales of highly durable goods show by far the greatest increase in 1922–28. The sales growth that occurred in the group of industries making consumers' goods of the highly durable type points significantly to the relatively high state of 'consumers' inventories' that prevailed at the time of the 1929–30 collapse.

CHAPTER 2

A GENERAL VIEW OF INDUSTRY

1. AVERAGE FIGURES FOR ALL CORPORATIONS

IN YEARS of prosperity American industry in the aggregate, as represented by all Manufacturing, Trading, Financial and Mining corporations, earns a net return of approximately 7 per cent upon the capital invested by its owners. This is just an average figure. It includes both the relatively profitable and unprofitable industries, the successful and unsuccessful corporations, the large and small enterprises. These several classes of industries and enterprises vary substantially in profitableness among themselves. What percentage of the corporations, what proportion of the separate industries, and what part of the total capital invested, earn profits at rates higher or lower than the average level will appear later. But for the moment, we may fasten our attention upon the general figures.

The average of 7 per cent presented is for the net return upon what may be termed 'entrepreneurial capital'. The net return includes both operating and non-operating income, after deducting all charges other than Federal income taxes, while the investment figure is the combined capital stock and surplus of the corporations in question.[1] Upon 'total capital', including under that head not only the sharehold-

---

[1] See Ch. 45 for a discussion of the meaning of book or stated capital figures, broadly viewed for industry and industrial groups at large.

ers' equity in the enterprise, but all of its funded debt as well, the return is fractionally lower, but still approximates 7 per cent. Throughout this volume the first investment concept, that of entrepreneurial capital, is termed *capitalization,* while the second concept, that of capital stock, surplus, and funded debt as well, is termed *total capital.* In correspondence with these two concepts of investment are the two concepts of earnings: *net income,* in an entrepreneurial sense, the return after all charges; *total profits,* in a more inclusive sense, the return before the subtraction of interest payments upon permanent but borrowed capital.

The data for both types of net return, for all corporations in Manufacturing, Trade, Finance and Mining combined, for the years 1924–28, are presented in Table 1.[2]

TABLE 1

ESTIMATED EARNINGS RATES, ALL CORPORATIONS IN MANUFACTURING, TRADE, FINANCE AND MINING, 1924–28

(before and after Federal income tax) [1]

	1924	1925	1926	1927	1928
Percentage income to capitalization					
before tax	6.0	7.8	7.4	6.5	7.6
after tax	5.2	6.8	6.4	5.7	6.7
Percentage profit to total capital					
before tax	5.9	7.5	7.2	6.4	7.3
after tax	5.2	6.6	6.4	5.6	6.6
Number of corporations	315,340	333,372	355,634	345,212	359,992

[1] See Appendix A for method of computation, and Appendix Table 1 for absolute figures.

The absolute figures on which the percentages are based are not given here in detail, but appear in Appendix B. The net income figures for all corporations in the four divi-

[2] This table, as well as Tables 3 and 4, is based upon data taken from *Statistics of Income* (Bureau of Internal Revenue), adjusted as described in Appendix A. See Ch. 46 for a discussion of the character of that publication as a source for industrial earnings data, broadly viewed.

A GENERAL VIEW OF INDUSTRY [51]

sions run from a little over five billion dollars in 1924 to a little over eight billion in 1928, whereas the capitalization figures show an aggregate investment of about 86 billion in 1924 and 108 billion in 1928.

It will be observed that the variation between different years, for either series during the period 1924–28, is but slight. But in years of deep depression such as 1921 or 1931 this general average return falls considerably below 7 per cent. For 1921, in the Manufacturing division it may be estimated at approximately 2½ per cent, and for 1931, at about 2⅓ per cent.[3]

2. A TEN-YEAR SERIES FOR LARGE CORPORATIONS

What, however, is the aggregate return over a continuous period long enough to include several good and bad years alike? In other words, what does industry earn during an eight- or ten-year succession of cyclical fluctuations? For this purpose no series of comparable figures that includes data for *all* American corporations in Manufacturing, Trade, Finance and Mining is available; but we do have a comprehensive and typical sample for the larger enterprises. The records of 3,144 companies that were engaged in business continuously from the beginning of 1919 to the end of 1928 comprise this series. Their capitalization, in most years of the period, amounts to more than 22 billion dollars, their net income to more than two and one-half billion. Including funded debt, their aggregate capital amounted to about 28 billion in 1924 and to over 35 billion in 1928.[4]

[3] These estimates are explained in Appendix A.
[4] As to the size of these companies, more specifically, it may be said that the lower decil for the array of total capitals in 1927, in the Manufacturing division, was about $500,000, while the median was about $2,000,000 (see Ch. 43).

The combined return of these large corporations, for the entire ten-year period, all gains and losses in good and bad years alike included, aggregated 10.5 per cent upon their combined capitalizations.[5] The three thousand odd corporations in question, to be sure, constitute but a small fraction of the total number of enterprises in the country, but their capitalization comprises approximately one-third of the entire corporate investment in the four broad industrial divisions that they represent. The series, as has been said, contains identical corporations throughout the ten-year period.[6]

In every year from 1922 through 1928 these corporations earned an aggregate net income of from 9.6 to 11.5 per cent upon capitalization. Upon total capital the return for 1924–28 ran between 9.2 and 10.9 per cent. Further details are given in Table 2. Basic data for this and similar tables are given in Appendix B.

3. AVERAGE FIGURES BY INDUSTRIAL DIVISIONS

For both the larger and the smaller groups of corporations discussed, however, the percentages of return vary among the four broad industrial divisions, Manufacturing, Trade, Finance and Mining. The general average ratio of

---

[5] This is a weighted average, in several senses: (1) it is automatically weighted by the respective sizes of the several firms' capitals (as it would have to be in order to ascertain the aggregate return upon the entire capital of industry as a whole); (2) it is unavoidably weighted by the trend of investment growth from year to year; (3) it is deliberately weighted by giving to both the investment and income figures for Manufacture, Trade, Finance and Mining, respectively, the same relative importance (in combining the sample data for these four divisions) as the investment figures of each bear to one another, in the actual data for the country as a whole, in years in which actual data are available. For amplification and a discussion of method see Appendix A.

[6] The investment figure given is for 1926. The 'entire corporate investment' figure is derived as explained in Appendix A. See Ch. 43 for a discussion of the 'representativeness' of these 3,144 corporations in this and other years.

A GENERAL VIEW OF INDUSTRY [53]

TABLE 2

EARNINGS RATES, 3,144 CORPORATIONS IN MANUFACTURING,
TRADE, FINANCE AND MINING, 1919–28 AND 1924–28
(before and after Federal income tax) [1]

	1919	1920	1921	1922	1923
Percentage income to capitalization					
before tax	17.1	11.6	4.4	10.6	10.9
after tax	12.8	9.3	3.4	9.6	9.8
	1924	1925	1926	1927	1928
Percentage income to capitalization					
before tax	9.6	11.3	11.5	9.8	10.7
after tax	8.6	10.0	10.2	8.7	9.6
Percentage profit to total capital					
before tax	9.2	10.7	10.9	9.4	10.2
after tax	8.3	9.6	9.7	8.4	9.2

[1] Absolute figures in Appendix Table 2.

net income to capitalization for all corporations in all divisions stands, as has been said, at around 7 per cent during the years 1924–28. But the Manufacturing division, which possesses roughly half of the four divisions' aggregate capitalization, runs close to 9 per cent in three of these five years. The eight to twelve billions of entrepreneurial capital invested in Mining, on the other hand, earn far less than in the general average—in only one year of the five is a return of more than 3 per cent shown.[7] In part, this low return is the result of large depletion charges which in the nature of the case are merely accounting and engineering estimates of the rates at which resources below the earth's surface are being exhausted. But to some extent also, the earnings rates of the Mining division are low for other

[7] It should, however, be noted that by no means all mining activity is included under 'Mining' in these data, as many large mining properties are wholly or partly owned by industrial concerns classified under 'Manufacturing'. See Ch. 8, sec. 4 for the pertinent data relating to the extent of such ownership, as evidenced by depletion charges.

reasons—are 'really' lower than those which prevail in Manufacturing, Trade and Finance (see Ch. 25).

In Finance and Trading, on the whole, the rate of return is around 6 or 7 per cent. Table 3 gives the detailed data.

TABLE 3

ESTIMATED EARNINGS RATES, ALL CORPORATIONS BY INDUSTRIAL DIVISIONS, 1924–28

(before and after Federal income tax) [1]

	1924	1925	1926	1927	1928
Manufacturing					
Percentage income to capitalization					
before tax	7.8	8.8	8.7	7.2	8.7
after tax	6.7	7.6	7.5	6.2	7.6
Percentage profit to total capital					
before tax	.7.6	8.5	8.4	7.1	8.3
after tax	6.6	7.5	7.4	6.1	7.4
Number of corporations	86,803	88,674	93,244	89,816	91,573
Trade					
Percentage income to capitalization					
before tax	7.1	8.5	7.1	6.6	7.3
after tax	6.1	7.3	6.0	5.5	6.4
Percentage profit to total capital					
before tax	7.1	8.2	7.0	6.5	7.2
after tax	6.1	7.2	6.0	5.5	6.3
Number of corporations	105,323	109,588	112,705	119,678	126,347
Finance					
Percentage income to capitalization					
before tax	5.5	8.0	6.8	6.9	7.5
after tax	5.0	7.2	6.1	6.3	6.9
Percentage profit to total capital					
before tax	5.5	7.5	6.5	6.7	7.1
after tax	5.1	6.9	6.0	6.1	6.6
Number of corporations	104,761	115,947	130,433	122,682	129,139
Mining					
Percentage income to capitalization					
before tax	−0.1	2.7	3.5	1.1	2.3
after tax	−0.3	2.2	2.9	0.7	1.8
Percentage profit to total capital					
before tax	0.7	2.9	3.7	1.5	2.6
after tax	0.5	2.6	3.2	1.2	2.2
Number of corporations	18,453	19,163	19,252	13,036	12,933

[1] See Chapter 43 for description of method.

A GENERAL VIEW OF INDUSTRY   [55]

The aggregate capitalization of the Finance division is from 21 to 33 billion dollars in the years 1924–28, while the entrepreneurial investment in Trade is from 12 to 14 billion.

The immediately foregoing figures are for the inclusive

CHART 1

PERCENTAGE OF NET INCOME TO CAPITALIZATION, 3,144 CORPORATIONS BY INDUSTRIAL DIVISIONS, 1919-28

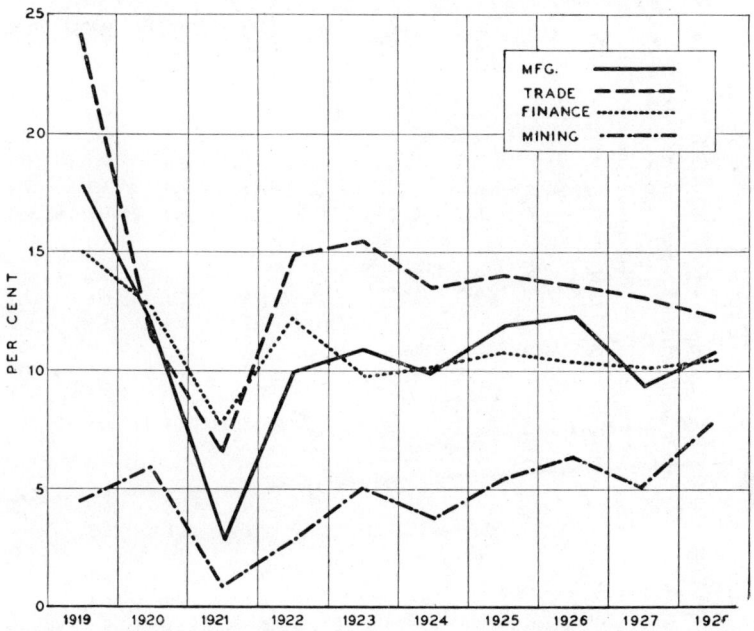

group: all of the country's corporations in the four fields in question, for the five years 1924–28. But for the 3,144 companies representing large-scale industry, we again have a ten-year series, running from 1919 through 1928. These data are presented in Table 4 and Chart 1. Here the Manufacturing division earns from 10 to 12 per cent in most

Table 4
EARNINGS RATES, 3,144 CORPORATIONS BY INDUSTRIAL DIVISIONS, 1919–28 and 1924–28
(before and after Federal income tax)

	1919	1920	1921	1922	1923	1924	1925	1926	1927	1928
	Percentage income to capitalization									
Manufacturing: 2,046 corporations										
before tax	18.3	12.3	2.9	10.2	11.2	10.0	12.1	12.4	9.5	11.0
after tax	13.1	9.6	1.9	9.1	10.0	8.9	10.7	11.0	8.4	9.8
Trade: 664 corporations										
before tax	24.2	11.4	6.6	14.9	15.4	13.4	14.0	13.6	13.1	12.3
after tax	17.1	8.6	4.9	13.3	13.7	11.8	12.2	11.8	11.4	10.9
Finance: 346 corporations										
before tax	15.0	12.6	7.8	12.2	9.8	10.2	10.8	10.4	10.2	10.4
after tax	13.2	10.9	7.0	11.3	9.2	9.4	9.8	9.5	9.3	9.5
Mining: 88 corporations										
before tax	4.5	6.0	.9	2.9	5.1	3.7	5.4	6.4	5.1	7.9
after tax	3.8	4.7	.5	2.5	4.6	3.2	4.8	5.7	4.5	7.2
	Percentage profit to total capital									
Manufacturing										
before tax						9.5	11.4	11.7	9.0	10.4
after tax						8.5	10.2	10.4	8.0	9.3
Trade										
before tax						13.0	13.4	13.1	12.6	11.7
after tax						11.4	11.7	11.4	11.0	10.5
Finance										
before tax						9.9	10.3	10.1	10.0	9.9
after tax						9.2	9.4	9.3	9.1	9.1
Mining										
before tax						3.9	5.3	6.2	5.1	7.5
after tax						3.5	4.8	5.6	4.5	6.9

A GENERAL VIEW OF INDUSTRY [57]

good years, Trade from 13 to 15 per cent, Finance about 10 per cent, and Mining 3 to 6 per cent.

Of especial interest in connection with the ten-year record of these large corporations is the aggregate result for each division over the entire period. This 'year-in-year-out' ratio of net income to capitalization for Manufacturing is 10.8 per cent, for Trade, 13.6 per cent, for Finance, 10.7 per cent, and for Mining, 4.9 per cent.

4. EARNINGS OF CORPORATIONS WITH NET INCOMES

For all of the country's corporations from 1924 through 1928, and for our 3,144 large corporations from 1919 through 1928, the average rates of earnings just discussed include the losses of the unsuccessful, subtracted from the gains of the successful. But in a competitive system of industry the number of corporations failing to earn net incomes in some years is almost as large as that with net incomes.[8] This is not to say that the total losses by any means equal the gains—or the aggregate rate of return on capital would of course be *nil*. Nor is it to say that either half the gross *business* done, or half the *capital* employed, fails to retain a 'net'.[9] It remains true, however, that the inclusion of data for the 'no net' firms with those for the 'with net' corporations greatly lowers the general figure, and that the rate of return as thus compiled is, like most broad arithmetic averages of this type, a somewhat abstract datum. For these reasons it is of interest to examine separately the higher rates of return which prevail for the corporations that do earn net incomes.

[8] More accurately, in prosperous years about two-fifths of the corporations engaged in competitive industry fail to return a net, at least as defined for purposes of the Federal income tax (see Ch. 43).
[9] See Ch. 43 and 47 for a discussion of these two points.

[58]   INDUSTRIAL PROFITS

In all four divisions combined the country's entire group of something over 200,000 corporations with net incomes earns, in prosperous years, about 11 per cent instead of 7 per cent upon capitalization. In each division the figure in round numbers is as follows: Manufacturing, 12 per cent instead of 9; Trade, 12 per cent instead of 7; Finance, 11 per cent instead of 7; Mining, 7 to 10 per cent instead of 2 or 3.[10] Details appear in Tables 5 and 6.

TABLE 5

ESTIMATED EARNINGS RATES, ALL CORPORATIONS WITH NET INCOMES IN MANUFACTURING, TRADE, FINANCE AND MINING, 1926–28

(before and after Federal income tax) [1]

	1926	1927	1928
Percentage income to capitalization			
before tax	11.8	10.7	11.4
after tax	10.5	9.6	10.3
Percentage profit to total capital			
before tax	11.2	10.2	10.7
after tax	10.0	9.2	9.8
Number of corporations	209,322	211,699	220,250

[1] See Chapter 43 for description of the method. Absolute figures in Appendix Table 3.

TABLE 6

ESTIMATED EARNINGS RATES, ALL CORPORATIONS WITH NET INCOMES IN MANUFACTURING, TRADE, FINANCE AND MINING, BY INDUSTRIAL DIVISIONS, 1926–28

(before and after Federal income tax) [1]

	1926	1927	1928
Manufacturing			
Percentage income to capitalization			
before tax	12.3	10.9	12.0
after tax	10.9	9.7	10.7

[10] The data for Mining fluctuate from year to year. It again is to be recalled that much mining activity is classed under manufacturing, as stated in Ch. 8, sec. 4.

A GENERAL VIEW OF INDUSTRY [59]

TABLE 6 *(continued)*

ESTIMATED EARNINGS RATES *(before and after Federal income tax)*[1]

	1926	1927	1928
Percentage profit to total capital			
before tax	11.8	10.5	11.4
after tax	10.4	9.3	10.2
Number of corporations	55,094	53,620	55,007

Trade

Percentage income to capitalization			
before tax	11.8	11.2	11.7
after tax	10.4	9.9	10.7
Percentage profit to total capital			
before tax	11.5	10.9	11.3
after tax	10.2	9.7	10.3
Number of corporations	71,403	74,747	79,745

Finance

Percentage income to capitalization			
before tax	11.0	10.9	11.0
after tax	10.1	10.0	10.1
Percentage profit to total capital			
before tax	10.1	10.0	10.1
after tax	9.4	9.3	9.4
Number of corporations	76,819	78,100	80,315

Mining

Percentage income to capitalization			
before tax	10.2	7.4	7.8
after tax	9.1	6.6	7.1
Percentage profit to total capital			
before tax	9.8	7.2	7.5
after tax	8.7	6.5	6.9
Number of corporations	6,006	5,232	5,183

[1] See Chapter 43 for description of the method.

A ten-year series for these same data is desirable, but is available only upon the basis of a sample representing corporations with absolute net incomes of over $2,000, and in the Manufacturing division only.[11] This series is shown in

[11] Ten-year series for corporations with net incomes in Trade, Finance and

[60] INDUSTRIAL PROFITS

Table 7. In all years except 1919 and 1921 the return is around 12 per cent. For the entire ten years aggregated it is 12.3 per cent.

TABLE 7

EARNINGS RATES, MANUFACTURING CORPORATIONS WITH NET INCOMES OF OVER $2,000, 1919–28 [1]

(before Federal income tax)

YEAR	PERCENTAGE INCOME TO CAPITALIZATION
1919	19.1
1920	13.8
1921	7.8
1922	11.4
1923	12.2
1924	10.7
1925	12.5
1926	12.9
1927	10.9
1928	12.2

[1] Absolute figures in Appendix Table 4. The number of corporations varies in different years as explained in Chapter 43.

5. FREQUENCY DISTRIBUTIONS OF INDIVIDUAL EARNINGS RATES

But all of the general data given thus far remain arithmetic means. They are weighted, to be sure, by the relative preponderance of capital and income prevailing between the several divisions, but they are still simply general averages. For numerous purposes far more precise information concerning the typical earnings of corporate enterprise is supplied by ranges, medians and other measures of the distribution of individual earnings rates among the multitude

Mining are shown in Ch. 21–26, but only for large corporations. In the series presented in Table 7 sample figures for large and small corporations are combined into a weighted average, as explained in Appendix A.

A GENERAL VIEW OF INDUSTRY [61]

of corporations which make up this general or composite picture; and we may now present in summary form these estimated frequency distributions.[12]

Take first the distribution for Manufacturing. About half of the 53,000 manufacturing corporations in the United States that enjoyed net incomes in 1925, 1926 or 1928 earned profits at individual rates of over 10 per cent upon their invested capitals. The lower fourth of these 53,000 companies earned under 5 per cent; the upper fourth, over 18 per cent. The figures hold about equally well for each of the three prosperous years in question, 1925, 1926 and 1928; and they are not greatly different even for 1927.

To recapitulate, in prosperous years the arithmetic mean return for all Manufacturing corporations is about 9 per cent, while for those 'with net' it is about 12 per cent. Of the concerns with net incomes, *half earn over 10 per cent*, while *one-fourth earn over 18 per cent*. The interquartile range [13] runs from 5 to 18 per cent. In absolute terms, about 27,000 manufacturing corporations earn over 10 per cent, 13,000 earn over 18 per cent, 5,000 earn over 30 per cent, but only 2,500 earn over 40 per cent. Further information

[12] Those for Manufacture and Trade have been developed upon the basis of data compiled from a total of some 25,000 individual corporate records in the four years 1925–28; that is to say, about 4,000 manufacturing and 2,000 trading corporations are included in the original samples of those divisions in each year. The final distributions are estimates in the sense that the frequencies of the original samples have been expanded or 'stepped up' to represent the entire group or 'universe' of the country's corporations with net incomes in the case of Manufacturing, and the entire group of Trading corporations with net incomes of over $2,000. The results, however, both in absolute and percentage terms, are probably subject to rather slight margins of error. See Ch. 43 for a full explanation of the 'stepping up' method employed. The distributions for Finance and Mining are less comprehensive; they represent only large corporations and are presented in their simple form—that is to say, no 'stepping up' of the frequencies is attempted.

[13] That is the distance or spread between the two figures ('quartiles') standing one-fourth of the way up or down from the top and bottom of the list respectively.

is given in Table 8, which shows the distributions of the absolute figures in detail, while Chart 2 presents them in the form of a block diagram.

CHART 2

FREQUENCY DISTRIBUTIONS OF EARNING RATES,
ALL MANUFACTURING CORPORATIONS WITH NET INCOMES, 1925-1928

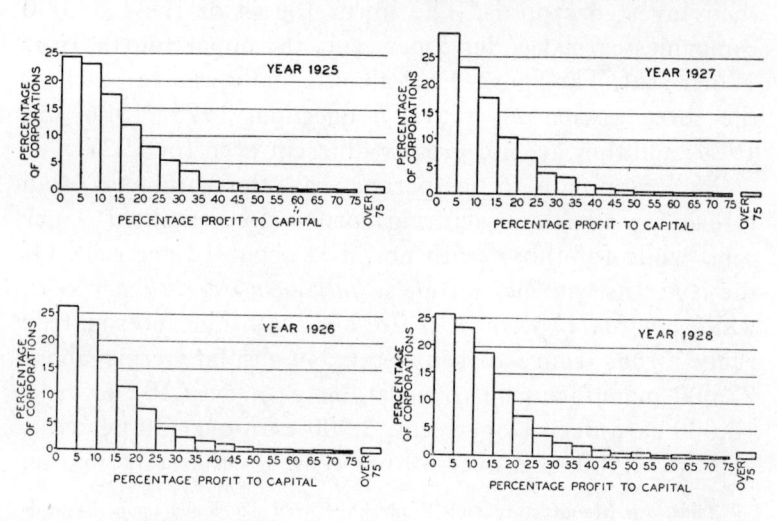

For Trade similar data are not available for all 'with net' corporations, but only for those with incomes over $2,000. For this group the lower quartile is regularly 8 per cent, the median is 13 per cent, and the upper quartile, in each year, either 20 or 21 per cent. To make possible a valid comparison of Trading with Manufacturing, the Manufacturing distribution has been recomputed so as also to include only corporations with net incomes of over $2,-000. When this is done, the three quartiles become almost exactly the same as those for Trade: 8 per cent, 13 per

TABLE 8
FREQUENCY DISTRIBUTIONS OF EARNINGS RATES, MANUFACTURING CORPORATIONS WITH NET INCOMES, 1925-28

(A) ABSOLUTE NUMBER OF CORPORATIONS SHOWING GIVEN RATES OF PROFIT
(B) PERCENTAGE OF CORPORATIONS SHOWING GIVEN RATES OF PROFIT

PERCENTAGE PROFIT TO TOTAL CAPITAL	1925	1926	1927	1928	1925 % in each class	1925 accum.	1926 % in each class	1926 accum.	1927 % in each class	1927 accum.	1928 % in each class	1928 accum.
Under 5	12,915	14,352	15,204	13,920	24.2	24.2	26.6	26.6	29.2	29.2	25.7	25.7
5 to 9	12,240	12,575	12,030	12,572	23.0	47.2	23.3	49.9	23.1	52.3	23.2	48.9
10 to 14	9,255	9,263	9,216	10,184	17.4	64.6	17.1	67.0	17.7	70.0	18.8	67.7
15 to 19	6,401	6,318	5,346	6,176	12.0	76.6	11.7	78.7	10.3	80.3	11.4	79.1
20 to 24	4,309	4,201	3,527	3,908	8.1	84.7	7.8	86.5	6.8	87.1	7.2	86.3
25 to 29	2,874	2,138	2,104	2,040	5.4	90.1	4.0	90.5	4.0	91.1	3.8	90.1
30 to 34	1,823	1,429	1,628	1,428	3.4	93.5	2.6	93.1	3.1	94.2	2.6	92.7
35 to 39	867	1,087	890	1,052	1.6	95.1	2.0	95.1	1.7	95.9	2.0	94.7
40 to 44	743	767	648	596	1.4	96.5	1.4	96.5	1.2	97.1	1.1	95.8
45 to 49	485	469	492	428	.9	97.4	.9	97.4	.9	98.0	.8	96.6
50 to 54	353	224	217	500	.7	98.1	.4	97.8	.4	98.4	.9	97.5
55 to 59	203	283	209	220	.4	98.5	.5	98.3	.4	98.8	.4	97.9
60 to 64	99	113	133	288	.2	98.7	.2	98.5	.3	99.1	.5	98.4
65 to 69	92	136	166	136	.2	98.9	.3	98.8	.3	99.4	.3	98.7
70 to 74	65	133	40	104	.1	99.0	.2	99.0	.1	99.5	.2	98.9
75 and over	533	532	301	620	1.0	100.0	1.0	100.0	.5	100.0	1.1	100.0
Total number of corporations	53,257	54,020	52,151	54,172								

cent (median) and 21 per cent respectively. Further details are afforded by Tables 9 and 10.

TABLE 9

FREQUENCY DISTRIBUTIONS OF EARNINGS RATES, TRADING CORPORATIONS WITH NET INCOMES OF OVER $2,000, 1925–28

(A) ABSOLUTE NUMBER OF CORPORATIONS SHOWING GIVEN RATES OF PROFIT

PERCENTAGE PROFIT TO TOTAL CAPITAL	1925	1926	1927	1928
Under 5	3,000	3,010	3,080	3,160
5 to 9	8,205	7,710	9,420	7,465
10 to 14	7,860	6,800	7,380	6,635
15 to 19	5,100	4,035	4,680	4,400
20 to 24	2,855	2,655	2,715	3,100
25 to 29	1,835	1,270	1,570	1,380
30 to 34	1,045	1,315	1,175	1,060
35 to 39	740	865	750	800
40 to 44	715	450	365	480
45 to 49	440	425	300	290
50 to 54	240	370	260	260
55 to 59	160	260	185	245
60 to 64	200	65	200	280
65 to 69	180	65	80	100
70 to 74	100	80	80	60
75 and over	450	425	580	280
Total number of corporations	33,125	29,800	32,820	29,995

(B) PERCENTAGE OF CORPORATIONS SHOWING GIVEN RATES OF PROFIT

PERCENTAGE PROFIT TO TOTAL CAPITAL	1925 PERCENTAGE IN EACH CLASS	1925 ACCUMULATED BY SUCCESSIVE CLASSES	1926 PERCENTAGE IN EACH CLASS	1926 ACCUMULATED BY SUCCESSIVE CLASSES	1927 PERCENTAGE IN EACH CLASS	1927 ACCUMULATED BY SUCCESSIVE CLASSES	1928 PERCENTAGE IN EACH CLASS	1928 ACCUMULATED BY SUCCESSIVE CLASSES
Under 5	9.1	9.1	10.1	10.1	9.4	9.4	10.5	10.5
5 to 9	24.8	33.9	25.9	36.0	28.7	38.1	24.9	35.4
10 to 14	23.7	57.6	22.8	58.8	22.5	60.6	22.1	57.5
15 to 19	15.4	73.0	13.5	72.3	14.2	74.8	14.7	72.2
20 to 24	8.6	81.6	8.9	81.2	8.3	83.1	10.3	82.5
25 to 29	5.5	87.1	4.3	85.5	4.8	87.9	4.6	87.1

TABLE 9 *(continued)*

(B) PERCENTAGE OF CORPORATIONS SHOWING GIVEN RATES OF PROFIT

PERCENTAGE PROFIT TO TOTAL CAPITAL	1925 PERCENTAGE IN EACH CLASS	1925 ACCUMULATED BY SUCCESSIVE CLASSES	1926 PERCENTAGE IN EACH CLASS	1926 ACCUMULATED BY SUCCESSIVE CLASSES	1927 PERCENTAGE IN EACH CLASS	1927 ACCUMULATED BY SUCCESSIVE CLASSES	1928 PERCENTAGE IN EACH CLASS	1928 ACCUMULATED BY SUCCESSIVE CLASSES
30 to 34	3.2	90.3	4.4	89.9	3.6	91.5	3.5	90.6
35 to 39	2.2	92.5	2.9	92.8	2.3	93.8	2.7	93.3
40 to 44	2.2	94.7	1.5	94.3	1.1	94.9	1.6	94.9
45 to 49	1.3	96.0	1.4	95.7	.9	95.8	1.0	95.9
50 to 54	.7	96.7	1.3	97.0	.8	96.6	.9	96.8
55 to 59	.5	97.2	.9	97.9	.6	97.2	.8	97.6
60 to 64	.6	97.8	.2	98.1	.6	97.8	.9	98.5
65 to 69	.5	98.3	.2	98.3	.2	98.0	.3	98.8
70 to 74	.3	98.6	.3	98.6	.2	98.2	.2	99.0
75 and over	1.4	100.0	1.4	100.0	1.8	100.0	1.0	100.0

TABLE 10

FREQUENCY DISTRIBUTIONS OF EARNINGS RATES, MANUFACTURING CORPORATIONS WITH NET INCOMES OF OVER $2,000, 1925–28

(A) ABSOLUTE NUMBER OF CORPORATIONS SHOWING GIVEN RATES OF PROFIT

PERCENTAGE PROFIT TO TOTAL CAPITAL	1925	1926	1927	1928
Under 5	3,412	4,388	4,804	4,944
5 to 9	8,155	8,561	8,580	8,220
10 to 14	7,664	7,625	7,616	8,184
15 to 19	5,756	5,310	4,696	5,312
20 to 24	3,922	3,697	3,052	3,412
25 to 29	2,358	1,796	1,804	1,672
30 to 34	1,608	1,267	1,428	1,140
35 to 39	824	907	740	892
40 to 44	614	677	548	500
45 to 49	356	433	392	412
50 to 54	353	188	192	420
55 to 59	203	229	184	188
60 to 64	99	77	108	288
65 to 69	92	118	116	104
70 to 74	65	115	40	88
75 and over	318	488	276	524
Total number of corporations	35,799	35,876	34,576	36,300

Table 10 (continued)

(B) PERCENTAGE OF CORPORATIONS SHOWING GIVEN RATES OF PROFIT

PERCENTAGE PROFIT TO TOTAL CAPITAL	1925 PERCENTAGE IN EACH CLASS	1925 ACCUMULATED BY SUCCESSIVE CLASSES	1926 PERCENTAGE IN EACH CLASS	1926 ACCUMULATED BY SUCCESSIVE CLASSES	1927 PERCENTAGE IN EACH CLASS	1927 ACCUMULATED BY SUCCESSIVE CLASSES	1928 PERCENTAGE IN EACH CLASS	1928 ACCUMULATED BY SUCCESSIVE CLASSES
Under 5	9.5	9.5	12.2	12.2	13.9	13.9	13.6	13.6
5 to 9	22.8	32.3	23.9	36.1	24.9	38.7	22.7	36.3
10 to 14	21.4	53.7	21.3	57.4	22.0	60.7	22.6	58.9
15 to 19	16.1	69.8	14.8	72.2	13.6	74.3	14.6	73.5
20 to 24	10.9	80.7	10.3	82.5	8.8	83.1	9.4	82.9
25 to 29	6.6	87.3	5.0	87.5	5.2	88.3	4.6	87.5
30 to 34	4.5	91.8	3.5	91.0	4.2	92.5	3.1	90.6
35 to 39	2.3	94.1	2.5	93.5	2.1	94.6	2.5	93.1
40 to 44	1.7	95.8	1.9	95.4	1.6	96.2	1.4	94.5
45 to 49	1.0	96.8	1.2	96.6	1.1	97.3	1.1	95.6
50 to 54	1.0	97.8	.5	97.1	.6	97.9	1.2	96.8
55 to 59	.6	98.4	.7	97.8	.6	98.5	.5	97.3
60 to 64	.3	98.7	.2	98.0	.3	98.8	.8	98.1
65 to 69	.2	98.9	.3	98.3	.3	99.1	.3	98.4
70 to 74	.2	99.1	.3	98.6	.1	99.2	.2	98.6
75 and over	.9	100.0	1.4	100.0	.8	100.0	1.4	100.0

For Finance and Mining sample data relating only to large corporations [14] are available. The quartiles for Finance, in each year of the period 1925–28, are approximately as follows: 7 per cent; 11 per cent (median); 14 per cent. For Mining they run (varying in different years) 5 to 7 per cent; 11 to 13 per cent (median); and 17 to 21 per cent.[15]

The several quartiles just enumerated pertain to the groups of corporations earning net incomes only, or to

---

[14] Those of the 3,144 corporations series for which arithmetic averages were previously presented. There are only 344 Financial and 82 Mining corporations in these two distributions (that is, in 1925; in other years some slight variation from these numbers occurs).

[15] The complete distributions are given in Ch. 26 and 25.

A GENERAL VIEW OF INDUSTRY [67]

parts of those groups. But it is, of course, to be remembered that in all instances these groups comprise only a portion of the total number of corporations if those with net losses as well as net incomes are considered. To facilitate the analysis of similar frequencies for 'all corporations', in this inclusive sense, Table 11 repeats the quartiles for Manufacturing and then gives in parallel columns these data converted into percentiles, for the 'with net' group alone and

TABLE 11

PERCENTAGES OF MANUFACTURING CORPORATIONS EARNING LESS THAN GIVEN RATES OF PROFIT UPON CAPITAL, 1925–28 [1]

RATE OF PROFIT UPON CAPITAL	PERCENTAGE OF CORPORATIONS WITH NET INCOMES	PERCENTAGE OF ALL CORPORATIONS
1925		
5.17%	25	54.7
10.80%	50	69.8
19.33%	75	84.8
Total number of corporations	53,527	88,674
1926		
4.71%	25	56.5
10.05%	50	71.0
18.43%	75	85.5
Total number of corporations	54,020	93,244
1927		
4.29%	25	56.4
9.52%	50	71.0
17.49%	75	85.5
Total number of corporations	52,151	89,816
1928		
4.87%	25	55.6
10.29%	50	70.4
18.20%	75	85.2
Total number of corporations	54,172	91,573

[1] The 'given rates of profit' are in each year the first, second and third quartiles for the distribution of the corporations with net incomes.

[68] INDUSTRIAL PROFITS

for 'all corporations'. The last column of the table shows, in other words, the proportions of *all* corporations earning either losses or net incomes at rates lower than the quartile figures for the 'with net' group.

This analysis—taking *all* corporations, whether they earned net incomes or not—shows that about two-fifths of the 90,000 companies engaged in Manufacturing suffer losses [16] in prosperous years such as 1925, 1926, 1927 and 1928. About one-half, including the two-fifths just mentioned, earn under 5 per cent. Nearly one-third of the total number earn over 10 per cent; but only about one-sixth earn over 18 per cent. Unfortunately, similar analyses cannot be made with any great exactness for Trade, Finance or Mining.

6. SUMMARY

In years of prosperity all corporations in Manufacture, Trade, Finance and Mining average a total net income of 7 per cent upon their capitalization. In years of severe depression this falls as low as two or two and one-half per cent. The larger corporations, those with capitals of over $500,000 [17] earn from 9 to 11 per cent in prosperous years.

[16] These, it should be remarked, are losses as shown in, and allowed by, Federal income tax schedules; that is to say, the number of Manufacturing corporations showing no net incomes is taken from *Statistics of Income* (Bureau of Internal Revenue) and is then combined with the expanded data of our several samples of corporations with positive total net incomes to yield the dispersion measurements (percentiles) for the entire universe, as shown in Table 11. The term 'net income' as here applied to the corporations showing losses is *taxable net income*, whereas applied to the corporations of our sample data it is *total net income*. In the main, however, and for the purpose at hand, the difference is not appreciable; see Ch. 43 for a full discussion of the point.

[17] This figure is approximately the ninth (lowest) decil of the array of individual total capital figures for the 2,046 manufacturing companies belonging to the 3,144 corporations series in 1927, as stated in note 4; see also Ch. 43.

In good years and bad alike the aggregate return for this group over the ten-year period 1919–28 is 10.5 per cent. Of all Manufacturing corporations with net incomes one-quarter earn profits of under 5 per cent upon their individual capitals in prosperous years; another two-quarters earn from 6 to 18 per cent, with a median of 10 per cent; while the highest quarter earn over 18 per cent.

CHAPTER 3

EARNINGS RATES IN DIFFERENT INDUSTRIES

1. VARIATION IN PARTICULAR YEARS

IF ONE takes any single year of the period 1919–28 and examines the rates of net income upon capitalization earned by the numerous specific industries into which Manufacture, Trade, Finance and Mining can be divided, he finds a substantial variation. The purpose of the present chapter is to examine the discrepancies that prevail in individual years and to see if they disappear over a period.

In 1919, a year of pronounced post-War prosperity, the average return for the 3,144 Manufacturing, Trading, Financial and Mining corporations belonging to our ten-year series[1] was 17.7 per cent.[2] Dividing Manufacture, Trade, Finance and Mining, however, into specific individual industries or trades such as Bakery Products, Castings and Forgings, or Department Stores, we obtain 73 groups in Manufacturing, 22 in Trade, 5 in Finance, and 6 in Mining, or 106 separate groups in all. These we may call either

---

[1] The larger corporations for which average figures were discussed in the preceding chapter.

[2] This is not precisely equal to the average given in Ch. 2, Table 2. That figure, 17.1 per cent, was a deliberately weighted average, applied to the sample for the four divisions (see note 5, Ch. 2). The present average of 17.7 per cent is weighted only because it is an aggregate, i.e., is weighted only in the first of the three senses described in note 6. Deliberate weighting of the present average was avoided because of the mathematical treatment to which data that were compared with it were subjected.

RATES IN DIFFERENT INDUSTRIES [71]

'industries' or 'minor groups'.[3] The number of corporations contained in each depends upon the nature of the group; it ranges from nine or ten in some groups to 100 or more in others.[4] But in every case, identical corporations are classified in the same groups from year to year. Corporations with losses as well as those with gains are thus included. The classification of industries is given in Table 12.[5]

Examining the average rates of return in these 106 industries during 1919, we find the median minor group earning 21.2 per cent, as compared with the arithmetic mean

[3] In contrast to the broader 'major groups', for example, Food Products, Metals or Retail Trade, to which they belong respectively and which are discussed in the next chapter.

[4] Three-quarters of the groups, however, contain 16 or more corporations each. The complete list is given in Table 12.

[5] *In toto,* of course, these 106 minor groups comprise the 3,144 companies series for which general averages were discussed in the preceding chapter. See, for qualifications, Ch. 43, 46.

It will also be noted in Table 12 that the numbering of the groups runs from 1 through 111. This is because of the necessity of combining several groups into miscellaneous categories in preparing the original *Source-Book* tables. The numbering scheme of the *Source-Book*, however, is retained in the present volume, although only 106 separate groups are available for analysis. (For illustration, consult Table 12 where Group 8 does not appear separately but is shown in combination with Group 11, as 'Group 11–8'.) The original Group 8 was Cane Sugar manufacturing, but the sample contained too few corporations to be significant as a separate classification, hence Cane Sugar was thrown into the Miscellaneous Food Products category.

It may here also be observed that in the analysis of these 106 groups, the term 'median industry' or 'median group' is often used because it has a less abstract connotation than merely 'the median' or 'median value'. By it is meant the industry that stands in the middle of the list when the 106 groups are arrayed according to their rates of return. To be sure, in an array containing an even number of items, such as 106, the mid-point is statistically not item 53 or 54 but 53½. But with the 53rd industry showing a return of perhaps 12.6 per cent and the 54th industry showing a return of 12.5, the median is taken as 12.6, which is the value obtained by rounding off 12.55 per cent.

When the upper or lower quarter of these 106 industries is discussed, reference is to the first 27 industries from the top or bottom of the list and not to an interpolated value.

Table 12

MINOR GROUP CLASSIFICATION, 3,144 CORPORATIONS, SHOWING SIZE OF SAMPLES

MINOR GROUP		NUMBER OF CORPO- RATIONS	MINOR GROUP		NUMBER OF CORPO- RATIONS
Manufacturing			35	Book and music publishing	17
1	Bakery products	17	36	Job printing	46
2	Flour	32	37	Miscellaneous printing and publishing	17
3	Confectionery	21			
4	Package foods	19	38	Crude chemicals	9
5	Dairying	26	39	Paints	42
6	Canned goods	16	40	Petroleum refining	52
7	Meat packing	23	41	Proprietary preparations	56
9	Beverages	11	42	Toilet preparations	9
10	Tobacco	23	43	Cleaning preparations	16
11–8	Miscellaneous food products	27	44	Miscellaneous chemicals	26
			45	Ceramics	48
12	Cotton spinning	12	46	Glass	18
13	Cotton converting	18	47	Portland cement	21
14	Cotton weaving	49	48	Miscellaneous stone and clay products	27
15	Weaving woolens	31			
16	Silk weaving	17	49	Casting and forgings	99
17	Carpets	18	50	Sheet metal	20
18	Men's clothing	25	51	Wire and nails	20
19	Knit goods	42	52	Heating machinery	42
20	Miscellaneous clothing	23	53	Electrical machinery	54
21	Miscellaneous textiles	54	54	Textile machinery	18
22	Boots and shoes	25	55	Printing machinery	12
23	Miscellaneous leather products	29	56	Road machinery	22
24	Rubber products	26	57	Engines	11
25	Lumber manufacture	64	58	Mining machinery	12
26	Planing mills	26	59	General factory machinery	23
27	Millwork	17			
28	Furniture (non-metal)	55	60	Office machinery	13
29	Miscellaneous lumber products	28	61	Railway equipment	25
			62	Motor vehicles	32
30	Blank paper	35	63	Firearms	11
31	Cardboard boxes	33	64	Hardware	40
32	Stationery	20	65	Tools	30
33	Miscellaneous paper products	23	66	Bolts and nuts	15
34	Newspapers and periodicals	20	67	Miscellaneous machinery	32
			68	Non-ferrous metals	48

TABLE 12 *(continued)*
MINOR GROUP CLASSIFICATION

MINOR GROUP		NUMBER OF CORPORATIONS	MINOR GROUP		NUMBER OF CORPORATIONS
Manufacturing (cont.)			91	Building material and hardware	13
69	Jewelry	24	92	Paper	18
70	Miscellaneous metal products	45	93–85	Miscellaneous wholesale trade	82
71	Scientific instruments	23	*Trade—Wholesale and Retatil*		
72	Toys	12	95	Commission dealers	
73	Pianos	11	96	Coal, wood and fuel	10
74	Miscellaneous special manufacturing	43	97	Hardware	16
Trade—Retail			98	Lumber	11
75	Automobiles	15	99–95	Miscellaneous wholesale and retail trade	52
76	Men's clothing	17	*Mining*		
77	Department stores	93	100	Bituminous coal	33
78	Drygoods	27	101	Gas and oil wells	11
79	Furniture	12	102	Stone quarrying	9
80	Groceries	14	103	Clay, sand and gravel	9
81	Jewelry	11	104	Metals, various	15
82	Building material and hardware	27	105	Miscellaneous mining, other than metal	11
83	Lumber and coal	15	*Finance*		
84	Miscellaneous retail trade	52	106	Savings banks	18
Trade—Wholesale			107	Commercial banks	30
85	Coal, fuel and wood		108	National banks	105
86	Drugs	25	109	Trust companies	56
87	Drygoods	29	110	Investments, various sorts	
88	Groceries	59	111–110	All other finance (except life insurance)	137
89	Hardware	43			
90	Importers and exporters	23			

figure of 17.7 per cent above cited. But some industries earn more than 40 per cent, while others earn less than 1 per cent. The upper quarter of these 106 industries all show rates of over 29 per cent; the lowest quarter, under 16 per cent. The average departure or 'spread' of all 106 minor groups above or below the median figure is 8.5 per cent[6]—

[6] The expression 'per cent' is here, of course, used in an absolute, not a

a spread equal to about two-fifths as much as the median itself. In appraising these figures, it is of course to be recalled that 1919 was an exceptionally prosperous year.

Turn, however, to a year of depression such as 1921. The median industry here earns only 7.1 per cent on its capitalization. Fifteen groups suffer actual losses. At the same time five others earn 20 per cent or more. The actual variation, in absolute terms, is less than in 1919; the average departure from the median is 5.2 per cent as against 8.5 per cent. But in relative terms the variation between these 106 industries in 1921 is substantially greater than in 1919; their average departure of about 5 per cent from the median represents an amount two-thirds as large as the median figure itself.

Finally, as a third example, take a prosperous year such as 1928. Here the median industry earns 11 per cent. The upper quarter earn 14.8 per cent or over; the lower quarter, 8.5 per cent or under. The average departure from the median is 3.8 per cent, a smaller figure than in either 1919 or 1921. Even so, it amounts to about one-third of the median figure.

These three distributions of earnings rates, together with those for other years, are shown in Chart 3. *In no year is anything approaching a uniformity of return seen between the different industries,* although it is true that in the last

relative, sense. The rate of return upon which attention is fastened in this chapter is the percentage of total net income to capitalization. In some ways, the rate of total profits to total capital (as these terms are defined in Ch. 2 and in the Glossary) would be preferable as a measure of comparative earning power. It is not employed in this chapter because our data show funded debt figures only for 1924–28, and ten-year comparisons are thus not available in terms other than those of total income upon capitalization. The two ratios, however, are not very different for the purpose in hand. On the close correspondence between them see Table 4, Ch. 2; also Ch. 8.

five years of the period the majority (slightly over half) of those 106 minor groups earn between 8 and 15 per cent.[7] The earnings rates of each individual industry, for 1921 and 1928, are given in Table 13.[8]

TABLE 13

EARNINGS RATES, 106 MINOR GROUPS IN 1921 AND 1928, RANGED IN ORDER OF PROFITABLENESS FROM THE LOWEST TO THE HIGHEST FIGURES

Trade Groups are Distinguished from Manufacturing by the Letters R (Retail), W (Wholesale) or W—R (Wholesale and Retail)

1921 PERCENTAGE INCOME TO CAPITALIZATION	1928 PERCENTAGE INCOME TO CAPITALIZATION
−12.6 Rubber products	1.3 Rubber products
−12.4 Sheet metals	1.5 Weaving woolens
−7.0 Meat packing	3.4 Railway equipment
−6.6 Miscellaneous leather products	4.5 W—Building material and hardware
−5.4 Miscellaneous food products	4.5 Bituminous coal
−3.1 Tools	4.6 Meat packing
−2.9 Miscellaneous metal products	4.7 Cotton weaving
−2.7 W—Paper	4.7 Silk weaving
−2.6 Miscellaneous machinery	5.1 Miscellaneous leather products
−2.5 Stationery	5.1 Blank paper
−2.3 Metals, various	5.1 W—R Lumber
−1.8 Bolts and nuts	5.8 Gas and oil wells
−1.5 W—Hardware	5.9 Pianos
−0.4 Castings and forgings	6.0 Castings and forgings
−0.4 Wire and nails	6.7 Carpets
0.8 Cardboard boxes	6.8 Lumber manufacture
0.9 Beverages	6.9 Engines
1.1 Gas and oil wells	7.4 Groceries
1.4 Miscellaneous R—Trade	

[7] The shape of the distributions varies somewhat from year to year, although in several years a rough approach to symmetry is approximated. Whether or not a symmetrical pattern would be approximated more closely if the samples were larger is debatable; but even so, the ranges of variation would scarcely be narrowed. As to the degree of reliability attaching to the present samples, see Ch. 43–45.

[8] Data for other years may be found in the chapters which contain detailed discussion of particular major and minor groups (the several chapters of Book II).

TABLE 13 *(continued)*

EARNINGS RATES, FROM THE LOWEST TO THE HIGHEST FIGURES

1921 PERCENTAGE INCOME TO CAPITALIZATION	1928 PERCENTAGE INCOME TO CAPITALIZATION
1.5 Miscellaneous stone and clay products	7.6 W—R Hardware
1.8 Millwork	7.7 Miscellaneous textiles
1.9 Blank paper	7.9 Miscellaneous mining, other than metal
1.9 Hardware	8.1 Commercial banks
1.9 Non-ferrous metals	8.3 Cotton converting
2.0 Miscellaneous W—Trade	8.3 Millwork
2.0 W—R Hardware	8.4 R—Building material and hardware
2.1 Firearms	8.4 W—Drygoods
2.1 Jewelry	8.5 Planing mills
2.3 Pianos	8.5 Ceramics
2.5 Lumber manufacture	8.5 Metals, various
2.5 W—Building material and hardware	8.6 Beverages
2.6 Groceries	8.6 W—Hardware
3.4 Mining machinery	8.7 Miscellaneous W—Trade
3.8 General factory machinery	9.0 Miscellaneous paper products
4.2 R—Lumber and coal	9.2 Heating machinery
4.3 Miscellaneous clothing	9.4 Miscellaneous food products
4.3 Railway equipment	9.4 R—Department stores
4.7 R—Jewelry	9.4 National banks
4.9 Paints	9.5 Cotton spinning
5.1 Heating machinery	9.7 Dairying
5.3 Miscellaneous paper products	9.7 Miscellaneous W—R Trade
5.3 Miscellaneous chemicals	9.8 Petroleum refining
5.9 Stone quarrying	9.8 R—Furniture
6.0 All other finance (except life insurance)	10.1 Miscellaneous lumber products
	10.2 Mining machinery
6.1 W—Drygoods	10.2 W—Paper
6.4 Ceramics	10.4 W—Drugs
6.4 Electrical machinery	10.5 Furniture (non-metal)
6.4 Office machinery	10.5 Stationery
6.6 Confectionery	10.6 R—Lumber and coal
6.6 Crude chemicals	10.7 W—Importers and exporters
6.7 Men's clothing	10.8 W—R Coal, wood and fuel
6.8 R—Building material and hardware	10.8 Stone quarrying
	10.9 Trust companies
7.0 W—R Coal, wood and fuel	11.0 Hardware
7.2 Trust companies	11.2 Knit goods
7.3 W—R Lumber	11.2 Savings banks

TABLE 13 (continued)
EARNINGS RATES, FROM THE LOWEST TO THE HIGHEST FIGURES

1921
PERCENTAGE INCOME TO CAPITALIZATION

- 7.6 W—Drugs
- 8.0 Miscellaneous lumber products
- 8.1 Portland cement
- 8.1 Clay, sand and gravel
- 8.3 Dairying
- 8.3 Silk weaving
- 8.3 Cleaning preparations
- 8.4 Furniture (non-metal)
- 8.4 Motor vehicles
- 8.5 Printing machinery
- 8.7 Road machinery
- 8.9 Flour
- 9.0 Bituminous coal
- 9.0 National banks
- 9.1 Canned goods
- 9.1 R—Men's clothing
- 9.2 W—Importers and exporters
- 9.4 Cotton weaving
- 9.4 Engines
- 9.5 Glass
- 9.9 Planing mills
- 10.3 R—Furniture
- 10.4 Cotton spinning
- 10.6 Miscellaneous special manufacturing
- 10.7 Miscellaneous W—R Trade
- 11.1 R—Automobiles
- 11.2 Toys
- 11.4 Weaving woolens
- 11.4 Boots and shoes
- 11.4 Proprietary preparations
- 11.4 Savings banks
- 11.6 Commercial banks
- 11.7 R—Drygoods
- 11.9 Cotton converting
- 12.2 Miscellaneous textiles
- 12.6 R—Department stores
- 13.0 Miscellaneous mining, other than metal
- 13.1 Tobacco

1928
PERCENTAGE INCOME TO CAPITALIZATION

- 11.4 Men's clothing
- 11.8 Glass
- 11.8 Sheet metal
- 11.9 Crude chemicals
- 11.9 R—Drygoods
- 11.9 All other finance (except life insurance)
- 12.0 Flour
- 12.1 Book and music publishing
- 12.1 Jewelry
- 12.3 Printing machinery
- 12.4 Miscellaneous clothing
- 12.4 Miscellaneous special manufacturing
- 12.5 Clay, sand and gravel
- 12.6 R—Men's clothing
- 12.7 Canned goods
- 12.8 Cardboard boxes
- 12.8 Portland cement
- 13.4 General factory machinery
- 13.5 Miscellaneous machinery
- 13.8 Wire and nails
- 13.9 Job printing
- 14.6 Textile machinery
- 14.8 Boots and shoes
- 14.8 Paints
- 14.8 Non-ferrous metals
- 15.1 Confectionery
- 15.1 R—Jewelry
- 15.2 Tools
- 15.2 Miscellaneous R—Trade
- 15.6 Tobacco
- 15.6 Miscellaneous metal products
- 16.1 Motor vehicles
- 16.1 Toys
- 16.5 Electrical machinery
- 17.0 Road machinery
- 17.1 Miscellaneous printing and publishing

TABLE 13 *(continued)*

EARNINGS RATES, FROM THE LOWEST TO THE HIGHEST FIGURES

1921 PERCENTAGE INCOME TO CAPITALIZATION	*1928* PERCENTAGE INCOME TO CAPITALIZATION
13.1 Job printing	17.1 Miscellaneous clay and stone products
13.1 Scientific instruments	
13.5 Book and music publishing	17.5 Bakery products
14.5 Petroleum refining	17.6 Package foods
14.9 Package foods	17.7 Office machinery
15.0 Bakery products	17.8 Miscellaneous chemicals
15.9 Carpets	18.2 R—Automobiles
16.5 Knit goods	19.0 Bolts and nuts
21.5 Newspapers and periodicals	19.4 Cleaning preparations
22.6 Textile machinery	19.6 Firearms
24.4 Miscellaneous printing and publishing	21.6 R—Groceries
	21.8 Proprietary preparations
26.1 R—Groceries	25.4 Toilet preparations
29.2 Toilet preparations	26.5 Newspapers and periodicals
	27.3 Scientific instruments

The degree of departure of the earnings rates of these 106 industries from the median figure, in particular years of the period 1919–28, is highest in 1919, 1920 and 1921. In all years subsequent to 1921 the relative variation remains almost constant from year to year, at a figure about equal to one-third of the median itself. These figures—'coefficients of variation'—are printed with the diagrams of Chart 3.[9] They indicate that, over the period 1922–28, no significant change in the extent of the variation between different industries took place. Chart 4 affords another measure of the relative variation of earnings in different years by presenting the 'interquartile ranges' to supplement the broader figures.

[9] The term 'coefficient of variation' is employed in the sense of the ratio of the arithmetic mean deviation to the median, and not to represent, as is more usual in statistics, the ratio of the standard deviation to the arithmetic mean.

2. VARIATION IN TEN-YEAR RATES

But neither the fact that the variation between industries is less in 1928 than in years before 1922, nor the fact that it remains much the same from 1922 to 1928 affords evidence as to the degree in which the alleged tendency of the return in different industries to approach an equality over a period is realized in practice. For it is conceivable that the several industries might constantly be changing their positions, yet the *average* amount or extent to which their rates varied from the median remains much the same. This might be true even were a pronounced tendency to equality indeed present; for it might be exactly *through* such a shifting of the high industries of one year into the low positions of another year, and *vice versa,* that the aggregate average earnings of a particular industry *for a period* would correspond with those of other industries for the same period. One industry might enjoy prosperity during one set of years, other industries earn above average rates in different years. To reiterate, a marked variation during any given year could conceivably be the mechanism through which approximate equality was realized in the long run.[10]

But is this what takes place? The available evidence would indicate that it is not—at least, over the ten-year period for which we have continuous data.

The 106 industries, the net incomes of each totalled for ten successive years and then divided by the aggregate capitalizations shown by each industry over the ten successive years, display a wide diversity indeed in their 'ten-year

---

[10] Were the frequency distributions entirely symmetrical, such shifting as would equalize earnings rates over a period could conceivably result not only in the absolute maintenance of a marked annual variation during the period but also in yearly variation coefficients of exactly the same magnitude.

INDUSTRIAL PROFITS

CHART 3
FREQUENCY DISTRIBUTIONS OF PERCENTAGE OF INCOME TO CAPITALIZATION, 106 MINOR GROUPS

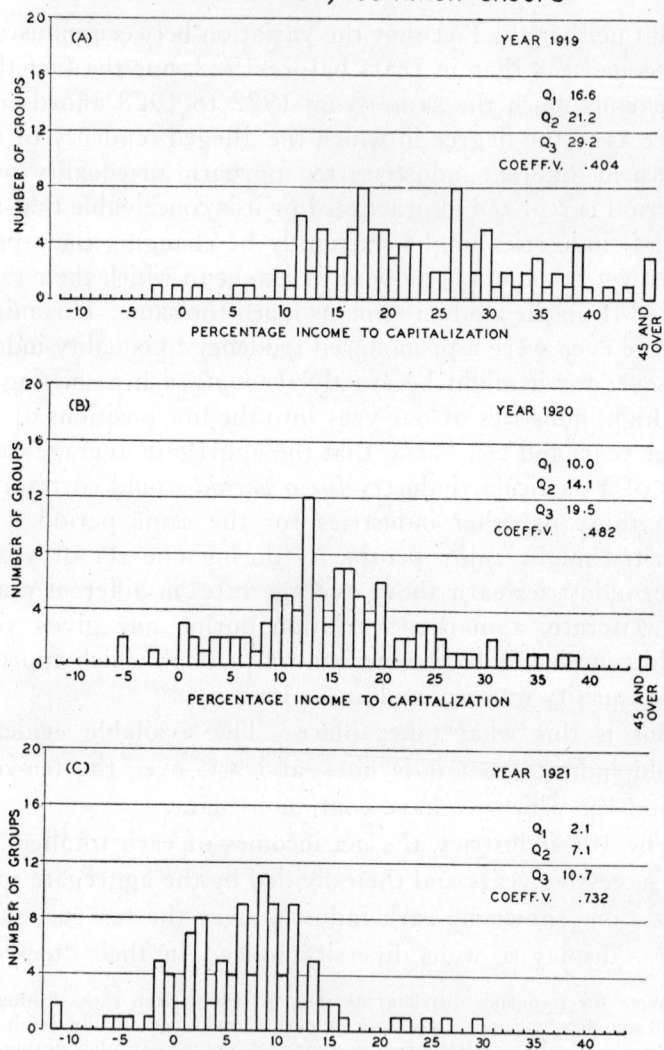

(A) YEAR 1919
Q_1 16.6
Q_2 21.2
Q_3 29.2
COEFF.V. .404

(B) YEAR 1920
Q_1 10.0
Q_2 14.1
Q_3 19.5
COEFF.V. .482

(C) YEAR 1921
Q_1 2.1
Q_2 7.1
Q_3 10.7
COEFF.V. .732

CHART 3 (CONT.)
FREQUENCY DISTRIBUTIONS OF PERCENTAGE OF INCOME TO CAPITALIZATION, 106 MINOR GROUPS

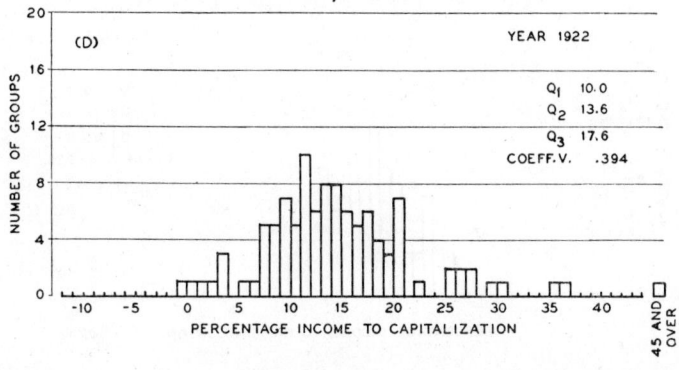

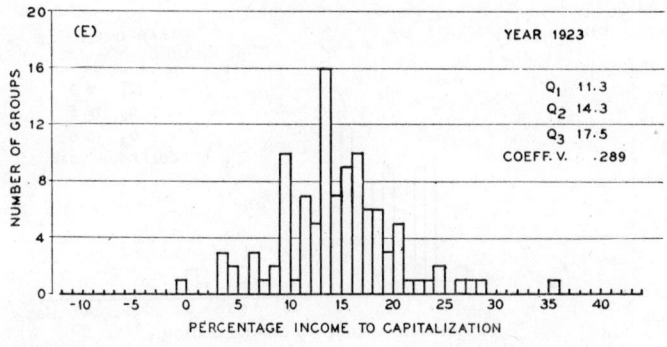

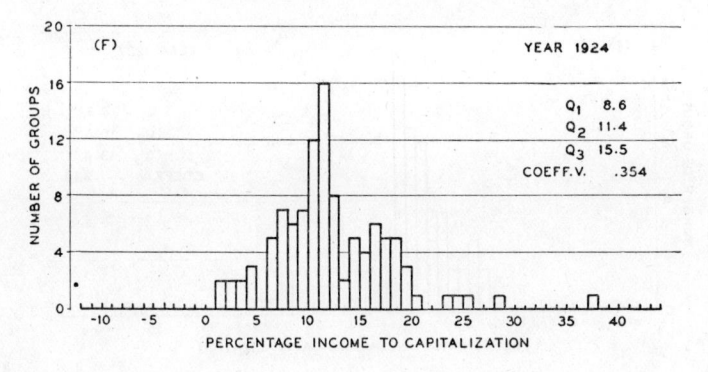

(D) YEAR 1922
Q_1 10.0
Q_2 13.6
Q_3 17.6
COEFF. V. .394

(E) YEAR 1923
Q_1 11.3
Q_2 14.3
Q_3 17.5
COEFF. V. .289

(F) YEAR 1924
Q_1 8.6
Q_2 11.4
Q_3 15.5
COEFF. V. .354

CHART 3 (CONT.)
FREQUENCY DISTRIBUTIONS OF PERCENTAGE OF INCOME TO CAPITALIZATION, 106 MINOR GROUPS

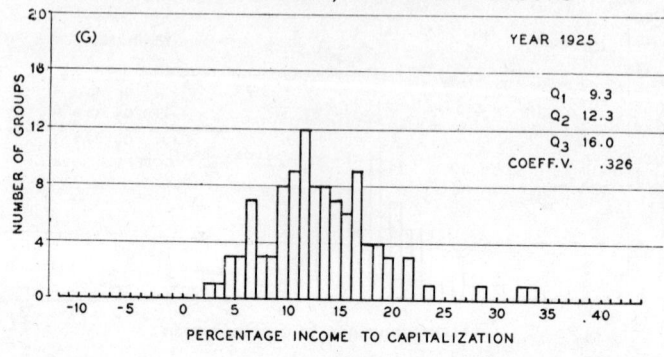

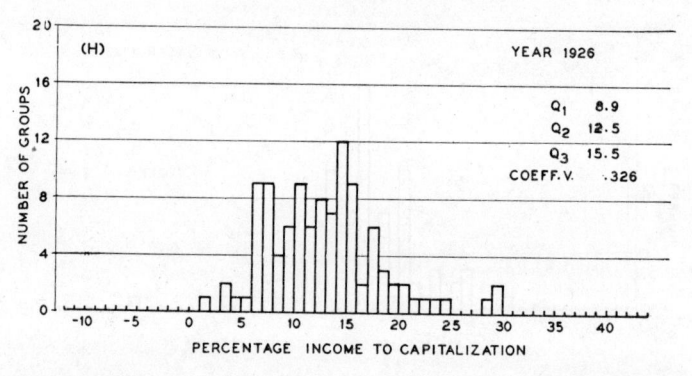

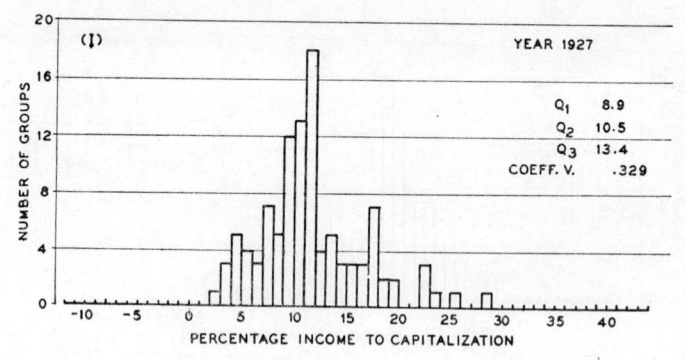

(G) YEAR 1925
Q_1 9.3
Q_2 12.3
Q_3 16.0
COEFF. V. .326

(H) YEAR 1926
Q_1 8.9
Q_2 12.5
Q_3 15.5
COEFF. V. .326

(I) YEAR 1927
Q_1 8.9
Q_2 10.5
Q_3 13.4
COEFF. V. .329

CHART 3 (CONT.)
FREQUENCY DISTRIBUTIONS OF PERCENTAGE OF INCOME TO CAPITALIZATION, 106 MINOR GROUPS

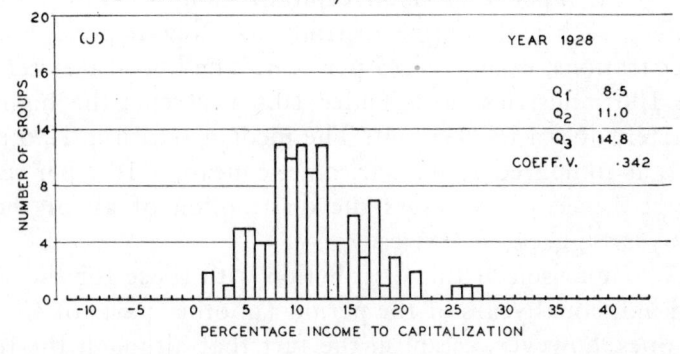

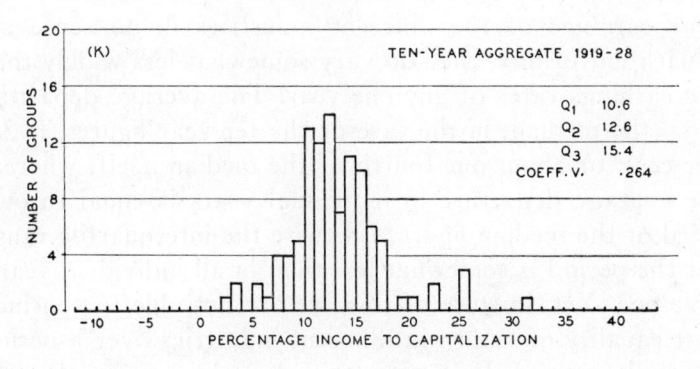

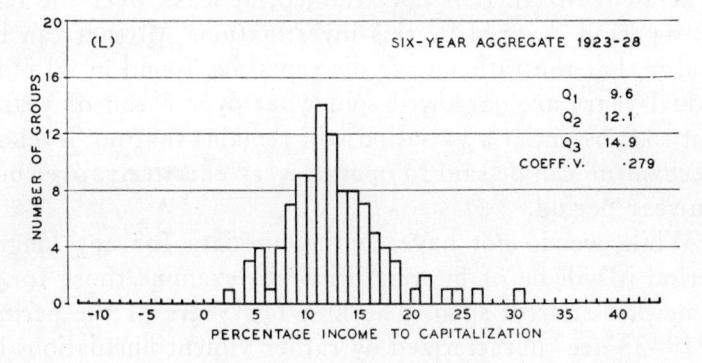

(J) YEAR 1928

Q_1	8.5
Q_2	11.0
Q_3	14.8
COEFF. V.	.342

(K) TEN-YEAR AGGREGATE 1919-28

Q_1	10.6
Q_2	12.6
Q_3	15.4
COEFF. V.	.264

(L) SIX-YEAR AGGREGATE 1923-28

Q_1	9.6
Q_2	12.1
Q_3	14.9
COEFF. V.	.279

rates' of earnings. Some industries, for example, Meat Packing, Castings and Forgings, or Rubber Products, earn less than 6 per cent upon capitalization for the period. Others, such as Scientific Instruments, Newspapers, Toilet Preparations, earn over 25 per cent. The lowest quarter of the 106 industries earns under 10.6 per cent; the highest quarter, over 15.4 per cent. The median return is 12.6 per cent, as compared with an arithmetic mean of 10.7 per cent. Chart 3, section K shows the distribution of all of these 'ten-year aggregate' figures.

A comparison of this distribution with those for the several individual years of the period (in other parts of Chart 3) does, however, establish the fact that although the ten-year earnings of the different industries in no sense approach uniformity, they do vary somewhat less widely than the earnings rates of any one year. The average departure from the median, in the case of the ten-year figures, is 3.3 per cent, or about one-fourth of the median itself, whereas the average departure in individual years is equal to one-third of the median figure. Likewise the interquartile range for the period is somewhat less than in all individual years, save one. Yet, in spite of this, we are not able to conclude that equality of return in different industries over a period is at all realized. It is not attained, at least, over the ten-year period covered by this investigation. All that can be said is that the rather *wide* discrepancies found in all individual years are narrowed somewhat over a run of years. But so substantial a variation still remains that no 'leveling mechanism' can be said to operate very effectively, over our ten-year period.

While we do not have continuous data for any longer period it will be of interest briefly to examine those for a somewhat shorter span. The first few years of the period 1919–28 are characterized by rather violent fluctuations in

CHART 4
INTERQUARTILE RANGE, PERCENTAGE INCOME TO CAPITALIZATION, 106 MINOR GROUPS

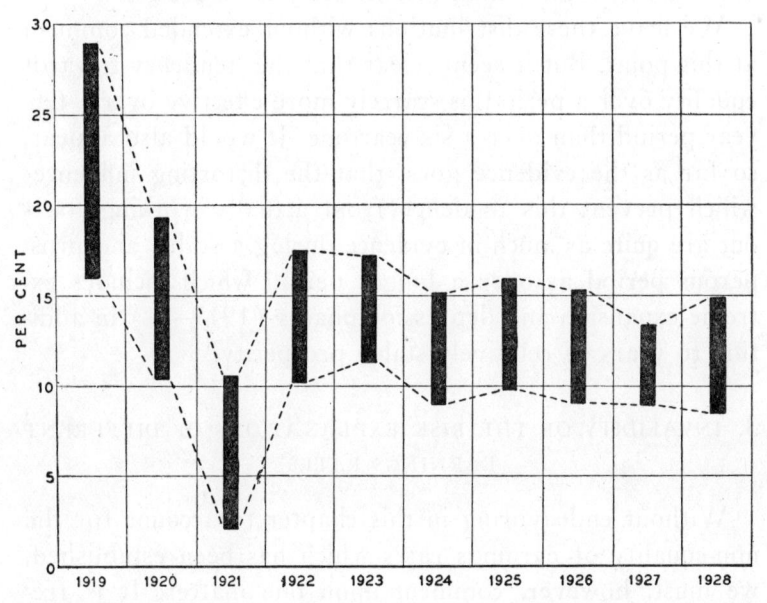

business conditions. On the other hand, the last six years, 1923–28, constitute a period of general expansion, broken by recessions far less severe than during the earlier period.[11] We may, therefore, survey the 'six-year rates' for this relatively stable period and observe to what extent they differ from those for the ten-year figures.

Chart 3, section L shows this distribution. It is to be compared with Chart 3, section K. The six-year distribution is roughly symmetrical: the 106 industries are grouped on either side of the median (which is 12.1 per cent) in a somewhat more regular pattern than in the case of the

[11] This statement refers, of course, to industrial activity and not to security speculation.

other distributions. The quartiles, however, are not very different, and the coefficient of variation from the median is only slightly higher than for the ten-year figures.

We leave these distributions without extended comment at this point. But it seems clear that the 'tendency towards equality over a period' is scarcely more effective over a ten-year period than over a six-year one. It would also appear, so far as the evidence goes, that the distorting influences which prevent this tendency from actually working itself out are quite as much in evidence during a stable and prosperous period as over a longer period which includes extreme expansion and depression phases (1919–21) in addition to years of relatively stable prosperity.[12]

3. INVALIDITY OF THE RISK EXPLANATIONS OF DIFFERENT EARNINGS RATES

Without endeavoring in this chapter to account for the non-equality of earnings rates which has been established, we must, however, comment upon one matter. It is fre-

[12] This conclusion contradicts the tentative hypothesis set forth by R. C. Epstein in Statistical Light Upon Profits, As Analyzed in Recent Literature, *Quarterly Journal of Economics*, February 1930, in which it was said: "Crum (in his *Corporate Earning Power*) alludes to 1926 as 'a fairly typical year' (p. 138). Probably he is right. In the sense of being relatively free from price fluctuations, and from customarily accepted boom or depression characteristics, 1926 was 'normal'. But profits and losses in business appear not merely during such normal years, but in years less typical as well. And it may indeed be that the principal distorting elements which perhaps prevent profits from reaching either relative equality or relative stability, as between different industries and trades, occur during the *non-typical* years which every business repeatedly goes through."

Distorting elements which prevent profits from reaching equality do indeed exist, as our present data show; but they are no more operative in the entire period under survey than in that portion which contains 'normal' years chiefly. In fact, upon the basis of the above ranges and coefficients, they seem even somewhat less operative during the shorter period; but the margins of possible error in the data prevent attaching much importance to this slight difference.

quently said that a tendency to equality between the several industries is operative, 'differences in risks considered'. Such statements are loose and betray a misconception of the problem.

Differences in the degree of risk to which industries are subject, to be sure, do exist. If the hazards are susceptible of close estimation in advance, they may be allowed for. The charge then becomes one for insurance and is deducted from gross income before net earnings appear. If, as is more often the case, no actuarial estimate of such risks is possible, then in the profits of any one (good) year there might appear a component that would properly be characterized as compensation for risk, or more accurately, for the uncertainty attaching to the economic circumstances of an industry in any particular year.[13] But here what holds true of the short run is emphatically not true of the long run. An excess of return in any one industry over the average rate in a good year, in so far as it constitutes a risk differential, would be received in order to offset a deficiency of return in a bad year; and if the principle which holds that differences in profits serve to equalize differences in risks were true, the 'differential surpluses' of the good years would, over a period, exactly equal the 'differential deficits' of the poor years.

If this did not occur, then it would always be advantageous to invest capital in the most risky, or rather the most 'uncertain', industries, for they would consistently return earnings (over a time period) at higher than average rates! In other words, the classical doctrine of compensation for risk can properly be applied in the explanation of such differences in earnings rates as exist in any one year, but not in the explanation of discrepancies that prevail over

[13] See Frank H. Knight, *Risk, Uncertainty and Profit* (1921).

a long period. Interpreted correctly, the principle of "the tendency towards an equality of profit rates in different industries differences in risk considered", in so far as it operated perfectly, would result in absolutely *no* differences in returns, extraordinary gains and losses combined, over a period sufficiently long to include years in which the hazards were realized.[14] Accordingly, 'differences in risk' can scarcely be said to account for the variation in earnings shown by the ten-year aggregate rates of the 106 industries here under examination.[15]

4. PERMANENCE OF THE POSITIONS OF 'HIGH' AND 'LOW' INDUSTRIES

The evidence afforded by the discrepancies found to exist among the 'ten-year earnings rates' of different industries may be supplemented by a somewhat less summary set of analyses. Earnings rates in general, we have found, fail to attain equality over a decade. But exactly how great and how continuous are the differences which specific minor

[14] Smith and Ricardo were perhaps not so explicit upon this score as might be desired, but a careful reading of Mill or a fair interpretation of Marshall leaves no doubt as to the logic of the position here taken: differences in risk, if compensated accurately, would equalize, not vary rates of return.

[15] This is not to say that capital is not withdrawn from industries in which, over a ten-year or longer period, it receives remuneration at substantially *less* than 'average' rates; in this sense, continued and recurrent uncertainties may affect the decisions of entrepreneurs just because they are not compensated for. The whole question of the calculation of risk is, however, involved, and in most discussions of it, gratuitous assumption and guesswork have played all too prominent parts. The question of the renewal or non-renewal of capital is again mentioned in Ch. 47.

Professor F. C. Mills, in commenting upon the general argument of the text, agrees that differences in risk do not account for the wide variations in earnings shown by our ten-year figures but suggests that the average return in a risky business might in the long run exceed that in a less risky enterprise, "the differential representing a reward for the high (year-to-year) variability of the return".

groups are able to maintain year by year? Do the influences which in some instances serve to reduce the extreme differential advantages enjoyed by specific industries operate steadily throughout a period or only at certain times? And do any industries manage to escape entirely the 'erosive' influences of competition upon persistently high profit rates?

Numerous statistical measures were applied to our data in an effort to answer these questions as completely as possible. From the several analyses made, two types of approach were finally selected as most suitable for the purpose at hand, in terms of fruitfulness and comparative simplicity alike. Neither method, however, avoids making some demand upon the reader's patience. For the benefit of the non-statistically minded reader, each is explained rather fully.

The first method of approach is to list the 106 industries, for each of the ten years separately, in the order of their respective rates of return upon capitalization in that year. Each list or array is then divided into four equal parts, the points of division being termed 'quartiles'. The 27 industries that are highest in point of net return may be said to stand 'above the first (or upper) quartile'. Similarly, in the list for any year the 27 lowest ranking industries occupy positions below the third (or lower) quartile. The industry at the second (or middle) quartile is the median industry and its rate of return is the median figure.[16]

Thus any particular industry, or set of industries, may

[16] In a series of 106 items the twenty-seventh item (counting from either end of the array) is theoretically merely a point of division between groups and does not, strictly speaking, belong to the group of items above or below it. In order, however, to include all of the 106 industries in the analysis, both the twenty-seventh item and the eightieth item have been included in the groups above the first quartile and below the third quartile. There are thus actually 27 items in each of these two groups, and 26 items in each of the two groups between the median and the upper and lower quartiles. See note 5, Ch. 3.

be compared with the median industry in any one year, or its position relative to the quartiles in any year may be traced throughout the period. The same industry might, of course, stand above the first quartile in one year but below it in another. Both with individual industries and with different sets of industries it is of interest to know not merely whether they consistently remain above the highest (or below the lowest) quartiles in position, but also the *extent* to which either their individual or their averaged rates of earnings regularly stand above or below the median figure. Our first method of measuring the degree and the permanence of profit differentials, therefore, consists of counting the changes in position, and examining the earnings rates, of the various minor groups that consistently remained above or below certain division points in the list.

Of the 106 industries four are to be found above the first quartile in all ten years: Scientific Instruments, Toilet Preparations, Miscellaneous Printing and Publishing, and Retail Automobiles. The first three are manufacturing groups, the last a trading group. The Scientific Instrument group includes 23 corporations, with an aggregate capitalization of 149 million dollars (annual average). Its net income upon capitalization ranges from 13.1 to 33.1 per cent per year. In six years of the ten its rate is equal to twice or more that of the median industry in the same year.[17] In no year does the return fail to exceed the median by about one-half.

In the case of Toilet Preparations the group includes only nine corporations. Their aggregate capitalization annually averages about nine million dollars. But on this capitalization three million dollars or over is earned in six of the ten years. The result is a rate of return that is ordinarily

[17] That is, the coefficient of variation for this one item is always 1.00 or more.

two or three times the median figure in each year. Beyond question, the great differentials enjoyed by the companies in this group rest upon the combination of low manufacturing expense and the high market prices that can be obtained for strongly advertised trade marked products.

The Retail Automobiles group comprises 15 corporations with a total investment of 13 million dollars (annual average). This group's variation from the median rate is in some years much like that of the Scientific Instruments group, but shows greater year-to-year fluctuation. Since 1925, however, its differential advantage has declined. Doubtless this is an instance in which the advantage would not be of permanent character if a period longer than ten years were taken, for we know that the secular trend of motor vehicle consumption has changed during the last half of the period. It is also to be noted that the corporations in question are relatively large for retail trading establishments and may not be very typical of motor car and distribution experience as a whole, even for this period.

Of the Miscellaneous Printing and Publishing group nothing need be said here other than to state that in most years the earnings of the 17 companies involved stood at a figure half as large again as the median.

Table 14 shows the ratios by which the earnings rates of the four groups in question exceeded the median rates. In each case the 'median difference coefficient' represents the difference between the group's earnings rate for the year and the median rate, divided by the median rate for the same year.

Although only four of the 106 minor groups are found above the first quartile in every year, two others, Newspapers and Retail Groceries, remained there in all years of the period save one. Details for these and other groups discussed in this section appear in Tables 14 and 15.

[92]   INDUSTRIAL PROFITS

TABLE 14

MEDIAN DIFFERENCE COEFFICIENTS, RELATIVELY PROFITABLE INDUSTRIES[1]

GROUP NAME	1919	1920	1921	1922	1923	1924	1925	1926	1927	1928
Above first quartile during ten years										
Miscellaneous printing and publishing	.47	2.23	2.44	.92	.31	.55	.74	.53	.66	.55
Toilet preparations	.85	.39	3.11	2.91	1.48	2.30	1.63	1.30	1.58	1.31
Scientific instruments	.56	.57	.85	1.26	1.00	.47	1.35	1.36	1.31	1.48
Retail automobiles	2.86	1.42	.56	1.15	.91	1.22	1.71	.85	.61	.65
Above first quartile during nine years										
Newspapers	..	1.13	2.03	1.64	.87	1.14	.48	1.38	1.17	1.41
Retail groceries	.40	..	2.68	1.01	.55	1.06	.71	.74	1.02	.96
Above median during ten years										
Boots and shoes	.56	.29	.61	.50	.13	.44	.31	.22	.61	.35
Newspapers	.25	1.13	2.03	1.64	.87	1.14	.48	1.38	1.17	1.41
Miscellaneous printing and publishing	.47	2.23	2.44	.92	.31	.55	.74	.53	.66	.55
Proprietary preparations	.31	.21	.61	.92	.35	.72	.71	.78	1.07	.98
Toilet preparations	.85	.39	3.11	2.91	1.48	2.30	1.63	1.30	1.58	1.31
Road machinery	.27	.56	.23	.03	.34	.66	.48	.40	.44	.55
Motor vehicles	.83	.30	.18	.86	.45	.52	.93	.66	.48	.46
Scientific instruments	.56	.57	.85	1.26	1.00	.47	1.35	1.36	1.31	1.48
Retail automobiles	2.86	1.42	.56	1.15	.91	1.22	1.71	.85	.61	.65
Retail groceries	.40	.14	2.68	1.01	.55	1.06	.71	.74	1.02	.96
Above median during nine years										
Furniture	.46	.73	.18	.49	.28	.32	.34	.22	.07	..
Job printing	..	.86	.85	.23	.09	.36	.21	.16	.17	.26
Paints	.28	.17	..	.47	.20	.30	.29	.24	.19	.35
Glass	.38	1.28	.34	.29	.66	.52	.26	.09	..	.07
Textile machinery	.29	.22	2.18	.64	.28	..	.20	.15	.46	.33
Toys	.24	.74	.58	..	.10	.38	.26	.12	.37	.46
Miscellaneous special manufacturing	.24	.28	.49	.49	.24	.04	..	.26	.21	.13

[1] See text for explanation.

The six groups just discussed all maintained positions *above the first* quartile for either nine or ten years. But what is the situation with respect to the groups that remained continuously, or almost continuously, *below the third* quartile?

Only one industry, Meat Packing, persistently retains sufficiently large (negative) differentials to place it below the lowest quartile in all ten years.[18] Regularly over the ten-year period the rate of return in this group falls far short of the median figure. For the ten-year period the aggregate rate of return in Meat Packing is 1.9 per cent as compared with the median group's ten-year aggregate rate of 12.6 per cent.

Four groups remained in the lowest division in every year except one. Two are manufacturing groups, Beverages and Castings and Forgings. The latter contains 99 corporations with an aggregate capital of about $3.4 billion (annual average). On this capital it earns in most years less than 8 per cent. From 1923 to 1928, the degree to which its earnings stand below the median changed hardly at all.

The other two industries that remained below the third quartile in all years except one are mining groups, Gas and Oil Wells, and Metals (ferrous and other). In the case of Gas and Oil Wells, however, the regularly low earnings may be more apparent than real because of the accounting practices in the matter of depletion that are peculiar to this field.[19] It is here somewhat difficult to distinguish the causes of low return due to the aleatory character of the industry from those due to the peculiar circumstances of accounting and valuation methods.

[18] In the case of these negative differentials the 'median difference coefficient' is, of course, the amount by which the group rate falls short of the median, divided by the median figure.

[19] See Ch. 25, where so-called 'discovery depletion' and related matters are discussed.

5. PERMANENT POSITIONS OF GROUPS ABOVE AND BELOW THE MEDIAN

A similar analysis may be made of the comparative profitableness of those industries that remained above the median in all years. This set of industries comprises ten groups. If we average their several median difference coefficients, we find that these ten industries regularly earned from about one and one-half to two times the median rate, and that, from 1924 to 1928, the differential scarcely narrowed at all.

If to these ten industries we add the seven that remained above the median in all years but one, we have 17 groups in the 'almost permanently-above-the-median' category.

Take now those groups that remained *below* the median in all years, as well as those which did so in all years but one. In the first category are seven groups, in the second, six. In some instances, for example, in Railway Equipment and in Rubber, declining secular rates of growth in the industry may partly account for the persistently poor showing, but in most instances such an obvious explanation is not apparent. The seven groups that remain below the median in all years average a 'median difference' which in most years amounts to at least 50 per cent of the median itself. Data for all groups discussed in this section appear in Tables 14 and 15.

6. SPECIFIC PROGRESS OF THE LEADING GROUPS OF EACH YEAR

Another method of analysis, in our search for measures of the permanence or non-permanence of differences in earnings rates, may now be employed. This is not to isolate the industries that remain above or below any quartile or

TABLE 15

MEDIAN DIFFERENCE COEFFICIENTS FOR RELATIVELY UNPROFITABLE INDUSTRIES [1]

GROUP NAME	1919	1920	1921	1922	1923	1924	1925	1926	1927	1928
Below third quartile during ten years										
Meat packing	1.17	.98	1.99	.86	.73	.61	.74	.50	.79	.58
Below third quartile during nine years										
Beverages	1.09	.99	.87	.76	.57	.74	.46	.48	.59	..
Castings and forgings	.46	..	1.06	.85	.52	.59	.54	.38	.59	.45
Gas and oil wells	.76	..	.85	1.08	1.13	.89	.84	.69	.72	.47
Metals (mining)	.93	.91	1.32	.96	.78	.78	.62	.61	.64	..
Below median during ten years										
Meat packing	1.17	.98	1.99	.86	.73	.61	.74	.50	.79	.58
Beverages	1.09	.99	.87	.76	.57	.74	.46	.48	.59	.22
Miscellaneous food products	.18	.51	1.76	.43	.35	.15	.45	.27	.35	.15
Castings and forgings	.46	.26	1.06	.85	.52	.59	.54	.38	.59	.45
Railway equipment	.20	.25	.39	.47	.06	.26	.57	.39	.49	.69
Gas and oil wells	.76	.23	.85	1.08	1.13	.89	.84	.69	.72	.47
Metals (mining)	.93	.91	1.32	.96	.78	.78	.62	.61	.64	.23
Below median during nine years										
Rubber products	.10	.85	2.77	.74	.58	.36	..	.31	.37	.88
Blank paper	.38	..	.73	.51	.31	.08	.44	.47	.48	.54
Wholesale drygoods	..	.62	.14	.15	.12	.35	.26	.45	.17	.24
Wholesale hardware	.01	..	1.21	.32	.98	.40	.30	.38	.29	.22
Wholesale paper	.15	..	1.38	.27	.07	.07	.15	.33	.23	.07
Wholesale groceries	..	.67	.63	.15	.23	.05	.24	.38	.11	.33

[1] See text for explanation.

other division point *throughout* successive years, but to take the highest or the lowest industries of each year and, whatever their positions in succeeding years, ascertain the degree to which they maintain or lose their advantage or disadvantage.

Specifically, we take the 27 highest ranking industries in, say, 1919 (those above the first quartile) and tabulate the amount by which the return in each exceeds the median rate. We then total these differences and divide by the number of industries (27). This gives us the average amount by which the return of the 27 industries exceeds the median rate. To illustrate, in 1919—a highly prosperous year—the median return is 21.2 per cent. Some of the highest 27 industries earn over 45 per cent, others around 30 per cent; they average an earnings rate of 37.5 per cent as compared with the median of 21.2 per cent. The average departure from the median, as we have termed it in another connection earlier in this chapter, we may now, in accordance with the language of statistics, term the *average deviation*.[20]

But for purposes of comparison with the deviations prevailing in other years, such an average deviation can best be expressed as a ratio to the median itself. In this instance we regard the difference of 16.29 not as 16.29 but as about three-quarters (.77) of the median rate, 21.2. Again in the language of statistics this figure of .77 we may term the coefficient of variation. It expresses the degree to which the several rates of earnings in the 27 highest industries

---

[20] Deviations may, of course, be based upon other averages than the median as statistically conversant readers are aware. To such readers much of the explanation contained in this and other chapters of Book I will prove somewhat tedious because of its elementary character. But in view of the needs of other readers, some prolixity of explanation as well as a relative simplicity of statistical methods seems desirable, at least throughout Book I. However, for the sake of accuracy of expression, it is perhaps wise to employ the terminology of statistics in most instances where repeated use is made of the same statistical device.

vary, on an average, from the median rate. It will be noted that this comparison is relative rather than absolute—the median is divided into the average of the deviations from it, and the resulting coefficient simply shows *the proportion of the median which the average deviation is*. For this reason, coefficients of average deviation afford better comparisons, between data of different years, than do the absolute deviations themselves, and will thus be employed throughout the remainder of this chapter.

We take, then, the industries that are the 27 highest in point of earnings in 1919, and analyze the earnings rates of *those same industries* in each of the succeeding nine years. If a tendency towards equality between different industries were effective, the coefficient of variation for these 27 industries would steadily decline, and to the extent that this tendency operated perfectly, would approach zero. Chart 5 shows that the coefficient does indeed decline at first; during the first five years the excessively large variation of these 27 groups' earnings from the median rate is reduced. The ratio falls from .77 in 1919 to .33 in 1923. But from 1923 through 1928 the average advantage of these 27 industries is consistently maintained; their earnings are always from .33 to .46 in excess of the median figure (that is, are from 1.33 to 1.46 times it). The course of these coefficients may be traced in Chart 5, while Table 16 gives them in numerical form.

In similar fashion coefficients are computed for the 27 industries that stood highest in 1920 (some of which were found above the first quartile in 1919, others not), and these same industries are then followed through the remaining years of the period.

Exactly the same analysis is applied to the highest industries of 1921, 1922, 1923 and 1924 respectively. The results of the several analyses, data for all of which are

CHART 5
COEFFICIENTS OF VARIATION OF 27 HIGHEST MINOR GROUPS IN EACH YEAR, 1919-24, FOLLOWED THROUGH SUCCESSIVE YEARS[1]

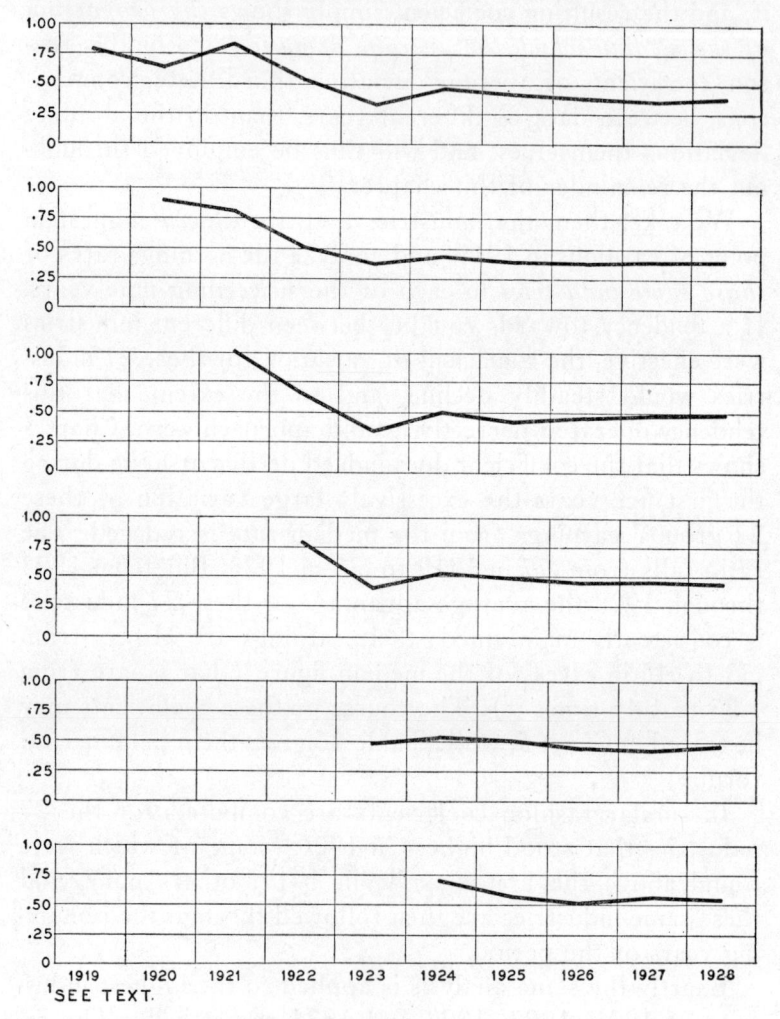

[1] SEE TEXT.

TABLE 16

AVERAGE DEVIATIONS AND COEFFICIENTS OF VARIATION FOR PERCENTAGES OF NET INCOME TO CAPITALIZATION, 27 HIGHEST MINOR GROUPS [1]

	1919	1920	1921	1922	1923	1924	1925	1926	1927	1928
Average deviation	16.289	8.863	5.878	7.259	4.737	5.241	5.211	4.856	3.930	4.230
Coefficient	.768	.629	.828	.534	.331	.460	.424	.388	.361	.385
Average deviation		12.759	5.659	7.000	5.541	4.985	5.026	4.833	4.319	4.470
Coefficient		.905	.797	.515	.387	.437	.409	.387	.396	.406
Average deviation			7.900	8.707	5.081	5.604	5.244	5.748	5.281	5.419
Coefficient			1.113	.640	.355	.492	.426	.460	.484	.493
Average deviation				10.741	5.778	5.930	5.933	5.719	5.070	4.978
Coefficient				.790	.404	.520	.482	.458	.465	.453
Average deviation					7.111	5.967	6.311	5.807	4.770	5.252
Coefficient					.497	.523	.513	.465	.438	.477
Average deviation						8.137	6.948	6.341	6.022	5.896
Coefficient						.714	.565	.507	.552	.536

[1] See text for explanation.

shown in Chart 5 and Table 16, are identical in that the earnings differentials are in all cases permanent. In the three series starting before 1922 a marked decline in the coefficient takes place after 1921, but in nearly all of the series the coefficients exhibit no appreciable fall from 1923 on.

That the coefficients in several instances do show a substantial decline after the first year or two might seem to indicate that competition, while not serving to equalize profit rates, reduces excessive discrepancies. But a careful examination of these figures, and other rather complicated data related to them, reveals that two fortuitous factors are mainly responsible for the initial, but really specious, declines in the coefficients. The first is the presence, in any given year, of a few very high earnings rates enjoyed by industries that are not persistently 'big money-makers'. The second is the excessively low average or median rate of earnings in 1921. A coefficient of variation affords a better measure of relative disparities than does the mere average deviation itself, but the coefficient may nevertheless be unstable and misleading if considered apart from fluctuations of the average on which it is based. In this case, that average is the median return for our 106 groups, and this figure fell from 21.2 in 1919 and 17.9 in 1920 to 7.1 per cent in 1921. It then jumped to 13.6 per cent in 1922.

In other words a large part of the explanation of the initial fall in the coefficients of Table 16 is that a year of depression such as 1921 brings about temporarily *greater* relative differentials in the standing of profitable industries relative to the median group because the latter in such a year shows a very much lower figure.[21] When recovery occurs the following year, the median return rises more sharply

[21] Mrs. John D. Sumner has given valuable criticism and aid in the interpretation of the misleading initial declines of these coefficients.

than the earnings rates of the most profitable groups (in general); and the relative differential between the median and the rates of the 'high groups' is reduced—not because the earnings rates of the latter (in general) *decline* but because the median rate rises. Competition does not greatly reduce the earning power of the high groups, but general cyclical improvement disproportionately enhances that of the others. This is evident if one glances at Table 17. The median increased from 7.1 in 1921 to 13.6 in 1922, or nearly doubled. (Similarly, the arithmetic mean of the 106 groups jumped from 4.4 to 10.6.) The average earnings rates of the 27 groups which were highest in 1921, however, increased only from 15.0 to 21.8, or by less than one-half.

As final evidence that the initial declines in the coefficients are largely spurious, so far as signifying any very effective tendency towards an equality of profit rates is concerned, we may 'run back' all of our computations into earlier years, that is, in the case of the ten industries that were highest in 1920, calculate their average deviations and coefficients for 1919; similarly, in the case of the highest industries for 1921, calculate their coefficients for 1920 and 1919, etc. When this is done, the 1919 coefficients for all series are much smaller than those for 1921; most of them are roughly half as large. And, roughly again, all of the 1919 coefficients are the same size as the 1928 figures. In other words, no marked reduction in the average deviation of any of these series from the median, in relative terms, took place over the ten years in question. Table 18 repeats the data of Table 16, but contains, in addition, data for the years preceding that in which the industries of each series are the ten highest. The figures for that year—the year of origin for each series, as it were—are shown in italics.

We are thus forced to conclude that the industries in which earnings exceed the median return by the largest rela-

TABLE 17

AVERAGE EARNINGS RATE, 27 HIGHEST MINOR GROUPS IN EACH YEAR 1919–28, TRACED THROUGH SUCCESSIVE YEARS AND RUN BACK THROUGH 1919

(Arithmetic mean and median figures shown first are for all 106 groups)

	1919	1920	1921	1922	1923	1924	1925	1926	1927	1928
1919										
Arithmetic mean	17.1									
Median	21.2									
Average rate, 27 groups	37.5	17.9	9.6	19.4	16.9	13.6	15.7	14.6	13.8	13.1
1920										
Arithmetic mean		11.6								
Median		14.1								
Average rate, 27 groups	27.0	26.9	8.7	17.9	17.3	14.2	15.1	14.5	12.5	13.1
1921										
Arithmetic mean			4.4							
Median			7.1							
Average rate, 27 groups	27.8	16.9	15.0	21.8	18.1	15.5	16.2	15.7	14.6	14.2
1922										
Arithmetic mean				10.6						
Median				13.6						
Average rate, 27 groups	29.8	17.8	13.4	24.3	19.7	17.0	17.2	16.8	15.0	14.8
1923										
Arithmetic mean					10.9					
Median					14.3					
Average rate, 27 groups	27.8	20.4	11.6	22.7	21.4	17.2	17.7	17.2	14.8	14.6

RATES IN DIFFERENT INDUSTRIES

1924											
Arithmetic mean						9.6					
Median						11.4					
Average rate, 27 groups	27.4	17.8	11.7	20.8	19.7	19.5	18.8	18.6	16.3		16.2
1925											
Arithmetic mean							11.3				
Median							12.3				
Average rate, 27 groups	27.0	16.7	10.5	21.1	19.1	18.0	19.7	19.0	16.7		16.3
1926											
Arithmetic mean								11.5			
Median								12.5			
Average rate, 27 groups	27.2	16.4	10.0	20.3	18.8	17.1	18.6	19.6	17.1		17.0
1927											
Arithmetic mean										9.8	
Median										10.9	
Average rate, 27 groups	27.0	17.0	10.9	20.0	18.5	17.2	19.0	19.2	18.3		17.5
1928											
Arithmetic mean											10.7
Median											11.0
Average rate, 27 groups	26.8	15.9	9.3	18.6	17.6	16.6	18.4	19.0	17.2		18.2

[103]

Table 18

AVERAGE DEVIATIONS AND COEFFICIENTS OF VARIATION FOR PERCENTAGES OF NET INCOME TO CAPITALIZATION, 27 HIGHEST MINOR GROUPS[1]

	1919	1920	1921	1922	1923	1924	1925	1926	1927	1928
Average deviation	16.289	8.863	5.878	7.259	4.737	5.241	5.211	4.856	3.930	4.230
Coefficient	.768	.629	.828	.534	.331	.460	.424	.388	.361	.385
Average deviation	10.322	12.759	5.659	7.000	5.541	4.985	5.026	4.833	4.319	4.470
Coefficient	.487	.905	.797	.515	.387	.437	.409	.387	.396	.406
Average deviation	9.422	6.837	7.900	8.707	5.081	5.604	5.244	5.748	5.281	5.419
Coefficient	.444	.485	1.113	.640	.355	.492	.426	.460	.484	.493
Average deviation	11.041	7.204	6.693	10.741	5.778	5.930	5.933	5.719	5.070	4.978
Coefficient	.521	.511	.943	.790	.404	.520	.482	.458	.465	.453
Average deviation	10.096	7.752	6.163	9.078	7.111	5.967	6.311	5.807	4.770	5.252
Coefficient	.476	.550	.868	.668	.497	.523	.513	.465	.438	.477
Average deviation	9.152	9.085	5.681	7.856	5.763	8.137	6.948	6.341	6.022	5.896
Coefficient	.432	.644	.800	.578	.403	.714	.565	.507	.552	.536

[1] See text for explanation.

tive amounts in any one year lose no significant part of their high relative earning power over a six-, eight- or even ten-year period. Indeed except for such temporary changes in average levels of earnings as accompany a year of marked depression, they retain a rather constant measure of advantage. This dictum does not necessarily apply to every individual industry that enjoys a large advantage in a particular year, but is based upon averages illustrative of the general situation.[22]

Much the same sort of process is at work in the case of the industries which stand, not highest, but lowest in each year. Taking the 27 minor groups standing under the lowest quartile in 1919, we find their coefficient of variation to be .50. By 1922 it falls to .37, but it continues regularly to stand at about that figure. Table 19 presents the data for the 1919 'low' groups and those starting with other years.

In the second and third of these cases, those of the industries standing lowest in 1920 and 1921 respectively, there is a sharp fall in the coefficient after one or two years—that is, the average return in the 'low' industries rises greatly. But for the remainder of the period this return remains definitely and steadily below the median rates. In the case of the last three series, those starting in 1922, 1923 and 1924 respectively, the fall (denoting an increase in the relative prosperity of the 'low' industries) is not so marked. Perhaps this is because 1922–24 were not as extreme years, cyclically speaking, after which readjustments could be expected to take place, as were 1919–21.

---

[22] Although these coefficients are derived from arithmetic means, they are not as non-typical as most arithmetic averages. It is to be noted that the selection of the items is such that *all* the components of each series stand above the first quartile in the initial year. Thus the mean of the deviations from the median is not so much influenced by the presence of extreme variants from the central figure, or by an extreme range, as it would be were all items of the entire range employed as components—as was done in some earlier sections of this chapter.

Table 19
AVERAGE DEVIATIONS AND COEFFICIENTS OF VARIATION FOR PERCENTAGES OF NET INCOME TO CAPITALIZATION, 27 *LOWEST* MINOR GROUPS[1]

	1919	1920	1921	1922	1923	1924	1925	1926	1927	1928
Average deviation	10.530	6.556	4.019	5.004	4.448	3.719	3.959	4.119	4.081	3.615
Coefficient	.497	.465	.566	.368	.311	.326	.322	.330	.374	.329
Average deviation		9.674	5.285	4.544	4.204	3.915	3.581	4.252	3.826	4.022
Coefficient		.686	.744	.334	.294	.343	.291	.340	.351	.366
Average deviation			8.763	5.737	4.993	3.570	4.185	3.819	3.504	3.856
Coefficient			1.234	.422	.349	.313	.340	.306	.321	.351
Average deviation				6.896	5.589	3.985	4.037	3.930	3.693	3.852
Coefficient				.507	.391	.350	.328	.314	.339	.350
Average deviation					6.485	4.207	4.141	4.122	3.304	3.622
Coefficient					.453	.369	.337	.330	.303	.329
Average deviation						5.367	4.470	4.881	3.589	4.215
Coefficient						.471	.363	.390	.329	.383

[1] See text for explanation.

Our conclusion here is thus more tempered than in the case of the highest ranking industries above discussed, but it remains true that the industries showing low earnings in any one year, while tending to lose *some* of their disadvantage, still permanently retain a substantial and rather constant measure of disadvantage.

If, as corroborative evidence of a more extreme sort, we perform similar analyses upon, not the 27 highest or lowest of our 106 industries, but upon the *ten* highest and lowest groups of each year, we again obtain approximately the same results. These are presented in Tables 20 and 21. The coefficients are, of course, larger. The initial declines that occur are sharper. But even towards the ends of the several spans of years in question the coefficients never go below .24, and the advantage or disadvantage of both sets of groups is permanent for the period. Here again the sharp initial declines suggest that competitive influences, cyclical readjustments, technological changes, and consumption shifts all do indeed force *some* reduction of extreme differentials, whether positive or negative. But the regular persistence of the coefficients above zero also affords clear evidence that competitive influences do not serve to bring about equality, over the period of years under survey, in different industries. Whether any greater tendency towards such an approximate equality would assert itself over longer than a ten-year period cannot, of course, be told.

Undoubtedly the highly specialized character of much fixed capital in modern industry, making it difficult if not impossible to withdraw all of the capital of an enterprise over a ten-year period, is one factor that prevents whatever 'tendencies towards equality' that may exist from becoming effective. Many enterprises that do not earn returns at rates that accord with the expectations of their owners still continue in business, for a smaller return is better than

Table 20

AVERAGE DEVIATIONS AND COEFFICIENTS OF VARIATION FOR PERCENTAGES OF NET INCOME TO CAPITALIZATION, 10 HIGHEST MINOR GROUPS [1]

	1919	1920	1921	1922	1923	1924	1925	1926	1927	1928
Average deviation	24.25	7.51	5.08	9.76	5.83	6.89	7.02	5.40	4.46	4.54
Coefficient	1.144	.533	.715	.718	.408	.604	.571	.432	.409	.413
Average deviation		19.86	6.73	8.46	6.15	5.26	5.38	5.07	4.71	4.41
Coefficient		1.409	.948	.622	.430	.461	.437	.406	.432	.401
Average deviation			12.96	14.88	7.47	8.02	6.06	7.49	7.61	6.90
Coefficient			1.825	1.094	.522	.704	.493	.599	.698	.627
Average deviation				18.21	10.02	9.35	10.02	9.43	8.38	8.79
Coefficient				1.339	.701	.820	.815	.754	.769	.799
Average deviation					11.27	9.41	8.79	8.08	6.69	7.34
Coefficient					.788	.825	.715	.646	.614	.667
Average deviation						12.24	8.83	8.40	8.22	8.02
Coefficient						1.074	.718	.672	.754	.729

[1] See text for explanation.

TABLE 21

AVERAGE DEVIATIONS AND COEFFICIENTS OF VARIATION FOR PERCENTAGES OF NET INCOME TO CAPITALIZATION, 10 *LOWEST* MINOR GROUPS [1]

	1919	1920	1921	1922	1923	1924	1925	1926	1927	1928
Average deviation	15.25	8.19	5.69	8.07	8.00	6.15	6.60	5.80	5.49	3.77
Coefficient	.719	.581	.801	.593	.559	.539	.537	.464	.504	.343
Average deviation		14.87	7.94	6.30	6.07	6.62	5.68	6.67	5.96	5.87
Coefficient		1.055	1.118	.453	.424	.581	.462	.534	.547	.534
Average deviation			12.88	6.92	5.43	3.24	3.66	3.71	2.62	3.70
Coefficient			1.814	.509	.380	.284	.298	.297	.240	.336
Average deviation				10.35	8.31	5.69	5.86	5.18	5.02	4.30
Coefficient				.761	.581	.499	.476	.414	.461	.391
Average deviation					9.86	6.14	5.95	5.34	4.84	3.89
Coefficient					.690	.539	.484	.427	.444	.354
Average deviation						8.00	6.99	6.78	5.06	4.51
Coefficient						.702	.568	.542	.464	.410

[1] See text for explanation.

none at all; were production entirely abandoned, all fixed capital investment of a specialized character might be completely lost. In extreme cases operations may be continued for considerable periods even though the product is sold at an absolute loss, if prices that repay something more than prime costs (direct labor and material) are realized.

Then, too, under the corporate form of enterprise, reorganization is far more frequent than liquidation. Old enterprises are not discontinued in one field and new ones readily started in another. The old shell—the framework of the enterprise—continues; but policies are drastically altered, methods are changed, executive personnel is replaced. The corporation may remain in the same industry, but its activities are reorganized and reoriented. New types of product within the same general field may be developed; and these new products or methods may prove no more successful competitively than their predecessors. At all events, it is often a long time before an unsuccessful corporation gives up the struggle entirely. Even then, the enterprise frequently disappears in name only; if the establishment is of any size, it may be absorbed by, or merged with, some other concern.

When reorganizations or mergers of this sort take place, 'capital values' are written down on the books of the unsuccessful corporation, or the fact of failure to earn a satisfactory return is recognized by the payment of far smaller amounts, in cash or stock, for the securities of the unsuccessful companies, than the sums that have been invested in them. In other words, declines in capital values are often formally recognized by owners or purchasers of unsuccessful enterprises, but the physical plant is not abandoned or even necessarily devoted to other uses. It may continue to produce the same products, but since book investment has been lowered, the same earnings as before will show as a higher rate of return on the capital as currently valued. Practices such as these do not affect our figures for industries of low return in the sense that the discrepancy between them and the median industry is accentuated, for, as just stated, the 'new' rate of return after capital values are written down is higher than the old and tends to raise the apparent earnings level of the industry in question. But such practices do throw light upon the reasons why ten-year differences in earnings rates prevail in spite of such recapitalizations: the recapitalization device is utilized just *because* large, specialized corporate capitals usually can *not* be withdrawn in the physical sense.

Finally, the imperfect character of competition—the prevalence of trade-marks, special designs of products, quasi-monopoly advantages of all sorts—serves also to explain why the tendency towards equality is not realized. Just as the classical doctrine of value—the standard explanation of the prices of individual commodities—assumed that the price of an article could not long remain much below cost of production because capital would be withdrawn from the field of enterprise, so did it also assume that new producers would soon enter the field were price long above cost of manufacture. It was thus tacitly assumed that what one producer could do, another could and would do; that identical products, in other words, are offered by different producers competing for the consumer's favor. The manufacture and sale of modern trade-marked products and specialty goods, however, do not fit this description. Great numbers of consumer goods commonly used today— automobiles, radios, vacuum cleaners, washing machines, electric cooking devices, furniture, even many articles of clothing and numerous food specialties—are given highly distinctive characters by virtue of their differentiated designs and particular specifications. The same is true of some producers' goods—machinery of different types designed to perform the same kinds of work. So long as different sets of purchasers either see or are led to believe they see advantages of the one product over the other, the markets for such products will not be fully competitive in the orthodox sense of that term. And competition, while preventing the very large net revenues that might accrue under conditions of real monopoly, will not necessarily equalize returns between either industries or enterprises.

The character of modern manufacturing and merchandising, therefore, furnishes some explanation of the lack of uniformity in the average profit rates of large corporations, when classed by industries, for two important conditions essential to perfect competition—a quick mobility of capital and a homogeneity of competing products—are absent in a large proportion of industries. To be sure, a substantial mobility of capital exists over a period of time. But, on the side of withdrawal, this mobility exists in the possibility of *not* creating *new* plant and organizations of particular types rather than in withdrawing from service those that at any given time are under way. We do not thus undertake to say that the classical doctrine of equality of profit rates is invalid as a 'tendency'; but we do say that under modern conditions, as they existed in 1919–28, the evidence seems clear that the tendency was scarcely effective over this ten-year period.[23]

[23] Whether or not a 'long-run tendency' ought to show an effect over a ten-year period depends upon one's definition of 'long-run'. The writer's feeling is that a fairly considerable effect ought to be noted within *ten* years if over, say, fifteen or twenty years the tendency really works out as alleged. But present data relate to ten years only.

Probably the persistence in an individual industry of an earnings rate far lower than the median figure would indeed not continue for several decades if the rate fell much short of the 'normal' interest rate or the cost of borrowed capital. Nor might an earnings rate in an individual industry, even if equal to this cost, persist for several decades at a level far below the median—*assuming that the median were known*. Either or both of these situations might cause the withdrawal of capital or its 'non-renewal' in one industry, and its investment in another. To grant deductively that secular trends in one industry may serve to cause the eventual withdrawal of capital is one thing; but to allege that this process results in an equality of the rate of earnings upon capital *between* industries over a period is quite another. Sometimes it results, as in the case of wagon manufacture, in a gradual collapse of the entire industry. And returns in the successor industry can hardly be added to losses of the capital employed in the predecessor and 'averaged' so as to see if equality with other industries over a quarter-century or more perhaps results.

Statistically it would be interesting to have data for twenty or thirty years running, but the problems of classification and analysis would be more difficult, and the results in some ways accordingly less significant, than with data covering only a ten-year period. See Ch. 46 on industrial classification; see also Ch. 47, where the question of the non-renewal of capital is again touched upon.

CHAPTER 4

RETURN UPON SALES IN DIFFERENT INDUSTRIES

1. SALES AND INVESTMENT: CAPITAL TURNOVER

THUS far, our discussion of earnings rates has been restricted either to the return on capitalization or to that on total capital. These indeed are the most fundamental measures of earning power. But another measure of profitableness that calls for examination, even though it is not of the same ultimate significance as the return upon capital, is that of the relation of net earnings to sales.

There is a close connection, of course, between the two measures. The one "expresses the rate of return on the investment, the other the margin of profit on the volume which produced that return".[1] If an industry or a company 'turns over' its capital exactly once during the year, that is, if the sales for the year are equal to the average investment of capital during that year, then its percentage of return upon sales exactly corresponds with that upon investment. Actually, however, the rate of capital turnover is seldom such that sales and investment precisely equal each other. Some enterprises and some industries, for example Meat Packing, turn over their capital four or five times in

[1] James H. Bliss, *Financial and Operating Ratios in Management* (1923), p. 65.

the course of a year; others, such as Factory Machinery, evidence annual sales of only about one-half or two-thirds the amount of their capital. Accordingly, differences between industries in the rates of return upon sales cannot be taken as indicative of differences in ultimate profitableness, although *changes* in the rate of return upon sales, if no substantial alteration in capital turnover takes place during the same period, of course *suggest* changes in the rate of earnings upon investment. As a measure of cyclical conditions, therefore, the return upon sales is of importance.[2] In any event, the business world commonly attaches sufficient importance to the relation between net earnings and sales to justify analysis of the ratio in this chapter. It is clearly to be borne in mind, however, that this measure of earning power is often more useful as an operating ratio to be employed in the current observation and control of particular enterprises than in general considerations relating to the theory of profits, and the qualifications that attach to such broader use should not be neglected.

This chapter will consider only the minor groups that make up the Manufacturing and Trade divisions. While sales and gross income (more accurately, aggregate receipts) figures are available for Mining and Finance respectively, those data [3] are either incomplete or else made up in a different way than the data for Manufacture and Trade, and are thus not really comparable with the sales

[2] This is largely the point of view from which William L. Crum's *Corporate Earning Power* (1929) is written. That volume presents a comprehensive and scholarly analysis of the rate of net income to aggregate receipts (which in Manufacturing and Trade are virtually tantamount to sales volume, sales in all manufacturing industries combined being about 60/63 of Crum's 'gross income'), both by industrial divisions and by what in this book are termed 'major groups' within the Manufacturing division, but not by specific industries or minor groups. The trends of absolute sales figures, by minor groups, are discussed in Ch. 7 of the present volume.

[3] See Ch. 25 and 26.

figures of the two latter divisions. Nor will any effort be made, even within the Manufacturing and Trade divisions, to carry out the same detailed analysis of the positions of the several minor groups as was undertaken in Chapter 3 in connection with the return upon investment. If the return on sales were of as great ultimate significance as that upon capital, such an elaborated analysis might be warranted. But since that is not the case, this chapter will present only the outline figures, will point out such discrepancies as regularly exist between rates of capital turnover, and will leave to the accountant or other interested reader any more extended analysis of these sales data, all of which are given in detailed tables either here or elsewhere in the book.[4] This comment concerning the limited significance of sales data, however, applies only to the *rate of return on sales* in one industry as compared with another, either at any one time or for an aggregate of years. With respect to year-to-year changes—or their absence—and the *rate of sales growth* in particular industries, much will be said in Chapter 7.

2. RETURN ON SALES AND CAPITAL: ALL MANUFACTURING

The 2,046 large manufacturing corporations for which we have a continuous ten-year series of data earn an average return which runs from 3.1 per cent upon sales in poor years to 10 or 11.5 per cent in good years. Chart 6 shows the annual rates. These general average figures for All Manufacture do not differ very strikingly from the ratios shown in Chapter 2 for the return upon capitalization. In 1924–28 they run fairly close to those for the percentage

[4] Under the headings of particular major and minor groups in Ch. 9–14, for the large corporations series, and Ch. 28–42, for the small corporations series.

of net profit to total capital, which for convenience are charted with them.

The ten-year aggregate figure for the rate of return on sales in Manufacture is 9.1 per cent, whereas that upon

CHART 6
EARNINGS RATES, 2,046 MANUFACTURING CORPORATIONS

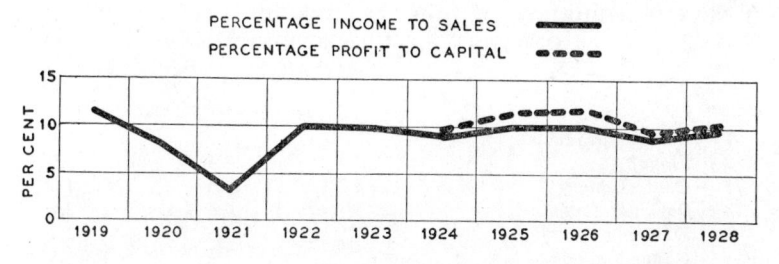

PERCENTAGE INCOME TO SALES
PERCENTAGE PROFIT TO CAPITAL

capitalization is 10.8. In 1928 the return on sales is 9.7 per cent, while that on total capital is 10.6. In other words, in the Manufacturing division *as a whole* the rate of capital turnover is roughly *one*.[5]

3. RETURN ON SALES AND CAPITAL: MINOR MANUFACTURING GROUPS

This average relationship, however, is very far from holding true in many of the 73 individual industries that compose the Manufacturing division. In these particular minor groups the return upon sales, in 1928, ranges from 0.8 per cent in Meat Packing to 28.8 per cent in Miscellaneous Chemicals. The median industry, which in that year

[5] This conclusion pertains to the large corporations series here discussed, but it also holds as a general statement. See note 7 for the definition of capital turnover, as the term is employed here. For all manufacturing corporations in the country sales in 1928 equalled $64,361,000,000 whereas capitalization as here defined equalled $53,919,000,000 and total capital, $59,790,-000,000 (the investment data are estimates as explained in Appendix A).

happens to be either Boots and Shoes or Toys (the return is the same in both industries), earns 10.3 per cent on its sales volume. Table 22 gives the data for 1928[6] as well as the capital turnover figures, that is, the quotients obtained by dividing the sales by the capitalization figures.[7]

TABLE 22

73 MANUFACTURING GROUPS, RETURN ON SALES AND RATE OF CAPITAL TURNOVER, 1928

MINOR GROUP		PERCENTAGE RETURN ON SALES	CAPITAL TURNOVER
1	Bakery products	12.9	1.4
2	Flour	3.4	3.5
3	Confectionery	14.5	1.0
4	Package foods	7.5	2.4
5	Dairying	4.5	2.2
6	Canned goods	8.6	1.5
7	Meat packing	.8	5.7
9	Beverages	15.8	.5
10	Tobacco	11.2	1.4
11–8	Miscellaneous food products	8.4	1.1
12	Cotton spinning	6.3	1.5
13	Cotton converting	6.9	1.2
14	Cotton weaving	4.6	1.0
15	Weaving woolens	1.8	.9
16	Silk weaving	3.8	1.2
17	Carpets	7.3	.9
18	Men's clothing	7.8	1.5
19	Knit goods	8.0	1.4
20	Miscellaneous clothing	7.1	1.7
21	Miscellaneous textiles	6.6	1.2
22	Boots and shoes	10.3	1.4
23	Miscellaneous leather products	3.1	1.7
24	Rubber products	.8	1.6
25	Lumber manufacture	10.5	.7

[6] Data for other years are given in Ch. 10–20.

[7] Sales divided by total capital would theoretically be a better way in which to calculate these ratios, but total capital figures are not available for the first five years of the period. The 'capital turnover' here arrived at is really the turnover of stockholders' equity; but since funded debt is relatively small in most of the minor groups of Manufacture in question, the difference between the two results is not appreciable. This would not be so in all instances if individual corporations were being compared, but here the comparison is between arithmetic means for different industries.

RETURN UPON SALES

TABLE 22 *(continued)*
73 MANUFACTURING GROUPS, RETURN ON SALES AND RATE OF CAPITAL TURNOVER, 1928

MINOR GROUP		PERCENTAGE RETURN ON SALES	CAPITAL TURNOVER
26	Planing mills	7.4	1.1
27	Millwork	9.2	.9
28	Furniture (non-metal)	8.4	1.2
29	Miscellaneous lumber products	6.5	1.5
30	Blank paper	7.2	.7
31	Cardboard boxes	10.0	1.3
32	Stationery	8.6	1.2
33	Miscellaneous paper products	9.2	1.0
34	Newspapers and periodicals	17.1	1.5
35	Book and music publishing	13.9	.9
36	Job printing	12.4	1.1
37	Miscellaneous printing and publishing	11.4	1.5
38	Crude chemicals	15.9	1.3
39	Paints	11.8	1.3
40	Petroleum refining	16.1	.6
41	Proprietary preparations	23.7	.9
42	Toilet preparations	20.4	.8
43	Cleaning preparations	10.2	1.9
44	Miscellaneous chemicals	28.8	.6
45	Ceramics	13.2	.6
46	Glass	10.4	1.1
47	Portland cement	23.4	.5
48	Miscellaneous stone and clay products	18.2	.9
49	Castings and forgings	7.8	.8
50	Sheet metal	9.5	1.2
51	Wire and nails	14.2	1.0
52	Heating machinery	9.4	1.0
53	Electrical machinery	15.6	1.1
54	Textile machinery	24.7	.6
55	Printing machinery	19.1	.6
56	Road machinery	14.9	1.1
57	Engines	13.2	.5
58	Mining machinery	9.3	1.1
59	General factory machinery	25.0	.5
60	Office machinery	17.0	1.0
61	Railway equipment	6.9	.5
62	Motor vehicles	8.6	1.9
63	Firearms	19.9	1.0
64	Hardware	10.4	1.1
65	Tools	19.0	.8

TABLE 22 *(continued)*

73 MANUFACTURING GROUPS, RETURN ON SALES AND RATE OF CAPITAL TURNOVER, 1928

MINOR GROUP		PERCENTAGE RETURN ON SALES	CAPITAL TURNOVER
66	Bolts and nuts	17.2	1.1
67	Miscellaneous machinery	12.9	1.0
68	Non-ferrous metals	12.2	1.2
69	Jewelry	9.7	1.3
70	Miscellaneous metal products	15.1	1.0
71	Scientific instruments	27.7	1.0
72	Toys	14.0	1.1
73	Pianos	7.8	.8
74	Miscellaneous special manufacturing	10.3	1.2

Turn, however, directly to the ten-year results. The five manufacturing industries showing the highest rates of return upon sales are Scientific Instruments, Textile Machinery, Portland Cement, General Factory Machinery and Proprietary Preparations. They all earn about 20 per cent or more on total business volume. In two groups, Scientific Instruments and Textile Machinery, this high return on sales is accompanied by a high return upon investment also; in Textile Machinery the return on capitalization, although substantially less than that on sales, is still high; but in Portland Cement and General Factory Machinery the returns on sales and investment differ widely. The latter group shows a return of 20.3 per cent on sales, but only 10.7 per cent upon investment, its capital turnover being only about one-half. The pertinent figures for these five minor groups (ten-year aggregate returns, 1919–28) are given below.

The five lowest groups, on the other hand, in point of their returns on sales for the ten-year period, are Meat Packing, Flour Milling, Rubber Products, Dairying, Miscellaneous Leather. Three show relatively low earnings upon

RETURN UPON SALES   [121]

	Percentage on sales	Rank in list of 73 groups		
Group		Percentage on capitalization	Earnings on sales	Earnings on capitalization
Scientific Instruments	26.5	25.1	1	3
Textile Machinery	22.6	17.1	2	11
Portland Cement	21.4	14.2	3	31
General Factory Machinery	20.3	10.7	4	52
Proprietary Preparations	19.8	20.8	5	5

investment also, but the other two, Flour Milling and Dairying, both show earnings rates three times as great upon investment as upon sales. The ten-year aggregate data are given below.

	Percentage on sales	Rank in list of 73 groups		
Group		Percentage on capitalization	Earnings on sales	Earnings on capitalization
Meat Packing	0.4	1.9	73	73
Flour Milling	3.1	11.4	72	54
Rubber Products	4.0	5.9	71	70
Dairying	4.1	12.7	70	39
Miscellaneous Leather Products	4.2	6.8	69	69

If all 73 Manufacturing industries are ranked in this manner, some general degree of correspondence between the rank in earnings on sales and that in earnings on investment appears. In general, however, it is far from exact, and in many instances very different returns and rankings alike prevail. Table 23 presents these arrays, together with the capital turnover figures which constitute the links of connection, so to speak, between the two rates of net return —that on sales and that on investment. For the general list the correspondence between the two is about one-half perfect: the coefficient of rank correlation is +.496, on a scale in which +1.0 would indicate exactly the same ranks throughout the entire list.

Table 23
73 MANUFACTURING GROUPS RANKED BY EARNINGS RATES

MINOR GROUP		RANK, RETURN ON SALES	RANK, RETURN ON INVESTMENT	RATE OF CAPITAL TURNOVER
1	Bakery products	35	13	1.49
2	Flour	72	50	3.66
3	Confectionery	22	7	1.30
4	Package foods	66	17	2.48
5	Dairying	70	41	3.12
6	Canned goods	52	35	1.46
7	Meat packing	73	73	4.99
9	Beverages	56	72	.46
10	Tobacco	39	33	1.36
11–8	Miscellaneous food products	67	66	1.22
12	Cotton spinning	47	23	1.58
13	Cotton converting	61	53	1.45
14	Cotton weaving	57	62	1.15
15	Weaving woolens	65	68	1.05
16	Silk weaving	60	57	1.38
17	Carpets	20	22	1.11
18	Men's clothing	58	46	1.52
19	Knit goods	53	16	1.75
20	Miscellaneous clothing	62	32	1.97
21	Miscellaneous textiles	51	38	1.38
22	Boots and shoes	50	10	1.80
23	Miscellaneous leather products	69	69	1.62
24	Rubber products	71	70	1.47
25	Lumber manufacture	13	59	.65
26	Planing mills	46	8	1.80
27	Millwork	44	60	.96
28	Furniture (non-metal)	30	15	1.34
29	Miscellaneous lumber products	55	36	1.59
30	Blank paper	41	64	.81
31	Carboard boxes	43	20	1.54
32	Stationery	68	67	1.16
33	Miscellaneous paper products	49	45	1.27
34	Newspapers and periodicals	6	2	1.31
35	Book and music publishing	19	25	1.08
36	Job printing	25	19	1.20
37	Miscellaneous printing and publishing	17	4	1.60
38	Crude chemicals	21	52	.80
39	Paints	38	21	1.45
40	Petroleum refining	34	63	.76
41	Proprietary preparations	5	5	1.06
42	Toilet preparations	9	1	1.75

RETURN UPON SALES [123]

TABLE 23 *(continued)*

73 MANUFACTURING GROUPS RANKED BY EARNINGS RATES

MINOR GROUP		RANK, RETURN ON SALES	RANK, RETURN ON INVESTMENT	RATE OF CAPITAL TURNOVER
43	Cleaning preparations	59	27	1.91
44	Miscellaneous chemicals	8	40	.70
45	Ceramics	11	51	.70
46	Glass	32	12	1.45
47	Portland cement	3	31	.66
48	Miscellaneous stone and clay products	15	14	1.10
49	Castings and forgings	64	71	.84
50	Sheet metal	63	61	1.32
51	Wire and nails	36	47	1.09
52	Heating machinery	24	34	1.06
53	Electrical machinery	18	26	1.07
54	Textile machinery	2	11	.76
55	Printing machinery	10	48	.65
56	Road machinery	14	9	1.18
57	Engines	7	39	.68
58	Mining machinery	45	37	1.34
59	General factory machinery	4	55	.52
60	Office machinery	23	28	1.09
61	Railway equipment	42	65	.80
62	Motor vehicles	33	6	1.71
63	Firearms	31	49	.97
64	Hardware	28	30	1.20
65	Tools	12	43	.77
66	Bolts and nuts	16	24	1.06
67	Miscellaneous machinery	29	44	1.00
68	Non-ferrous metals	48	56	1.09
69	Jewelry	54	42	1.39
70	Miscellaneous metal products	27	58	.81
71	Scientific instruments	1	3	.96
72	Toys	26	18	1.21
73	Pianos	37	54	.98
74	Miscellaneous special manufacturing	40	29	1.41

4. RETURN ON SALES IN TRADING GROUPS

In Trade we have 664 companies in our large corporations series. Their combined return upon sales runs from under 3 per cent in a poor year, such as 1921, to 6 or 7 per cent in good years. But because Trade as a whole turns over its capital about two and one-half or more times a year (in contrast to the average turnover of roughly 1.00 in Manufacture), the rate on investment runs far higher than that on sales. For the ten-year period, the aggregate return on sales in Trading is 5.1 per cent, whereas upon capitalization it is 13.6 per cent. The average turnover of capitaliza-

CHART 7
PERCENTAGE OF NET INCOME TO SALES AND PERCENTAGE OF TOTAL PROFIT TO TOTAL CAPITAL
664 TRADING CORPORATIONS

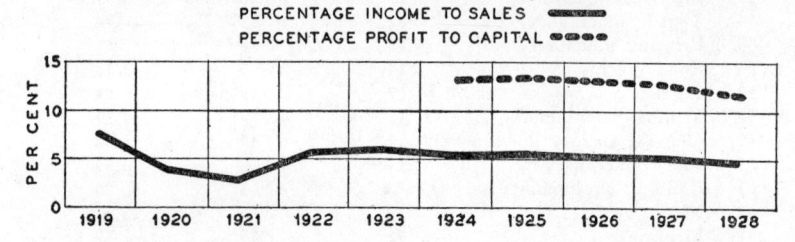

PERCENTAGE INCOME TO SALES
PERCENTAGE PROFIT TO CAPITAL

tion, over the same period, is thus two and six-tenths times per year. Chart 7 shows the percentage of net income to sales in Trading for the ten years 1919–28, and that of total profits to total capital for the five years 1924–28.

The Trade division, however, may be separated into 22 minor groups. As in the case of the 73 groups of the Manufacturing division, these vary widely in both the return upon sales and the degree of correspondence between that rate and the return upon capital investment. There is, however, generally less variation in the percentage of earnings upon sales than in that upon investment. Table 24 gives the data for 1928: the return on sales, and the rate of capital turnover.

Table 24
22 TRADING GROUPS, RETURN ON SALES AND RATE OF CAPITAL TURNOVER, 1928

MINOR GROUP		PERCENTAGE RETURN ON SALES	RATE OF CAPITAL TURNOVER
Retail			
75	Automobiles	3.4	4.4
76	Men's clothing	7.4	1.7
77	Department stores	4.6	1.7
78	Drygoods	6.0	1.6
79	Furniture	6.0	1.6
80	Groceries	3.1	6.8
81	Jewelry	13.6	1.0
82	Building material and lumber	7.0	1.2
83	Lumber and coal	9.0	1.2
84	Miscellaneous retail trade	7.9	1.8
Wholesale			
85	Coal, fuel and wood		
86	Drugs	4.3	2.4
87	Drygoods	3.6	2.3
88	Groceries	2.0	3.6
89	Hardware	4.5	1.8
90	Importers and exporters	4.7	2.1
91	Building material and lumber	2.0	2.3
92	Paper	2.7	3.6
93–85	Miscellaneous wholesale trade	3.2	2.6
Retail and Wholesale			
96	Coal, wood and fuel	6.2	1.7
97	Hardware	3.9	1.9
98	Lumber	4.0	1.2
99–95	Miscellanous retail and wholesale trade	6.0	1.5

But again we may fasten attention upon the distribution of the ten-year aggregate figures.[8] The diversity of capital turnover relationships may be illustrated by three minor groups: Retail Jewelry, Retail Dry Goods[9] and Wholesale Paper. Retail Jewelry stands highest of the 22 trading groups in its profit margin upon sales: 10.7 per cent. Its turnover is, however, low for a trading group, and its re-

[8] The detailed data are given in the tables of the various chapters of Book II.
[9] Including ladies' ready-to-wear goods.

turn upon investment is 12.7 per cent, which places it only ninth highest in the list. Retail Drygoods, on the other hand, earns a lower rate upon sales: 6 per cent. But a high turnover gives it a 14.3 per cent return upon capitalization, which places it fourth in that list as against only ninth in the percentage-on-sales column. Finally, take the case of Wholesale Paper. It earns only 2.3 per cent on sales, but with a turnover of more than four, shows 11.3 per cent on its investment.

For all 22 Trading groups the general correspondence between their ranks in earnings on sales and earnings on investment is less marked than in the Manufacturing groups, the coefficient of rank correlation for the ten-year aggregate figures being +.347. Table 25 gives the array for these ten-year aggregate data, together with the capital turnover figures.

TABLE 25
22 TRADING GROUPS RANKED BY EARNINGS RATES

MINOR GROUP		RANK, RETURN ON SALES	RANK, RETURN ON INVESTMENT	RATE OF CAPITAL TURNOVER
Retail				
75	Automobiles	14	1	6.3
76	Men's clothing	6	3	2.1
77	Department stores	10	6	2.3
78	Drygoods	9	4	2.3
79	Furniture	4	11	1.7
80	Groceries	20	2	6.5
81	Jewelry	1	9	1.2
82	Building material and lumber	3	14	1.5
83	Lumber and coal	2	10	1.5
84	Miscellaneous retail trade	5	5	2.0
Wholesale				
86	Drugs	16	13	3.0
87	Drygoods	15	17	2.7
88	Groceries	22	21	4.0
89	Hardware	13	20	2.1
90	Importers and exporters	19	16	3.2
91	Building material and lumber	18	22	2.3
92	Paper	21	15	4.3
93–85	Miscellaneous wholesale trade	17	12	3.0

TABLE 25 *(continued)*
22 TRADING GROUPS RANKED BY EARNINGS RATES

MINOR GROUP		RANK, RETURN ON SALES	RANK, RETURN ON INVESTMENT	RATE OF CAPITAL TURNOVER
Retail and Wholesale				
96	Coal, wood and fuel	11	7	2.8
97	Hardware	12	19	2.2
98	Lumber	8	18	1.7
99–95	Miscellaneous retail and wholesale trade	7	8	1.9

Chapter 5

SIZE AND GEOGRAPHICAL LOCATION OF CORPORATIONS

1. THE SIZE OF ENTERPRISE AND ITS MEASUREMENT

IT IS frequently contended that larger corporations earn profits at higher rates than smaller ones. Indeed, this alleged greater efficiency of large-scale enterprise is held, by some persons, to constitute the *raison d'être* of the trend towards concentration which so markedly characterized post-War industrial development through 1929.[1] Others, while agreeing in their impressions as to the greater profitableness of

[1] See, for descriptions of this trend, Gardiner C. Means, *American Economic Review,* March 1931, The Large Corporation in American Economic Life; Charles S. Tippetts and Shaw Livermore, *Business Organization and Control* (1932), especially Ch. XVI, The Recent Modern Merger Movement; and Harry W. Laidler, *Concentration of Control in American Industry* (1931). Statistical measures of the relation between size and the rate of return on sales volume in various retail trades have been given in the several bulletins of both the Harvard and Northwestern University Bureaus of Business Research; and data on size of capital and the return upon investment in certain manufacturing industries, of limited scope, in papers by Ralph C. Epstein: Industrial Profits in 1917, *Quarterly Journal of Economics* (February 1925); Profits and the Size of Firm in the Automobile Industry, *American Economic Review* (December 1931). More recently, in an admirable paper in the May 1932 *Quarterly Journal of Economics,* A Comparison of the Rates of Large-Scale and Small-Scale Industries, H. B. Summers gives data for manufacturing industries that lead him to the conclusion reached in this chapter. Summers' data are compared below with our own.

On geographical location, see W. L. Crum, *Corporate Earning Power* (1929).

the larger firms, have asserted that not superior productive effectiveness but monopolistic advantages—resulting in the ability to charge 'good prices'—underlie the higher relative earnings of the larger establishments.

Nevertheless, many observers have urged that although in many industries, plants of *certain* sizes are undoubtedly more efficient than smaller ones, this affords no evidence that there do not exist limits beyond which further growth becomes relatively less profitable. In any particular industry such an optimum might be either tangible or intangible; it might pertain to the size of the actual plant or to a financial or corporate unit which operates or controls several establishments.

The data which we shall analyze in this chapter afford no definite answers to these questions, either in terms of what this optimum may be in any particular branch of industry or as to the causes of varying profitableness in enterprises of different size. They do, however, offer both for Manufacturing as a whole, and for three of its major groups—Foods, Chemicals and Metals—fairly comprehensive facts as to the size of the corporate unit and the rate of earnings. It is to be noted that the data pertain simply to *corporate* units, not to *physical production* units. While a large number of the corporations included perhaps do operate only single plants, many others own two or several establishments. Our comparisons, therefore, are of financial and not necessarily physical or engineering magnitudes.

The measure of size employed, in all cases, is the fundamental one of the amount of total capital invested. This, it will be noted,[2] includes the capital contributed by bondholders as well as by shareholders, and is a better index of size, for most comparative purposes of this sort, than would

[2] See Ch. 2; also Glossary.

be capitalization alone. Although from the accountant's point of view, interest upon borrowed capital is regarded as a cost, while that upon owned capital is not, both returns are income upon a corporation's capital in an economic sense; and differences of capital structure between enterprises, even though less marked on the whole in Manufacturing than in other industrial divisions (notably public utilities), ought not to be allowed to influence size comparisons.[3] For this reason, total capital and not capitalization is employed as the basis of all our size classifications; but for corporations of any given size of total capital, the net return upon either total capital or simply capitalization can, of course, be shown.

It might be possible to employ as a still more inclusive measure of size, total assets instead of total capital. Such data, however, are not here available. Were they at hand, they would provide a somewhat better measure of size in some ways, and a poorer one in others, than do total capital figures. From the point of view of managerial accounting, total assets afford a somewhat better basis for comparison —they include working capital borrowed for short periods from the banks, etc. But from the point of view of the permanent investment of capital in the business by its owners

[3] If only capitalization were considered as the measurement of size (and the ratio of net income *after* interest payments on long-term debt were then related to it) most misleading results might ensue. Of two corporations, one might have its total capital all in the form of common stock; another, with exactly the same investment, might have one-third of its capital represented by a bonded debt bearing 5 per cent interest. Both might earn, say 10 per cent on total capital, but the corporation with the bond issue would show a net return of 12.5 per cent upon its capitalization exclusive of bonded debt. It may be desirable to show the return upon capitalization, after charges, for corporations of different sizes, as well as that upon total capital before fixed charges; but, both to avoid difficulties arising from variations in capital structure and also because the capital contributed by bondholders is as much a part of the corporation's capital as that supplied by stockholders, the basic *classification* by size rests upon the total capital of each corporation, as above stated.

or other security-holders, total capital figures give a more realistic picture than do total assets; for in a balance sheet of either an enterprise or an industry, short-time advances cancel out—that is, the 'receivables' of one corporation constitute the 'payables' of another. For our purposes, therefore, total capital probably provides the most satisfactory measure of the size of the corporate unit in terms of the permanent investment made by those who receive incomes upon it, whether they be stockholders or bondholders.

2. EARNINGS RATES BY SIZE OF CORPORATIONS: ALL MANUFACTURING

Our data as to size consist of the 2,046 large manufacturing corporations series for which other analyses have been made in previous chapters. The data are available only for the two years 1924 and 1928. In each of these years these 2,046 concerns have been grouped into seven classes, according to the amount of total capital possessed by each company. The lowest class includes those with capitals of less than half a million dollars; the highest, those with capitals of over fifty million. The number of corporations falling into any one class in either year ranges from about 65 to 600.

The results seem rather conclusive. In both years, in Manufacturing as a whole, by far the highest percentage of profit to capital is earned by the smallest corporations— those with investments of less than $500,000. In 1924 the 230 companies belonging to this class show aggregate profits of 20.3 per cent, upon an aggregate investment of 82 million dollars. (The average investment per firm of the corporations in this class, it should be noted, is substantially less than $500,000, the mean figure being about $350,000).

In 1928 almost exactly the same rate of return, as well as the same average investment figure, characterizes this group.

Conversely, the largest corporations of all—those with capitals of over fifty million each—earn the very lowest rate of return in 1924 and almost the lowest rate of all in 1928. In the former year the concerns in this highest class—66 in all—show an aggregate return of only 8.1 per cent, upon their aggregate investment of over 14 billion dollars, as against 20.3 per cent for the smallest concerns.

In 1928 the very largest companies—now numbering 82, all with capitals over fifty million each—earn 9.8 per cent, as compared with 20.2 per cent for the smallest concerns. Thus, in both years the companies with capitals of under half a million dollars show earnings rates that are double or more those of the companies with capitals of over fifty million.

A less extreme comparison of sizes, however, is to lump together the two classes having capitals under one million, and likewise to consolidate all classes containing firms with capitals of over one million. When this is done, the 'Under $1,000,000' group in 1924 shows earnings of about 18 per cent while the '$1,000,000 or over' group shows profits of only 9 per cent. In 1928 the first group earns about 15 per cent, the second group 10 per cent.

So much for the general summary. Beyond question, among manufacturing corporations of all sizes of capital from $250,000 [4] to over $50,000,000, the smaller corporations earn profits at higher rates than the larger ones. Table 26 gives these results in detail. It will be noted that the rate of return regularly falls as the capital class in-

[4] The frequency distributions of total capital for the 2,046 corporations (see Appendix C) show that less than 2 per cent have capitals of under $250,000; but in 1924 and 1928 about 12 per cent and 10 per cent, respectively, have capitals of under $500,000.

TABLE 26

EARNINGS RATES, 2,046 MANUFACTURING CORPORATIONS BY CAPITAL CLASSES, 1924 AND 1928

SIZE OF CAPITAL (in dollars)	NUMBER OF CORPORATIONS	PERCENTAGE INCOME TO CAPITALIZATION	PERCENTAGE PROFIT TO TOTAL CAPITAL	NUMBER OF CORPORATIONS	PERCENTAGE INCOME TO CAPITALIZATION	PERCENTAGE PROFIT TO TOTAL CAPITAL
		1924			1928	
Under 500,000	230	20.4	20.3	187	20.3	20.2
500,000 to 999,999	461	17.9	17.7	376	13.5	13.4
1,000,000 to 2,499,999	596	15.6	15.4	607	13.8	13.6
2,500,000 to 4,999,999	310	13.1	12.9	351	14.3	14.0
5,000,000 to 24,999,999	315	9.8	9.5	376	10.0	9.7
25,000,000 to 49,999,999	68	13.0	12.6	67	12.3	11.8
50,000,000 and over	66	8.6	8.1	82	10.5	9.8

creases, with the exception of but one class interval, in which a slight recovery occurs.[5] For comparative purposes, the percentages of net income to capitalization are given in the table together with those for the rate upon total profits to total capital. That the two do not greatly differ is because of the relatively small amount of funded debt that characterizes manufacturing generally. Certain individual corporations, of course, possess enormous funded debts; that is the reason for having made total capital and not capitalization the basis of our size classification. But in the aggregate the combined long-term borrowed capital of our 2,046 companies constitutes slightly less than 10 per cent of their combined total capital figures, in both 1924 and 1928.

With these results for our 2,046 manufacturing corporations we may compare the broad findings of a similar analysis undertaken by H. B. Summers[6] for a smaller

---

[5] It is to be observed that the class intervals are unequal and that the somewhat broad range covered by the limits of this particular class may not disclose some variation within these limits themselves.

[6] *Op. cit.*

sample of 1,130 companies. His data are based on published reports as presented in Moody's and Poor's Manuals and not upon Government data; but broadly speaking, his definition of income and investment are the same as our own. His investigation, however, covers the twenty-year period 1910–29 inclusive, and his series is not one of identical corporations. The earnings rates that he develops are averages for this twenty-year period. With these reservations in mind, we may note that his results show a higher earnings rate for the corporations with capitals of under $2 million than either for those with capitals from 50 to 100 million or for those with capitals of 100 million and over. The discrepancy—the figures are 11.6 per cent as compared with 9.8 and 9.5 per cent respectively—is not nearly so large as that between our size groups, but the two samples, drawn from different sources as they are, serve to confirm each other.[7]

3. EARNINGS RATES BY SIZE OF CORPORATIONS: MAJOR GROUPS

Unfortunately, we are not able to present these size data by minor industrial groups or even by all major groups. For three major fields—Foods, Chemicals, Metals—separate figures are, however, available.

a. Foods

In both 1924 and 1928 the largest corporations of the

---

[7] The less decisive discrepancy in Summers' results may well be due not only to the fact that his sample is half the size of ours, but also, because, as stated in his paper, it contains an inadequate representation of the smaller companies among the enterprises which we have termed 'large corporations'. Relatively few corporations with capitals of under $500,000 have published financial statements; and beyond question, Summers' 'under two million' group, which is his lowest separate category, contains few if any corporations possessing capitals of from $250,000 to $500,000.

Foods group show earnings rates of less than half those shown by the smallest concerns. In 1924 the companies with capitals of over $50 million earned 8.8 per cent on their investment, while those with capitals of under $500,000 earned 24.3 per cent. The 1928 figures are almost the same —9.5 per cent for the larger companies, 22.6 per cent for the smaller ones.

When narrowed by major groups and further divided into class intervals, the number of corporations in the sample, however, sometimes becomes small. Thus there are in the Foods group only 12 corporations with capitals of over $50,000,000 in the sample for 1924, and 14 in 1928. Our broad results for this major group, therefore, will be more certain if we enlarge the comparison by combining the two classes with capitals of under one million, and likewise the six classes with capitals of over that amount. This gives, in 1924 for example, 74 Food Corporations in the 'small' companies group and 141 companies in the 'large' group. The 'small' group, thus defined, in 1924 earns 21.0 per cent, while the 'large' one earns only 9.9 per cent. In 1928, the one group earns 16.3 per cent, the other 10.3. Full data for these two broad sizes of capital classes are presented in Table 27.

b. Chemicals

The Chemical corporations with capitals of less than $500,000 in 1924 earned 42.1 per cent upon their investments, while those with capitals of over $500,000 earned 7.9 per cent. In 1928 the figures were 68.4 and 10.6 per cent respectively. The exceptional figure of 68 per cent for the 14 smaller companies with capitals of less than $500,000 suggests that something may be wrong with the sample. On the other hand, it is quite conceivable that certain small chemical concerns, possessing secret formulae or patented

Table 27
EARNINGS RATES IN FOODS, CHEMICALS AND METALS, BY BROAD CAPITAL CLASSES

MAJOR GROUP AND CAPITAL CLASS	1924 NUMBER OF CORPORATIONS	1924 PERCENTAGE PROFIT TO TOTAL CAPITAL	1928 NUMBER OF CORPORATIONS	1928 PERCENTAGE PROFIT TO TOTAL CAPITAL
1: Foods				
Under $1,000,000	74	21.0	59	16.3
$1,000,000 and over	141	9.9	156	10.3
8: Chemicals				
Under $1,000,000	62	31.5	48	26.0
$1,000,000 and over	148	8.7	162	11.1
10: Metals				
Under $1,000,000	187	16.2	151	14.6
$1,000,000 and over	461	9.1	497	10.4

processes, might in some years earn 100 per cent or more upon their investments, and thus raise the average rate for those 14 concerns to something over 50 or 60 per cent. Very probably this is indeed the case, for a frequency distribution of the *individual* rates of profit to capital earned by the 210 corporations of our entire Chemical group sample actually shows, for 1928, 8 Chemical companies with profit rates of over 68 per cent, 6 with rates of over 90 per cent, and 3 with rates of over 200 per cent each; and, if these happen to be included in our 14 companies with capitals of under $500,000, an average rate of 68 per cent upon investment in 1928 is entirely possible.[8]

But to be more certain of the broad tendencies involved, we may again combine the 'under one million' classes and

[8] These individual frequencies, for the higher earnings rates brackets in Chemicals in 1928, are shown on p. 40 of the *Source-Book*. They appear, but with classes of '30 per cent and over' lumped together, in Ch. 17 of the present volume. It may be added that Summers presents data for the chemical industry in the paper previously cited, and his results show chemical corporations of under two million dollar capitals as earning 24.5 per cent (average for a 20 year period) whereas for all those with capitals of over that amount, the average rate is 12.0 per cent.

also merge the several classes with capitals of over that amount. The result, in 1924, is that the 62 smaller Chemical companies belonging to the first group earn 31.5 per cent while the 148 concerns of the second group earn only 8.7 per cent. In 1928 the figures are 26.0 and 11.1 per cent respectively.

c. Metals

The Metals group sample contains 648 corporations, a far greater number than either of the two major groups already discussed. Of these 648 companies 61 had capitals of less than $500,000. Upon their investment these 61 companies earned 16.9 per cent. In the same year the Metals corporations with capitals of over $50 million—29 in number—earned only 8 per cent. About the same situation prevailed in 1928, the figures being 16.7 per cent and 9.6 per cent respectively.

Combining the capital classes of 'under one million' and similarly combining all those of over that amount, in 1924 we see the 187 smaller Metals companies of the first group earning 16.2 per cent, while the 461 larger concerns of the second group earn but 9.1 per cent. In 1928 the figures for the two groups are 14.6 and 10.4 per cent respectively.

Complete data for all three major groups are presented in Table 28.

4. CONCENTRATION OF CAPITAL AND INCOME

In a recent study Gardiner C. Means estimated that the 200 largest non-financial corporations of the country control 44 per cent of all non-financial corporate gross assets. Our figures upon corporate size will not enable us to develop, for the Manufacturing division or for any of its specific major groups, such striking evidence as this con-

TABLE 28
EARNINGS RATES IN FOODS, CHEMICALS AND METALS, BY DETAILED CAPITAL CLASSES

MAJOR GROUP AND CAPITAL CLASS (in dollars)	NUMBER OF CORPORATIONS	PERCENTAGE INCOME TO CAPITALIZATION	PERCENTAGE PROFIT TO TOTAL CAPITAL	NUMBER OF CORPORATIONS	PERCENTAGE INCOME TO CAPITALIZATION	PERCENTAGE PROFIT TO TOTAL CAPITAL
		1924			*1928*	
1: Foods						
Under 500,000	28	25.0	24.3	27	22.9	22.6
500,000 to 999,999	46	20.2	20.0	32	13.9	13.6
1,000,000 to 2,499,999	57	16.5	16.1	55	12.4	12.2
2,500,000 to 4,999,999	30	10.7	10.5	39	15.3	14.9
5,000,000 to 24,999,999	29	10.5	10.3	37	9.2	8.8
25,000,000 to 49,999,999	13	13.3	12.7	11	14.3	13.6
50,000,000 and over	12	9.6	8.8	14	10.4	9.5
8: Chemicals						
Under 500,000	19	42.5	42.1	14	69.1	68.4
500,000 to 999,999	43	30.0	29.4	34	18.5	18.0
1,000,000 to 2,499,999	68	17.9	17.7	71	15.9	15.7
2,500,000 to 4,999,999	24	11.8	11.7	33	20.9	20.6
5,000,000 to 24,999,999	33	12.2	11.8	30	13.8	13.6
25,000,000 to 49,999,999	8	12.6	12.2	9	11.8	11.5
50,000,000 and over	15	8.0	7.9	19	11.1	10.6
10: Metals						
Under 500,000	61	16.9	16.9	47	16.8	16.7
500,000 to 999,999	126	16.2	16.0	104	14.3	14.2
1,000,000 to 2,499,999	196	14.8	14.7	185	15.9	15.7
2,500,000 to 4,999,999	107	15.4	15.2	124	15.8	15.4
5,000,000 to 24,999,999	99	9.2	9.1	123	11.0	10.6
25,000,000 to 49,999,999	30	13.2	12.9	29	13.0	12.6
50,000,000 and over	29	8.6	8.0	36	10.3	9.6

cerning the degree of concentration existing in Manufacturing; but we may nevertheless utilize the data of the preceding sections for what they are worth in this connection.

For Manufacturing as a whole the 82 corporations in our sample with capitals of over $50 million each in 1928 possessed a combined capital of about $19 billion. In number, these 82 corporations constitute only 0.1 per cent of all manufacturing corporations in the country, but their capital equals 31 per cent, and their total profit amounts to 39 per cent of the aggregate figure for the country. That the share of the total profit received by these 82 corporations is somewhat larger than their share of the total capital does not contradict our previous figures showing that large corporations earn lower rates of return than smaller companies. In our size comparisons, we considered companies that had capitals of over $250,000 (with but few exceptions) and compared them with one another. Here, in discussing concentration, the comparison is of these 82 largest companies with *all* corporations in the country, many of which, of course, have capitals of much less than $250,000.

For the three major groups—Foods, Chemicals, Metals—separate data are available. In Foods the 14 corporations of the sample with capitals of over $50 million in 1928 number 0.1 per cent of all Food manufacturing corporations in the country. They possess, however, 26 per cent of all the capital and receive 30 per cent of the total profit. In Chemicals 19 corporations with capitals of over $50 million constitute 0.3 per cent of all Chemical corporations by number, but account for 52 per cent of the capital and 59 per cent of the income. Finally, in Metals the 36 corporations of the sample having capitals of over $50 million constitute only 0.2 per cent of all Metal manufacturing companies in number but possess 42 per cent of the total capital and 44 per cent of the total income.

These measures, it should be noted, are not necessarily indicative of the maximum degree of concentration in each group, that is, the 14 Food corporations of our sample with capitals of over $50,000,000 may not include *every* Food company in the country having a capital of that amount. All we can say is that 14 of the larger Food companies (or 0.1 per cent of the total number) own *at least* 26 per cent of the country's corporate investment in the Food manufacturing industry, that 0.3 per cent of the Chemical firms have *at least* 52 per cent of the aggregate investment, and that 0.2 per cent of the Metals corporations possess *at least* 42 per cent of the country's total investment in that industry; while for Manufacturing as a whole (which includes such other major groups as Textiles, Rubber and Leather, as well as Foods, Chemicals and Metals), 0.1 per cent of all the corporations in the country own *at least* 31 per cent of the aggregate corporate investment in all manufacturing industry, and receive *at least* 38.5 per cent of the total profit. In some major groups for which separate data are not available, however, concentration is not so high as the average figures for Manufacturing as a whole imply.

5. EARNINGS BY GEOGRAPHICAL REGIONS

The companies belonging to our large manufacturing and trading corporations series may be classified upon the basis of geographical location, and the earnings rates for these several regions compared. While such a classification is subject to substantial qualification because a given corporation, whether consolidated or otherwise, may possess production units located in two or more geographical regions, it is nevertheless of interest to note whatever broad differences prevail between those regions for which the sample contains a sufficient number of corporations to seem at all significant. But it is to be borne in mind that classification is based upon the place at which the corporation has its head office.[9] The country is divided into seven regions

[9] See Ch. 46 for further discussion of this important qualification.

based upon the classification employed by the Census: New England, Middle Atlantic, East North Central, West North Central, South Atlantic, East South Central, West South Central, Mountain and Pacific. The states included in these regions are shown in Table 29. Our data pertain to the years 1924 and 1928.

TABLE 29
CODE FOR GEOGRAPHICAL REGIONS

New England
  Maine
  New Hampshire
  Vermont
  Massachusetts
  Rhode Island
  Connecticut
Middle Atlantic
  New York
  New Jersey
  Pennsylvania
East North Central
  Ohio
  Indiana
  Illinois
  Michigan
  Wisconsin
West North Central
  Minnesota
  Iowa
  Missouri
  North Dakota
  South Dakota
  Nebraska
  Kansas
South Atlantic
  Delaware
  Maryland
  District of Columbia

South Atlantic (continued)
  Virginia
  West Virginia
  North Carolina
  South Carolina
  Georgia
  Florida
East South Central
  Kentucky
  Tennessee
  Alabama
  Mississippi
West South Central
  Arkansas
  Louisiana
  Oklahoma
  Texas
Mountain
  Montana
  Idaho
  Wyoming
  Colorado
  New Mexico
  Arizona
  Utah
  Nevada
Pacific
  Washington
  Oregon
  California

For Manufacture the West South Central region in both years shows the highest rates of return upon capitalization: 14.4 per cent in 1924 and 14.7 per cent in 1928.

The region showing the lowest return in 1924 is New England with an earnings rate of 8.3 per cent, while the lowest rate in 1928 is for the Pacific region, 6.3 per cent. The number of corporations contained in the sample for the Pacific region is less than 100, so the figures may be accepted with some reservation.

In both years, however, certain disparities persist. The New England region is near the bottom of the list and shows earnings rates of about 8 or 9 per cent, while the East North Central region, for example, shows rates of nearer 12 per cent. It is, of course, to be remarked that these disparities in part reflect differences in the industrial composition of the several sections of the country. Much New England manufacturing consists of Textiles in which the trend of earnings rates has been downward, while the East North Central region (containing the state of Michigan) has a large number of Metals establishments and includes virtually the entire automobile industry, in which the earnings rates were relatively high during the years in question. Table 30 gives the data, except for the Mountain

TABLE 30

EARNINGS RATES, 2,046 MANUFACTURING CORPORATIONS CLASSIFIED BY GEOGRAPHICAL REGIONS, 1924 AND 1928 [1]

REGION	1924 NUMBER OF CORPORATIONS	1924 PERCENTAGE INCOME TO CAPITALIZATION	1928 NUMBER OF CORPORATIONS	1928 PERCENTAGE INCOME TO CAPITALIZATION
New England	268	8.3	269	8.7
Middle Atlantic	681	8.8	680	11.3
East North Central	648	12.7	651	11.2
West North Central	126	12.7	121	13.4
South Atlantic	133	9.5	134	13.4
East South Central	50	13.3	49	8.4
West South Central	57	14.4	57	14.7
Pacific	74	9.2	75	6.3

[1] Mountain region omitted, see text.

SIZE OF CORPORATIONS [143]

region. Earnings rates for that region have not been computed because of the small number of corporations contained in the sample.

In Trade somewhat different results prevail. New England does not appear towards the bottom of the list in either year. The highest rate of return in both years is earned by the Middle Atlantic region: 15.5 per cent in 1924 and 12.2 per cent in 1928. The lowest rates of return are earned by the West North Central section: 7.1 per cent in 1924 and 9.6 per cent in 1928. For 1928, however, the several differences in these earnings rates for Trade are much slighter than in Manufacturing. Table 31 makes pos-

TABLE 31

EARNINGS RATES, 664 TRADING CORPORATIONS CLASSIFIED
BY GEOGRAPHICAL REGIONS, 1924 AND 1928 [1]

	1924		1928	
REGION	NUMBER OF CORPORATIONS	PERCENTAGE INCOME TO CAPITALIZATION	NUMBER OF CORPORATIONS	PERCENTAGE INCOME TO CAPITALIZATION
New England	60	12.6	59	11.9
Middle Atlantic	152	15.5	152	12.2
East North Central	148	13.5	147	12.0
West North Central	94	7.1	96	9.6
West South Central	61	11.5	61	10.8
Pacific	64	13.5	65	11.3

[1] South Atlantic, East South Central and Mountain regions omitted, see text.

sible a detailed comparison. Three of the nine regions, however, are here omitted: the South Atlantic, the East South Central and the Mountain sections. In the first case the figures contained in the *Source-Book* suggested errors in either the original data or the tabulation, while in each of the last two cases the number of corporations contained in the sample is too small to be significant.

CHAPTER 6

CYCLICAL FLUCTUATIONS IN PROFITS

1. EARNINGS RATES FROM 1919 THROUGH 1928

THIS chapter will examine, in somewhat broad terms and from a somewhat different point of view, data which are presented in more specific detail in other parts of the volume. Our interest here is not in the particular industry that may be named in the discussion, but in its behavior along with, or relative to, certain other groups during the up- and down-swings of the business cycle. The analysis will be restricted to Manufacturing and its various branches; nothing will be said of Trade, Mining or Finance. These three divisions, to be sure, exhibit cyclical variations which it is important to examine; but the smallness of the Mining sample (see Ch. 25), and the fact that in Finance somewhat different accounting procedures are the rule than in Manufacturing, make it inadvisable to compare these four divisions in the present chapter. Data for Trade, Mining and Finance, with a limited discussion of their cyclical character, will be found in Chapters 21, 25 and 26.

Considered as a whole, the period 1919–28 indeed afforded opportunities for profit to many manufacturing enterprises. Our list of 2,046 large corporations, in all manufacturing fields together, shows an aggregate net return of 10.8 per cent upon capitalization for the ten years in question. Even the severe depression year 1921 did not

CYCLICAL FLUCTUATIONS [145]

greatly lower this average. If that poor year, 1921, is eliminated by taking figures for only the years 1922–28, the return is almost the same, 10.9 per cent.[1] While there exist no data for other periods with which to compare these figures, it would seem that, judged absolutely, the series of profit ratios presented in Chart 8 confirms our general knowledge that 1919–28 was a prosperous decade (the underlying table for Chart 8 is Table 42). The Trading

CHART 8

**PERCENTAGE OF NET INCOME TO CAPITALIZATION
2,046 CORPORATIONS**

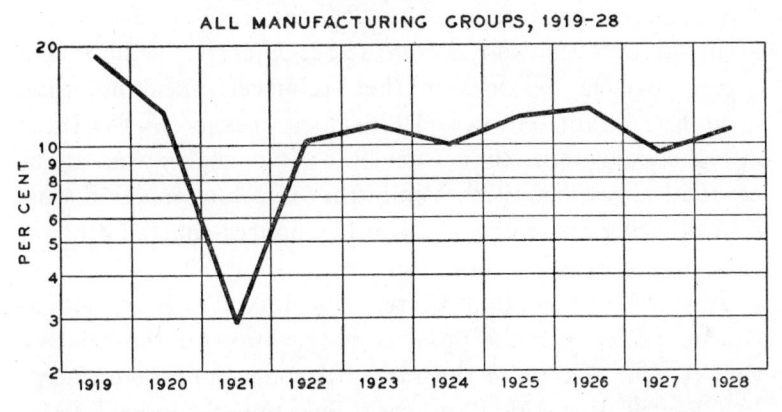

ALL MANUFACTURING GROUPS, 1919-28

[1] The concept of investment here employed, it will be noted, is that of capitalization as earlier defined. This assumes, for valid comparison in a time series, that no substantial alterations in capital structure have taken place (see Ch. 5). Even apart from this, it would be better from some points of view to include funded debt as well as stockholders' equity in order to show the total return on the full investment of capital in an economic sense. Funded debt figures for this series are not, however, available over more than the last half of the 1919–28 period and are therefore not used in most portions of the present analysis. While in analyses that seek to determine the rate of return as between establishments or enterprises of different *sizes* (such as appear in Ch. 5), the capital figures employed should preferably be those which include funded debt (and the income figures, those before instead of after fixed charges on such debt), for purposes both of *time* comparison and of the comparison of different branches *of industry* over a

field was even more profitable than Manufacturing, showing an average (aggregate) net return of 13.6 per cent upon capitalization for the ten years 1919–28 and one of 13.7 per cent for the seven years 1922–28.

But the year-to-year variation in earnings is substantial. The year 1919 afforded manufacturing industry an 18.3 per cent return; 1920 saw this reduced to 12.3 per cent, and the harsh year 1921 cut the figure down to 2.9 per cent. Recovery came in 1922. From that time through 1928 fluctuations in the rate of net income were less severe, between 9.5 and 12.4 per cent being earned in every year.

Examining Chart 8 further, it is surprising to note that the peak of profits, in terms of the rate upon capital, occurred in 1926 and not in 1928. Clearly, 1928 was a better year in the stock market, relatively speaking, than in industry. Not only was 1926 more prosperous for these 2,046 corporations than was 1928; it probably was about as good a year as 1929. While the data now under discussion do not run beyond 1928, other figures charted later in this chapter justify this inference.

It will be noted that Chart 8 is drawn to a semi-logarithmic scale, to make possible observation of the relative year-to-year change in the rate of profits upon investment. In Chart 9, the same data are shown upon a natural scale, but in the form of an index with 1927 as the base year.

That 1926 was as prosperous as 1928, or even more prosperous, can be seen again in the actual percentages of total profit to total capital enjoyed by the 2,046 individual

ten-year period, one set of figures probably serves almost as well as the other, if alterations in capital structure are not generally great. That the difference between the two sets of figures in the aggregate is not large may be seen by comparing the two ratios for all manufacturing for 1928: net profits after interest payments on funded debt to invested capital excluding funded debt, 11.0 per cent; the same before interest charges upon funded debt to capital including funded debt, 10.4 per cent.

corporations comprising the series. Frequency distributions affording knowledge of the range of individual earnings are presented graphically in Chart 10. In 1926, 2.5 per cent

CHART 9
PERCENTAGES OF NET INCOME TO CAPITALIZATION
AS RELATIVES ON 1927 BASE, 2,046 CORPORATIONS
ALL MANUFACTURING GROUPS, 1919-28

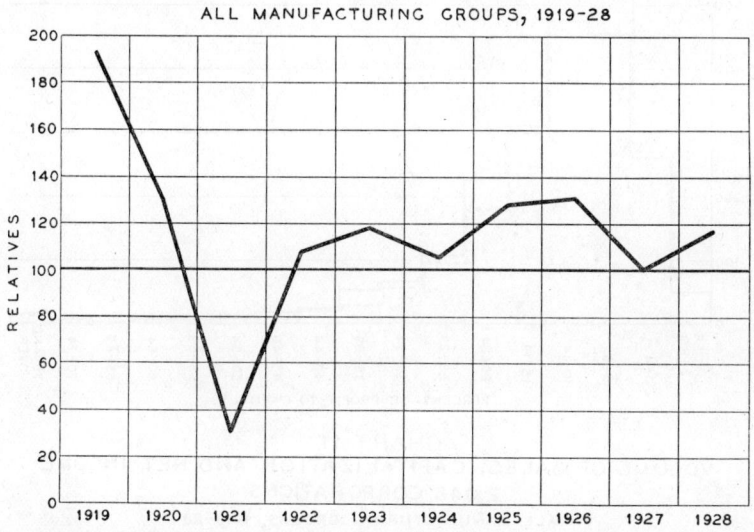

of the 2,046 companies suffered losses; in 1928, 3.7 per cent. In 1926, 33 per cent earned profits at less than 10 per cent; in 1928, 38 per cent. Then, jumping to the higher brackets, in 1926 over one-quarter of the total earned 20 per cent or over upon their capitals, whereas in 1928 only one-fifth did so.[2]

The absolute figures for net income, for capital investment and for dollar volume of sales are given in Chart 11.

[2] The distributions are given in detail in Ch. 9. The figures in these distributions are for total profits upon total capital, i.e., they include funded debt and the interest thereon. But distributions of the rates of net income to capitalization would yield about the same results; see Appendix Table 8.

[148] INDUSTRIAL PROFITS

CHART 10
FREQUENCY DISTRIBUTION OF INDIVIDUAL PERCENTAGES
OF TOTAL PROFIT TO TOTAL CAPITAL,
2,046 MANUFACTURING CORPORATIONS, 1926 AND 1928
——1926   ---1928

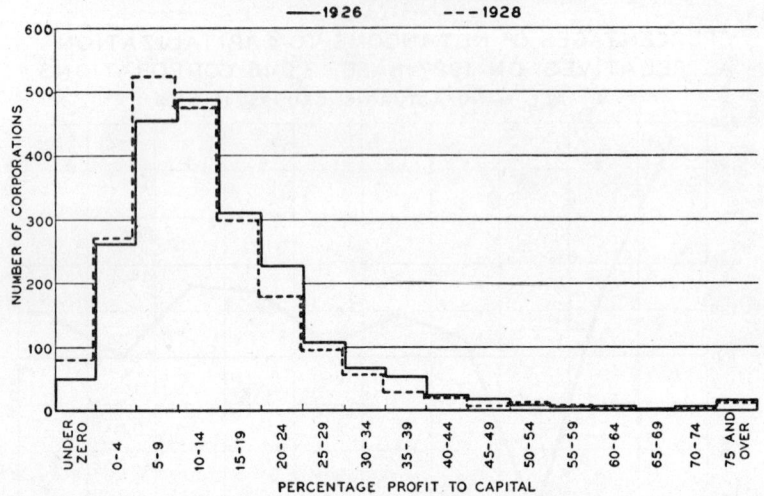

CHART 11
VOLUME OF SALES, CAPITALIZATION AND NET INCOME
2,046 CORPORATIONS
ALL MANUFACTURING GROUPS, 1919-28
——— SALES —·—· CAPITALIZATION ······ INCOME

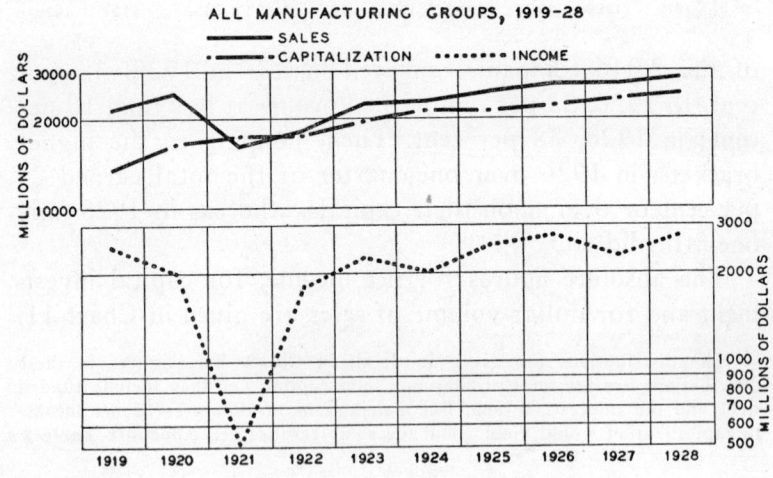

CYCLICAL FLUCTUATIONS   [149]

It will be noted that the rate of growth in sales volume (the scale is semi-logarithmic)[3] exceeds that in capital investment from 1922 through 1926; thereafter, the reverse is true. Comparing 1928 and 1923, however, the growth in the two series is almost exactly the same. Of the relation between sales and investment something will be said below, when the analysis of trends in particular industries is essayed.

2. RELATION OF PROFITS TO TOTAL VALUE OF PRODUCT

One point in connection with these aggregate sales figures commands especial attention. It is often contended that the cause of an industrial collapse is the increase of profits at such a rate that the mounting incomes of entrepreneurs and capitalists, during the period of expansion, leave a progressively smaller proportion of the total industrial product in the hands of wage earners and other income receivers. This is admittedly difficult to measure, but some clue can be obtained from data such as these by taking the absolute amounts of net incomes of these manufacturing corporations, adding to them the interest paid on bonded debt, and comparing the growth of those combined figures with the gross value of the product as represented by total sales volume.

This is done in Chart 12.[4] It will be observed that while

[3] Semi-logarithmic, or 'ratio', scales will be used in most of the charts of this chapter, since interest in these data centers more on their relative changes than in absolute amounts.

[4] This analysis is based only on the period 1924-28 because funded debt figures are not available for earlier years. Interest charges were estimated by assuming an average rate of 5 per cent on the issues of large industrial corporations (see Appendix A). The income figures are before Federal taxes, but the relative differences, were taxes subtracted, would be slight for this period, and the trend of the series not be altered.

It is also true that sales do not represent the entire receipts of these

total profits, including interest payments to bondholders, increased somewhat more rapidly than did total volume of product, as measured by sales, the disparity is not great. The discrepancy between the increase in the amount of income actually disbursed to security-holders and total sales indeed looms somewhat larger. It indicates a more liberal dividend policy towards the peak of the cycle; relatively less of earnings is 'ploughed back' into industry, at least less is directly so reinvested.

CHART 12
TOTAL PROFIT, TOTAL SALES AND TOTAL DISBURSEMENTS TO SECURITY-HOLDERS
ALL MANUFACTURING GROUPS, 1924-28

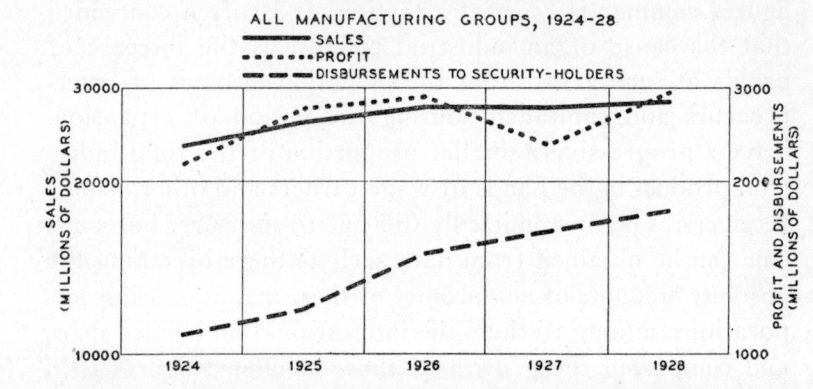

corporations; non-operating income of various kinds frequently appears as well. But the aggregate of gross non-operating revenue in manufacturing as a whole is small in comparison with that received from sales, however large the former may be in certain individual cases; and unless the ratio of the one to the other changed very markedly over the period under examination, sales serve quite as well as would a more refined total gross revenue figure for purposes of *time* comparison. Of course, for certain other purposes this might not be so. The question of 'value of products' *versus* 'value added' is likewise pertinent; but for the immediate purpose at hand its discussion does not seem essential. In the flow of money income through manufacturing industry at least, the volume of sales best represents industry's aggregate product in terms of purchasing power received and passed on again to the one or the other productive factor. What is not disbursed to security-owners or retained in the surplus account is (apart from taxes) spent for wages, materials, supplies or rentals.

CYCLICAL FLUCTUATIONS [151]

But the total net earnings of all capital—the aggregate of income ploughed back and income disbursed to both stock- and bondholders—*bore no very different relation to the total product of manufacturing industry in 1928 than in 1925 or 1926.* The bars of Chart 13 show these ratios,

CHART 13

TOTAL PROFIT AS A PERCENTAGE OF SALES, ALL MANUFACTURING GROUPS, 1924-1928

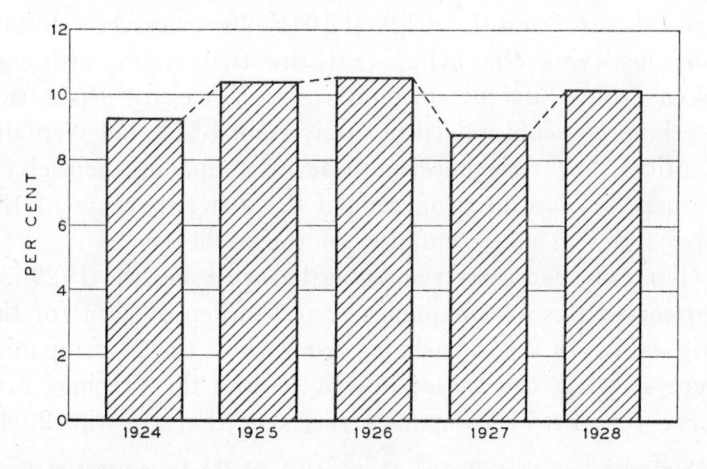

those for the three years just mentioned standing at about 10 per cent. We shall discuss this matter further in the concluding section of this chapter.

3. CYCLICAL FLUCTUATIONS THROUGH 1931

Although it is not possible to obtain 1929 and 1930 figures for all of the 2,046 manufacturing companies just analyzed, a somewhat restricted but still closely representative sample of that group can be constructed and carried straight through from 1919 to the end of 1931. This has been done by selecting from the list of 2,046 companies, through an empirical process of trial and error, 71 corporations in various industries for which the consolidated income and balance sheet accounts in 1927 and 1928 showed ratios quite the same as those characterizing the larger group from which they were drawn. Then, for these 71 corporations, data drawn from other than Government sources were obtained[5] for 1927 through 1931.

In 1927 and 1928 the new figures 'fit' the data for these years drawn from the original 1919–28 series very closely, thus justifying the belief that the two series, although taken from different original sources, are for these two overlapping years indeed not only comparable but virtually identical. So far as concerns these 71 companies themselves, we may beyond question regard the last two years of the later series as a continuation of the earlier one.[6]

The only questions remaining before using the 1929–31 portion of this 71 companies series, in lieu of data for the original list of 2,046 concerns from which the 71 companies were selected, are these: how well does the earnings rate curve for the 71 companies series fit that for the 2,046

[5] See notes in Tables 50 and 52, pp. 60–1, of the Department of Commerce document previously cited.

[6] For 1927, the ratio of net income to capitalization shown for these 71 companies, when data are taken from the original 1919–28 series, is 9.6 per cent; when taken from the new 1927–31 series, 10.3 per cent. For 1928 the two figures are 10.4 and 11.4 per cent respectively. (These figures are all for net income after Federal taxes). This correspondence in ratios is quite as close when individual major industrial groups are taken in the two series as for all manufacturing groups together. It is not, as will be pointed out below, possible to divide these 71 companies into quite as many major groups as the original 2,046 concerns, since in certain groups too small numbers would result; but when classified into eight (instead of 11) such groups, the 'old' and 'new' series respectively show, for 1927, net income percentages upon invested capital as follows: Foods, 8.4, 9.3; Textiles, 7.6, 9.1; Chemicals, 7.5, 8.0; Metals, 11.2, 11.5; Paper and Printing combined, 23.6, 23.7; Stone and Lumber combined, 8.4, 9.2; Leather and Rubber combined, 6.1, 8.6; Special Manufacturing Industries, 18.5, 18.2.

CYCLICAL FLUCTUATIONS [153]

concerns over the entire period *prior* to 1927; and how representative industrially is the smaller list? Chart 14 shows that the two curves follow each other, on the whole,

CHART 14

**PERCENTAGE OF NET INCOME TO CAPITALIZATION
AFTER TAX, 1919-28**

2,046 MANUFACTURING CORPORATIONS AND A SAMPLE
OF 71 COMPANIES
——— 2,046 CORPORATIONS
— — — 71 COMPANIES

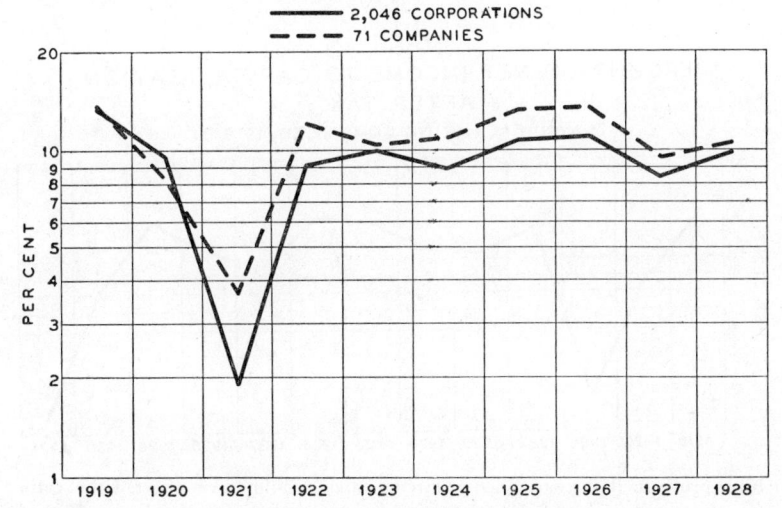

quite closely; in only one year is there an absolute difference of much over 2 per cent between the earnings ratios of the two series.[7] The other test, that of representativeness by

---

[7] The expression 'per cent' is here used in an absolute sense, i.e., '2 per cent' meaning the two points spread between, say, 11.2 per cent and 13.2 per cent. For a discussion of the significance of such differences, and for their interpretation upon a sliding scale of permissible amounts of difference, see Ch. 43. Here it may merely be said that the amount of discrepancy present, in view of the inaccuracies to which the data are subject, is not serious (*cf.* note 6, Ch. 7). The only exception to this statement occurs in 1922, and could readily have been caused by some dominantly large concern in one group or the other having enjoyed an inordinately

the relative amounts of capital investment in the different major groups, is fairly met also. The proportions of total capitalization shown in each of the various groups correspond fairly well in the sample and the larger list; however, because of the small number of companies in some groups, three combinations of groups had to be effected.[8]

We have then, in Chart 15, a tested series representing manufacturing industry from 1919 through 1931.[9] For the

CHART 15
PERCENTAGE NET INCOME TO CAPITALIZATION AFTER TAX
71 MANUFACTURING COMPANIES, 1919-31

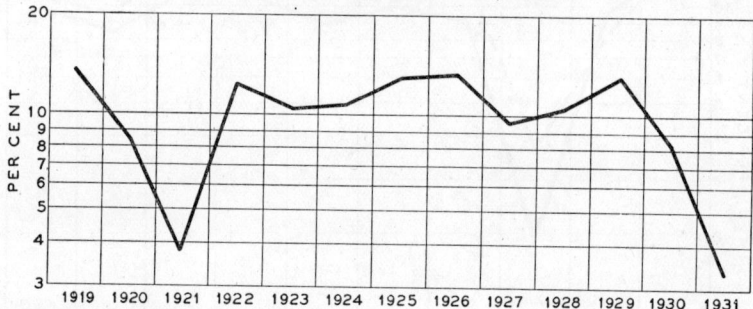

high profit in that year. Such a circumstance would have affected the ratio for the smaller list of 71 companies far more than for the larger list of 2,046 concerns. But even here, the discrepancy is not tremendous; the two figures are 12.1 and 9.1 per cent respectively.

[8] These percentages for the amount of capitalization in each major group (in 1927) for the list of 71 companies and for the list of 2,046 companies respectively are as follows: Food, 14.6, 11.1; Textiles, 4.2, 5.2; Chemicals, 24.3, 26.1; Metals, 41.1, 42.8; Paper and Printing, 1.9, 4.9; Stone and Lumber, 4.2, 4.1; Leather and Rubber, 7.8, 3.8; Special Manufacturing Industries, 1.9, 2.0. It should also be said that just as the capital percentages in Paper and Printing, and Leather and Rubber are somewhat 'off', so is the earnings ratio in Paper and Printing. For the group in the list of 71 companies (in 1927) it is 23.6 per cent, while for the same two groups combined in the list of 2,046 companies the figure is only 13.1 per cent.

[9] The 71 companies included have an aggregate capital of $5.3 billion in 1927, which is 22.4 per cent of the aggregate capital of the 2,046 concerns.

CYCLICAL FLUCTUATIONS [155]

thirteen-year period as a whole, the aggregate return was 10.0 per cent. Taking only the 1921-29 portion of the period—which gives a 9-year span from the trough of a serious depression to the crisis in which the 'new era' prosperity culminated—the figure becomes 10.9 per cent. Table 32 gives the series divided into eight major manufacturing groups.

The most surprising thing about these figures, on the whole, is that no great or sustained upward trend characterizes them between 1922 and 1929. The period was one of relative prosperity, to be sure, but in industry (as distinguished from the stock market) no generally higher level of profits was attained during the last few years of the expansion than during its earlier phases. And the recession of 1927, commonly viewed as merely a ripple on the sea of general business prosperity, is seen to have had a more severe effect upon profits than has been realized. *Manufacturing industry on the whole earned almost as high a return in 1930 as in 1927.* The 1931 figure, of course, registers a tremendous drop. It stands at 3.6 per cent, or at almost exactly the 1921 level. But it is worthy of note that 1927, regarded generally as a year of very slight recession, was actually one of scarcely greater profitableness than 1930, regarded properly as a year of poor business activity and great unemployment. (The 1932 figure indeed *is* lower than 1921—a preliminary computation shows it to be nearly zero, 0.8 per cent).[10]

That the 1931 figure is virtually the exact rate recorded for 1921 is a rather interesting coincidence. One would have expected it to be lower. (It is fractionally lower, that is, 3.6 instead of 3.8 per cent, but this difference is negligible

[10] This figure rests upon a slightly (but not significantly) different basis of computation than the 1919-31 figures. See *Bulletin 44,* National Bureau of Economic Research, January 27, 1933.

TABLE 32
EARNINGS RATES, 71 COMPANIES BY MAJOR GROUPS, 1919-31

YEAR	FOODS	TEXTILES	LEATHER AND RUBBER	LUMBER AND STONE	PAPER AND PRINTING	CHEMICALS	METALS	SPECIAL MANU-FACTURING INDUSTRIES
1919	−.2	18.0	13.4	12.7	10.5	14.0	22.3	17.2
1920	4.5	5.0	2.7	14.3	14.7	8.3	12.3	9.2
1921	4.9	7.4	−7.4	6.7	6.4	2.4	7.0	5.3
1922	8.3	11.7	5.7	12.5	17.0	9.3	18.4	18.4
1923	8.3	12.2	4.6	17.3	15.4	5.4	14.4	19.3
1924	7.9	5.7	6.7	12.4	19.9	8.5	13.7	17.0
1925	8.3	7.4	12.2	11.3	20.9	11.7	16.2	16.4
1926	9.8	7.0	10.2	10.9	21.0	12.2	16.2	17.8
1927	8.4	7.6	6.1	8.4	23.6	7.5	11.2	18.5
1928	9.2	5.7	2.3	9.1	29.0	12.2	11.1	16.5
1929	10.5	7.2	4.5	11.5	26.7	11.6	16.8	11.9
1930	11.6	−.7	−3.7	3.7	22.3	7.5	10.4	8.2
1931	9.5	−2.3	−3.4	−.5	13.7	3.1	3.2	4.3
1919-31	8.0	6.7	4.1	9.6	18.8	8.5	12.7	14.2

CYCLICAL FLUCTUATIONS [157]

in view of the character of the data; see note 8.) Economic conditions in general were worse in 1931; certainly unemployment was greater, and the several indexes of general business activity all dipped much lower.[11] Yet the average rate of net income to capitalization earned by large manufacturing corporations was virtually the same as in 1921.

This is not, to be sure, true of every manufacturing group. Some major groups are seen to have made relatively better showings in 1931 than in 1921 while others appear in a relatively worse light. Table 33 gives the earnings

TABLE 33

71 COMPANIES SERIES, PERCENTAGE INCOME TO CAPITALIZATION AFTER TAX, BY MAJOR GROUPS
(as relatives on 1927 base)

GROUP	RELATIVES			
	1921	1927	1928	1931
Foods	58	100	110	113
Textiles	97	100	75	−30
Chemicals	32	100	163	41
Metals	63	100	99	29
Paper and printing	27	100	123	58
Stone and lumber	80	100	108	−1[1]
Leather and rubber	121	100	29	−56
Special manufacturing industries	29	100	89	23
All groups	40	100	108	38

[1] Estimated; see Appendix A.

rates of the groups in several years, expressed as relatives with the year 1927 taken as 100.

Returning to the composite figures, in which the rate of return for all manufacturing groups stands at 3.6 per cent in 1931 as compared with 3.8 per cent in 1921, we may

[11] For example, the *Annalist* index stood at 65.0 in November, the 1931 low, as against 81.6 per cent in March, the 1921 low. The index of the American Telephone and Telegraph Company in December 1931, stood at −47.4, whereas in July 1921, it was only −27.4.

note the relationships prevailing between the general net income curve and the indexes of general business activity. Chart 16 presents three series of relative or index figures. The curve showing by far the largest fluctuations is that for

CHART 16
RELATIVES FOR EARNINGS RATES FOR 71 MANUFACTURING COMPANIES AND FOR ANNALIST AND A. T. AND T. INDEXES OF BUSINESS ACTIVITY, 1919-31

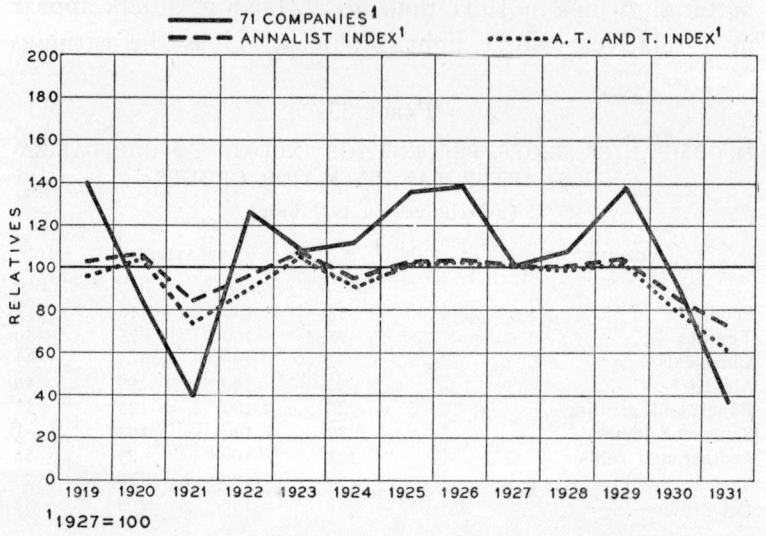

——— 71 COMPANIES[1]
— — — ANNALIST INDEX[1]   ········ A. T. AND T. INDEX[1]

[1] 1927 = 100

the rate of net income. The two business activity series are the *Annalist* and American Telephone and Telegraph Company indexes, converted into relatives with the same base as that of all the net income series, the year 1927 being taken as 100 in all three series.

The index of corporate net income, or rather of the rate of return for large corporations in Manufacturing industries, is seen to fluctuate from about 140 to 40, while the two indexes of general business activity move only from about 107 or 104 to about 70 or 60 respectively. In other words, the amplitude of the extreme swing is roughly twice as great in the rate of net corporate incomes as in general business activity.

In closing this chapter, we revert to a point made earlier. This last series of figures, like a preceding one that was examined, fails to show any continuous increase in the earnings rates of large corporations[12] during the five years leading up to the 1929–30 collapse. The data thus do not lend support to explanations of recession that hold that cumulatively increasing profit rates in industry at large are the fundamental cause of general overexpansion, eventual crisis and subsequent liquidation. If anything, closer examination of the figures suggests that the collapse of 1929 was *not* caused principally by generally high earnings rates prevailing in the period immediately preceding.[13]

It has been remarked that the curve for all manufacturing fell about as low in 1927 as in 1930. It is also true that *it stood as high in 1926 as in 1929*. This is likewise true of the showing of most of the major groups themselves. The rate of return in Metals was virtually as high in 1926 as in 1929. The same is true in every other group with the sole exception of Paper and Printing; and here the adequacy of the sample is somewhat questionable (see note 9). Most of the series, it may be repeated, show no sharp upswing whatever in the rate of profits upon investment during the three or four years ending in 1929; no more so than during the three or four years prior to 1926.

Observe carefully the data for Metals and Chemicals for 1926 and 1927; and again for 1929 and 1930. Ex-

---

[12] That is, in terms of their ratio to investment, which is the proper way to measure the profitableness of industry. In absolute amounts, of course, profits increased greatly.

[13] *Cf.* Gordon Hayes, Profits Destroy Prosperity, *New Republic,* June 3, 1931, pp. 67–9.

amine the Food figures; then turn back to the curve for All Manufacturing (Chart 15). The declines in the important Metals and Chemicals groups are about as severe between 1926 and 1927 as from 1929 to 1930. In Foods, also an important group, a decline occurred in 1927, but none in 1930. In All Manufacturing together the 1926–27 decline is from 13.3 to 9.6 per cent while that in 1929–30 is from 13.2 to but 8.3 per cent—a difference not at all striking.

Why, then, did not 1927 turn into a year of pronounced recession such as 1930; or 1928 become a year of deep depression such as 1921 or 1931? Certainly the answer is not that the profits situation was essentially different in 1928–29 from that in 1925–26. As a matter of fact, aggregate earnings upon investment for the three years 1924–26, for All Manufacturing, actually stand at a higher level than do those of the three years 1927–29. If 'profits destroyed prosperity' in 1929, as has been said, they should have done so equally in 1926.

But to say that *generally* high earnings in industry (or even in large major groups of industries) exerted no causative influence upon the cessation of prosperity does not mean that the large net incomes enjoyed by *particular branches* of manufacturing may not have resulted in an overexpansion of investment in those specific industries during the years 1927–29, and thus contributed to bring about a general collapse. To examine the evidence for or against this somewhat different point, we may next, returning to the data for the 2,046 companies from 1919–28, analyze the rates of earnings and the growth of capital in 73 sub-branches of the several major groups just discussed.

CHAPTER 7

CYCLICAL FLUCTUATIONS *(Continued)*

1. RATE OF EARNINGS IN MINOR MANUFACTURING GROUPS

THE 71 corporations series analyzed in the latter part of the preceding chapter, containing data that run through 1931, cannot be subdivided into individual industries or minor groups. Our 2,046 large manufacturing corporations series running from 1919 through 1928, can, however, be so treated. Furthermore, it will be recalled that we have sales data available for this series as well as income and investment figures. This chapter seeks to examine these three items, sales, income and investment, in terms of comparative growth or decline, by individual minor groups of industry. The reader is referred to Table 12 if he wishes to refresh his recollection of the full classification of 73 industries into which the several major manufacturing groups have been divided.[1] Our purpose at this point is not to discuss or even to mention in turn each one of these groups as is done in Book II, but rather to summarize the situation concerning the types of behavior shown by their several curves, and to chart the series that deserve particular attention.

Before commencing the analysis, some remarks about the nature of the period are pertinent. While business men often

[1] These 73 *industries* should not be confused with the 71 *companies* discussed in the preceding chapter.

termed 1922–29 a period of 'profitless prosperity', the expression was a misnomer. In nearly all industries, some years were quite profitable, some less so, but for no industry was the period as a whole 'profitless'. The expression was derived from the fact that although the volume of business increased in many lines, commodity prices failed to advance appreciably—indeed, in comparison with the War and immediate post-War years, prices were remarkably stable during the entire 1922–28 period. However, the volume of production in most lines showed a general increase between 1922 and 1928. Although this growth was in no sense steady, in many industries it was persistent; the checks administered in 1924 and 1927 were more than overcome in succeeding years. This growth of general business, particularly towards the end of the period when it became confused with a concomitant and more dramatic expansion of stock market speculation and a rise in stock prices, then caused the period as a whole to be popularly thought of as one of marked prosperity. Talk of 'profitless prosperity' subsided, and towards the end of 1928, only 'prosperity' was mentioned. And after the crisis of 1929–30, it became common to regard an alleged 'increasing profitableness' of industry during the years 1922–29 as a cause of the 1929–30 collapse.

We have in this chapter to examine the course of profit rates, of sales and of investment in manufacturing industries during the years in question. Our interest is not only in seeing what were the cyclical fluctuations of 1923–24, 1926–27 or 1929–30, but also in examining the 1922–28 period as a unit. (For our 2,046 corporations, the 1929 data, unfortunately, are not available.)

In terms of strict business cycle theory, the years 1922–28 are not, of course, a unit. They begin with a year of recovery from severe depression, cover one full cycle (1924–27),

CYCLICAL FLUCTUATIONS [163]

and end with a year of recovery from mild depression. Nevertheless, from the point of view of the business man interested in the expansion or contraction of the fixed capital investment in his enterprise or industry, the years 1922–28 possess certain characteristics which stamp them as 'good years'. For many products, the market grew greatly. For many lines of production, new and markedly cheaper processes, often involving greatly increased mechanization, were developed. And finally during 1922–28, despite the cyclically low years of 1924 and 1927, no severe and sustained general depression was encountered. For these reasons it seems to us desirable to examine the period as a unit as well as to note its year-to-year cyclical aspects; and it seems not inaccurate, likewise, to describe it as a period of good times, bearing in mind, of course, that the prevailing prosperity was in no sense unbroken.[2]

During 1922–28, then, we find that most of our 73 manufacturing industries showed no general increases in earnings upon investment.[3] Fifteen industries, or about one-fifth of

[2] The recessions of 1924 and 1927, while sharp in their effects on corporate earnings, were not so violent as to belie the statement that 1922–28 constituted 'a prosperous 7-year period'. Dr. Mitchell points out that the data analyzed in this chapter are annual, not monthly, figures and therefore do not match the cyclical turning points very well. He observes that what he would expect is not an increase in 1922–28, but a sharp rise in '22–'23, fall in '23–'24, rise in '24–'25 or '26, fall in '26–'27, and rise in '27–'28. In many industries such movements, of course, occurred. Granting the correctness of these observations, it still seems proper for the present purpose to regard 1922–28 as a unit. To find a satisfactory term to describe such a period is difficult; 'cyclical upswing' does not serve because the period contains parts of three cycles; years of *generally* (although not consistently) sustained industrial expansion' seems fairly accurate, though cumbersome. Another expression, also imperfect, might be 'period between holocaustic depressions'. The problem of different 'wave-lengths' in cycle theory is, of course, one on which much work is now being done.

[3] In this chapter 'investment' is mainly used in the sense of capitalization. Similarly, 'rate of earnings' or 'earnings rate' means the percentage of total net income to capitalization and is employed as a briefer substitute for that expression.

the total number, show a rise in earnings rates. Thirty more, or about two-fifths of the total number, show scarcely any trends whatever. And in the 28 others, or the remaining two-fifths, definitely declining trends are shown. The term 'trend' is used loosely to denote the general slope of the curves in question—reference is not to computed, mathematically fitted curves. Nor is the term ever employed (unless specifically so stated) in the sense of long-time or secular trend; reference is only to the period under discussion. The footnotes of the next section explain this more fully.

These findings merit further analysis. How great were the increases in earnings rates in those industries which did record gains? How large were the losses in the group that actually showed declining trends? And what were the courses of sales and investment, in comparison with one another, and with earnings rates, in various industries?

2. INDUSTRIES WITH RISING EARNINGS RATES, 1922–1928

The 15 industries that enjoyed a general increase in their rates of return may be divided into two sets: those in which earnings rates, generally rising after 1922–23, reached their peaks in 1926; and those in which earnings rates reached their peaks in 1928.[4] Rates of earnings in the following industries reached their peaks in 1926 (or 1925):

[4] In all of the 'trends' now discussed either 1922 or 1923 (whichever is lower) is taken as the initial year from which the growth in the profits rates and the ranges of these rates over the period are determined. In a few cases the peaks in the one set of curves are reached in 1925; these are classified with the 1926 peak group. In a few cases also, when expansion continues beyond 1926, the peak is reached in 1927; these are classed with the 1928 peak group.

As previously stated, the word 'trend' is used loosely throughout this chapter, in the sense of general slope—not as a mathematical derivative. See footnote 6 for discussion of the determination of 'general slope'.

CYCLICAL FLUCTUATIONS [165]

Meat Packing
Cleaning Preparations
Castings
Electrical Machinery
Miscellaneous Machinery

Similarly, earnings rates reached their peaks in 1928 (or 1927) in the following industries:

Beverages
Stationery
Crude Chemicals
Miscellaneous Chemicals
General Factory Machinery

Office Machinery
Firearms
Tools
Non-ferrous Metals
Miscellaneous Metals

Of course, were figures available for 1929 the dating of these peaks might be changed.

It will be noted that most of these industries showing increases are engaged in the manufacture of producers' rather than consumers' goods. The 15 industries combined show earnings of about 5 per cent in 1922, and of about 11 per cent in both 1926 and 1928, or approximately a doubling in the rate of return over the period. Chart 17

CHART 17

PERCENTAGE OF NET INCOME TO CAPITALIZATION
15 INDUSTRIES SHOWING INCREASING
EARNINGS RATES, 1922-28

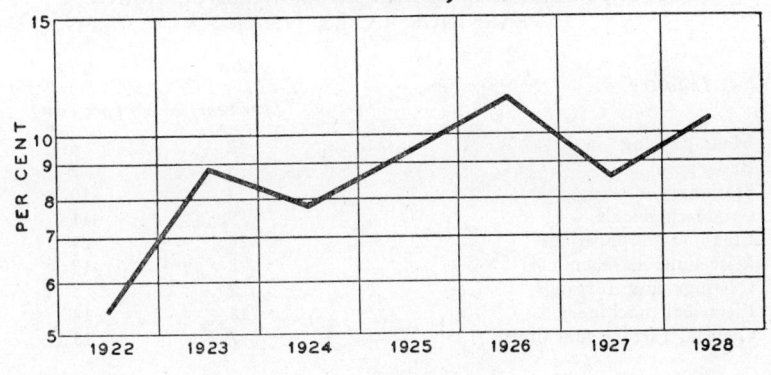

presents the averages for the group. Sales in this group about doubled also, while capital investment rose about 23 per cent. These growths are observable in Chart 18. The

CHART 18

SALES AND CAPITALIZATION, 15 INDUSTRIES SHOWING INCREASING EARNINGS RATES, 1922-28

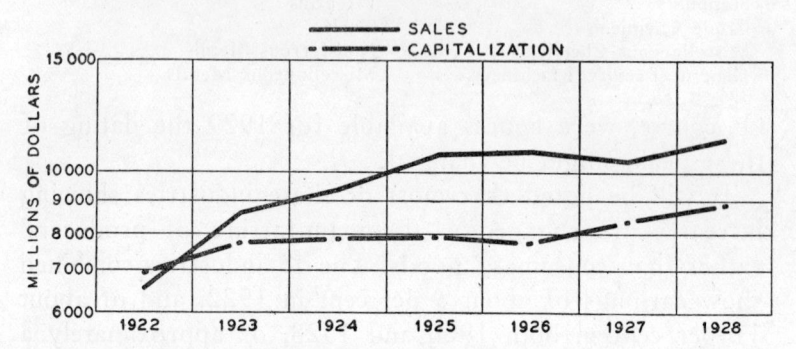

individual ranges for the period (high and low earnings years) for each industry are presented in Table 34.

TABLE 34

RANGES IN PERCENTAGES OF NET INCOME TO CAPITALIZATION, FOR 15 INDUSTRIES SHOWING INCREASING EARNINGS RATES, 1922-28

Industry	LOW 1922 (or 1923) (per cent)	HIGH 1928 (or 1926) (per cent)
Meat packing	2	6
Beverages	5	7
Stationery	4	10
Crude chemicals	9	11
Cleaning preparations	16	24
Miscellaneous chemicals	8	18
Castings and forgings	2	8
Electrical machinery	13	18
General factory machinery	7	13

TABLE 34 *(continued)*
RANGES IN PERCENTAGES OF NET INCOME TO CAPITALIZATION, FOR 15 INDUSTRIES SHOWING INCREASING EARNINGS RATES, 1922–28

Industry	LOW 1922 (or 1923) (per cent)	HIGH 1928 (or 1926) (per cent)
Office machinery	9	19
Firearms	10	19
Tools	8	15
Miscellaneous machinery	10	15
Non-ferrous metals	9	15
Miscellaneous metals	3	16

3. INDUSTRIES WITH FALLING EARNINGS RATES, 1922–28

The 28 industries in which earnings rates showed definitely declining trends are given below:

Dairy Products
Canned Foods
Cotton Converting
Weaving Woolens
Silk Weaving
Carpets
Knit Goods
Miscellaneous Textiles
Lumber Manufacturing
Planing Mills
Millwork
Furniture (non-metal)
Miscellaneous Lumber
Pianos
Blank Paper
Miscellaneous Paper
Book and Music Publishing
Paints
Toilet Preparations
Ceramics
Glass
Portland Cement
Heating Machinery
Textile Machinery
Engines
Railroad Equipment
Hardware
Miscellaneous Special Manufacturing Industries

It will be noted that no great preponderance of clearly definable producers' goods over consumers' goods industries is here apparent, at least not in sufficient measure to warrant any significant conclusions in this connection.

How great actually is the decline in earnings in these industries during 1922–28? The ranges for the individual industries vary greatly, as shown in Table 35; but the com-

Table 35

RANGES IN PERCENTAGES OF NET INCOME TO CAPITALIZATION, FOR 28 INDUSTRIES SHOWING DECLINING EARNINGS RATES, 1922–28

Industry	HIGH 1922 (or 1923) (per cent)	LOW 1928 (or 1927) (per cent)
Dairying	20	10
Canned goods	20	12
Cotton converting	15	8
Weaving woolens	15	1.5
Silk weaving	13	5
Carpets	35	6
Knit goods	25	10
Miscellaneous textiles	20	8
Lumber manufacture	25	7
Planing mills	26	7
Millwork	25	8
Furniture (non-metal)	19	10
Miscellaneous lumber	17	10
Blank paper	10	5
Miscellaneous paper	11	8
Book and music publishing	19	11
Paints	20	9
Toilet preparations	50	25
Ceramics	15	8
Glass	23	12
Portland cement	20	12
Heating machinery	21	9
Textile machinery	21	14
Engines	14	6
Railway equipment	13	3
Hardware	20	11
Pianos	12	5
Miscellaneous special manufacturing	20	12

bined figures for the group, as presented in Chart 19, evidence a drop of from 14.5 per cent in 1922 (and 16.4 per cent in 1923) to 8.5 per cent in 1928. Doubtless in several of these industries declining secular trends in the consumption of the product are one cause of the fall in the rate of return: in certain of them the volume of sales shows an absolute decrease. But in others sales show a substantial

CHART 19

PERCENTAGE OF NET INCOME TO CAPITALIZATION 28 INDUSTRIES SHOWING DECLINING EARNINGS RATES, 1922-28

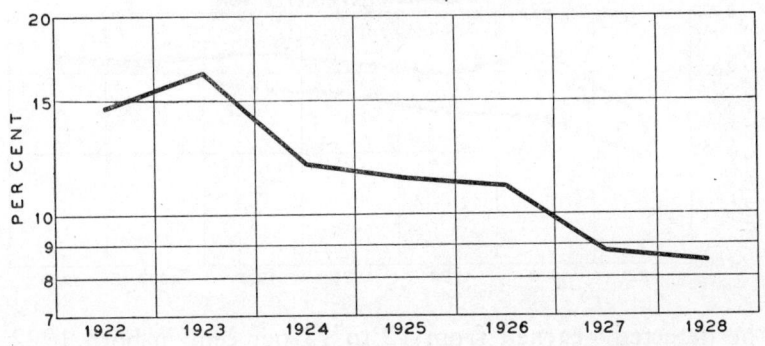

increase; here different factors primarily cause the relative profitableness to shrink. The word 'relative' is used advisedly, for the average (aggregate) return for this group in 1927 and 1928 still stood at about 9 per cent. Only 11 of the 28 industries, by 1928, fell to a point lower than that; and of these 11, only 4 fell below 6 per cent (Woolen Weaving, Silk Weaving, Blank Paper, Railway Equipment). Aggregate sales, for this declining profits trend group, remained virtually constant from 1923 through 1928; they are shown in Chart 20. Capital investment after 1923, however, increased steadily.

4. INDUSTRIES SHOWING NO TRENDS IN EARNINGS RATES

The final group, that of the 30 industries for which the rates of return either remained practically stable over the period or else showed such fluctuations that no trend could

CHART 20

SALES AND CAPITALIZATION, 28 INDUSTRIES
SHOWING DECLINING EARNINGS RATES, 1922-28

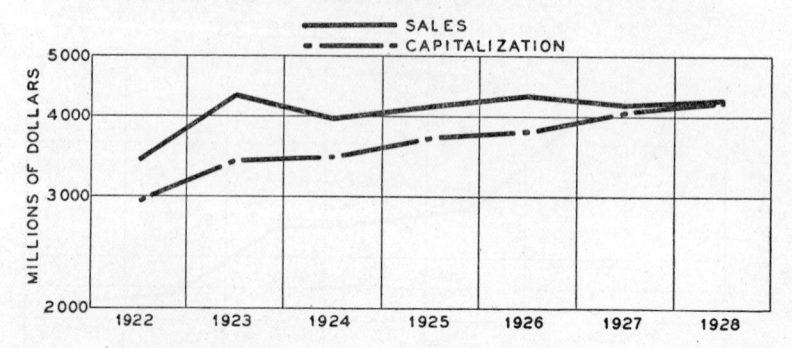

be detected,[5] earned from 12 to 13 per cent in both 1922

[5] In grouping the earnings ratio curves for these 73 industries a common sense interpretation in terms of reasonable approximation was used, rather than an abstract or refined mathematical technique. Some of the curves classified either as 'stable' or as 'no trends' showed small general increases over the period, but at best relatively slight ones; e.g., a change from a return of 11.3 per cent in 1922 to one of 12.2 per cent in 1928. This cannot be regarded, by anyone who possesses a sense of humor along with a slide-rule, as clearly constituting an increasing trend in the rate of net income for the period: there are altogether too many possible sources of error in the original data of individual companies, in the dropping of decimal points from the millions figures during the processes of computation, etc., to regard absolute variations of 1 per cent or less, in ratios such as these, as having any significance. When mere inspection of the curves (all were plotted on the same semi-logarithmic scales) failed to yield satisfactory knowledge as to the direction of the trend, then three-year moving averages were computed and their slopes over the period were allowed to influence the decision. In no instance were terminal values alone allowed to determine the classification; general slope or contour was always considered. One other factor was considered: where the slope established by inspection was so slight that a 1929 figure (which was not available) might readily have made questionable the direction of the trend—were it added to the series and did it chance to run counter to the 1922-28 result—then, too, the chart was placed in the 'no trend' group. (I.e., if the slope of the 1922-28 curve was downward, but so slightly that a *high* 1929 figure might readily have made the *1922-29* curve not clearly downward in general slope, then the chart was relegated to the no-trend category; if the 1922-28 curve showed

CYCLICAL FLUCTUATIONS [171]

and 1928, although, as Chart 21 discloses, the curve fluc-

CHART 21

PERCENTAGE OF NET INCOME TO CAPITALIZATION
30 INDUSTRIES SHOWING NO TREND IN
EARNINGS RATES, 1922-28

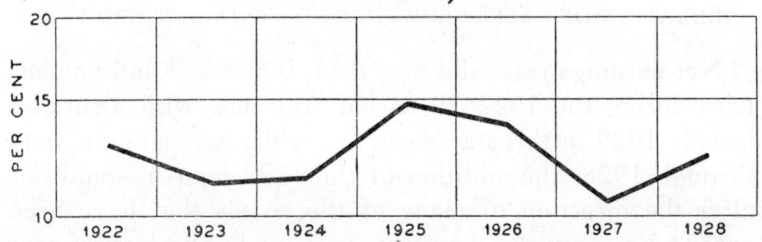

tuated about this level during the period. Sales for this group, however, increased at about as rapid a rate as did those of the group in which earnings rates for the period increased. Chart 22 shows the steady upswing in sales and

CHART 22

SALES AND CAPITALIZATION, 30 INDUSTRIES
SHOWING NO TREND IN EARNINGS RATES, 1922-28

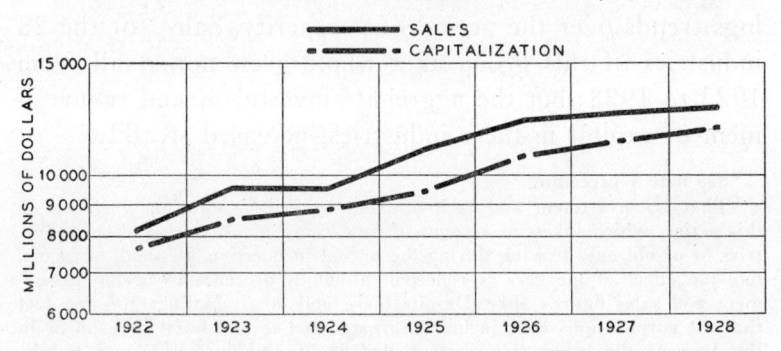

an upward slope, but a very *low* 1929 figure might have made the 1922–29 curve not clearly upward in general slope, then too the chart was cast aside.)

investment for this stationary or 'no trend' group, which includes several leading industries, among them Motor Vehicles, Rubber Goods, Petroleum Refining and Sheet Metal Products.

5. SUMMARY:
RELATION OF SALES GROWTH TO INVESTMENT GROWTH

Net earnings rates did not, then, increase in most industries during the 1922–29 period. We may with assurance include 1929 in this statement, for while our data run only through 1928, the addition of the 1929 figures would not alter the direction of many of the trends that have been noted.[6] Earnings did, however, increase in absolute amount in slightly over one-half of the 73 branches of manufacture; and in their percentage upon capital investment in about one-fifth of the total number of manufacturing industries.

In most of the individual industries that exhibit *rising rates* of earnings in 1922–28, this rise does not seem to call forth additional capital investment at a rate more rapid than that of the increase in sales. But the case is different with certain of the industries that manifest *declining* earnings trends over the period of prosperity. Sales for the 28 industries of this group as a whole grew not at all from 1923 to 1928; but the aggregate investment and re-investment of capital in these industries increased steadily.[7]

[6] See note 5 preceding.

[7] That is, investment and re-investment by the corporations included in this series, which takes no account of new companies entering these industries or of old ones leaving during the period in question. In some instances, too, the effect of mergers is reflected, although presumably in the investment and sales figures alike. Despite these and other qualifications the fact that the corporations here included so expanded their capital investment in the face of the other trends mentioned is of significance. These trends, however, as will be suggested below, probably were unknown to those responsible for the expansion.

CYCLICAL FLUCTUATIONS [173]

Circumstances in the following 13 of these 28 industries were responsible for this result:

Dairy Products
Knit Goods
Miscellaneous Textiles
Miscellaneous Lumber
Miscellaneous Paper
Book and Music Publishing
Toilet Preparations

Glass
Portland Cement
Textile Machinery
Engines
Railroad Equipment
Pianos

These 13 groups will repay study. In each the rate of earnings declined. In some sales remained stationary, in some they declined, in some they grew. But in every instance additions to capital investment were made, either as sales declined or remained stationary, *at a faster rate* than sales increased.

It is no part of the present analysis to survey the detailed circumstances of each industry, although analyses by persons familiar with such details might yield explanations of the situation that do not appear on the surface. The aggregate situation, however, is shown in Charts 23 and 24. Between

CHART 23

PERCENTAGE OF NET INCOME TO CAPITALIZATION 13 INDUSTRIES IN WHICH CAPITALIZATION GREW FASTER THAN SALES, 1922-28

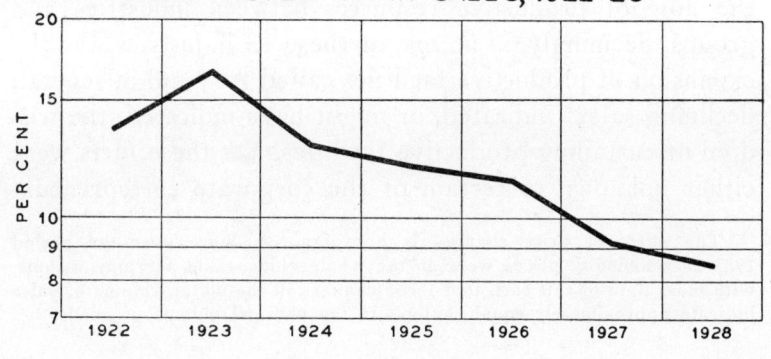

CHART 24

SALES AND CAPITALIZATION
13 INDUSTRIES IN WHICH CAPITALIZATION
GREW FASTER THAN SALES, 1922-28

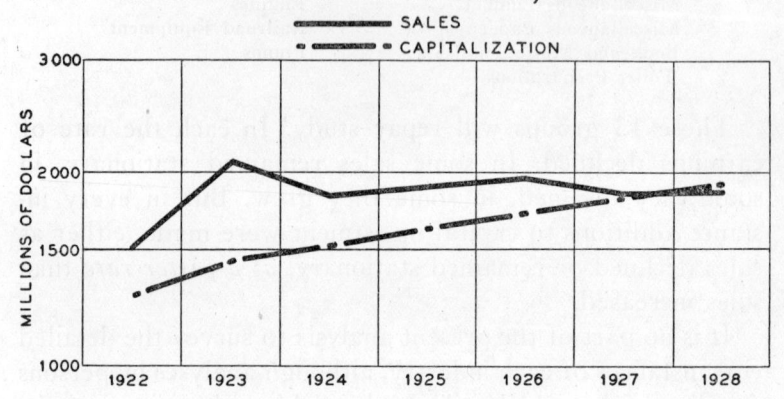

1923 and 1928 the aggregate sales of these 13 industries declined by 10 per cent. The rate of return fell from 16.7 to 8.5 per cent. Investment grew from nearly one and one-half billion dollars to almost two billion, the exact increase being 32 per cent.

This illustrates, it seems fair to remark, the failure of competition to function, as is often assumed, in directing the flow of productive resources between industries and groups. Seemingly, in no one of these 13 industries was the expansion of productive facilities called for; and in several, declining sales [8] indicated, or might have indicated, the wisdom of curtailing productive facilities. Yet these facts were either unknown to certain of the corporate entrepreneurs

[8] The effect of price changes is here ignored. Since over the period 1923-28 commodity prices were on the whole quite stable, we may assume, with mass data of this sort, that large changes in the dollar volume of sales indicate approximately equal changes in the physical volume of goods.

involved, or else they were not heeded. So long, apparently, as there is a substantial profit to be made, or the promise of one exists, the fact that a particular industry already has more than sufficient equipment to satisfy the demand for its products need make no difference to the individual business establishment. Even a generally declining trend of earnings may still yield an absolutely high return to the successful producer, especially if the rate is well above the cost of new capital,[9] and under these conditions, apparently, the industrial capacities of particular branches of manufacture are freely expanded.

In Charts 25 to 28, four examples of unwise industrial expansion are given; that is, presumably unwise in the light of subsequent maladjustments in production and employment in these industries as a whole. The expansion of any individual concern may or may not be wise for itself, of course, depending upon the given conditions in each case. But even additions to investment that result in profits to individual producers may cause losses and in some instances disaster for other producers, as well as for large numbers of workers employed in the industries. There are no accepted or standardized criteria for the wise and unwise investment of capital by individual producers in a competitive system. But in the absence of such criteria, a rate of investment expansion that clearly outstrips the rate of market expansion (as represented by the growth of sales) seems presumptive evidence of future economic difficulty, from the point of view of the industry as a whole.

To the four examples of such expansion already cited—Book and Music Publishing, Toilet Preparations, Portland Cement, and Railway Equipment—we may now add a

[9] Either the direct expense of interest payments upon working or fixed capital, if it is borrowed, or the opportunity cost involved in investing one's own, or one's shareholders', capital.

fifth, one taken not from the declining earnings trend group but from the stationary or 'no-trend' group discussed earlier. This is Motor Vehicles. It is included with the other four

CHART 25

PERCENTAGE OF NET INCOME TO CAPITALIZATION IN TWO MINOR GROUPS, 1922-28

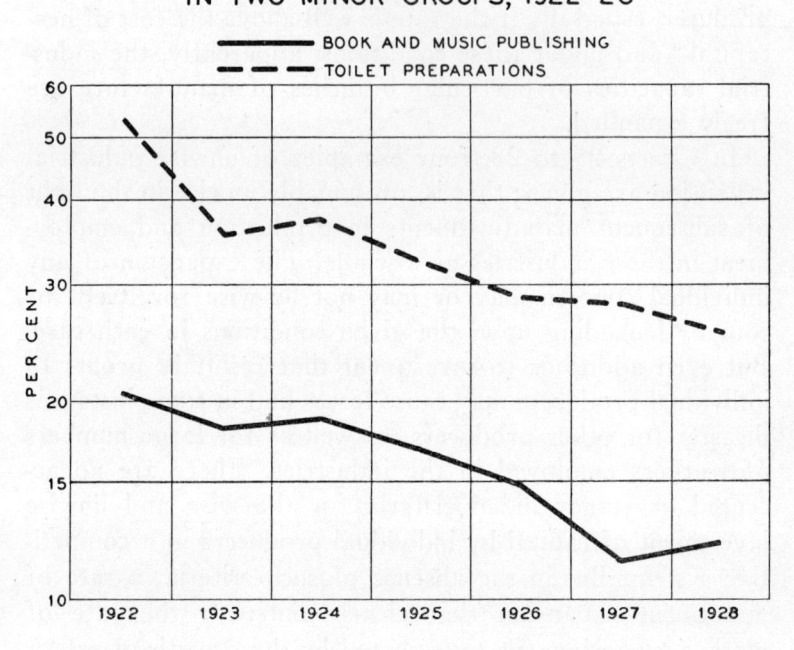

——— BOOK AND MUSIC PUBLISHING
— — — TOILET PREPARATIONS

because while its rate of return from 1922 to 1928 did not decline sufficiently to place it in the group exhibiting definitely falling trends for that entire period, its earnings rates from 1925 onward manifest a clearly falling course: from 24 per cent in 1925 to 16 per cent in 1928.

Yet because either 24 or 16 per cent is more than a satisfactory return upon capital, and with a competitive situation under which no producer is restrained from expanding

CYCLICAL FLUCTUATIONS [177]

his capacity, each felt that he had a better chance than his competitor to capture a larger portion of the market, and

CHART 26

SALES AND CAPITALIZATION
IN TWO MINOR GROUPS, 1922-28

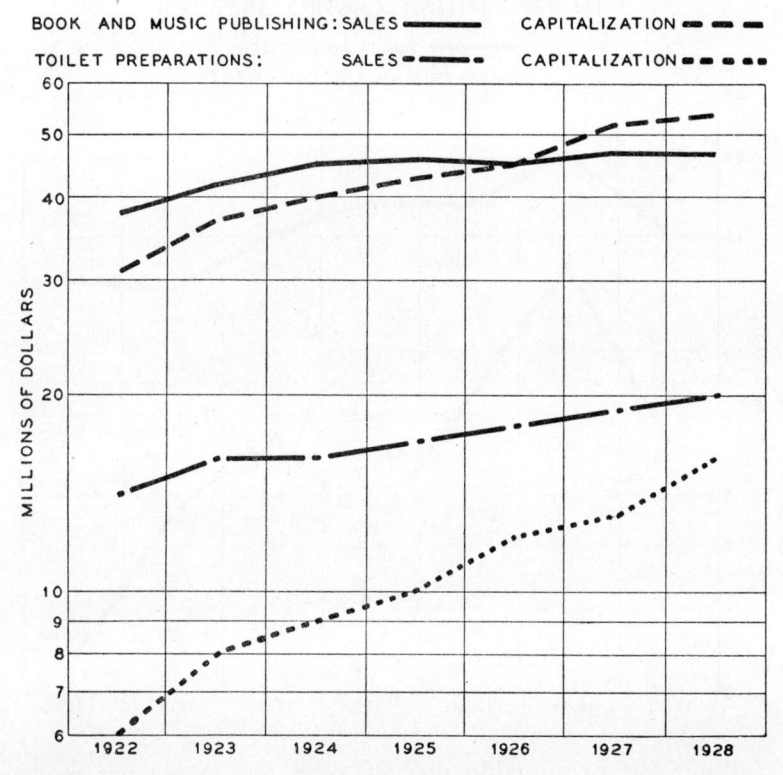

BOOK AND MUSIC PUBLISHING: SALES ——— CAPITALIZATION — — —
TOILET PREPARATIONS: SALES •—•—• CAPITALIZATION • • • •

additions to plant capacity in Motor Vehicles continued to be made. Frequently, of course, the general trends of the earnings upon capital and the growth of aggregate investments are not really known to the business executive concerned. And in some instances, further capital investment may be socially desirable in an industry yielding profits decidedly above the average even if the rate of profit is

CHART 27

PERCENTAGE OF NET INCOME TO CAPITALIZATION IN TWO MINOR GROUPS, 1922-28

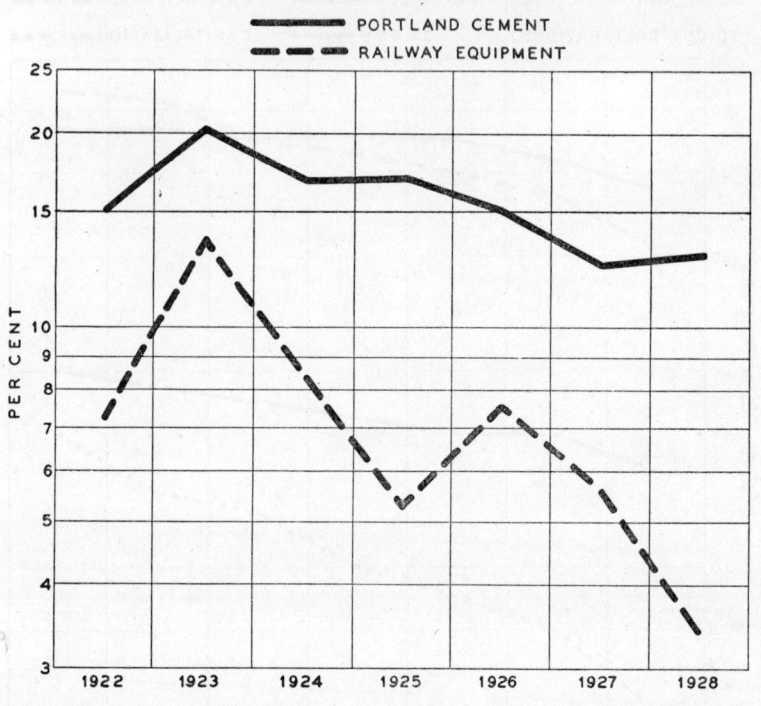

————— PORTLAND CEMENT
— — — RAILWAY EQUIPMENT

falling, but presumably only if sales are increasing more rapidly than productive capacity.

It is in this sense that the lure of profits over-rides the so-called law of supply and demand during a period of prosperity. Ultimately, a reckoning comes. But it comes

CYCLICAL FLUCTUATIONS [179]

neither automatically nor quickly enough to prevent enormous investments of capital being made, over a period of six or eight years, in quarters where they are not really

CHART 28

SALES AND CAPITALIZATION IN TWO MINOR GROUPS, 1922-28

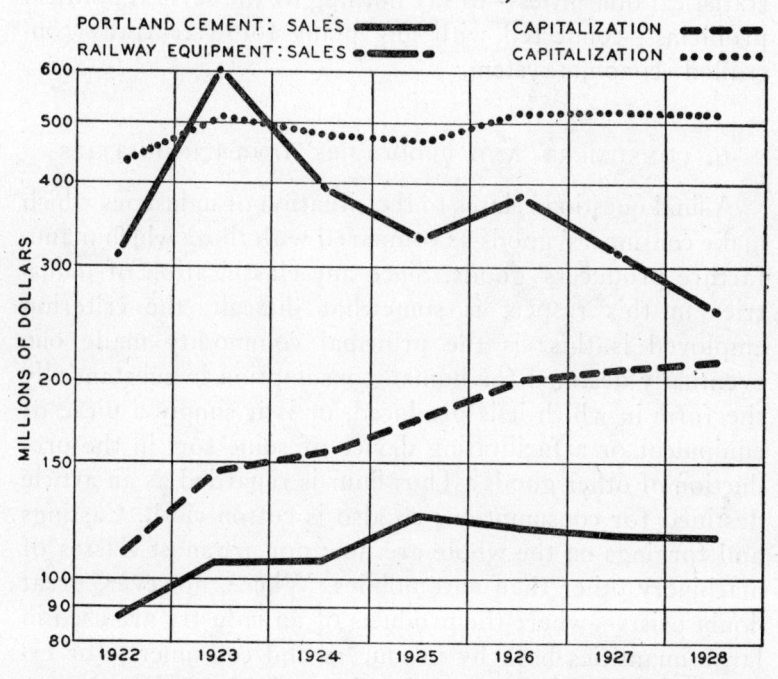

PORTLAND CEMENT: SALES ━━━   CAPITALIZATION ━ ━ ━
RAILWAY EQUIPMENT: SALES ●━━●   CAPITALIZATION ●●●●●●

needed and where they later serve to reduce profits below levels which, again under a competitive system, allow anything like the full employment of the capital so invested. It is, in other words, the possibility of absolutely high rates of income that causes overinvestment, relative to market needs, in *particular industries*. This overinvestment in productive facilities for *particular* products, rather than increasing rates of earnings *in general,* is what later occasions difficulty so far as the profits situation is concerned. How, under a fully competitive system of industry, such investments can be checked, save by fuller disclosures and current publication of the figures and trends involved, it is difficult to see. On the other hand, our final chapter points out the statistical difficulties—to say nothing of the several political problems—connected with any plans for a centrally controlled economic system.

6. CONSUMERS' AND PRODUCERS' GOODS INDUSTRIES

A final question relates to the situation of industries which make consumers' goods as compared with those which manufacture producers' goods. Since any classification of industries in this respect is somewhat difficult, the criterion employed is this: is the principal commodity made one eventually destined for human consumption in substantially the form in which it is produced, or is it simply a piece of equipment or a facilitating device of some sort in the production of other goods? Thus flour is regarded as an article destined for consumption; so also is cotton cloth. Castings and forgings on the whole are not; nor are most classes of machinery other than automobiles. Where, however, great doubt exists—where the products of an industry are used in large quantities both by producers and consumers, for example, Lumber, Electrical Machinery, Scientific Instruments —the industry is put into neither class but is omitted from the calculations.

Thus classed, the 18 industries manufacturing producers' goods show an aggregate earnings rate that runs from 6 per cent in 1922 to 10 per cent in both 1923 and 1926, and stands at 8 per cent in 1928. The group making consumers'

CYCLICAL FLUCTUATIONS [181]

goods (26 industries) enjoys much higher and much steadier earnings—from 12 to 16 per cent in all years of the same period. The two curves are shown in Chart 29.

CHART 29

PERCENTAGE OF NET INCOME TO CAPITALIZATION
PRODUCERS' GOODS AND CONSUMERS' GOODS
INDUSTRIES, 1922-28

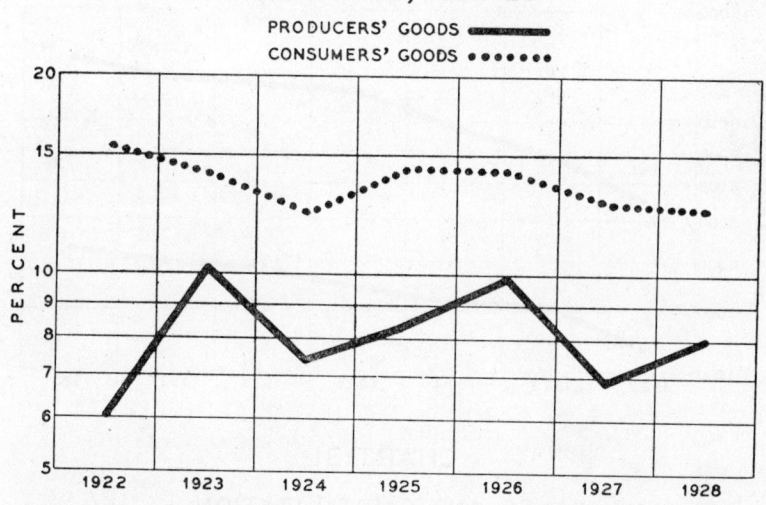

PRODUCERS' GOODS
CONSUMERS' GOODS

Sales in the consumers' goods group grew somewhat more rapidly than did capital investment (Chart 30). In the producers' goods, sales grew more rapidly from 1922 to 1926; thereafter, the growth of capital invested greatly exceeded that of sales (Chart 31). This relatively excessive investment of capital by producers' goods industries just prior to the peak of a cycle is a significant phenomenon. It accounts, for one thing, for the great distress of the 'heavy industries' in the ensuing period of depression. And it emphasizes the 'roundabout' character of modern methods of production, under which enormous commitments of capital are regularly made solely *in anticipation* of a demand

CHART 30

**SALES AND CAPITALIZATION
CONSUMERS' GOODS INDUSTRIES, 1922-28**

——— SALES
• • • • CAPITALIZATION

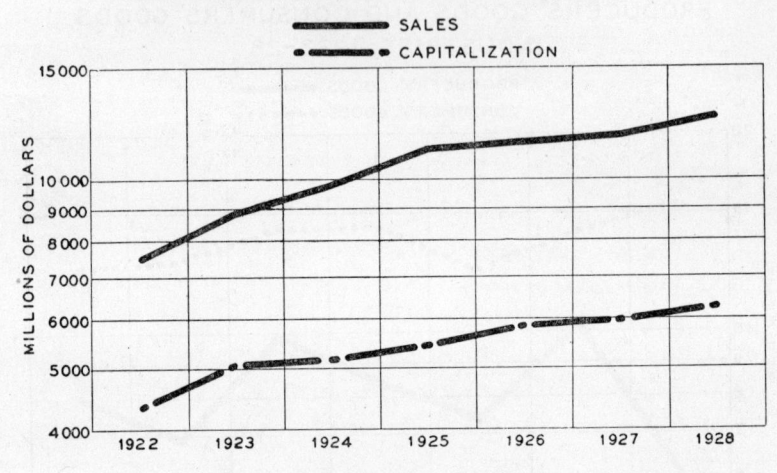

CHART 31

**SALES AND CAPITALIZATION
PRODUCERS' GOODS INDUSTRIES, 1922-28**

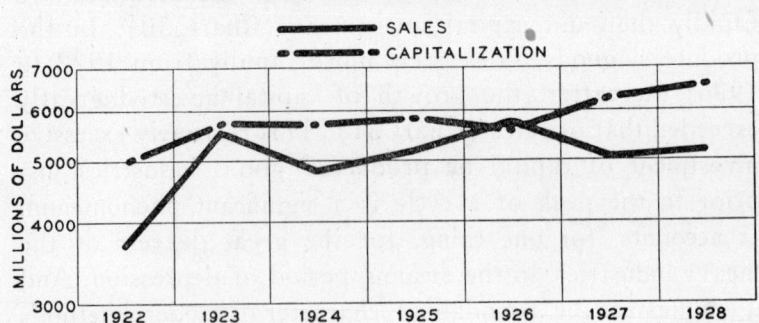

——— SALES
• • • • CAPITALIZATION

which, in either an absolute or a relative sense, is already declining even as the investments of capital made to satisfy it are increased.

The consumers' goods group, however, in which no such overinvestment—in the sense of a capital expansion altogether disproportionate to the growth of sales—took place towards the peak of the cycle, may be analyzed further. Producers' goods industries, after all, exist basically in order to feed or to maintain the industries that make consumers' goods; and the rates at which sales, profits and the like grow in various classes of consumers' goods industries are deserving of further attention.

The numerous consumers' goods industries for which aggregate data were just presented may arbitrarily be divided into three classes: those making goods that are quickly consumed; those making durable goods; and those making goods of intermediate durability. In the Quick consumption group have been placed all Food products, including Tobacco; Proprietary Preparations; Toilet Preparations. In the Intermediate consumption group have been placed all types of Clothing. Finally, in the Durable group have been put Furniture, non-metal; Motor Vehicles; Jewelry; Toys;[10] Pianos.

The volume of sales in each of these groups from 1922 through 1928 is shown in Chart 32. The annual sales of Durable goods more than doubled between 1922 and 1928, the degree of this increase greatly exceeding that of either of the other two types of commodity. Again, the growth in the capital investment devoted to the production of Durable

[10] One may question the inclusion of Toys in the Durable group; however, what is in mind is not the length of life, or the article's physical condition as it ages, so much as the greater or lesser degree of necessity for replacement as it becomes old. Most large toys, at least, are probably not articles for which the 'replacement' demand is elastic.

goods proceeded at a far more rapid rate than in the other two groups (Chart 33).

Finally, however, it is to be observed that the rate of

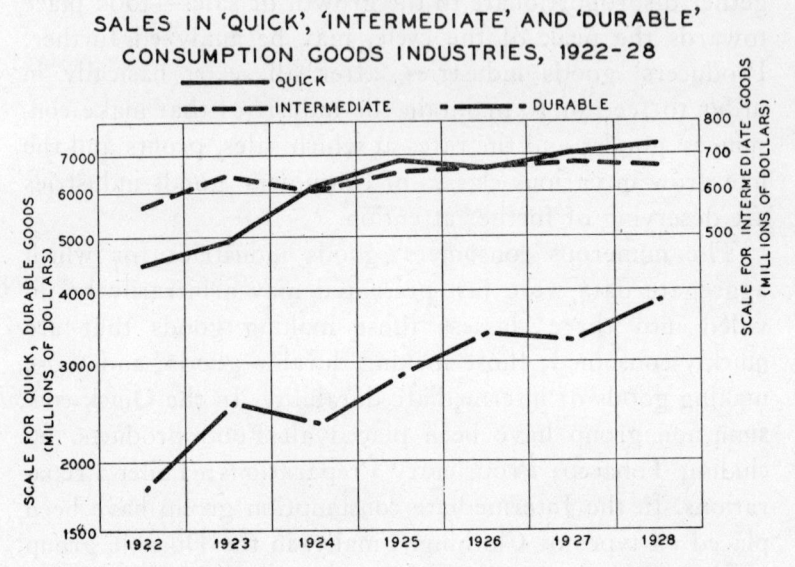

CHART 32

SALES IN 'QUICK', 'INTERMEDIATE' AND 'DURABLE' CONSUMPTION GOODS INDUSTRIES, 1922-28

earnings did not take the same course (Chart 34). In Durable goods, it fell; in Intermediate consumption goods, it fell too; in Quick consumption goods the rate showed a very slight increase. But even at the 1928 low point (of the period 1922–28), the return in Durable consumption goods stood higher than that in either of the other two groups. This illustrates again how falling earnings rates fail to check the investment of capital as long as their downward slope remains absolutely high—or at least high relative to other industries. In this instance, however, there is present no striking lack of proportion between the growth of sales and

CYCLICAL FLUCTUATIONS [185]

the expansion of investment. The Durable consumption

CHART 33

CAPITALIZATION IN 'QUICK', 'INTERMEDIATE' AND 'DURABLE' CONSUMPTION GOODS INDUSTRIES, 1922-28

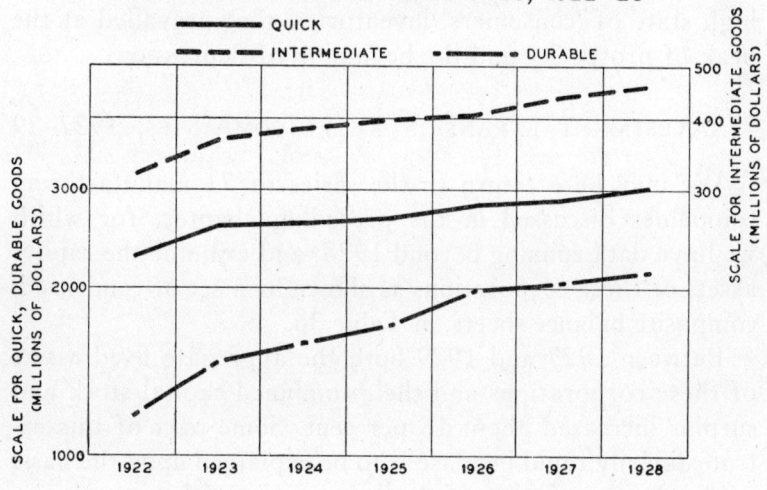

CHART 34

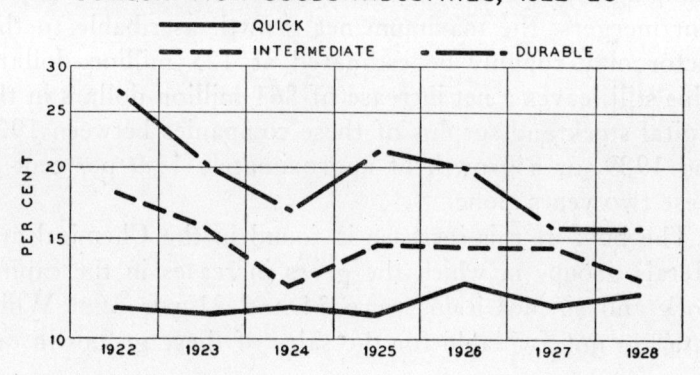

PERCENTAGE OF NET INCOME TO CAPITALIZATION IN 'QUICK', 'INTERMEDIATE' AND 'DURABLE' CONSUMPTION GOODS INDUSTRIES, 1922-28

goods industries merely became increasingly important in the national economy between 1922 and 1928. The increase that took place in their sales over this period, however, was greatly out of proportion to the growth of sales in other consumption goods industries and points to the relatively high state of 'consumers' inventories' that prevailed at the peak of prosperity and the beginning of depression.

7. INVESTMENT EXPANSION BY 71 COMPANIES, 1927–29

We may here return to the series of 71 manufacturing companies discussed in the preceding chapter, for which we have data running beyond 1928, and examine the capital assets of these corporations as shown by a set of condensed, composite balance sheets, in Table 36.

Between 1927 and 1929 both the aggregate fixed assets of these corporations and their combined capital stock and surplus increased about 18 per cent. Some part of this extraordinarily rapid increase is to be explained upon the basis of the merger of some of these companies with corporations not included in the list as of the end of 1927. But inquiry has disclosed that few of these corporations increased their assets by any very large relative amount for this reason. Lumping together the increases due to the effect of important mergers, the maximum net growth ascribable to this factor may roughly be estimated at 125 million dollars. This still leaves a net increase of 861 million dollars in the capital stock and surplus of these companies between 1927 and 1929, or a growth of approximately 15.9 per cent in these two years alone.

The bulk of this increase is found in the Chemical and Metals groups in which the gross increases in the capital stock and surplus items were 34 and 21 per cent. While data are not available for the sales of these groups in our

TABLE 36
CONDENSED COMPOSITE BALANCE SHEETS OF 71 COMPANIES IN ALL MAJOR MANUFACTURING GROUPS AS OF DECEMBER 31, 1927–30

	1927 Millions of dollars	1927 Percentage of total	1928 Millions of dollars	1928 Percentage of total	1929 Millions of dollars	1929 Percentage of total	1930 Millions of dollars	1930 Percentage of total
Assets								
Cash and equivalent	1185	17.1	1255	17.3	1269	15.9	1289	16.5
Inventories	1338	19.2	1424	19.6	1512	19.0	1395	17.8
Other current assets	543	7.8	576	7.9	600	7.5	544	7.0
Total current assets	3066	44.1	3255	44.8	3381	42.4	3228	41.3
Fixed assets	3879	55.9	4010	55.2	4596	57.6	4586	58.7
Total assets	6945	100.0	7265	100.0	7977	100.0	7814	100.0
Liabilities								
Total current liabilities	610	8.8	694	9.6	677	8.5	459	5.9
Funded debt	722	10.4	715	9.8	656	8.2	696	8.9
Capital stock and surplus	5416	78.0	5655	77.8	6402	80.3	6494	83.1
Other liabilities	197	2.8	201	2.8	242	3.0	165	2.1
Total liabilities	6945	100.0	7265	100.0	7977	100.0	7814	100.0

71 companies series, we may note that in our larger samples (which include the corporations of the 71 companies series) sales in the Chemical group fell off substantially between 1927 and 1928 and in the Metals group showed only an 11 per cent increase. Sales data for 1929 are not available for either series, but it seems fairly certain that whatever increase occurred between 1927 and 1929 was not nearly so great as the increases in investment just noted.

NOTE UPON
ABSOLUTE SALES AND INCOME CHANGES

DECLINE IN SALES, 1920–1921

IN THIS and the preceding chapter, interest was centered chiefly upon the general course of sales, income and investment in different industries over the period 1922–28. This note summarizes an examination of some shorter-run phenomena: the decline of sales and income, in each industry, from the cyclical peak to the trough which, within a year or two, follows; and the recovery from the bottom of the trough to the immediately succeeding point of recovery. Which industries suffer the severest, which the mildest, drops? Which soon recover to a greater, which to a lesser extent? How does a decline in sales affect the amount of net income in one industry as compared with another? The discussion is couched in terms of *absolute amounts* of income and sales and their relative changes—not *rates* of return upon either sales or investment. For, over so short a period as from one year to the next, it may be assumed that investment does not ordinarily vary sufficiently to make adjustments in the data essential. By and large, the typical manufacturing plant or retail store possessed roughly the same total capital or capitalization at the beginning of 1920 as a year later in 1921; it is thus roughly accurate to compare the sales made or incomes received during 1920 with those of 1921. The procedure, then, is to measure the percentage by which actual sales in a prosperous year such as 1920 are 'off' in a depression year such as 1921; and similarly to compare the actual amounts of net income earned, or lost in such years. The cycles through which all, or nearly all, individual industries pass, however, are not exactly the same. While most of our 73 manufacturing minor groups have sales peaks in 1920, some show peaks in 1919. In such cases, 1921 is com-

[190]   INDUSTRIAL PROFITS

pared not with 1920 but with 1919. This is also, of course, true of the volume of income; and there the same procedure is followed.[1]

Examining the contraction in sales volume that took place in the 73 manufacturing industries from 1920 (or 1919) to 1921, we find a wide variation in the percentages of decline. Two industries show not declines but increases; in 16 others the declines range from 4 to 25 per cent, while 44 more suffer declines of from 25 to 50 per cent. In the remaining 11 groups, decreases of from 50 to 82 per cent occurred. The quartiles are shown in Chart 35.

CHART 35

DISPERSION OF PERCENTAGE DECLINES IN SALES AND INCOME IN 73 MANUFACTURING INDUSTRIES, 1921 COMPARED WITH 1920 (OR 1919)
(WITH QUARTILES OF THE DISTRIBUTION INDICATED)

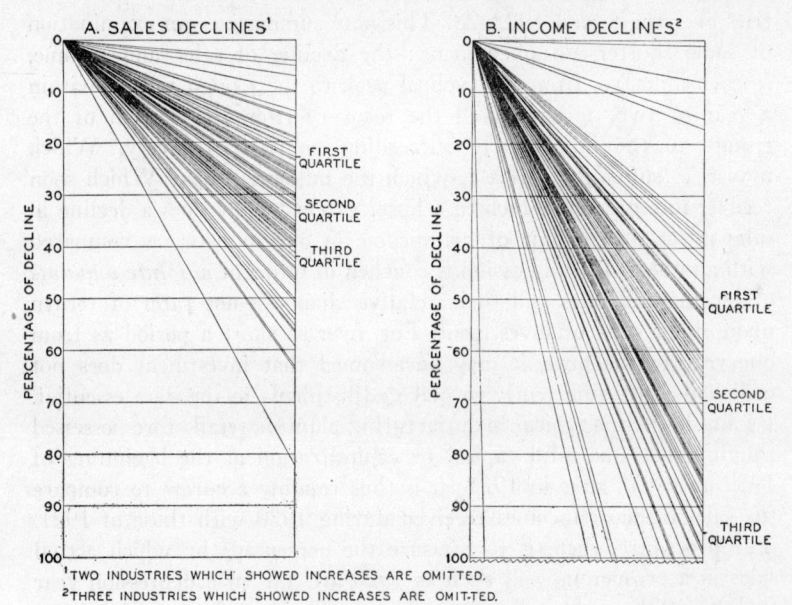

A. SALES DECLINES[1]

B. INCOME DECLINES[2]

[1] TWO INDUSTRIES WHICH SHOWED INCREASES ARE OMITTED.
[2] THREE INDUSTRIES WHICH SHOWED INCREASES ARE OMITTED.

[1] In the case of net income, in certain instances when the peak occurs in 1919, the low point is reached in 1920 and recovery is evidenced in 1921. In such instances the 1920 low is the figure that is compared with the peak. Appendix Table 6 gives the absolute data, which may be consulted or charted by the reader who cares to extend the analysis.

DECLINE IN NET INCOMES, 1920–21

The same procedure may be followed in analyzing the amounts of net incomes received by the 73 manufacturing groups in 1920 and 1921. Of the 73 industries 3 showed increases in income and 4 had declines of less than 25 per cent. Eight industries underwent declines of from 25 to 50 per cent, while 58 industries suffered declines of 50 per cent or over. Of these, 44 showed income shrinkages of from 50 to 100 per cent, while 14 declined over 100 per cent, that is, they had deficits in 1921.

COMPARISON, 1921 SALES AND INCOME DECLINES

The fact that sales declined by 50 per cent or more in only 11 of the 73 industries, while income fell by 50 per cent or over in 58, vividly corroborates the oft-repeated statement that a "small drop in gross revenues may cause a large drop in net". In all 73 manufacturing groups combined, sales fell, roughly 33 per cent between 1920 and 1921, from 25 billion dollars to 16 billion. But total net income fell 75 per cent from exactly two billion to almost precisely one-half billion. This, of course, is because overhead expense remains relatively constant over short periods, or at least seldom contracts in proportion to the reduction in sales. The discrepancy is emphasized graphically in Chart 35. The two sections of the chart are drawn to the same scale, but in the income diagram the available space prevents carrying down fully the lines representing drops of over 100 per cent.

Although certain industries are conspicuous in the degree to which given declines in sales cause disproportionate shrinkages in net earnings, there is nevertheless a fairly close general correspondence between the relative standing of the different industries with respect to their declines in sales and in income.[2] If we compare specifically the list of the ten industries showing the smallest declines in sales from 1920 to 1921 with that of the ten showing the slightest falling off in incomes, we find that seven industries are common to both lists.

Similarly, if we compare the industries that suffer the largest sales

[2] Only the industries occupying extreme positions are analyzed here, but a general measurement of the correlation in ranks is undertaken later.

declines with those undergoing the greatest income curtailment, we find a high degree of correspondence in the two lists. Here, however, the industries with the greatest declines in incomes suffered actual deficits—13 industries in all. Comparing with this list, then, not the 10 but the 13 industries in which sales declined the most, we find 10 names common to both lists.

SALES AND INCOME DECLINES, 1923–1924

The year 1924, while not nearly so depressed as 1921, recorded a general drop in business activity. The *Annalist* index fell from 108 in 1923 to 97 in 1924 and the index of the American Telephone

CHART 36
DISPERSION OF PERCENTAGE DECLINES OR INCREASES IN SALES AND INCOME IN 73 MANUFACTURING INDUSTRIES, 1924 COMPARED WITH 1923
(WITH QUARTILES OF THE DISTRIBUTION INDICATED)

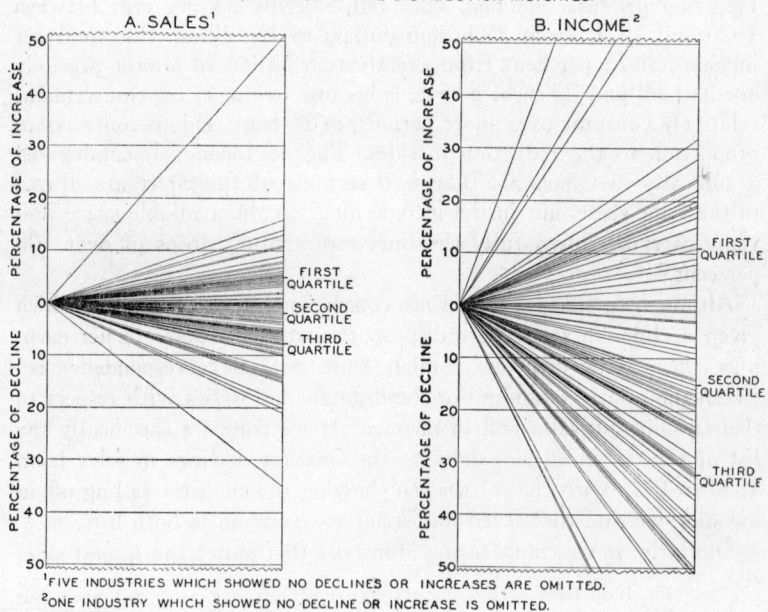

[1] FIVE INDUSTRIES WHICH SHOWED NO DECLINES OR INCREASES ARE OMITTED.
[2] ONE INDUSTRY WHICH SHOWED NO DECLINE OR INCREASE IS OMITTED.

CYCLICAL FLUCTUATIONS [193]

and Telegraph Company from 108 to 95.[3] The 1921 figures for the two indexes respectively were 85 and 76. Although annual figures by no means indicate the full extent of the drop, it is nevertheless of interest to examine the 1923–24 recessions in sales and income in the 73 manufacturing industries and to compare them with the 1920–21 situation. Nearly half of these industries showed no sales declines at all in 1924 (more accurately, 32 failed to show declines). Rather, in 27, sales increased. In 5 others, sales equalled the 1923 figures. Only in the remaining 41 minor groups did sales fall off. More than ever, one is impressed with the fact that what we term 'general business' (however useful a concept) is a composite, an abstraction.

The 1923–24 declines in the 41 manufacturing groups where sales fell off are not large as compared with the declines of 1920–21. In 28 groups they are less than 10 per cent; in 9 more they run from 10 to 15 per cent; in only 4 groups are they 20 per cent or more.

Net income, 1923–24, either remains constant or increases in about one-third of the 73 industries. Of these 25 groups, one shows the same income in 1924 as in 1923, while the other 24 all register gains ranging from 3 to more than 100 per cent. In the 48 groups that show declines in income, the drops range from 1 to 89 per cent.

SALES AND INCOME DECLINES, 1926–1927

The year 1927 is customarily regarded as one of mildest recession. While the general drop of that year was hardly felt in comparison with either that of 1921 or even 1924, data for the rate of net earnings upon capital presented in Chapters 6 and 7 have suggested that 1927 recorded a more severe business contraction than is ordinarily thought to have been the case. A survey of the absolute declines in sales and income, 1926–27, seemingly corroborates this earlier conclusion, although again annual figures do not tell the entire story. Of the 73 manufacturing industries, 39 show declines in sales. Most of the declines are of almost the same magnitude as the declines shown by the 1923–24 list. In 1924, 28 groups showed declines ranging from 1 to 10 per cent; in 1927, 31 groups fell into the same category.

In 1924, 13 groups showed declines of 10 per cent or over, while in 1927, 8 groups did so.

[3] These figures are annual averages of the monthly data.

[194] INDUSTRIAL PROFITS

As regards net income, the number of groups showing declines in 1927 is almost the same as that for 1923–24, 47 in one case and 48 in the other. The range is not greatly different, although a smaller proportion of industries suffers extreme changes: in 1927, 3 groups show income drops of 50 per cent or over, as against 8 groups in 1924.

CHART 37
DISPERSION OF PERCENTAGE DECLINES OR INCREASES IN SALES AND INCOME IN 73 MANUFACTURING INDUSTRIES, 1927 COMPARED WITH 1926
(WITH QUARTILES OF THE DISTRIBUTION INDICATED)

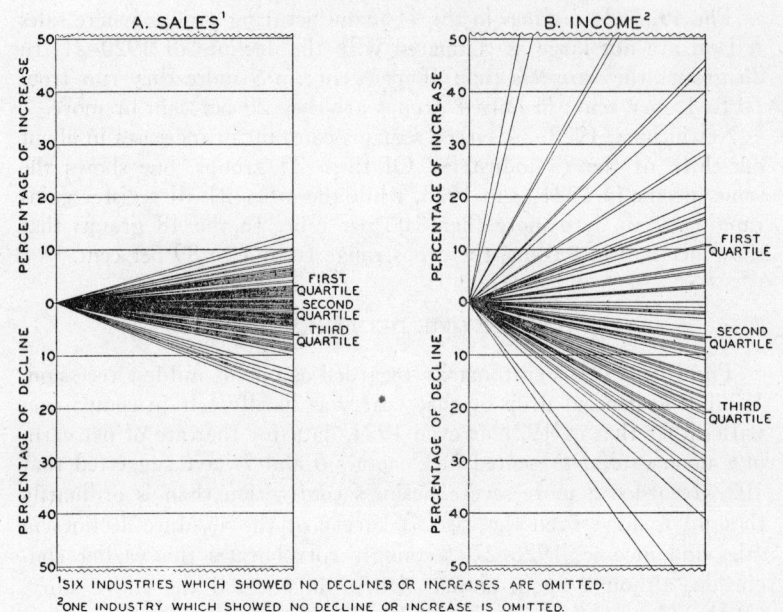

[1] SIX INDUSTRIES WHICH SHOWED NO DECLINES OR INCREASES ARE OMITTED.
[2] ONE INDUSTRY WHICH SHOWED NO DECLINE OR INCREASE IS OMITTED.

INCREASES IN SALES AND INCOME, 1921–22

We may now inquire how the rate of recovery in sales and incomes varied.

The 1922 upswing in sales ranges from 1 to 82 per cent over the

CYCLICAL FLUCTUATIONS   [195]

1921 figures.[4] In 15 industries the gains were under 10 per cent; in 25, from 10 to 19 per cent; in 30, from 20 to 49 per cent; in 3, 50 per cent or over.

Increases in net income, 1921–22, range from 6 to several hundred and even more than a thousand per cent; in some of the industries, however, actual deficits prevailed in 1921. Fifty-eight show gains of 50 per cent or over; 44, of 100 per cent or over.

GENERAL RELATIONSHIPS BETWEEN INCOME AND SALES CHANGES

Thus far, this note has dealt broadly with the character of the variation in income and sales changes. There remain to be given certain measurements of the general degree to which decreases and increases in income and sales correspond.

a. *High Correspondence in Sales and Income Declines*

If the 73 industries be arrayed (or ranked) according to their percentages of sales decline, and then, in parallel columns, are entered their positions in terms of their income declines, we obtain the two lists presented in Table 37. The general correspondence in ranks prevailing between these two lists is close, about 70 per cent perfect.

TABLE 37

RANK OF 73 MANUFACTURING GROUPS IN SALES DECLINE COMPARED WITH RANK IN INCOME DECLINE, 1920–21

MINOR GROUP	RANK IN SALES DECLINE	RANK IN INCOME DECLINE
26 Planing mills	1	45
65 Tools	2	10
66 Bolts and nuts	3	12
12 Cotton spinning	4	39
50 Sheet metal	5	2
70 Miscellaneous metals	6	8
23 Miscellaneous leather	7	4
31 Cardboard boxes	8	17
51 Wire and nails	9	14
11 Miscellaneous foods	10	6

[4] In 10 industries out of the 73, the increases are for 1923 over 1922, the latter year being in those 10 industries lower than 1921. In 3 other industries, the comparison is also that of 1923 over 1922 because the latter is as low as 1921.

TABLE 37 *(continued)*

RANK OF 73 MANUFACTURING GROUPS IN SALES DECLINE

MINOR GROUP		RANK IN SALES DECLINE	RANK IN INCOME DECLINE
49	Castings and forgings	11	13
32	Stationery	12	9
24	Rubber products	13	3
68	Non-ferrous metals	14	28
4	Package foods	15	7
61	Railway equipment	16	38
48	Miscellaneous clay and stone products	17	21
38	Crude chemicals	18	57
25	Lumber manufacture	19	25
63	Firearms	20	31
27	Millwork	21	23
58	Mining machinery	22	26
67	Miscellaneous machinery	23	11
14	Cotton weaving	24	40
30	Blank paper	25	15
64	Hardware	26	22
69	Jewelry	27	19
7	Meat packing	28	1
33	Miscellaneous paper	29	33
62	Motor vehicles	30	36
44	Miscellaneous chemicals	31	53
21	Miscellaneous textiles	32	49
46	Glass	33	42
52	Heating machinery	34	37
3	Confectionery	35	32
13	Cotton converting	36	24
57	Engines	37	55
29	Miscellaneous lumber	38	56
39	Paints	39	34
2	Flour	40	27
6	Canned goods	41	44
20	Miscellaneous clothing	42	29
45	Ceramics	43	54
59	General factory machinery	44	35
72	Toys	45	65
37	Miscellaneous printing and publishing	46	63
18	Men's clothing	47	41
19	Knit goods	48	51
73	Pianos	49	30
28	Furniture (non-metal)	50	47
40	Petroleum refining	51	20
16	Silk weaving	52	18

CYCLICAL FLUCTUATIONS [197]

TABLE 37 *(continued)*

RANK OF 73 MANUFACTURING GROUPS IN SALES DECLINE

MINOR GROUP	RANK IN SALES DECLINE	RANK IN INCOME DECLINE
17 Carpets	53	61
53 Electrical machinery	54	48
55 Printing machinery	55	64
36 Job printing	56	62
43 Cleaning preparations	57	5
60 Office machinery	58	43
1 Bakery products	59	72
56 Road machinery	60	50
71 Scientific instruments	61	58
41 Proprietary preparations	62	59
15 Weaving woolens	63	16
74 Miscellaneous special manufacturing	64	60
5 Dairying	65	46
22 Boots and shoes	66	52
54 Textile machinery	67	67
47 Portland cement	68	69
34 Newspapers	69	68
35 Book and music publishing	70	70
10 Tobacco	71	71
9 Beverages	72	73
42 Toilet preparations	73	66

Coefficient of rank correlation +0.71

That is to say, the coefficient of rank correlation is +0.71, on a scale in which 1.00 would express perfect correspondence of positions. With due allowance for individual exceptions, we may therefore say that in general the industries that show the larger *sales declines* are also those which show the greater *net income declines*.

b. Lack of Correspondence in Sales and Income Increases

Similarly arraying the 1921–22 percentages of sales and income increase, we obtain the lists given in Table 38. The general correspondence in ranks is very slight and does not justify a conclusion similar to that concerning the two sets of decreases previously discussed. On the whole, it cannot be said that the industries which enjoy the larger *increases* in sales in the year of recovery following one of severe depression are those which also show the greater increases in net income. The coefficient of rank correlation here is only

+0.13, expressing little more than a chance relationship between the two sets of ranks.

Table 38

RANK OF 73 MANUFACTURING GROUPS IN SALES INCREASE COMPARED WITH RANK IN INCOME INCREASE, 1921–22

MINOR GROUP	RANK IN SALES INCREASE	RANK IN INCOME INCREASE
66 Bolts and nuts	1	4
50 Sheet metal	2	35
57 Engines	3	71
65 Tools	4	17
29 Miscellaneous lumber	5	39
12 Cotton spinning	6	63
17 Carpets	7	61
56 Road machinery	8	55
25 Lumber manufacture	9	19
62 Motor vehicles	10	27
26 Planing mills	11	32
27 Millwork	12	7
53 Electrical machinery	13	47
58 Mining machinery	14	22
64 Hardware	15	8
68 Non-ferrous metals	16	16
51 Wire and nails	17	2
48 Miscellaneous clay and stone products	18	5
45 Ceramics	19	50
19 Knit goods	20	67
21 Miscellaneous textiles	21	73
31 Cardboard boxes	22	3
63 Firearms	23	15
38 Crude chemicals	24	31
39 Paints	25	21
47 Portland cement	26	48
52 Heating machinery	27	33
59 General factory machinery	28	45
9 Beverages	29	26
23 Miscellaneous leather	30	25
28 Furniture (non-metal)	31	38
72 Toys	32	64
73 Pianos	33	14
49 Castings and forgings	34	6
6 Canned goods	35	42
46 Glass	36	51
5 Dairying	37	62
18 Men's clothing	38	54

TABLE 38 *(continued)*

RANK OF 73 MANUFACTURING GROUPS IN SALES INCREASE

MINOR GROUP	RANK IN SALES INCREASE	RANK IN INCOME INCREASE
24 Rubber products	39	41
33 Miscellaneous paper	40	44
70 Miscellaneous metals	41	30
69 Jewelry	42	11
3 Confectionery	43	37
13 Cotton converting	44	29
44 Miscellaneous chemicals	45	56
15 Weaving woolens	46	1
55 Printing machinery	47	59
71 Scientific instruments	48	36
42 Toilet preparations	49	52
1 Bakery products	50	65
14 Cotton weaving	51	66
22 Boots and shoes	52	46
32 Stationery	53	18
41 Proprietary preparations	54	43
11 Miscellaneous foods	55	23
61 Railway equipment	56	60
7 Meat packing	57	40
34 Newspapers	58	53
36 Job printing	59	69
60 Office machinery	60	58
67 Miscellaneous machinery	61	13
37 Miscellaneous printing and publishing	62	72
54 Textile machinery	63	68
74 Miscellaneous special manufacturing	64	49
4 Package foods	65	10
20 Miscellaneous clothing	66	20
35 Book and music publishing	67	57
10 Tobacco	68	70
16 Silk weaving	69	12
30 Blank paper	70	28
43 Cleaning preparations	71	24
2 Flour	72	34
40 Petroleum refining	73	9

Coefficient of rank correlation +0.13

c. *Correspondence in Sales Declines and Sales Increases*

We now may, in the same way, ask whether the industries that experienced the greater *sales declines* in 1921 were those which enjoyed the larger *sales increases* in 1922. The two lists of ranks are

Table 39

RANK OF 73 MANUFACTURING GROUPS IN SALES DECLINE, 1920–21, COMPARED WITH RANK IN SALES INCREASE, 1921–22

MINOR GROUP		RANK IN SALES DECLINE	RANK IN SALES INCREASE
26	Planing mills	1	11
65	Tools	2	4
66	Bolts and nuts	3	1
12	Cotton spinning	4	6
50	Sheet metal	5	2
70	Miscellaneous metals	6	41
23	Miscellaneous leather	7	30
31	Cardboard boxes	8	22
51	Wire and nails	9	17
11	Miscellaneous foods	10	55
49	Castings and forgings	11	34
32	Stationery	12	53
24	Rubber products	13	39
68	Non-ferrous metals	14	16
4	Package foods	15	65
61	Railway equipment	16	56
48	Miscellaneous clay and stone products	17	18
38	Crude chemicals	18	24
25	Lumber manufacture	19	9
63	Firearms	20	23
27	Millwork	21	12
58	Mining machinery	22	14
67	Miscellaneous machinery	23	61
14	Cotton weaving	24	51
30	Blank paper	25	70
64	Hardware	26	15
69	Jewelry	27	42
7	Meat packing	28	57
33	Miscellaneous paper	29	40
62	Motor vehicles	30	10
44	Miscellaneous chemicals	31	45
21	Miscellaneous textiles	32	21
46	Glass	33	36
52	Heating machinery	34	27
3	Confectionery	35	43
13	Cotton converting	36	44
57	Engines	37	3
29	Miscellaneous lumber	38	5
39	Paints	39	25
2	Flour	40	72
6	Canned goods	41	35
20	Miscellaneous clothing	42	66

TABLE 39 *(continued)*
RANK OF 73 MANUFACTURING GROUPS IN SALES DECLINE

MINOR GROUP	RANK IN SALES DECLINE	RANK IN SALES INCREASE
45 Ceramics	43	19
59 General factory machinery	44	28
72 Toys	45	32
37 Miscellaneous printing and publishing	46	62
18 Men's clothing	47	38
19 Knit goods	48	20
73 Pianos	49	33
28 Furniture (non-metal)	50	31
40 Petroleum refining	51	73
16 Silk weaving	52	69
17 Carpets	53	7
53 Electrical machinery	54	13
55 Printing machinery	55	47
36 Job printing	56	59
43 Cleaning preparations	57	71
60 Office machinery	58	60
1 Bakery products	59	50
56 Road machinery	60	8
71 Scientific instruments	61	48
41 Proprietary preparations	62	54
15 Weaving woolens	63	46
74 Miscellaneous special manufacturing	64	64
5 Dairying	65	37
22 Boots and shoes	66	52
54 Textile machinery	67	63
47 Portland Cement	68	26
34 Newspapers	69	58
35 Book and music publishing	70	67
10 Tobacco	71	68
9 Beverages	72	29
42 Toilet preparations	73	49

Coefficient of rank correlation +0.41

given in Table 39. The correspondence is only about 40 per cent perfect, the coefficient of rank correlation being +0.41.

d. *High Correspondence in Income Declines and Increases*

Finally, and in like manner, we ask whether the industries in which income *declined* most, 1920–21, are in general the industries in which it *increased* most, 1921–22. The correspondence here is high—over 70 per cent perfect. The two sets of ranks are shown in

TABLE 40

RANK OF 73 MANUFACTURING GROUPS IN INCOME DECLINE, 1920–21, COMPARED WITH RANK IN INCOME INCREASE, 1921–22

MINOR GROUP		RANK IN INCOME DECLINE	RANK IN INCOME INCREASE
7	Meat packing	1	40
50	Sheet metal	2	35
24	Rubber products	3	41
23	Miscellaneous leather	4	25
43	Cleaning preparations	5	24
11	Miscellaneous foods	6	23
4	Package foods	7	10
70	Miscellaneous metals	8	30
32	Stationery	9	18
65	Tools	10	17
67	Miscellaneous machinery	11	13
66	Bolts and nuts	12	4
49	Castings and forgings	13	6
51	Wire and nails	14	2
30	Blank paper	15	28
15	Weaving woolens	16	1
31	Cardboard boxes	17	3
16	Silk weaving	18	12
69	Jewelry	19	11
40	Petroleum refining	20	9
48	Miscellaneous clay and stone products	21	5
64	Hardware	22	8
27	Millwork	23	7
13	Cotton converting	24	29
25	Lumber manufacture	25	19
58	Mining machinery	26	22
2	Flour	27	34
68	Non-ferrous metals	28	16
20	Miscellaneous clothing	29	20
73	Pianos	30	14
63	Firearms	31	15
3	Confectionery	32	37
33	Miscellaneous paper	33	44
39	Paints	34	21
59	General factory machinery	35	45
62	Motor vehicles	36	27
52	Heating machinery	37	33
61	Railway equipment	38	60
12	Cotton spinning	39	63
14	Cotton weaving	40	66
18	Men's clothing	41	54
46	Glass	42	51

TABLE 40 *(continued)*
RANK OF 73 MANUFACTURING GROUPS IN INCOME DECLINE

MINOR GROUP		RANK IN INCOME DECLINE	RANK IN INCOME INCREASE
60	Office machinery	43	58
6	Canned goods	44	42
26	Planing mills	45	32
5	Dairying	46	62
28	Furniture (non-metal)	47	38
53	Electrical machinery	48	47
21	Miscellaneous textiles	49	73
56	Road machinery	50	55
19	Knit goods	51	67
22	Boots and shoes	52	46
44	Miscellaneous chemicals	53	56
45	Ceramics	54	50
57	Engines	55	71
29	Miscellaneous lumber	56	39
38	Crude chemicals	57	31
71	Scientific instruments	58	36
41	Proprietary preparations	59	43
74	Miscellaneous special manufacturing	60	49
17	Carpets	61	61
36	Job printing	62	69
37	Miscellaneous printing and publishing	63	72
55	Printing machinery	64	59
72	Toys	65	64
42	Toilet preparations	66	52
54	Textile machinery	67	68
34	Newspapers	68	53
47	Portland cement	69	48
35	Book and music publishing	70	57
10	Tobacco	71	70
1	Bakery products	72	65
9	Beverages	73	26

Coefficient of rank correlation +0.72

Table 40, the coefficient of rank correlation being +0.72. This correspondence between the ranks in income declines and increases is just about the same as that found in a preceding section for sales declines and income declines, and justifies the statement that, on the whole, the manufacturing groups that suffer the severest curtailment of income in depression enjoy the greatest relative enhancement of income upon the return of prosperity. At least, this was the case in the period 1920–22. Whether the generalization holds, in the same strong measure, for all periods of decline, depression and revival cannot, of course, be said; but one is inclined to suspect that some substantial degree of positive correlation, at least, in this respect prevails for other periods as well.

Finally by way of summary it may be of interest to have a more refined and yet not too abstract measure of the extent to which sales and income declines are correlated than that afforded by the coefficient of rank correlation and the other devices employed in the preceding sections. It has been pointed out that because of the presence of either fixed or relatively fixed overhead costs in nearly all manufacturing industries, a comparatively small drop in gross revenues will cause a large shrinkage in net earnings. It was also shown graphically that the general dispersion in net income declines, 1920–21, was far greater than that in sales declines. We did not, however, undertake to measure the varying degrees to which declines of a given magnitude in the one factor were accompanied by proportionately greater declines in the other. This could be done in several ways, but the simplest as well as the most illuminating for our purpose is to classify the sales decline percentages by given intervals, and to compute the average income declines of the industries so ranged.

Specifically, we find that 2 industries out of the 73 manufacturing groups had *sales* declines of from 1 to 10 per cent. Their average decline (simple mean of the individual percentages) was 6 per cent. But the average of their *income* declines was 8 per cent. Dividing the latter by the former figure, we have a ratio of 1.3 between the income decline and the sales decline.

Going to the next higher bracket, 6 industries suffered *sales* declines of from 10 to 19 per cent, their average being 15 per cent. But their average *income* decline was 47 per cent. Here the ratio between the two figures is 3.1, that is, sales declines ranging from 10 to 19 per cent are accompanied by income declines about three times as large.

Table 41 gives the entire distribution by 10 per cent class intervals, while the bars of Chart 38 make possible a quick comparison of the several ratios. (The total number of frequencies is only 67 instead of 73 because of the omission of four industries that showed sales increases, and two that showed declines in sales but increases in income).

CYCLICAL FLUCTUATIONS [205]

TABLE 41

AVERAGE INCOME AND SALES DECLINES, 1920–21, RANGED BY SALES DECLINE CLASSES, 67 MANUFACTURING INDUSTRIES (SAMPLES OF IDENTICAL CORPORATIONS IN BOTH YEARS)

(1) AMOUNT OF SALES DECLINE	(2) NUMBER OF INDUSTRIES	(3) AVERAGE SALES DECLINE	(4) AVERAGE INCOME DECLINE	(5) RATIO OF (4) TO (3)
1 to 9%	2	6	8	1.3
10 to 19%	6	15	47	3.1
20 to 29%	18	23	61	2.6
30 to 39%	21	35	197	5.7
40 to 49%	12	43	97	2.3
50 to 59%	8	54	124	2.3

CHART 38

RATIO OF INCOME DECLINES TO SALES DECLINES, RANGED BY SALES DECLINE CLASSES, 1921 COMPARED WITH 1920

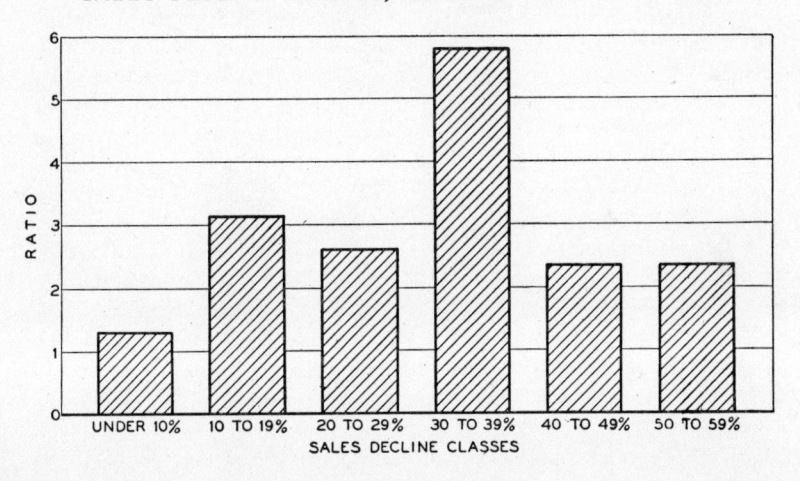

Book II
Earnings of Large Corporations

CHAPTER 8

INTRODUCTION

1. CHARACTER OF THE DATA

THE chapters in Book II are concerned with detailed information on the earnings, sales and capital investment of the various major and minor groups that make up the Manufacturing, Trading, Mining and Financial divisions. Data only for fairly large corporations [1] are given here; those for smaller enterprises appear in Book III. In Book II, all of the companies included in each group are identical from year to year. That is to say, each of the minor group tables for Manufacture will contain a portion of the 2,046 corporations for which aggregate data have been presented in various parts of Book I; each of the Trading minor groups contains a portion of the 664 Trading corporations that have been previously discussed; and the Mining and Financial minor groups deal with the subdivisions of the 88 Mining and 346 Financial corporations for which we possess identical data over the ten-year period 1919–28.

With the exception of two broader chapters—Chapter 9, Manufacture and Its Major Groups, and Chapter 14, Trading and Its Minor Groups—each of the chapters that follow presents tabular data in the same general form.

The first table of each chapter describes the size and character of the minor groups that make up the major group; for example, in the major group Food Products, data for such minor groups as Bakery Products and Package Foods appear. Next come the earnings rates for each minor group. Then the proportion of earnings

[1] The arithmetic average and median sizes of the corporations in each group in terms of capital investment will be found in the tables at the close of each chapter. Additional data and comment on their size will be found in Ch. 43, sec. 3.

paid out in cash dividends is given. Finally, frequency distributions of the earnings rates of individual corporations are presented.

These chapters obviously are intended for reading or reference on the part of persons interested in any particular industry or major industrial group. They are not designed primarily for the use of statistical specialists whose concern is rather with more technical questions such as frequency distribution patterns, average deviations and ranges of dispersion. While the data of these chapters invite such extended analyses, what has been undertaken in this direction is placed in Appendix A. Likewise, the more technical questions involving the character of the various samples involved are discussed in Chapters 43–46.

2. DEFINITIONS OF TERMS

When the phrase, 'the period as a whole', is used without any specification of dates, the expression refers to the ten years 1919–28. The 'first half of the period' thus refers to the years 1919–23, and the 'second half' to 1924–28. By 'first part' of the period is meant the two or three years starting with 1919, and by 'last part', the years 1926–28. The context will make clear the occasional slight departures from this practice.

The phrase 'earnings upon investment', and the expression 'rate' or 'return' upon capital investment are used indiscriminately to refer either to the percentage of *net income to capitalization* or to the percentage of *total profits to total capital*. It will be recalled that the two latter terms have been defined as involving the rate of earnings before and after fixed charges upon capital respectively, the capital in the one case including, in the other case excluding, funded debt.[2] The reason in these chapters for not distinguishing these two concepts (apart from a few places in which attention is specifically called to the desirability of so doing) is that, in nearly all of the minor groups of the several industrial divisions here under discussion, the difference between the two rates of return is negligible. This would not be true generally of Railroads or Public Utilities; nor is it true of some individual corporations in the industrial divisions here under survey. But, in the main, even with frequency distributions of individual earnings rates, the two ratios amount to one

[2] See Ch. 2 and Glossary.

and the same thing in the fields of Manufacture, Trade, Mining and Finance. (The evidence for this statement is given in Appendix Table 8.) In discussing the average rate of net return upon invested capital in the various minor groups, therefore, the expression 'percentage of net income to capitalization' is avoided because it implies that a difference exists between this return and the 'percentage of total profit to total capital', whereas our findings show that no appreciable difference is evident. The reason is that most Manufacturing, Trading, Mining and Financial groups are characterized by a very low ratio of funded debt to total capital—in sharp contrast to the railroad and public utility fields. The amount of funded debt in each minor group is given in Appendix B, while the rates of earnings upon capital including such debt are shown in the tables at the end of each chapter and may be compared with the 'after charges' figures by any interested reader.

The term 'all', when employed in such phrases as 'all Manufacturing', 'all Food Products corporations', or 'all Trading enterprises', refers to all of the corporations of our sample—not to all corporations in the United States. When in rare instances the latter meaning is intended, the phrase 'all corporations in the country' is used.

Likewise, and this it is hardly necessary to remark, the use of the word 'earned' implies no judgment as to an income, whatever its rate, being deserved or not deserved as a reward for services performed or for any other reason; the word is used simply to denote an amount or rate of income received by the corporations in question or shown by the figures of their profit and loss and balance sheet accounts.

3. RELATIVE VERSUS ABSOLUTE CHANGE

The charts on which percentages are plotted are drawn to ordinary or natural scales. Those showing absolute amounts, however, are drawn to semi-logarithmic or ratio scales in which equal vertical distances represent unequal absolute amounts, but equal percentages, of increase or decrease. In these absolute figures it is the comparative rates of change that are important. As a matter of fact, the actual size of these data themselves in some instances are not significant because the corporations in any particular group represent only a sample of the entire industry. Over a period the significance of the relations between the several series of data involved is not, however, thereby impaired. Again, if these charts, which do not always give a clear picture of the absolute amounts involved, fail to serve the reader's purpose, the actual data can always be found in Appendix B.

While the text discusses the comparative course of these figures rather than their absolute amounts, in the case of each group an actual sales or investment figure is given for at least one year of the period in order to afford some indication of the approximate size of the sample. Incidentally, the word 'actual' is occasionally employed in the text as a synonym for 'absolute'. In this sense it merely affords a contrast to the term comparative or relative but is not intended to imply that the figure in question, especially if it be an investment amount, is necessarily valid, correct, 'real' or final in any basic or ultimate sense. The investment figures in most instances are simply to be taken for what they may be worth. For any individual corporation they reflect, or at least are subject to, the vagaries of corporation accounting. Taken *en masse,* either in aggregate amounts or as the individual data of a frequency distribution, they are probably subject to no error great enough to vitiate the figures with respect to any purposes for which they are here employed; but on this subject the critical reader must consult other portions of the volume.[3]

Then, too, all the sales, income and investment data given as absolute amounts are, of course, expressed in dollars; and a dollar of sales represented more goods in 1921 than it did in 1919 or 1920. No effort is made to correct or adjust the data because of such price changes. To do so for each of the 106 minor groups would involve the use of different index numbers for the commodities of every group, and even then no great accuracy could be attained. It seems wiser, as regards the first part of the period, not to attempt any such wholesale revision of the data; but it is to be borne in mind that declines of dollar sales between 1919 and 1921 do not represent equivalent declines in the physical volume of goods produced and marketed. As regards the last five or six years of the period, price changes are far less important, and fluctuations in sales volume probably represent changes in the course of physical volume with fair accuracy in most instances.

All earnings figures are for net income or profits before the pay-

[3] See Ch. 43–46.

ment of Federal income taxes. The 'after taxes' data were available, but to have given all of the ratios in each form, that is, both before and after taxes, would have entailed the presentation of just twice as much tabular material and it was not believed that, for most purposes of analysis, this would have been justified. The reasons for this decision are given in Appendix A. The amount of Federal income tax paid by each minor group is also shown there; and the reader interested in any particular group or year may readily perform the necessary subtractions and compute the desired percentages.

4. LIMITATIONS OF MINING AND FINANCE SAMPLES

While all of the data represent samples, those for the Manufacturing and Trading groups constitute better samples, on the whole, than those for Mining and Finance. The aggregate capital investments of the corporations in both the Manufacturing and Trading samples are far larger parts of the investment of all the corporations in the country engaged in these fields than is the Finance sample.[4] In Mining, this is not technically true; nevertheless the sample falls far short of representing much typical large-scale mining activity. The reason is that a very large portion of ferrous, as well as non-ferrous, metal mining is carried on by iron and steel companies and by brass, zinc, lead and copper enterprises, which own their own mines. Similarly, many companies classified in Manufacturing, under the head of Petroleum Refining, operate their own oil wells. The extent to which figures for Mining, as carried on by corporations which engage only or predominantly in mining activities, fall short of typifying the entire business of extracting ores, oil, etc., from the earth is shown by comparing the total amount of depletion reported to the Bureau of Internal Revenue by Manufacturing corporations and by corporations classified under Mining and Quarrying. In 1928 the corporations which reported that they were engaged in Mining

[4] The proportions which the investment (capitalization) of the companies in the four samples discussed in Book II bear to the total investment of all of the country's capitalization in these four fields are as follows in 1928: Manufacture, 46 per cent; Trade, 17 per cent; Mining, 17 per cent; Finance, 8 per cent. The absolute investment figures are as follows: our samples—Manufacture, 25 billion; Trade, two and one-half billion; Mining, one and seven-tenths billion; Finance, three billion; all corporations (estimated as explained in Appendix A)—Manufacture, 54 billion; Trade, 15 billion; Mining, 10 billion; Finance, 36 billion.

and Quarrying show total depletion charges of 212 million dollars; while under the head of Manufacturing, total depletion charges of 254 million were reported. Because such companies as the United States Steel Corporation are really mining as well as manufacturing enterprises, there is no good way to accumulate total figures for Mining which would represent all such activity.[5] We obtain a better picture of steel *manufacturing,* as a completely integrated undertaking, because such companies merge their accounts, but a poorer picture of *mining.* A more cumbersome caption but one better descriptive of our Mining division would thus be: 'Mining carried on by corporations which engage only or primarily in mining, but excluding a probably larger volume of mining activity which is carried on by corporations in which mining is integrated with manufacturing operations.' Other comment upon the nature of the Mining data, particularly in respect of qualifications surrounding charges for depletion, appears in Chapter 46.

In the Finance groups no figures for sales or the return upon sales are, of course, given. Instead, the figure employed is 'total gross income'. This is defined more carefully in the Finance chapter, but here it may be said that the term is tantamount to gross profits from sales or turnover, or from services billed as would be sales in a Manufacturing or Trading business, plus profits, both gross and net, from other operations. It excludes, however, the items of interest upon government bonds or other securities which are not taxable under the Federal income tax law. Except in the case of certain individual corporations, this omission is not serious, as the total of such non-taxable interest is probably less than 5 per cent of total gross income.[6]

A final and more serious qualifying factor is the fact that in one of the Finance groups (minor group No. 110, Investments, etc.) the cost of securities purchased for customers may in certain instances be included in total gross income. This practice—to the extent that it prevails—is both unfortunate for our purposes and an utterly incorrect accounting use of the term 'income'. The rate of net re-

[5] See Ch. 46, on classification.

[6] For all Financial corporations reporting to the Bureau of Internal Revenue in 1928 total gross income plus tax exempt interest (termed 'total compiled receipts' in the Bureau's report *Statistics of Income* for that year) amounted to over 20 billion dollars, while non-taxable interest reported by these same corporations was 371 million dollars or less than 2 per cent of the first figure.

turn upon total gross income in Financial groups is clearly not to be compared with that on sales in Manufacturing or Trading groups. And more serious, as an impairment of the representativeness of the data for Finance as a major group, is that the sample excludes all life insurance companies.

CHAPTER 9

MANUFACTURE AND ITS MAJOR GROUPS

1. RETURNS ON SALES AND INVESTMENT: ALL MANUFACTURE

THE corporations included in our series of 2,046 large manufacturing companies, while constituting only about a 2 per cent sample, in number, of all manufacturing corporations in the country, in 1928 enjoyed sales of 28 billion dollars, possessed an invested capital of 25 billion, and received a net income of 2¾ billion. In other words, their business was nearly one-half of the total business done by the country's 95,000 manufacturing corporations, and, as pointed out in the preceding chapter, they possessed about half of the total invested capital.

In the prosperous year 1919 these 2,046 corporations showed net earnings of 12 per cent upon sales volume. In 1920 this was cut to 8 per cent; and in the depression year 1921, to 3 per cent. Chart 39 shows the severe decline in the rate of net return on sales that took place from 1919 to 1921, and the recovery in 1922, when 10 per cent was earned. But the curve of this chart also shows the absence of similar fluctuations during the seven years 1922–28. In each year except 1927 the return was either 9 or 10 per cent; in 1927 it was 8 per cent. The data are given in numerical form in Table 42 at the end of the chapter.

Upon investment the return for Manufacture as a whole was 18 per cent in 1919. This fell to 12 per cent in 1920, and in 1921 to 3 per cent, the rate earned also upon sales in that year. The annual turnover of the capital investment of these 2,046 Manufacturing corporations, in other words, averaged just one.

In 1922, earnings upon investment amounted to 10 per cent. Between 1923 and 1928 the turnover of investment was in several

MANUFACTURE AND MAJOR GROUPS [217]

years slightly more than one. The return on investment, in other words, somewhat exceeded that on sales. But it showed about the same degree of stability: from 10 to 12 per cent (rounding off the figures) was earned consistently during the seven years 1922–28. The most profitable of these years, it will be observed, was 1926, when 12.4 per cent was earned. The figure fell to 9.5 per cent in 1927, and stood at 11 per cent in 1928.

The relative stability which both the return on sales and on investment show in the years 1922–28 should not, of course, be taken to suggest that this same stability characterizes the individual major and minor groups that make up Manufacture as a whole. As has been pointed out, some manufacturing industries during these same years show generally increasing earnings rates, others declining earnings rates, others stable rates, and still others highly fluctuating rates in which no trends are apparent (see Ch. 7). This is one reason why the average figure for All Manufacture is so stable—some industries decline in their rates from one year to the next, others increase and roughly offset the first set of changes; thus, except in periods of severe depression or exceptional price upheaval, a comparative stability in the broad *average* rate for Manufacturing industry as a whole prevails. The detailed figures for the 73 Manufacturing industries, presented in the next ten chapters, show clearly these varying specific situations.

2. ABSOLUTE EARNINGS, SALES AND INVESTMENT: ALL MANUFACTURE

The variations in the actual amounts of sales, investment and net income for the Manufacturing sample as a whole over these same years are next of interest, although again it must be remembered that the data here plotted are composite figures, from which the trends in any particular branch of manufacture may differ greatly.

Chart 39 shows these absolute data. Sales volume stood at about 21 billion dollars in 1919, then jumped to 25¼ billion in 1920. But in 1921 declining physical volume accompanied by lower prices reduced the figure to 16 billion.

Recovery in 1922 and 1923 brought the figure to 22½ billion in the latter year. The 1924 figure was only fractionally higher. But between 1924 and 1928 sales grew from slightly under 23 billion to

CHART 39
IDENTICAL CORPORATIONS SERIES, 1919-28
ALL MANUFACTURE

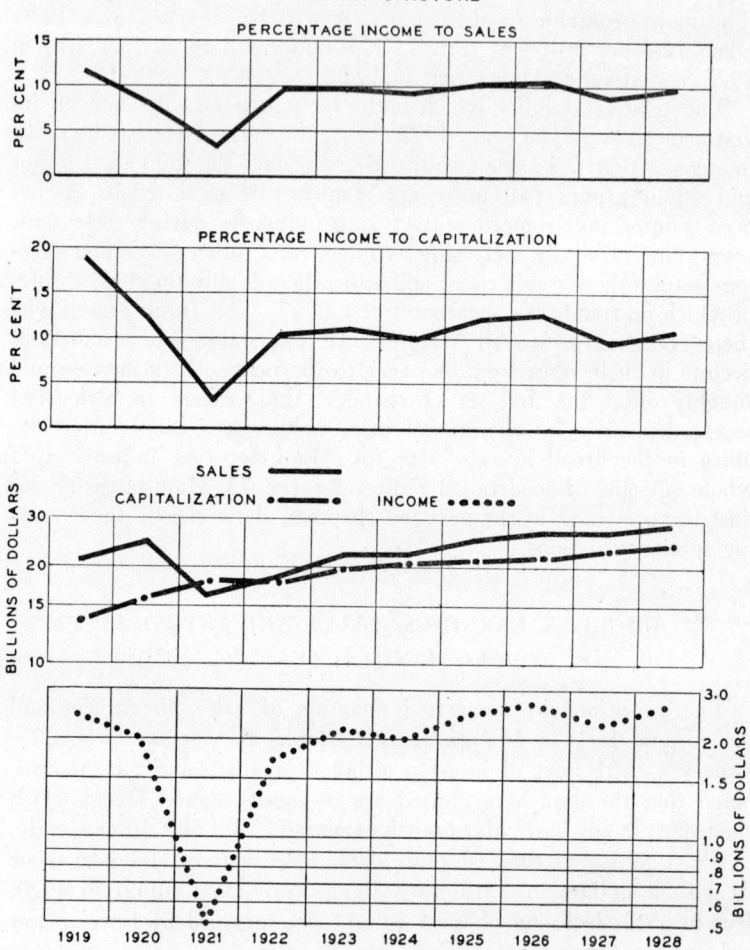

slightly over 28 billion a year. This 1928 figure of 28 billion represented an increase of 33 per cent over the 1919 level, and of 12 per cent over the 1920 peak.

Investment showed a somewhat steadier, and for the entire period a greater, rate of growth—from 13 billion dollars in 1919 to 16 billion in 1920, and 25 billion in 1928. From 1924 to 1928, however, investment increased at only a slightly greater rate than sales. With the margin of possible error to which the investment data are subject, this difference between a 25 and a 22 per cent increase is not to be regarded as possessing any significance.[1] Indeed the two series may be regarded as having grown at approximately the same rate during the last five years of the period. This close correspondence in the *general* growth of sales and investment affords an illuminating contrast to the specific situation prevailing in particular industries.[2]

The course of net income over the ten years, as would be expected, is far less regular than that of either sales or investment. From about 2½ billion in 1919, income fell to just 2 billion in 1920, then to half a billion in 1921. Thus while the volume of sales, as we have seen, declined by only 33 per cent between 1920 and 1921, net income was reduced by 75 per cent.

Recovery in 1922 brought the income figure to 1¾ billion. From then to 1928 a general upward trend was evident, although a temporary decline of 9 per cent occurred in 1924, and of 18 per cent in 1927. In 1928 net income stood at about 2¾ billion, as compared with 2½ billion in 1919. The data for all ten years are plotted in Chart 39, while the absolute figures may be found in Appendix B.

3. SURVEY OF THE MAJOR MANUFACTURING GROUPS

a. *Foods and Food Products*

In the Food and Food Products group are 215 corporations. They averaged a net return of about 4 per cent on sales in 1919, about 2 per cent in 1920 and slightly less than 2 per cent in 1921. Between 1922 and 1928 the return ran between 4 and 5 per cent in every year, about half the figure for All Manufacturing during the same period.

The return on investment in the Food group is much higher than on sales by reason of a capital turnover of two to two and one-half times a year. In 1919 the return on investment was 12 per cent.

---

[1] Attention is again called to the valuation of capital assets, etc., discussed in Ch. 45; see also Ch. 7.
[2] Discussed in Ch. 7 (the second of the two chapters on cyclical fluctuations) and also in Ch. 47.

[220] INDUSTRIAL PROFITS

This was cut in half in 1920, and again cut in half in 1921, when it reached 3 per cent. Recovery in 1922 brought the return up to 10 per cent and it remained on a level of 10 or 11 per cent in every year from then until the end of the period, except for 1926, when it approached 12 per cent. These rates represent approximately the same level as that for All Manufacturing.

Sales in the Food group declined from about 6 billion dollars in

CHART 40
IDENTICAL CORPORATIONS SERIES, 1919-28
MAJOR GROUP 1: FOODS

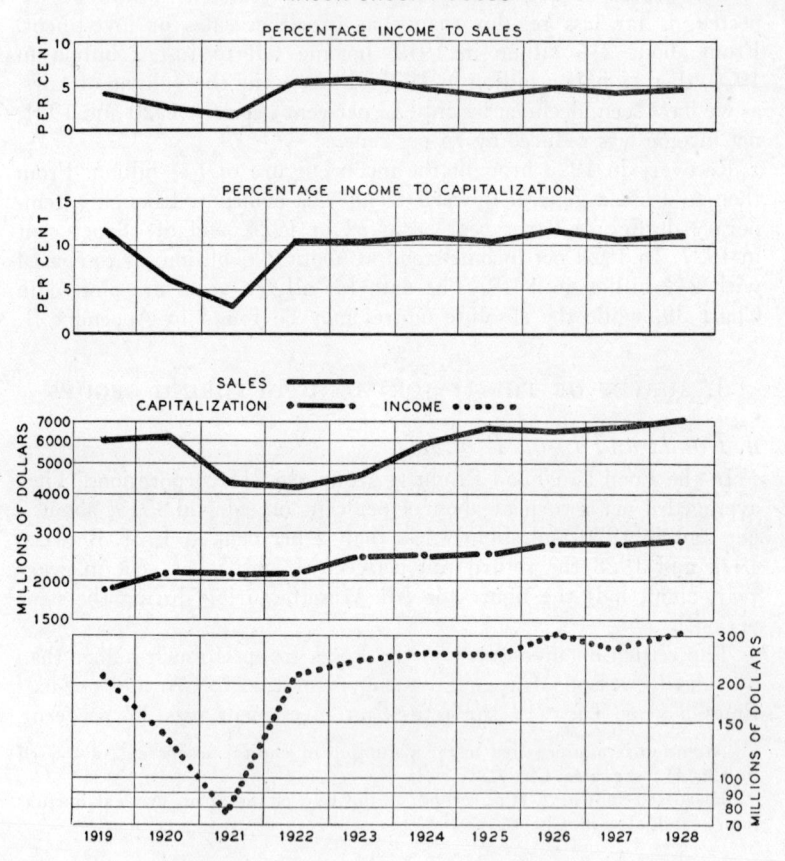

MANUFACTURE AND MAJOR GROUPS

both 1919 and 1920 to a little over 4 billion in 1921 and 1922. They then expanded until they reached almost 7 billion in 1925 and remained approximately upon that level, or somewhat above it, until the end of the period. Investment showed general growth from 1919 to 1926 and then remained stable. In 1928 it stood at 2¾ billion dollars as compared with somewhat less than 2 billion in 1919. Net income fell from about 220 million in 1919 to about 75 million in 1921; then recovered to about 220 million again in 1922, and showed a general although irregular growth to the end of the period, when it stood at slightly over 300 million.

Tabular data for the Food and other major groups appear in the chapters following.

b. *Textiles*

In the Textile group are 289 corporations. The peak for this group occurred in 1919, when the net return upon sales was 17 per cent. This fell to a low point of 5 per cent in 1920, but with the recovery of 1921 the rate rose to 9 per cent. In 1922 it rose still more, reaching 13 per cent. In 1923, at the end of the first half of the period, it was 11 per cent. From 1924 on it fluctuated between 6 and 8 per cent in every year.

Upon investment the return was in all years higher. It fell from 30 per cent in 1919 to 8 per cent in 1920; then rose to 17 per cent by 1922. But after that year earnings declined to a much lower level. Between 1924 and 1928 the return ranged from 7 to 9 per cent, standing at the end of the period at 7 per cent.

Sales volume shows a substantial decline in 1921 and recovery in 1922 and 1923, but no growth for the period as a whole. In 1919 sales were about 1400 million; in 1928, they were almost exactly the same figure.

Investment shows a general increase over the period, growing from about 800 million in 1919 to 1200 million in 1928. The 1928 figure, however, represents a very slight decline from that of 1927. Net income shows excessive oscillation for the entire period, but fluctuates about a lower level during the last five years than during the first five. The 1927 figure was about 110 million, the 1928 figure 80 million. Unlike most groups, the Textile industry as a whole showed a higher net income, both in absolute terms and relative to capital investment, in 1927 than in 1928.

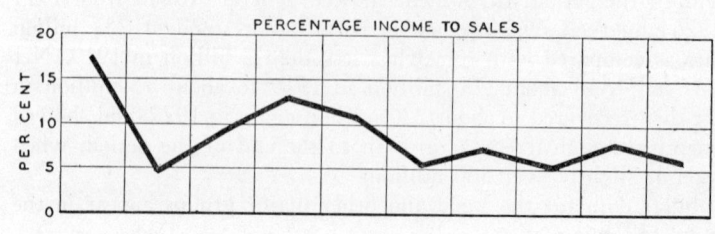

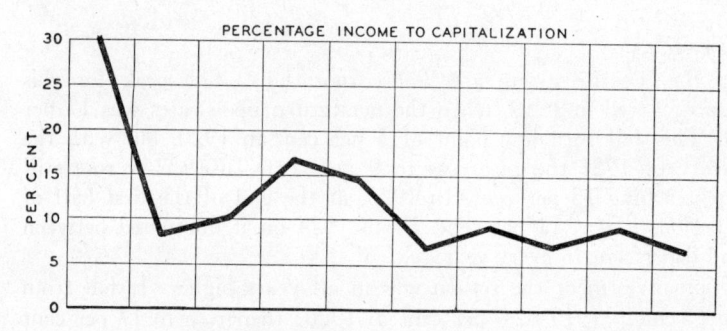

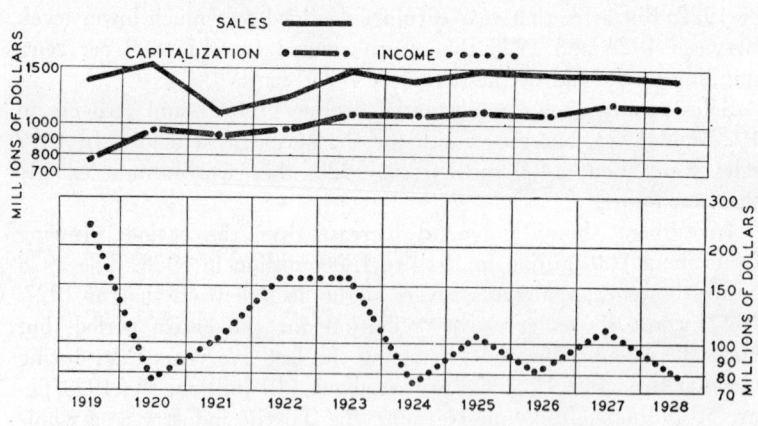

CHART 41
IDENTICAL CORPORATIONS SERIES, 1919-28
MAJOR GROUP 2: TEXTILES

MANUFACTURE AND MAJOR GROUPS [223]

CHART 42
IDENTICAL CORPORATIONS SERIES, 1919-28
MAJOR GROUP 3: LEATHER

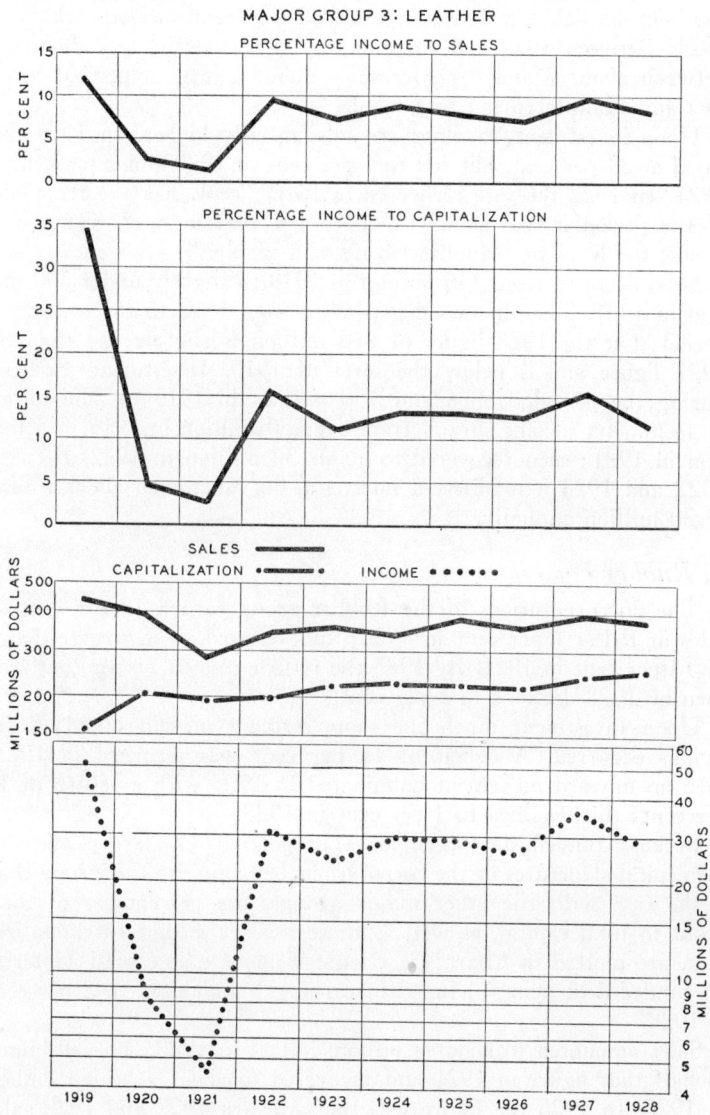

c. Leather

The 54 corporations belonging to the Leather group earned 12 per cent on sales in 1919, but only 2 per cent in both 1920 and 1921. Between 1922 and the end of the period the rate fluctuated between about 7 and 9 per cent, or about a level somewhat below that for Manufacturing as a whole.

Upon investment, earnings are substantially higher. In 1919 they stood at 34 per cent, but fell to 4 per cent in 1920 and 2 per cent in 1921. In 1922 the rate recovered to 16 per cent. For the remainder of the period it was about 12 or 13 per cent in most years, or at almost the level for Manufacturing as a whole.

Sales declined from 436 million in 1919 to slightly under 300 million in 1921. They increased gradually from 1921 to the end of the period; but the 1928 figure of 380 million is slightly less than the 1927 figure and is below the level of 1919. Investment increased during the period, from about 150 million in 1919 to 250 million in 1928. Net income shrank from over 50 million in 1919 to 5 million in 1921; then recovered to about 30 million in 1922. Between 1922 and 1928 it manifested no trend, but fluctuated about a level of 30 million annually.

d. Rubber

The 26 corporations of the Rubber group earned 12 per cent on sales in 1919; 1 per cent in 1920; and suffered an aggregate deficit of 13 per cent in 1921. By 1925 the return rose to 11 per cent, and then by 1928 declined to 1 per cent.

Upon investment much the same striking upswings and downswings occurred. A deficit of 13 per cent was recorded in 1921; then an upward movement culminated in 1925 with a return of 19 per cent; this declined to 1 per cent in 1928.

Because funded debt occupies a proportionately larger place in the capital structures of the corporations belonging to this group than is the case with the other major groups, the percentages of total profit to total capital, as well as those for net income to capitalization, are plotted in Chart 43. Earnings upon total capital (interest on funded debt being included in earnings) amounted to 2 per cent in 1928.

Sales amounted to about a billion dollars in 1920. They declined to half that figure in 1921 and recovered to about a billion dollars in 1925. In 1926 the figure was the same. In 1927 and 1928 sales

MANUFACTURE AND MAJOR GROUPS [225]

declined somewhat, standing at 935 million at the end of the period. Investment increased from 489 million in 1919 to 660 million in 1927, but dropped to 583 million in 1928. Net income fluctuated enormously, declining from over 90 million in 1919 to a deficit of 77 million in 1921. It then increased to 115 million in 1925, and fell off to eight million in 1928.

e. Lumber

The 190 corporations of the Lumber group showed a return on sales that oscillated between 6 and 15 per cent during the years

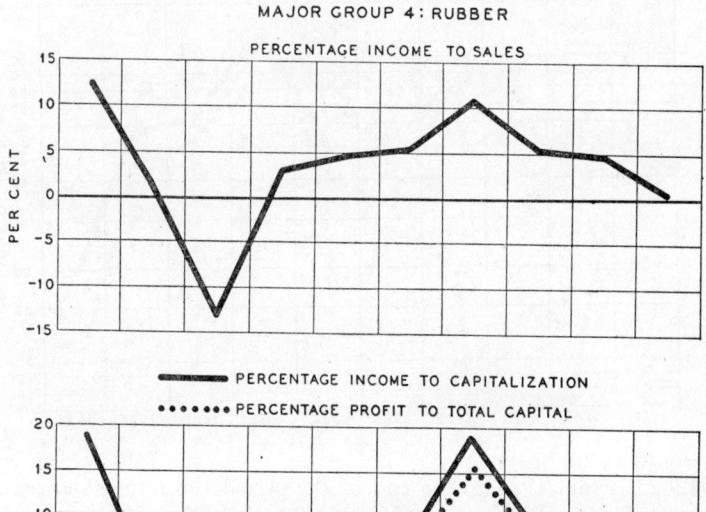

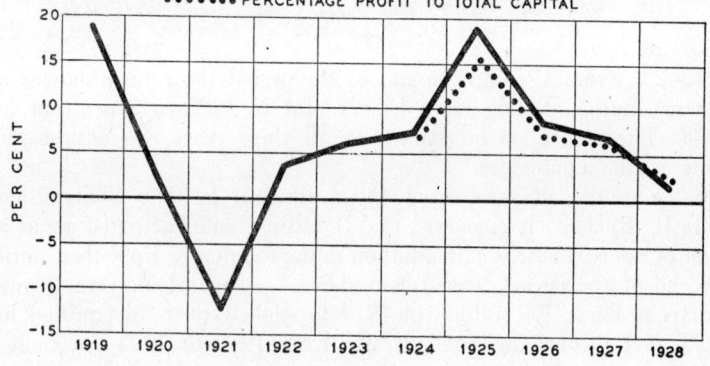

CHART 43
IDENTICAL CORPORATIONS SERIES, 1919-28
MAJOR GROUP 4: RUBBER

[226] INDUSTRIAL PROFITS

CHART 43 (CONT.)
IDENTICAL CORPORATIONS SERIES, 1919-28
MAJOR GROUP 4: RUBBER

― SALES
― • CAPITALIZATION
― ― TOTAL CAPITAL
• • • • • INCOME
▬ ▬ TOTAL PROFIT

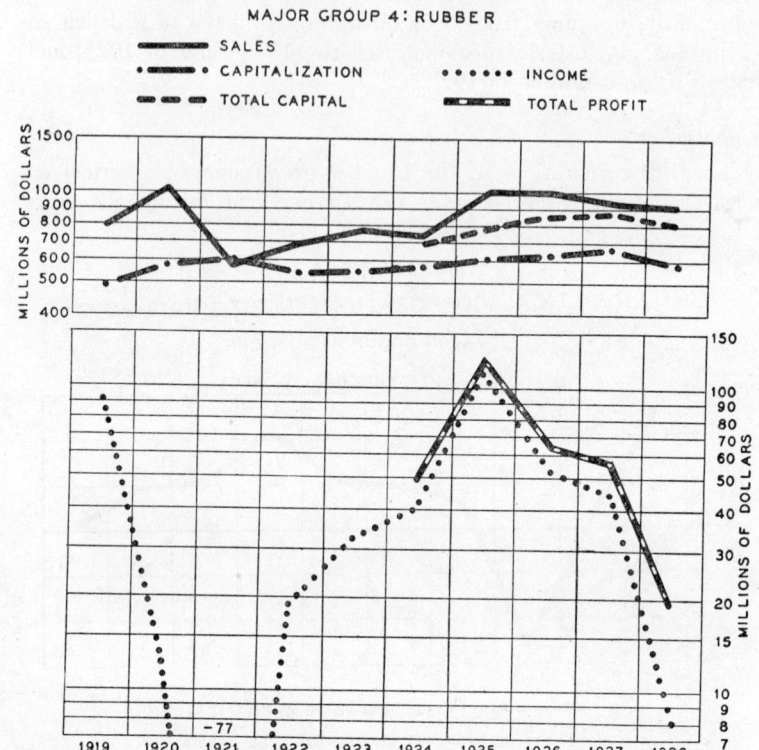

1919–23. From 1923 to the end of the period the return showed a general decline, falling from 15 per cent in 1923 to 8 per cent in 1928. The return on investment in all these years was almost the same as that upon sales.

Sales volume declined from 456 million in 1919 to 286 million in 1921. By 1925 it recovered to 531 million and fluctuated about a level of approximately half a billion dollars annually from then until the end of the period. Investment showed a general increase, growing from about 300 million in 1919 to slightly over 500 million in 1928. Net income oscillated greatly from 1919 to 1923 but there-

CHART 44
IDENTICAL CORPORATIONS SERIES, 1919-28
MAJOR GROUP 5: LUMBER

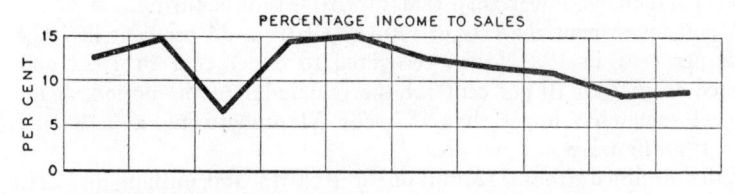

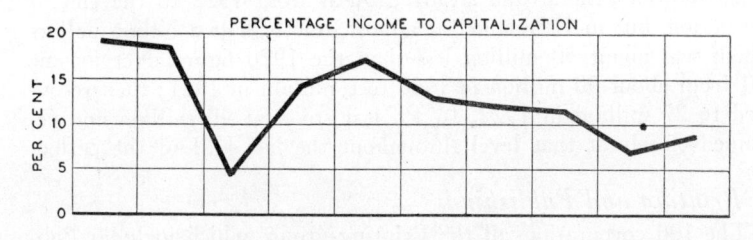

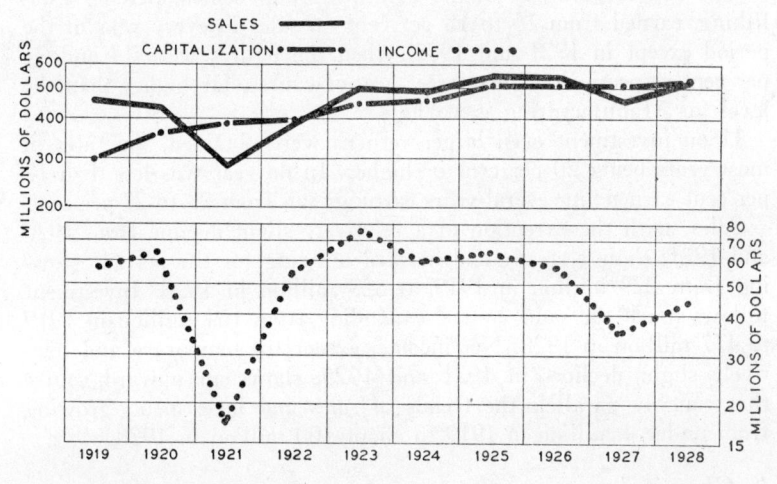

after showed a general decline, falling from 77 million in that year to 44 million in 1928.

f. Paper

The 111 corporations of the Paper group earned 13 per cent upon sales in 1919 and 16 per cent in 1920. This return was cut to 2 per cent in 1921, but recovered to 8 per cent in 1922 and for the remainder of the period was either 8 or 9 per cent in every year, a level somewhat lower than that for All Manufacturing.

Upon investment the rate of return fell from 28 per cent in 1920 to 2 per cent in 1921; then recovered to 8 per cent in 1922 and ranged from 7 to 10 per cent for the remainder of the period, again a level somewhat lower than that for Manufacturing as a whole. The 1928 figure was 7 per cent.

Sales declined from 552 million in 1920 to 300 million in 1921. They showed general and steady growth from 1922 to the end of the period, but in 1928 stood at almost exactly half a billion dollars which was about 50 million less than the 1920 figure. Net income fell from about 90 million in 1920 to 6 million in 1921; then recovered to 27 million in 1922. In 1924 it stood at 40 million and remained closely at that level throughout the last half of the period.

g. Printing and Publishing

The 100 corporations of the Printing group, which includes Publishing, earned from 16 to 18 per cent on sales in every year of the period except in 1921 and 1922, when the figures were 14 and 21 per cent respectively. These rates are, of course, far higher than the level for Manufacturing as a whole.

Upon investment even larger returns were obtained, the rates in most years being 20 per cent or higher. In no year was less than 17 per cent earned; in several years earnings ran from 23 to 27 per cent.

Sales, with the exception of a relatively slight decline from 1920 and 1921, show a steady and marked upswing for the period, growing from 229 million in 1919 to 623 million in 1928. Investment follows much the same course, expanding from 164 million in 1919 to 457 million in 1928. Net income, except for temporary and relatively slight declines in 1921 and 1925, shows an upward course that roughly parallels the trends of sales and investment, growing from under 4 million in 1919 to about 100 million in 1928.

h. Chemicals

The 210 corporations of the Chemicals group show a return on sales that fluctuates from 14 to 4 per cent between 1919 and 1922. From 1923 to the end of the period the trend might be said to be generally upward were it not for a substantial fluctuation between

MANUFACTURE AND MAJOR GROUPS [229]

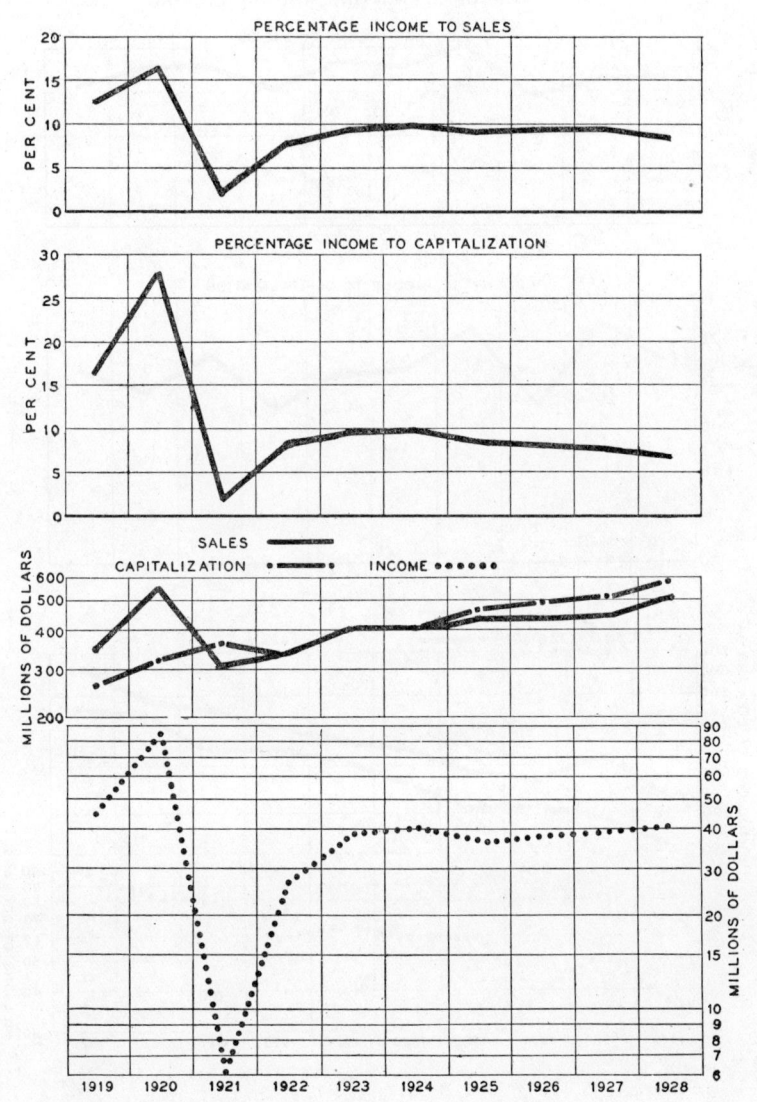

CHART 45
IDENTICAL CORPORATIONS SERIES, 1919-28
MAJOR GROUP 6: PAPER

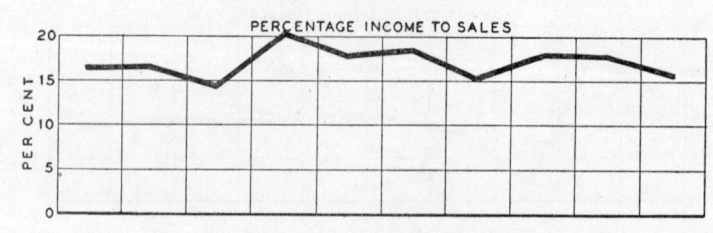

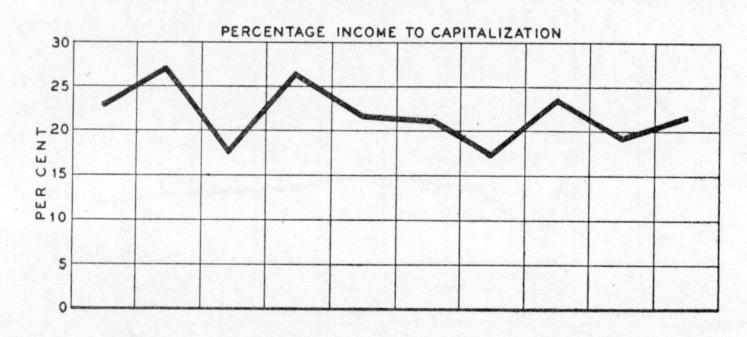

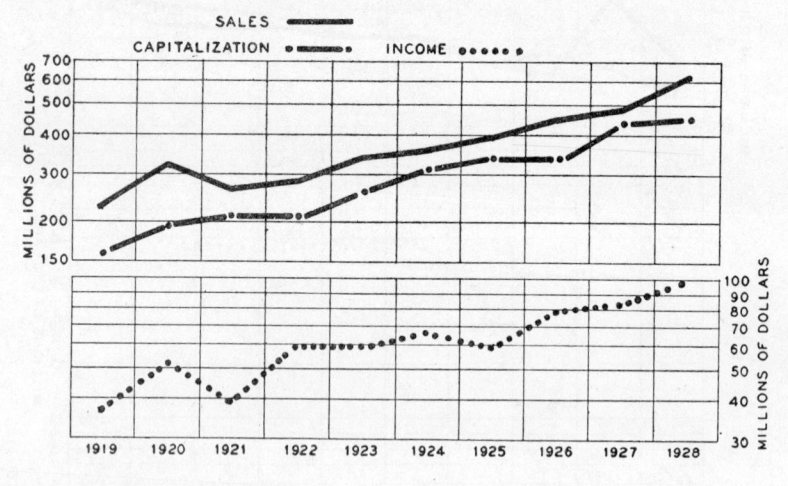

CHART 46
IDENTICAL CORPORATIONS SERIES, 1919-28
MAJOR GROUP 7: PRINTING AND PUBLISHING

CHART 47
IDENTICAL CORPORATIONS SERIES, 1919-28
MAJOR GROUP 8: CHEMICALS

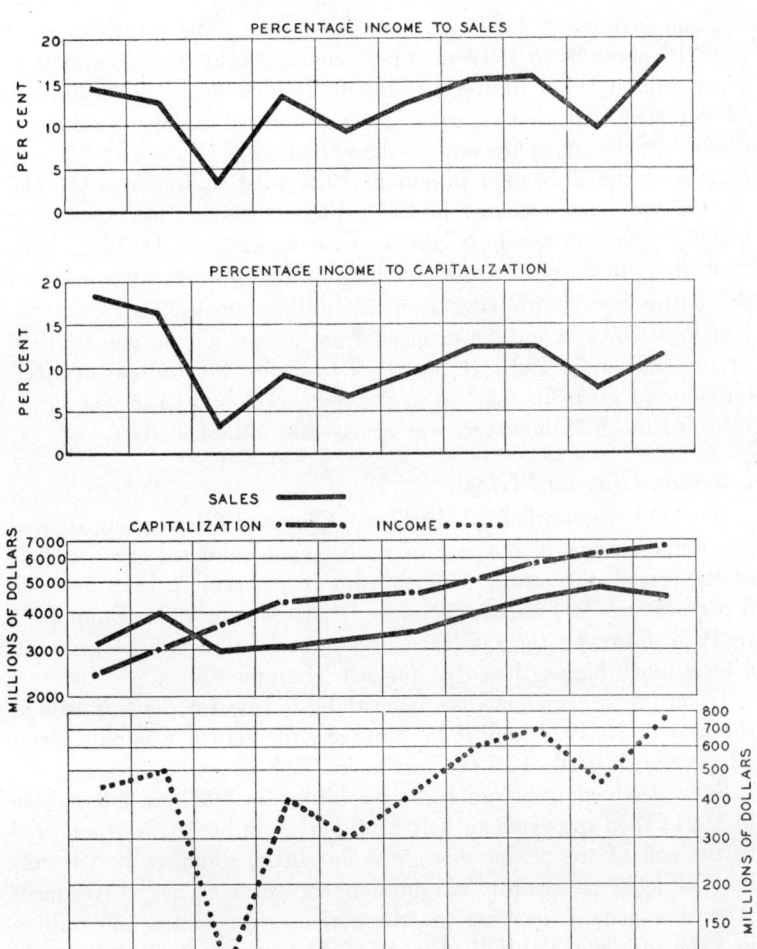

1926 and 1928. The 1926 return was 16 per cent; 1927, 10 per cent, and 1928, 18 per cent. During the second half of the period the return on sales thus fluctuated between 10 and 18 per cent, or upon a level substantially higher than that for Manufacture as a whole.

Upon investment lower earnings are shown. The return dropped from 18 per cent in 1919 to 3 per cent in 1921; then recovered to 9 per cent in 1922. Between 1922 and 1928 it fluctuated from 7 to 12 per cent, but showed some general upward sweep, standing at about 12 per cent at the end of the period.

Sales declined from 4 billion in 1920 to 3 billion in 1921 and showed but scant recovery in 1922. From 1922 to 1927 they grew steadily, reaching nearly 5 billion in the latter year. In 1928, however, they declined to about 4.5 billion. Investment expanded over the entire period, growing from 2.5 billion in 1919 to 6.75 billion in 1928. Net income dropped from about 500 million in 1920 to 109 million in 1921. It recovered to about 400 million in 1922, but showed great fluctuations in succeeding years. The income figure recorded in 1928, however, was nearly 800 million dollars.

i. Stone, Clay and Glass

The 114 corporations of the Stone, Clay and Glass group showed great fluctuations in the rate of return upon sales for the first half of the period, the return ranging from 16 per cent in 1919 down to 8 per cent in 1921 and up again to 19 per cent in 1923. From 1924 to 1928, however, the rate varied only between 15 and 17 per cent, a level much higher than that for All Manufacture.

Upon investment much the same thing is true for the first half of the period. In 1927 and 1928, however, the return was only about 12 per cent instead of 16 per cent as in 1924–26.

Sales declined from nearly half a billion in 1920 to 330 million in 1921; then recovered to half a billion again by 1923; from 1923 to the end of the period they grew but little, standing at 550 million in 1928 as against 525 million six years earlier. Investment showed a general increase for the period, rising from 320 million in 1919 to about 700 million in 1928. Net income oscillated greatly during the first half of the period but remained relatively stable at between about 85 and 100 million annually during the last half.

CHART 48
IDENTICAL CORPORATIONS SERIES, 1919-28
MAJOR GROUP 9: STONE, CLAY AND GLASS

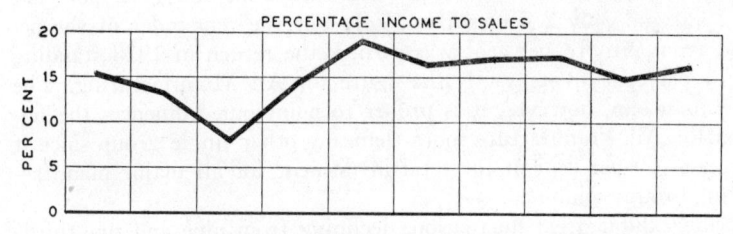

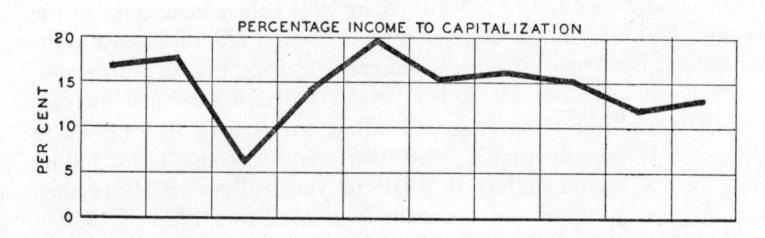

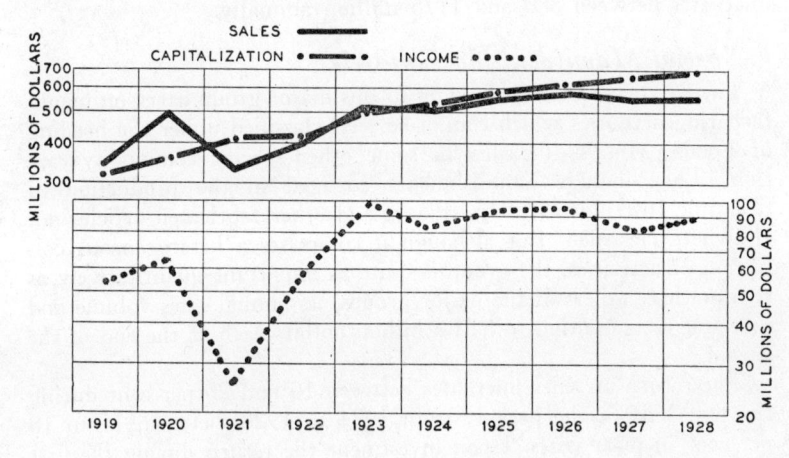

j. Metals

The 648 corporations of the Metals group showed a return of 15 per cent upon sales in 1919, 10 per cent in 1920, and 3 per cent in 1921. With recovery in 1922 the rate rose to 10 per cent, and remained at either 10 or 11 per cent in every year from 1922 to 1928.

Upon investment 18 per cent was earned in 1919, 12 per cent in 1920 and only 2 per cent in 1921. For the remainder of the period from 9 to 13 per cent was earned, the return in 1928 standing at 11 per cent or at exactly the figure for All Manufacturing. The Metals group, however, it is proper to point out, influences the figures for All Manufacture more than any other single group since it possesses 60 per cent of the total investment for all major manufacturing groups combined.

Sales exhibit great fluctuation, declining from nine and two-thirds billion dollars in 1920 to 5.5 billion in 1921; then increasing to the previous figure again by 1923. From 1923 to 1928 they show some fluctuation, but record a general increase of about 17 per cent, standing at 11.25 billion in 1928. Investment shows a sustained increase over the period, growing from 6.5 billion in 1919 to 10.5 billion in 1928. Net income fluctuates greatly between 1919 and 1923, falling from over a billion dollars in 1919 to 166 million in 1921; then reaching over a billion dollars again in 1923. From 1923 to 1928 it fluctuates between 880 and 1175 million annually.

k. Special Manufacturing Industries

The 89 corporations belonging to this major group carry on manufacturing activities which cannot be well classified under the heading of Foods, Metals, Textiles, or some other specific commodity caption. They include establishments engaged in the production of Scientific Instruments, Toys, Pianos and other fabricated articles not elsewhere classified. But although it comprises a heterogeneous collection of activities, the group is quite as important quantitatively as two or three others of the major groups, its annual sales volume and investment amounting to half a billion dollars each at the end of the period.

The return on sales fluctuates between 10 and 20 per cent during the first half of the period; from 1924 to 1928, between 15 to 18 per cent in most years. Upon investment the return during the first half of the period varies between 11 and 28 per cent; during the last half of the period, between 17 and 20 per cent in most years.

CHART 49
IDENTICAL CORPORATIONS SERIES, 1919-28
MAJOR GROUP 10: METALS

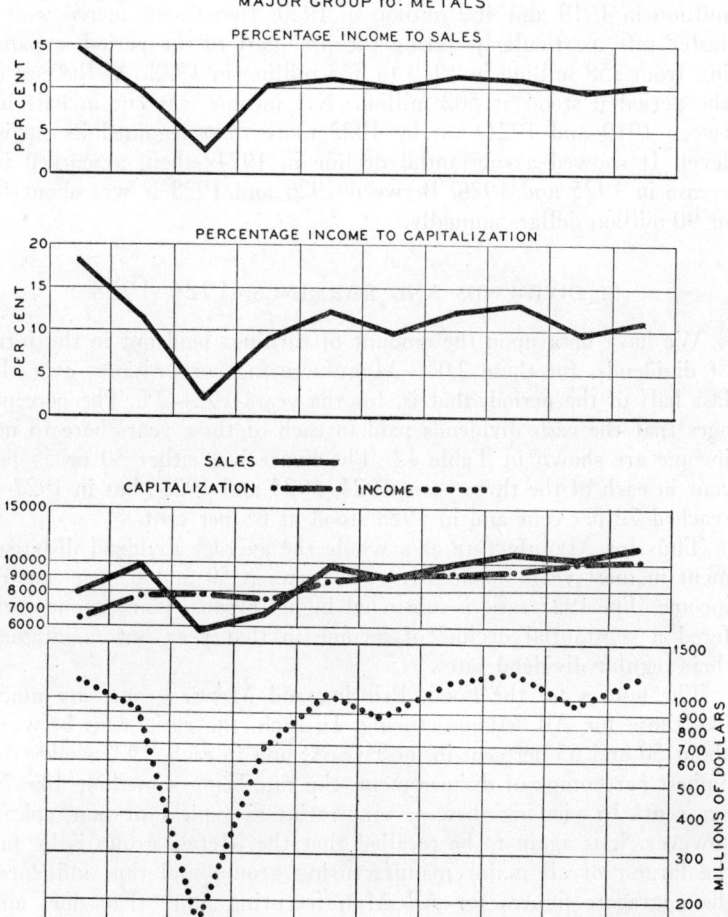

In both 1927 and 1928 earnings on investment stand at 17 per cent, which is a substantially higher figure than that for All Manufacture.

Sales show a decline in 1921 but show growth for the period as a whole, the 1928 figure being 539 million as compared with 394 million in 1919 and 469 million in 1920. Investment increases at a faster rate, particularly during the first part of the period, expanding from 258 million in 1919 to 353 million in 1922. At the end of the period it stood at 502 million. Net income was cut in half between 1919 and 1921, but by 1922 more than regained its earlier level. It showed a substantial decline in 1924; then, a marked increase in 1925 and 1926. Between 1926 and 1928 it was about 80 or 90 million dollars annually.

4. DIVIDENDS AND EARNINGS, 1924–1928

We have data upon the amount of earnings paid out in the form of dividends, for these 2,046 Manufacturing corporations, over the last half of the period, that is, for the years 1924–28. The percentages that the cash dividends paid in each of these years bore to net income are shown in Table 42. The figure was either 50 or 55 per cent in each of the three years 1924, 1925 and 1926; but in 1927 it reached 72 per cent and in 1928 stood at 65 per cent.

Thus for Manufacture as a whole the average dividend disbursement in most years apparently runs between 50 and 65 per cent of income. The 1927 ratio is somewhat higher because many groups suffered a substantial decline of income in that year but maintained their regular dividend rates.

The figures for the Food, Printing and Metals groups are much like those for All Manufacturing. In each, the ratio runs between about 50 and 65 per cent in most years; and in each, 1927 shows the highest percentage of disbursement, the rate being something like 70 per cent. In viewing these several ratios as typical or non-typical, however, it is again to be recalled that the Metals group is by far the largest of all major manufacturing groups and thus influences the aggregate figures for All Manufacturing more than does any other single group, or even any two groups, combined.

The other eight major groups show figures that do not conform so closely with those for All Manufacturing. Details for all groups are given in Table 42.

MANUFACTURE AND MAJOR GROUPS [237]

CHART 50
IDENTICAL CORPORATIONS SERIES, 1919-28
MAJOR GROUP 11: SPECIAL MANUFACTURING INDUSTRIES

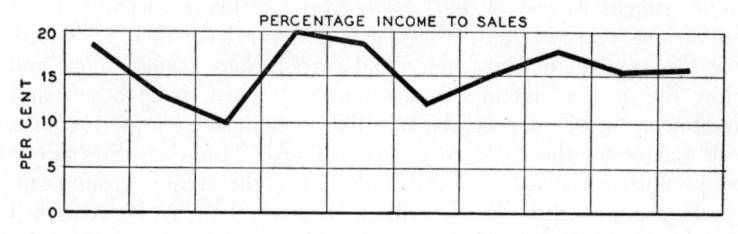

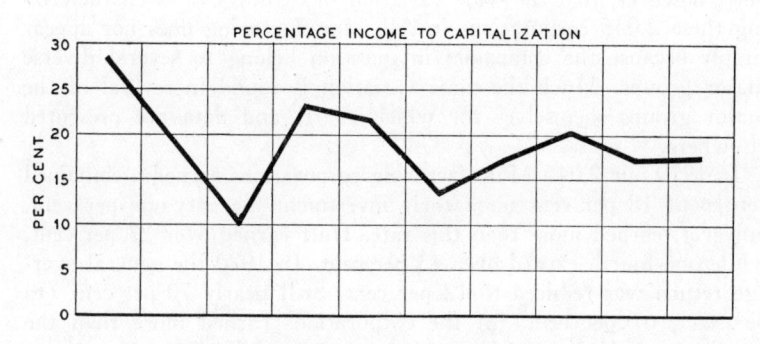

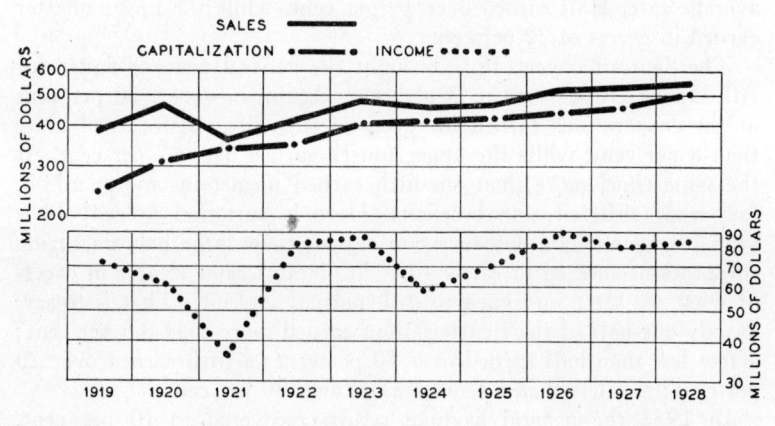

5. EARNINGS OF INDIVIDUAL CORPORATIONS

In the first section we discussed the general average rates of return on investment earned by our 2,046 Manufacturing corporations in the various years of the period 1919–28. We have now to inquire how the earnings of these individual corporations ranged above and below the general average figures obtained when their income and investment figures are combined. The present section will discuss these ranges for the 2,046 corporations in All Manufacturing as one large industrial division. Similar data for the major groups separately are presented in succeeding chapters. It may be remarked here, however, that the wide variation in earnings rates characterizing these 2,046 corporations in All Manufacturing does not appear simply because the companies in question belong to several diverse major groups. Much the same variation is found in several of the major groups themselves for which charts and data are presented elsewhere.

In 1919 our 2,046 Manufacturing corporations earned a combined return of 18 per cent upon their investment. Seventy-one per cent, however, earned more than this rate. Half earned over 27 per cent, while one-fourth earned over 43 per cent. In 1920 the general average return was reduced to 12 per cent. Still nearly 70 per cent (to be exact, 67 per cent) of the corporations earned more than the average rate. Half earned over 19 per cent, while the upper quarter earned in excess of 32 per cent.

The depression year 1921 brought the general average figure for All Manufacture down to 3 per cent. Again, however, 70 per cent of the corporations earned in excess of this rate; half earned more than 8 per cent, while the upper fourth earned over 17 per cent. At the same time, more than one-fifth earned no net income at all; in fact, they suffered actual deficits. Here is variation indeed! In a year of undeniably deep depression half of these large manufacturing corporations succeed in earning net incomes at rates clearly in excess of what we are accustomed to call 'normal interest'. That is to say, exactly one-half of these corporations earned more than 8.6 per cent; a few less than half earned over 10 per cent; a fifth earned over 20 per cent; and less than a tenth earned over 30 per cent.

In 1922 the general average return recovered to 10 per cent. Again, however, almost three-quarters of the corporations earned in

MANUFACTURE AND MAJOR GROUPS [239]

excess of this figure; half earned over 17 per cent; the upper quarter earned over 28 per cent; while the lower quarter earned under 9 per cent. Over a fifth, in this year of recovery, earned over 30 per cent.

Between 1922 and 1928 the distribution of the earnings of individual corporations, while continuing to show substantial variation, exhibited a general decline in the number of companies receiving the highest earnings (and a corresponding increase in the number receiving the lowest). Chart 51 presents these changes in the distribution by broad classes of earnings rates.[3] It will be observed that while in 1922 and 1923 something like a fourth of the corporations earned under 10 per cent, about 40 per cent did so in 1928. Examining the highest bracket of the chart, we see that whereas almost two-thirds of the corporations earned 20 per cent or over in 1922 and 1923, only about one-fifth did so in 1928. The proportion of companies occupying the middle of the three brackets of the chart—the 10 to 19 per cent class of earnings rates—remains roughly constant between 1923 and 1928, that is, approximately two-fifths of the corporations in most years earned between 10 and 19 per cent upon their investment. Detailed figures for the distribution in each year are given in Table 42.

---

[3] The four broad class intervals of this chart, and of those like it in succeeding chapters, are shown as 'Under Zero', '1 to 9 per cent', '10 to 19 per cent', and '20 per cent and over' respectively. This appears to omit the range from zero to one per cent. Actually it does not. The theoretically possible case of an exact zero income was never encountered in the original calculations. The original data themselves, on which the *Source-Book* is based, had been rounded off to the nearest dollar. All calculated percentages for income to capitalization were thus either positive or negative. But these calculated percentages themselves were rounded off to the nearest whole per cent. In the case of all positive percentages falling in the 0.1 to 0.9 class, these were regarded as belonging to the 'one per cent' category. Thus 'Under Zero' means negative earnings rates of any size, and '1 to 9' per cent includes the positive rates which may have been fractional before they were rounded off in the preparation of the *Source-Book*.

CHART 51
FREQUENCY DISTRIBUTION OF EARNINGS RATES, INDIVIDUAL COMPANIES (IDENTICAL CORPORATIONS SERIES)
ALL MANUFACTURE

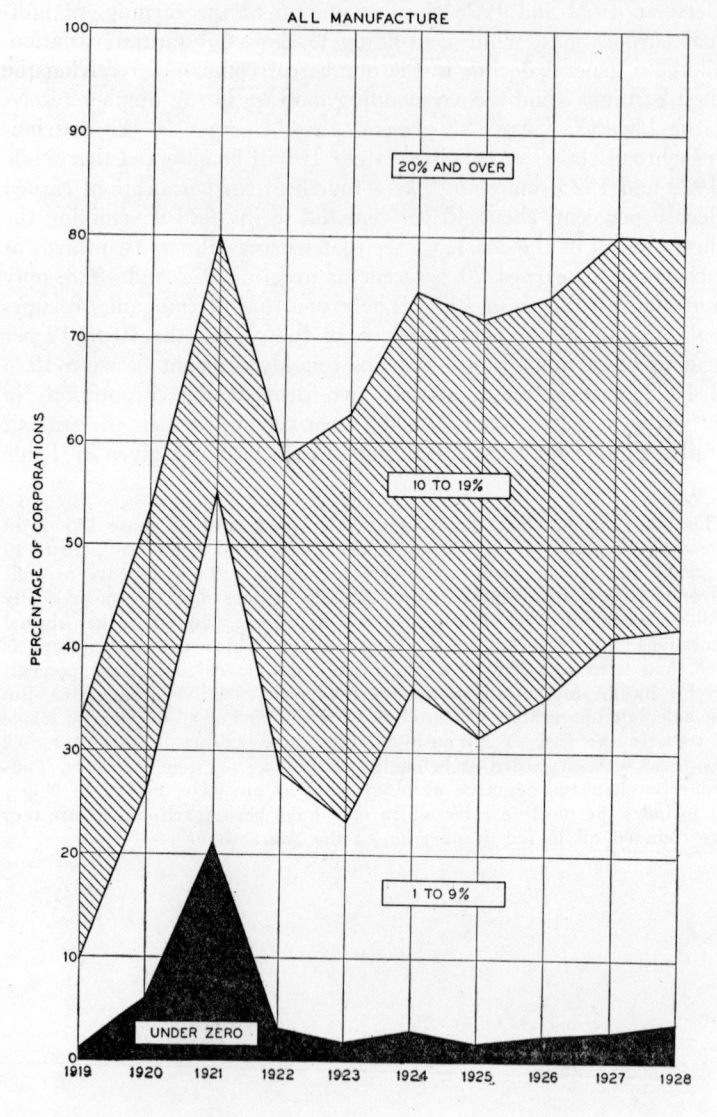

Table 42

MANUFACTURING AND ITS MAJOR GROUPS, LARGE IDENTICAL CORPORATIONS SERIES

(A) SIZE AND CHARACTER OF SAMPLE

	NUMBER OF CORPORATIONS	AVERAGE CAPITAL PER CORPORATION [1] *(millions of dollars)* ARITHMETIC MEAN	MEDIAN
All manufacturing	2,046	13.50	1.97
Major group			
1 Foods	215	14.76	2.17
2 Textiles	289	4.30	1.73
3 Leather	54	4.85	2.40
4 Rubber	26	31.03	2.83
5 Lumber	190	2.95	1.15
6 Paper	111	6.00	1.58
7 Printing and publishing	100	5.69	1.36
8 Chemicals	210	34.44	2.22
9 Stone, clay and glass	114	6.48	2.08
10 Metals	648	18.31	2.38
11 Special manufacturing industries	89	5.75	2.32

[1] Total capital (i.e., includes funded debt) as of December 31, 1928.

TABLE 42 (continued)

(B) PERCENTAGE INCOME TO SALES

	1919	1920	1921	1922	1923	1924	1925	1926	1927	1928	1919-1928[a]
All manufacturing	11.5	7.9	3.1	9.9	9.8	8.9	10.0	10.1	8.3	9.7	9.1
Major group											
1 Foods	3.7	2.3	1.7	5.1	5.3	4.4	3.8	4.8	4.1	4.4	4.0
2 Textiles	16.9	4.9	9.0	12.6	11.0	5.4	7.2	5.5	7.7	5.8	8.5
3 Leather	12.1	2.2	1.6	9.2	6.8	8.4	7.6	7.3	9.5	7.6	7.4
4 Rubber	12.1	1.1	−13.2	2.9	4.3	5.6	11.2	5.2	4.8	0.8	4.0
5 Lumber	12.4	14.7	6.3	14.3	15.2	12.3	11.7	10.8	7.8	8.2	11.5
6 Paper	12.5	16.1	1.9	7.6	9.2	9.9	8.6	8.9	8.9	8.1	9.5
7 Printing and publishing	16.5	16.5	14.4	20.7	17.8	18.4	15.2	17.7	17.5	15.8	17.0
8 Chemicals	14.0	12.5	3.7	12.9	9.4	12.3	15.4	15.6	9.6	17.5	12.6
9 Stone, clay and glass	15.5	13.1	7.9	14.4	18.9	16.5	16.9	16.8	15.0	16.2	15.4
10 Metals	14.7	9.7	3.0	10.2	11.1	10.1	11.4	11.1	9.8	10.4	10.4
11 Special manufacturing industries	18.3	12.9	10.0	19.9	18.1	12.2	15.0	17.6	15.4	15.9	15.6

(C) PERCENTAGE INCOME TO CAPITALIZATION

	1919	1920	1921	1922	1923	1924	1925	1926	1927	1928	1919-1928[a]
All manufacturing	18.3	12.3	2.9	10.2	11.2	10.0	12.1	12.4	9.5	11.0	10.8
Major group											
1 Foods	11.9	6.5	3.4	10.3	10.4	10.9	10.1	11.7	10.5	11.1	9.8
2 Textiles	30.2	8.1	10.6	16.5	14.5	6.7	9.2	7.1	9.0	6.7	11.2
3 Leather	34.1	4.3	2.4	15.5	11.2	12.8	12.7	12.1	15.4	11.5	12.7
4 Rubber	19.0	2.1	−12.6	3.6	6.0	7.3	18.9	8.6	6.9	1.3	5.9
5 Lumber	19.1	18.0	4.6	14.2	16.9	12.8	12.3	11.6	7.1	8.5	12.1
6 Paper	16.6	27.6	1.7	7.8	9.5	9.9	8.1	7.9	7.6	6.9	9.6
7 Printing and publishing	23.0	26.9	17.6	26.6	21.7	21.0	17.2	23.0	19.4	21.5	21.4
8 Chemicals	18.0	16.5	2.9	9.2	6.7	9.1	12.2	12.1	7.5	11.6	10.2

MANUFACTURE AND MAJOR GROUPS [243]

	1924	1925	1926	1927	1928
9 Stone, clay and glass	16.7	17.4	6.3	14.1	19.6	15.6
10 Metals	18.0	12.0	2.1	8.8	12.1	9.8
11 Special manufacturing industries	28.0	19.4	10.6	23.1	21.5	13.9

[1] Ten-year aggregate.

(D) PERCENTAGE PROFIT TO TOTAL CAPITAL

	1924	1925	1926	1927	1928
All manufacturing	9.5	11.4	11.7	9.0	10.4
Major group					
1 Foods	10.1	9.3	10.9	9.7	10.3
2 Textiles	6.6	9.1	7.0	8.9	6.6
3 Leather	12.6	12.5	12.0	15.0	12.2
4 Rubber	6.8	15.7	7.6	6.4	2.3
5 Lumber	12.4	11.9	11.4	7.0	8.2
6 Paper	9.4	7.5	7.3	7.0	6.7
7 Printing and publishing	19.4	15.6	20.2	16.5	18.3
8 Chemicals	8.9	11.8	11.6	7.3	11.1
9 Stone, clay and glass	15.3	15.9	15.0	12.1	12.3
10 Metals	9.2	11.3	12.2	9.3	10.4
11 Special manufacturing industries	13.7	16.7	20.1	16.9	16.8

	1924	1925	1926	1927	1928
	16.2	15.2	12.3	12.8	14.5
	12.1	13.1	9.8	11.1	10.8
	16.9	20.2	17.0	17.0	18.4

(E) PERCENTAGE OF INCOME PAID OUT IN CASH DIVIDENDS

	1924	1925	1926	1927	1928
	55.0	50.0	55.0	72.0	65.0
	58.3	64.7	59.4	76.7	61.2
	82.3	58.6	72.6	52.6	71.0
	26.7	33.0	33.7	24.4	58.4
	24.1	21.4	56.4	114.1	270.1
	53.4	60.3	73.7	97.8	66.1
	45.7	56.5	48.6	66.4	76.4
	44.3	58.3	59.0	69.9	48.6
	66.8	54.0	60.5	88.7	70.5
	42.3	45.8	59.7	60.0	49.9
	49.2	44.2	48.4	67.5	62.7
	71.9	74.5	61.5	47.5	72.3

TABLE 42 (*continued*)

(F) FREQUENCY DISTRIBUTIONS OF PERCENTAGES OF TOTAL NET INCOME TO CAPITALIZATION, INDIVIDUAL CORPORATIONS, 1919–23. ALL MANUFACTURING

PERCENTAGE INCOME TO CAPITALIZATION	1919 PERCENTAGE IN EACH CLASS	1919 ACCUMULATED BY SUCCESSIVE CLASSES	1920 PERCENTAGE IN EACH CLASS	1920 ACCUMULATED BY SUCCESSIVE CLASSES	1921 PERCENTAGE IN EACH CLASS	1921 ACCUMULATED BY SUCCESSIVE CLASSES	1922 PERCENTAGE IN EACH CLASS	1922 ACCUMULATED BY SUCCESSIVE CLASSES	1923 PERCENTAGE IN EACH CLASS	1923 ACCUMULATED BY SUCCESSIVE CLASSES
Under zero	1.0	1.0	6.0	6.0	21.2	21.2	3.2	3.2	1.9	1.9
Zero to 4	2.2	3.2	7.1	13.1	15.5	36.7	9.2	12.4	6.3	8.2
5 to 9	6.5	9.7	13.3	26.4	18.4	55.1	15.4	27.8	15.1	23.3
10 to 14	10.9	20.6	14.0	40.4	14.8	69.9	16.5	44.3	19.4	42.7
15 to 19	12.6	33.2	13.0	53.4	10.2	80.1	14.2	58.5	20.0	62.7
20 to 24	12.4	45.6	9.9	63.3	6.3	86.4	10.9	69.4	13.2	75.9
25 to 29	9.4	55.0	8.5	71.8	4.2	90.6	9.2	78.6	9.3	85.2
30 and over	45.0	100.0	28.2	100.0	9.4	100.0	21.4	100.0	14.8	100.0

(G) FREQUENCY DISTRIBUTIONS OF PERCENTAGES OF TOTAL PROFIT TO TOTAL CAPITAL, INDIVIDUAL CORPORATIONS, 1924–28. ALL MANUFACTURING

	1924 PERCENTAGE IN EACH CLASS	1924 ACCUMULATED BY SUCCESSIVE CLASSES	1925 PERCENTAGE IN EACH CLASS	1925 ACCUMULATED BY SUCCESSIVE CLASSES	1926 PERCENTAGE IN EACH CLASS	1926 ACCUMULATED BY SUCCESSIVE CLASSES	1927 PERCENTAGE IN EACH CLASS	1927 ACCUMULATED BY SUCCESSIVE CLASSES	1928 PERCENTAGE IN EACH CLASS	1928 ACCUMULATED BY SUCCESSIVE CLASSES
Under zero	2.9	2.9	1.8	1.8	2.4	2.4	3.0	3.0	3.7	3.7
Zero to 4	10.0	12.9	8.3	10.1	10.6	13.0	12.4	15.4	13.0	16.7
5 to 9	23.3	36.2	21.4	31.5	22.2	35.2	25.7	41.1	25.4	42.1
10 to 14	22.0	58.2	25.9	57.4	23.8	59.0	23.5	64.6	23.0	65.1

15 to 19	16.4	74.6	14.6	72.0	15.2	74.2	15.5	80.1	14.6	79.7
20 to 24	10.0	84.6	10.3	82.3	11.0	85.2	8.2	88.3	8.7	88.4
25 to 29	5.6	90.2	7.0	89.3	5.2	90.4	4.2	92.5	4.5	92.9
30 and over	9.8	100.0	10.7	100.0	9.6	100.0	7.5	100.0	7.1	100.0

CHAPTER 10

FOODS AND FOOD PRODUCTS

THE major group, Food Products, is made up of 11 minor groups, each in turn consisting of smaller, but in the main rather closely related, sets of food manufacturing activities: Bakery Products; Flour, Feed and Grist Mills; Confectionery; Package Foods; Dairying; Canned Goods; Meat Packing; Beverages; Tobacco; Miscellaneous Food Products. The last-mentioned is shown mainly in order to round out the sample so that the major group is representative of food manufacturing activities as a whole. The number of corporations in each group and their average size are shown in Table 43. The groups are described briefly:

Bakery Products: Bread, ice cream cones, pie, cakes, etc.
Flour, Feed and Grist Mills: All sorts of milling activity concerned with the processing of grains and cereals. Bran, alfalfa, grits, hominy, buckwheat, corn, oats, rye and their products, are all included, as well as wheat and wheat flour.
Confectionery: Candy, chewing gum, cocoa, glacé fruits, icings, etc.
Package Foods: A long list of items makes up this group of branded and trade-marked products. Breakfast foods, bouillon cubes, spaghetti, starch, egg noodles, shredded cocoanut, tea and coffee are among them.
Dairying and Dairy Products: Butter and cheese, evaporated, condensed, malted and pasteurized milk.
Canned Goods: Canned sea food, canned fruit and vegetables; pickles, relishes, catsup, sauerkraut, flavoring extracts and fruit juices. Canned meats are excluded.
Meat Packing: All sorts of meats whether fresh or canned, beef and pork products, and slaughtering.
Beverages: These beverages are non-alcoholic; liquors are classified under Miscellaneous Food Products. Here are mineral waters, grape juice, cereal beverages and near-beer, and other soft drinks.
Tobacco: Cigarettes, cigars, snuff, smoking and chewing tobacco.
Miscellaneous Food Products: Butter substitutes, poultry, distilled and vinous liquors, ice, ice cream, beet sugar, and cane sugar.

Table 43

FOODS GROUPS: LARGE IDENTICAL MANUFACTURING CORPORATIONS SERIES

(A) SIZE AND CHARACTER OF SAMPLE

	NUMBER OF CORPORATIONS	AVERAGE CAPITAL PER CORPORATION [1] (millions of dollars) ARITHMETIC MEAN	MEDIAN
Major group			
1 Foods	215	14.76	2.17
Minor group			
1 Bakery products	17	14.27	
2 Flour	32	2.07	
3 Confectionery	21	5.34	
4 Package foods	19	5.05	
5 Dairying	26	8.06	
6 Canned goods	16	7.17	
7 Meat packing	23	41.65	
9 Beverages	11	4.22	
10 Tobacco	23	33.68	
11-8 Miscellaneous food products	27	20.45	

[1] Total capital (i.e., includes funded debt) as of December 31, 1928.

TABLE 43 (continued)

(B) PERCENTAGE INCOME TO SALES

	1919	1920	1921	1922	1923	1924	1925	1926	1927	1928	1919–1928[a]
Major group											
1 Foods	3.7	2.3	1.7	5.1	5.3	4.4	3.8	4.8	4.1	4.4	4.0
Minor group											
1 Bakery products	8.5	6.1	10.2	12.2	11.2	12.5	11.9	12.9	13.5	12.9	11.3
2 Flour	4.8	.7	2.6	2.5	3.3	5.1	2.8	2.9	3.4	3.4	3.1
3 Confectionery	18.7	8.0	5.7	13.7	13.7	15.8	15.1	14.8	15.4	14.5	13.7
4 Package foods	4.8	–1.2	7.5	10.2	7.5	8.4	6.2	8.7	8.0	7.5	6.5
5 Dairying	4.1	1.5	2.5	5.0	4.8	3.7	4.7	4.8	4.6	4.5	4.1
6 Canned goods	12.6	5.6	6.7	12.7	10.5	11.6	9.2	8.5	7.7	8.6	9.4
7 Meat packing	–.5	.1	–1.9	.5	1.1	.9	.6	1.2	.4	.8	.4
9 Beverages	–4.6	.2	1.9	9.7	14.6	6.8	13.0	13.1	9.6	15.8	8.2
10 Tobacco	10.0	7.9	9.7	11.0	10.9	10.0	10.9	11.2	11.3	11.2	10.5
11–8 Miscellaneous food products	10.3	4.1	5.4	7.4	8.5	8.4	6.0	8.1	6.1	8.4	6.4

(C) PERCENTAGE INCOME TO CAPITALIZATION

	1919	1920	1921	1922	1923	1924	1925	1926	1927	1928	1919–1928[a]
Major group											
1 Foods	11.9	6.5	3.4	10.3	10.4	10.9	10.1	11.7	10.5	11.1	9.8
Minor group											
1 Bakery products	15.2	12.1	15.0	18.0	15.0	18.6	16.2	18.8	19.0	17.5	16.8
2 Flour	25.3	3.2	8.9	9.0	9.4	16.2	9.9	9.9	11.9	12.0	11.4
3 Confectionery	41.9	13.2	6.6	17.1	17.9	19.2	18.4	17.4	17.0	15.1	17.8
4 Package foods	19.8	–3.5	14.9	20.7	16.7	20.7	16.0	20.2	17.9	17.6	16.2
5 Dairying	20.7	6.7	8.3	15.6	20.6	12.1	13.0	13.2	12.8	9.7	12.7
6 Canned goods	29.2	8.7	9.1	20.5	13.3	14.7	12.4	12.2	10.1	12.7	13.8
7 Meat packing	–3.6	.3	–7.0	1.9	3.8	4.4	3.2	6.3	2.3	4.6	1.9
9 Beverages	–1.9	.1	.9	3.2	6.1	3.0	6.7	6.5	4.5	8.6	3.8
10 Tobacco	14.0	11.7	13.1	14.2	13.4	13.5	15.0	14.7	16.0	15.6	14.2
11–8 Miscellaneous food products	17.4	6.9	–5.4	7.7	9.3	9.7	6.8	9.1	7.1	9.4	7.9

[a] Ten-year aggregate.

TABLE 43 *(continued)*
FOODS GROUPS: LARGE IDENTICAL MANUFACTURING CORPORATION SERIES

(D) PERCENTAGE PROFIT TO TOTAL CAPITAL

		1924	1925	1926	1927	1928
Major group						
1	Foods	10.1	9.3	10.9	9.7	10.3
Minor group						
1	Bakery products	17.9	15.6	18.3	18.6	17.1
2	Flour	16.2	9.9	9.8	11.7	11.8
3	Confectionery	18.7	17.9	17.0	16.6	14.9
4	Package foods	20.1	15.6	19.7	17.1	16.8
5	Dairying	11.8	12.3	13.0	12.5	9.5
6	Canned goods	14.7	12.4	12.1	10.1	12.7
7	Meat packing	4.5	3.8	6.0	3.0	4.7
9	Beverages	3.0	6.6	6.5	4.5	8.6
10	Tobacco	12.7	14.1	14.2	15.0	14.6
11–8	Miscellaneous food products	9.3	6.6	8.7	6.9	8.9

(E) PERCENTAGE OF INCOME PAID OUT IN CASH DIVIDENDS

		1924	1925	1926	1927	1928
Major group						
1	Foods	58.3	64.7	59.4	76.7	61.2
Minor group						
1	Bakery products	54.9	52.5	62.4	63.6	75.3
2	Flour	50.2	70.8	72.2	71.3	106.0
3	Confectionery	44.2	53.3	62.7	65.1	65.4
4	Package foods	52.5	55.6	43.5	57.3	71.2
5	Dairying	52.7	41.4	53.0	60.5	51.0
6	Canned goods	39.7	49.0	53.0	59.8	40.4
7	Meat packing	130.5	150.9	56.2	175.2	75.0
9	Beverages	89.9	53.3	74.8	133.8	67.6
10	Tobacco	43.2	59.3	55.2	70.8	57.8
11–8	Miscellaneous food products	57.0	64.0	77.2	95.5	44.9

[250]   INDUSTRIAL PROFITS

TABLE 43 (*continued*)

(F) FREQUENCY DISTRIBUTIONS OF PERCENTAGES OF TOTAL NET INCOME TO CAPITALIZATION, INDIVIDUAL CORPORATIONS, 1919–23. MAJOR GROUP 1: FOODS

PERCENTAGE INCOME TO CAPITALIZATION	1919 PERCENTAGE IN EACH CLASS	1919 ACCUMULATED BY SUCCESSIVE CLASSES	1920 PERCENTAGE IN EACH CLASS	1920 ACCUMULATED BY SUCCESSIVE CLASSES	1921 PERCENTAGE IN EACH CLASS	1921 ACCUMULATED BY SUCCESSIVE CLASSES	1922 PERCENTAGE IN EACH CLASS	1922 ACCUMULATED BY SUCCESSIVE CLASSES	1923 PERCENTAGE IN EACH CLASS	1923 ACCUMULATED BY SUCCESSIVE CLASSES
Under zero	3.7	3.7	11.6	11.6	12.1	12.1	3.7	3.7	1.4	1.4
Zero to 4	1.9	5.6	12.1	23.7	8.8	20.9	6.5	10.2	8.8	10.2
5 to 9	5.1	10.7	17.7	41.4	13.5	34.4	14.0	24.2	16.3	26.5
10 to 14	15.3	26.0	16.3	57.7	17.2	51.6	16.3	40.5	24.2	50.7
15 to 19	12.1	38.1	12.1	69.8	13.0	64.6	11.6	52.1	15.8	66.5
20 to 24	10.2	48.3	7.4	77.2	9.3	73.9	14.4	66.5	12.1	78.6
25 to 29	13.0	61.3	6.5	83.7	5.6	79.5	11.2	77.7	8.8	87.4
30 and over	38.7	100.0	16.3	100.0	20.5	100.0	22.3	100.0	12.6	100.0

(G) FREQUENCY DISTRIBUTIONS OF PERCENTAGES OF TOTAL PROFIT TO TOTAL CAPITAL, INDIVIDUAL CORPORATIONS, 1924–28 MAJOR GROUP 1: FOODS

	1924	1924	1925	1925	1926	1926	1927	1927	1928	1928
Under zero	2.8	2.8	3.7	3.7	3.3	3.3	4.2	4.2	1.9	1.9
Zero to 4	5.1	7.9	9.8	13.5	8.3	11.6	9.3	13.5	10.7	12.6
5 to 9	15.4	23.3	20.9	34.4	20.0	31.6	24.7	38.2	25.1	37.7

FOODS

10 to 14	24.2	47.5	23.3	57.7	26.5	58.1	20.9	59.1	26.1	63.8
15 to 19	20.0	67.5	16.7	74.4	12.5	70.6	17.7	76.8	16.7	80.5
20 to 24	15.8	83.3	12.1	86.5	19.1	89.7	13.5	90.3	10.2	90.7
25 to 29	6.5	89.8	5.6	92.1	3.3	93.0	3.7	94.0	3.7	94.4
30 and over	10.2	100.0	7.9	100.0	7.0	100.0	6.0	100.0	5.6	100.0

Chapter 11

TEXTILES AND TEXTILE PRODUCTS

The Textile Products group is made up of ten minor groups: Cotton Spinning; Cotton Converting; Cotton Weaving; Weaving Woolens; Silk Weaving; Carpets; Men's Clothing; Knit Goods, including Sweaters, Bathing Suits, Gloves, etc; Miscellaneous Clothing, Men's and Women's; Miscellaneous Textiles and Textile Products. The number of corporations included in each group and their average size are shown in Table 44. The groups are described briefly:

Cotton Spinning: Both coarse and medium yarns.
Cotton Converting: Cloths, threads and tape.
Cotton Weaving: Cloths.
Weaving Woolens: Cloths.
Silk Weaving: Includes rayon and other artificial silks.
Carpets: Carpet yarns, ropes and cordage are included.
Men's Clothing: Includes suits, shirts, bathrobes, vests and all boys' clothing.
Knit Goods: Sweaters, bathing suits, gloves, etc.
Miscellaneous Clothing: Custom made clothing, ladies' clothing, men's and women's hats, and underwear other than knit goods.
Miscellaneous Textile Products: Includes some 24 different types of Textile manufacture, such as cotton bags, cotton upholstery, dyeing woolens, silk ribbons and labels, felt, fur goods and moss gins.

Table 44

TEXTILE GROUPS, LARGE IDENTICAL MANUFACTURING CORPORATIONS SERIES

(A) SIZE AND CHARACTER OF SAMPLE

	NUMBER OF CORPORATIONS	AVERAGE CAPITAL PER CORPORATION [1] (millions of dollars) ARITHMETIC MEAN	MEDIAN
Major group			
2 Textiles	289	4.30	1.73
Minor group			
12 Cotton spinning	12	.83	

TEXTILES

Table 44 *(continued)*
TEXTILE GROUPS, LARGE IDENTICAL MANUFACTURING CORPORATIONS SERIES

(A) SIZE AND CHARACTER OF SAMPLE

		NUMBER OF CORPORATIONS	AVERAGE CAPITAL PER CORPORATION [1] *(millions of dollars)* ARITHMETIC MEAN	MEDIAN
Minor group				
13	Cotton converting	18	3.01	
14	Cotton weaving	49	5.46	
15	Weaving woolens	31	6.47	
16	Silk weaving	17	6.95	
17	Carpets	18	4.63	
18	Men's clothing	25	5.09	
19	Knit goods	42	2.88	
20	Miscellaneous clothing	23	2.36	
21	Miscellaneous textiles	54	3.84	

[1] Total capital (i.e., includes funded debt) as of December 31, 1928.

TABLE 44 (continued)

	1919	1920	1921	1922	1923	1924	1925	1926	1927	1928	1919-1928[a]
(B) PERCENTAGE INCOME TO SALES
Major group
2 Textiles	16.9	4.9	9.0	12.6	11.0	5.4	7.2	5.5	7.7	5.8	8.5
Minor group
12 Cotton spinning	18.1	15.4	11.9	10.2	8.9	4.7	7.7	7.2	8.0	6.3	9.8
13 Cotton converting	13.9	1.7	8.2	11.7	9.9	5.1	7.4	4.5	8.2	6.9	7.6
14 Cotton weaving	19.4	7.6	9.4	10.9	10.5	1.3	3.8	3.0	9.9	4.6	8.1
15 Weaving woolens	16.0	.3	11.8	14.5	10.5	2.1	4.1	1.4	4.2	1.8	6.9
16 Silk weaving	18.9	1.0	6.9	10.7	9.5	5.6	9.7	5.8	3.6	3.8	7.6
17 Carpets	20.9	9.2	17.4	26.0	21.1	11.8	10.2	8.1	9.7	7.3	14.1
18 Men's clothing	13.1	5.3	4.8	8.1	9.3	6.5	8.3	7.8	9.0	7.8	8.0
19 Knit goods	15.9	5.2	9.3	12.7	8.3	6.7	10.6	9.9	7.7	8.0	9.2
20 Miscellaneous clothing	12.6	2.9	2.4	8.9	8.5	5.9	7.6	8.1	8.4	7.1	7.2
21 Miscellaneous textiles	17.5	6.0	10.1	13.5	12.8	9.1	8.4	5.2	7.8	6.6	9.5
(C) PERCENTAGE INCOME TO CAPITALIZATION
Major group
2 Textiles	30.2	8.1	10.6	16.5	14.5	6.7	9.2	7.1	9.0	6.7	11.2
Minor group
12 Cotton spinning	47.0	37.4	10.4	16.0	13.8	7.6	12.3	10.1	10.4	9.5	15.5
13 Cotton converting	27.7	3.6	11.9	14.8	16.8	6.7	9.8	5.9	10.1	8.3	11.1
14 Cotton weaving	32.5	12.1	9.4	11.4	11.0	1.3	4.3	3.2	10.2	4.7	9.3
15 Weaving woolens	22.5	.4	11.4	15.2	11.6	2.1	4.1	1.5	3.8	1.5	7.2
16 Silk weaving	38.4	1.2	8.3	14.3	13.2	8.1	14.3	8.3	4.8	4.7	10.5
17 Carpets	26.5	12.2	15.9	36.3	24.6	12.2	11.4	8.9	10.0	6.7	15.6
18 Men's clothing	25.3	9.4	6.7	11.3	14.2	9.1	12.0	11.7	13.3	11.4	12.1
19 Knit goods	38.1	12.6	16.5	25.7	15.9	11.0	16.8	16.4	11.7	11.2	16.2

TEXTILES

	1924	1925	1926	1927	1928
20 Miscellaneous clothing	34.7	7.6	4.3	18.4	16.5	10.9
21 Miscellaneous textiles	34.3	11.1	12.2	19.7	18.5	12.2

¹ Ten-year aggregate.

(D) PERCENTAGE PROFIT TO TOTAL CAPITAL

	1924	1925	1926	1927	1928
Major group					
2 Textiles	6.6	9.1	7.0	8.9	6.6
Minor group					
12 Cotton spinning	7.6	12.3	10.1	10.4	9.5
13 Cotton converting	6.6	9.6	5.9	9.9	8.1
14 Cotton weaving	1.3	4.3	3.4	9.7	4.7
15 Weaving woolens	2.1	4.1	1.6	3.8	1.6
16 Silk weaving	7.8	14.2	8.1	4.8	4.7
17 Carpets	12.2	11.4	8.9	10.0	6.7
18 Men's clothing	9.0	11.8	11.6	13.2	11.4
19 Knit goods	10.8	15.8	15.6	11.3	10.8
20 Miscellaneous clothing	10.7	13.5	14.9	14.4	12.2
21 Miscellaneous textiles	11.9	11.1	6.8	8.6	7.6

(E) PERCENTAGE OF INCOME PAID OUT IN CASH DIVIDENDS

	1924	1925	1926	1927	1928
Major group					
2 Textiles	82.3	58.6	72.6	52.6	71.0
Minor group					
12 Cotton spinning	65.6	35.0	58.4	64.4	57.9
13 Cotton converting	79.6	56.1	94.7	53.7	61.3
14 Cotton weaving	344.7	91.8	100.8	32.0	91.8
15 Weaving woolens	236.7	106.0	308.5	73.4	155.9
16 Silk weaving	69.7	36.1	67.5	91.4	90.2
17 Carpets	73.0	70.3	78.2	59.8	93.7
18 Men's clothing	61.2	51.6	64.6	57.0	50.1
19 Knit goods	45.9	28.9	28.4	44.9	51.3
20 Miscellaneous clothing	45.1	35.2	39.2	38.8	48.1
21 Miscellaneous textiles	52.1	66.1	82.1	68.2	72.6

TABLE 44 (*continued*)

(F) FREQUENCY DISTRIBUTIONS OF PERCENTAGES OF TOTAL NET INCOME TO CAPITALIZATION, INDIVIDUAL CORPORATIONS, 1919–23. MAJOR GROUP 2: TEXTILES

PERCENTAGE INCOME TO CAPITALIZATION	1919 PERCENTAGE IN EACH CLASS	1919 ACCUMULATED BY SUCCESSIVE CLASSES	1920 PERCENTAGE IN EACH CLASS	1920 ACCUMULATED BY SUCCESSIVE CLASSES	1921 PERCENTAGE IN EACH CLASS	1921 ACCUMULATED BY SUCCESSIVE CLASSES	1922 PERCENTAGE IN EACH CLASS	1922 ACCUMULATED BY SUCCESSIVE CLASSES	1923 PERCENTAGE IN EACH CLASS	1923 ACCUMULATED BY SUCCESSIVE CLASSES
Under zero	.0	.0	14.9	14.9	9.3	9.3	1.4	1.4	2.1	2.1
Zero to 4	.7	.7	10.7	25.6	10.7	20.0	4.5	5.9	2.1	4.2
5 to 9	.7	1.4	18.0	43.6	20.1	40.1	14.5	20.4	14.2	18.4
10 to 14	3.8	5.2	8.6	52.2	18.4	58.5	16.3	36.7	22.5	40.9
15 to 19	8.7	13.9	11.1	63.3	11.4	69.9	16.6	53.3	27.0	67.9
20 to 24	12.1	26.0	7.6	70.9	10.7	80.6	11.8	65.1	13.5	81.4
25 to 29	10.0	36.0	8.0	78.9	6.2	86.8	11.1	76.2	7.9	89.3
30 and over	64.0	100.0	21.1	100.0	13.2	100.0	23.8	100.0	10.7	100.0

(G) FREQUENCY DISTRIBUTIONS OF PERCENTAGES OF TOTAL PROFIT TO TOTAL CAPITAL, INDIVIDUAL CORPORATIONS, 1924–28. MAJOR GROUP 2: TEXTILES

	1924	1924	1925	1925	1926	1926	1927	1927	1928	1928
Under zero	8.0	8.0	1.7	1.7	5.5	5.5	1.4	1.4	5.5	5.5
Zero to 4	12.5	20.5	9.3	11.0	18.4	23.9	11.4	12.8	24.6	30.1
5 to 9	28.0	48.5	28.0	39.0	27.7	51.6	26.0	38.8	28.4	58.5

TEXTILES

10 to 14	20.4	68.9	26.0	65.0	20.1	71.7	27.0	65.8	21.4	79.9
15 to 19	17.3	86.2	13.2	78.2	11.4	83.1	20.4	86.2	11.1	91.0
20 to 24	4.8	91.0	9.7	87.9	6.9	90.0	7.6	93.8	3.5	94.5
25 to 29	3.5	94.5	5.9	93.8	4.5	94.5	3.1	96.9	3.8	98.3
30 and over	5.5	100.0	6.2	100.0	5.5	100.0	3.1	100.0	1.7	100.0

Chapter 12

LEATHER AND LEATHER PRODUCTS

THE major group, Leather and Leather Products, is made up of but two smaller groups: Boots and Shoes, and Leather and Miscellaneous Leather Products. The number of corporations in each and their average size are shown in Table 45. The groups are described briefly:

Boots and Shoes: All footwear made of leather.
Miscellaneous Leather Products: Saddlery, trunks, gaiters, gloves, leather substitutes, etc.

TABLE 45
LEATHER AND LEATHER PRODUCTS, LARGE IDENTICAL MANUFACTURING CORPORATIONS SERIES

(A) SIZE AND CHARACTER OF SAMPLE

	NUMBER OF CORPORATIONS	AVERAGE CAPITAL PER CORPORATION [1] (millions of dollars) ARITHMETIC MEAN	MEDIAN
Major group			
3 Leather	54	4.85	2.40
Minor group			
22 Boots and shoes	25	6.68	
23 Miscellaneous leather products	29	3.27	

[1] Total capital (i.e., includes funded debt) as of December 31, 1928.

LEATHER [259]

TABLE 45 (continued)

(B) PERCENTAGE INCOME TO SALES

	1919	1920	1921	1922	1923	1924	1925	1926	1927	1928	1919-1928[1]
Major group											
3 Leather	12.1	2.2	1.6	9.2	6.8	8.4	7.6	7.3	9.5	7.6	7.4
Minor group											
22 Boots and shoes	11.8	7.7	6.1	10.6	9.1	10.4	8.7	9.2	11.1	10.3	9.5
23 Miscellaneous leather products	12.2	−4.2	−6.0	6.9	2.9	5.2	5.4	4.2	7.0	3.1	4.2

(C) PERCENTAGE INCOME TO CAPITALIZATION

	1919	1920	1921	1922	1923	1924	1925	1926	1927	1928	1919-1928[1]
Major group											
3 Leather	34.1	4.3	2.4	15.5	11.2	12.8	12.7	12.1	15.4	11.5	12.7
Minor group											
22 Boots and shoes	33.1	18.2	11.4	20.4	16.2	16.4	16.1	15.2	17.6	14.8	17.3
23 Miscellaneous leather products	35.0	−6.8	−6.6	9.7	4.3	7.4	7.9	6.9	11.6	5.1	6.8

[1] Ten-year aggregate.

(D) PERCENTAGE PROFIT TO TOTAL CAPITAL

	1924	1925	1926	1927	1928
Major Group					
3 Leather	12.6	12.5	12.0	15.0	12.2
Minor group					
22 Boots and shoes	16.2	15.9	15.0	17.3	14.7
23 Miscellaneous leather products	7.2	7.8	6.9	11.3	5.1

(E) PERCENTAGE OF INCOME PAID OUT IN CASH DIVIDENDS

	1924	1925	1926	1927	1928
Major Group					
3 Leather	26.7	33.0	33.7	24.4	58.4
Minor group					
22 Boots and shoes	16.6	25.4	26.8	15.9	49.3
23 Miscellaneous leather products	60.3	55.4	59.4	46.5	108.3

TABLE 45 (*continued*)

(F) FREQUENCY DISTRIBUTIONS OF PERCENTAGES OF TOTAL NET INCOME TO CAPITALIZATION, INDIVIDUAL CORPORATIONS, 1919–23. MAJOR GROUP 3: LEATHER AND LEATHER PRODUCTS

PERCENTAGE INCOME TO CAPITALIZATION	1919 PERCENTAGE IN EACH CLASS	1919 ACCUMULATED BY SUCCESSIVE CLASSES	1920 PERCENTAGE IN EACH CLASS	1920 ACCUMULATED BY SUCCESSIVE CLASSES	1921 PERCENTAGE IN EACH CLASS	1921 ACCUMULATED BY SUCCESSIVE CLASSES	1922 PERCENTAGE IN EACH CLASS	1922 ACCUMULATED BY SUCCESSIVE CLASSES	1923 PERCENTAGE IN EACH CLASS	1923 ACCUMULATED BY SUCCESSIVE CLASSES
Under zero	.0	.0	25.9	25.9	25.9	25.9	3.7	3.7	9.3	9.3
Zero to 4	.0	.0	11.1	37.0	18.5	44.4	5.5	9.2	.0	9.3
5 to 9	1.8	1.8	20.4	57.4	14.8	59.2	24.0	33.2	24.0	42.6
10 to 14	1.8	3.6	16.7	74.1	16.7	75.9	13.0	46.2	22.2	64.8
15 to 19	13.0	16.6	7.4	81.5	11.1	87.0	22.3	68.5	14.8	79.6
20 to 24	14.8	31.4	3.7	85.2	5.6	92.6	7.4	75.9	13.0	92.6
25 to 29	5.6	37.0	7.4	92.6	.0	92.6	11.1	87.0	.0	92.6
30 and over	63.0	100.0	7.4	100.0	7.4	100.0	13.0	100.0	7.4	100.0

(G) FREQUENCY DISTRIBUTIONS OF PERCENTAGES OF TOTAL PROFIT TO TOTAL CAPITAL, INDIVIDUAL CORPORATIONS, 1924–28. MAJOR GROUP 3: LEATHER AND LEATHER PRODUCTS

	1924 PERCENTAGE IN EACH CLASS	1924 ACCUMULATED BY SUCCESSIVE CLASSES	1925 PERCENTAGE IN EACH CLASS	1925 ACCUMULATED BY SUCCESSIVE CLASSES	1926 PERCENTAGE IN EACH CLASS	1926 ACCUMULATED BY SUCCESSIVE CLASSES	1927 PERCENTAGE IN EACH CLASS	1927 ACCUMULATED BY SUCCESSIVE CLASSES	1928 PERCENTAGE IN EACH CLASS	1928 ACCUMULATED BY SUCCESSIVE CLASSES
Under zero	1.9	1.9	1.9	1.9	1.9	3.7	1.9	1.9	9.3	9.3
Zero to 4	13.0	14.9	16.6	18.5	24.1	27.8	9.3	11.2	11.1	20.4
5 to 9	27.7	42.6	25.9	44.4	16.6	44.4	20.3	31.5	27.8	48.2

… LEATHER

10 to 14	33.3	75.9	22.2	66.6	27.7	72.1	29.6	61.1	29.6	77.8
15 to 19	11.1	87.0	18.5	85.1	13.0	85.1	24.0	85.1	18.5	96.3
20 to 24	7.4	94.4	5.6	90.7	9.3	94.4	9.3	94.4	3.7	100.0
25 to 29	3.7	98.1	5.6	96.3	3.7	98.1	3.7	98.1	.0	100.0
30 and over	1.9	100.0	3.7	100.0	1.9	100.0	1.9	100.0	.0	100.0

Chapter 13

RUBBER AND RUBBER PRODUCTS

UNLIKE the other major groups, the Rubber group is not susceptible of division into several minor groups. Its 26 corporations, which in 1928 possessed a total capital of about 600 million dollars, manufacture rubber clothing, mechanical rubber goods such as belting, hose, tires and tubes, celluloid novelties, insulation, bakelite, bone, ivory and shell products. By far the principal product is mechanical rubber goods, consisting mainly of motor car tires.

TABLE 46
RUBBER AND RUBBER PRODUCTS, LARGE IDENTICAL MANUFACTURING CORPORATIONS SERIES

(A) SIZE AND CHARACTER OF SAMPLE

	NUMBER OF CORPORATIONS	AVERAGE CAPITAL PER CORPORATION [1] (millions of dollars) ARITHMETIC MEAN	MEDIAN
Major group 4 (minor group 24)			
Rubber and rubber products	26	31.03	2.83

[1] Total capital (i.e., includes funded debt) as of December 31, 1928.

RUBBER

TABLE 46 (continued)

(B) PERCENTAGE INCOME TO SALES

	1919	1920	1921	1922	1923	1924	1925	1926	1927	1928	1919–28[1]
Major group 4 (minor group 24) Rubber and rubber products	12.1	1.1	−13.2	2.9	4.3	5.6	11.2	5.2	4.8	.8	4.0

(C) PERCENTAGE INCOME TO CAPITALIZATION

	1919	1920	1921	1922	1923	1924	1925	1926	1927	1928	1919–28[1]
Major group 4 (minor group 24) Rubber and rubber products	19.0	2.1	−12.6	3.6	6.0	7.3	18.9	8.6	6.9	1.3	5.9

[1] Ten-year aggregate.

(D) PERCENTAGE PROFIT TO TOTAL CAPITAL

	1924	1925	1926	1927	1928
Major group 4 (minor group 24) Rubber and rubber products	6.8	15.7	7.6	6.4	2.3

(E) PERCENTAGE OF INCOME PAID OUT IN CASH DIVIDENDS

	1924	1925	1926	1927	1928
Major group 4 (minor group 24) Rubber and rubber products	24.1	21.4	56.4	114.1	270.1

TABLE 46 (*continued*)

(F) FREQUENCY DISTRIBUTIONS OF PERCENTAGES OF TOTAL NET INCOME TO CAPITALIZATION, INDIVIDUAL CORPORATIONS, 1919–23. MAJOR GROUP 4: RUBBER AND RUBBER PRODUCTS

PERCENTAGE INCOME TO CAPI- TALIZATION	1919 PERCENT- AGE IN EACH CLASS	1919 ACCU- MULATED BY SUC- CESSIVE CLASSES	1920 PERCENT- AGE IN EACH CLASS	1920 ACCU- MULATED BY SUC- CESSIVE CLASSES	1921 PERCENT- AGE IN EACH CLASS	1921 ACCU- MULATED BY SUC- CESSIVE CLASSES	1922 PERCENT- AGE IN EACH CLASS	1922 ACCU- MULATED BY SUC- CESSIVE CLASSES	1923 PERCENT- AGE IN EACH CLASS	1923 ACCU- MULATED BY SUC- CESSIVE CLASSES
Under zero	.0	.0	23.1	23.1	46.2	46.2	7.7	7.7	7.7	7.7
Zero to 4	.0	.0	19.2	42.3	7.7	53.9	7.7	15.4	7.7	15.4
5 to 9	.0	.0	15.4	57.7	11.5	65.4	23.1	38.5	15.4	30.8
10 to 14	19.2	19.2	11.5	69.2	19.2	84.6	7.7	46.2	34.7	65.5
15 to 19	15.4	34.6	15.4	84.6	7.7	92.3	23.1	69.3	23.1	88.6
20 to 24	11.6	46.2	7.7	92.3	7.7	100.0	15.4	84.7	3.8	92.4
25 to 29	19.2	65.4	7.7	100.0	.0	100.0	3.8	88.5	3.8	96.2
30 and over	34.6	100.0	.0	100.0	.0	100.0	11.5	100.0	3.8	100.0

(G) FREQUENCY DISTRIBUTIONS OF PERCENTAGES OF TOTAL PROFIT TO TOTAL CAPITAL, INDIVIDUAL CORPO- RATIONS, 1924–28. MAJOR GROUP 4: RUBBER AND RUBBER PRODUCTS

	1924 PERCENT- AGE IN EACH CLASS	1924 ACCU- MULATED BY SUC- CESSIVE CLASSES	1925 PERCENT- AGE IN EACH CLASS	1925 ACCU- MULATED BY SUC- CESSIVE CLASSES	1926 PERCENT- AGE IN EACH CLASS	1926 ACCU- MULATED BY SUC- CESSIVE CLASSES	1927 PERCENT- AGE IN EACH CLASS	1927 ACCU- MULATED BY SUC- CESSIVE CLASSES	1928 PERCENT- AGE IN EACH CLASS	1928 ACCU- MULATED BY SUC- CESSIVE CLASSES
Under zero	7.7	7.7	.0	.0	15.4	15.4	19.2	19.2	23.1	23.1
Zero to 4	7.7	15.4	3.8	3.8	15.4	30.8	3.8	23.0	15.4	38.5
5 to 9	26.9	42.3	11.5	15.3	11.5	42.3	15.4	38.4	19.2	57.7

10 to 14	19.2	61.5	27.0	42.3	23.1	65.4	27.0	65.4	27.0	84.7
15 to 19	30.8	92.3	27.0	69.3	23.1	88.5	15.4	80.8	7.7	92.4
20 to 24	7.7	100.0	23.1	92.4	3.8	92.3	3.8	84.6	.0	92.4
25 to 29	.0	100.0	3.8	96.2	7.7	100.0	7.7	92.3	3.8	96.2
30 and over	.0	100.0	3.8	100.0	.0	100.0	7.7	100.0	3.8	100.0

Chapter 14

LUMBER AND LUMBER PRODUCTS

THE Lumber Products group is composed of five minor groups: Lumber Manufacture; Planing Mill Products; Millwork; Furniture and Miscellaneous Lumber Products. The number of corporations included in each group and their average size are shown in Table 47. The groups are described briefly:

Lumber Manufacture: Includes establishments which produce piling, pulp wood, railroad ties, sawdust, shingles, and various other saw mill products.
Planing Mill Products: Doors, sashes, flooring, veneer, etc.
Millwork
Furniture: Includes all types of furniture, whether household, store, school or office, except those made of metal.
Miscellaneous Lumber Products: Includes numerous types of lumber products, such as automobile bodies, wagons, boxboard, cork, coffins, foundry patterns and shoe lasts.

TABLE 47

LUMBER GROUPS, LARGE IDENTICAL MANUFACTURING CORPORATIONS SERIES

(A) SIZE AND CHARACTER OF SAMPLE

	NUMBER OF CORPORATIONS	AVERAGE CAPITAL PER CORPORATION [1] (millions of dollars) ARITHMETIC MEAN	MEDIAN
Major group			
5 Lumber	190	2.95	1.15
Minor group			
25 Lumber manufacture	64	3.91	
26 Planing mills	26	1.05	
27 Millwork	17	2.30	
28 Furniture	55	1.47	
29 Miscellaneous lumber	28	5.82	

[1] Total capital (i.e., includes funded debt) as of December 31, 1928.

LUMBER

TABLE 47 (continued)

	1919	1920	1921	1922	1923	1924	1925	1926	1927	1928	1919-1928[1]
(B) PERCENTAGE INCOME TO SALES											
Major group											
5 Lumber	12.4	14.7	6.3	14.3	15.2	12.3	11.7	10.8	7.8	8.2	11.5
Minor group											
25 Lumber manufacture	18.5	21.9	5.7	17.0	22.6	14.0	14.0	13.6	10.6	10.5	15.3
26 Planing mills	2.8	16.9	8.6	17.4	16.4	14.8	12.9	10.1	8.1	7.4	9.8
27 Millwork	15.6	11.8	2.4	13.1	15.0	8.2	7.0	8.1	8.9	9.2	10.2
28 Furniture	17.1	14.2	7.6	15.0	14.2	11.8	12.4	11.6	9.2	8.4	12.0
29 Miscellaneous lumber	11.6	6.3	6.7	10.7	9.1	11.6	10.3	9.1	4.7	6.5	8.6
(C) PERCENTAGE INCOME TO CAPITALIZATION											
Major group											
5 Lumber	19.1	18.0	4.6	14.2	16.9	12.8	12.3	11.6	7.1	8.5	12.1
Minor group											
25 Lumber manufacture	16.0	17.7	2.5	10.2	15.8	9.0	8.8	9.4	5.9	6.8	10.0
26 Planing mills	26.7	35.9	9.9	27.5	24.3	18.6	17.0	12.3	9.6	8.5	17.7
27 Millwork	18.6	15.5	1.8	13.1	15.7	7.8	6.4	7.1	7.3	8.3	9.8
28 Furniture	31.0	24.4	8.4	20.3	18.3	15.0	16.5	15.3	11.7	10.5	16.2
29 Miscellaneous lumber	18.5	11.3	8.0	18.3	17.2	19.2	17.4	14.3	6.1	10.1	13.7

[1] Ten-year aggregate.

INDUSTRIAL PROFITS

TABLE 47 (continued)

(D) PERCENTAGE PROFIT TO TOTAL CAPITAL

	1924	1925	1926	1927	1928
Major group					
5 Lumber	12.4	11.9	11.4	7.0	8.2
Minor group					
25 Lumber manufacture	8.7	8.5	9.3	5.9	6.7
26 Planing mills	18.5	17.0	12.2	9.5	8.5
27 Millwork	7.8	6.3	7.0	7.3	8.2
28 Furniture	14.8	16.4	14.8	11.1	10.0
29 Miscellaneous lumber	18.4	16.6	13.8	6.1	9.7

(E) PERCENTAGE OF INCOME PAID OUT IN CASH DIVIDENDS

	1924	1925	1926	1927	1928
Major group					
5 Lumber	53.4	60.3	73.7	97.8	66.1
Minor group					
25 Lumber manufacture	79.1	72.2	86.7	115.1	92.7
26 Planing mills	56.2	63.0	88.1	110.8	96.9
27 Millwork	93.1	98.8	178.0	91.6	71.3
28 Furniture	41.5	41.9	48.7	65.4	59.8
29 Miscellaneous lumber	29.4	53.8	57.0	100.0	35.7

(F) FREQUENCY DISTRIBUTIONS OF PERCENTAGES OF TOTAL NET INCOME TO CAPITALIZATION, INDIVIDUAL CORPORATIONS, 1919–23. MAJOR GROUP 5: LUMBER

PERCENTAGE INCOME TO CAPITALIZATION	1919 PERCENTAGE IN EACH CLASS	1919 ACCUMULATED BY SUCCESSIVE CLASSES	1920 PERCENTAGE IN EACH CLASS	1920 ACCUMULATED BY SUCCESSIVE CLASSES	1921 PERCENTAGE IN EACH CLASS	1921 ACCUMULATED BY SUCCESSIVE CLASSES	1922 PERCENTAGE IN EACH CLASS	1922 ACCUMULATED BY SUCCESSIVE CLASSES	1923 PERCENTAGE IN EACH CLASS	1923 ACCUMULATED BY SUCCESSIVE CLASSES
Under zero	0.5	0.5	2.6	2.6	14.2	14.2	2.1	2.1	.0	.0
Zero to 4	1.6	2.1	3.7	6.3	21.1	35.3	3.7	5.8	3.7	3.7
5 to 9	7.4	9.5	5.3	11.6	22.1	57.4	13.7	19.5	10.0	13.7
10 to 14	9.5	19.0	13.2	24.8	17.9	75.3	16.3	35.8	14.7	28.4
15 to 19	13.7	32.7	13.7	38.5	13.7	89.0	12.6	48.4	22.6	51.0

20 to 24	13.2	45.9	10.0	48.5	4.2	93.2	16.3	64.7	17.4	68.4
25 to 29	9.5	55.4	12.1	60.6	3.2	96.4	8.4	73.1	13.7	82.1
30 and over	44.6	100.0	39.4	100.0	3.6	100.0	26.9	100.0	17.9	100.0

(G) FREQUENCY DISTRIBUTIONS OF PERCENTAGES OF TOTAL PROFIT TO TOTAL CAPITAL, INDIVIDUAL CORPORATIONS, 1924–28. MAJOR GROUP 5: LUMBER

	1924		*1925*		*1926*		*1927*		*1928*	
Under zero	1.1	1.1	1.6	1.6	1.1	1.1	1.6	1.6	1.1	1.1
Zero to 4	9.5	10.6	11.6	13.2	12.6	13.7	17.4	19.0	18.9	20.0
5 to 9	17.4	28.0	14.7	27.9	24.2	37.9	33.7	52.7	27.9	47.9
10 to 14	26.3	54.3	30.0	57.9	26.3	64.2	19.5	72.2	25.3	73.2
15 to 19	16.8	71.1	14.2	72.1	11.6	75.8	11.5	83.7	13.1	86.3
20 to 24	14.2	85.3	8.9	81.0	13.2	89.0	5.7	89.4	7.9	94.2
25 to 29	4.7	90.0	9.5	90.5	6.8	95.8	5.3	94.7	3.2	97.4
30 and over	10.0	100.0	9.5	100.0	4.2	100.0	5.3	100.0	2.6	100.0

Chapter 15

PAPER AND PAPER PRODUCTS

The Paper Products group consists of four minor groups: Blank Paper, Cardboard Boxes, Stationery, and Miscellaneous Paper Products. The number of corporations in each group and their average size are shown in Table 48. The Miscellaneous Group includes paper utensils, wall paper, wrapping paper, fibre, paper pulp, etc.

Table 48
PAPER GROUPS, LARGE IDENTICAL MANUFACTURING CORPORATIONS SERIES

(A) SIZE AND CHARACTER OF SAMPLE

	NUMBER OF CORPORATIONS	AVERAGE CAPITAL PER CORPORATION [1] *(millions of dollars)* ARITHMETIC MEAN	MEDIAN
Major group			
6 Paper	111	6.00	1.58
Minor group			
30 Blank paper	35	12.83	
31 Cardboard boxes	33	1.58	
32 Stationery	20	3.08	
33 Miscellaneous paper	23	4.49	

[1] Total capital (i.e., includes funded debt) as of December 31, 1928.

TABLE 48 (*continued*)

(B) PERCENTAGE INCOME TO SALES

	1919	1920	1921	1922	1923	1924	1925	1926	1927	1928	1919-1928[a]
Major group											
6 Paper	12.5	16.1	1.9	7.6	9.2	9.9	8.6	8.9	8.9	8.1	9.5
Minor group											
30 Blank paper	12.4	19.4	2.5	7.6	11.9	13.2	9.2	9.4	8.5	7.2	10.4
31 Cardboard boxes	1.4	15.0	.8	9.2	10.2	8.1	8.8	8.4	12.2	10.0	10.2
32 Stationery	9.5	10.9	−2.9	5.9	3.6	4.5	5.7	5.8	8.4	8.6	6.4
33 Miscellaneous paper	13.9	14.3	4.6	8.2	7.6	8.6	9.1	10.0	7.9	9.2	9.5

(C) PERCENTAGE INCOME TO CAPITALIZATION

	1919	1920	1921	1922	1923	1924	1925	1926	1927	1928	1919-1928[a]
Major group											
6 Paper	16.6	27.6	1.7	7.8	9.5	9.9	8.1	7.9	7.6	6.9	9.6
Minor group											
30 Blank paper	13.2	27.3	1.9	6.6	9.8	10.5	6.9	6.6	5.7	5.1	8.4
31 Cardboard boxes	30.8	38.0	.8	12.1	16.1	11.8	13.4	13.1	17.9	12.8	15.7
32 Stationery	11.3	19.4	−2.5	5.4	3.9	4.9	6.1	6.5	11.2	10.5	7.4
33 Miscellaneous paper	26.3	30.7	5.3	11.8	10.1	11.0	10.7	10.5	7.7	9.0	12.1

[a] Ten-year aggregate.

(D) PERCENTAGE PROFIT TO TOTAL CAPITAL

	1924	1925	1926	1927	1928
Major group					
6 Paper	9.4	7.5	7.3	7.0	6.7

(E) PERCENTAGE OF INCOME PAID OUT IN CASH DIVIDENDS

	1924	1925	1926	1927	1928
Major group					
6 Paper	45.7	56.5	48.6	66.4	76.4

TABLE 48 (*continued*)

(D) PERCENTAGE PROFIT TO TOTAL CAPITAL

Minor group	1924	1925	1926	1927	1928
30 Blank paper	9.8	6.5	6.2	5.5	5.1
31 Cardboard boxes	11.5	13.1	13.0	17.6	12.6
32 Stationery	4.9	6.0	6.3	10.5	9.9
33 Miscellaneous paper	10.5	10.1	10.0	7.4	8.7

(E) PERCENTAGE OF INCOME PAID OUT IN CASH DIVIDENDS

	1924	1925	1926	1927	1928
30 Blank paper	44.1	64.5	47.0	82.1	102.8
31 Cardboard boxes	43.2	52.6	67.4	56.4	50.6
32 Stationery	60.7	48.4	52.5	33.3	39.2
33 Miscellaneous paper	46.7	45.2	39.5	61.3	60.1

(F) FREQUENCY DISTRIBUTIONS OF PERCENTAGES OF TOTAL NET INCOME TO CAPITALIZATION, INDIVIDUAL CORPORATIONS, 1919–23. MAJOR GROUP 6: PAPER

PERCENTAGE INCOME TO CAPITALIZATION	1919 PERCENTAGE IN EACH CLASS	1919 ACCUMULATED BY SUCCESSIVE CLASSES	1920 PERCENTAGE IN EACH CLASS	1920 ACCUMULATED BY SUCCESSIVE CLASSES	1921 PERCENTAGE IN EACH CLASS	1921 ACCUMULATED BY SUCCESSIVE CLASSES	1922 PERCENTAGE IN EACH CLASS	1922 ACCUMULATED BY SUCCESSIVE CLASSES	1923 PERCENTAGE IN EACH CLASS	1923 ACCUMULATED BY SUCCESSIVE CLASSES
Under zero	0.9	0.9	0.9	0.9	32.4	32.4	5.4	5.4	0.9	0.9
Zero to 4	2.7	3.6	0.9	1.8	15.3	47.7	9.0	14.4	10.8	11.7
5 to 9	8.1	11.7	1.8	3.6	14.4	62.1	18.0	32.4	22.5	34.2
10 to 14	12.6	24.3	5.4	9.0	15.3	77.4	16.2	48.6	22.5	56.7
15 to 19	9.9	34.2	10.8	19.8	12.7	90.1	19.8	68.4	13.5	70.2
20 to 24	16.2	50.4	10.8	30.6	4.5	94.6	5.4	73.8	11.7	81.9
25 to 29	5.4	55.8	9.0	39.6	0.9	95.5	9.0	82.8	4.6	86.5
30 and over	44.2	100.0	60.4	100.0	4.5	100.0	17.2	100.0	13.5	100.0

(G) FREQUENCY DISTRIBUTIONS OF PERCENTAGES OF TOTAL PROFIT TO TOTAL CAPITAL, INDIVIDUAL CORPORATIONS, 1924–28. MAJOR GROUP 6: PAPER

	1924		1925		1926		1927		1928	
Under zero	0.9	0.9	1.8	1.8	1.8	1.8	0.9	0.9	1.8	1.8
Zero to 4	9.9	10.8	10.8	12.6	11.7	13.5	12.6	13.5	12.6	14.4
5 to 9	29.7	40.5	24.3	36.9	29.7	43.2	26.1	39.6	35.1	49.5
10 to 14	25.2	65.7	32.4	69.3	22.5	65.7	25.2	64.8	24.3	73.8
15 to 19	13.5	79.2	13.5	82.8	15.3	81.0	18.0	82.8	9.9	83.7
20 to 24	6.3	85.5	4.6	87.4	9.0	90.0	5.4	88.2	7.3	91.0
25 to 29	3.6	89.1	6.3	93.7	3.6	93.6	5.4	93.6	4.5	95.5
30 and over	10.9	100.0	6.3	100.0	6.4	100.0	6.4	100.0	4.5	100.0

Chapter 16

PRINTING AND PUBLISHING

Four industries make up the Printing group: Newspaper and Periodical Publishing, Book and Music Publishing, Job Printing, and Miscellaneous Printing and Publishing. The number of corporations in each group and their average size are given in Table 49. The groups are described briefly:

Newspaper and Periodical Publishing
Book and Music Publishing: Includes various types of books, also sheet music and bound music volumes.
Job Printing: Advertising novelties, signs, art calendars, tickets, bonds and notes, sales books, catalogues, stationery, playing cards, etc.
Miscellaneous Printing and Publishing: Bookbinding, photo-engraving, typefounding, etc.

Table 49

PRINTING AND PUBLISHING GROUPS, LARGE IDENTICAL MANUFACTURING CORPORATIONS SERIES

(A) SIZE AND CHARACTER OF SAMPLE

	NUMBER OF CORPORATIONS	AVERAGE CAPITAL PER CORPORATION [1] (millions of dollars) ARITHMETIC MEAN	MEDIAN
Major group			
7 Printing and publishing	100	5.69	1.36
Minor group			
34 Newspapers	20	19.23	
35 Books and music	17	3.18	
36 Job printing	46	2.57	
37 Miscellaneous printing and publishing	17	.72	

[1] Total capital (i.e., includes funded debt) as of December 31, 1928.

[274]

TABLE 49 (continued)

(B) PERCENTAGE INCOME TO SALES

	1919	1920	1921	1922	1923	1924	1925	1926	1927	1928	1919-1928[1]
Major group											
7 Printing and publishing	16.5	16.5	14.4	20.7	17.8	18.4	15.2	17.7	17.5	15.8	17.0
Minor group											
34 Newspapers	19.4	18.8	17.2	25.9	20.5	21.8	16.4	20.5	21.1	17.1	19.6
35 Books and music	12.6	10.5	11.2	16.7	16.1	16.8	15.8	14.9	12.6	13.9	14.2
36 Job printing	14.2	15.1	11.4	14.6	14.2	13.4	12.9	12.7	11.1	12.4	13.2
37 Miscellaneous printing and publishing	17.0	20.3	16.9	16.8	13.4	11.8	13.4	12.4	11.1	11.4	14.3

(C) PERCENTAGE INCOME TO CAPITALIZATION

	1919	1920	1921	1922	1923	1924	1925	1926	1927	1928	1919-1928[1]
Major group											
7 Printing and publishing	23.0	26.9	17.6	26.6	21.7	21.0	17.2	23.0	19.4	21.5	21.4
Minor group											
34 Newspapers	26.4	30.1	21.5	35.9	26.8	24.4	18.2	29.7	23.6	26.5	25.6
35 Books and music	17.6	13.8	13.5	20.4	18.3	18.9	16.9	14.9	11.4	12.1	15.4
36 Job printing	19.8	26.2	13.1	16.7	15.6	15.5	14.9	14.5	12.7	13.9	15.8
37 Miscellaneous printing and publishing	31.2	45.6	24.4	26.1	18.8	17.7	21.4	19.1	18.1	17.1	22.9

[1] Ten-year aggregate.

TABLE 49 (continued)

(D) PERCENTAGE PROFIT TO TOTAL CAPITAL

	1924	1925	1926	1927	1928
Major group					
7 Printing and publishing	19.4	15.6	20.2	16.5	18.3
Minor group					
34 Newspapers	21.5	15.6	23.8	18.7	20.7
35 Books and music	18.7	16.6	14.6	11.2	12.1
36 Job printing	15.1	14.4	14.2	11.9	13.2
37 Miscellaneous printing and publishing	17.7	21.3	19.1	17.9	16.8

(E) PERCENTAGE OF INCOME PAID OUT IN CASH DIVIDENDS

	1924	1925	1926	1927	1928
7 Printing and publishing	44.3	58.3	59.0	69.9	48.6
34 Newspapers	42.1	61.9	61.0	71.1	45.4
35 Books and music	36.5	51.0	46.0	54.7	51.6
36 Job printing	52.6	52.3	57.0	73.1	62.4
37 Miscellaneous printing and publishing	65.5	59.8	60.5	57.8	53.2

(F) FREQUENCY DISTRIBUTIONS OF PERCENTAGES OF TOTAL NET INCOME TO CAPITALIZATION, INDIVIDUAL CORPORATIONS, 1919–23. MAJOR GROUP 7: PRINTING AND PUBLISHING

PERCENTAGE INCOME TO CAPITALIZATION	1919 PERCENTAGE IN EACH CLASS	1919 ACCUMULATED BY SUCCESSIVE CLASSES	1920 PERCENTAGE IN EACH CLASS	1920 ACCUMULATED BY SUCCESSIVE CLASSES	1921 PERCENTAGE IN EACH CLASS	1921 ACCUMULATED BY SUCCESSIVE CLASSES	1922 PERCENTAGE IN EACH CLASS	1922 ACCUMULATED BY SUCCESSIVE CLASSES	1923 PERCENTAGE IN EACH CLASS	1923 ACCUMULATED BY SUCCESSIVE CLASSES
Under zero	1.0	1.0	.0	.0	5.0	5.0	1.0	1.0	1.0	1.0
Zero to 4	.0	1.0	3.0	3.0	4.0	9.0	2.0	3.0	5.0	6.0
5 to 9	11.0	12.0	8.0	11.0	15.0	24.0	14.0	17.0	13.0	19.0
10 to 14	14.0	26.0	7.0	18.0	17.0	41.0	14.0	31.0	18.0	37.0
15 to 19	11.0	37.0	9.0	27.0	13.0	54.0	13.0	44.0	22.0	59.0
20 to 24	15.0	52.0	11.0	38.0	10.0	64.0	17.0	61.0	11.0	70.0
25 to 29	9.0	61.0	7.0	45.0	16.0	80.0	4.0	65.0	11.0	81.0
30 and over	39.0	100.0	55.0	100.0	20.0	100.0	35.0	100.0	19.0	100.0

PRINTING

(G) FREQUENCY DISTRIBUTIONS OF PERCENTAGES OF TOTAL PROFIT TO TOTAL CAPITAL, INDIVIDUAL CORPORATIONS, 1924–28. MAJOR GROUP 7: PRINTING AND PUBLISHING

	1924		1925		1926		1927		1928	
Under zero	0.0	0.0	0.0	0.0	1.0	1.0	0.0	0.0	0.0	0.0
Zero to 4	4.0	4.0	6.0	6.0	9.0	10.0	15.0	15.0	6.0	6.0
5 to 9	18.0	22.0	20.0	26.0	13.0	23.0	22.0	37.0	18.0	24.0
10 to 14	20.0	42.0	17.0	43.0	23.0	46.0	20.0	57.0	30.0	54.0
15 to 19	19.0	61.0	18.0	61.0	20.0	66.0	16.0	73.0	21.0	75.0
20 to 24	15.0	76.0	15.0	76.0	10.0	76.0	8.0	81.0	6.0	81.0
25 to 29	10.0	86.0	8.0	84.0	9.0	85.0	8.0	89.0	8.0	89.0
30 and over	14.0	100.0	16.0	100.0	15.0	100.0	11.0	100.0	11.0	100.0

Chapter 17

CHEMICALS

THE Chemical group is made up of seven minor groups: Crude Chemicals; Paints; Petroleum Refining; Proprietary Preparations; Toilet Preparations; Cleaning Preparations; Miscellaneous Chemicals and Products. The number of corporations in each group and their average size are shown in Table 50. The groups are described briefly:

Crude Chemicals: Sulphuric and other acids, camphor, cyanide, chlorine, lye, zinc and other oxides are among the products of this group. All fertilizers are included.

Paints: House paints, varnishes, lacquers and shellac, putty, shoe polish, dyes and inks.

Petroleum Refining: Processing of gasoline, benzine, kerosene, fuel, cutting and lubricating oils, vaseline and paraffin.

Proprietary Preparations: All sorts of druggist compounds, pills, powders, ointments, tonics and patent medicines.

Toilet Preparations: Cosmetics, cold creams, hair dyes, perfumery, etc.

Cleaning Preparations: Includes soaps, bleaching powder, furniture and metal polish, and glycerine.

Miscellaneous Chemicals: Includes baking powder, boiler compound, artificial fuel, adhesives, etc. Also contains some large general chemical enterprises, each making paints, crude chemicals, etc., in such roughly equal proportions (in respect of total volume of business done), that no clearly predominant activity made feasible their assignment to the Paint or Crude Chemicals group specifically.

TABLE 50

CHEMICAL GROUPS, LARGE IDENTICAL MANUFACTURING CORPORATIONS SERIES

(A) SIZE AND CHARACTER OF SAMPLE

	NUMBER OF CORPORATIONS	AVERAGE CAPITAL PER CORPORATION [1] (millions of dollars) ARITHMETIC MEAN	MEDIAN
Major group			
8 Chemicals	210	34.44	2.22
Minor group			
38 Crude chemicals	9	14.89	
39 Paints	42	2.91	
40 Petroleum refining	52	109.96	
41 Proprietary preparations	56	4.24	
42 Toilet preparations	9	1.78	
43 Cleaning preparations	16	8.95	
44 Miscellaneous chemicals	26	33.14	

[1] Total capital (i.e., includes funded debt) as of December 31, 1928.

TABLE 50 (*continued*)

(B) PERCENTAGE INCOME TO SALES

	1919	1920	1921	1922	1923	1924	1925	1926	1927	1928	1919–28[1]
Major group											
8 Chemicals	14.0	12.5	3.7	12.9	9.4	12.3	15.4	15.6	9.6	17.5	12.6
Minor group											
38 Crude chemicals	15.0	10.9	10.5	22.7	12.3	11.9	13.8	12.0	13.9	15.9	13.9
39 Paints	12.9	8.6	4.1	13.0	12.4	10.8	11.2	11.1	9.8	11.8	10.7
40 Petroleum	14.8	14.4	1.9	11.8	6.9	10.8	15.3	14.7	6.5	16.1	11.5
41 Proprietary preparations	19.0	13.0	11.5	22.7	19.6	19.4	20.5	21.8	22.8	23.7	19.8
42 Toilet preparations	17.4	7.5	12.5	22.8	17.8	21.1	19.1	19.2	19.2	20.4	18.0
43 Cleaning preparations	5.0	−3.9	5.7	10.1	8.9	9.4	9.0	10.7	9.9	10.2	7.9
44 Miscellaneous chemicals	13.8	8.2	10.3	14.3	16.5	19.4	18.9	23.5	23.8	28.8	18.4

(C) PERCENTAGE INCOME TO CAPITALIZATION

	1919	1920	1921	1922	1923	1924	1925	1926	1927	1928	1919–28[1]
Major group											
8 Chemicals	18.0	16.5	2.9	9.2	6.7	9.1	12.2	12.1	7.5	11.6	10.2
Minor group											
38 Crude chemicals	15.0	11.9	6.6	18.3	9.7	8.6	10.5	9.6	10.3	11.9	11.1
39 Paints	27.2	16.5	4.9	20.0	17.2	14.8	15.9	15.5	13.0	14.8	15.6
40 Petroleum	18.4	19.8	14.5	7.9	4.6	7.3	11.0	10.3	4.8	9.8	8.7
41 Proprietary preparations	27.7	17.1	11.4	26.1	19.3	19.6	21.0	22.2	22.6	21.8	20.8
42 Toilet preparations	39.3	19.6	29.2	53.2	35.5	37.6	32.4	28.8	28.1	25.4	31.6
43 Cleaning preparations	13.9	−6.0	8.3	13.6	15.7	18.5	19.5	24.4	22.6	19.4	15.1
44 Miscellaneous chemicals	14.1	8.1	5.3	8.1	9.9	12.6	14.1	18.0	17.0	17.8	12.9

[1] Ten-year aggregate.

CHEMICALS

(D) PERCENTAGE PROFIT TO TOTAL CAPITAL

(E) PERCENTAGE OF INCOME PAID OUT IN CASH DIVIDENDS

	1924	1925	1926	1927	1928	1924	1925	1926	1927	1928
Major group										
8 Chemicals	8.9	11.8	11.6	7.3	11.1	66.8	54.0	60.5	88.7	70.5
Minor group										
38 Crude chemicals	8.6	10.5	9.6	10.3	11.9	71.2	56.1	64.4	57.7	40.6
39 Paints	14.4	15.6	15.4	13.0	14.8	47.7	47.9	56.8	84.4	59.4
40 Petroleum	7.2	10.7	9.9	4.8	9.4	70.5	50.1	56.0	104.5	70.2
41 Proprietary preparations	19.0	20.3	21.8	22.1	21.4	58.0	57.3	61.2	63.2	65.5
42 Toilet preparations	37.4	32.4	28.8	28.1	25.4	62.7	38.6	31.6	60.3	47.7
43 Cleaning preparations	18.4	19.4	24.4	22.6	19.4	54.8	56.9	59.6	57.3	55.1
44 Miscellaneous chemicals	12.2	14.0	17.7	16.8	17.3	65.4	71.6	78.4	80.4	81.5

(F) FREQUENCY DISTRIBUTIONS OF PERCENTAGES OF TOTAL NET INCOME TO CAPITALIZATION, INDIVIDUAL CORPORATIONS, 1919–23. MAJOR GROUP 8: CHEMICALS

PERCENTAGE INCOME TO CAPITAL	1919 PERCENTAGE IN EACH CLASS	1919 ACCUMULATED BY SUCCESSIVE CLASSES	1920 PERCENTAGE IN EACH CLASS	1920 ACCUMULATED BY SUCCESSIVE CLASSES	1921 PERCENTAGE IN EACH CLASS	1921 ACCUMULATED BY SUCCESSIVE CLASSES	1922 PERCENTAGE IN EACH CLASS	1922 ACCUMULATED BY SUCCESSIVE CLASSES	1923 PERCENTAGE IN EACH CLASS	1923 ACCUMULATED BY SUCCESSIVE CLASSES
Under zero	1.0	1.0	2.9	2.9	19.5	19.5	2.9	2.9	6.2	6.2
Zero to 4	4.3	5.3	11.9	14.8	18.1	37.6	11.4	14.3	10.0	16.2
5 to 9	8.6	13.9	16.6	31.4	19.5	57.1	14.3	28.6	17.6	33.8
10 to 14	11.0	24.9	14.8	46.2	12.9	70.0	12.4	41.0	18.1	51.9

TABLE 50 (*continued*)

(F) FREQUENCY DISTRIBUTIONS OF PERCENTAGES OF TOTAL NET INCOME TO CAPITALIZATION, INDIVIDUAL CORPORATIONS, 1919–23. MAJOR GROUP 8: CHEMICALS

PERCENTAGE INCOME TO CAPITALIZATION	1919 PERCENTAGE IN EACH CLASS	1919 ACCUMULATED BY SUCCESSIVE CLASSES	1920 PERCENTAGE IN EACH CLASS	1920 ACCUMULATED BY SUCCESSIVE CLASSES	1921 PERCENTAGE IN EACH CLASS	1921 ACCUMULATED BY SUCCESSIVE CLASSES	1922 PERCENTAGE IN EACH CLASS	1922 ACCUMULATED BY SUCCESSIVE CLASSES	1923 PERCENTAGE IN EACH CLASS	1923 ACCUMULATED BY SUCCESSIVE CLASSES
15 to 19	14.2	39.1	14.3	60.5	7.1	77.1	13.3	54.3	14.3	66.2
20 to 24	12.4	51.5	9.0	69.5	6.7	83.8	11.0	65.3	10.5	76.7
25 to 29	10.0	61.5	6.7	76.2	2.4	86.2	7.6	72.9	5.2	81.9
30 and over	38.5	100.0	23.8	100.0	13.8	100.0	27.1	100.0	18.1	100.0

(G) FREQUENCY DISTRIBUTIONS OF PERCENTAGES OF TOTAL PROFIT TO TOTAL CAPITAL, INDIVIDUAL CORPORATIONS, 1924–28. MAJOR GROUP 8: CHEMICALS

	1924 PERCENTAGE IN EACH CLASS	1924 ACCUMULATED BY SUCCESSIVE CLASSES	1925 PERCENTAGE IN EACH CLASS	1925 ACCUMULATED BY SUCCESSIVE CLASSES	1926 PERCENTAGE IN EACH CLASS	1926 ACCUMULATED BY SUCCESSIVE CLASSES	1927 PERCENTAGE IN EACH CLASS	1927 ACCUMULATED BY SUCCESSIVE CLASSES	1928 PERCENTAGE IN EACH CLASS	1928 ACCUMULATED BY SUCCESSIVE CLASSES
Under zero	3.8	3.8	1.4	1.4	2.9	2.9	6.2	6.2	3.3	3.3
Zero to 4	9.0	12.8	8.6	10.0	7.1	10.0	13.3	19.5	12.4	15.7
5 to 9	24.2	37.0	22.8	32.8	19.0	29.0	17.2	36.7	18.1	33.8
10 to 14	18.6	55.6	20.5	53.3	23.3	52.3	21.4	58.1	22.4	56.2
15 to 19	8.6	64.2	12.8	66.1	14.8	67.1	14.8	72.9	11.4	67.6
20 to 24	12.4	76.6	8.6	74.7	10.0	77.1	7.1	80.0	12.9	80.5
25 to 29	4.8	81.4	6.2	80.9	4.3	81.4	4.3	84.3	4.3	84.8
30 and over	18.6	100.0	19.1	100.0	18.6	100.0	15.7	100.0	15.2	100.0

Chapter 18

STONE, CLAY AND GLASS

The four minor groups comprising the Stone, Clay and Glass Products industry are: Ceramics; Glass; Portland Cement; and Miscellaneous Clay and Stone Products. The number of corporations in each and their average size are shown in Table 51. The groups are described briefly:

Ceramics: Includes the manufacture of both building and paving brick, terra cotta, china, crockery, porcelain ware and specialties of all sorts, tile and tile drain, refractory materials of various kinds, etc.
Glass: Includes window glass, plate glass, glassware.
Portland Cement
Miscellaneous Clay and Stone Products: Includes corporations making abrasives, concrete, lime plaster, asbestos, etc., and a few engaged in stone cutting.

Table 51

STONE, CLAY AND GLASS GROUPS, LARGE IDENTICAL MANUFACTURING CORPORATIONS SERIES

(A) SIZE AND CHARACTER OF SAMPLE

	NUMBER OF CORPORATIONS	AVERAGE CAPITAL PER CORPORATION [1] *(millions of dollars)* ARITHMETIC MEAN	MEDIAN
Major group			
9 Stone, clay and glass	114	6.48	2.08
Minor group			
45 Ceramics	48	3.46	
46 Glass	18	7.51	
47 Portland cement	21	11.73	
48 Miscellaneous clay and stone	27	7.08	

[1] Total capital (i.e., includes funded debt) as of December 31, 1928.

TABLE 51 (*continued*)

	1919	1920	1921	1922	1923	1924	1925	1926	1927	1928	1919–28[1]
(B) PERCENTAGE INCOME TO SALES
Major group
9 Stone, clay and glass	15.5	13.1	7.9	14.4	18.9	16.5	16.9	16.8	15.0	16.2	15.4
Minor group
45 Ceramics	19.8	17.0	11.4	16.3	19.3	16.2	16.1	16.3	14.7	13.2	16.0
46 Glass	15.0	13.3	7.3	11.2	15.8	12.5	11.3	10.3	8.2	10.4	11.7
47 Portland cement	14.6	12.1	12.5	19.4	26.5	23.7	24.5	25.1	21.8	23.4	21.4
48 Miscellaneous clay and stone	14.2	11.0	1.9	12.6	16.3	15.2	17.4	17.3	16.3	18.2	14.8
(C) PERCENTAGE INCOME TO CAPITALIZATION
Major group
9 Stone, clay and glass	16.7	17.4	6.3	14.1	19.6	15.6	16.2	15.2	12.3	12.8	14.5
Minor group
45 Ceramics	12.3	14.6	6.4	10.8	15.2	11.9	12.1	12.2	10.0	8.5	11.3
46 Glass	29.2	32.1	9.5	17.5	23.8	17.3	15.5	13.6	10.0	11.8	16.9
47 Portland cement	9.3	9.7	8.1	15.1	20.8	17.0	17.1	15.2	12.4	12.8	14.2
48 Miscellaneous clay and stone	20.7	17.2	1.5	14.2	19.1	16.3	19.7	19.6	16.0	17.1	16.4

[1] Ten-year aggregate.

STONE, CLAY AND GLASS [285]

(D) PERCENTAGE PROFIT TO TOTAL CAPITAL

	1924	1925	1926	1927	1928
Major group					
9 Stone, clay and glass	15.3	15.9	15.0	12.1	12.3
Minor group					
45 Ceramics	11.7	12.0	12.0	9.7	8.4
46 Glass	16.9	15.3	13.5	9.9	11.8
47 Portland cement	16.3	16.6	14.8	12.0	11.9
48 Miscellaneous clay and stone	16.3	19.6	19.5	15.9	16.8

(E) PERCENTAGE OF INCOME PAID OUT IN CASH DIVIDENDS

	1924	1925	1926	1927	1928
Major group					
9 Stone, clay and glass	42.3	45.8	59.7	60.0	49.9
Minor group					
45 Ceramics	50.4	53.6	50.9	72.4	67.2
46 Glass	56.5	63.1	73.4	79.7	42.7
47 Portland cement	29.9	43.0	63.3	57.1	52.9
48 Miscellaneous clay and stone	39.1	31.9	53.5	47.0	43.4

(F) FREQUENCY DISTRIBUTIONS OF PERCENTAGES OF TOTAL NET INCOME TO CAPITALIZATION, INDIVIDUAL CORPORATIONS, 1919–23. MAJOR GROUP 9: STONE, CLAY AND GLASS

PERCENTAGE INCOME TO CAPI-TALIZATION	1919 PERCENT-AGE IN EACH CALSS	1919 ACCU-MULATED BY SUC-CESSIVE CLASSES	1920 PERCENT-AGE IN EACH CLASS	1920 ACCU-MULATED BY SUC-CESSIVE CLASSES	1921 PERCENT-AGE IN EACH CLASS	1921 ACCU-MULATED BY SUC-CESSIVE CLASSES	1922 PERCENT-AGE IN EACH CLASS	1922 ACCU-MULATED BY SUC-CESSIVE CLASSES	1923 PERCENT-AGE IN EACH CLASS	1923 ACCU-MULATED BY SUC-CESSIVE CLASSES
Under zero	.0	.0	.9	.9	14.0	14.0	.0	.0	.0	.0
Zero to 4	6.1	6.1	3.5	4.4	21.9	35.9	10.5	10.5	2.6	2.6
5 to 9	17.5	23.6	12.3	16.7	16.7	52.6	17.5	28.0	11.4	14.0
10 to 14	18.4	42.0	21.9	38.6	14.9	67.5	19.3	47.3	14.0	28.0
15 to 19	13.2	55.2	15.8	54.4	14.0	81.5	8.8	56.1	17.5	45.5
20 to 24	9.6	64.8	7.9	62.3	6.1	87.6	6.1	62.2	17.5	63.0
25 to 29	7.0	71.8	7.0	69.3	7.0	94.6	16.7	78.9	13.3	76.3
30 and over	28.2	100.0	30.7	100.0	5.4	100.0	21.1	100.0	23.7	100.0

[286] INDUSTRIAL PROFITS

TABLE 51 (*continued*)

(G) FREQUENCY DISTRIBUTIONS OF PERCENTAGES OF TOTAL PROFIT TO TOTAL CAPITAL, INDIVIDUAL CORPORATIONS, 1924–28. MAJOR GROUP 9: STONE, CLAY AND GLASS

PERCENTAGE PROFIT TO TOTAL CAPITAL	1924 PERCENTAGE IN EACH CLASS	1924 ACCUMULATED BY SUCCESSIVE CLASSES	1925 PERCENTAGE IN EACH CLASS	1925 ACCUMULATED BY SUCCESSIVE CLASSES	1926 PERCENTAGE IN EACH CLASS	1926 ACCUMULATED BY SUCCESSIVE CLASSES	1927 PERCENTAGE IN EACH CLASS	1927 ACCUMULATED BY SUCCESSIVE CLASSES	1928 PERCENTAGE IN EACH CLASS	1928 ACCUMULATED BY SUCCESSIVE CLASSES
Under zero	0.9	0.9	0.9	0.9	.0	.0	0.9	0.9	2.6	2.6
Zero to 4	7.9	8.8	5.3	6.2	5.3	5.3	12.3	13.2	11.4	14.0
5 to 9	16.7	25.5	16.7	22.9	22.8	28.1	28.9	42.1	28.9	42.9
10 to 14	18.4	43.9	21.9	44.8	21.2	49.3	26.3	68.4	20.2	63.1
15 to 19	24.6	68.5	19.3	64.1	24.6	73.9	11.4	79.8	13.2	76.3
20 to 24	11.4	79.9	14.0	78.1	10.4	84.3	8.8	88.6	8.8	85.1
25 to 29	7.9	87.8	8.8	86.9	6.1	90.4	2.6	91.2	5.3	90.4
30 and over	12.2	100.0	13.1	100.0	9.6	100.0	8.8	100.0	9.6	100.0

Chapter 19

METALS

The Metals group is made up of 22 minor groups: Castings and Forgings; Sheet Metal; Wire and Nails; Heating and Ventilating Machinery; Electrical Machinery; Textile Machinery; Printing Machinery; Road Machinery; Engines; Mining Machinery; Factory Machinery; Office Machinery; Railway Equipment; Motor Vehicles; Firearms; Hardware; Tools; Bolts and Nuts; Miscellaneous Machinery; Non-ferrous Metals; Jewelry; and Miscellaneous Metals. The number of corporations in each group and their average size are shown in Table 52. The groups are described briefly:

Castings and Forgings: Foundries, rolling mills, iron and steel plants of all sorts are included. Among their products are anchors, anvils, bars, chains, steel plates, pipes, springs and rails. Blast furnaces, sheet metals, machinery, and tools appear, however, in other minor groups; likewise, all non-ferrous metals are shown elsewhere.

Sheet Metals: Includes corrugated iron, cornices, pipes, gutters, stove and furnace parts, barrels, etc.

Wire and Nails: Includes wire, nails, fences, screens, and springs.

Heating and Ventilating Machinery: Blowers, boilers, furnaces, ovens, stoves, radiators, incinerators, air conditioning apparatus.

Electrical Machinery: Motors, dynamos, pumps, furnaces, stoves, fixtures, conduit wires, vacuum cleaners, washing machines, fans, flashlights, light bulbs, etc.

Textile Machinery: Carding and spinning machines, looms, dyeing machines and other textile manufacturing equipment.

Printing Machinery: Includes typesetting machines, printing presses, newspaper presses, lithographing machines, etc.

Road Machinery: Includes hoisting and excavating machinery and tractors as well as road machinery; also cranes, derricks, elevators, steam shovels, dredges, concrete mixers, graders and street sprinklers.

Engines and Parts: Stationary and marine engines, but not automobile motors.

Mining Machinery: Coal chutes, cars, tools, drills, drilling equipment, etc.

Factory Machinery: Includes flour and grist mill machinery, metal working machinery such as drill-presses, forges, planers, gear-cutters, and general plant machinery for shoe factories, paper mills, laundries, etc., that is, all machinery *other* than textile, railroad equipment, and printing, electrical, and automotive machinery, which are classified in minor groups of their own.

Office Machinery: Cash registers, accounting machines, typewriters, mimeographing devices and all office appliances other than furniture.

Railway Equipment: Railroad cars, car wheels, locomotives, air brakes, couplings, parts and supplies.

Motor Vehicles: Passenger automobiles, trucks, trailers, and all automobile parts and accessories.

Firearms: Guns, rifles, gunpowder and explosives.

Hardware: Includes plumbers' supplies as well as hardware.

Tools: All manner of hand and shop tools, as well as machine tools are included: awls, axes, chucks, chisels, drills, files, hammers, jacks, jigs, pliers, shovels, saws, vises, wrenches, etc.

Bolts and Nuts: Includes related small iron and steel articles as screws, gaskets, rivets, taps and turnbuckles.

Miscellaneous Machinery: Includes machinery and machining processes not otherwise classified, such as ice machinery; air, oil and steam pumps, gasoline service station equipment; sewing machinery shops, blacksmith, machine and boiler shops, bottle capping machines; condensers and meat cutters.

Non-ferrous Metals: Aluminum, copper, lead, zinc and tin refining activities, as well as the refining of precious metals. Products made with precious metals (gold, iridium, platinum and silver) are not included;[1] but both the products of the other non-ferrous metals themselves and articles made of brass, bronze, nickel, babbitt and other alloys are here classified.

Jewelry: Precious stones, precious metal products of various sorts, watch cases (but not watches), bags, emblems, and novelty jewelry.

Miscellaneous Metals: Includes metals and metal processes not elsewhere classified: the principal activities and products are blast furnaces, agricultural implements, ornamental iron and steel, safes and vaults, cutlery and enameled granit ware.

[1] These are shown in the next group, together with jewelry.

METALS

Table 52

METALS GROUPS, LARGE IDENTICAL MANUFACTURING CORPORATIONS SERIES

(A) SIZE AND CHARACTER OF SAMPLE

	NUMBER OF CORPORATIONS	AVERAGE CAPITAL PER CORPORATION [1] (millions of dollars) ARITHMETIC MEAN	MEDIAN
Major group			
10 Metals	648	18.31	2.38
Minor group			
49 Castings and forgings	99	49.27	
50 Sheet metal	20	3.09	
51 Wire and nails	20	4.31	
52 Heating machinery	42	4.91	
53 Electrical machinery	54	16.68	
54 Textile machinery	18	4.95	
55 Printing machinery	12	4.97	
56 Road machinery	22	6.09	
57 Engines	11	5.98	
58 Mining machinery	12	10.75	
59 Factory machinery	23	8.32	
60 Office machinery	13	9.38	
61 Railway equipment	25	21.71	
62 Motor vehicles	32	61.95	
63 Firearms	11	4.74	
64 Hardware	40	8.60	
65 Tools	30	3.85	
66 Bolts and nuts	15	1.93	
67 Miscellaneous machinery	32	4.58	
68 Non-ferrous metals	48	20.34	
69 Jewelry	24	1.53	
70 Miscellaneous metals	45	15.89	

[1] Total capital (i.e., includes funded debt) as of December 31, 1928.

TABLE 52 (*continued*)

(B) PERCENTAGE INCOME TO SALES

	1919	1920	1921	1922	1923	1924	1925	1926	1927	1928	1919–28[1]
Major group											
10 Metals	14.7	9.7	3.0	10.2	11.1	10.1	11.4	11.1	9.8	10.4	10.4
Minor group											
49 Castings and forgings	11.6	9.7	−7.0	3.3	7.3	5.9	6.5	7.4	5.9	7.8	6.9
50 Sheet metal	9.8	7.7	−18.3	6.5	9.2	7.9	7.9	9.1	7.0	9.5	7.1
51 Wire and nails	12.7	9.9	−.6	12.2	13.8	11.1	10.7	10.7	10.3	14.2	10.9
52 Heating machinery	17.4	9.8	6.5	14.6	18.3	15.6	15.0	14.4	10.3	9.4	13.2
53 Electrical machinery	17.1	9.8	7.2	14.6	16.8	15.3	15.9	15.6	13.3	15.6	14.2
54 Textile machinery	25.3	15.3	23.0	29.4	20.4	19.0	23.2	23.1	25.3	24.7	22.6
55 Printing machinery	25.5	18.5	16.5	21.6	20.9	15.6	12.1	16.5	16.0	19.1	17.9
56 Road machinery	17.0	16.5	8.5	14.7	17.2	16.4	15.4	13.8	12.9	14.9	14.8
57 Engines	21.0	16.0	13.3	15.1	17.1	35.0	17.1	20.6	21.8	13.2	19.1
58 Mining machinery	15.1	12.6	3.4	9.9	11.2	5.5	9.1	11.4	10.1	9.3	10.1
59 Factory machinery	22.3	13.9	8.1	18.8	24.2	18.9	25.8	24.3	21.9	25.0	20.3
60 Office machinery	18.2	12.5	6.9	9.6	10.6	11.1	14.6	14.3	17.7	17.0	13.6
61 Railway equipment	13.5	10.6	7.4	9.9	11.6	10.4	7.4	10.3	9.1	6.9	10.2
62 Motor vehicles	18.6	9.3	6.6	16.1	11.6	11.5	13.9	11.8	9.8	8.6	11.5
63 Firearms	12.0	7.5	2.7	11.4	13.0	10.6	11.1	13.0	13.2	19.9	11.9
64 Hardware	17.5	13.6	2.3	12.9	16.7	13.0	12.8	10.9	9.4	10.4	12.2
65 Tools	25.3	18.8	−8.3	14.1	16.5	11.5	15.1	16.5	13.4	19.0	15.9
66 Bolts and nuts	15.5	15.3	−3.4	17.5	16.6	11.0	14.5	16.0	13.4	17.2	14.4
67 Miscellaneous machinery	18.4	10.5	−3.8	12.2	14.4	11.6	13.0	14.7	11.1	12.9	12.1
68 Non-ferrous metals	10.0	4.8	2.5	10.0	9.9	9.9	11.6	10.6	10.7	12.2	9.6
69 Jewelry	14.0	7.9	1.8	9.5	10.4	8.5	7.5	8.3	9.5	9.7	9.0
70 Miscellaneous metals	16.4	9.0	−6.3	5.2	13.4	11.5	15.7	16.6	15.3	15.1	12.4

[1] Ten-year aggregate.

METALS

(c) PERCENTAGE INCOME TO CAPITALIZATION

	1919	1920	1921	1922	1923	1924	1925	1926	1927	1928	1919–28[1]
Major group											
10 Metals	18.0	12.0	2.1	8.8	12.1	9.8	12.1	13.1	9.8	11.1	10.8
Minor group											
49 Castings and forgings	11.5	10.5	.4	2.1	6.8	4.7	5.6	7.7	4.5	6.0	5.8
50 Sheet metal	16.1	12.6	−12.4	7.2	13.2	10.4	11.8	13.1	8.9	11.8	9.3
51 Wire and nails	17.9	15.6	.4	12.4	16.1	11.4	11.4	11.7	9.9	13.8	11.9
52 Heating machinery	20.5	12.8	5.1	15.0	21.8	17.3	15.5	17.0	9.5	9.2	14.0
53 Electrical machinery	21.8	12.1	6.4	13.4	16.5	16.7	16.8	17.9	14.2	16.5	15.2
54 Textile machinery	27.4	17.2	22.6	22.3	18.3	10.6	14.8	14.4	15.9	14.6	17.1
55 Printing machinery	17.8	13.3	8.5	13.8	13.8	10.3	9.1	10.9	9.6	12.3	11.6
56 Road machinery	26.9	22.0	8.7	14.0	19.2	18.9	18.2	17.5	15.7	17.0	17.5
57 Engines	28.0	19.2	9.4	10.6	14.6	28.0	9.2	14.1	11.1	6.9	12.9
58 Mining machinery	36.3	25.1	3.4	13.9	15.2	6.2	11.2	16.0	11.6	10.2	13.6
59 Factory machinery	15.8	9.5	3.8	7.7	11.3	8.2	13.0	13.3	11.2	13.4	10.7
60 Office machinery	22.5	15.8	6.4	9.0	12.9	11.5	17.3	15.8	19.1	17.7	14.9
61 Railway equipment	17.0	10.6	4.3	7.2	13.5	8.4	5.3	7.6	5.6	3.4	8.1
62 Motor vehicles	38.8	18.4	8.4	25.3	20.8	17.3	23.7	20.7	16.1	16.1	19.7
63 Firearms	11.7	9.4	2.1	11.4	12.4	10.4	10.4	12.3	11.9	19.6	11.5
64 Hardware	29.0	21.7	1.9	15.7	20.9	15.1	15.9	13.6	10.4	11.0	14.7
65 Tools	29.8	19.5	−3.1	8.5	12.4	7.9	11.5	14.6	9.6	15.2	12.3
66 Bolts and nuts	19.6	21.8	−1.8	17.5	18.6	10.6	16.9	17.2	13.4	19.0	15.4
67 Miscellaneous machinery	24.2	12.8	−2.6	9.9	13.5	10.9	13.4	15.5	11.5	13.5	12.1
68 Non-ferrous metals	12.5	5.9	1.9	8.6	11.1	9.8	14.2	12.6	11.3	14.8	10.5
69 Jewelry	36.7	15.5	2.1	12.6	13.7	10.1	9.0	10.3	11.7	12.1	12.5
70 Miscellaneous metals	17.0	9.6	−2.9	3.0	9.0	8.1	12.9	14.7	13.3	15.6	10.1

[1] Ten-year aggregate.

TABLE 52 (*continued*)

	(D) PERCENTAGE PROFIT TO TOTAL CAPITAL					(E) PERCENTAGE OF INCOME PAID OUT IN CASH DIVIDENDS				
	1924	1925	1926	1927	1928	1924	1925	1926	1927	1928
Major group										
10 Metals	9.2	11.3	12.2	9.3	10.4	49.2	44.2	48.4	67.5	62.7
Minor group										
49 Castings and forgings	4.8	5.5	7.1	4.6	5.8	69.9	53.4	44.6	76.4	58.7
50 Sheet metal	9.9	11.0	12.1	8.7	10.8	46.6	38.5	38.7	54.3	40.3
51 Wire and nails	11.3	11.4	11.7	9.9	13.7	76.4	60.8	79.9	108.9	67.3
52 Heating machinery	16.8	15.1	16.7	9.1	8.9	44.7	48.8	52.0	84.0	79.8
53 Electrical machinery	15.9	16.2	17.2	13.6	15.8	38.1	43.7	41.2	65.7	58.2
54 Textile machinery	10.6	14.1	14.2	15.1	13.9	68.5	56.0	67.3	66.5	61.6
55 Printing machinery	9.6	8.6	10.3	9.1	10.9	49.4	43.6	48.5	57.1	36.1
56 Road machinery	18.9	18.2	17.5	15.3	16.5	36.7	39.5	44.1	55.5	49.6
57 Engines	27.5	9.2	14.0	11.0	6.9	28.6	71.1	50.5	58.8	87.3
58 Mining machinery	6.1	11.1	15.8	11.6	10.2	69.8	48.8	41.2	50.0	43.1
59 Factory machinery	8.1	12.8	13.1	11.1	13.3	63.6	62.8	57.1	70.1	66.4
60 Office machinery	11.4	17.1	15.6	19.0	17.6	49.6	37.5	60.3	54.2	54.4
61 Railway equipment	8.3	5.3	7.5	5.6	3.4	69.2	152.6	85.6	123.1	195.0
62 Motor vehicles	17.0	23.3	20.4	15.9	16.0	32.6	34.6	47.3	66.5	82.3
63 Firearms	10.4	10.4	12.3	11.9	19.5	59.5	63.6	56.8	50.1	34.6
64 Hardware	14.9	15.3	13.2	10.1	10.7	47.2	49.9	57.3	85.5	63.6
65 Tools	7.9	11.4	14.5	9.5	14.9	84.0	60.0	57.0	66.8	50.4
66 Bolts and nuts	10.6	16.9	17.2	13.4	19.0	72.8	66.0	59.4	63.5	44.6
67 Miscellaneous machinery	10.9	13.3	15.2	11.0	12.7	112.3	39.8	55.0	68.7	63.4
68 Non-ferrous metals	9.4	13.5	12.0	10.8	13.8	48.1	39.9	57.0	57.5	49.9
69 Jewelry	10.1	9.0	10.3	11.6	12.0	54.3	61.4	60.9	56.3	42.8
70 Miscellaneous metals	7.9	12.4	14.3	12.8	15.0	48.9	21.1	33.1	45.2	24.3

METALS [293]

(F) FREQUENCY DISTRIBUTIONS OF PERCENTAGES OF TOTAL NET INCOME TO CAPITALIZATION, INDIVIDUAL CORPORATIONS, 1919–23. MAJOR GROUP 10: METALS

PERCENTAGE INCOME TO CAPITALIZATION	1919 PERCENTAGE IN EACH CLASS	1919 ACCUMULATED BY SUCCESSIVE CLASSES	1920 PERCENTAGE IN EACH CLASS	1920 ACCUMULATED BY SUCCESSIVE CLASSES	1921 PERCENTAGE IN EACH CLASS	1921 ACCUMULATED BY SUCCESSIVE CLASSES	1922 PERCENTAGE IN EACH CLASS	1922 ACCUMULATED BY SUCCESSIVE CLASSES	1923 PERCENTAGE IN EACH CLASS	1923 ACCUMULATED BY SUCCESSIVE CLASSES
Under zero	1.2	1.2	3.2	3.2	33.5	33.5	4.9	4.9	0.9	0.9
Zero to 4	2.6	3.8	5.4	8.6	18.4	51.9	14.4	19.3	7.4	8.3
5 to 9	6.3	10.1	13.4	22.0	20.1	72.0	17.0	36.3	15.1	23.4
10 to 14	11.6	21.7	16.1	38.1	10.9	82.9	17.3	53.6	17.4	40.8
15 to 19	13.9	35.6	13.4	51.5	7.1	90.0	13.0	66.6	20.5	61.3
20 to 24	11.7	47.3	12.5	64.0	3.4	93.4	8.6	75.2	13.6	74.9
25 to 29	8.7	56.0	8.8	72.8	2.0	95.4	8.3	83.5	10.4	85.3
30 and over	44.0	100.0	27.2	100.0	4.6	100.0	16.5	100.0	14.7	100.0

(G) FREQUENCY DISTRIBUTIONS OF PERCENTAGES OF TOTAL PROFIT TO TOTAL CAPITAL, INDIVIDUAL CORPORATIONS, 1924–28. MAJOR GROUP 10: METALS

	1924 PERCENTAGE IN EACH CLASS	1924 ACCUMULATED BY SUCCESSIVE CLASSES	1925 PERCENTAGE IN EACH CLASS	1925 ACCUMULATED BY SUCCESSIVE CLASSES	1926 PERCENTAGE IN EACH CLASS	1926 ACCUMULATED BY SUCCESSIVE CLASSES	1927 PERCENTAGE IN EACH CLASS	1927 ACCUMULATED BY SUCCESSIVE CLASSES	1928 PERCENTAGE IN EACH CLASS	1928 ACCUMULATED BY SUCCESSIVE CLASSES
Under zero	2.2	2.2	1.7	1.7	1.5	1.5	3.9	3.9	4.5	4.5
Zero to 4	12.8	15.0	6.5	8.2	8.5	10.0	12.2	16.1	8.8	13.3
5 to 9	25.9	40.9	21.5	29.7	21.9	31.9	27.0	43.1	25.1	38.4
10 to 14	21.3	62.2	27.5	57.2	24.1	56.0	23.9	67.0	19.9	58.3

TABLE 52 (*continued*)

(G) FREQUENCY DISTRIBUTIONS OF PERCENTAGES OF TOTAL PROFIT TO TOTAL CAPITAL, INDIVIDUAL CORPORATIONS, 1924–28. MAJOR GROUP 10: METALS

PERCENTAGE PROFIT TO TOTAL CAPITAL	1924 PERCENTAGE IN EACH CLASS	1924 ACCUMULATED BY SUCCESSIVE CLASSES	1925 PERCENTAGE IN EACH CLASS	1925 ACCUMULATED BY SUCCESSIVE CLASSES	1926 PERCENTAGE IN EACH CLASS	1926 ACCUMULATED BY SUCCESSIVE CLASSES	1927 PERCENTAGE IN EACH CLASS	1927 ACCUMULATED BY SUCCESSIVE CLASSES	1928 PERCENTAGE IN EACH CLASS	1928 ACCUMULATED BY SUCCESSIVE CLASSES
15 to 19	15.1	77.3	13.7	70.9	16.4	72.4	13.6	80.6	17.6	75.9
20 to 24	8.2	85.5	10.3	81.2	10.5	82.9	7.2	87.8	9.9	85.8
25 to 29	5.7	91.2	6.9	88.1	5.1	88.0	3.9	91.7	5.1	90.9
30 and over	8.8	100.0	11.9	100.0	12.0	100.0	8.3	100.0	9.1	100.0

Chapter 20

SPECIAL MANUFACTURING INDUSTRIES

FOUR minor groups which do not well fit into any other major manufacturing group are classified under the head of Special Manufacturing. They are: Professional and Scientific Instruments, including Optical Goods; Toys, Stationery Goods and School Supplies; Pianos, Organs and Parts; and Miscellaneous Special Manufacturing. The number of corporations contained in each group and their average size are shown in Table 53. The groups are described briefly:

Scientific Instruments: Included are not only bacteriological, X-ray, dental and optical apparatus, slide-rules, gyroscopes, thermometers, pyrometers, nautical and surveying instruments, cameras, eye glasses and binoculars, but also many kinds of medical, dental and optical supplies such as surgical gauze, elastic bandages, trusses, artificial eyes and teeth.

Toys: Includes not only dolls, games, sleds, velocipedes, but also stationers' supplies such as pencils, pens and school supplies.

Pianos: Pianos, player pianos, organs, keys, strings, sounding boards and other parts.

Miscellaneous Special Manufacturing: Contains branches of manufacture which could not be classed with Textiles Metals or with some other well-defined major group. The list of products includes artificial flowers, athletic goods, brooms, clocks, watches, hair goods, fire apparatus, soda fountains and umbrellas. (Since, however, 45 corporations comprise the group and in the pursuit of these diverse activities marketed nearly 300 million dollars worth of goods in 1928, the inclusion of their data is essential to complete the sample of large corporations engaged in manufacturing pursuits.)

Table 53

SPECIAL MANUFACTURING INDUSTRIES GROUPS, LARGE IDENTICAL MANUFACTURING CORPORATIONS SERIES

(A) SIZE AND CHARACTER OF SAMPLE

	NUMBER OF CORPORATIONS	AVERAGE CAPITAL PER CORPORATION [1] (millions of dollars) ARITHMETIC MEAN	MEDIAN
Major group			
11 Special manufacturing industries	89	5.75	2.32
Minor group			
71 Scientific instruments	23	7.77	
72 Toys	12	2.36	
73 Pianos	11	5.38	
74 Miscellaneous special manufacturing industries	43	5.71	

[1] Total capital (i.e., includes funded debt) as of December 31, 1928.

SPECIAL MANUFACTURING

Table 53 (continued)

	1919	1920	1921	1922	1923	1924	1925	1926	1927	1928	1919–28[1]
(B) PERCENTAGE INCOME TO SALES											
Major group											
11 Special manufacturing industries	18.3	12.9	10.0	19.9	18.1	12.2	15.0	17.6	15.4	15.9	15.6
Minor group											
71 Scientific instruments	26.2	20.2	16.5	35.5	31.3	18.1	30.6	29.9	26.6	27.7	26.5
72 Toys	16.4	12.9	11.2	12.4	13.7	12.6	12.6	12.0	13.3	14.0	13.1
73 Pianos	13.6	11.0	2.7	12.0	13.7	11.7	12.5	12.1	9.0	7.8	10.8
74 Miscellaneous special manufacturing industries	14.2	9.5	7.8	13.6	12.1	8.9	5.9	11.9	10.2	10.3	10.4
(C) PERCENTAGE INCOME TO CAPITALIZATION											
Major group											
11 Special manufacturing industries	28.0	19.4	10.6	23.1	21.5	13.9	16.9	20.2	17.0	17.0	18.4
Minor group											
71 Scientific instruments	33.1	22.1	13.1	30.8	28.6	16.8	28.9	29.5	25.2	27.3	25.5
72 Toys	26.3	24.6	11.2	13.1	15.7	15.7	15.5	14.0	14.9	16.1	15.9
73 Pianos	17.2	13.9	2.3	12.0	14.3	11.7	13.2	11.9	7.5	5.9	10.7
74 Miscellaneous special manufacturing industries	26.2	18.0	10.6	20.3	17.8	11.8	7.6	15.7	13.2	12.4	14.7

[1] Ten-year aggregate.

TABLE 53 (continued)

(D) PERCENTAGE PROFIT TO TOTAL CAPITAL

	1924	1925	1926	1927	1928
Major group					
11 Special manufacturing industries	13.7	16.7	20.1	16.9	16.8
Minor group					
71 Scientific instruments	16.8	28.9	29.5	25.2	26.8
72 Toys	15.7	15.5	14.0	14.4	15.6
73 Pianos	11.5	12.9	11.9	7.4	5.8
74 Miscellaneous special manufacturing industries	11.5	7.5	15.5	13.2	12.3

(E) PERCENTAGE INCOME PAID OUT IN CASH DIVIDENDS

	1924	1925	1926	1927	1928
Major group					
11 Special manufacturing industries	71.9	74.5	61.5	47.5	72.3
Minor group					
71 Scientific instruments	89.7	82.0	84.3	51.9	83.9
72 Toys	36.3	46.2	43.3	46.5	35.9
73 Pianos	43.2	30.1	39.6	53.9	72.5
74 Miscellaneous special manufacturing industries	63.1	77.2	33.6	40.1	59.2

(F) FREQUENCY DISTRIBUTIONS OF PERCENTAGES OF TOTAL NET INCOME TO CAPITALIZATION, INDIVIDUAL CORPORATIONS, 1919–23. MAJOR GROUP 11: SPECIAL MANUFACTURING INDUSTRIES

PERCENTAGE INCOME TO CAPITALIZATION	1919 PERCENTAGE IN EACH CLASS	1919 ACCUMULATED BY SUCCESSIVE CLASSES	1920 PERCENTAGE IN EACH CLASS	1920 ACCUMULATED BY SUCCESSIVE CLASSES	1921 PERCENTAGE IN EACH CLASS	1921 ACCUMULATED BY SUCCESSIVE CLASSES	1922 PERCENTAGE IN EACH CLASS	1922 ACCUMULATED BY SUCCESSIVE CLASSES	1923 PERCENTAGE IN EACH CLASS	1923 ACCUMULATED BY SUCCESSIVE CLASSES
Under zero	.0	.0	1.1	1.1	14.6	14.6	.0	.0	1.1	1.1
Zero to 4	.0	.0	3.4	4.5	14.6	29.2	10.1	10.1	1.1	2.2
5 to 9	7.9	7.9	13.5	18.0	18.0	47.2	5.6	15.7	12.4	14.6
10 to 14	9.0	16.9	19.1	37.1	18.0	65.2	27.0	42.7	22.5	37.1
15 to 19	13.5	30.4	20.2	57.3	11.2	76.4	20.2	62.9	23.6	60.7
20 to 24	15.7	46.1	10.1	67.4	7.9	84.3	10.1	73.0	11.2	71.9
25 to 29	10.1	56.2	12.4	79.8	6.7	91.0	6.8	79.8	13.5	85.4
30 and over	43.8	100.0	20.2	100.0	9.0	100.0	20.2	100.0	14.6	100.0

(G) FREQUENCY DISTRIBUTIONS OF PERCENTAGES OF TOTAL PROFIT TO TOTAL CAPITAL, INDIVIDUAL CORPORATIONS, 1924–28. MAJOR GROUP 11: SPECIAL MANUFACTURING INDUSTRIES

	1924		1925		1926		1927		1928	
Under zero	1.1	1.1	2.2	2.2	.0	.0	.0	.0	2.2	2.2
Zero to 4	5.6	6.7	5.6	7.8	6.8	6.8	12.4	12.4	11.2	13.4
5 to 9	20.2	26.9	15.7	23.5	21.3	28.1	25.8	38.2	22.5	35.9
10 to 14	23.6	50.5	32.6	56.1	25.8	53.9	21.3	59.5	29.3	65.2
15 to 19	20.3	70.8	11.3	67.4	15.8	69.7	15.8	75.3	9.0	74.2
20 to 24	10.1	80.9	11.3	78.7	14.6	84.3	14.6	89.9	15.7	89.9
25 to 29	11.2	92.1	10.1	88.8	9.0	93.3	5.6	95.5	6.7	96.6
30 and over	7.9	100.0	11.2	100.0	6.7	100.0	4.5	100.0	3.4	100.0

Chapter 21

TRADE AND ITS MAJOR GROUPS

1. EARNINGS RATES ON SALES AND INVESTMENT: ALL TRADE

THE 664 companies included in our series of large Trading corporations in 1928 possessed a combined capitalization of $2.5 billion dollars. This investment was 'turned over' about two and one-half times, so that sales amounted to nearly $6.5 billion, while the net income amounted to about one-third of a billion. In the first few sections of this chapter, we shall examine the earnings, sales and capital investment of these companies over the period 1919–28, both in the All Trade group as a whole and in each of the three major groups that compose it; then we shall consider the income disbursed as dividends and the earnings of individual companies, in the three latter groups combined.

In 1919, a year of marked prosperity, these 664 companies earned a net return of 7.4 per cent upon their sales volume. In 1920, this was reduced to 3.7 per cent and in 1921 to 2.7 per cent. Recovery in 1922 brought the figure to 5.9 per cent. Between 1923 and 1928, however, the return figure showed a slight general decline, falling from 6 per cent in 1923 to 4.8 per cent in 1928. Chart 52 shows the course of this gradual decline.

Upon investment the return dropped from 24 per cent in 1919 to 7 per cent in 1921. Earnings recovered to 15 per cent in 1922; but from 1923 on showed a general fall, dropping from 15.4 per cent to 12.3 per cent in 1928. It is to be noted that the return upon investment is in all years two or three times as high as that upon sales. The capital turnover of these 664 large Trading corporations, in other words, is approximately 2.5 times a year. This general average, however, should not be assumed to hold for many of the specific

TRADE AND MAJOR GROUPS [301]

CHART 52
IDENTICAL CORPORATIONS SERIES, 1919-28
ALL TRADING CORPORATIONS

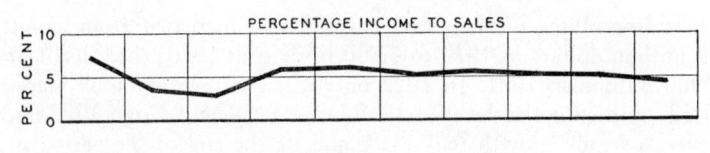

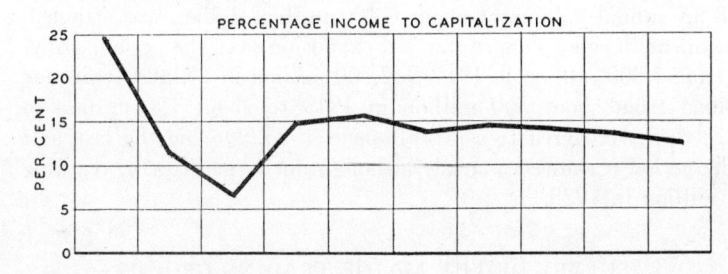

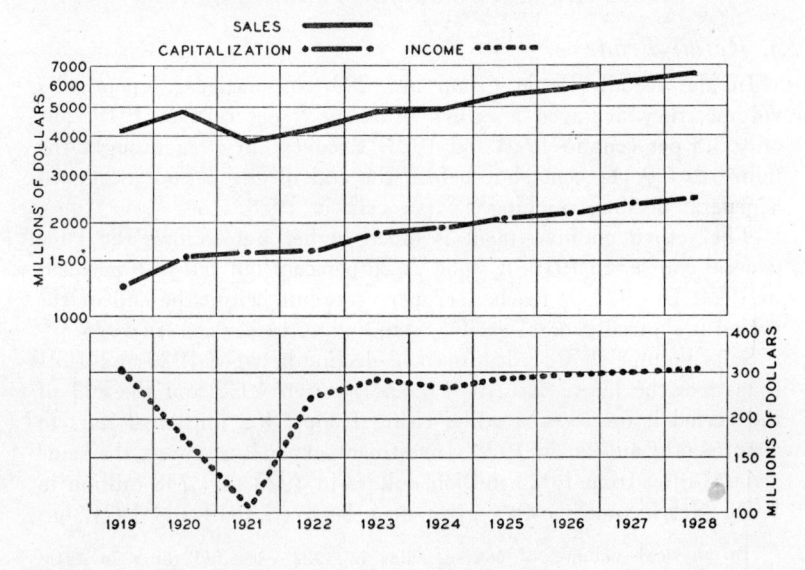

minor groups in Trade, the figures for a number of which deviate markedly from this ratio.

2. ABSOLUTE INCOME, SALES AND INVESTMENT: ALL TRADE

The sales volume of these 664 corporations increased from about 4,100 million dollars in 1919 to 4,800 million in 1920; then declined to 3,900 million in 1921. In 1922 only a slight recovery took place, the 4,121 million dollar level of 1919 being regained.[1] From 1922 on, however, a steady growth took place and by the end of the period in 1928 an annual volume of about 6,400 million dollars was attained. Investment likewise showed marked expansion over the period, growing from 1,300 million in 1919 to 2,500 million in 1928. Net income declined from about 300 million in 1919 to about 100 million in 1921; then, recovered to 288 million in 1923. During the last half of the period it showed a steady although not large growth, reaching 307 million in 1928.

3. SURVEY OF THE MAJOR TRADING GROUPS

a. *Retail Trade*

In the Retail Trade group are 283 corporations. Upon sales volume, they averaged a return of about 9 per cent in 1919, but only 3.5 per cent in 1920 and 1921. Recovery in 1922 brought the figure to 6.9 per cent; but before the end of the period it showed a general decline, reaching 5.3 per cent in 1928.

The return on investment is much higher but follows the same general course. In 1919, it stood at 26 per cent but fell to 8 per cent in 1921. In 1922, it reached 17 per cent, but before the end of the period it showed general decline, standing at 14 per cent in 1928.

Sales volume shows a less marked decline between 1920 and 1921 than does the figure for All Trade. Between 1922 and the end of the period it increases steadily, rising from 2,462 million dollars to about 4,600 million in 1928. Investment expands at much the same general rate, from 1,022 million dollars in 1922 to 1,758 million in 1928. Net income shows a great drop between 1919 and 1921, but

[1] In physical volume, of course, sales in 1922 exceeded those in 1919, e.g., commodity prices were substantially lower in the latter year.

CHART 53
IDENTICAL CORPORATIONS SERIES, 1919-28
MAJOR GROUP 12: RETAIL TRADE

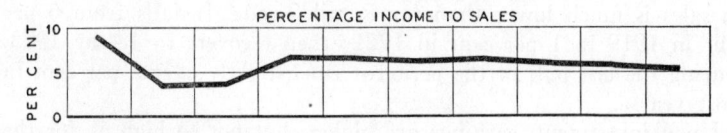

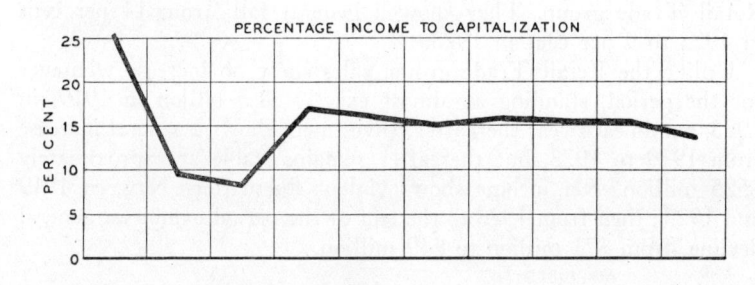

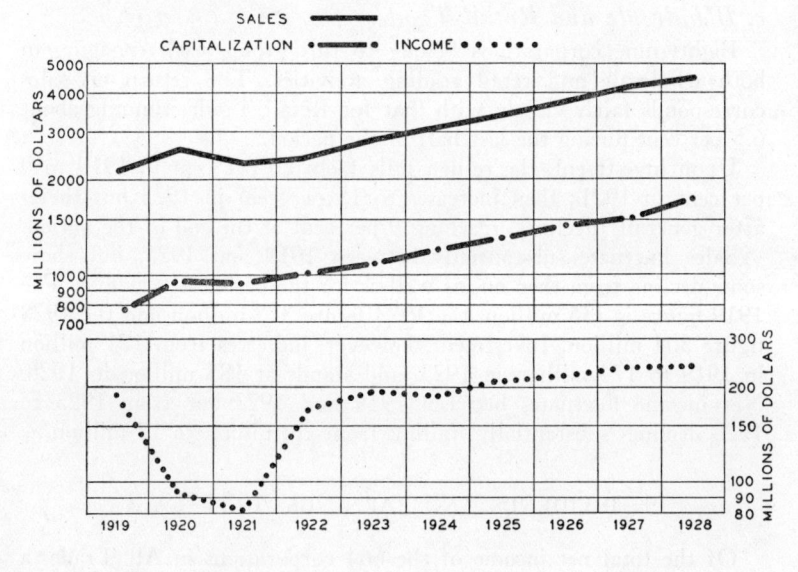

recovers in 1922 and shows a fairly steady growth for the remainder of the period, standing at about 204 million in 1927 and 1928.

b. Wholesale Trade

The Wholesale Trade group contains 292 corporations. The return on sales is much lower than for Retail Trade. It falls from 6 per cent in 1919 to 1 per cent in 1921; then recovers to 4.4 by 1923. During the last half of the period it runs slightly over 3 per cent in most years.

Upon investment, earnings are higher, but not so high as for the Retail Trade group. They show a general fall, from 14 per cent in 1923 to 9 per cent in 1928.

Unlike the Retail Trade group, sales show no increase whatever for the period, standing at almost exactly $1.5 billion in 1919, in 1923, and in each year thereafter. Investment shows a general increase from 1919 to 1923, but thereafter remains stable at approximately $525 million. Net income shows violent fluctuations between 1919 and 1923; then from 1923 to the end of the period exhibits a general decline, from $71 million to $49 million.

c. Wholesale and Retail Trade

Eighty-nine corporations belong to this group, each engaging in both wholesale and retail trading activities. The return on sales corresponds fairly closely with that for Retail Trade, running about 6.5 per cent during the last half of the period.

Upon investment, the return falls from 20 per cent in 1919 to 9 per cent in 1921; then increases to 15 per cent in 1923 but thereafter generally declines, reaching 9 per cent at the end of the period.

Sales fluctuate substantially between 1919 and 1923, but show some decline from then on, as well as for the period as a whole. The 1919 figure is 335 million, the 1923 figure 375 million and the 1928 figure 304 million. Investment, however, increases from 121 million in 1919 to 174 million in 1923, and stands at 185 million in 1928. Net income fluctuates between 1919 and 1923 but from 1923 to 1928 declines substantially, falling from 26 million to 17 million.

4. DIVIDENDS AND EARNINGS, 1924–1928

Of the total net income of the 664 corporations in All Trade, a somewhat varying proportion was paid out in the form of cash divi-

TRADE AND MAJOR GROUPS [305]

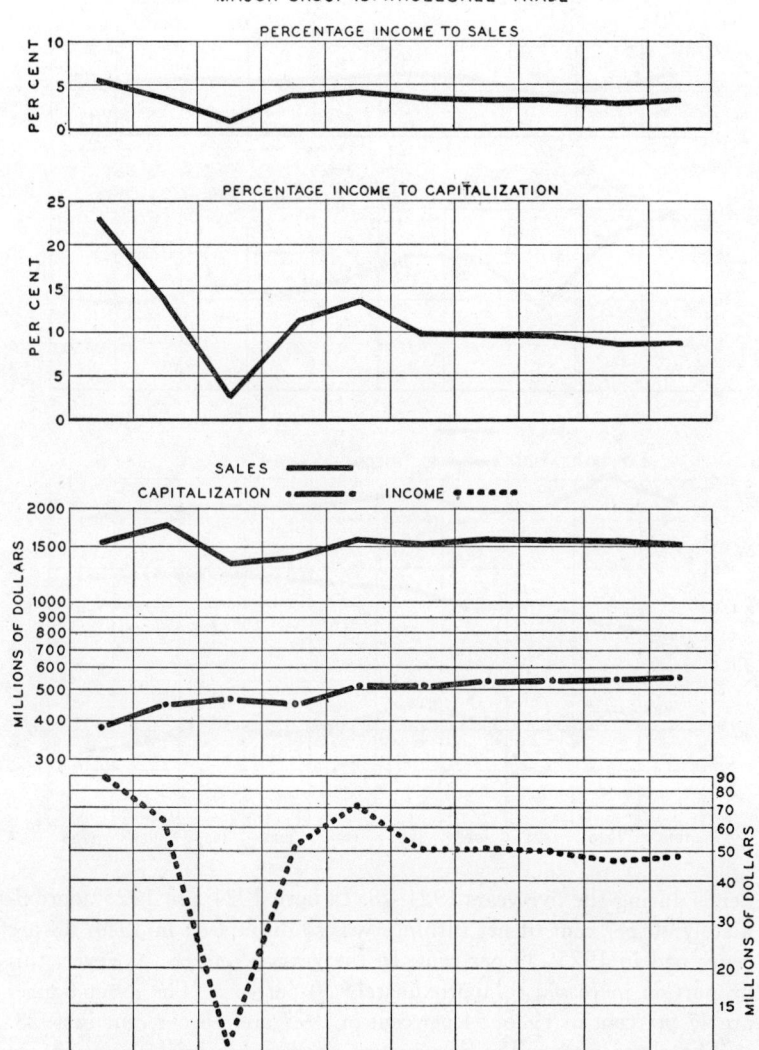

CHART 54
IDENTICAL CORPORATIONS SERIES, 1919-28
MAJOR GROUP 13: WHOLESALE TRADE

CHART 55
IDENTICAL CORPORATIONS SERIES, 1919-28
MAJOR GROUP 14: WHOLESALE AND RETAIL TRADE

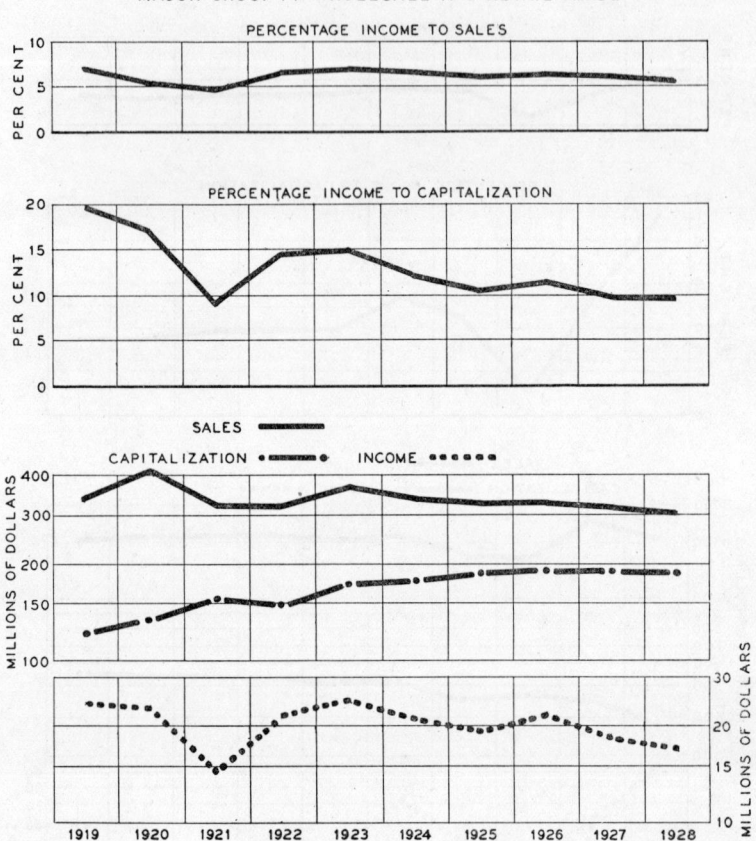

dends during the five years 1924–28. In both 1924 and 1925 approximately 40 per cent of net earnings was so disbursed; in 1924, 38 per cent; and in 1925, 39 per cent. In the years 1926–28, however, this proportion increased to approximately 50 per cent. The exact figures are 47 per cent in 1926, 54 per cent in 1927 and 48 per cent in 1928.

The three major Trading groups show substantial variations in these ratios of dividend disbursements to total net income. The Retail Trade group shows ratios of only about 30 per cent in 1924 and 1925 and about 40 or 45 per cent in the other years. The Wholesale Trade group shows much higher ratios, the figures being about 60 per cent in 1924 and 1925 and over 65 per cent in the other years. The Wholesale and Retail Trade group exhibits ratios of approximately 50 per cent in 1924 and 1925, but higher ones in the other years, the figure reaching 78 per cent in 1928. Complete data are given in Table 54.

5. EARNINGS OF INDIVIDUAL CORPORATIONS: ALL TRADE

The 664 large corporations in All Trade averaged a return of 24 per cent upon their combined investment in 1919. About 70 per cent, however, earned more than this rate. Half earned over 31 per cent. The highest quarter earned over 45 per cent, the lowest quarter, under 22 per cent. In this extremely prosperous post-War year, however, only 3 per cent of these companies earned less than 10 per cent.

In 1920, the average return was cut to 11 per cent. Again, however, about 70 per cent of the companies earned more than the average figure. Half earned over 17 per cent. A quarter earned over 27 per cent, while the lowest quarter earned under 10 per cent—a sharp contrast to the preceding year.

The year 1921 saw the general average figure decline to under 7 per cent; but 60 per cent of the companies earned in excess of this average rate, and half earned under 8 per cent. The upper quarter earned in excess of 14 per cent, but the lowest quarter earned under 2 per cent.

Between 1922 and 1928 the number of corporations occupying the upper brackets declined greatly. In 1922 almost a third earned more than 20 per cent upon their investments, but by 1928 less than a tenth did so. Conversely, in 1922 less than a third earned under 10 per cent but by 1928 half did so. The proportion of companies earning between 10 and 19 per cent remained approximately constant, about two-fifths of the total number being in this middle bracket in both of the years in question. Chart 56 shows the year-to-year course of this distribution, the trends of which in general corresponds with those for the All Manufacturing division.

CHART 56

FREQUENCY DISTRIBUTION OF EARNINGS RATES, INDIVIDUAL COMPANIES (IDENTICAL CORPORATIONS SERIES)

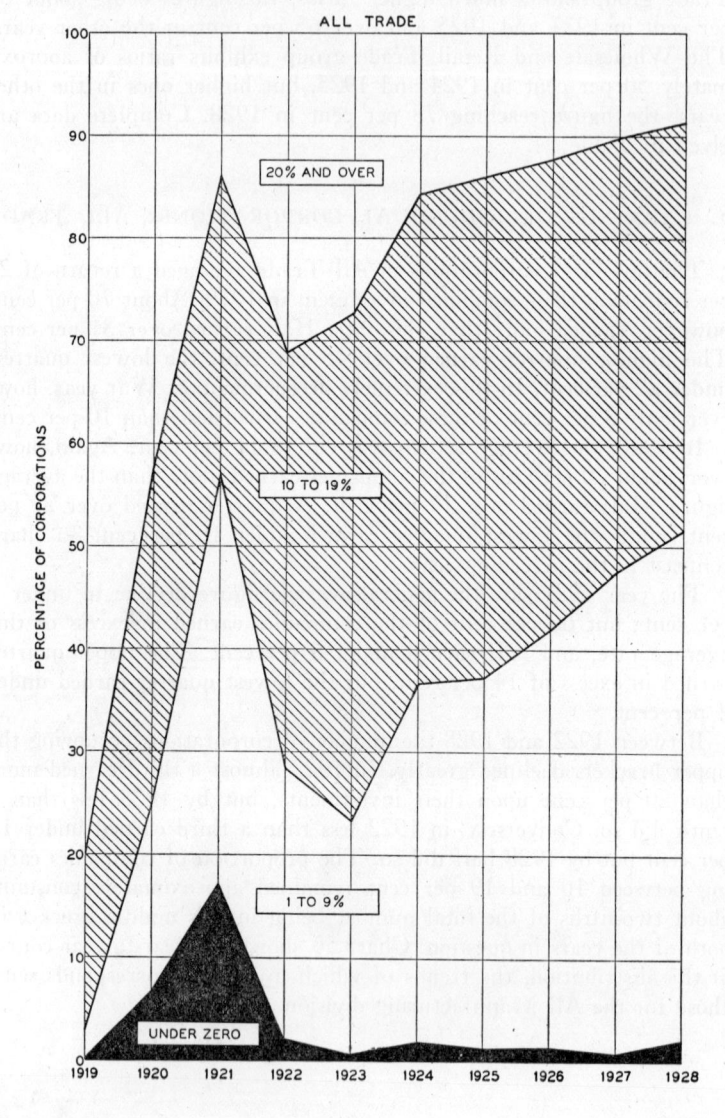

ALL TRADE

Table 54
TRADE AND ITS MAJOR GROUPS, LARGE IDENTICAL CORPORATIONS SERIES

(A) SIZE AND CHARACTER OF SAMPLE

	NUMBER OF CORPORATIONS	AVERAGE CAPITAL PER CORPORATION [1] *(millions of dollars)* ARITHMETIC MEAN	MEDIAN
All trade	664	4.07	1.24
Major group			
12 Retail trade	283	6.81	1.59
13 Wholesale trade	292	1.99	.99
14 Wholesale and retail trade	89	2.15	1.01

[1] Total capital (i.e., includes funded debt) as of December 31, 1928.

TABLE 54 (*continued*)

	1919	1920	1921	1922	1923	1924	1925	1926	1927	1928	1919–28[1]
(B) PERCENTAGE INCOME TO SALES
All trade	7.4	3.7	2.7	5.9	6.0	5.3	5.5	5.2	5.0	4.8	5.1
Major group
12 Retail trade	8.7	3.6	3.5	6.9	6.7	6.2	6.4	5.9	5.7	5.3	5.8
13 Wholesale trade	5.7	3.6	.9	3.8	4.4	3.4	3.3	3.2	3.0	3.2	3.5
14 Wholesale and retail trade	7.2	5.6	4.5	6.6	6.9	6.4	6.0	6.7	5.9	5.7	6.1
(C) PERCENTAGE INCOME TO CAPITALIZATION
All trade	24.2	11.4	6.6	14.9	15.4	13.4	14.0	13.6	13.1	12.3	13.6
Major group
12 Retail trade	25.5	9.5	8.3	16.7	16.2	15.1	16.1	15.3	15.2	13.7	14.9
13 Wholesale trade	23.0	13.8	2.4	11.2	13.7	10.0	9.6	9.5	8.6	8.7	10.7
14 Wholesale and retail trade	19.8	17.0	9.4	14.3	14.9	12.0	10.6	11.5	9.8	9.3	12.5
(D) PERCENTAGE PROFIT TO TOTAL CAPITAL
All trade						13.0	13.4	13.1	12.6	11.7	
Major group
12 Retail trade						14.4	15.2	14.6	14.3	12.9	
13 Wholesale trade						9.8	9.5	9.4	8.5	8.5	
14 Wholesale and retail trade						11.6	10.3	11.2	9.6	9.1	
(E) PERCENTAGE OF INCOME PAID OUT IN CASH DIVIDENDS
All trade						38.0	39.4	47.3	53.5	48.1	
Major group
12 Retail trade						30.4	33.6	41.7	46.1	42.2	
13 Wholesale trade						59.8	58.9	67.9	86.2	66.9	
14 Wholesale and retail trade						52.2	53.5	57.2	64.6	78.1	

(F) FREQUENCY DISTRIBUTIONS OF PERCENTAGES OF TOTAL NET INCOME TO CAPITALIZATION, INDIVIDUAL CORPORATIONS, 1919–23. ALL TRADE

PERCENTAGE INCOME TO CAPITALIZATION	1919 PERCENTAGE IN EACH CLASS	1919 ACCUMULATED BY SUCCESSIVE CLASSES	1920 PERCENTAGE IN EACH CLASS	1920 ACCUMULATED BY SUCCESSIVE CLASSES	1921 PERCENTAGE IN EACH CLASS	1921 ACCUMULATED BY SUCCESSIVE CLASSES	1922 PERCENTAGE IN EACH CLASS	1922 ACCUMULATED BY SUCCESSIVE CLASSES	1923 PERCENTAGE IN EACH CLASS	1923 ACCUMULATED BY SUCCESSIVE CLASSES
Under zero	0.1	0.1	6.6	6.6	17.2	17.2	2.0	2.0	0.5	0.5
Zero to 4	0.5	0.6	7.5	14.1	15.5	32.7	6.6	8.6	5.3	5.8
5 to 9	2.1	2.7	10.7	24.8	24.2	56.9	19.7	28.3	17.5	23.3
10 to 14	6.3	9.0	16.7	41.5	18.1	75.0	24.1	52.4	27.7	51.0
15 to 19	11.0	20.0	16.4	57.9	11.1	86.1	16.3	68.7	21.7	72.7
20 to 24	13.6	33.6	10.9	68.8	5.0	91.1	11.6	80.3	12.7	85.4
25 to 29	13.1	46.7	9.5	78.3	2.9	94.0	6.6	86.9	6.8	92.2
30 and over	58.3	100.0	21.7	100.0	6.0	100.0	13.1	100.0	7.8	100.0

(G) FREQUENCY DISTRIBUTIONS OF PERCENTAGES OF TOTAL PROFIT TO TOTAL CAPITAL, INDIVIDUAL CORPORATIONS, 1924–28. ALL TRADE

	1924 % IN EACH CLASS	1924 ACCUM.	1925 % IN EACH CLASS	1925 ACCUM.	1926 % IN EACH CLASS	1926 ACCUM.	1927 % IN EACH CLASS	1927 ACCUM.	1928 % IN EACH CLASS	1928 ACCUM.
Under zero	1.8	1.8	1.1	1.1	1.2	1.2	0.6	0.6	2.0	2.0
Zero to 4	8.7	10.5	9.6	10.7	11.7	12.9	13.3	13.9	15.7	17.7
5 to 9	26.1	36.6	26.6	37.3	29.2	42.1	33.7	47.6	33.9	51.6
10 to 14	32.7	69.3	30.1	67.4	28.9	71.0	29.5	77.1	27.6	79.2

TABLE 54 (*continued*)

(G) FREQUENCY DISTRIBUTIONS OF PERCENTAGES OF TOTAL PROFIT TO TOTAL CAPITAL, INDIVIDUAL CORPORATIONS, 1924–28. ALL TRADE

PERCENTAGE PROFIT TO TOTAL CAPITAL	1924 PERCENTAGE IN EACH CLASS	1924 ACCUMULATED BY SUCCESSIVE CLASSES	1925 PERCENTAGE IN EACH CLASS	1925 ACCUMULATED BY SUCCESSIVE CLASSES	1926 PERCENTAGE IN EACH CLASS	1926 ACCUMULATED BY SUCCESSIVE CLASSES	1927 PERCENTAGE IN EACH CLASS	1927 ACCUMULATED BY SUCCESSIVE CLASSES	1928 PERCENTAGE IN EACH CLASS	1928 ACCUMULATED BY SUCCESSIVE CLASSES
15 to 19	15.1	84.4	18.7	86.1	16.7	87.7	12.6	89.7	12.0	91.2
20 to 24	6.9	91.3	5.9	92.0	5.9	93.6	4.1	93.8	4.8	96.0
25 to 29	4.2	95.5	3.5	95.5	2.8	96.4	3.3	97.1	2.4	98.4
30 and over	4.5	100.0	4.5	100.0	3.6	100.0	2.9	100.0	1.6	100.0

CHAPTER 22

RETAIL TRADE

THE major group, Retail Trade, is subdivided into ten minor trading groups: Automobiles; Men's Clothing; Department Stores; Drygoods; Furniture; Groceries; Jewelry; Building Material and Hardware; Lumber and Coal; Miscellaneous Retail Trade. The number of corporations in each group and their average size are shown in Table 55. The groups are described briefly:

Automobiles: Includes corporations selling and servicing either passenger cars or trucks. This sample is not typical of the trade which it represents in that the average size of the corporations included is unusually large.
Men's Clothing
Department Stores
Drygoods
Furniture
Groceries: The 14 enterprises belonging to this group are exceptionally large in comparison with the typical firms engaged in the retailing of groceries, as chain store corporations are included. Average sales per company in 1928 were about 100 million dollars.
Jewelry
Building Material and Hardware: Stores which merchandise building supplies and hardware, some also selling lumber at retail.
Lumber and Coal
Miscellaneous Retail Trade: Includes all manner of articles sold at retail but not classified under any other minor group. Among them are: Boots and Shoes; Millinery; Music and Instruments; Notions; Cigars; Tobacco and Smokers' Supplies; also, the miscellany of products sold by mail-order houses.

Table 55
RETAIL TRADE GROUPS, LARGE IDENTICAL TRADING CORPORATIONS SERIES

(A) SIZE AND CHARACTER OF SAMPLE

	NUMBER OF CORPORATIONS	AVERAGE CAPITAL PER CORPORATION [1] *(millions of dollars)* ARITHMETIC MEAN	MEDIAN
Major group			
12 Retail trade	283	6.81	1.59
Minor group			
75 Automobiles	15	1.64	
76 Men's clothing	17	2.01	
77 Department stores	93	7.39	
78 Drygoods	27	3.24	
79 Furniture	12	1.59	
80 Groceries	14	16.06	
81 Jewelry	11	1.25	
82 Building material and hardware	27	1.03	
83 Lumber and coal	15	1.20	
84 Miscellaneous retail trade	52	15.22	

[1] Total capital (i.e., includes funded debt) as of December 31, 1928.

RETAIL TRADE [315]

TABLE 55 (continued)

	1919	1920	1921	1922	1923	1924	1925	1926	1927	1928	1919–28[1]
(B) PERCENTAGE INCOME TO SALES											
Major group											
12 Retail trade	8.7	3.6	3.5	6.9	6.7	6.2	6.4	5.9	5.7	5.3	5.8
Minor group											
75 Automobiles	7.5	4.9	1.8	4.1	4.6	4.3	4.9	3.8	3.1	3.4	4.1
76 Men's clothing	12.9	3.7	3.8	7.6	7.7	7.2	8.0	6.0	6.8	7.4	7.1
77 Department stores	10.7	4.3	5.0	7.3	7.4	5.9	5.9	5.6	5.4	4.6	6.1
78 Drygoods	10.6	6.1	5.3	7.1	6.6	5.3	6.1	6.0	5.2	6.0	6.3
79 Furniture	7.3	11.1	6.3	15.7	9.2	7.5	5.6	4.3	5.7	6.0	7.4
80 Groceries	3.5	2.0	4.1	4.1	4.0	4.3	3.7	3.4	3.2	3.1	3.5
81 Jewelry	20.0	9.2	4.4	9.0	8.2	6.4	9.2	12.3	10.0	13.6	10.7
82 Building material and hardware	5.6	9.5	5.0	8.5	8.2	7.7	8.1	7.4	6.2	7.0	7.4
83 Lumber and coal	10.4	11.4	3.3	8.9	6.7	7.4	8.1	7.1	8.1	9.0	8.2
84 Miscellaneous retail trade	8.1	2.1	.8	8.2	7.7	8.0	9.1	8.3	8.6	7.9	7.2
(C) PERCENTAGE INCOME TO CAPITALIZATION											
Major group											
12 Retail trade	25.5	9.5	8.3	16.7	16.2	15.1	16.1	15.3	15.2	13.7	14.9
Minor group											
75 Automobiles	81.8	34.1	11.1	29.2	27.3	25.3	33.3	23.1	17.5	18.2	25.8
76 Men's clothing	47.4	10.4	9.1	19.5	16.7	13.9	14.6	10.9	11.4	12.6	14.9
77 Department stores	34.0	12.0	12.6	17.4	14.3	12.6	12.7	12.2	11.7	9.4	14.1
78 Drygoods	38.0	15.8	11.7	16.1	11.3	11.1	12.9	12.7	12.2	11.9	14.3
79 Furniture	13.1	23.0	10.3	19.1	16.4	14.4	7.9	7.5	8.9	9.8	12.2
80 Groceries	29.6	16.1	26.1	27.3	22.1	23.5	21.0	21.7	22.0	21.6	22.5
81 Jewelry	43.8	12.8	4.7	10.0	8.9	6.6	10.1	14.2	11.2	15.1	12.7

[1] Ten-year aggregate.

TABLE 55 (continued)

(C) PERCENTAGE INCOME TO CAPITALIZATION (continued)

	1919	1920	1921	1922	1923	1924	1925	1926	1927	1928	1919–28[1]
82 Building material and hardware	13.3	23.1	6.8	13.6	13.6	10.7	11.6	10.0	8.2	8.4	11.4
83 Lumber and coal	26.7	24.1	4.2	11.9	9.1	9.7	11.4	10.1	10.7	10.6	12.2
84 Miscellaneous retail trade	16.3	4.0	1.4	14.2	14.9	16.3	19.0	17.5	17.3	15.2	14.1

(D) PERCENTAGE PROFIT TO TOTAL CAPITAL

	1924	1925	1926	1927	1928
Major group					
12 Retail trade	14.4	15.2	14.6	14.3	12.9
Minor group					
75 Automobiles	24.2	27.9	20.0	15.7	15.6
76 Men's clothing	13.9	14.6	10.9	11.4	12.6
77 Department stores	11.9	11.7	11.4	10.7	8.8
78 Drygoods	9.8	11.2	11.1	11.0	10.6
79 Furniture	14.3	7.9	7.4	8.9	9.6
80 Groceries	23.5	21.0	21.7	21.8	21.3
81 Jewelry	6.5	9.6	13.2	10.6	14.3
82 Building material and hardware	10.7	11.6	10.0	8.2	8.4
83 Lumber and coal	9.7	11.4	10.1	10.7	10.5
84 Miscellaneous retail trade	16.0	18.5	17.0	16.8	14.7

(E) PERCENTAGE OF INCOME PAID OUT IN CASH DIVIDENDS

	1924	1925	1926	1927	1928
Major group					
12 Retail trade	30.4	33.6	41.7	46.1	42.2
Minor group					
75 Automobiles	38.4	28.7	36.7	54.7	45.3
76 Men's clothing	28.3	35.7	50.8	51.8	54.7
77 Department stores	34.3	35.6	38.7	45.6	42.8
78 Drygoods	53.5	48.3	47.0	45.0	39.9
79 Furniture	61.0	65.7	85.4	58.8	47.8
80 Groceries	21.9	37.6	41.3	38.2	35.5
81 Jewelry	77.1	60.0	44.4	62.3	30.0
82 Building material and hardware	49.2	38.1	46.8	65.2	45.7
83 Lumber and coal	55.0	52.4	68.7	54.1	70.0
84 Miscellaneous retail trade	26.0	28.9	42.1	48.0	43.8

RETAIL TRADE [317]

(F) FREQUENCY DISTRIBUTIONS OF PERCENTAGES OF TOTAL NET INCOME TO CAPITALIZATION, INDIVIDUAL CORPORATIONS, 1919–23. MAJOR GROUP 12: RETAIL TRADE

PERCENTAGE INCOME TO CAPITALIZATION	1919 PERCENTAGE IN EACH CLASS	1919 ACCUMULATED BY SUCCESSIVE CLASSES	1920 PERCENTAGE IN EACH CLASS	1920 ACCUMULATED BY SUCCESSIVE CLASSES	1921 PERCENTAGE IN EACH CLASS	1921 ACCUMULATED BY SUCCESSIVE CLASSES	1922 PERCENTAGE IN EACH CLASS	1922 ACCUMULATED BY SUCCESSIVE CLASSES	1923 PERCENTAGE IN EACH CLASS	1923 ACCUMULATED BY SUCCESSIVE CLASSES
Under zero	0.4	0.4	2.5	2.5	9.2	9.2	0.4	0.4	0.0	0.0
Zero to 4	0.4	0.8	6.7	9.2	10.6	19.8	3.9	4.3	6.0	6.0
5 to 9	1.4	2.2	12.7	21.9	24.7	44.5	15.5	19.8	13.1	19.1
10 to 14	4.9	7.1	20.1	42.0	20.5	65.0	23.3	43.1	21.9	41.0
15 to 19	9.5	16.6	15.6	57.6	14.7	79.7	15.5	58.6	23.3	64.3
20 to 24	9.2	25.8	11.7	69.3	7.7	87.4	15.5	74.1	18.0	82.3
25 to 29	10.6	36.4	10.2	79.5	4.9	92.3	9.2	83.3	8.1	90.4
30 and over	63.6	100.0	20.5	100.0	7.7	100.0	16.7	100.0	9.6	100.0

(G) FREQUENCY DISTRIBUTIONS OF PERCENTAGES OF TOTAL PROFIT TO TOTAL CAPITAL, INDIVIDUAL CORPORATIONS, 1924–28. MAJOR GROUP 12: RETAIL TRADE

	1924 PERCENTAGE IN EACH CLASS	1924 ACCUMULATED BY SUCCESSIVE CLASSES	1925 PERCENTAGE IN EACH CLASS	1925 ACCUMULATED BY SUCCESSIVE CLASSES	1926 PERCENTAGE IN EACH CLASS	1926 ACCUMULATED BY SUCCESSIVE CLASSES	1927 PERCENTAGE IN EACH CLASS	1927 ACCUMULATED BY SUCCESSIVE CLASSES	1928 PERCENTAGE IN EACH CLASS	1928 ACCUMULATED BY SUCCESSIVE CLASSES
Under zero	1.1	1.1	0.0	0.0	1.1	1.1	1.1	1.1	1.8	1.8
Zero to 4	7.8	8.9	5.7	5.7	6.0	7.1	11.3	12.4	11.3	13.1
5 to 9	19.4	28.3	20.8	26.5	21.5	28.6	27.6	40.0	30.0	43.1
10 to 14	32.9	61.2	28.3	54.8	31.1	59.7	28.6	68.6	26.5	69.6
15 to 19	17.3	78.5	23.7	78.5	22.3	82.0	16.6	85.2	16.6	86.2
20 to 24	9.2	87.7	8.1	86.6	9.2	91.2	5.3	90.5	7.4	93.6
25 to 29	6.4	94.1	4.6	91.2	3.5	94.7	4.6	95.1	4.2	97.8
30 and over	5.9	100.0	8.8	100.0	5.3	100.0	4.9	100.0	2.2	100.0

CHAPTER 23

WHOLESALE TRADE

EIGHT minor groups comprise Wholesale Trade. Two—Drygoods and Groceries—are the wholesale equivalents of two minor groups bearing these names in the Retail Trade sample already discussed. Two others—Hardware, and Building Material and Lumber—correspond in part with two other Retail Trade groups. Three groups of this Wholesale Trade sample, however, were not found separately in Retail Trade. These are Drugs, Importers and Exporters, and Paper. The eighth group is the Miscellaneous category. The number of corporations in each group and their average size are shown in Table 56. Except for the Miscellaneous group, descriptions are unnecessary here.

Miscellaneous Wholesale Trade: Comprises 82 corporations engaged in all sorts of wholesale trading activities. Principal trades included are: Coal; Fuel and Wood; Cigars; Tobacco and Smokers' Supplies; Jewelry; Music and Instruments; and Jobbers of Electrical and Plumbing Supplies.

TABLE 56

WHOLESALE TRADE GROUPS, LARGE IDENTICAL TRADING CORPORATIONS SERIES

(A) SIZE AND CHARACTER OF SAMPLE

		NUMBER OF CORPORATIONS	AVERAGE CAPITAL PER CORPORATION [1] (millions of dollars)	
			ARITHMETIC MEAN	MEDIAN
Major group				
13	Wholesale trade	292	1.99	.99 *
Minor group				
86	Drugs	25	1.25	
87	Drygoods	29	1.53	
88	Groceries	59	1.56	
89	Hardware	43	2.25	

[318]

TABLE 56 *(continued)*
WHOLESALE TRADE GROUPS, LARGE IDENTICAL TRADING CORPORATIONS SERIES

		NUMBER OF CORPORATIONS	AVERAGE CAPITAL PER CORPORATION [1] *(millions of dollars)* ARITHMETIC MEAN	MEDIAN
Minor group				
90	Importers and exporters	23	2.34	
91	Building material and lumber	13	1.39	
92	Paper	18	2.32	
93–85	Miscellaneous wholesale trade	82	2.49	

[1] Total capital (i.e., includes funded debt) as of December 31, 1928.

TABLE 56 (*continued*)

(B) PERCENTAGE INCOME TO SALES

		1919	1920	1921	1922	1923	1924	1925	1926	1927	1928	1919–28[a]
Major group												
13	Wholesale trade	5.7	3.6	.9	3.8	4.4	3.4	3.3	3.2	3.0	3.2	3.5
Minor group												
86	Drugs	4.5	5.0	2.7	3.7	4.5	4.2	4.1	3.8	3.5	4.3	4.0
87	Drygoods	10.2	1.6	2.3	4.3	4.5	3.0	3.6	2.8	3.8	3.6	4.0
88	Groceries	3.9	.9	.7	3.2	2.9	2.7	2.4	2.0	2.1	2.0	2.3
89	Hardware	7.6	6.3	–.8	4.5	6.1	3.5	4.3	3.9	4.0	4.5	4.5
90	Importers and exporters	7.1	3.1	2.2	4.0	3.9	3.7	2.0	2.5	3.5	4.7	3.5
91	Building material and lumber	5.0	6.2	2.0	5.4	3.4	3.0	2.8	2.9	2.2	2.0	3.5
92	Paper	3.5	4.6	–.1	2.3	3.0	2.4	2.5	2.2	2.1	2.7	2.6
93–85	Miscellaneous wholesale trade	5.8	4.2	.8	4.0	5.5	3.9	3.8	4.2	3.2	3.2	3.9

(C) PERCENTAGE INCOME TO CAPITALIZATION

		1919	1920	1921	1922	1923	1924	1925	1926	1927	1928	1919–28[a]
Major group												
13	Wholesale trade	23.0	13.8	2.4	11.2	13.7	10.0	9.6	9.5	8.6	8.7	10.7
Minor group												
86	Drugs	18.0	19.7	7.6	10.2	13.2	11.8	11.5	11.0	9.9	10.4	11.9
87	Drygoods	37.2	5.4	6.1	11.6	12.6	7.4	9.1	6.9	9.1	8.4	10.9
88	Groceries	21.7	4.7	2.6	11.5	11.0	10.8	9.3	7.7	7.8	7.4	9.2
89	Hardware	21.1	16.8	–1.5	9.2	12.9	6.8	8.6	7.7	7.7	8.6	9.5
90	Importers and exporters	24.9	12.2	9.2	16.3	13.5	11.1	6.5	6.8	9.7	10.7	11.3
91	Building material and lumber	28.1	14.2	2.5	11.0	8.5	6.7	6.2	6.7	4.8	4.5	7.9
92	Paper	18.1	28.4	–2.7	9.9	13.3	10.6	10.5	8.4	8.4	10.2	11.3
93–85	Miscellaneous wholesale trade	22.3	15.6	2.0	11.4	16.6	11.5	11.2	12.9	9.3	8.7	11.9

[a] Ten-year aggregate.

WHOLESALE TRADE

(D) PERCENTAGE PROFIT TO TOTAL CAPITAL

	1924	1925	1926	1927	1928
Major group					
13 Wholesale trade	9.8	9.5	9.4	8.5	8.5
Minor group					
86 Drugs	11.7	11.4	10.9	9.8	10.3
87 Drygoods	7.4	9.1	7.0	9.1	8.4
88 Groceries	10.8	9.3	7.7	7.8	7.3
89 Hardware	6.7	8.5	7.6	7.6	8.5
90 Importers and exporters	10.5	6.3	6.6	9.3	10.2
91 Building material and lumber	6.7	6.2	6.6	4.8	4.5
92 Paper	10.3	10.4	8.3	8.3	10.0
93–85 Miscellaneous wholesale trade	11.4	11.1	12.7	9.2	8.5

(E) PERCENTAGE OF INCOME PAID OUT IN CASH DIVIDENDS

	1924	1925	1926	1927	1928
Major group					
13 Wholesale trade	59.8	58.9	67.9	86.2	66.9
Minor group					
86 Drugs	47.3	48.4	54.3	52.5	41.9
87 Drygoods	59.1	51.8	64.0	39.5	57.6
88 Groceries	54.8	58.3	60.3	66.9	64.3
89 Hardware	69.2	57.4	96.5	237.0	58.6
90 Importers and exporters	46.7	63.1	69.3	34.9	29.6
91 Building material and lumber	58.6	56.2	58.5	100.0	93.8
92 Paper	58.2	77.5	78.4	83.4	60.2
93–85 Miscellaneous wholesale trade	64.4	58.6	62.5	61.9	90.7

(F) FREQUENCY DISTRIBUTIONS OF PERCENTAGES OF TOTAL NET INCOME TO CAPITALIZATION, INDIVIDUAL CORPORATIONS, 1919–23. MAJOR GROUP 13 : WHOLESALE TRADE

PERCENTAGE INCOME TO CAPI-TALIZATION	1919 PERCENT-AGE IN EACH CLASS	1919 ACCU-MULATED BY SUC-CESSIVE CLASSES	1920 PERCENT-AGE IN EACH CLASS	1920 ACCU-MULATED BY SUC-CESSIVE CLASSES	1921 PERCENT-AGE IN EACH CLASS	1921 ACCU-MULATED BY SUC-CESSIVE CLASSES	1922 PERCENT-AGE IN EACH CLASS	1922 ACCU-MULATED BY SUC-CESSIVE CLASSES	1923 PERCENT-AGE IN EACH CLASS	1923 ACCU-MULATED BY SUC-CESSIVE CLASSES
Under zero	0.0	0.0	12.0	12.0	25.0	25.0	3.4	3.4	1.0	1.0
Zero to 4	0.0	0.0	9.2	21.2	20.9	45.9	8.9	12.3	5.1	6.1
5 to 9	2.1	2.1	8.9	30.1	23.3	69.2	24.7	37.0	20.6	26.7
10 to 14	7.9	10.0	15.4	45.5	16.4	85.6	25.7	62.7	33.9	60.6
15 to 19	12.3	22.3	16.1	61.6	8.6	94.2	14.0	76.7	20.6	81.2
20 to 24	16.4	38.7	8.2	69.8	2.1	96.3	8.9	85.6	7.9	88.1
25 to 29	15.4	54.1	9.2	79.0	1.0	97.3	4.5	90.1	5.8	94.9
30 and over	45.9	100.0	21.0	100.0	2.7	100.0	9.9	100.0	5.1	100.0

TABLE 56 (continued)

(G) FREQUENCY DISTRIBUTIONS OF PERCENTAGES OF TOTAL PROFIT TO TOTAL CAPITAL, INDIVIDUAL CORPORATIONS, 1924–28. MAJOR GROUP 13: WHOLESALE TRADE

PERCENTAGE PROFIT TO TOTAL CAPITAL	1924 PERCENTAGE IN EACH CLASS	1924 ACCUMULATED BY SUCCESSIVE CLASSES	1925 PERCENTAGE IN EACH CLASS	1925 ACCUMULATED BY SUCCESSIVE CLASSES	1926 PERCENTAGE IN EACH CLASS	1926 ACCUMULATED BY SUCCESSIVE CLASSES	1927 PERCENTAGE IN EACH CLASS	1927 ACCUMULATED BY SUCCESSIVE CLASSES	1928 PERCENTAGE IN EACH CLASS	1928 ACCUMULATED BY SUCCESSIVE CLASSES
Under zero	2.4	2.4	2.1	2.1	1.7	1.7	0.3	0.3	2.4	2.4
Zero to 4	9.9	12.3	13.4	15.5	16.4	18.1	14.4	14.7	18.2	20.6
5 to 9	33.6	45.9	31.8	47.3	36.3	54.4	41.1	55.8	38.3	58.9
10 to 14	32.9	78.8	31.5	78.8	27.1	81.5	28.8	84.6	28.4	87.3
15 to 19	12.7	91.5	15.1	93.9	13.0	94.5	8.9	93.5	8.9	96.2
20 to 24	3.8	95.3	3.1	97.0	1.7	96.2	2.7	96.2	2.1	98.3
25 to 29	2.0	97.3	2.7	99.7	2.1	98.3	2.4	98.6	1.0	99.3
30 and over	2.7	100.0	0.3	100.0	1.7	100.0	1.4	100.0	0.7	100.0

Chapter 24

RETAIL AND WHOLESALE TRADE

THE major group designated as Retail and Wholesale Trade does not include corporations engaged in either retail or wholesale trade alone, but only enterprises which carry on *both* wholesaling and retailing activities. The major group is subdivided into only four such trades, one a miscellaneous category: Coal; Hardware; Building Material and Lumber; Miscellaneous Retail and Wholesale Trade. The number of corporations in each group and their average size are shown in Table 57. Only the Miscellaneous group need here be described, since the others have been treated in the two preceding chapters.

Miscellaneous Retail and Wholesale Trade: The 52 corporations of this group are engaged in all sorts of trading activities, the principal pursuits followed or commodities dealt in being: Commission Dealers; Boots and Shoes; Drugs and Chemicals; Furniture; Glass, Paints and Oils; Stationery.

TABLE 57
WHOLESALE AND RETAIL TRADE GROUPS, LARGE IDENTICAL TRADING CORPORATIONS SERIES

(A) SIZE AND CHARACTER OF SAMPLE

		NUMBER OF CORPORATIONS	AVERAGE CAPITAL PER CORPORATION [1] *(millions of dollars)* ARITHMETIC MEAN	MEDIAN
Major group				
14	Wholesale and retail trade	89	2.15	1.01
Minor group				
96	Coal, wood and fuel	10	2.24	
97	Hardware	16	1.16	
98	Lumber	11	1.10	
99–95	Miscellaneous wholesale and retail trade	52	2.66	

[1] Total capital (i.e., includes funded debt) as of December 31, 1928.

TABLE 57 (continued)

	1919	1920	1921	1922	1923	1924	1925	1926	1927	1928	1919–28[1]
(B) PERCENTAGE INCOME TO SALES
Major group
14 Wholesale and retail trade	7.2	5.6	4.5	6.6	6.9	6.4	6.0	6.7	5.9	5.7	6.1
Minor group
96 Coal, wood and fuel	3.1	3.6	2.1	4.5	5.0	5.2	5.9	6.3	5.5	6.2	4.8
97 Hardware	8.0	6.5	1.1	4.3	5.0	3.6	4.9	4.5	3.8	3.9	4.7
98 Lumber	3.5	9.0	4.3	8.2	8.5	7.5	5.6	5.0	5.0	4.0	6.3
99–95 Miscellaneous wholesale and retail trade	7.8	5.5	5.3	7.2	7.5	7.0	6.2	7.3	6.5	6.0	6.6
(C) PERCENTAGE INCOME TO CAPITALIZATION
Major group
14 Wholesale and retail trade	19.8	17.0	9.4	14.3	14.9	12.0	10.6	11.5	9.8	9.3	12.5
Minor group
96 Coal, wood and fuel	11.7	16.4	7.0	15.0	17.8	14.8	13.7	15.5	10.7	10.8	13.3
97 Hardware	22.6	17.6	2.0	8.7	11.4	8.0	10.3	9.6	7.7	7.6	10.2
98 Lumber	6.7	25.4	7.3	17.3	17.5	11.4	8.3	7.1	6.8	5.1	10.7
99–95 Miscellaneous wholesale and retail trade	21.2	16.4	10.7	14.8	14.8	12.1	10.4	11.5	10.2	9.7	12.8

[1] Ten-year aggregate.

RETAIL AND WHOLESALE TRADE [325]

(D) PERCENTAGE PROFIT TO TOTAL CAPITAL

	1924	1925	1926	1927	1928
Major group					
14 Retail and wholesale trade	11.6	10.3	11.2	9.6	9.1
Minor group					
96 Coal	14.6	13.7	15.5	10.7	10.7
97 Hardware	8.0	10.3	9.5	7.6	7.5
98 Lumber	11.4	8.3	7.2	6.9	5.1
99–95 Miscellaneous retail and wholesale trade	11.7	10.0	11.1	9.9	9.5

(E) PERCENTAGE OF INCOME PAID OUT IN CASH DIVIDENDS

	1924	1925	1926	1927	1928
Major group					
14 Retail and wholesale trade	52.2	53.5	57.2	64.6	78.1
Minor group					
96 Coal	23.0	35.9	40.0	42.9	90.8
97 Hardware	66.2	50.0	57.1	69.3	75.0
98 Lumber	43.3	62.2	70.0	66.3	98.3
99–95 Miscellaneous retail and wholesale trade	56.7	56.8	60.2	67.7	75.2

(F) FREQUENCY DISTRIBUTIONS OF PERCENTAGES OF TOTAL NET INCOME TO CAPITALIZATION, INDIVIDUAL CORPORATIONS, 1919–23. MAJOR GROUP 14: RETAIL AND WHOLESALE TRADE

PERCENTAGE INCOME TO CAPITALIZATION	1919 PERCENTAGE IN EACH CLASS	1919 ACCUMULATED BY SUCCESSIVE CLASSES	1920 PERCENTAGE IN EACH CLASS	1920 ACCUMULATED BY SUCCESSIVE CLASSES	1921 PERCENTAGE IN EACH CLASS	1921 ACCUMULATED BY SUCCESSIVE CLASSES	1922 PERCENTAGE IN EACH CLASS	1922 ACCUMULATED BY SUCCESSIVE CLASSES	1923 PERCENTAGE IN EACH CLASS	1923 ACCUMULATED BY SUCCESSIVE CLASSES
Under zero	0.0	0.0	2.2	2.2	16.9	16.9	2.2	2.2	0.0	0.0
Zero to 4	2.2	2.2	4.5	6.7	13.5	30.4	7.9	10.1	3.4	3.4
5 to 9	4.5	6.7	10.1	16.8	25.8	56.2	16.9	27.0	21.4	24.8
10 to 14	5.6	12.3	10.1	26.9	15.7	71.9	21.3	48.3	25.8	50.6
15 to 19	11.2	23.5	20.2	47.1	9.0	80.9	25.8	74.1	20.2	70.8
20 to 24	18.0	41.5	16.9	64.0	5.6	86.5	7.9	82.0	11.2	82.0
25 to 29	13.5	55.0	7.9	71.9	2.2	88.7	5.6	87.6	6.8	88.8
30 and over	45.0	100.0	28.1	100.0	11.3	100.0	12.4	100.0	11.2	100.0

Table 57 (continued)

(G) FREQUENCY DISTRIBUTIONS OF PERCENTAGES OF TOTAL PROFIT TO TOTAL CAPITAL, INDIVIDUAL CORPORATIONS, 1924–28. MAJOR GROUP 14: RETAIL AND WHOLESALE TRADE

PERCENTAGE PROFIT TO TOTAL CAPITAL	1924 PERCENTAGE IN EACH CLASS	1924 ACCUMULATED BY SUCCESSIVE CLASSES	1925 PERCENTAGE IN EACH CLASS	1925 ACCUMULATED BY SUCCESSIVE CLASSES	1926 PERCENTAGE IN EACH CLASS	1926 ACCUMULATED BY SUCCESSIVE CLASSES	1927 PERCENTAGE IN EACH CLASS	1927 ACCUMULATED BY SUCCESSIVE CLASSES	1928 PERCENTAGE IN EACH CLASS	1928 ACCUMULATED BY SUCCESSIVE CLASSES
Under zero	2.2	2.2	1.1	1.1	0.0	0.0	0.0	0.0	1.1	1.1
Zero to 4	7.9	10.1	10.1	11.2	14.6	14.6	15.7	15.7	21.3	22.4
5 to 9	22.5	32.6	28.1	39.3	30.3	44.9	29.2	44.9	31.5	53.9
10 to 14	31.5	64.1	31.5	70.8	28.1	73.0	34.8	79.7	28.1	82.0
15 to 19	15.7	79.8	14.6	85.4	11.2	84.2	12.4	92.1	7.9	89.9
20 to 24	10.1	89.9	7.9	93.3	9.0	93.2	4.6	96.7	5.6	95.5
25 to 29	4.5	94.4	2.2	95.5	2.2	95.4	2.2	98.9	1.1	96.6
30 and over	5.6	100.0	4.5	100.0	4.6	100.0	1.1	100.0	3.4	100.0

Chapter 25

MINING AND ITS MINOR GROUPS

1. THE MINING GROUP AS A WHOLE

IN the terminology which we have been employing, the industrial division Mining may be regarded as one major group. Included in it are all types of extractive operations: coal mining, oil drilling and gas producing; ferrous and non-ferrous metal mining, including gold and silver; the quarrying of stone, salt, clay, sand and gravel, etc.

As previously pointed out, some of the Mining minor groups are not such representative samples of the extractive activities carried on by these industries as is the case with the various Manufacturing and Trading groups discussed in preceding chapters.[1] It is also to be observed that not only are the samples rather small in several instances, but that neither the investment nor net income figures are to be taken as possessing as high a degree of validity as in the case of the Manufacturing or Trading samples.[2] The qualifications which attach to most accounting appraisals—which in the nature of things are never more than close estimates—apply with peculiar cogency to figures for the Mining industry. Investment, in the case of a mine, means the cost of acquisition and development, rather than of construction in the ordinary sense of original cost or 'prudent investment'. As carried on the books, it may even involve a 'discovery value'—the engineers' appraisal of the extent and market value of veins or deposits as yet unworked. The computation of net income is likewise in some instances beclouded—so far as a valid comparison with Manufacturing or Trade incomes is concerned—because of the inclusion of depletion charges as a large proportion of total deduction from revenues. To what extent depletion charges represent deductions accurately based upon the exhaustion of an original investment, to what degree they represent, beyond this, an attempt to show

[1] See Ch. 8, sec. 4.
[2] As to the general reliability of the two latter, see Ch. 44 and 45.

lower net earnings figures for one reason or another—these are questions not easily solved. Particularly in the case of gas and oil wells are net income figures to be accepted only provisionally for any comparative purposes. The fact that the income tax law, in its several revisions, has changed the provisions affecting the charging of depletion [3] undoubtedly has influenced the accounting practices of certain mining enterprises; and in any minor industrial groups for which the samples are as small as those discussed in this chapter, such variations in accounting practice on the part of even a few corporations might well affect the comparability of the income series over a time period.

With these preliminary remarks of warning, the tabular data for Mining may be presented. In computing the return on sales, however, data for one of the six minor groups, Gas and Oil Wells, are omitted from the total Mining figures because of incompleteness in the sample (see section 2 below). Data for the return on investment, however, include all six minor groups.

The return on sales declines from 13 per cent in 1920 to 3 per cent in 1921; then increases to 8 per cent in 1922. Although temporary declines occur in 1924 and 1927, the trend is upward during the years from 1922 to 1928, the figure standing at 16 per cent at the end of the period.

Upon investment, much lower earnings are the rule. The return declines from 6 per cent in 1920 to barely 1 per cent in 1921; then recovers to 5 per cent by 1923. During the second half of the period,

[3] For example, the Revenue Acts of 1919, 1921 and 1924 all provided for depletion charges based on either original cost, valuation as of March 1, 1913, or discovery value; but where discovery value was employed, the Act of 1921 limited the depletion charge to the amount of net income (reckoned before depletion). The Act of 1924, however, where discovery value was employed, limited the charge to 50 per cent of the net income. These provisions applied to all types of mining. But the Act of 1926 provided that, in the case of gas and oil wells, the depletion charged upon any valuation had to be limited to 27.5 per cent of the amount of sales volume and to 50 per cent of the net income. But whereas previous acts had permitted the annual depletion charges on any given mining property to accumulate only to the aggregate amount of the investment (cost, March 1913 value, or discovery value), the Act of 1926 imposed no limit whatever upon the accumulation of charges in the case of gas and oil wells, i.e., the entire cost of a gas or oil property could be written off and depletion could still be charged on the same property in subsequent years, subject only to the 27.5 per cent of current sales and 50 per cent of current net income limits above mentioned.

MINING GROUPS

CHART 57
IDENTICAL CORPORATIONS SERIES, 1919-28
MAJOR GROUP 15: MINING

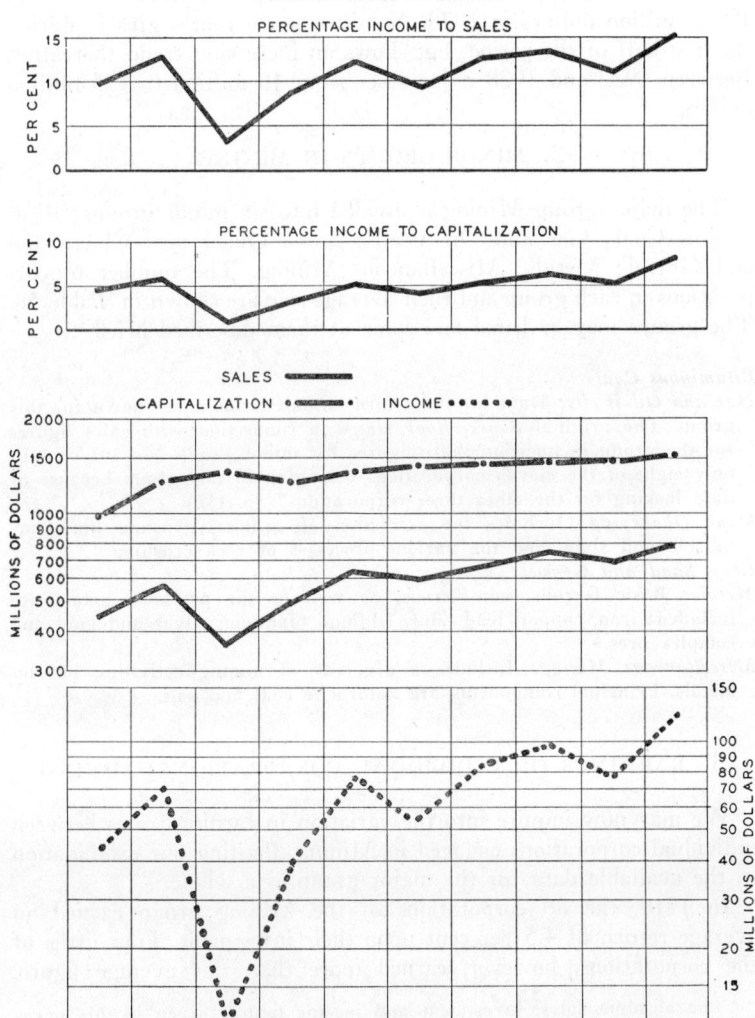

it runs between 4 and 8 per cent, the latter figure prevailing in 1928.

Sales [4] show a generally rising trend, expanding from 435 million in 1919 to 783 million dollars in 1928. Investment grows at a somewhat slower rate, increasing from 972 million dollars in 1919 to 1,539 million dollars in 1928. Net income fluctuates greatly during the first half of the period, but shows an increasing trend thereafter. Between 1922 and 1928 it increases from 40 million to 125 million dollars.

2. MINOR GROUPS IN MINING

The major group Mining is divided into six minor groups: Bituminous Coal; Gas and Oil Wells; Stone Quarrying; Clay, Sand and Gravel; Metals; Miscellaneous Mining. The number of corporations in each group and their average size are shown in Table 58. The groups may be listed and some of them described briefly:

Bituminous Coal
Gas and Oil Wells: Data for the return on sales cannot be shown for this group. The original *Source-Book* states in connection with sales figures for the group in question that "figures for minor group No. 101 contain only eight of the eleven corporations belonging to this group because of data lacking for the other three corporations" (p. 152).
Stone Quarrying: Includes the extraction of granite, gypsum, limestone, marble and slate, and the various processes of rock crushing.
Clay, Sand and Gravel
Metals: Basic ferrous, non-ferrous, as well as the precious metals are included: iron, copper, lead, zinc, iridium, platinum, silver and gold and complex ores.
Miscellaneous Mining: Includes a diversity of mining activities, but no metals. Principal components are anthracite coal and salt.

3. EARNINGS OF INDIVIDUAL CORPORATIONS: MINING

We may now inquire into the variation in earnings rates between individual corporations engaged in Mining, limiting our examination to the available data for the major group as a whole.

In 1919, the 88 corporations of the Mining group earned an average return of 4.5 per cent upon their investment. Four-fifths of the corporations, however, earned more than this average figure,

---

[4] The absolute sales, investment and income figures given in this paragraph omit the Gas and Oil Wells group, for the reason given in sec. 2 below.

CHART 58

FREQUENCY DISTRIBUTION OF EARNINGS RATES, INDIVIDUAL COMPANIES (IDENTICAL CORPORATIONS SERIES)

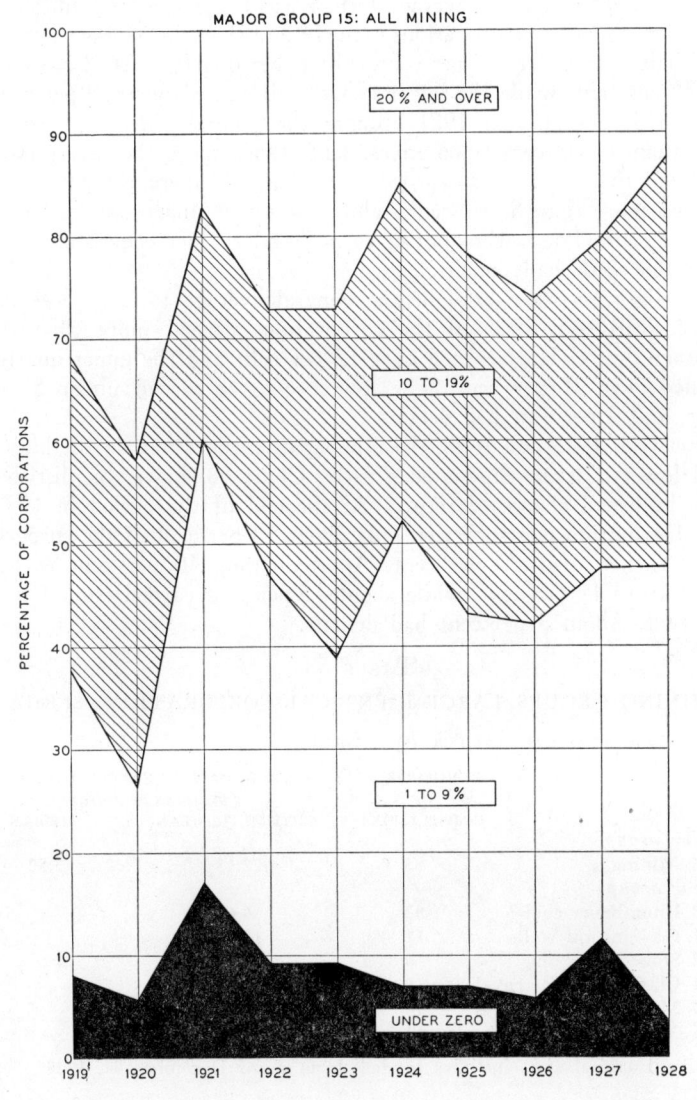

MAJOR GROUP 15: ALL MINING

while half earned over 13 per cent. The upper quarter earned over 26 per cent, while the lower quarter earned under 7 per cent. At the same time 8 per cent recorded deficits.

In 1920, the general average return was 6 per cent. Again, about four-fifths of these corporations earned more than the average return; and half earned over 18 per cent. The upper quarter earned in excess of 35 per cent, while the lower quarter all earned under 9 per cent.

The depression year 1921 brought the general average return to less than 1 per cent upon investment. Once more, however, four-fifths of the corporations earned more than the average figure. Half earned more than 8 per cent, while the upper quarter earned over 16 per cent. The lower quarter earned under 2 per cent, and a few over one-sixth had deficits.

A slight recovery brought the general average to 3 per cent in 1922. Still four-fifths of the corporations earned more than the average figure. Half earned over 12 per cent and the upper quarter earned over 22 per cent. The lowest quarter earned under 5 per cent, and 9 per cent had deficits.

Between 1923 and 1928, the number of corporations in the higher and lower brackets fluctuated greatly. Chart 58 shows this distribution by broad classes of return. At the end of the period in 1928, the distribution was such that only about 13 per cent of the corporations earned over 20 per cent. Approximately 40 per cent earned from 10 to 19 per cent, while about 45 per cent earned from 1 to 9 per cent. About 3 per cent had deficits.

TABLE 58

MINING GROUPS, LARGE IDENTICAL CORPORATIONS SERIES

(A) SIZE AND CHARACTER OF SAMPLE

	NUMBER OF CORPORATIONS	AVERAGE CAPITAL PER CORPORATION [1] (millions of dollars) ARITHMETIC MEAN	MEDIAN
Major group			
15 Mining	88	22.15	3.50
Minor group			
100 Bituminous coal	33	6.60	
101 Gas and oil wells	11	12.93	
102 Stone quarrying	9	6.66	
103 Clay, sand and gravel	9	4.91	
104 Metals	15	87.67	
105 Miscellaneous mining	11	15.45	

[1] Total capital (i.e., includes funded debt) as of December 31, 1928.

MINING GROUPS [333]

TABLE 58 (continued)

	1919	1920	1921	1922	1923	1924	1925	1926	1927	1928	1919–28[1]
(B) PERCENTAGE INCOME TO SALES											
Major group											
15 Mining[2]	9.9	12.6	3.2	8.2	12.0	9.4	12.6	13.0	11.3	15.9	11.4
Minor group											
100 Bituminous coal	14.8	25.4	14.5	18.0	15.5	8.2	11.4	13.4	10.8	10.2	14.8
101[3]											
102 Stone quarrying	18.1	15.7	10.0	18.9	20.5	20.0	23.2	21.7	21.8	15.9	18.9
103 Clay, sand and gravel	20.0	20.0	18.9	31.0	23.6	24.6	32.7	31.7	32.9	26.3	27.2
104 Metals	4.1	4.1	−15.2	1.9	7.7	6.9	11.2	10.5	9.0	16.7	8.0
105 Miscellaneous mining	21.9	20.1	18.8	18.6	22.8	16.4	14.5	20.6	15.6	14.2	11.4
(C) PERCENTAGE INCOME TO CAPITALIZATION											
Major group											
15 Mining	4.5	6.0	0.9	2.9	5.1	3.8	5.4	6.4	5.1	7.9	4.9
Minor group											
100 Bituminous coal	10.5	23.5	9.0	8.1	9.0	3.6	5.2	7.7	5.4	4.5	8.2
101 Gas and oil wells	5.0	10.9	1.1	−1.1	−1.8	1.3	2.0	3.9	3.0	5.8	2.9
102 Stone quarrying	13.2	12.9	5.9	11.0	13.2	12.2	14.5	14.3	15.7	10.8	12.6
103 Clay, sand and gravel	9.3	10.0	8.1	14.1	13.2	11.9	16.9	18.4	18.1	12.5	13.8
104 Metals	1.4	1.3	−2.3	0.6	3.1	2.5	4.7	4.9	3.9	8.5	3.0
105 Miscellaneous mining	16.8	16.9	13.0	17.6	20.8	14.2	10.9	14.6	10.0	7.9	13.8

[1] Ten-year aggregate.
[2] In this calculation, major group 15 contains data for only 77 corporations instead of 88, minor group 101 being entirely omitted (see following note).
[3] Sales figures for minor group 101 contains only 8 of the 11 corporations belonging to this group, because of lack of data for the other three corporations, therefore no percentages have been worked.

TABLE 58 *(continued)*

MINING GROUPS, LARGE IDENTICAL CORPORATIONS SERIES

(D) PERCENTAGE PROFIT TO TOTAL CAPITAL

	1924	1925	1926	1927	1928
Major group					
15 Mining	3.9	5.3	6.2	5.1	7.5
Minor group					
100 Bituminous coal	3.8	5.2	7.5	5.4	4.5
101 Gas and oil wells	1.3	2.2	4.0	3.1	5.7
102 Stone quarrying	11.7	14.0	13.4	14.3	9.8
103 Clay, sand and gravel	11.6	16.7	18.2	17.6	11.8
104 Metals	2.9	4.7	4.9	4.1	7.9
105 Miscellaneous mining	11.6	9.4	12.8	9.1	7.4

MINING GROUPS

TABLE 58 (*continued*)

(E) FREQUENCY DISTRIBUTIONS OF PERCENTAGES OF TOTAL NET INCOME TO CAPITALIZATION, INDIVIDUAL CORPORATIONS, 1919–23. MAJOR GROUP 15: MINING

PERCENTAGE INCOME TO CAPITALIZATION	1919 PERCENTAGE IN EACH CLASS	1919 ACCUMULATED BY SUCCESSIVE CLASSES	1920 PERCENTAGE IN EACH CLASS	1920 ACCUMULATED BY SUCCESSIVE CLASSES	1921 PERCENTAGE IN EACH CLASS	1921 ACCUMULATED BY SUCCESSIVE CLASSES	1922 PERCENTAGE IN EACH CLASS	1922 ACCUMULATED BY SUCCESSIVE CLASSES	1923 PERCENTAGE IN EACH CLASS	1923 ACCUMULATED BY SUCCESSIVE CLASSES
Under zero	8.0	8.0	5.7	5.7	17.0	17.0	9.1	9.1	9.1	9.1
Zero to 4	11.4	19.4	11.4	17.1	21.6	38.6	14.8	23.9	11.4	20.5
5 to 9	18.2	37.6	9.1	26.2	21.6	60.2	22.7	46.6	18.2	38.7
10 to 14	20.4	58.0	15.9	42.1	12.5	72.7	8.0	54.6	21.6	60.3
15 to 19	10.2	68.2	15.9	58.0	10.2	82.9	18.2	72.8	12.5	72.8
20 to 24	5.7	73.9	9.1	67.1	9.1	92.0	8.0	80.8	6.8	79.6
25 to 29	9.1	83.0	3.4	70.5	2.3	94.3	5.7	86.5	5.7	85.3
30 and over	17.0	100.0	29.5	100.0	5.7	100.0	13.5	100.0	14.7	100.0

(F) FREQUENCY DISTRIBUTIONS OF PERCENTAGES OF TOTAL PROFIT TO TOTAL CAPITAL, INDIVIDUAL CORPORATIONS, 1924–28. MAJOR GROUP 15: MINING

	1924 PERCENTAGE IN EACH CLASS	1924 ACCUMULATED BY SUCCESSIVE CLASSES	1925 PERCENTAGE IN EACH CLASS	1925 ACCUMULATED BY SUCCESSIVE CLASSES	1926 PERCENTAGE IN EACH CLASS	1926 ACCUMULATED BY SUCCESSIVE CLASSES	1927 PERCENTAGE IN EACH CLASS	1927 ACCUMULATED BY SUCCESSIVE CLASSES	1928 PERCENTAGE IN EACH CLASS	1928 ACCUMULATED BY SUCCESSIVE CLASSES
Under zero	6.8	6.8	6.8	6.8	5.7	5.7	11.4	11.4	3.4	3.4
Zero to 4	18.2	25.0	13.6	20.4	14.8	20.5	13.6	25.0	22.7	26.1
5 to 9	27.3	52.3	22.7	43.1	21.6	42.1	22.7	47.7	21.6	47.7

TABLE 58 (*continued*)

(F) FREQUENCY DISTRIBUTIONS OF PERCENTAGES OF TOTAL PROFIT TO TOTAL CAPITAL, INDIVIDUAL CORPORATIONS, 1924–28. MAJOR GROUP 15: MINING

PERCENTAGE PROFIT TO TOTAL CAPITAL	1924 PERCENTAGE IN EACH CLASS	1924 ACCUMULATED BY SUCCESSIVE CLASSES	1925 PERCENTAGE IN EACH CLASS	1925 ACCUMULATED BY SUCCESSIVE CLASSES	1926 PERCENTAGE IN EACH CLASS	1926 ACCUMULATED BY SUCCESSIVE CLASSES	1927 PERCENTAGE IN EACH CLASS	1927 ACCUMULATED BY SUCCESSIVE CLASSES	1928 PERCENTAGE IN EACH CLASS	1928 ACCUMULATED BY SUCCESSIVE CLASSES
10 to 14	19.3	71.6	21.6	64.7	18.2	60.3	15.9	63.6	21.6	69.3
15 to 19	13.6	85.2	13.6	78.3	13.6	73.9	15.9	79.5	18.2	87.5
20 to 24	9.1	94.3	10.2	88.5	10.2	84.1	8.0	87.5	6.8	94.3
25 to 29	4.6	98.9	2.3	90.8	10.2	94.3	6.8	94.3	4.6	98.9
30 and over	1.1	100.0	9.2	100.0	5.7	100.0	5.7	100.0	1.1	100.0

CHAPTER 26

FINANCE AND ITS MINOR GROUPS

1. THE FINANCE GROUP AS A WHOLE

THE industrial division, Finance, may be regarded as one major group in the terminology which we have been employing. Included in it are all financial activities, such as commercial banking, trust companies, with the important exception of life insurance companies. The Finance group therefore differs from other divisions and major groups which have been considered in preceding chapters. In Textiles, or in Retail Trade, for example, *all* textile manufacturing activities or *all* retail trading activities were represented, whereas in Finance no life insurance activity whatever is included. Other forms of insurance, however, such as casualty or fire, appear in the Miscellaneous Finance category.

The 346 identical Financial corporations for which we have continuous data from 1919 through 1928 possessed an aggregate capitalization of over a billion dollars in 1919 and almost three billion dollars in 1928. No measure of the total volume of business which they carry on is as readily available as in the case of Manufacturing or Trading groups, where sales figures afford an accurate index of operating volume. However, a provisional index of the amount of activity is to be had in the figures for *total gross income*. This may be defined as the sum of three categories: (1) gross profit from sales or turnover (or services billed as would be sales in a manufacturing or trading business); (2) gross profits from other operations; (3) such other gross or net items of income as are not included in the first two categories (that is, all non-operating income), with the exception of interest receipts upon tax-exempt securities. Because of the varied character of the services provided by different financial groups, for example, a brokerage house as compared with a savings bank, the absolute significance of this gross income figure is not so consistent a concept as is the sales figure in the case of manufacturing or trading enterprises. Assuming that there has been no very great *change* in accounting practices in the one financial field or the other during the period under examination, however, year-to-year comparisons of the amount of gross income—or in the percentages of net to gross—are not necessarily invalidated because of the varying significance of the term as between different types of financial enterprise. With these qualifications in mind, it may be stated that the total gross income of the 346 corporations of the Finance group in 1919 was somewhat over half a billion dollars, as compared with the investment figure of something over a billion above cited, while in 1928 the gross income was a little over one billion dollars as compared with an investment of approximately three billion. So much for the character of the major group and the absolute magnitudes of the sample involved.[1]

Upon gross income, net earnings run between about 25 and 32 per cent a year, except in 1921 when the rate fell to 20 per cent. Chart 59 shows these rates plotted upon both natural and semi-logarithmic (ratio) scales. Since the year-to-year fluctuations occur about a much higher absolute level than was the case with the data for the return upon sales in Manufacturing and Trading groups which we considered in previous chapters, the ratio scale serves some purposes of analysis better than does the simpler diagram.

Upon investment, the return is much lower, running around 10 or 11 per cent in all years since 1923. The rates for all ten years are plotted in Chart 59, again upon both types of scale.

Total gross income, net income, and investment all show general and rather steady growth over the period. Gross income fell off by about only 3 per cent between 1920 and 1921 and by 6 per cent from 1921 to 1922. Net income, however, declined by about 30 per cent between 1920 and 1921.

Between 1922 and the end of the period, gross income grew from 661 million to over a billion dollars; investment, from about one and one-half to three billion; net income from 200 to 300 million.

It is to be noted that the rate of return upon investment showed no general upswing during the last few years of the period. This is interesting in view of the widespread impression that the financial

[1] For the discussion of the relative magnitude of the sample, see Ch. 43.

FINANCE GROUPS [339]

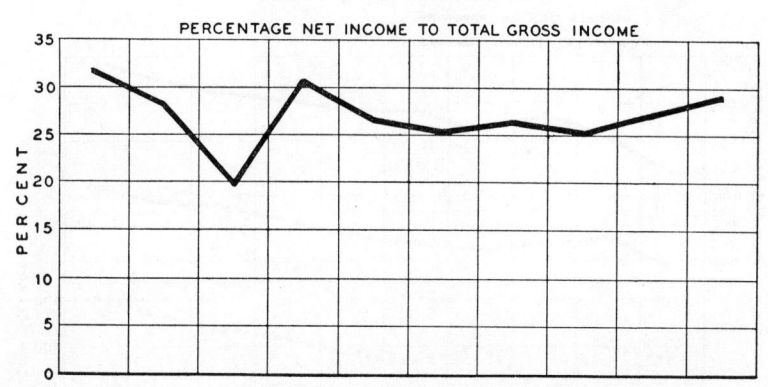

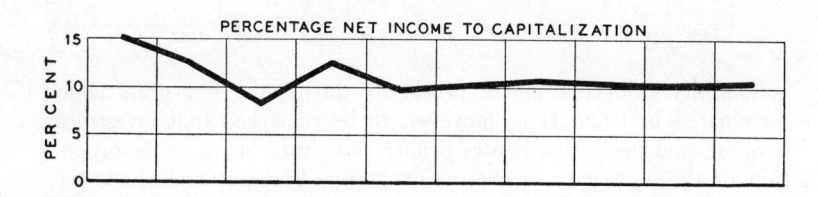

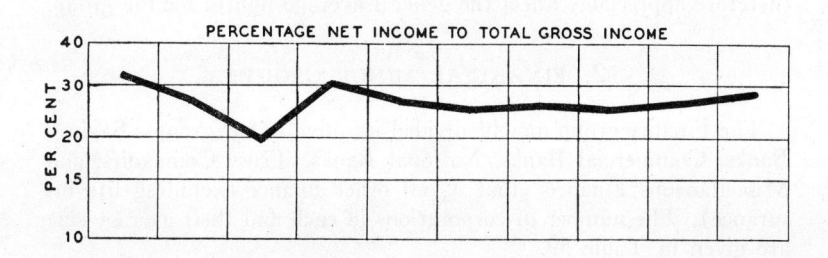

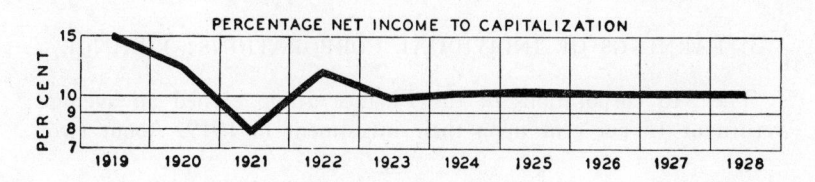

CHART 59
IDENTICAL CORPORATIONS SERIES, 1919-28
MAJOR GROUP 16: FINANCE

PERCENTAGE NET INCOME TO TOTAL GROSS INCOME

PERCENTAGE NET INCOME TO CAPITALIZATION

PERCENTAGE NET INCOME TO TOTAL GROSS INCOME

PERCENTAGE NET INCOME TO CAPITALIZATION

CHART 59 (CONT.)
IDENTICAL CORPORATIONS SERIES, 1919-28
MAJOR GROUP 16: FINANCE

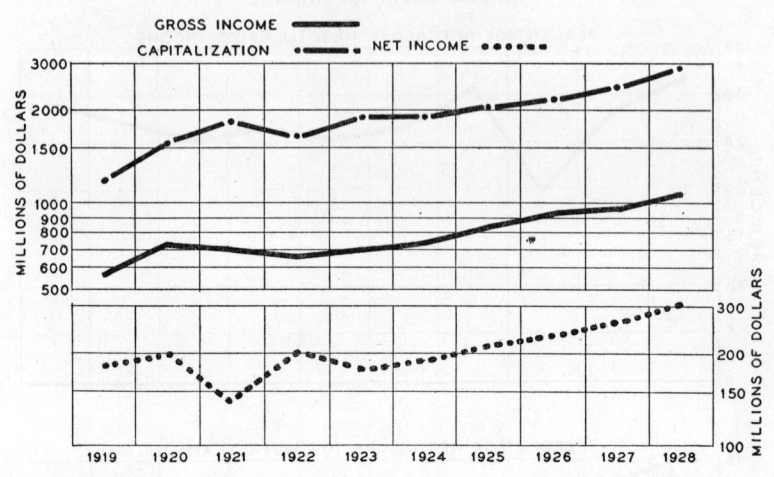

community enjoyed rampant prosperity during the few years which terminated in 1929. It is, however, to be remarked that investment banking and brokerage houses proper constitute but a small proportion of the aggregate of the major group, Finance, and the exceptional earnings which they enjoyed in such a year as 1928 does not therefore appreciably affect the general average figures for the group.

2. FINANCIAL MINOR GROUPS

The Finance group may be divided into five minor groups: Savings Banks, Commercial Banks, National Banks, Trust Companies, and Miscellaneous Finance (that is, all other finance excluding life insurance). The number of corporations in each and their average size are given in Table 59.

3. EARNINGS OF INDIVIDUAL CORPORATIONS: FINANCE

The 346 corporations of the Finance group earned an average return of 15 per cent upon their investment in 1919. About two-

FINANCE GROUPS [341]

CHART 60

FREQUENCY DISTRIBUTION OF EARNINGS RATES,
INDIVIDUAL COMPANIES (IDENTICAL CORPORATIONS SERIES)

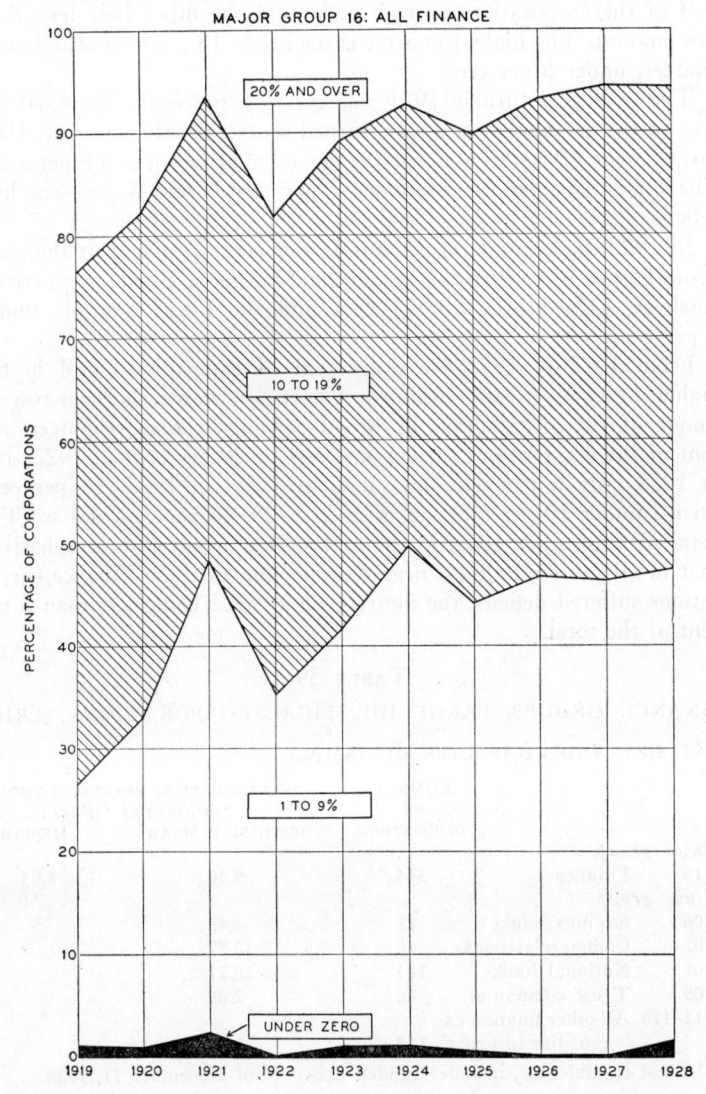

MAJOR GROUP 16: ALL FINANCE

fifths, however, earned more than the average figure. The highest fourth earned over 20 per cent; the lowest fourth, under 8 per cent.

In 1920, the general average rate was 13 per cent. Approximately half of the corporations earned more, and the other half less, than this amount. The highest quarter earned over 18 per cent; the lowest quarter, under 8 per cent.

The average return in 1921 was cut to 8 per cent. About 70 per cent of the companies, however, earned more than this amount. Half earned over 10 per cent; and the upper quarter, over 14 per cent. The lowest quarter earned under 7 per cent. Only 3 per cent had deficits.

In 1922 the average return was 12 per cent. Just half of the companies earned more than this amount and half less. The upper quarter, however, earned over 18 per cent and the lower quarter, under 8 per cent.

From 1922 to 1928 the proportion of companies found in the higher brackets greatly declined. Chart 60 shows the year-to-year course of this distribution by broad earnings classes. Eighteen per cent of the corporations earned in excess of 20 per cent in 1922; but in 1928 only 6 per cent did so. Conversely, in 1922, 35 per cent earned under 10 per cent; whereas in 1928, 48 per cent did so. The detailed figures are given in the tables. It is again to be emphasized that in all years an almost negligible portion of these Finance corporations suffered deficits, the figure even in 1921 being less than 3 per cent of the total.

TABLE 59

FINANCE GROUPS, LARGE IDENTICAL CORPORATIONS SERIES

(A) SIZE AND CHARACTER OF SAMPLE

		NUMBER OF CORPORATIONS	AVERAGE CAPITAL PER CORPORATION [1] (millions of dollars) ARITHMETIC MEAN	MEDIAN
Major group				
16	Finance	346	9.30	3.05
Minor group				
106	Savings banks	18	4.46	
107	Commercial banks	30	12.77	
108	National banks	105	10.21	
109	Trust companies	56	7.60	
111–110	All other finance, except life insurance	137	9.18	

[1] Total capital (i.e., includes funded debt) as of December 31, 1928.

FINANCE GROUPS [343]

TABLE 59 (*continued*)

(B) PERCENTAGE NET INCOME TO TOTAL GROSS INCOME

		1919	1920	1921	1922	1923	1924	1925	1926	1927	1928	1919–28[1]
Major group												
16	Finance	31.5	27.7	19.9	30.3	26.5	25.7	26.3	25.3	26.9	28.6	26.8
Minor group												
106	Savings banks	29.6	27.2	22.9	32.2	26.7	23.8	26.8	26.5	20.8	25.6	25.8
107	Commercial banks	35.1	26.6	23.1	30.7	32.5	26.2	26.0	19.8	29.2	28.1	27.3
108	National banks	39.9	37.1	24.0	37.2	34.4	30.4	28.9	30.6	28.6	30.1	31.8
109	Trust companies	26.6	28.3	16.6	25.7	21.8	26.9	29.1	25.5	29.8	31.0	26.4
111–110	All other finance, except life insurance	25.1	18.7	16.4	26.6	21.4	22.4	23.7	22.7	24.5	27.0	23.1

(C) PERCENTAGE INCOME TO CAPITALIZATION

		1919	1920	1921	1922	1923	1924	1925	1926	1927	1928	1919–28[1]
Major group												
16	Finance	15.0	12.6	7.8	12.2	9.8	10.2	10.8	10.4	10.2	10.4	10.7
Minor group												
106	Savings banks	11.9	14.0	11.4	16.3	13.3	12.0	13.4	13.3	9.8	11.2	12.5
107	Commercial banks	19.5	15.3	11.6	13.5	14.0	11.2	11.6	7.9	9.9	8.1	10.8
108	National banks	17.7	16.7	9.0	12.1	9.9	9.2	9.1	9.7	9.1	9.4	10.7
109	Trust companies	16.0	13.8	7.2	9.3	7.6	9.8	10.6	10.0	11.9	10.9	10.5
111–110	All other finance, except life insurance	11.7	8.0	6.0	12.9	9.6	11.0	12.2	11.6	11.0	11.9	10.6

[1] Ten-year aggregate.

TABLE 59 *(continued)*

(D) PERCENTAGE PROFIT TO TOTAL CAPITAL

		1924	1925	1926	1927	1928
Major group						
16	Finance	9.9	10.3	10.1	10.0	9.9
Minor group						
106	Savings banks	11.9	13.4	13.2	9.8	11.2
107	Commercial banks	11.1	11.5	7.8	9.9	8.1
108	National banks	9.2	9.1	9.7	9.1	9.4
109	Trust companeis	9.8	10.5	10.0	11.9	10.9
111–110	All other finance, except life insurance	10.2	10.8	10.9	10.3	10.4

TABLE 59 (continued)

(E) FREQUENCY DISTRIBUTIONS OF PERCENTAGES OF TOTAL NET INCOME TO CAPITALIZATION, INDIVIDUAL CORPORATIONS, 1919–23. MAJOR GROUP 16: FINANCE

PERCENTAGE INCOME TO CAPITALIZATION	1919 PERCENTAGE IN EACH CLASS	1919 ACCUMULATED BY SUCCESSIVE CLASSES	1920 PERCENTAGE IN EACH CLASS	1920 ACCUMULATED BY SUCCESSIVE CLASSES	1921 PERCENTAGE IN EACH CLASS	1921 ACCUMULATED BY SUCCESSIVE CLASSES	1922 PERCENTAGE IN EACH CLASS	1922 ACCUMULATED BY SUCCESSIVE CLASSES	1923 PERCENTAGE IN EACH CLASS	1923 ACCUMULATED BY SUCCESSIVE CLASSES
Under zero	1.2	1.2	0.9	0.9	2.6	2.6	0.3	0.3	1.2	1.2
Zero to 4	6.1	7.3	8.1	9.0	6.9	9.5	5.5	5.8	4.3	5.5
5 to 9	19.4	26.7	24.0	33.0	39.0	48.5	29.5	35.3	36.4	41.9
10 to 14	32.6	59.3	26.9	59.9	32.6	81.1	31.8	67.1	35.8	77.7
15 to 19	17.3	76.6	22.3	82.2	12.4	93.5	14.7	81.8	11.6	89.3
20 to 24	10.7	87.3	9.2	91.4	4.1	97.6	8.4	90.2	4.3	93.6
25 to 29	3.2	90.5	4.9	96.3	0.9	98.5	2.9	93.1	1.7	95.3
30 and over	9.5	100.0	3.7	100.0	1.5	100.0	6.9	100.0	4.7	100.0

(F) FREQUENCY DISTRIBUTIONS OF PERCENTAGES OF TOTAL PROFIT TO TOTAL CAPITAL, INDIVIDUAL CORPORATIONS, 1924–28. MAJOR GROUP 16: FINANCE

	1924 PERCENTAGE IN EACH CLASS	1924 ACCUMULATED BY SUCCESSIVE CLASSES	1925 PERCENTAGE IN EACH CLASS	1925 ACCUMULATED BY SUCCESSIVE CLASSES	1926 PERCENTAGE IN EACH CLASS	1926 ACCUMULATED BY SUCCESSIVE CLASSES	1927 PERCENTAGE IN EACH CLASS	1927 ACCUMULATED BY SUCCESSIVE CLASSES	1928 PERCENTAGE IN EACH CLASS	1928 ACCUMULATED BY SUCCESSIVE CLASSES
Under zero	1.2	1.2	0.6	0.6	0.3	0.3	0.3	0.3	1.7	1.7
Zero to 4	6.6	7.8	6.4	7.0	5.8	6.1	8.1	8.4	7.2	8.9
5 to 9	41.9	49.7	37.3	44.3	40.7	46.8	38.1	46.5	38.7	47.6
10 to 14	30.6	80.3	35.0	79.3	37.0	83.8	37.3	83.8	37.3	84.9
15 to 19	12.4	92.7	10.4	89.7	9.3	93.1	10.7	94.5	9.5	94.4
20 to 24	3.2	95.9	4.3	94.0	2.0	95.1	3.2	97.7	2.7	97.1
25 to 29	1.2	97.1	2.3	96.3	2.3	97.4	0.3	98.0	0.9	98.0
30 and over	2.9	100.0	3.7	100.0	2.6	100.0	2.0	100.0	2.0	100.0

Book III
Earnings of Small Corporations

Chapter 27

INTRODUCTION

LIKE several chapters of Book II, the succeeding chapters of Book III present detailed information on the earnings rates of corporations engaged in various branches of Manufacture and Trade. But unlike those of Book II, the present chapters contain data for no series of identical corporations, that is, the sample does not contain exactly the same companies from year to year. Furthermore, the non-identical corporations about to be discussed are small enterprises compared with those belonging to the series already analyzed. In 1928 the average (arithmetic mean) size of the corporations in All Manufacture for the large corporations series discussed above is $13,500,000 whereas for the small corporations to be presented, the average size of capital is only $171,000.[1] About nine-tenths of the corporations with net incomes in the large corporations series have incomes of over $50,000, whereas nearly 90 per cent of those in the small corporations series have incomes under $50,000.

These smaller corporations are termed 'non-identical' not because there is no repetition whatever of the same companies from year to year, but because the extent of such repetition is uncertain. The samples in the several Manufacturing minor groups vary considerably in size from year to year. In a very few instances there are less than 20 corporations in a minor group in any one year; in other instances there are as many as 100. Most of the minor groups, in most years, contain between 25 and 50 companies each; but in any

---

[1] The median figure for total capital in 1928 for the large corporations is $1,972,222, while for the small corporations, it is probably under $200,000. The mean and median capitals in each major group, for the small corporations of this Book, are given in the tables at the close of each chapter. Corresponding data for the large corporations series have already been presented in the tables at the ends of the several chapters of Book II.

one group the number of companies might, for example, be 30 in one year and 40 or 45 in another.

Since no small corporations series for either Mining or Finance are available, our analysis is limited to the Manufacture and Trade divisions.

A second important distinction between the data of the present chapters and those of Book II is that these samples of non-identical corporations contain only companies with net incomes; that is to say, these small corporations, while varying in their rates of earnings, include in no year any enterprises that suffered deficits. The data therefore do not show average rates of earnings for 'small corporations in general' but only for 'small corporations that earn profits'.

When comparisons are sought, in any minor group, between the arithmetic mean figures for these small corporations and the larger corporations of the preceding series, it is thus to be borne in mind that the arithmetic average earnings rates of the minor groups include only corporations with net incomes in one case and corporations with both net incomes and negative incomes in the other case. For the years 1922–29, however, the inclusion of some corporations with negative incomes in the large corporations series is not, in most instances, at all serious because of the relatively slight number and extent of such deficits. It will be recalled that in the large corporations series for All Manufacture the number of corporations with deficits between 1922 and 1928 amounted to little more than 3 per cent in any one year.[2]

In the several major groups, data for median earnings are available —or more precisely, the rate of net income earned by the median corporation in the major group. These medians are used in preference to general averages (arithmetic means) in the analysis of major groups; and whenever major group figures for the small corporations are compared—in charts or discussion—with those for the large corporations, *the data for the latter are recast so as to exclude corporations with deficits from that series.*[3] The median figures, as well as the complete frequency distributions of the earnings of individual

---

[2] In most years the figure was less than this; in only one year, 1928, was it as high as 3.7 per cent.

[3] This can be done in the computation of the medians, by major groups, but not in that of arithmetic means by minor groups. Frequency distributions for the earnings rates of individual corporations by minor groups are available for neither sample.

corporations, for the two series are therefore directly comparable.[4]

The general plan of the chapters is the same as that of Book II, save that no chapters for Mining or Finance are included. It is not, however, possible to present detailed data for as many minor groups as in the case of the large corporations series of Book II because in some minor groups the corporations were too few either to afford significant samples or to conceal the identity of the individual corporations. In either case the group is not shown separately, but the corporations that belonged to it nevertheless are carried in the major group data.

But a further distinction now needs to be drawn between the data of the several major groups and those of the minor groups contained in this Book. In Book II the large corporations constituting each minor group, when aggregated, directly made up the respective major groups, that is, the total of any set of figures for the minor groups gave the major group figure. In Book III, however, this is not always necessarily so. In some sets of minor groups it has been found possible to provide a more complete coverage, and frequently a better series of minor group samples, by showing, for certain minor groups, data from samples that were originally drawn independently of the major groups under which they fall. In other words, any one minor group here is to be regarded as a sample in itself—some more adequate than others, but all of them together not comprising a typical major group sample.[5] The various frequency distributions of earnings rates for the several major groups, however, are constructed in the same manner as those of Book II, that is, are samples containing as well rounded a representation of the various minor groups as in the earlier cases.

The description of the component activities of each minor group, for example, such statements as "the Bakery group includes such products as bread, ice cream cones, pie and cakes", are omitted in these chapters. The general descriptions of all minor groups correspond with those given under the same headings in the various chapters of Book II, and since the captions are given in the same

[4] For qualifications concerning the character of the two sets of samples in other respects, however, see Ch. 43.

[5] That is to say, both to obtain better minor group samples and to avoid burying as many minor groups under 'Miscellaneous' as would otherwise have been necessary, resort has been had to separate 'sub-code' samples of the sort explained more fully in Ch. 44, sec. 2.

order here as there, the previously presented statements may readily be consulted when desired.

The use of terms is in general the same as in Book II, and the reader who has not already done so is asked to read the introductory chapter of that Book.

No absolute data upon sales, investment and net income are presented in Book III, because the corporations are non-identical and the samples vary too greatly in size from year to year. The reader who wishes to investigate the character of the samples more closely may, however, find all of the absolute data in the *Source-Book*.

CHAPTER 28

MANUFACTURE AND ITS MAJOR GROUPS

1. ALL MANUFACTURE: EARNINGS ON SALES

THE small manufacturing corporations sample contains approximately 1,500 corporations in each year of the period 1919–28.[1] As remarked in the preceding chapter, not all of the corporations contained in the series are identical from year to year, nor are any companies with deficits included.

The percentage of net income to sales earned by these small Manufacturing corporations is shown in Chart 61. The rate is quite stable, and during the last half of the period varies only between 5.5 and 5.7 per cent. It is, however, to be remarked that this is just a general average rate and that many of the groups contributing to it show quite different figures.

With these percentages for the average return on sales received by these small Manufacturing corporations are plotted in Chart 61 the earnings on sales volume for the large Manufacturing corporations series discussed in preceding chapters. These data are shown only from 1922 on because in all years they contain figures for a few corporations with deficits. The proportion of such corporations is almost negligible between 1922 and 1928; but this is not so in 1921, hence the exclusion of figures for the first few years.

It is to be observed that the return on sales for the large corporations series runs very much higher than that for the small corporations, being roughly 8 to 10 per cent in nearly all years as compared with 5.5 to 7 per cent for the small companies. The inclusion, in the

[1] The exact number in each year is: 1919, 1,562; 1920, 1,487; 1921, 1,539; 1922, 1,440; 1923, 1,545; 1924, 1,560; 1925, 1,461; 1926, 1,468; 1927, 1,665; 1928, 1,421.

large corporations series, of some companies with deficits accentuates this difference, for otherwise the large corporations series figures would be somewhat higher.

This discrepancy between the figures for the two series in terms of their return on sales is not, however, characteristic of the two sets of figures in terms of the return upon investment. Full treatment of

CHART 61

PERCENTAGE NET INCOME TO SALES
ALL MANUFACTURE

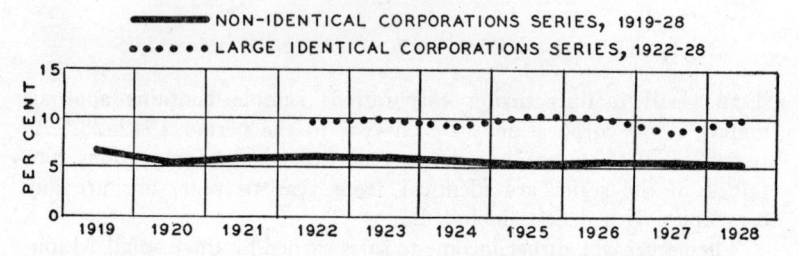

— NON-IDENTICAL CORPORATIONS SERIES, 1919-28
• • • • • LARGE IDENTICAL CORPORATIONS SERIES, 1922-28

this return is reserved for a later section; but it may here be noted that, whether general arithmetic mean figures or medians of the sort to be presented later are taken, the large corporations series shows no markedly higher return upon investment than does the small corporations series. The great difference in the rates of return on sales that exists is therefore to be attributed to a very much higher average turnover of capital on the part of the smaller corporations. The annual capital turnover figures [2] for the years 1924–28 for the two series are given below.

Years	Large corporations	Small corporations
1924	1.0	1.8
1925	1.1	1.9
1926	1.1	2.0
1927	1.0	1.9
1928	1.0	2.0

[2] Total capital divided into sales as explained in Ch. 4. The figures used here are for all the companies in the large corporations series, i.e., those with deficits as well as those with net incomes.

MANUFACTURE: SMALL CORPORATIONS [355]

2. SURVEY OF MANUFACTURING GROUPS: EARNINGS ON SALES

We may now divide All Manufacture into 11 major groups just as has been done in previous chapters and examine the net return upon sales in each group as shown in Table 60. The treatment of the return upon investment is reserved for a later section since the character of the data makes it desirable to employ a different type of analysis.

a. Foods

The return on sales runs between 3 and 4 per cent in all years. In six of the ten years it stands somewhat lower than in the case of the large corporations series.

b. Textiles

Earnings on sales run between 4 and 7 per cent during the first half of the period and between 4 and 5 per cent during the last half. In all years the return is substantially lower than for the large corporations series.

c. Leather

The return on sales runs from 4 to 6 per cent during the first half of the period and between 4 and 5 per cent during the last half. It stands well below the level of the large corporations series.

d. Rubber

The return on sales rises from about 5 per cent in 1919 to 6 per cent in 1922. During the last half of the period it also shows a general increase, rising from 4 per cent in 1924 to 8 per cent in 1928. For reasons given previously, no comparison with the large corporations series is attempted in this group.

e. Lumber

The return on sales fluctuates between 6 and 8 per cent in most years. It stands consistently below that for the large corporations series, but does not exhibit the generally falling trend of the latter between 1923 and 1928.

f. Paper

The return on sales fluctuates from 5 to 8 per cent, standing at about 5 or 6 per cent in most years. It is below that for the large corporations series in nine years.

g. Printing

Earnings upon sales vary only between 9 and 11 per cent from 1919 through 1926; but in 1927 and 1928, stand at 8 and 7 per cent respectively. In all years these ratios are far below those for the large corporations series.

h. Chemicals

The return on sales runs between 6 and 9 per cent over the period. It stands at a lower level than that for the large corporations series, but shows far less fluctuation.

i. Stone, Clay and Glass

Earnings upon sales fluctuate between 7 and 11 per cent during the first half of the period but stand at 9 per cent throughout the last half, except in 1928 when they fall to 7 per cent. In all years the figure is much lower than that for the large corporations series.

j. Metals

The return on sales varies between 6 and 8 per cent throughout the period. It is consistently lower than that for the large corporations series.

k. Special Manufacturing Industries

The return on sales fluctuates between 6 and 8 per cent. In all years it is below the level for the large corporations series.

3. ALL MANUFACTURE: EARNINGS ON INVESTMENT

In analyzing the return upon investment received by the small corporations series as a whole we may make use both of the general average (arithmetic mean) figures and the median returns derived from the frequency distributions for the earnings of individual corporations presented in a later section. In both, these data may be com-

MANUFACTURE: SMALL CORPORATIONS [357]

pared directly with those for the large corporations series for the entire period, it here being possible to exclude in each year those large corporations which did not earn net incomes.

The arithmetic mean return upon investment for the small corporations series is shown in Chart 62. Comparable data for the large

CHART 62
ARITHMETIC MEAN PERCENTAGE NET INCOME TO CAPITALIZATION
ALL MANUFACTURE

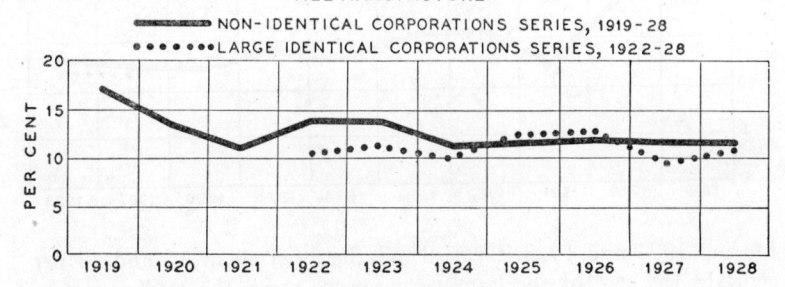

— NON-IDENTICAL CORPORATIONS SERIES, 1919-28
• • • • LARGE IDENTICAL CORPORATIONS SERIES, 1922-28

corporations series are also shown in Chart 62, from 1922 on. It will be noted that from 1924 to 1928 the large corporations series evidences greater fluctuation in the rate of earnings than does the small corporations series, although the two figures are never very far apart. It is of interest to observe that in the aggregate the business recession of 1927 was felt to an appreciable extent by the large corporations but not at all by the small corporations, that is, so far as general average figures for the rate of earnings upon investment go.[3]

We have, however, available for comparison with these data the earnings rates of the median corporations in the case of each series, the data for the large corporations series again being computed for the companies with net incomes only. These figures are shown in Chart 63. The median return upon investment for the small corporations fell from about 20 per cent in 1919 to 13 per cent in 1921. It recovered to 16 per cent in 1922 but declined to 13 per cent by 1924.

[3] This is not, however, true of the median rates of return, as will appear in a moment.

CHART 63
MEDIAN EARNINGS RATES
ALL MANUFACTURE
── NON-IDENTICAL CORPORATIONS SERIES, 1919-28
••••• LARGE IDENTICAL CORPORATIONS SERIES, 1919-28

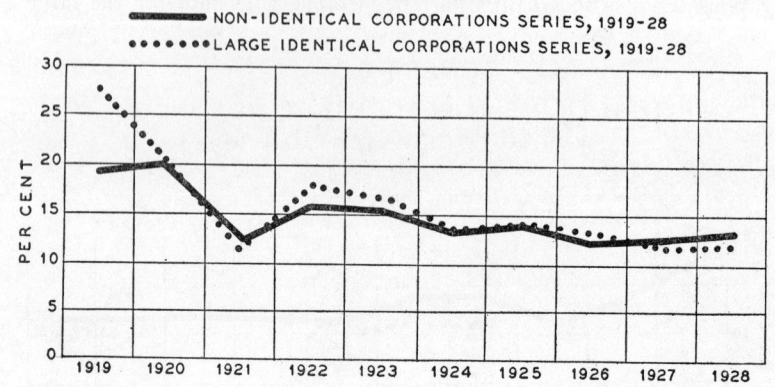

During 1924 and 1928 it varied only between about 13 and 14 per cent. In the case of the large corporations series the median return showed a far greater drop between 1919 and 1921, falling from 28 to 12 per cent. It then increased to 18 per cent in 1922 but declined to 13.5 per cent in 1924. During the five years from 1923 to 1928 the median return for the large corporations followed very closely that for the small corporations, the 1928 figure being 12.1 per cent for the one series and 13.4 per cent for the other.

In both series a substantial difference between the arithmetic mean and the median figures prevails during the first half of the period, the medians being markedly higher in every year. But these discrepancies are narrowed after 1923. During the last part of the period the difference between the two figures is not significant in the large corporations series; but for the small corporations the medians are somewhat greater than the means.

4. SURVEY OF THE MAJOR MANUFACTURING GROUPS: EARNINGS ON INVESTMENT

Our analysis of the return upon investment for the small corporations in the Food group as well as in the other major groups which are treated in this section can best be undertaken, as already explained, in terms of the median corporation's earnings rate instead of the group's arithmetic mean return which we customarily have had in mind in speaking of 'the general average'. In referring to the large corporations series for comparison, medians are also used, these being made directly comparable with those for the small corporations series by calculating them for the large corporations with net incomes only.

a. Foods

The return on investment in the Food group declines from 19 per cent in 1919 to 15 per cent in 1921. It varies between 14 and 16 per cent in the years 1922–25 and then falls to about 13 per cent for the remainder of the period. These rates roughly coincide with those for the large corporations series except in 1919 and 1922, when those for the latter stand substantially higher.

b. Textiles

Earnings upon investment in the Textile group decline from 22 per cent in 1919 to 15 per cent in 1920. Between 1920 and 1923 they fluctuate closely about 15 per cent. During the last half of the period earnings fluctuate about a somewhat lower level, varying from 12 to 14 per cent. The return for the large corporations series stands higher in some years and lower in others, and evidences both greater fluctuation and a sharper general decline over the period.

c. Leather

In this group, the return on investment declines from 22 per cent in 1919 to 13 per cent in 1920; then fluctuates between 10 and 17 per cent during the remainder of the period. In several years it stands lower, in others higher, than that for the large corporations series, but during the last three years of the period the two practically coincide.

d. Rubber

The return on investment in this group declines from 25 per cent in 1919 to 10 per cent in 1920. It recovers slightly in 1921 and then falls to 8 per cent in 1922. It rises to 16 per cent in 1923 and then fluctuates widely from this level during the remainder of the period, standing at 10 per cent in 1927 and 21 per cent in 1928. The figures are not greatly different from those for the large corporations series, save in 1922 when the return is much lower, and in 1928 when it is far higher. Again the reader is to be reminded that in both the small corporations and the large corporations series, the Rubber group sample consists of a small number of companies.

e. Lumber

The return on investment declines from about 20 per cent in 1919 and 1920 to 13 per cent in 1921; then recovers to 18 per cent in 1923. Between 1923 and 1928, however, it shows a general decline, falling from 18 to 13 per cent. In most years the curve follows that for the large corporations series quite closely.

f. Paper

Earnings on investment in this group fall from 24 per cent in 1920 to 13 per cent in 1921; then oscillate between 9 and 16 per cent for the remainder of the period. Broadly speaking, the rates of return are not greatly different from those for the large corporations series, but less fluctuation is shown during the first part of the period and more during the last part.

g. Printing

In this group earnings on investment decline from 25 per cent in 1920 to 17 per cent in 1921 and 16 per cent in 1922. Between 1922 and the end of the period they run from 13 to 16 per cent. In most years these rates stand somewhat lower than those for the large corporations series.

h. Chemicals

Earnings on investment in this group decline from 19 per cent in 1919 to 13 per cent in 1921. They then recover to 16 per cent in 1922 and fluctuate between 13 and 16 per cent for the remainder of the period. During the first half of the period these rates are below for three years and above for two years those for the large corporations series, but during the last half the two nearly coincide.

i. Stone, Clay and Glass

In this group the return upon investment declines from 18 per cent in 1919 to 12 per cent in 1921, then recovers to 16 per cent

MANUFACTURE: SMALL CORPORATIONS [361]

in 1923. From 1923 to 1928, it shows a gradual decline, falling to 12 per cent by the end of the period. In most years the return is below that for the large corporations series, although in 1928 scarcely any difference prevails.

j. Metals

In this group the return on investment declines from 17 per cent in 1919 to 11 per cent in 1921; then recovers to 16 per cent by 1923. During the last half of the period, it fluctuates between 12 and 14 per cent. In all years other than 1919 and 1920, these rates are virtually identical with those for the large corporations series.

k. Special Manufacturing Industries

The return on investment in this group declines from 21 per cent in 1919 to 14 per cent in 1921. It then rises to 19 per cent in 1922 and declines to 14 per cent in 1923. During the last half of the period it fluctuates between 12 and 16 per cent. These rates of return are sometimes somewhat above, and sometimes somewhat below, those for the large corporations series.

5. ALL MANUFACTURE: EARNINGS OF INDIVIDUAL CORPORATIONS

The small manufacturing corporations series may now be analyzed in terms of the earnings of its individual corporations upon their invested capitals in the several years from 1919 through 1928. The term 'general average' will here be used in the sense of the arithmetic mean return, with which the range of individual corporations' earnings may be compared.

In 1919, the general average rate of return was 17 per cent. About three-fifths of all the corporations, however, earned more than this amount; about half earned over 20 per cent; the upper quarter earned over 31 per cent, while the lowest quarter earned under 12 per cent.

In 1920, the average return was 14 per cent. Nearly two-thirds of the companies, however, earned more than this amount; the highest quarter earned over 29 per cent and the lowest quarter, under 10 per cent.

The year 1921 saw the general average reduced to 11 per cent, but again nearly two-thirds of the corporations earned in excess of

CHART 64

FREQUENCY DISTRIBUTION OF EARNINGS RATES, INDIVIDUAL COMPANIES
ALL MANUFACTURE
—— NON-IDENTICAL CORPORATIONS
---- IDENTICAL CORPORATIONS

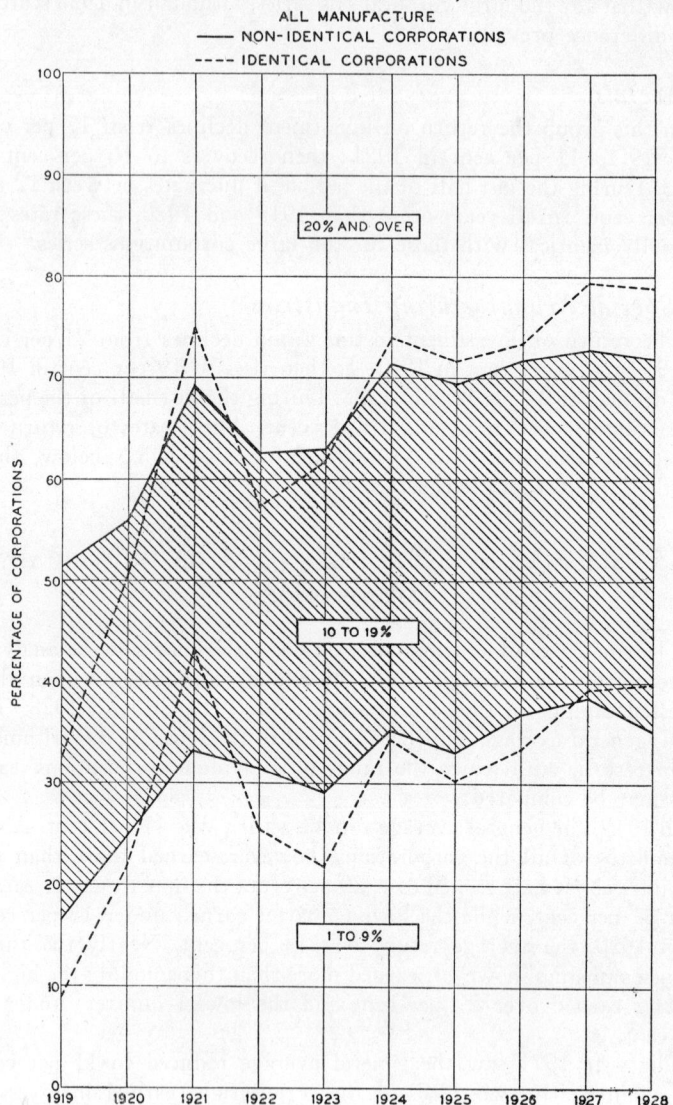

MANUFACTURE: SMALL CORPORATIONS [363]

this rate. The highest quarter earned over 23 per cent; the lowest quarter, under 8 per cent.

Between 1922 and 1928 a general decline took place in the number of corporations occupying the higher earnings rates brackets. In 1922, more than a third earned over 20 per cent upon their invested capitals, but in 1928 less than a third did so. Conversely, in 1922, just under a third earned under 10 per cent, whereas in 1928, just over a third did so. The year-to-year course of the distribution by broad classes of earnings rates is shown in Chart 64, while detailed data are given in the tables.

TABLE 60

MANUFACTURING AND ITS MAJOR GROUPS, SMALL NON-IDENTICAL CORPORATIONS SERIES

(A) SIZE AND CHARACTER OF SAMPLE

	\multicolumn{10}{c}{NUMBER OF CORPORATIONS}	AVERAGE CAPITAL PER CORPORATION [1] (thousands of dollars)
	1919	1920	1921	1922	1923	1924	1925	1926	1927	1928	ARITHMETIC MEAN
All manufacturing	1562	1487	1539	1440	1545	1560	1461	1468	1665	1421	171
Major group											
1 Foods	275	222	305	231	264	293	255	258	293	220	168
2 Textiles	247	161	232	200	215	199	209	206	247	191	194
3 Leather	57	36	45	42	48	39	44	40	49	40	154
4 Rubber	12	8	11	11	9	15	13	11	12	11	139
5 Lumber	206	207	194	189	204	205	169	112	177	146	175
6 Paper	44	49	41	42	48	54	36	48	57	44	161
7 Printing and publishing	144	184	203	162	152	154	145	146	179	153	126
8 Chemicals	77	76	61	84	86	108	91	84	109	110	213
9 Stone, clay and glass	70	83	94	76	84	88	81	91	83	67	214
10 Metals	357	387	271	332	359	336	352	372	373	369	166
11 Special manufacturing industries	73	74	82	71	76	69	66	100	86	70	153

MANUFACTURE: SMALL CORPORATIONS [365]

(B) PERCENTAGE INCOME TO SALES

	1919	1920	1921	1922	1923	1924	1925	1926	1927	1928
All manufacturing	6.7	5.6	5.8	6.5	6.3	5.7	5.6	5.6	5.7	5.5
Major group										
1 Foods	4.0	3.1	3.8	3.7	4.1	3.8	3.6	3.7	4.2	3.6
2 Textiles	6.8	4.4	5.4	5.6	5.1	4.3	4.3	3.6	4.1	3.7
3 Leather	6.3	3.7	5.5	5.5	4.0	3.7	5.3	3.5	4.5	4.0
4 Rubber	4.5	2.1	4.6	5.6	3.9	3.5	5.9	6.8	6.0	8.3
5 Lumber	9.0	7.7	6.8	7.9	7.6	6.6	6.2	5.9	6.0	6.8
6 Paper	7.3	6.9	6.2	7.0	8.1	5.0	5.4	6.8	5.9	6.6
7 Printing and publishing	10.9	10.8	9.1	11.1	9.1	9.6	9.9	10.9	8.0	6.8
8 Chemicals	6.2	6.1	6.4	7.3	5.7	7.6	7.1	8.6	8.2	6.5
9 Stone, clay and glass	10.2	8.2	7.4	9.9	11.0	8.7	8.6	8.7	8.6	7.4
10 Metals	7.6	6.3	7.8	7.7	8.1	7.7	6.5	7.1	7.0	7.5
11 Special manufacturing industries	7.9	6.8	7.3	7.7	6.7	5.7	7.8	6.1	7.7	5.5

(C) PERCENTAGE INCOME TO CAPITALIZATION

	1919	1920	1921	1922	1923	1924	1925	1926	1927	1928
All manufacturing	16.8	13.7	10.9	13.5	13.6	11.1	11.4	11.7	11.6	11.5
Major group										
1 Foods	16.7	10.8	11.5	12.0	12.8	12.3	14.3	12.5	10.4	10.7
2 Textiles	20.0	12.5	12.6	14.5	12.8	11.0	11.5	9.6	11.7	9.8
3 Leather	23.3	9.9	12.7	17.0	11.0	14.4	18.9	9.2	14.6	11.0
4 Rubber	10.4	10.0	8.2	7.4	8.4	10.0	15.0	16.2	12.3	12.7
5 Lumber	18.2	17.0	11.0	13.8	16.8	10.4	7.9	10.7	11.0	11.6
6 Paper	19.0	23.2	11.3	16.6	13.3	6.4	8.4	13.0	10.1	14.9
7 Printing and publishing	22.1	21.1	16.2	16.3	14.4	14.2	13.2	14.4	13.2	12.3
8 Chemicals	18.4	13.9	11.4	13.0	11.8	15.6	13.3	14.0	13.3	9.8
9 Stone, clay and glass	9.0	13.3	7.4	13.9	15.0	10.1	12.7	13.2	11.6	8.8
10 Metals	14.8	12.7	10.6	12.4	14.4	10.8	10.8	11.3	11.4	13.5
11 Special manufacturing industries	16.8	13.1	6.1	15.8	10.7	10.3	13.1	11.7	13.4	12.7

TABLE 60 (*continued*)

	1919	1920	1921	1922	1923	1924	1925	1926	1927	1928
(D) PERCENTAGE PROFIT TO TOTAL CAPITAL
All manufacturing	19.6	20.1	12.5	15.9	15.5	10.8	11.1	11.4	11.3	11.3
Major group
1 Foods	19.1	16.6	15.0	15.8	14.5	12.1	13.9	12.0	10.1	10.5
2 Textiles	22.1	14.7	14.7	15.8	14.5	10.7	11.3	9.6	11.6	9.8
3 Leather	22.1	13.3	15.7	16.9	12.5	13.9	18.7	9.0	14.5	10.9
4 Rubber	25.0	10.0	12.5	7.5	16.3	9.7	14.7	16.2	12.0	12.4
5 Lumber	19.7	20.7	13.2	15.9	18.4	10.3	7.8	10.5	10.8	11.3
6 Paper	19.3	24.2	13.3	16.4	15.0	6.4	8.2	12.5	9.7	14.1
7 Printing and publishing						14.0	12.6	13.9	12.8	11.9
8 Chemicals	24.3	25.4	17.3	16.2	15.9	15.3	13.2	13.8	12.0	9.7
9 Stone, clay and glass						9.9	11.9	12.6	11.3	8.6
10 Metals	18.7	17.1	12.7	16.4	14.4	10.6	10.6	11.2	11.1	13.1
11 Special manufacturing industries						10.1	12.7	11.5	13.0	12.3
(E) MEDIAN PERCENTAGE INCOME TO CAPITALIZATION[1]
All manufacturing						13.4	14.1	12.8	12.6	13.4
Major group
1 Foods						13.5	15.8	12.4	13.1	12.9
2 Textiles						12.5	14.1	12.7	11.7	12.6
3 Leather						13.9	16.6	10.0	13.6	11.9
4 Rubber						12.5	13.9	15.6	10.0	20.8
5 Lumber						13.7	13.1	13.1	10.6	13.3
6 Paper						9.2	14.2	14.0	11.8	15.0
7 Printing and publishing						14.1	14.0	15.0	14.0	12.9
8 Chemicals						15.8	15.8	13.1	15.4	13.7

MANUFACTURE: SMALL CORPORATIONS [367]

9 Stone, clay and glass	17.7	16.3	12.4	15.0	16.0	13.9	14.9	13.4	13.6	13.8	12.5	11.6
10 Metals	17.2	16.0	11.4	14.8	16.1	12.8	13.4		13.8		12.3	13.8
11 Special manufacturing industries	21.0	19.3	14.0	18.8	14.4	13.0	13.3		12.2		16.1	15.3

[1] For 1924–28, total profit to total capital.

(F) FREQUENCY DISTRIBUTIONS OF PERCENTAGES OF TOTAL NET INCOME TO CAPITALIZATION, INDIVIDUAL CORPORATIONS, 1919–23. ALL MANUFACTURING

PERCENTAGE INCOME TO CAPITALIZATION	1919 PERCENTAGE IN EACH CLASS	1919 ACCUMULATED BY SUCCESSIVE CLASSES	1920 PERCENTAGE IN EACH CLASS	1920 ACCUMULATED BY SUCCESSIVE CLASSES	1921 PERCENTAGE IN EACH CLASS	1921 ACCUMULATED BY SUCCESSIVE CLASSES	1922 PERCENTAGE IN EACH CLASS	1922 ACCUMULATED BY SUCCESSIVE CLASSES	1923 PERCENTAGE IN EACH CLASS	1923 ACCUMULATED BY SUCCESSIVE CLASSES
Zero to 4	4.7	4.7	8.0	8.0	12.4	12.4	10.2	10.2	9.8	9.8
5 to 9	11.7	16.4	16.7	24.7	20.7	33.1	21.2	31.4	19.3	29.1
10 to 14	18.9	35.3	16.3	41.0	20.7	53.8	16.3	47.7	19.6	48.7
15 to 19	15.8	51.1	14.8	55.8	15.5	69.3	14.9	62.6	14.2	62.9
20 to 24	12.2	63.3	11.6	67.4	9.6	78.9	9.6	72.2	11.2	74.1
25 to 29	9.9	73.2	8.3	75.7	6.1	85.0	6.3	78.5	6.6	80.7
30 and over	26.8	100.0	24.3	100.0	15.0	100.0	21.5	100.0	19.3	100.0

TABLE 60 (*continued*)

(G) FREQUENCY DISTRIBUTIONS OF PERCENTAGES OF TOTAL PROFIT TO TOTAL CAPITAL, INDIVIDUAL CORPORATIONS, 1924–28. ALL MANUFACTURING

PERCENTAGE PROFIT TO TOTAL CAPITAL	1924 PERCENTAGE IN EACH CLASS	1924 ACCUMULATED BY SUCCESSIVE CLASSES	1925 PERCENTAGE IN EACH CLASS	1925 ACCUMULATED BY SUCCESSIVE CLASSES	1926 PERCENTAGE IN EACH CLASS	1926 ACCUMULATED BY SUCCESSIVE CLASSES	1927 PERCENTAGE IN EACH CLASS	1927 ACCUMULATED BY SUCCESSIVE CLASSES	1928 PERCENTAGE IN EACH CLASS	1928 ACCUMULATED BY SUCCESSIVE CLASSES
Zero to 4	12.6	12.6	9.9	9.9	12.7	12.7	14.2	14.2	13.6	13.6
5 to 9	22.6	35.2	23.1	33.0	24.2	36.9	24.3	38.5	21.6	35.2
10 to 14	22.7	57.9	20.0	53.0	20.3	57.2	21.4	59.9	22.2	57.4
15 to 19	13.4	71.3	16.4	69.4	14.6	71.8	12.9	72.8	14.5	71.9
20 to 24	10.1	81.4	11.1	80.5	10.0	81.8	8.9	81.7	9.5	81.4
25 to 29	5.2	86.6	6.4	86.9	4.9	86.7	5.5	87.2	4.6	86.0
30 and over	13.4	100.0	13.1	100.0	13.3	100.0	12.8	100.0	14.0	100.0

TABLE 61

MANUFACTURING AND ITS MAJOR GROUPS, LARGE IDENTICAL CORPORATIONS SERIES

(companies with net incomes only)

(A) MEDIAN PERCENTAGE INCOME TO CAPITALIZATION [1]

	1919	1920	1921	1922	1923	1924	1925	1926	1927	1928
All manufacturing	27.6	19.8	11.8	17.5	17.1	13.5	13.8	14.0	12.2	12.1
Major group										
1 Foods	26.4	14.4	16.8	20.0	15.0	16.0	13.8	13.8	13.3	12.6
2 Textiles	37.0	17.3	14.0	19.3	16.9	11.4	12.3	10.3	12.2	9.0
3 Leather	34.0	11.6	11.1	16.2	12.9	11.3	11.5	11.3	13.3	11.1
4 Rubber	26.0	11.6	12.0	16.6	13.3	13.0	16.4	13.3	13.9	10.7
5 Lumber	27.5	26.3	10.0	20.8	19.5	14.3	13.8	14.4	9.7	10.5
6 Paper	25.0	37.9	11.5	16.1	13.6	12.0	12.2	11.7	12.1	10.3
7 Printing and publishing	24.5	32.8	19.4	21.9	18.1	17.1	16.9	16.1	13.2	14.3
8 Chemicals	24.6	16.8	11.0	18.9	19.2	14.0	14.4	14.8	13.8	14.0
9 Stone, clay and glass	18.0	18.8	11.5	16.5	21.3	16.3	16.5	15.2	11.3	12.1
10 Metals	26.9	20.0	8.7	14.7	17.3	12.4	13.9	13.9	11.9	13.5
11 Special manufacturing industries	26.9	18.3	12.8	16.8	17.9	12.6	14.2	14.2	12.8	12.6

[1] For 1924–28, total profit to total capital.

TABLE 61 (*continued*)

(B) FREQUENCY DISTRIBUTIONS OF PERCENTAGES OF TOTAL NET INCOME TO CAPITALIZATION, INDIVIDUAL CORPORATIONS, 1919–23. ALL MANUFACTURING

PERCENTAGE INCOME TO CAPITALIZATION	1919 PERCENTAGE IN EACH CLASS	1919 ACCUMULATED BY SUCCESSIVE CLASSES	1920 PERCENTAGE IN EACH CLASS	1920 ACCUMULATED BY SUCCESSIVE CLASSES	1921 PERCENTAGE IN EACH CLASS	1921 ACCUMULATED BY SUCCESSIVE CLASSES	1922 PERCENTAGE IN EACH CLASS	1922 ACCUMULATED BY SUCCESSIVE CLASSES	1923 PERCENTAGE IN EACH CLASS	1923 ACCUMULATED BY SUCCESSIVE CLASSES
Zero to 4	2.2	2.2	7.6	7.6	19.7	19.7	9.5	9.5	6.4	6.4
5 to 9	6.6	8.8	14.2	21.8	23.4	43.1	15.9	25.4	15.4	21.8
10 to 14	11.0	19.8	14.9	36.7	18.8	61.9	17.1	42.5	19.7	41.5
15 to 19	12.7	32.5	13.8	50.5	13.0	74.9	14.6	57.1	20.4	61.9
20 to 24	12.5	45.0	10.5	61.0	8.0	82.9	11.2	68.3	13.5	75.4
25 to 29	9.5	54.5	9.0	70.0	5.3	88.2	9.5	77.8	9.5	84.9
30 and over	45.5	100.0	30.0	100.0	11.8	100.0	22.2	100.0	15.1	100.0

(C) FREQUENCY DISTRIBUTIONS OF PERCENTAGES OF TOTAL PROFIT TO TOTAL CAPITAL, INDIVIDUAL CORPORATIONS, 1924–28. ALL MANUFACTURING

	1924 PERCENTAGE IN EACH CLASS	1924 ACCUMULATED BY SUCCESSIVE CLASSES	1925 PERCENTAGE IN EACH CLASS	1925 ACCUMULATED BY SUCCESSIVE CLASSES	1926 PERCENTAGE IN EACH CLASS	1926 ACCUMULATED BY SUCCESSIVE CLASSES	1927 PERCENTAGE IN EACH CLASS	1927 ACCUMULATED BY SUCCESSIVE CLASSES	1928 PERCENTAGE IN EACH CLASS	1928 ACCUMULATED BY SUCCESSIVE CLASSES
Zero to 4	10.3	10.3	8.4	8.4	10.8	10.8	12.7	12.7	13.5	13.5
5 to 9	24.0	34.3	21.8	30.2	22.7	33.5	26.5	39.2	26.4	39.9
10 to 14	22.7	57.0	26.3	56.5	24.4	57.9	24.2	63.4	23.9	63.8
15 to 19	16.9	73.9	14.9	71.4	15.6	73.5	16.0	79.4	15.1	78.9
20 to 24	10.3	84.2	10.5	81.9	11.3	84.8	8.4	87.8	9.0	87.9
25 to 29	5.8	90.0	7.1	89.0	5.4	90.2	4.4	92.2	4.8	92.7
30 and over	10.0	100.0	11.0	100.0	9.8	100.0	7.8	100.0	7.3	100.0

Chapter 29

FOODS AND FOOD PRODUCTS

THE major group Food Products is made up of eleven minor groups. Each in turn consists of smaller, but in the main rather closely related, sets of Manufacturing activity. For several, however, no small corporations samples are available. Descriptions of the groups appeared in Ch. 10.

TABLE 62

FOODS GROUPS, SMALL NON-IDENTICAL MANUFACTURING CORPORATIONS SERIES

(A) SIZE AND CHARACTER OF SAMPLE

	1919	1920	1921	1922	1923	1924	1925	1926	1927	1928	AVERAGE CAPITAL PER CORPORATION [1] (thousands of dollars) ARITHMETIC MEAN
Major group											
1 Foods	275	222	305	231	264	293	255	258	293	220	168
Minor group											
1 Bakery products	84	86	87	90	94	88	80	92	96	95	166
2 Flour	90	98	95	92	94	88	79	93	92	86	225
3 Confectionery	21	16	17	8	20	21	15	14	15	15	316
5 Dairying	82	92	93	82	91	86	84	92	93	89	96
7 Meat packing	48	45	43	39	45	44	45	48	46	46	219
11–8 Miscellaneous food products	56	40	67	53	49	64	50	79	73	53	145

[1] Total capital (i.e., includes funded debt) as of December 31, 1928.

FOODS: SMALL CORPORATIONS

	1919	1920	1921	1922	1923	1924	1925	1926	1927	1928
(B) PERCENTAGE INCOME TO SALES										
Major group										
1 Foods	4.0	3.1	3.8	3.7	4.1	3.8	3.6	3.7	4.2	3.6
Minor group										
1 Bakery products	4.0	3.5	4.7	4.8	4.9	4.8	4.9	5.4	5.7	5.5
2 Flour	3.1	1.6	2.4	2.9	2.3	2.7	2.0	2.1	2.4	2.2
3 Confectionery	6.7	4.6	4.5	5.6	5.0	5.5	4.5	1.9	6.1	4.3
5 Dairying	1.7	1.7	1.9	2.4	2.6	2.5	2.5	2.4	2.6	2.3
7 Meat packing	1.6	1.8	2.9	2.1	2.5	2.4	2.5	1.7	2.6	1.5
11–8 Miscellaneous food products	3.8	4.8	4.5	6.1	4.5	6.1	9.1	6.8	5.5	4.7
(C) PERCENTAGE INCOME TO CAPITALIZATION										
Major group										
1 Foods	16.7	10.8	11.5	12.0	12.8	12.3	14.3	12.5	10.4	10.7
Minor group										
1 Bakery products	13.3	16.0	11.0	12.4	15.3	12.8	12.3	13.7	14.7	20.8
2 Flour	21.5	9.4	9.2	10.8	9.2	10.7	9.8	8.9	8.9	10.3
3 Confectionery	32.7	15.7	11.1	11.8	19.0	16.2	12.1	7.5	16.7	8.1
5 Dairying	17.9	13.3	14.9	15.2	14.8	15.3	14.6	13.7	12.8	11.7
7 Meat packing	13.0	12.9	11.4	9.6	13.1	11.9	11.3	9.2	12.2	10.0
11–8 Miscellaneous food products	12.5	9.9	17.2	14.7	13.5	13.7	17.9	12.1	12.3	11.6
(D) PERCENTAGE PROFIT TO TOTAL CAPITAL										
Minor group										
1 Foods						12.1	13.9	12.0	10.1	10.5
Major group										
1 Bakery products						12.5	11.9	13.3	14.1	13.8
2 Flour						10.6	9.7	8.9	8.8	10.1

TABLE 62 (*continued*)

(D) PERCENTAGE PROFIT TO TOTAL CAPITAL

Major group	1919	1920	1921	1922	1923	1924	1925	1926	1927	1928
3 Confectionery						16.7	11.9	7.5	16.4	8.0
5 Dairying						15.0	14.0	13.2	12.4	11.4
7 Meat packing						11.6	11.1	9.1	11.8	9.7
11–8 Miscellaneous food products						13.2	17.0	11.3	11.9	11.5

(E) FREQUENCY DISTRIBUTIONS OF PERCENTAGES OF TOTAL NET INCOME TO CAPITALIZATION, INDIVIDUAL CORPORATIONS, 1919–23. MAJOR GROUP 1: FOODS

PERCENTAGE INCOME TO CAPI- TALIZATION	1919 PERCENT- AGE IN EACH CLASS	1919 ACCU- MULATED BY SUC- CESSIVE CLASSES	1920 PERCENT- AGE IN EACH CLASS	1920 ACCU- MULATED BY SUC- CESSIVE CLASSES	1921 PERCENT- AGE IN EACH CLASS	1921 ACCU- MULATED BY SUC- CESSIVE CLASSES	1922 PERCENT- AGE IN EACH CLASS	1922 ACCU- MULATED BY SUC- CESSIVE CLASSES	1923 PERCENT- AGE IN EACH CLASS	1923 ACCU- MULATED BY SUC- CESSIVE CLASSES
Zero to 4	3.6	3.6	11.7	11.7	10.2	10.2	8.7	8.7	9.8	9.8
5 to 9	12.0	15.6	18.9	30.6	18.7	28.9	25.5	34.2	21.6	31.4
10 to 14	22.2	37.8	14.0	44.6	21.3	50.2	13.4	47.6	20.8	52.2
15 to 19	14.9	52.7	17.1	61.7	15.7	65.9	15.6	63.2	12.9	65.1
20 to 24	9.1	61.8	11.7	73.4	8.5	74.4	10.4	73.6	12.5	77.6
25 to 29	10.2	72.0	4.5	77.9	5.9	80.3	6.1	79.7	11.0	88.6
30 and over	28.0	100.0	22.1	100.0	19.7	100.0	20.3	100.0	11.4	100.0

(F) FREQUENCY DISTRIBUTIONS OF PERCENTAGES OF TOTAL PROFIT TO TOTAL CAPITAL, INDIVIDUAL CORPORATIONS, 1924–28. MAJOR GROUP 1: FOODS

	1924		1925		1926		1927		1928	
Zero to 4	9.6	9.6	9.4	9.4	11.6	11.6	13.0	13.0	16.8	16.8
5 to 9	22.2	31.8	20.4	29.8	28.3	39.9	23.9	26.9	21.4	38.2
10 to 14	25.9	57.7	17.3	47.1	21.4	61.3	21.2	58.1	20.4	58.6
15 to 19	12.6	70.3	18.8	65.9	14.3	75.6	14.0	72.1	12.7	71.3
20 to 24	13.0	83.3	13.7	79.6	8.9	84.5	9.2	81.3	12.3	83.6
25 to 29	6.1	89.4	7.5	87.1	2.7	87.2	5.1	86.4	5.0	88.6
30 and over	10.6	100.0	12.9	100.0	12.8	100.0	13.6	100.0	11.4	100.0

[376]   INDUSTRIAL PROFITS

Table 63

DISTRIBUTIONS OF EARNINGS RATES, FOODS, LARGE IDENTICAL MANUFACTURING CORPORATIONS SERIES

(companies with net incomes only)

(A) FREQUENCY DISTRIBUTIONS OF PERCENTAGES OF TOTAL NET INCOME TO CAPITALIZATION, INDIVIDUAL CORPORATIONS, 1919–23. MAJOR GROUP 1: FOODS

PERCENTAGE INCOME TO CAPITALIZATION	1919 PERCENTAGE IN EACH CLASS	1919 ACCUMULATED BY SUCCESSIVE CLASSES	1920 PERCENTAGE IN EACH CLASS	1920 ACCUMULATED BY SUCCESSIVE CLASSES	1921 PERCENTAGE IN EACH CLASS	1921 ACCUMULATED BY SUCCESSIVE CLASSES	1922 PERCENTAGE IN EACH CLASS	1922 ACCUMULATED BY SUCCESSIVE CLASSES	1923 PERCENTAGE IN EACH CLASS	1923 ACCUMULATED BY SUCCESSIVE CLASSES
Zero to 4	1.9	1.9	13.7	13.7	10.1	10.1	6.8	6.8	9.0	9.0
5 to 9	5.3	7.2	20.0	33.7	15.3	25.4	14.5	21.3	16.5	25.5
10 to 14	15.9	23.1	18.4	52.1	19.6	45.0	16.9	38.2	24.5	50.0
15 to 19	12.6	35.7	13.7	65.8	14.8	59.8	12.1	50.3	16.0	66.0
20 to 24	10.6	46.3	8.4	74.2	10.6	70.4	15.0	65.3	12.3	78.3
25 to 29	13.5	59.8	7.4	81.6	6.3	76.7	11.6	76.9	9.0	87.3
30 and over	40.2	100.0	18.4	100.0	23.3	100.0	23.1	100.0	12.7	100.0

(B) FREQUENCY DISTRIBUTIONS OF PERCENTAGES OF TOTAL PROFIT TO TOTAL CAPITAL, INDIVIDUAL CORPORATIONS, 1924–28. MAJOR GROUP 1: FOODS

	1924 PERCENTAGE IN EACH CLASS	1924 ACCUMULATED	1925 PERCENTAGE	1925 ACCUMULATED	1926 PERCENTAGE	1926 ACCUMULATED	1927 PERCENTAGE	1927 ACCUMULATED	1928 PERCENTAGE	1928 ACCUMULATED
Zero to 4	5.2	5.2	10.1	10.1	8.6	8.6	9.7	9.7	10.9	10.9
5 to 9	15.8	21.0	21.7	31.8	20.7	29.3	25.7	35.4	25.6	36.5
10 to 14	24.9	45.9	24.2	56.0	27.4	56.7	21.8	57.2	26.5	63.0

FOODS: SMALL CORPORATIONS [377]

15 to 19	20.6	66.5	17.4	73.4	13.0	69.7	18.5	75.7	17.1	80.1
20 to 24	16.3	82.8	12.6	86.0	19.7	89.4	14.1	89.8	10.4	90.5
25 to 29	6.7	89.5	5.8	91.8	3.4	92.8	3.9	93.7	3.8	94.3
30 and over	10.5	100.0	8.2	100.0	7.2	100.0	6.3	100.0	5.7	100.0

Chapter 30

TEXTILES AND TEXTILE PRODUCTS

The major group Textiles is composed of ten minor groups. For several, however, no small corporations are available. Descriptions of the groups appeared in Ch. 11.

TEXTILES: SMALL CORPORATIONS [379]

TABLE 64
TEXTILE GROUPS, SMALL NON-IDENTICAL MANUFACTURING CORPORATIONS SERIES

(A) SIZE AND CHARACTER OF SAMPLE

	\multicolumn{10}{c}{NUMBER OF CORPORATIONS}	AVERAGE CAPITAL PER CORPORATION [1] (thousands of dollars)
	1919	1920	1921	1922	1923	1924	1925	1926	1927	1928	1928 ARITHMETIC MEAN
Major group											
2 Textiles	247	161	232	200	215	199	209	206	247	191	194
Minor group											
18 Men's clothing	20	13	20	18	29	18	7	15	30	21	224
19 Knit goods	89	82	93	84	96	88	85	91	97	89	213
20 Miscellaneous clothing	59	45	49	41	66	58	43	66	71	54	98
21 Miscellaneous textiles	73	40	62	56	53	59	55	51	68	71	216

[1] Total capital (i.e., includes funded debt) as of December 31, 1928.

(B) PERCENTAGE INCOME TO SALES

	1919	1920	1921	1922	1923	1924	1925	1926	1927	1928
Major group										
2 Textiles	6.8	4.4	5.4	5.6	5.1	4.3	4.3	3.6	4.1	3.7
Minor group										
18 Men's clothing	6.1	3.4	4.3	3.9	3.1	2.2	4.8	1.9	3.0	2.9
19 Knit goods	6.1	3.7	5.0	5.4	4.8	4.5	5.2	5.4	4.5	5.6
20 Miscellaneous clothing	6.0	2.9	3.5	4.3	3.8	4.2	4.5	3.7	3.2	3.8
21 Miscellaneous textiles	6.4	4.6	5.9	6.4	6.4	5.1	4.1	3.7	5.2	4.0

TABLE 64 (*continued*)

(C) PERCENTAGE INCOME TO CAPITALIZATION

	1919	1920	1921	1922	1923	1924	1925	1926	1927	1928
Major group										
2 Textiles	20.0	12.5	12.6	14.5	12.8	11.0	11.5	9.6	11.7	9.8
Minor group										
18 Men's clothing	24.8	14.4	11.9	13.3	8.9	6.2	14.5	8.6	9.8	8.9
19 Knit goods	15.0	11.0	12.9	14.0	11.0	10.3	12.1	13.6	10.5	13.7
20 Miscellaneous clothing	30.3	13.7	12.9	18.8	14.6	16.9	18.6	15.7	12.1	17.7
21 Miscellaneous textiles	20.9	14.4	14.3	16.3	16.5	12.6	11.1	10.9	14.5	8.1

(D) PERCENTAGE PROFIT TO TOTAL CAPITAL

	1924	1925	1926	1927	1928
Major group					
2 Textiles	10.7	11.3	9.6	11.6	9.8
Minor group					
18 Men's clothing	6.2	14.3	8.6	9.7	8.9
19 Knit goods	10.0	11.8	13.4	10.4	13.5
20 Miscellaneous clothing	16.7	18.6	15.7	12.1	17.7
21 Miscellaneous textiles	11.9	11.0	10.8	14.2	8.0

(E) FREQUENCY DISTRIBUTIONS OF PERCENTAGES OF TOTAL NET INCOME TO CAPITALIZATION, INDIVIDUAL CORPORATIONS, 1919–23. MAJOR GROUP 2: TEXTILES

PERCENTAGE INCOME TO CAPITALIZATION	1919 PERCENTAGE IN EACH CLASS	1919 ACCUMULATED BY SUCCESSIVE CLASSES	1920 PERCENTAGE IN EACH CLASS	1920 ACCUMULATED BY SUCCESSIVE CLASSES	1921 PERCENTAGE IN EACH CLASS	1921 ACCUMULATED BY SUCCESSIVE CLASSES	1922 PERCENTAGE IN EACH CLASS	1922 ACCUMULATED BY SUCCESSIVE CLASSES	1923 PERCENTAGE IN EACH CLASS	1923 ACCUMULATED BY SUCCESSIVE CLASSES
Zero to 4	3.6	3.6	9.9	9.9	13.4	13.4	10.5	10.5	7.9	7.9
5 to 9	7.7	11.3	19.3	29.2	18.5	31.9	18.5	19.0	21.4	29.3
10 to 14	17.0	28.3	22.4	51.6	19.4	51.3	18.5	37.5	22.8	52.1
15 to 19	15.4	43.7	14.9	66.5	14.2	65.5	16.0	53.5	13.0	65.1
20 to 24	15.0	58.7	8.1	74.6	10.4	75.9	7.5	61.0	13.5	78.6
25 to 29	10.5	69.2	9.3	83.9	7.3	83.2	5.0	66.0	2.8	81.4
30 and over	30.8	100.0	16.1	100.0	16.8	100.0	24.0	100.0	18.6	100.0

(F) FREQUENCY DISTRIBUTIONS OF PERCENTAGES OF TOTAL PROFIT TO TOTAL CAPITAL, INDIVIDUAL CORPORATIONS, 1924–28. MAJOR GROUP 2: TEXTILES

PERCENTAGE INCOME TO CAPITALIZATION	1924 PERCENTAGE IN EACH CLASS	1924 ACCUMULATED BY SUCCESSIVE CLASSES	1925 PERCENTAGE IN EACH CLASS	1925 ACCUMULATED BY SUCCESSIVE CLASSES	1926 PERCENTAGE IN EACH CLASS	1926 ACCUMULATED BY SUCCESSIVE CLASSES	1927 PERCENTAGE IN EACH CLASS	1927 ACCUMULATED BY SUCCESSIVE CLASSES	1928 PERCENTAGE IN EACH CLASS	1928 ACCUMULATED BY SUCCESSIVE CLASSES
Zero to 4	14.1	14.1	9.6	9.6	17.0	17.0	14.6	14.6	13.6	13.6
5 to 9	24.1	38.2	26.8	36.4	21.8	38.8	27.1	41.7	24.1	37.7
10 to 14	23.6	61.8	16.7	53.1	20.9	59.7	23.9	65.6	24.1	61.8
15 to 19	14.6	76.4	18.7	71.8	12.6	72.3	12.1	77.7	14.7	76.5
20 to 24	10.1	86.5	10.0	81.8	9.7	82.0	6.9	84.6	6.8	83.3
25 to 29	5.0	91.5	6.2	88.0	4.4	86.4	5.3	89.9	5.2	88.5
30 and over	8.5	100.0	12.0	100.0	13.6	100.0	10.1	100.0	11.5	100.0

Table 65

DISTRIBUTIONS OF EARNINGS RATES, TEXTILES, LARGE IDENTICAL MANUFACTURING CORPORATIONS SERIES

(companies with net incomes only)

(A) FREQUENCY DISTRIBUTIONS OF PERCENTAGES OF TOTAL NET INCOME TO CAPITALIZATION, INDIVIDUAL CORPORATIONS, 1919–23. MAJOR GROUP 2: TEXTILES

PERCENTAGE INCOME TO CAPITALIZATION	1919 PERCENTAGE IN EACH CLASS	1919 ACCUMULATED BY SUCCESSIVE CLASSES	1920 PERCENTAGE IN EACH CLASS	1920 ACCUMULATED BY SUCCESSIVE CLASSES	1921 PERCENTAGE IN EACH CLASS	1921 ACCUMULATED BY SUCCESSIVE CLASSES	1922 PERCENTAGE IN EACH CLASS	1922 ACCUMULATED BY SUCCESSIVE CLASSES	1923 PERCENTAGE IN EACH CLASS	1923 ACCUMULATED BY SUCCESSIVE CLASSES
Zero to 4	0.7	0.7	12.6	12.6	11.8	11.8	4.6	4.6	2.1	2.1
5 to 9	0.7	1.4	21.1	33.7	22.1	33.9	14.8	19.4	14.5	16.6
10 to 14	3.8	5.2	10.2	43.9	20.2	54.1	16.5	35.9	23.0	39.6
15 to 19	8.7	13.9	13.0	56.9	12.6	66.7	16.8	52.7	27.6	67.2
20 to 24	12.1	26.0	9.0	65.9	11.8	78.5	11.9	64.6	13.8	81.0
25 to 29	10.0	36.0	9.3	75.2	6.9	85.4	11.2	75.8	8.1	89.1
30 and over	64.0	100.0	24.8	100.0	14.6	100.0	24.2	100.0	10.9	100.0

(B) FREQUENCY DISTRIBUTIONS OF PERCENTAGES OF TOTAL PROFIT TO TOTAL CAPITAL, INDIVIDUAL CORPORATIONS, 1924–28. MAJOR GROUP 2: TEXTILES

	1924 PERCENTAGE IN EACH CLASS	1924 ACCUMULATED	1925 PERCENTAGE IN EACH CLASS	1925 ACCUMULATED	1926 PERCENTAGE IN EACH CLASS	1926 ACCUMULATED	1927 PERCENTAGE IN EACH CLASS	1927 ACCUMULATED	1928 PERCENTAGE IN EACH CLASS	1928 ACCUMULATED
Zero to 4	13.5	13.5	9.5	9.5	19.4	19.4	11.6	11.6	26.0	26.0
5 to 9	30.4	43.9	28.5	38.0	29.3	48.7	26.3	38.9	30.0	56.0
10 to 14	22.2	66.1	26.4	64.4	21.2	69.9	27.4	65.3	22.7	78.7

TEXTILES: SMALL CORPORATIONS

15 to 19	18.8	84.9	13.4	77.8	12.1	82.0	20.7	86.0	11.8	90.5
20 to 24	5.3	90.2	9.9	87.7	7.3	89.3	7.7	93.7	3.7	94.2
25 to 29	3.8	94.0	6.0	93.7	4.8	94.1	3.2	96.9	4.0	98.2
30 and over	6.0	100.0	6.3	100.0	5.9	100.0	3.1	100.0	1.8	100.0

Chapter 31

LEATHER AND LEATHER PRODUCTS

THE major group Leather is made up of but two minor groups, Boots and Shoes, and Leather and Miscellaneous Leather Products. In the latter only can the data for small corporations be shown separately. A description of the groups appeared in Ch. 12.

TABLE 66
LEATHER AND LEATHER PRODUCTS, SMALL NON-IDENTICAL MANUFACTURING CORPORATIONS SERIES

(A) SIZE AND CHARACTER OF SAMPLE

				NUMBER OF CORPORATIONS						AVERAGE CAPITAL PER CORPORATION [1] (thousands of dollars) 1928 ARITHMETIC MEAN
	1919	1920	1921	1922	1923	1924	1925	1926	1927	1928	
Major group											
3 Leather	57	36	45	42	48	39	44	40	49	40	154
Minor group											
23 Miscellaneous leather products	29	23	21	22	31	6	19	17	23	21	144

[1] Total capital (i.e., includes funded debt) as of December 31, 1928.

(B) PERCENTAGE INCOME TO SALES

	1919	1920	1921	1922	1923	1924	1925	1926	1927	1928
Major group										
3 Leather		6.3	3.7	5.5	5.5	4.0	5.3	3.5	4.5	4.0
Minor group										
23 Miscellaneous leather		7.9	3.6	6.3	6.4	5.1	1.5	5.5	3.9	5.1	5.7

(C) PERCENTAGE INCOME TO CAPITALIZATION

	1919	1920	1921	1922	1923	1924	1925	1926	1927	1928
Major group										
3 Leather		23.3	9.9	12.7	17.0	11.0	14.4	18.9	9.2	14.6	11.0
Minor group										
23 Miscellaneous leather		22.6	9.1	11.0	13.3	9.6	3.6	18.9	7.9	13.9	13.3

Table 66 (continued)

(D) PERCENTAGE PROFIT TO TOTAL CAPITAL

	1924	1925	1926	1927	1928
Major group					
3 Leather	13.9	18.7	9.0	14.5	10.9
Minor group					
23 Miscellaneous leather	3.8	18.4	7.8	13.8	13.2

(E) FREQUENCY DISTRIBUTIONS OF PERCENTAGES OF TOTAL NET INCOME TO CAPITALIZATION, INDIVIDUAL CORPORATIONS, 1919–23. MAJOR GROUP 3: LEATHER AND LEATHER PRODUCTS

PERCENTAGE INCOME TO CAPI- TALIZATION	1919 PERCENT- AGE IN EACH CLASS	1919 ACCU- MULATED BY SUC- CESSIVE CLASSES	1920 PERCENT- AGE IN EACH CLASS	1920 ACCU- MULATED BY SUC- CESSIVE CLASSES	1921 PERCENT- AGE IN EACH CLASS	1921 ACCU- MULATED BY SUC- CESSIVE CLASSES	1922 PERCENT- AGE IN EACH CLASS	1922 ACCU- MULATED BY SUC- CESSIVE CLASSES	1923 PERCENT- AGE IN EACH CLASS	1923 ACCU- MULATED BY SUC- CESSIVE CLASSES
Zero to 4	0.0	0.0	2.8	2.8	17.8	17.8	7.2	7.2	12.5	12.5
5 to 9	3.5	3.5	30.5	33.3	17.8	35.6	19.0	26.2	27.1	39.6
10 to 14	14.0	17.5	25.0	58.3	11.1	46.7	16.7	42.9	20.8	60.4
15 to 19	24.6	42.1	5.6	63.9	24.4	71.1	19.0	61.9	14.6	75.0
20 to 24	19.3	61.4	2.8	66.7	15.5	86.6	2.4	64.3	2.1	77.1
25 to 29	1.8	62.2	11.1	77.8	6.7	93.3	14.3	78.6	4.1	81.2
30 and over	36.8	100.0	22.2	100.0	6.7	100.0	21.4	100.0	18.8	100.0

(F) FREQUENCY DISTRIBUTION OF PERCENTAGES OF TOTAL PROFIT TO TOTAL CAPITAL, INDIVIDUAL CORPORATIONS, 1924–28. MAJOR GROUP 3: LEATHER AND LEATHER PRODUCTS

PERCENTAGE PROFIT TO TOTAL CAPITAL	1924 PERCENTAGE IN EACH CLASS	1924 ACCUMULATED BY SUCCESSIVE CLASSES	1925 PERCENTAGE IN EACH CLASS	1925 ACCUMULATED BY SUCCESSIVE CLASSES	1926 PERCENTAGE IN EACH CLASS	1926 ACCUMULATED BY SUCCESSIVE CLASSES	1927 PERCENTAGE IN EACH CLASS	1927 ACCUMULATED BY SUCCESSIVE CLASSES	1928 PERCENTAGE IN EACH CLASS	1928 ACCUMULATED BY SUCCESSIVE CLASSES
Zero to 4	10.3	10.3	6.8	6.8	20.0	20.0	8.1	8.1	12.5	12.5
5 to 9	25.6	35.9	20.5	27.3	30.0	50.0	28.6	36.7	30.0	42.5
10 to 14	17.9	53.8	13.6	40.9	20.0	70.0	18.4	55.1	20.0	62.5
15 to 19	23.1	76.9	27.3	68.2	7.5	77.5	18.4	73.5	20.0	82.5
20 to 24	7.7	84.6	6.8	75.0	2.5	80.0	14.3	87.8	5.0	87.5
25 to 29	5.1	89.7	6.8	81.8	5.0	85.0	4.1	91.9	2.5	90.0
30 and over	10.3	100.0	18.2	100.0	15.0	100.0	8.1	100.0	10.0	100.0

TABLE 67

DISTRIBUTIONS OF EARNINGS RATES, LEATHER, LARGE IDENTICAL MANUFACTURING CORPORATIONS SERIES

(companies with net incomes only)

(A) FREQUENCY DISTRIBUTIONS OF PERCENTAGES OF TOTAL NET INCOME TO CAPITALIZATION, INDIVIDUAL CORPORATIONS, 1919–23. MAJOR GROUP 3: LEATHER AND LEATHER PRODUCTS

PERCENTAGE INCOME TO CAPITALIZATION	1919 PERCENTAGE IN EACH CLASS	1919 ACCUMULATED BY SUCCESSIVE CLASSES	1920 PERCENTAGE IN EACH CLASS	1920 ACCUMULATED BY SUCCESSIVE CLASSES	1921 PERCENTAGE IN EACH CLASS	1921 ACCUMULATED BY SUCCESSIVE CLASSES	1922 PERCENTAGE IN EACH CLASS	1922 ACCUMULATED BY SUCCESSIVE CLASSES	1923 PERCENTAGE IN EACH CLASS	1923 ACCUMULATED BY SUCCESSIVE CLASSES
Zero to 4	0.0	0.0	15.0	15.0	25.0	25.0	5.8	5.8	10.2	10.2
5 to 9	1.8	1.8	27.5	42.5	20.0	45.0	25.0	30.8	26.5	36.7
10 to 14	1.8	3.6	22.5	65.0	22.5	67.5	13.5	44.3	24.5	61.2
15 to 19	13.0	16.6	10.0	75.0	15.0	82.5	23.1	67.4	16.3	77.5
20 to 24	14.8	31.4	5.0	80.0	7.5	90.0	7.7	75.1	14.3	91.8
25 to 29	5.6	37.0	10.0	90.0	0.0	90.0	11.5	86.6	0.0	91.8
30 and over	63.0	100.0	10.0	100.0	10.0	100.0	13.4	100.0	8.2	100.0

(B) FREQUENCY DISTRIBUTIONS OF PERCENTAGES OF TOTAL PROFIT TO TOTAL CAPITAL, INDIVIDUAL CORPORATIONS, 1924–28. MAJOR GROUP 3: LEATHER AND LEATHER PRODUCTS

	1924 PERCENTAGE IN EACH CLASS	1924 ACCUMULATED BY SUCCESSIVE CLASSES	1925 PERCENTAGE IN EACH CLASS	1925 ACCUMULATED BY SUCCESSIVE CLASSES	1926 PERCENTAGE IN EACH CLASS	1926 ACCUMULATED BY SUCCESSIVE CLASSES	1927 PERCENTAGE IN EACH CLASS	1927 ACCUMULATED BY SUCCESSIVE CLASSES	1928 PERCENTAGE IN EACH CLASS	1928 ACCUMULATED BY SUCCESSIVE CLASSES
Zero to 4	13.2	13.2	17.0	17.0	25.0	25.0	9.4	9.4	12.2	12.2
5 to 9	28.3	41.5	26.4	43.4	17.3	42.3	20.8	30.2	30.6	42.8
10 to 14	34.0	75.5	22.6	66.0	28.8	71.1	30.2	60.4	32.7	75.5

LEATHER: SMALL CORPORATIONS

15 to 19	11.3	86.8	18.8	84.8	13.5	84.6	24.5	84.9	20.4	95.9
20 to 24	7.5	94.3	5.7	90.5	9.6	94.2	9.4	94.3	4.1	100.0
25 to 29	3.8	98.1	5.7	96.2	3.9	98.1	3.8	98.1	0.0	100.0
30 and over	1.9	100.0	3.8	100.0	1.9	100.0	1.9	100.0	0.0	100.0

CHAPTER 32

RUBBER AND RUBBER PRODUCTS

THE major group Rubber is not susceptible of division into smaller groups. The corporations included produce both wearing apparel, such as overshoes and raincoats, and mechanical rubber goods, such as tires and garden hose.

TABLE 68

RUBBER AND RUBBER PRODUCTS, SMALL NON-IDENTICAL MANUFACTURING CORPORATIONS SERIES

(A) SIZE AND CHARACTER OF SAMPLE

NUMBER OF CORPORATIONS

	1919	1920	1921	1922	1923	1924	1925	1926	1927	1928	AVERAGE CAPITAL PER CORPORATION[1] (thousands of dollars) 1928 ARITHMETIC MEAN
Major group 4 (minor group 24)											
Rubber and rubber products	12	8	11	11	9	15	13	11	12	11	139

[1] Total capital (i.e., includes funded debt) as of December 31, 1928.

(B) PERCENTAGE INCOME TO SALES

	1919	1920	1921	1922	1923	1924	1925	1926	1927	1928
Major group 4 (minor group 24)										
Rubber and rubber products			4.5	2.1	4.6	5.6	3.9	3.5	5.9	8.3

(C) PERCENTAGE INCOME TO CAPITALIZATION

	1919	1920	1921	1922	1923	1924	1925	1926	1927	1928
Major group 4 (minor group 24)										
Rubber and rubber products			10.4	10.0	8.2	7.4	8.4	10.0	15.0	12.7

(D) PERCENTAGE PROFIT TO TOTAL CAPITAL

	1919	1920	1921	1922	1923	1924	1925	1926	1927	1928
Major group 4 (minor group 24)										
Rubber and rubber products							9.7	14.7	16.2	12.4

TABLE 68 (*continued*)

(E) FREQUENCY DISTRIBUTIONS OF PERCENTAGES OF TOTAL NET INCOME TO CAPITALIZATION, INDIVIDUAL CORPORATIONS, 1919–23. MAJOR GROUP 4: RUBBER AND RUBBER PRODUCTS

PERCENTAGE INCOME TO CAPITALIZATION	1919 PERCENTAGE IN EACH CLASS	1919 ACCUMULATED BY SUCCESSIVE CLASSES	1920 PERCENTAGE IN EACH CLASS	1920 ACCUMULATED BY SUCCESSIVE CLASSES	1921 PERCENTAGE IN EACH CLASS	1921 ACCUMULATED BY SUCCESSIVE CLASSES	1922 PERCENTAGE IN EACH CLASS	1922 ACCUMULATED BY SUCCESSIVE CLASSES	1923 PERCENTAGE IN EACH CLASS	1923 ACCUMULATED BY SUCCESSIVE CLASSES
Zero to 4	8.3	8.3	12.5	12.5	27.2	27.2	36.4	36.4	11.1	11.1
5 to 9	8.3	16.6	37.5	50.0	18.2	45.4	27.2	63.6	11.1	22.2
10 to 14	16.7	33.3	25.0	75.0	9.1	54.5	0.0	63.6	22.2	44.4
15 to 19	8.3	41.6	12.5	87.5	9.1	63.6	9.1	72.7	22.2	66.6
20 to 24	8.3	49.9	0.0	87.5	9.1	72.7	9.1	81.8	22.2	88.8
25 to 29	16.7	66.6	12.5	100.0	18.2	90.9	0.0	81.8	0.0	88.8
30 and over	33.4	100.0	0.0	100.0	9.1	100.0	18.2	100.0	11.2	100.0

(F) FREQUENCY DISTRIBUTIONS OF PERCENTAGES OF TOTAL PROFIT TO TOTAL CAPITAL, INDIVIDUAL CORPORATIONS, 1924–28. MAJOR GROUP 4: RUBBER AND RUBBER PRODUCTS

	1924 PERCENTAGE IN EACH CLASS	1924 ACCUMULATED BY SUCCESSIVE CLASSES	1925 PERCENTAGE IN EACH CLASS	1925 ACCUMULATED BY SUCCESSIVE CLASSES	1926 PERCENTAGE IN EACH CLASS	1926 ACCUMULATED BY SUCCESSIVE CLASSES	1927 PERCENTAGE IN EACH CLASS	1927 ACCUMULATED BY SUCCESSIVE CLASSES	1928 PERCENTAGE IN EACH CLASS	1928 ACCUMULATED BY SUCCESSIVE CLASSES
Zero to 4	13.3	13.3	0.0	0.0	18.2	18.2	25.0	25.0	9.1	9.1
5 to 9	13.3	26.6	7.7	7.7	9.1	27.3	25.0	50.0	9.1	18.2
10 to 14	46.7	73.3	53.8	61.5	18.2	45.5	8.3	58.3	27.3	45.5
15 to 19	13.3	86.6	15.4	76.9	36.3	81.8	25.0	83.3	0.0	45.5
20 to 24	0.0	86.6	7.7	84.6	9.1	90.9	0.0	83.3	27.3	72.8
25 to 29	0.0	86.6	0.0	84.6	0.0	90.9	8.3	91.6	0.0	72.8
30 and over	13.4	100.0	15.4	100.0	9.1	100.0	8.4	100.0	27.2	100.0

TABLE 69

DISTRIBUTIONS OF EARNINGS RATES, RUBBER, LARGE
IDENTICAL MANUFACTURING CORPORATIONS SERIES

(companies with net incomes only)

(A) FREQUENCY DISTRIBUTIONS OF PERCENTAGES OF TOTAL NET INCOME TO CAPITALIZATION, INDIVIDUAL CORPORATIONS, 1919–23. MAJOR GROUP 4: RUBBER AND RUBBER PRODUCTS

PERCENTAGE INCOME TO CAPITALIZATION	1919 PERCENTAGE IN EACH CLASS	1919 ACCUMULATED BY SUCCESSIVE CLASSES	1920 PERCENTAGE IN EACH CLASS	1920 ACCUMULATED BY SUCCESSIVE CLASSES	1921 PERCENTAGE IN EACH CLASS	1921 ACCUMULATED BY SUCCESSIVE CLASSES	1922 PERCENTAGE IN EACH CLASS	1922 ACCUMULATED BY SUCCESSIVE CLASSES	1923 PERCENTAGE IN EACH CLASS	1923 ACCUMULATED BY SUCCESSIVE CLASSES
Zero to 4	0.0	0.0	25.0	25.0	14.3	14.3	8.3	8.3	8.3	8.3
5 to 9	0.0	0.0	20.0	45.0	21.4	35.7	25.0	33.3	16.6	24.9
10 to 14	19.2	19.2	15.0	60.0	35.7	71.4	8.3	41.6	37.5	62.4
15 to 19	15.4	34.6	20.0	80.0	14.3	85.7	25.0	66.6	25.0	87.4
20 to 24	11.6	46.2	10.0	90.0	14.3	100.0	16.7	83.3	4.2	91.6
25 to 29	19.2	65.4	10.0	100.0	0.0	100.0	4.2	87.5	4.2	95.8
30 and over	34.6	100.0	0.0	100.0	0.0	100.0	12.5	100.0	4.2	100.0

(B) FREQUENCY DISTRIBUTIONS OF PERCENTAGES OF TOTAL PROFIT TO TOTAL CAPITAL, INDIVIDUAL CORPORATIONS, 1924–28. MAJOR GROUP 4: RUBBER AND RUBBER PRODUCTS

	1924 PERCENTAGE IN EACH CLASS	1924 ACCUMULATED BY SUCCESSIVE CLASSES	1925 PERCENTAGE IN EACH CLASS	1925 ACCUMULATED BY SUCCESSIVE CLASSES	1926 PERCENTAGE IN EACH CLASS	1926 ACCUMULATED BY SUCCESSIVE CLASSES	1927 PERCENTAGE IN EACH CLASS	1927 ACCUMULATED BY SUCCESSIVE CLASSES	1928 PERCENTAGE IN EACH CLASS	1928 ACCUMULATED BY SUCCESSIVE CLASSES
Zero to 4	8.3	8.3	3.8	3.8	18.2	18.2	4.8	4.8	20.0	20.0
5 to 9	29.2	37.5	11.5	15.3	13.6	31.8	19.0	23.8	25.0	45.0
10 to 14	20.8	58.3	27.0	42.3	27.3	59.1	33.3	57.1	35.0	80.0
15 to 19	33.4	91.7	27.0	69.3	27.3	86.4	19.0	76.1	10.0	90.0
20 to 24	8.3	100.0	23.1	92.4	4.5	90.9	4.8	80.9	0.0	90.0
25 to 29	0.0	100.0	3.8	96.2	9.1	100.0	9.5	90.4	5.0	95.0
30 and over	0.0	100.0	3.8	100.0	0.0	100.0	9.6	100.0	5.0	100.0

Chapter 33

LUMBER AND LUMBER PRODUCTS

The major group Lumber is made up of 5 minor groups, although no small corporations samples are available for several. Descriptions appeared in Ch. 14.

Table 70

LUMBER GROUPS, SMALL NON-IDENTICAL MANUFACTURING CORPORATIONS SERIES

(A) SIZE AND CHARACTER OF SAMPLE

	1919	1920	1921	1922	1923	1924	1925	1926	1927	1928	AVERAGE CAPITAL PER CORPORATION [1] (thousands of dollars) ARITHMETIC MEAN
				NUMBER OF CORPORATIONS							
Major group											
5 Lumber	206	207	194	189	204	205	169	112	177	146	175
Minor group											
25 Lumber manufacture	81	90	89	88	87	91	89	93	90	86	208
28 Furniture	90	96	96	87	97	87	100	94	95	98	247

[1] Total capital (i.e, includes funded debt) as of December 31, 1928.

(B) PERCENTAGE INCOME TO SALES

	1919	1920	1921	1922	1923	1924	1925	1926	1927	1928
Major group										
5 Lumber	9.0	7.7	6.8	7.9	7.6	6.6	6.2	5.9	6.0	6.8
Minor group										
25 Lumber manufacture	8.8	6.7	5.3	6.5	7.1	7.4	9.0	4.9	5.8	6.1
28 Furniture	10.6	6.9	6.2	7.7	7.3	6.2	6.3	5.5	5.5	4.9

TABLE 70 (*continued*)

(C) PERCENTAGE INCOME TO CAPITALIZATION

	1919	1920	1921	1922	1923	1924	1925	1926	1927	1928
Major group										
5 Lumber	18.2	17.0	11.0	13.8	16.8	10.4	7.9	10.7	11.0	11.6
Minor group										
25 Lumber manufacture	15.1	12.4	5.7	6.4	11.7	10.5	8.5	8.3	10.1	10.0
28 Furniture	22.6	19.6	10.2	15.3	16.6	11.5	13.0	11.4	9.9	8.4

(D) PERCENTAGE PROFIT TO TOTAL CAPITAL

	1924	1925	1926	1927	1928
Major group					
5 Lumber	10.3	7.8	10.5	10.8	11.3
Minor group					
25 Lumber manufacture	10.4	8.1	8.1	10.0	9.9
28 Furniture	11.3	12.7	11.0	9.7	8.3

(E) FREQUENCY DISTRIBUTIONS OF PERCENTAGES OF TOTAL NET INCOME TO CAPITALIZATION, INDIVIDUAL CORPORATIONS, 1919–23. MAJOR GROUP 5: LUMBER

PERCENTAGE INCOME TO CAPI- TALIZATION	1919 PERCENT- AGE IN EACH CLASS	1919 ACCU- MULATED BY SUC- CESSIVE CLASSES	1920 PERCENT- AGE IN EACH CLASS	1920 ACCU- MULATED BY SUC- CESSIVE CLASSES	1921 PERCENT- AGE IN EACH CLASS	1921 ACCU- MULATED BY SUC- CESSIVE CLASSES	1922 PERCENT- AGE IN EACH CLASS	1922 ACCU- MULATED BY SUC- CESSIVE CLASSES	1923 PERCENT- AGE IN EACH CLASS	1923 ACCU- MULATED BY SUC- CESSIVE CLASSES
Zero to 4	3.9	3.9	8.7	8.7	9.8	9.8	6.9	6.9	8.3	8.3
5 to 9	15.0	18.9	15.0	23.7	17.5	27.3	23.8	30.7	15.7	24.0
10 to 14	18.0	36.9	10.1	33.8	20.1	57.2	16.9	47.6	15.2	39.2
15 to 19	14.1	51.0	14.0	37.8	18.5	75.7	13.7	61.3	15.7	54.9

LUMBER: SMALL CORPORATIONS

(continuation of preceding table)

	1924 PERCENTAGE IN EACH CLASS	1924 ACCUMULATED BY SUCCESSIVE CLASSES	1925 PERCENTAGE IN EACH CLASS	1925 ACCUMULATED BY SUCCESSIVE CLASSES	1926 PERCENTAGE IN EACH CLASS	1926 ACCUMULATED BY SUCCESSIVE CLASSES	1927 PERCENTAGE IN EACH CLASS	1927 ACCUMULATED BY SUCCESSIVE CLASSES	1928 PERCENTAGE IN EACH CLASS	1928 ACCUMULATED BY SUCCESSIVE CLASSES
20 to 24	12.6	63.6	15.5	53.3	5.7	81.4	8.5	69.8	11.8	66.7
25 to 29	10.7	74.3	6.8	60.1	5.7	87.1	6.9	76.7	8.8	75.5
30 and over	25.7	100.0	29.9	100.0	12.9	100.0	23.3	100.0	24.5	100.0

(F) FREQUENCY DISTRIBUTIONS OF PERCENTAGES OF TOTAL PROFIT TO TOTAL CAPITAL, INDIVIDUAL CORPORATIONS, 1924–28. MAJOR GROUP 5: LUMBER

PERCENTAGE PROFIT TO TOTAL CAPITAL	1924 PERCENTAGE IN EACH CLASS	1924 ACCUMULATED BY SUCCESSIVE CLASSES	1925 PERCENTAGE IN EACH CLASS	1925 ACCUMULATED BY SUCCESSIVE CLASSES	1926 PERCENTAGE IN EACH CLASS	1926 ACCUMULATED BY SUCCESSIVE CLASSES	1927 PERCENTAGE IN EACH CLASS	1927 ACCUMULATED BY SUCCESSIVE CLASSES	1928 PERCENTAGE IN EACH CLASS	1928 ACCUMULATED BY SUCCESSIVE CLASSES
Zero to 4	13.2	13.2	11.2	11.2	14.3	14.3	17.5	17.5	16.4	16.4
5 to 9	18.0	31.2	28.4	39.6	25.9	40.2	29.4	46.9	16.4	32.8
10 to 14	25.4	56.6	16.6	56.2	16.1	56.3	24.9	71.8	26.0	58.8
15 to 19	18.0	74.6	14.8	71.0	17.9	74.2	9.6	81.4	15.8	74.6
20 to 24	8.8	83.4	9.5	80.5	9.8	84.0	6.8	88.2	9.6	84.2
25 to 29	2.9	86.3	8.9	89.4	6.2	90.2	4.5	92.7	5.5	89.7
30 and over	13.7	100.0	10.6	100.0	9.8	100.0	7.3	100.0	10.3	100.0

TABLE 71

DISTRIBUTIONS OF EARNINGS RATES, LUMBER, LARGE IDENTICAL MANUFACTURING CORPORATIONS SERIES

(companies with net incomes only)

(A) FREQUENCY DISTRIBUTIONS OF PERCENTAGES OF TOTAL NET INCOME TO CAPITALIZATION, INDIVIDUAL CORPORATIONS, 1919–23. MAJOR GROUP 5: LUMBER

PERCENTAGE INCOME TO CAPITALIZATION	1919 PERCENTAGE IN EACH CLASS	1919 ACCUMULATED BY SUCCESSIVE CLASSES	1920 PERCENTAGE IN EACH CLASS	1920 ACCUMULATED BY SUCCESSIVE CLASSES	1921 PERCENTAGE IN EACH CLASS	1921 ACCUMULATED BY SUCCESSIVE CLASSES	1922 PERCENTAGE IN EACH CLASS	1922 ACCUMULATED BY SUCCESSIVE CLASSES	1923 PERCENTAGE IN EACH CLASS	1923 ACCUMULATED BY SUCCESSIVE CLASSES
Zero to 4	1.6	1.6	3.8	3.8	24.5	24.5	3.8	3.8	3.7	3.7
5 to 9	7.4	9.0	5.4	9.2	25.7	50.2	14.0	17.8	10.0	13.7
10 to 14	9.5	18.5	13.5	22.7	20.9	71.1	16.7	34.5	14.7	28.4
15 to 19	13.8	32.3	14.1	36.8	16.0	87.1	12.9	47.4	22.6	51.0
20 to 24	13.2	45.5	10.3	47.1	4.9	92.0	16.7	64.1	17.4	68.4
25 to 29	9.5	55.0	12.4	59.5	3.7	95.7	8.6	72.7	13.7	82.1
30 and over	45.0	100.0	40.5	100.0	4.3	100.0	27.3	100.0	17.9	100.0

(B) FREQUENCY DISTRIBUTIONS OF PERCENTAGES OF TOTAL PROFIT TO TOTAL CAPITAL, INDIVIDUAL CORPORATIONS, 1924–28. MAJOR GROUP 5: LUMBER

	1924 PERCENTAGE IN EACH CLASS	1924 ACCUMULATED	1925 PERCENTAGE IN EACH CLASS	1925 ACCUMULATED	1926 PERCENTAGE IN EACH CLASS	1926 ACCUMULATED	1927 PERCENTAGE IN EACH CLASS	1927 ACCUMULATED	1928 PERCENTAGE IN EACH CLASS	1928 ACCUMULATED
Zero to 4	9.6	9.6	11.8	11.8	12.8	12.8	17.6	17.6	19.1	19.1
5 to 9	17.6	27.2	15.0	26.8	24.5	37.3	34.3	51.9	28.2	47.3

10 to 14	26.6	53.8	30.5	57.3	26.6	63.9	19.8	71.7	25.5	72.8
15 to 19	17.0	70.8	14.4	71.7	11.7	75.6	11.8	83.5	13.3	86.1
20 to 24	14.3	85.1	9.1	80.8	13.3	88.9	5.9	89.4	8.0	94.1
25 to 29	4.8	89.9	9.6	90.4	6.9	95.8	5.3	94.7	3.2	97.3
30 and over	10.1	100.0	9.6	100.0	4.2	100.0	5.3	100.0	2.7	100.0

Chapter 34

PAPER AND PAPER PRODUCTS

The major group Paper and Paper Products is made up of four minor groups. Descriptions appeared in Ch. 15.

TABLE 72
PAPER GROUPS, SMALL NON-IDENTICAL MANUFACTURING CORPORATIONS SERIES

(A) SIZE AND CHARACTER OF SAMPLE

	\multicolumn{10}{c}{NUMBER OF CORPORATIONS}	AVERAGE CAPITAL PER CORPORATION[1] (thousands of dollars)
	1919	1920	1921	1922	1923	1924	1925	1926	1927	1928	1928 ARITHMETIC MEAN
Major group											
6 Paper	44	49	41	42	48	54	36	48	57	44	161
Minor group											
30 Blank paper	45	47	46	44	43	41	41	49	48	48	278
31 Cardboard boxes	45	46	47	46	47	45	47	45	49	48	156
32 Stationery	49	45	47	46	46	49	47	47	49	48	224

[1] Total capital, (i.e., includes funded debt) as of December 31, 1928.

(B) PERCENTAGE INCOME TO SALES

	1919	1920	1921	1922	1923	1924	1925	1926	1927	1928
Major group										
6 Paper	7.3	6.9	6.2	7.0	8.1	5.0	5.4	6.8	5.9	6.6
Minor group										
30 Blank paper	5.5	4.7	5.8	5.3	5.0	4.0	3.6	4.2	5.4	5.3
31 Cardboard boxes	8.5	6.4	8.5	8.5	7.0	7.2	6.1	4.4	6.9	5.8
32 Stationery	5.8	6.9	4.7	5.6	5.2	5.0	5.4	5.7	5.1	6.5

TABLE 72 (*continued*)

(C) PERCENTAGE INCOME TO CAPITALIZATION

	1919	1920	1921	1922	1923	1924	1925	1926	1927	1928
Major group										
6 Paper	19.0	23.2	11.3	16.6	13.3	6.4	8.4	13.0	10.1	14.9
Minor group										
30 Blank paper	10.9	12.0	6.2	11.7	8.8	5.9	7.5	7.0	9.6	10.2
31 Cardboard boxes	18.5	23.6	14.7	13.2	15.9	11.4	12.3	7.3	11.7	12.4
32 Stationery	17.3	25.5	8.3	12.0	10.4	8.9	9.9	11.5	9.6	12.2

(D) PERCENTAGE PROFIT TO TOTAL CAPITAL

						1924	1925	1926	1927	1928
Major group										
6 Paper						6.4	8.2	12.5	9.7	14.1
Minor group										
30 Blank paper						5.9	7.4	6.8	9.5	10.0
31 Cardboard boxes						11.3	11.8	7.2	11.4	11.9
32 Stationery						8.6	9.7	11.3	9.3	11.6

(E) FREQUENCY DISTRIBUTIONS OF PERCENTAGES OF TOTAL NET INCOME TO CAPITALIZATION, INDIVIDUAL CORPORATIONS, 1919–23. MAJOR GROUP 6: PAPER

PERCENTAGE INCOME TO CAPI- TALIZATION	1919 PERCENT- AGE IN EACH CLASS	1919 ACCU- MULATED BY SUC- CESSIVE CLASSES	1920 PERCENT- AGE IN EACH CLASS	1920 ACCU- MULATED BY SUC- CESSIVE CLASSES	1921 PERCENT- AGE IN EACH CLASS	1921 ACCU- MULATED BY SUC- CESSIVE CLASSES	1922 PERCENT- AGE IN EACH CLASS	1922 ACCU- MULATED BY SUC- CESSIVE CLASSES	1923 PERCENT- AGE IN EACH CLASS	1923 ACCU- MULATED BY SUC- CESSIVE CLASSES
Zero to 4	9.1	9.1	8.2	8.2	12.2	12.2	9.5	9.5	12.5	12.5
5 to 9	6.8	15.9	10.2	18.4	21.9	34.1	11.9	21.4	25.0	37.5

	1924		1925		1926		1927		1928	
10 to 14	20.5	36.4	2.0	20.4	24.4	58.5	23.8	45.2	12.5	50.0
15 to 19	15.9	52.3	14.3	34.7	17.1	75.6	16.7	61.9	18.8	68.8
20 to 24	6.8	59.1	18.4	53.1	12.2	87.8	11.9	73.8	6.2	75.0
25 to 29	9.1	68.2	10.2	63.3	4.9	92.7	4.8	78.6	10.4	85.4
30 and over	31.8	100.0	36.7	100.0	7.3	100.0	21.4	100.0	14.6	100.0

(F) FREQUENCY DISTRIBUTIONS OF PERCENTAGES OF TOTAL PROFIT TO TOTAL CAPITAL, INDIVIDUAL CORPORATIONS, 1924–28. MAJOR GROUP 6: PAPER

	1924		1925		1926		1927		1928	
Zero to 4	22.2	22.2	5.5	5.5	2.1	2.1	10.5	10.5	2.3	2.3
5 to 9	33.3	55.5	30.6	36.1	31.2	33.3	29.8	40.3	18.2	20.5
10 to 14	18.5	74.0	16.7	53.8	20.8	54.1	26.3	66.6	29.5	50.0
15 to 19	9.3	83.3	16.7	70.5	12.5	66.6	15.8	82.4	18.2	68.2
20 to 24	3.7	87.0	5.5	76.0	12.5	79.1	8.8	91.2	15.9	84.1
25 to 29	7.4	94.4	2.8	78.8	4.2	83.3	1.8	93.0	2.3	86.4
30 and over	5.6	100.0	22.2	100.0	16.7	100.0	7.0	100.0	13.6	100.0

[404] INDUSTRIAL PROFITS

Table 73
DISTRIBUTIONS OF EARNINGS RATES, PAPER, LARGE IDENTICAL MANUFACTURING CORPORATIONS SERIES
(companies with net incomes only)

(A) FREQUENCY DISTRIBUTIONS OF PERCENTAGES OF TOTAL NET INCOME TO CAPITALIZATION, INDIVIDUAL CORPORATIONS, 1919–23. MAJOR GROUP 6: PAPER

PERCENTAGE INCOME TO CAPI-TALIZATION	1919 PERCENT-AGE IN EACH CLASS	1919 ACCU-MULATED BY SUC-CESSIVE CLASSES	1920 PERCENT-AGE IN EACH CLASS	1920 ACCU-MULATED BY SUC-CESSIVE CLASSES	1921 PERCENT-AGE IN EACH CLASS	1921 ACCU-MULATED BY SUC-CESSIVE CLASSES	1922 PERCENT-AGE IN EACH CLASS	1922 ACCU-MULATED BY SUC-CESSIVE CLASSES	1923 PERCENT-AGE IN EACH CLASS	1923 ACCU-MULATED BY SUC-CESSIVE CLASSES
Zero to 4	2.7	2.7	0.9	0.9	22.7	22.7	9.5	9.5	10.9	10.9
5 to 9	8.2	10.9	1.8	2.7	21.3	44.0	19.0	28.5	22.7	33.6
10 to 14	12.7	23.6	5.5	8.2	22.7	66.7	17.2	45.7	22.7	56.3
15 to 19	10.0	33.6	10.9	19.1	18.7	85.4	21.0	66.7	13.6	69.9
20 to 24	16.4	50.0	10.9	30.0	6.7	92.1	5.7	72.4	11.8	81.7
25 to 29	5.5	55.5	9.1	39.1	1.3	93.4	9.5	82.9	4.6	86.3
30 and over	44.5	100.0	60.9	100.0	6.6	100.0	18.1	100.0	13.7	100.0

(B) FREQUENCY DISTRIBUTIONS OF PERCENTAGES OF TOTAL PROFIT TO TOTAL CAPITAL, INDIVIDUAL CORPORATIONS, 1924–28. MAJOR GROUP 6: PAPER

	1924 PERCENT-AGE IN EACH CLASS	1924 ACCU-MULATED BY SUC-CESSIVE CLASSES	1925 PERCENT-AGE IN EACH CLASS	1925 ACCU-MULATED BY SUC-CESSIVE CLASSES	1926 PERCENT-AGE IN EACH CLASS	1926 ACCU-MULATED BY SUC-CESSIVE CLASSES	1927 PERCENT-AGE IN EACH CLASS	1927 ACCU-MULATED BY SUC-CESSIVE CLASSES	1928 PERCENT-AGE IN EACH CLASS	1928 ACCU-MULATED BY SUC-CESSIVE CLASSES
Zero to 4	10.0	10.0	11.0	11.0	11.9	11.9	12.7	12.7	12.8	12.8
5 to 9	30.0	40.0	24.8	35.8	30.3	42.2	26.3	39.0	35.8	48.6
10 to 14	25.5	65.5	33.0	68.8	22.9	65.1	25.5	64.5	24.8	73.4

15 to 19	13.6	79.1	13.8	82.6	15.6	80.7	18.2	82.7	10.1	83.5
20 to 24	6.4	85.5	4.6	87.2	9.2	89.9	5.5	88.2	7.3	90.8
25 to 29	3.6	89.1	6.4	93.6	3.7	93.6	5.5	93.7	4.6	95.4
30 and over	10.9	100.0	6.4	100.0	6.4	100.0	6.3	100.0	4.6	100.0

Chapter 35

PRINTING AND PUBLISHING

THE major group Printing and Publishing is made up of four minor groups. Descriptions appeared in Ch. 16.

TABLE 74
PRINTING AND PUBLISHING GROUPS, SMALL NON-IDENTICAL MANUFACTURING CORPORATIONS SERIES

(A) SIZE AND CHARACTER OF SAMPLE

	\multicolumn{10}{c}{NUMBER OF CORPORATIONS}	AVERAGE CAPITAL PER CORPORATION [1] (thousands of dollars)
	1919	1920	1921	1922	1923	1924	1925	1926	1927	1928	ARITHMETIC MEAN
Major group											
7 Printing and publishing	144	184	203	162	152	154	145	146	179	153	126
Minor group											
34 Newspapers	38	88	89	89	61	64	56	119	54	59	117
35 Job printing	93	90	96	88	93	88	85	93	96	95	136
37 Miscellaneous printing and publishing	29	29	26	8	18	12	26	27	31	36	129

[1] Total capital (i.e., includes funded debt) as of December 31, 1928.

(B) PERCENTAGE INCOME TO SALES

	1919	1920	1921	1922	1923	1924	1925	1926	1927	1928
Major group										
7 Printing and publishing	10.9	10.8	9.1	11.1	9.1	9.6	9.9	10.9	8.0	6.8
Minor group										
34 Newspapers	18.5	17.6	13.3	15.4	11.4	20.0	16.5	11.4	11.6	9.2
36 Job printing	7.5	7.7	5.5	7.6	7.0	7.4	5.7	6.7	7.2	6.8
37 Miscellaneous printing and publishing	9.3	10.5	4.3	6.7	12.6	7.8	6.4	9.2	6.2	7.1

[408] INDUSTRIAL PROFITS

TABLE 74 (continued)

	1919	1920	1921	1922	1923	1924	1925	1926	1927	1928
(c) PERCENTAGE INCOME TO CAPITALIZATION
Major group
7 Printing and publishing	22.1	21.1	16.2	16.3	14.4	14.2	13.2	14.4	13.2	12.3
Minor group
34 Newspapers	18.5	22.2	18.4	19.0	16.0	15.3	15.5	13.6	13.8	15.0
36 Job printing	16.6	22.9	12.6	15.1	14.6	12.4	11.2	13.9	13.8	14.5
37 Miscellaneous printing and publishing	35.0	30.0	13.3	20.0	25.3	20.0	13.6	20.4	16.4	11.8
(d) PERCENTAGE PROFIT TO TOTAL CAPITAL
Major group
7 Printing and publishing						14.0	12.6	13.9	12.8	11.9
Minor group
34 Newspapers						15.2	15.2	13.1	13.0	14.3
36 Job printing						12.0	10.9	13.6	13.4	14.3
37 Miscellaneous printing and publishing						20.0	13.6	19.8	16.4	11.6

(e) FREQUENCY DISTRIBUTIONS OF PERCENTAGES OF TOTAL NET INCOME TO CAPITALIZATION, INDIVIDUAL CORPORATIONS, 1919–23. MAJOR GROUP 7: PRINTING AND PUBLISHING

PERCENTAGE INCOME TO CAPITALIZATION	1919 PERCENT-AGE IN EACH CLASS	1919 ACCU-MULATED BY SUCCESSIVE CLASSES	1920 PERCENT-AGE IN EACH CLASS	1920 ACCU-MULATED BY SUCCESSIVE CLASSES	1921 PERCENT-AGE IN EACH CLASS	1921 ACCU-MULATED BY SUCCESSIVE CLASSES	1922 PERCENT-AGE IN EACH CLASS	1922 ACCU-MULATED BY SUCCESSIVE CLASSES	1923 PERCENT-AGE IN EACH CLASS	1923 ACCU-MULATED BY SUCCESSIVE CLASSES
Zero to 4	1.4	1.4	3.3	3.3	4.4	4.4	7.4	7.4	9.2	9.2
5 to 9	9.7	11.1	4.9	8.2	11.3	15.7	17.9	25.3	15.1	24.3

	1924		1925		1926		1927		1928	
10 to 14	16.0	27.1	13.0	21.2	25.2	40.9	21.0	46.3	23.7	48.0
15 to 19	13.9	41.0	13.6	34.8	19.7	60.6	16.1	62.4	11.2	59.2
20 to 24	10.4	51.4	14.1	48.9	12.8	73.4	9.9	72.3	13.2	72.4
25 to 29	9.7	61.1	14.1	63.0	7.4	80.8	8.6	80.9	5.9	78.3
30 and over	38.9	100.0	37.0	100.0	19.2	100.0	19.1	100.0	21.7	100.0

(F) FREQUENCY DISTRIBUTIONS OF PERCENTAGES OF TOTAL PROFIT TO TOTAL CAPITAL, INDIVIDUAL CORPORATIONS, 1924–28. MAJOR GROUP 7: PRINTING AND PUBLISHING

	1924		1925		1926		1927		1928	
Zero to 4	5.2	5.2	6.9	6.9	8.9	8.9	8.9	8.9	12.4	12.4
5 to 9	27.3	32.5	24.1	31.0	19.9	28.8	23.5	32.4	23.5	35.9
10 to 14	21.4	53.9	23.4	54.4	21.2	50.0	21.8	54.2	24.2	60.1
15 to 19	11.7	65.6	14.5	68.9	16.4	66.4	15.1	69.3	13.7	73.8
20 to 24	14.3	79.9	8.3	77.2	13.7	80.1	9.5	78.8	7.9	81.7
25 to 29	3.2	83.1	6.9	84.1	6.9	87.0	8.4	87.2	3.3	85.0
30 and over	16.9	100.0	15.9	100.0	13.0	100.0	12.8	100.0	15.0	100.0

Table 75

DISTRIBUTIONS OF EARNINGS RATES, PRINTING AND PUBLISHING, LARGE IDENTICAL MANUFACTURING CORPORATIONS SERIES

(companies with net incomes only)

(A) FREQUENCY DISTRIBUTIONS OF PERCENTAGES OF TOTAL NET INCOME TO CAPITALIZATION, INDIVIDUAL CORPORATIONS, 1919–23. MAJOR GROUP 7: PRINTING AND PUBLISHING

PERCENTAGE INCOME TO CAPITALIZATION	1919 PERCENTAGE IN EACH CLASS	1919 ACCUMULATED BY SUCCESSIVE CLASSES	1920 PERCENTAGE IN EACH CLASS	1920 ACCUMULATED BY SUCCESSIVE CLASSES	1921 PERCENTAGE IN EACH CLASS	1921 ACCUMULATED BY SUCCESSIVE CLASSES	1922 PERCENTAGE IN EACH CLASS	1922 ACCUMULATED BY SUCCESSIVE CLASSES	1923 PERCENTAGE IN EACH CLASS	1923 ACCUMULATED BY SUCCESSIVE CLASSES
Zero to 4	0.0	0.0	3.0	3.0	4.2	4.2	2.0	2.0	5.1	5.1
5 to 9	11.1	11.1	8.0	11.0	15.8	20.0	14.1	16.1	13.1	18.2
10 to 14	14.1	25.2	7.0	18.0	17.9	37.9	14.1	30.2	18.2	36.4
15 to 19	11.1	36.3	9.0	27.0	13.7	51.6	13.1	43.3	22.2	58.6
20 to 24	15.2	51.5	11.0	38.0	10.5	62.1	17.2	60.5	11.1	69.7
25 to 29	9.1	60.6	7.0	45.0	16.8	78.9	4.1	64.6	11.1	80.8
30 and over	39.4	100.0	55.0	100.0	21.1	100.0	35.4	100.0	19.2	100.0

(B) FREQUENCY DISTRIBUTIONS OF PERCENTAGES OF TOTAL PROFIT TO TOTAL CAPITAL, INDIVIDUAL CORPORATIONS, 1924–28. MAJOR GROUP 7: PRINTING AND PUBLISHING

	1924 PERCENTAGE IN EACH CLASS	1924 ACCUMULATED	1925 PERCENTAGE IN EACH CLASS	1925 ACCUMULATED	1926 PERCENTAGE IN EACH CLASS	1926 ACCUMULATED	1927 PERCENTAGE IN EACH CLASS	1927 ACCUMULATED	1928 PERCENTAGE IN EACH CLASS	1928 ACCUMULATED
Zero to 4	4.0	4.0	6.0	6.0	9.1	9.1	15.0	15.0	6.0	6.0
5 to 9	18.0	22.0	20.0	26.0	13.1	22.2	22.0	37.0	18.0	24.0

PRINTING: SMALL CORPORATIONS

10 to 14	20.0	42.0	17.0	43.0	23.2	45.4	20.0	57.0	30.0	54.0
15 to 19	19.0	61.0	18.0	61.0	20.2	65.6	16.0	73.0	21.0	75.0
20 to 24	15.0	76.0	15.0	76.0	10.1	75.7	8.0	81.0	6.0	81.0
25 to 29	10.0	86.0	8.0	84.0	9.1	84.8	8.0	89.0	8.0	89.0
30 and over	14.0	100.0	16.0	100.0	15.2	100.0	11.0	100.0	11.0	100.0

Chapter 36

CHEMICALS

The major group Chemicals is made up of seven minor groups Descriptions appeared in Ch. 17.

CHEMICALS: SMALL CORPORATIONS

TABLE 76
CHEMICAL GROUPS, SMALL NON-IDENTICAL MANUFACTURING CORPORATIONS SERIES

(A) SIZE AND CHARACTER OF SAMPLE

	NUMBER OF CORPORATIONS										AVERAGE CAPITAL PER CORPORATION [1] (thousands of dollars) 1928 ARITHMETIC MEAN
	1919	1920	1921	1922	1923	1924	1925	1926	1927	1928	
Major group											
8 Chemicals	77	76	61	84	86	108	91	84	109	110	213
Minor group											
39 Paints	46	47	47	41	48	46	47	46	48	50	192
40 Petroleum	45	47	41	40	44	43	41	42	47	43	256

[1] Total capital (i.e., includes funded debt) as of December 31, 1928.

(B) PERCENTAGE INCOME TO SALES

	1919	1920	1921	1922	1923	1924	1925	1926	1927	1928
Major group										
8 Chemicals		6.2	6.1	6.4	7.3	5.7	7.6	7.1	8.6	8.2	6.5
Minor group										
39 Paints		9.3	5.7	6.0	7.5	7.5	6.9	5.2	5.9	6.2	7.0
40 Petroleum		5.4	3.1	1.9	4.0	6.4	4.0	8.3	4.8	4.9	5.6

TABLE 76 (continued)

(c) PERCENTAGE INCOME TO CAPITALIZATION

	1919	1920	1921	1922	1923	1924	1925	1926	1927	1928
Major group										
8 Chemicals	18.4	13.9	11.4	13.0	11.8	15.6	13.3	14.0	13.3	9.8
Minor group										
39 Paints	23.5	15.4	10.9	19.7	15.0	11.2	11.5	12.3	13.0	11.9
40 Petroleum	10.9	9.5	5.0	7.9	9.0	7.0	9.0	9.1	6.1	10.5

(d) PERCENTAGE PROFIT TO TOTAL CAPITAL

	1919	1920	1921	1922	1923	1924	1925	1926	1927	1928
Major group										
8 Chemicals						15.3	13.2	13.8	12.0	9.7
Minor group										
39 Paints						10.6	11.3	11.8	12.7	11.6
40 Petroleum						7.0	9.0	8.7	6.1	10.3

(e) FREQUENCY DISTRIBUTIONS OF PERCENTAGES OF TOTAL NET INCOME TO CAPITALIZATION, INDIVIDUAL CORPORATIONS, 1919–23. MAJOR GROUP 8: CHEMICALS

PERCENTAGE INCOME TO CAPI- TALIZATION	1919 PERCENT- AGE IN EACH CLASS	1919 ACCU- MULATED BY SUC- CESSIVE CLASSES	1920 PERCENT- AGE IN EACH CLASS	1920 ACCU- MULATED BY SUC- CESSIVE CLASSES	1921 PERCENT- AGE IN EACH CLASS	1921 ACCU- MULATED BY SUC- CESSIVE CLASSES	1922 PERCENT- AGE IN EACH CLASS	1922 ACCU- MULATED BY SUC- CESSIVE CLASSES	1923 PERCENT- AGE IN EACH CLASS	1923 ACCU- MULATED BY SUC- CESSIVE CLASSES
Zero to 4	2.6	2.6	10.5	10.5	16.4	16.4	16.7	16.7	14.0	14.0
5 to 9	16.9	19.5	13.2	23.7	22.9	39.3	21.4	38.1	18.6	32.6
10 to 14	18.2	37.7	18.4	42.1	19.7	59.0	8.3	46.4	19.8	52.4

	1924		1925		1926		1927		1928	
15 to 19	16.9	54.6	18.4	60.5	18.0	77.0	13.1	59.5	16.3	68.7
20 to 24	15.6	70.2	15.8	76.3	4.9	81.9	14.3	73.8	8.1	76.8
25 to 29	11.6	81.8	6.6	82.9	6.6	88.5	6.0	79.8	2.3	79.1
30 and over	18.2	100.0	17.1	100.0	11.5	100.0	20.2	100.0	20.9	100.0

(F) FREQUENCY DISTRIBUTIONS OF PERCENTAGES OF TOTAL PROFIT TO TOTAL CAPITAL, INDIVIDUAL CORPORATIONS, 1924–28. MAJOR GROUP 8: CHEMICALS

	1924		1925		1926		1927		1928	
Zero to 4	13.9	13.9	6.6	6.6	19.0	19.0	11.0	11.0	15.5	15.5
5 to 9	17.6	31.5	18.7	25.3	21.4	40.4	16.5	27.5	17.3	32.8
10 to 14	16.7	48.2	21.9	47.2	15.5	55.9	21.1	48.6	23.6	56.4
15 to 19	11.1	59.3	16.5	63.7	11.9	67.8	17.4	66.0	12.7	69.1
20 to 24	12.0	71.3	13.2	76.9	8.3	76.1	13.8	79.8	12.7	81.8
25 to 29	8.3	79.6	4.4	81.3	7.2	83.3	3.7	83.5	2.7	84.5
30 and over	20.4	100.0	18.7	100.0	16.7	100.0	16.5	100.0	15.5	100.0

TABLE 77

DISTRIBUTIONS OF EARNINGS RATES, CHEMICALS, LARGE IDENTICAL MANUFACTURING CORPORATIONS SERIES

(*companies with net incomes only*)

(A) FREQUENCY DISTRIBUTIONS OF PERCENTAGES OF TOTAL NET INCOME TO CAPITALIZATION, INDIVIDUAL CORPORATIONS, 1919–23. MAJOR GROUP 8: CHEMICALS

PERCENTAGE INCOME TO CAPI- TALIZATION	1919 PERCENT- AGE IN EACH CLASS	1919 ACCU- MULATED BY SUC- CESSIVE CLASSES	1920 PERCENT- AGE IN EACH CLASS	1920 ACCU- MULATED BY SUC- CESSIVE CLASSES	1921 PERCENT- AGE IN EACH CLASS	1921 ACCU- MULATED BY SUC- CESSIVE CLASSES	1922 PERCENT- AGE IN EACH CLASS	1922 ACCU- MULATED BY SUC- CESSIVE CLASSES	1923 PERCENT- AGE IN EACH CLASS	1923 ACCU- MULATED BY SUC- CESSIVE CLASSES
Zero to 4	4.3	4.3	12.2	12.2	22.5	22.5	11.8	11.8	10.6	10.6
5 to 9	8.7	13.0	17.2	29.4	24.2	46.7	14.7	26.5	18.8	29.4
10 to 14	11.1	24.1	15.2	44.6	16.0	62.7	12.8	39.3	19.3	48.7
15 to 19	14.4	38.5	14.7	59.3	8.9	71.6	13.7	53.0	15.2	63.9
20 to 24	12.5	51.0	9.3	68.6	8.3	79.9	11.3	64.3	11.2	75.1
25 to 29	10.1	61.1	6.9	75.5	3.0	82.9	7.8	72.8	5.6	80.7
30 and over	38.9	100.0	24.5	100.0	17.1	100.0	27.9	100.0	19.3	100.0

(B) FREQUENCY DISTRIBUTIONS OF PERCENTAGES OF TOTAL PROFIT TO TOTAL CAPITAL, INDIVIDUAL CORPO- RATIONS, 1924–28. MAJOR GROUP 8: CHEMICALS

	1924 PERCENT- AGE IN EACH CLASS	1924 ACCU- MULATED BY SUC- CESSIVE CLASSES	1925 PERCENT- AGE IN EACH CLASS	1925 ACCU- MULATED BY SUC- CESSIVE CLASSES	1926 PERCENT- AGE IN EACH CLASS	1926 ACCU- MULATED BY SUC- CESSIVE CLASSES	1927 PERCENT- AGE IN EACH CLASS	1927 ACCU- MULATED BY SUC- CESSIVE CLASSES	1928 PERCENT- AGE IN EACH CLASS	1928 ACCU- MULATED BY SUC- CESSIVE CLASSES
Zero to 4	9.4	9.4	8.7	8.7	7.4	7.4	14.2	14.2	12.8	12.8
5 to 9	25.2	34.6	23.2	31.9	19.6	27.0	18.3	32.5	18.7	31.5
10 to 14	19.3	53.9	20.8	52.7	24.0	51.0	22.8	55.3	23.2	54.7

CHEMICALS: SMALL CORPORATIONS

15 to 19	8.9	62.8	13.0	65.7	15.2	66.2	15.7	71.0	11.8	66.5
20 to 24	12.9	75.7	8.7	74.4	10.3	76.5	7.6	78.6	13.3	79.8
25 to 29	5.0	80.7	6.3	80.7	4.4	80.9	4.6	83.2	4.4	84.2
30 and over	19.3	100.0	19.3	100.0	19.1	100.0	16.8	100.0	15.8	100.0

CHAPTER 37

STONE, CLAY AND GLASS

THE major group Stone, Clay and Glass is made up of four minor groups. Descriptions appeared in Ch. 18.

TABLE 78
STONE, CLAY AND GLASS GROUPS, SMALL NON-IDENTICAL MANUFACTURING CORPORATIONS SERIES

(A) SIZE AND CHARACTER OF SAMPLE

	\multicolumn{10}{c}{NUMBER OF CORPORATIONS}	AVERAGE CAPITAL PER CORPORATION [1] (thousands of dollars)
	1919	1920	1921	1922	1923	1924	1925	1926	1927	1928	1928 ARITHMETIC MEAN
Major group											
9 Stone, clay and glass	70	83	94	76	84	88	81	91	83	67	214
Minor group											
45 Ceramics	90	95	85	93	93	96	90	88	97	92	286
48 Miscellaneous clay and stone products	31	37	38	39	41	36	55	47	50	34	192

[1] Total capital (i.e., includes funded debt) as of December 31, 1928.

(B) PERCENTAGE INCOME TO SALES

	1919	1920	1921	1922	1923	1924	1925	1926	1927	1928
Major group										
9 Stone, clay and glass	10.2	8.2	7.4	9.9	11.0	8.7	8.6	8.7	8.6	7.4
Minor group										
45 Ceramics	11.4	11.1	8.7	10.9	12.6	9.8	9.2	8.6	8.9	9.4
48 Miscellaneous clay and stone products	10.0	6.6	6.1	11.0	11.9	7.5	8.5	8.6	9.3	6.9

TABLE 78 (*continued*)

(c) PERCENTAGE INCOME TO CAPITALIZATION

	1919	1920	1921	1922	1923	1924	1925	1926	1927	1928
Major group										
9 Stone, clay and glass	9.0	13.3	7.4	13.9	15.0	10.1	12.7	13.2	11.6	8.8
Minor group										
45 Ceramics	12.8	14.5	11.5	13.0	14.5	11.6	10.1	12.0	8.9	9.6
48 Miscellaneous clay and stone products	16.5	15.0	17.1	14.2	18.2	8.6	13.3	13.4	15.3	6.9

(D) PERCENTAGE PROFIT TO TOTAL CAPITAL

	1924	1925	1926	1927	1928
Major group					
9 Stone, clay and glass	9.9	11.9	12.6	11.3	8.6
Minor group					
45 Ceramics	11.5	10.0	11.7	8.7	9.3
48 Miscellaneous clay and stone products	8.5	12.9	13.2	14.8	6.9

(E) FREQUENCY DISTRIBUTIONS OF PERCENTAGES OF TOTAL NET INCOME TO CAPITALIZATION, INDIVIDUAL CORPORATIONS, 1919–23. MAJOR GROUP 9: STONE, CLAY AND GLASS

PERCENTAGE INCOME TO CAPITALIZATION	1919 PERCENTAGE IN EACH CLASS	ACCUMULATED BY SUCCESSIVE CLASSES	1920 PERCENTAGE IN EACH CLASS	ACCUMULATED BY SUCCESSIVE CLASSES	1921 PERCENTAGE IN EACH CLASS	ACCUMULATED BY SUCCESSIVE CLASSES	1922 PERCENTAGE IN EACH CLASS	ACCUMULATED BY SUCCESSIVE CLASSES	1923 PERCENTAGE IN EACH CLASS	ACCUMULATED BY SUCCESSIVE CLASSES
Zero to 4	11.4	11.4	2.4	2.4	19.2	19.2	5.3	5.3	8.3	8.3
5 to 9	15.8	27.2	21.7	24.1	22.3	41.5	23.7	29.0	21.4	29.7

	1924		1925		1926		1927		1928	
10 to 14	11.4	38.6	20.5	44.6	18.1	59.6	21.0	50.0	17.9	47.6
15 to 19	21.4	60.0	20.5	65.1	8.5	68.1	11.8	61.8	11.9	59.5
20 to 24	10.0	70.0	6.0	71.1	12.8	80.9	9.2	71.0	13.1	72.6
25 to 29	10.0	80.0	8.4	79.5	7.4	88.3	5.3	76.3	7.2	79.8
30 and over	20.0	100.0	20.5	100.0	11.7	100.0	23.7	100.0	20.2	100.0

(F) FREQUENCY DISTRIBUTIONS OF PERCENTAGES OF TOTAL PROFIT TO TOTAL CAPITAL, INDIVIDUAL CORPORATIONS, 1924–28. MAJOR GROUP 9: STONE, CLAY AND GLASS

	1924		1925		1926		1927		1928	
Zero to 4	15.9	15.9	9.9	9.9	12.1	12.1	15.7	15.7	20.9	20.9
5 to 9	17.0	32.9	19.7	29.6	23.0	35.1	21.7	37.4	23.9	44.8
10 to 14	21.6	54.5	21.0	50.6	20.9	56.0	25.3	62.7	16.4	61.2
15 to 19	9.1	63.6	21.0	71.6	14.3	70.3	12.0	74.7	4.5	65.7
20 to 24	9.1	72.7	9.9	81.5	8.8	79.1	6.0	80.7	11.9	77.6
25 to 29	9.1	81.8	6.2	87.7	7.7	86.8	3.6	84.3	6.0	83.6
30 and over	18.2	100.0	12.3	100.0	13.2	100.0	15.7	100.0	16.4	100.0

Table 79

DISTRIBUTIONS OF EARNINGS RATES, STONE, CLAY AND GLASS, LARGE IDENTICAL MANUFACTURING CORPORATIONS SERIES

(companies with net incomes only)

(A) FREQUENCY DISTRIBUTIONS OF PERCENTAGES OF TOTAL NET INCOME TO CAPITALIZATION, INDIVIDUAL CORPORATIONS, 1919–23. MAJOR GROUP 9: STONE, CLAY AND GLASS

PERCENTAGE INCOME TO CAPITALIZATION	1919 PERCENT-AGE IN EACH CLASS	1919 ACCU-MULATED BY SUCCESSIVE CLASSES	1920 PERCENT-AGE IN EACH CLASS	1920 ACCU-MULATED BY SUCCESSIVE CLASSES	1921 PERCENT-AGE IN EACH CLASS	1921 ACCU-MULATED BY SUCCESSIVE CLASSES	1922 PERCENT-AGE IN EACH CLASS	1922 ACCU-MULATED BY SUCCESSIVE CLASSES	1923 PERCENT-AGE IN EACH CLASS	1923 ACCU-MULATED BY SUCCESSIVE CLASSES
Zero to 4	6.1	6.1	3.5	3.5	25.5	25.5	10.5	10.5	2.7	2.7
5 to 9	17.5	23.6	12.4	15.9	19.4	44.9	17.5	28.0	11.4	14.1
10 to 14	18.4	42.0	22.1	38.0	17.3	62.2	19.3	47.3	14.0	28.1
15 to 19	13.2	55.2	15.9	53.9	16.3	78.5	8.8	56.1	17.5	45.6
20 to 24	9.7	64.9	8.0	61.9	7.2	85.7	6.1	62.2	17.5	63.1
25 to 29	7.0	71.9	7.1	69.0	8.2	93.9	16.7	78.9	13.2	76.3
30 and over	28.1	100.0	31.0	100.0	6.1	100.0	21.1	100.0	23.7	100.0

(B) FREQUENCY DISTRIBUTIONS OF PERCENTAGES OF TOTAL PROFIT TO TOTAL CAPITAL, INDIVIDUAL CORPORATIONS, 1924–28. MAJOR GROUP 9: STONE, CLAY AND GLASS

	1924 PERCENT-AGE IN EACH CLASS	1924 ACCU-MULATED	1925 PERCENT-AGE IN EACH CLASS	1925 ACCU-MULATED	1926 PERCENT-AGE IN EACH CLASS	1926 ACCU-MULATED	1927 PERCENT-AGE IN EACH CLASS	1927 ACCU-MULATED	1928 PERCENT-AGE IN EACH CLASS	1928 ACCU-MULATED
Zero to 4	8.0	8.0	5.3	5.3	5.3	5.3	12.4	12.4	11.7	11.7
5 to 9	16.8	24.8	16.8	22.1	22.8	28.1	29.2	41.6	29.7	41.4
10 to 14	18.6	43.4	22.1	44.2	21.1	49.2	26.6	68.2	20.7	62.1

15 to 19	24.7	68.1	19.5	63.7	24.6	73.8	11.5	79.7	13.6	75.7
20 to 24	11.5	79.6	14.2	77.9	10.5	84.3	8.8	88.5	9.0	84.7
25 to 29	8.0	87.6	8.8	86.7	6.1	90.4	2.7	91.2	5.4	90.1
30 and over	12.4	100.0	13.3	100.0	9.6	100.0	8.8	100.0	9.9	100.0

Chapter 38

METALS

The major group Metals is made up of twenty-two minor groups. Descriptions appeared in Ch. 19.

TABLE 80

METALS GROUPS, SMALL NON-IDENTICAL MANUFACTURING CORPORATIONS SERIES

(A) SIZE AND CHARACTER OF SAMPLE

	\multicolumn{10}{c}{NUMBER OF CORPORATIONS}	AVERAGE CAPITAL PER CORPORATION [1] (thousands of dollars)
	1919	1920	1921	1922	1923	1924	1925	1926	1927	1928	1928 ARITHMETIC MEAN
Major group											
10 Metals	357	387	271	332	359	336	352	372	373	369	166
Minor group											
49 Castings and forgings	99	98	96	92	93	88	91	93	97	95	234
50 Sheet metal	90	93	95	90	93	97	92	90	96	94	162
52 Heating machinery	49	48	48	46	46	46	45	46	47	43	186
53 Electrical machinery	19	21	34	29	31	30	19	31	40	36	156
62 Motor vehicles	90	88	90	84	87	90	79	91	95	82	147
65 Tools	46	49	47	46	48	42	48	45	49	46	236
67 Miscellaneous machinery	35	59	23	23	48	22	64	50	35	35	148
70 Miscellaneous metals	41	40	25	37	39	55	24	33	39	22	220

[1] Total capital (i.e., includes funded debt) as of December 31, 1928.

(B) PERCENTAGE INCOME TO SALES

	1919	1920	1921	1922	1923	1924	1925	1926	1927	1928
Major group										
10 Metals	7.6	6.3	7.8	7.7	8.1	7.7	6.5	7.1	7.0	7.5

TABLE 80 (continued)

	1919	1920	1921	1922	1923	1924	1925	1926	1927	1928
Minor group										
49 Castings and forgings	8.2	5.2	6.0	9.2	6.6	5.9	6.4	6.9	6.4	6.2
50 Sheet metal	8.4	6.6	5.1	6.8	6.4	6.3	7.1	5.9	6.0	6.6
52 Heating and ventilating machinery	9.0	6.3	6.5	10.1	10.1	6.1	7.3	6.1	5.3	6.1
53 Electrical machinery	7.3	5.8	5.7	6.5	8.3	5.5	6.9	4.8	6.6	8.0
62 Motor vehicles	5.5	3.8	4.5	5.8	7.4	6.5	7.0	5.9	6.1	6.4
65 Tools	9.7	10.0	6.9	5.7	7.5	7.1	9.3	6.9	7.5	8.6
67 Miscellaneous machinery	10.6	7.4	7.2	10.7	8.2	10.9	10.8	8.7	6.2	8.6
70 Miscellaneous metals	7.5	4.9	10.4	11.4	8.5	6.8	6.0	7.7	7.7	11.3

(c) PERCENTAGE INCOME TO CAPITALIZATION

	1919	1920	1921	1922	1923	1924	1925	1926	1927	1928
Major group										
10 Metals	14.8	12.7	10.6	12.4	14.4	10.8	10.8	11.3	11.4	13.5
Minor group										
49 Castings and forgings	16.0	12.4	8.6	16.4	11.7	10.0	13.1	14.6	12.3	10.9
50 Sheet metal	19.7	16.6	9.1	13.5	12.3	13.1	14.7	11.9	12.9	12.7
52 Heating and ventilating machinery	17.4	13.9	9.6	16.0	17.1	9.6	12.4	9.3	8.9	9.4
53 Electrical machinery	15.9	13.5	9.8	11.1	18.0	12.3	19.2	11.1	13.8	15.0
62 Motor vehicles	10.2	9.7	6.9	6.7	13.8	12.9	10.5	11.9	12.5	15.5
65 Tools	18.2	17.2	6.6	8.8	11.1	11.9	12.4	11.6	10.9	12.8
67 Miscellaneous machinery	20.8	15.5	9.3	13.3	10.2	9.1	9.6	12.4	8.7	12.0
70 Miscellaneous metals	12.8	8.9	11.5	10.7	12.5	10.7	13.6	13.9	9.2	16.2

METALS: SMALL CORPORATIONS [427]

(D) PERCENTAGE PROFIT TO TOTAL CAPITAL

	1924	1925	1926	1927	1928
Major group					
10 Metals	10.6	10.6	11.2	11.1	13.1
Minor group					
49 Castings and forgings	9.8	12.6	14.1	12.1	10.3
50 Sheet metal	12.9	14.3	11.6	12.3	12.4
52 Heating and ventilating machinery	9.5	12.3	9.2	8.7	9.4
53 Electrical machinery	12.1	18.8	10.8	13.0	14.6
62 Motor vehicles	12.5	10.3	11.5	12.3	15.1
65 Tools	11.5	12.2	11.3	10.7	11.2
67 Miscellaneous machinery	9.1	9.6	12.1	8.7	11.0
70 Miscellaneous metals	10.5	12.9	13.5	8.9	15.9

(E) FREQUENCY DISTRIBUTIONS OF PERCENTAGES OF TOTAL NET INCOME TO CAPITALIZATION, INDIVIDUAL CORPORATIONS, 1919–23. MAJOR GROUP 10: METALS

PERCENTAGE INCOME TO CAPI-TALIZATION	1919 PERCENT-AGE IN EACH CLASS	1919 ACCU-MULATED BY SUC-CESSIVE CLASSES	1920 PERCENT-AGE IN EACH CLASS	1920 ACCU-MULATED BY SUC-CESSIVE CLASSES	1921 PERCENT-AGE IN EACH CLASS	1921 ACCU-MULATED BY SUC-CESSIVE CLASSES	1922 PERCENT-AGE IN EACH CLASS	1922 ACCU-MULATED BY SUC-CESSIVE CLASSES	1923 PERCENT-AGE IN EACH CLASS	1923 ACCU-MULATED BY SUC-CESSIVE CLASSES
Zero to 4	7.0	7.0	7.8	7.8	17.4	17.4	13.8	13.8	10.8	10.8
5 to 9	12.9	19.9	19.6	27.4	26.9	44.3	20.5	34.3	15.9	26.7
10 to 14	22.7	42.6	19.6	47.0	19.9	64.2	16.3	50.6	19.8	46.5
15 to 19	16.5	59.1	14.5	61.5	11.1	75.3	14.8	65.4	15.9	62.4
20 to 24	11.7	70.8	10.8	72.3	8.5	83.8	9.3	74.7	9.5	71.9
25 to 29	9.0	79.8	7.8	80.1	3.7	87.5	5.7	80.4	5.0	76.9
30 and over	20.2	100.0	19.9	100.0	12.5	100.0	19.6	100.0	23.1	100.0

TABLE 80 (*continued*)

(F) FREQUENCY DISTRIBUTIONS OF PERCENTAGES OF TOTAL PROFIT TO TOTAL CAPITAL, INDIVIDUAL CORPORATIONS, 1924–28. MAJOR GROUP 10: METALS

PERCENTAGE PROFIT TO TOTAL CAPITAL	1924 PERCENTAGE IN EACH CLASS	1924 ACCUMULATED BY SUCCESSIVE CLASSES	1925 PERCENTAGE IN EACH CLASS	1925 ACCUMULATED BY SUCCESSIVE CLASSES	1926 PERCENTAGE IN EACH CLASS	1926 ACCUMULATED BY SUCCESSIVE CLASSES	1927 PERCENTAGE IN EACH CLASS	1927 ACCUMULATED BY SUCCESSIVE CLASSES	1928 PERCENTAGE IN EACH CLASS	1928 ACCUMULATED BY SUCCESSIVE CLASSES
Zero to 4	14.0	14.0	12.8	12.8	9.7	9.7	17.7	17.7	11.4	11.4
5 to 9	23.5	37.5	22.2	35.0	23.4	33.1	23.3	41.0	23.0	34.4
10 to 14	22.0	59.5	21.9	56.9	22.6	55.7	19.3	60.3	20.3	54.7
15 to 19	12.8	72.3	14.8	71.7	14.0	69.7	9.4	69.7	15.2	69.9
20 to 24	8.9	81.2	11.9	83.6	11.5	81.2	8.6	78.3	7.9	77.8
25 to 29	5.1	86.3	5.1	88.7	4.0	85.2	6.4	84.7	4.9	82.7
30 and over	13.7	100.0	11.3	100.0	14.8	100.0	15.3	100.0	17.3	100.0

METALS: SMALL CORPORATIONS [429]

TABLE 81

DISTRIBUTIONS OF EARNINGS RATES, METALS, LARGE IDENTICAL MANUFACTURING CORPORATIONS SERIES

(*companies with net incomes only*)

(A) FREQUENCY DISTRIBUTIONS OF PERCENTAGES OF TOTAL NET INCOME TO CAPITALIZATION, INDIVIDUAL CORPORATIONS, 1919–23. MAJOR GROUP 10: METALS

PERCENTAGE INCOME TO CAPI- TALIZATION	1919 PERCENT- AGE IN EACH CLASS	1919 ACCU- MULATED BY SUC- CESSIVE CLASSES	1920 PERCENT- AGE IN EACH CLASS	1920 ACCU- MULATED BY SUC- CESSIVE CLASSES	1921 PERCENT- AGE IN EACH CLASS	1921 ACCU- MULATED BY SUC- CESSIVE CLASSES	1922 PERCENT- AGE IN EACH CLASS	1922 ACCU- MULATED BY SUC- CESSIVE CLASSES	1923 PERCENT- AGE IN EACH CLASS	1923 ACCU- MULATED BY SUC- CESSIVE CLASSES
Zero to 4	2.7	2.7	5.6	5.6	27.6	27.6	15.1	15.1	7.5	7.5
5 to 9	6.4	9.1	13.9	19.5	30.2	57.8	17.8	32.9	15.3	22.8
10 to 14	11.7	20.8	16.6	36.1	16.4	74.2	18.2	51.1	17.6	40.4
15 to 19	14.1	34.9	13.9	50.0	10.7	84.9	13.6	64.7	20.7	61.1
20 to 24	11.9	46.8	12.9	62.9	5.1	90.0	9.1	73.8	13.7	74.8
25 to 29	8.7	55.5	9.1	72.0	3.0	93.0	8.8	82.6	10.4	85.2
30 and over	44.5	100.0	28.0	100.0	7.0	100.0	17.4	100.0	14.8	100.0

(B) FREQUENCY DISTRIBUTIONS OF PERCENTAGES OF TOTAL PROFIT TO TOTAL CAPITAL, INDIVIDUAL CORPO- RATIONS, 1924–28. MAJOR GROUP 10: METALS

	1924 PERCENT- AGE IN EACH CLASS	1924 ACCU- MULATED BY SUC- CESSIVE CLASSES	1925 PERCENT- AGE IN EACH CLASS	1925 ACCU- MULATED BY SUC- CESSIVE CLASSES	1926 PERCENT- AGE IN EACH CLASS	1926 ACCU- MULATED BY SUC- CESSIVE CLASSES	1927 PERCENT- AGE IN EACH CLASS	1927 ACCU- MULATED BY SUC- CESSIVE CLASSES	1928 PERCENT- AGE IN EACH CLASS	1928 ACCU- MULATED BY SUC- CESSIVE CLASSES
Zero to 4	13.1	13.1	6.6	6.6	8.6	8.6	12.7	12.7	9.2	9.2
5 to 9	26.5	39.6	21.8	28.4	22.3	30.9	28.1	40.8	26.3	35.5
10 to 14	21.8	61.4	27.9	56.3	24.4	55.3	24.9	65.7	20.9	56.4
15 to 19	15.4	76.8	14.0	70.3	16.6	71.9	14.1	79.8	18.4	74.8
20 to 24	8.4	85.2	10.5	80.8	10.7	82.6	7.5	87.3	10.4	85.2
25 to 29	5.8	91.0	7.1	87.9	5.2	87.8	4.0	91.3	5.3	90.5
30 and over	9.0	100.0	12.1	100.0	12.2	100.0	8.7	100.0	9.5	100.0

Chapter 39

SPECIAL MANUFACTURING INDUSTRIES

The major group Special Manufacturing Industries is made up of four minor groups. Descriptions appeared in Ch. 20. For only one group, however, can a small corporations sample be presented.

Table 82
SPECIAL MANUFACTURING INDUSTRIES GROUPS, SMALL NON-IDENTICAL CORPORATIONS SERIES

(A) SIZE AND CHARACTER OF SAMPLE

	_____ NUMBER OF CORPORATIONS _____										AVERAGE CAPITAL, PER CORPORATION[1] (thousands of dollars)
	1919	1920	1921	1922	1923	1924	1925	1926	1927	1928	1928 ARITHMETIC MEAN
Major group											
11 Special manufacturing industries	73	74	82	71	76	69	66	100	86	70	153
Minor group											
74 Miscellaneous special manufacturing	42	41	49	32	49	57	41	74	59	56	149

[1] Total capital (i.e., includes funded debt) as of December 31, 1928.

(B) PERCENTAGE INCOME TO SALES

	1919	1920	1921	1922	1923	1924	1925	1926	1927	1928
Major group										
11 Special manufacturing industries	7.9	6.8	7.3	7.7	6.7	5.7	7.8	6.1	7.7	5.5
Minor group										
74 Miscellaneous special manufacturing	8.6	6.9	7.1	8.6	7.4	5.3	9.3	5.7	7.8	5.0

TABLE 82 (*continued*)

	1919	1920	1921	1922	1923	1924	1925	1926	1927	1928
(C) PERCENTAGE INCOME TO CAPITALIZATION										
Major group										
11 Special manufacturing industries	16.8	13.1	6.1	15.8	10.7	10.3	13.1	11.7	13.4	12.7
Minor group										
74 Miscellaneous special manufacturing	17.7	13.9	9.2	20.0	13.3	9.0	13.6	11.8	12.3	12.5
(D) PERCENTAGE PROFIT TO TOTAL CAPITAL										
Major group										
11 Special manufacturing industries						10.1	12.7	11.5	13.0	12.3
Minor group										
74 Miscellaneous special manufacturing						9.0	12.9	11.6	12.0	12.2

(E) FREQUENCY DISTRIBUTIONS OF PERCENTAGES OF TOTAL NET INCOME TO CAPITALIZATION, INDIVIDUAL CORPORATIONS, 1919–23, MAJOR GROUP 11: SPECIAL MANUFACTURING INDUSTRIES

PERCENTAGE INCOME TO CAPITALIZATION	1919 PERCENTAGE IN EACH CLASS	1919 ACCUMULATED BY SUCCESSIVE CLASSES	1920 PERCENTAGE IN EACH CLASS	1920 ACCUMULATED BY SUCCESSIVE CLASSES	1921 PERCENTAGE IN EACH CLASS	1921 ACCUMULATED BY SUCCESSIVE CLASSES	1922 PERCENTAGE IN EACH CLASS	1922 ACCUMULATED BY SUCCESSIVE CLASSES	1923 PERCENTAGE IN EACH CLASS	1923 ACCUMULATED BY SUCCESSIVE CLASSES
Zero to 4	5.5	5.5	9.5	9.5	11.0	11.0	8.4	8.4	7.9	7.9
5 to 9	12.3	17.8	17.5	27.0	19.5	30.5	21.1	29.5	30.3	38.2
10 to 14	15.1	32.9	14.9	41.9	24.4	54.9	9.9	39.4	14.5	52.7

	1924		1925		1926		1927		1928	
15 to 19	13.7	46.6	9.5	51.4	17.1	72.0	14.1	53.5	11.8	64.5
20 to 24	16.4	63.0	8.1	59.5	12.2	84.2	14.1	67.6	11.8	76.3
25 to 29	13.7	76.7	8.1	67.6	6.1	90.3	5.6	73.2	10.5	86.8
30 and over	23.3	100.0	32.4	100.0	9.7	100.0	26.8	100.0	13.2	100.0

(F) FREQUENCY DISTRIBUTIONS OF PERCENTAGES OF TOTAL PROFIT TO TOTAL CAPITAL, INDIVIDUAL CORPORATIONS, 1924–28. MAJOR GROUP 11: SPECIAL MANUFACTURING INDUSTRIES

	1924		1925		1926		1927		1928	
Zero to 4	15.9	15.9	10.6	10.6	18.0	18.0	14.0	14.0	11.4	11.4
5 to 9	24.6	40.5	21.2	31.8	25.0	43.0	19.7	33.7	18.6	30.0
10 to 14	15.9	56.4	27.3	59.1	16.0	59.0	12.8	46.5	18.6	48.6
15 to 19	13.1	69.5	4.5	63.6	19.0	78.0	16.3	63.8	24.3	72.9
20 to 24	5.8	75.3	15.2	78.8	7.0	85.0	14.0	77.8	8.6	81.5
25 to 29	4.4	79.7	9.1	87.9	7.0	92.0	5.8	83.6	5.7	87.2
30 and over	20.3	100.0	12.1	100.0	8.0	100.0	17.4	100.0	12.8	100.0

TABLE 83

DISTRIBUTIONS OF EARNINGS RATES, SPECIAL MANUFACTURING INDUSTRIES GROUPS, LARGE IDENTICAL CORPORATIONS SERIES

(companies with net incomes only)

(A) FREQUENCY DISTRIBUTIONS OF PERCENTAGES OF TOTAL NET INCOME TO CAPITALIZATION, INDIVIDUAL CORPORATIONS, 1919–23. MAJOR GROUP 11: SPECIAL MANUFACTURING INDUSTRIES

PERCENTAGE INCOME TO CAPITALIZATION	1919 PERCENTAGE IN EACH CLASS	1919 ACCUMULATED BY SUCCESSIVE CLASSES	1920 PERCENTAGE IN EACH CLASS	1920 ACCUMULATED BY SUCCESSIVE CLASSES	1921 PERCENTAGE IN EACH CLASS	1921 ACCUMULATED BY SUCCESSIVE CLASSES	1922 PERCENTAGE IN EACH CLASS	1922 ACCUMULATED BY SUCCESSIVE CLASSES	1923 PERCENTAGE IN EACH CLASS	1923 ACCUMULATED BY SUCCESSIVE CLASSES
Zero to 4	0.0	0.0	3.4	3.4	17.1	17.1	10.1	10.1	1.1	1.1
5 to 9	7.9	7.9	13.6	17.0	21.1	38.2	5.6	15.7	12.5	13.6
10 to 14	9.0	16.9	19.3	36.3	21.1	59.3	27.0	42.7	22.7	36.3
15 to 19	13.5	30.4	20.5	56.8	13.1	72.4	20.2	62.9	23.9	60.2
20 to 24	15.7	46.1	10.2	67.0	9.2	81.6	10.1	73.0	11.4	71.6
25 to 29	10.1	56.2	12.5	79.5	7.9	89.5	6.8	79.8	13.6	85.2
30 and over	43.8	100.0	20.5	100.0	10.5	100.0	20.2	100.0	14.8	100.0

(B) FREQUENCY DISTRIBUTIONS OF PERCENTAGES OF TOTAL PROFIT TO TOTAL CAPITAL, INDIVIDUAL CORPORATIONS, 1924–28. MAJOR GROUP 11: SPECIAL MANUFACTURING INDUSTRIES

	1924 PERCENTAGE IN EACH CLASS	1924 ACCUMULATED	1925 PERCENTAGE	1925 ACCUMULATED	1926 PERCENTAGE	1926 ACCUMULATED	1927 PERCENTAGE	1927 ACCUMULATED	1928 PERCENTAGE	1928 ACCUMULATED
Zero to 4	5.7	5.7	5.7	5.7	6.7	6.7	12.4	12.4	11.5	11.5
5 to 9	20.5	26.2	16.1	21.8	21.4	28.1	25.8	38.2	23.0	34.5
10 to 14	23.9	50.1	33.3	55.1	25.8	53.9	21.4	59.6	29.9	64.4

SPECIAL: SMALL CORPORATIONS

15 to 19	20.4	70.5	11.5	66.6	15.8	69.7	15.7	75.3	9.2	73.6
20 to 24	10.2	80.7	11.5	78.1	14.6	84.3	14.6	89.9	16.1	89.7
25 to 29	11.3	92.0	10.4	88.5	9.0	93.3	5.6	95.5	6.9	96.6
30 and over	8.0	100.0	11.5	100.0	6.7	100.0	4.5	100.0	3.4	100.0

Chapter 40

TRADE AND ITS MAJOR GROUPS

1. EARNINGS UPON INVESTMENT

THE small Trading corporations sample contains between approximately 1,300 and 1,500 corporations in different years of the period 1924–28. Frequency distributions for the earnings of individual corporations are available for the last four of these five years, but general arithmetic mean figures for the return upon investment are to be had for only two major groups separately and for only 1924 and 1928.[1] No data are available for the return upon sales for the Trade division or its major groups.

In 1924 the return upon investment for All Trade was 12.1 per cent; in 1928 the figure was almost exactly the same: 12.0 per cent. These returns correspond closely with comparable figures for the large Trading corporations sample in the same years: 13.6 per cent and 12.6 per cent respectively.[2]

Only very slight deviations from these figures for All Trade are evidenced by Retail Trade and Wholesale Trade. In Retail Trade the small corporations series shows a net return of 12.5 per cent on investment in 1924 and 12.4 per cent in 1928. In Wholesale Trade, the two figures are 12.6 per cent and 11 per cent respectively. Table 84 shows the number of corporations in each group as well as their average size.

[1] The five-year series for the several minor groups in Retail Trade and Wholesale Trade given in Ch. 41 and 42 are based upon samples that do not 'add up' so as to form major groups. The reasons for this are given in Ch. 27 and 44.

[2] These figures for the large corporations series are for corporations with net incomes only.

2. EARNINGS OF INDIVIDUAL CORPORATIONS

We may now inquire into the variation of individual rates of income received upon investment by the companies belonging to the small Trading corporations series in the years 1925–28. No general arithmetic mean return figures are available, however, for the first three of these four years: thus the comparisons will be of the median return with the rates earned by the corporations standing at the upper and lower quartiles of the distribution.

In all three years the median return was approximately 13 per cent. But, in all three years, a quarter of all the corporations earned in excess of 21 per cent while the lowest quarter earned under 8 per cent.

In 1928, the arithmetic mean return for All Trade was 12 per cent. About three-fifths of the companies, however, earned in excess of this amount. One-quarter of them earned over 22 per cent, while the lowest quarter again earned under 8 per cent. Chart 65 shows the distribution from year to year by broad classes of earnings rates.

CHART 65
FREQUENCY DISTRIBUTION OF EARNINGS RATES, INDIVIDUAL COMPANIES
ALL TRADE
—— NON-IDENTICAL CORPORATIONS
---- IDENTICAL CORPORATIONS

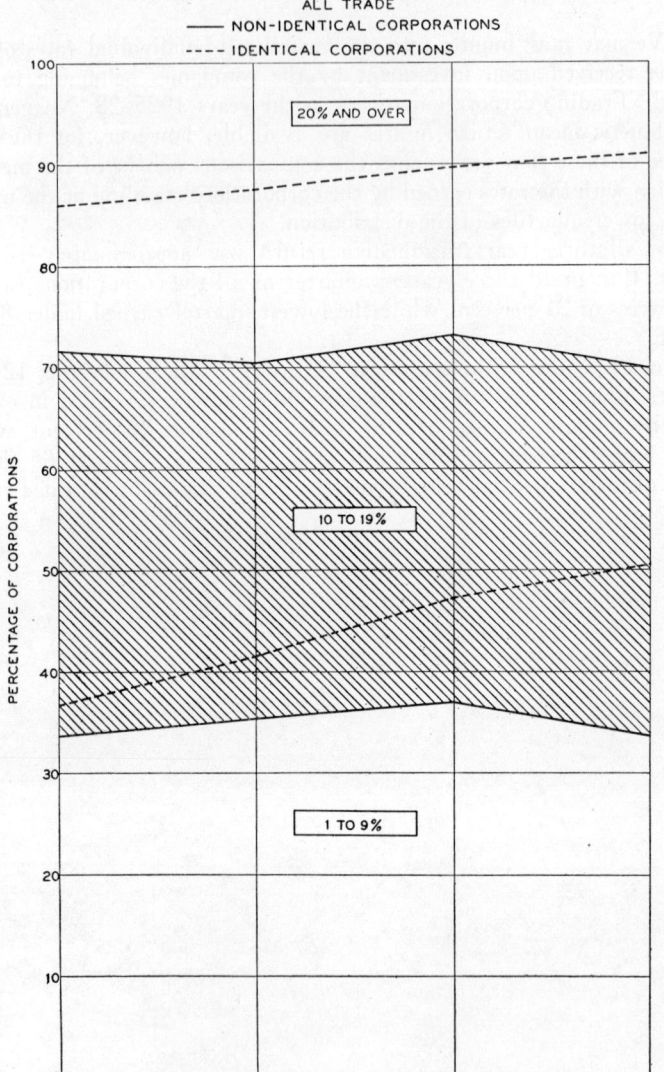

TRADE: SMALL CORPORATIONS [439]

TABLE 84

TRADE AND ITS MAJOR GROUPS, SMALL NON-IDENTICAL
CORPORATIONS SERIES

(A) SIZE AND CHARACTER OF SAMPLE

	NUMBER OF CORPORATIONS		AVERAGE CAPITAL PER CORPORATION [1] *(thousands of dollars)*
	1924	*1928*	ARITHMETIC MEAN
All trade	1,350	1,537	111
Major group			
12 Retail trade	742	858	89
13 Wholesale trade	397	308	138

[1] Total capital (i.e., includes funded debt) as of December 31, 1928.

	1924	*1928*
(B) PERCENTAGE INCOME TO CAPITALIZATION		
All trade	12.1	12.0
Major group		
12 Retail trade	12.5	12.4
13 Wholesale trade	12.6	11.0
(C) PERCENTAGE PROFIT TO TOTAL CAPITAL		
All trade	11.9	11.7
Major group		
12 Retail trade	12.3	12.0
13 Wholesale trade	12.4	10.9

TABLE 84 (continued)

(D) FREQUENCY DISTRIBUTIONS OF PERCENTAGES OF TOTAL PROFIT TO TOTAL CAPITAL, INDIVIDUAL CORPORATIONS, 1925–28. ALL TRADE

PERCENTAGE PROFIT TO TOTAL CAPITAL	1925 PERCENTAGE IN EACH CLASS	1925 ACCUMULATED BY SUCCESSIVE CLASSES	1926 PERCENTAGE IN EACH CLASS	1926 ACCUMULATED BY SUCCESSIVE CLASSES	1927 PERCENTAGE IN EACH CLASS	1927 ACCUMULATED BY SUCCESSIVE CLASSES	1928 PERCENTAGE IN EACH CLASS	1928 ACCUMULATED BY SUCCESSIVE CLASSES
Zero to 4	9.0	9.0	9.9	9.9	8.9	8.9	9.9	9.9
5 to 9	24.5	33.5	25.4	35.3	28.1	37.0	23.7	33.6
10 to 14	23.0	56.5	22.0	57.3	21.7	58.7	21.4	55.0
15 to 19	15.0	71.5	13.1	70.4	14.4	73.1	14.9	69.9
20 to 24	8.9	80.4	9.3	79.7	8.7	81.8	11.0	80.9
25 to 29	5.8	86.2	4.5	84.2	5.0	86.8	4.9	85.8
30 and over	13.8	100.0	15.8	100.0	13.2	100.0	14.2	100.0

TRADE: SMALL CORPORATIONS [441]

TABLE 85

FREQUENCY DISTRIBUTIONS OF PERCENTAGES OF TOTAL PROFIT TO TOTAL CAPITAL, INDIVIDUAL CORPORATIONS, 1925–28. ALL TRADE

(large identical trading corporations with net incomes)

PERCENTAGE PROFIT TO TOTAL CAPITAL	1925 PERCENT- AGE IN EACH CLASS	1925 ACCU- MULATED BY SUCCESSIVE CLASSES	1926 PERCENT- AGE IN EACH CLASS	1926 ACCU- MULATED BY SUCCESSIVE CLASSES	1927 PERCENT- AGE IN EACH CLASS	1927 ACCU- MULATED BY SUCCESSIVE CLASSES	1928 PERCENT- AGE IN EACH CLASS	1928 ACCU- MULATED BY SUCCESSIVE CLASSES
Zero to 4	9.7	9.7	11.9	11.9	13.3	13.3	16.0	16.0
5 to 9	27.0	36.7	29.6	41.5	34.0	47.3	34.5	50.5
10 to 14	30.4	67.1	29.3	70.8	29.7	77.0	28.1	78.6
15 to 19	18.9	86.0	16.9	87.7	12.7	89.7	12.3	90.9
20 to 24	5.9	91.9	5.9	93.6	4.1	93.8	4.9	95.8
25 to 29	3.5	95.4	2.7	96.3	3.3	97.1	2.5	98.3
30 and over	4.6	100.0	3.7	100.0	2.9	100.0	1.7	100.0

CHAPTER 41

RETAIL TRADE

THE major group Retail Trade is divided into ten minor groups: Automobiles; Men's Clothing; Department Stores; Drygoods; Furniture; Groceries; Jewelry; Building Material and Hardware; Lumber and Coal; Miscellaneous Retail Trade. In addition to these ten divisions, it is possible in one case, Miscellaneous Retail Trade, to effect a further subdivision into several subgroups.

In both the minor groups and subgroups, however, the data for the small corporations series are available only for the five years 1924–28. The small corporations data for each minor group, as in preceding chapters, are compared with the data for the large corporations series over the same period, although in the several subgroups into which Miscellaneous Retail Trade is divided, this procedure is not possible.

TABLE 86
RETAIL TRADE GROUPS, SMALL NON-IDENTICAL CORPORATIONS SERIES

(A) SIZE AND CHARACTER OF SAMPLE

	\multicolumn{5}{c	}{NUMBER OF CORPORATIONS}	AVERAGE CAPITAL PER CORPORATION [1] (thousands of dollars) ARITHMETIC MEAN
	1924	1925	1926	1927	1928	
Major group						
12 Retail trade [2]	742	..	..	..	858	89
Minor group						
75 Automobiles	106	77	100	105	82	68
76 Men's clothing	39	37	43	48	44	86
77 Department stores	87	91	93	93	90	236
78 Drygoods	91	90	81	96	88	91
79 Furniture	41	41	43	48	46	160
80 Groceries	85	79	82	92	81	87
81 Jewelry	45	46	44	48	46	115
84 Miscellaneous retail trade						
i Automobile accessories	58	81	74	82	89	91
ii Boots and shoes	46	44	44	47	41	70
iii Drugs	86	77	81	86	88	42
iv Haberdashery	36	44	43	49	46	83
v Hardware	41	48	44	46	45	81

[1] Total capital (i.e., includes funded debt) as of December 31, 1928.
[2] Data available only for 1924 and 1928 (see text).

[444] INDUSTRIAL PROFITS

TABLE 86 (continued)

(B) PERCENTAGE INCOME TO SALES

	1924	1925	1926	1927	1928
Major group					
12 Retail trade	...[1]	...[1]	...[1]	...[1]	...[1]
Minor group					
75 Automobiles	3.4	3.0	2.2	2.5	2.0
76 Men's clothing	5.1	5.1	4.5	4.9	4.0
77 Department stores	3.6	4.2	3.6	3.5	3.4
78 Drygoods	4.5	4.5	4.6	5.1	3.6
79 Furniture	7.1	7.5	7.0	6.1	5.2
80 Groceries	2.4	1.7	1.9	1.9	2.3
81 Jewelry	8.1	7.2	6.9	6.7	6.7
84 Miscellaneous retail trade					
i Automobile accessories	4.5	5.0	2.9	3.0	3.9
ii Boots and shoes	5.2	4.6	4.0	5.2	4.6
iii Drugs	3.8	3.7	5.3	5.8	6.2
iv Haberdashery	3.3	4.6	4.2	4.5	3.5
v Hardware	3.8	5.7	5.6	4.8	5.5

(C) PERCENTAGE INCOME TO CAPITALIZATION

	1924	1925	1926	1927	1928
Major group					
12 Retail trade	12.5[2]	...	...	...	12.4[2]
Minor group					
75 Automobiles	21.7	19.6	15.8	17.0	14.6
76 Men's clothing	14.1	9.9	13.4	10.2	10.5
77 Department stores	8.5	9.4	9.1	8.0	8.6
78 Drygoods	14.9	15.9	14.8	14.2	13.3
79 Furniture	10.8	10.1	11.7	10.4	7.3
80 Groceries	16.2	9.0	13.2	9.3	13.4
81 Jewelry	10.9	10.7	11.7	10.4	12.0
84 Miscellaneous retail trade					
i Automobile accessories	17.6	22.6	14.2	9.7	14.2
ii Boots and shoes	15.9	15.3	13.9	19.9	18.9
iii Drugs	10.1	11.7	18.3	16.6	19.5
iv Haberdashery	7.7	11.9	11.8	10.8	10.2
v Hardware	8.7	11.4	11.0	9.5	10.6

[1] Data not available.
[2] Data available only for 1924 and 1928 (see text).

(D) PERCENTAGE PROFIT TO TOTAL CAPITAL

	1924	1925	1926	1927	1928
Major group					
12 Retail trade[1]	12.3	...	...	...	12.0

RETAIL TRADE: SMALL CORPORATIONS [445]

Minor group	1925	1926	1927	1928
75 Automobiles	20.6	18.7	14.9	16.1	14.3
76 Men's clothing	13.8	9.9	13.3	10.1	10.1
77 Department stores	8.4	9.1	8.8	7.8	8.4
78 Drygoods	14.7	15.5	14.4	14.1	13.3
79 Furniture	10.7	10.2	11.2	10.4	7.2
80 Groceries	16.0	8.9	13.0	9.1	13.1
81 Jewelry	10.9	10.6	11.7	10.2	11.9
84 Miscellaneous retail trade					
i Automobile accessories	17.2	21.9	13.6	9.3	13.8
ii Boots and shoes	15.0	15.2	13.6	19.5	18.6
iii Drugs	9.9	11.5	18.1	16.4	19.2
iv Haberdashery	7.8	11.0	11.6	10.9	10.3
v Hardware	8.7	11.3	11.1	9.5	10.6

[1] Data available only for 1924 and 1928 (see text).

(E) FREQUENCY DISTRIBUTIONS OF PERCENTAGES OF TOTAL PROFIT TO TOTAL CAPITAL, INDIVIDUAL CORPORATIONS, 1925–28. MAJOR GROUP 12: RETAIL TRADE

PERCENTAGE PROFIT TO TOTAL CAPITAL	1925 PERCENTAGE IN EACH CLASS	1925 ACCUMULATED BY SUCCESSIVE CLASSES	1926 PERCENTAGE IN EACH CLASS	1926 ACCUMULATED BY SUCCESSIVE CLASSES	1927 PERCENTAGE IN EACH CLASS	1927 ACCUMULATED BY SUCCESSIVE CLASSES	1928 PERCENTAGE IN EACH CLASS	1928 ACCUMULATED BY SUCCESSIVE CLASSES
Zero to 4	8.1	8.1	8.8	8.8	6.8	6.8	8.0	8.0
5 to 9	23.1	31.2	25.1	33.9	26.9	33.7	22.8	30.8
10 to 14	23.0	54.2	22.6	56.5	23.6	57.3	22.0	52.8
15 to 19	15.0	69.2	14.0	70.5	14.5	71.8	15.2	68.0
20 to 24	9.5	78.7	10.5	81.0	9.0	80.8	11.3	79.3
25 to 29	5.7	84.4	4.4	85.4	5.3	86.1	5.4	84.7
30 and over	15.6	100.0	14.6	100.0	13.9	100.0	15.3	100.0

TABLE 87

FREQUENCY DISTRIBUTIONS OF PERCENTAGES OF TOTAL
PROFIT TO TOTAL CAPITAL, INDIVIDUAL CORPORATIONS,
1925–28. MAJOR GROUP 12: RETAIL TRADE

(large identical trading corporations with net incomes)

PERCENTAGE PROFIT TO TOTAL CAPITAL	1925 PERCENTAGE IN EACH CLASS	1925 ACCUMULATED BY SUCCESSIVE CLASSES	1926 PERCENTAGE IN EACH CLASS	1926 ACCUMULATED BY SUCCESSIVE CLASSES	1927 PERCENTAGE IN EACH CLASS	1927 ACCUMULATED BY SUCCESSIVE CLASSES	1928 PERCENTAGE IN EACH CLASS	1928 ACCUMULATED BY SUCCESSIVE CLASSES
Zero to 4	5.7	5.7	6.1	6.1	11.4	11.4	11.5	11.5
5 to 9	20.8	26.5	21.8	27.9	27.9	39.3	30.5	42.0
10 to 14	28.3	54.8	31.4	59.3	28.9	68.2	27.0	69.0
15 to 19	23.7	78.5	22.5	81.8	16.8	85.0	16.9	85.9
20 to 24	8.1	86.6	9.3	91.1	5.4	90.4	7.6	93.5
25 to 29	4.6	91.2	3.6	94.7	4.6	95.0	4.3	97.8
30 and over	8.8	100.0	5.3	100.0	5.0	100.0	2.2	100.0

Chapter 42

WHOLESALE TRADE

The major group Wholesale Trade contains eight minor groups: Drugs; Drygoods; Groceries; Hardware; Importers and Exporters; Building Material and Lumber; Paper; Miscellaneous Wholesale Trade. In addition to these eight divisions, it is possible in one case, Miscellaneous Wholesale Trade, to effect a further division into subgroups. Again, in both the minor groups and subgroups, data for the small corporations series are available only for the five years 1924–28.

TABLE 88

WHOLESALE TRADE GROUPS, SMALL NON-IDENTICAL CORPORATIONS SERIES

(A) SIZE AND CHARACTER OF SAMPLE

		NUMBER OF CORPORATIONS					AVERAGE CAPITAL PER CORPORATION [1] (thousands of dollars) ARITHMETIC MEAN
		1924	1925	1926	1927	1928	
Major group							
13	Wholesale trade [2]	397	..	..	..	308	138
Minor group							
86	Drugs	43	29	42	49	43	316
87	Drygoods	39	45	47	49	47	241
88	Groceries	84	78	85	97	91	157
89	Hardware	49	49	48	48	48	229
99–85	Miscellaneous wholesale trade						
	i Furniture	26	46	48	47	46	185
	ii Jewelry	46	48	48	50	46	152

[1] Total capital (i.e., includes funded debt) as of December 31, 1928.
[2] Data available only for 1924 and 1928 (see text).

WHOLESALE: SMALL CORPORATIONS

TABLE 88 (continued)

(B) PERCENTAGE INCOME TO SALES

		1924	1925	1926	1927	1928
Major group						
13	Wholesale Trade [1]	...	...	...	...	...
Minor group						
86	Drugs	2.5	3.3	2.9	3.3	2.9
87	Drygoods	2.8	2.7	2.0	3.3	2.2
88	Groceries	1.9	1.9	1.3	1.7	1.5
89	Hardware	3.3	3.0	2.9	3.0	4.0
93–85	Miscellaneous wholesale trade					
	i Furniture	3.7	3.4	3.9	2.4	4.1
	ii Jewelry	4.2	4.2	4.4	3.7	3.2

(C) PERCENTAGE INCOME TO CAPITALIZATION

		1924	1925	1926	1927	1928
Major group						
13	Wholesale trade [2]	12.6	...	...	...	11.0
Minor group						
86	Drugs	7.8	10.4	10.6	12.6	8.9
87	Drygoods	10.1	11.4	7.6	8.7	6.8
88	Groceries	9.9	10.3	9.0	8.8	11.0
89	Hardware	8.9	8.3	7.8	8.1	9.6
93–85	Miscellaneous wholesale trade					
	i Furniture	9.8	11.6	14.7	7.9	11.8
	ii Jewelry	10.7	9.6	12.5	9.6	9.1

(D) PERCENTAGE PROFIT TO TOTAL CAPITAL

		1924	1925	1926	1927	1928
Major group						
13	Wholesale trade [2]	12.4	...	...	...	10.9
Minor group						
86	Drugs	7.7	10.4	10.5	12.4	8.8
87	Drygoods	10.1	11.4	7.6	8.6	6.8
88	Groceries	9.9	10.3	9.0	8.7	10.9
89	Hardware	8.9	8.2	7.7	8.0	9.4
93–85	Miscellaneous wholesale trade					
	i Furniture	9.6	11.6	14.5	7.9	11.2
	ii Jewelry	10.7	9.6	12.4	9.6	9.0

[1] Data not available.
[2] Data available only for 1924 and 1928 (see text).

TABLE 88 (continued)

(E) FREQUENCY DISTRIBUTIONS OF PERCENTAGES OF TOTAL PROFIT TO TOTAL CAPITAL, INDIVIDUAL CORPORATIONS, 1925–28. MAJOR GROUP 13: WHOLESALE TRADE

PERCENTAGE PROFIT TO TOTAL CAPITAL	1925 PERCENTAGE IN EACH CLASS	1925 ACCUMULATED BY SUCCESSIVE CLASSES	1926 PERCENTAGE IN EACH CLASS	1926 ACCUMULATED BY SUCCESSIVE CLASSES	1927 PERCENTAGE IN EACH CLASS	1927 ACCUMULATED BY SUCCESSIVE CLASSES	1928 PERCENTAGE IN EACH CLASS	1928 ACCUMULATED BY SUCCESSIVE CLASSES
Zero to 4	12.2	12.2	11.9	11.9	14.4	14.4	15.0	15.0
5 to 9	26.5	38.7	25.9	37.8	29.7	44.1	26.3	41.3
10 to 14	23.4	62.1	20.1	57.9	17.6	61.7	18.8	60.1
15 to 19	15.7	77.8	12.8	70.7	14.1	75.8	12.3	72.4
20 to 24	7.7	85.5	5.5	76.2	8.1	83.9	9.4	81.8
25 to 29	3.7	89.2	4.3	80.5	4.0	87.9	3.2	85.0
30 and over	10.8	100.0	19.5	100.0	12.1	100.0	15.0	100.0

TABLE 89

FREQUENCY DISTRIBUTIONS OF PERCENTAGES OF TOTAL PROFIT TO TOTAL CAPITAL, INDIVIDUAL CORPORATIONS, 1925–28. MAJOR GROUP 13: WHOLESALE TRADE

(large identical trading corporations with net incomes)

PERCENTAGE PROFIT TO TOTAL CAPITAL	1925 PERCENTAGE IN EACH CLASS	1925 ACCUMULATED BY SUCCESSIVE CLASSES	1926 PERCENTAGE IN EACH CLASS	1926 ACCUMULATED BY SUCCESSIVE CLASSES	1927 PERCENTAGE IN EACH CLASS	1927 ACCUMULATED BY SUCCESSIVE CLASSES	1928 PERCENTAGE IN EACH CLASS	1928 ACCUMULATED BY SUCCESSIVE CLASSES
Zero to 4	13.7	13.7	16.7	16.7	14.4	14.4	18.6	18.6
5 to 9	32.5	46.2	37.0	53.7	41.2	55.6	39.3	57.9
10 to 14	32.2	78.4	27.5	81.2	28.9	84.5	29.1	87.0
15 to 19	15.4	93.8	13.3	94.5	9.0	93.5	9.1	96.1
20 to 24	3.1	96.9	1.7	96.2	2.7	96.2	2.1	98.2
25 to 29	2.8	99.7	2.1	98.3	2.4	98.6	1.1	99.3
30 and over	.3	100.0	1.7	100.0	1.4	100.0	0.7	100.0

Book IV
PROBLEMS OF ESTIMATION AND INTERPRETATION

CHAPTER 43

PROBLEMS OF SAMPLING AND WEIGHTING

1. NECESSITY OF RESORTING TO SAMPLES

THERE are in the United States about half a million corporations—the exact number reporting to the Bureau of Internal Revenue in 1928 was 495,892.[1] Of these, some 95,000 engage in Manufacture, 130,000 in Trade, 19,000 in Mining, 120,000 in Finance. The remainder are classified in industrial divisions not treated in this volume, such as Railroads and Public Utilities, Agriculture, Construction, and Service (for example, laundries, hotels and moving picture theatres).

Of the 365,000 engaged in Manufacture, Trade, Finance and Mining in 1928, about 25,000 were 'inactive', that is, they reported no income data. For the remaining 340,000 active corporations in these four fields, no complete tabulations, involving the types of data presented in this volume, have ever been made. Whether based upon Government data or materials collected by other agencies, every statistical study of profits that has essayed to divide such a field as Manufacture into numerous minor industrial groups, to cover more than a one- or two-year period, and to present frequency distributions for the earnings rates of individual

[1] This figure really is for the number of corporate income tax returns, which varies from about 320,000 to 495,000 in the different years between 1919 and 1928. The number of corporations is somewhat larger, since some of these tax returns are for consolidated companies. See Ch. 46.

[455]

corporations, has had to rely upon samples of one sort or another. We have done likewise throughout the greater part of this volume. Accordingly, even though our data constitute a more comprehensive set of detailed materials than those heretofore available, we still have to ask, how large, both absolutely and relatively, how representative, how typical, are our several samples?

In doing so, it will be necessary not only to discuss the samples already presented, but also to introduce others which because of their smaller size, or for technical reasons, have not been discussed in the parts of the volume intended for general readers. In some instances, these new sets of samples either correspond with or overlap upon some portions of those previously presented, and may thus serve as a check upon their validity. Also, the methods by which some of the earlier samples already presented have in several instances been combined, in order to yield certain estimates and results contained in other parts of the volume, need here to be explained.

2. DIVISION OF TOTAL FIELD OR UNIVERSE: MANUFACTURING AS AN ILLUSTRATION

The 90,000 active corporations in the country engaged in manufacture, of course, include enterprises that are large or small, that in a given year have net incomes or deficits, that have been engaged in business for many years or for only a few years, that are consistently successful or unsuccessful, or that have enjoyed neither conspicuously good nor conspicuously bad fortune.

Of this hybrid and complex universe or total, the corporations of our samples constitute but a small percentage by number. But the manner in which each sample has been drawn, or the relation it bears to the general aggregate of the original materials, affects greatly its representativeness and significance. For no one of the samples is so heterogeneous as is the whole of which each is a part. Each typifies rather, to a degree more or less accurate, a particular portion or segment of the entire universe of manufacturing corporations, meaning by 'entire universe' the approximately 70,000 to 90,000 manufacturing corporations of the country in each year between 1919 and 1928. It will be desirable first to comment more specifically upon the character of this 'general universe', then to relate our samples quantitatively, as best we can, to its several segments.

For this purpose, we first divide the entire universe of manufacturing corporations into two broad portions: corporations with net incomes and those without net incomes. The 'with net' group amounts to roughly 60 per cent of the total number. Thus in all years from 1919 to 1928 the number of manufacturing corporations with net incomes runs from about 50,000 to 55,000 a year, except in 1921 when the figure was slightly less than 40,000.

We may further divide the 'with net' group into various segments according to the amount of income received by each of the corporations comprising it. Absolute amount of net income is not by any means the best index of size—amount of sales, capital or even total assets would be a better basis—but it is the only one available in the data for all of the country's corporations.[2] However, while not the best index of *size,* it affords one important criterion by which the representativeness of our samples may be judged; and for this purpose the corporations earning net incomes

[2] In the analysis in this chapter the data for all corporations in the country, or broad segments thereof, are taken from the annual reports of the Bureau of Internal Revenue, *Statistics of Income.* The 1931 volume happily has begun the practice of classifying income and balance sheet data by size of assets; that volume, however, became available only at the end of 1933.

may be further divided into three broad groups: those with incomes of less than $2,000; those with incomes between $2,000 and $50,000; and those with incomes of over $50,000.[3]

These net incomes, as classified in the data for all corporations in the country, are *taxable net incomes*.[4] They thus exclude both interest receipts upon tax-exempt securities and intercorporate dividends, that is, dividends received by one corporation upon the capital stocks that it owns in other corporations. The net income items in our several samples, however, are so computed as to include these tax-exempt items: interest on Government, state and municipal securities and dividends received from other corporations (exempted from taxation under the income tax law because the tax on such dividends is already paid by the corporation earning the income originally). Thus our income comparisons in later sections will be of somewhat different items. But the discrepancy here, while great in the case of certain individual corporations having substantial intercorporate

[3] Strictly speaking, incomes of from $2,000 to $49,999, and of $50,000 or over. The reports of the Bureau of Internal Revenue, however, in some years show class intervals in which the upper limit of one class appears as the lower limit of the next class; with respect to this point there is here no need to be meticulous.

[4] This statement is subject to two qualifications, neither of which is important for our purposes here. One is that the incomes contained in the frequency distributions of *Statistics of Income* for any year are actual or current year net earnings, and in the case of corporations which had *net losses* in the year previous, the whole of the current year income is not taxable, but only the amount of the income after deduction of the 'prior year loss'. In some years, the losses of more than one year back have been deductible. Another qualification is that domestic corporations with net incomes of $25,000 or less may deduct $2,000 as a special credit or exemption, before determining the income on which a tax liability is incurred. But except for these two types of case, the net incomes shown in the *Statistics of Income* distributions discussed in this chapter are taxable incomes, i.e., unlike the net incomes shown for corporations of our various samples, they exclude non-taxable items, chiefly those of dividends received and interest on tax-exempt securities.

holdings, is probably not serious by and large. It is certainly not serious, at least, so far as our general arithmetic mean calculations of the return upon investment are concerned. For the entire universe of manufacturing corporations of the country with net incomes, the sum of tax-exempt interest and dividends received amounted (in 1928) to 11.3 per cent of the net income reckoned without those two items. Thus, related to an investment base of 46 billion dollars, the return without the inclusion of the two items is 10.4 per cent as compared with 11.6 per cent when they are included.

As said, in considering the return earned by any particular corporation, the inclusion or exclusion of tax-exempt income may make a large difference. But it probably makes slight difference with respect to the frequency distributions of the rates of earnings upon investment received by individual corporations; for the proportion of individual corporations receiving tax-exempt incomes that are at all substantial relative to their taxable incomes is quite small. That this is so follows from the generally low ratio of aggregate tax-exempt income to the aggregate taxable income of all corporations combined. The proportion is so small that for any list of even a few dozen companies the relative standing in terms of earnings rates is probably about the same taking either set of figures.[5] Evidence supporting this *a priori* reasoning is available in data for two manufacturing groups, chosen quite at random and in which an experiment was undertaken to check upon this point. For the group, Bakery Products,[6] containing 18 corporations each possessing some tax-exempt income, but each having a

[5] This could, of course, also be so, theoretically, if all corporations received tax-exempt incomes in exactly the same proportion to the taxable incomes—but we know this is not the case.

[6] Sub-code No. 0290 in the *Source-Book,* corresponding in classification with Minor group No. 1, the experimental data for which are given on p. 201 of that volume.

total net income of over $100,000, there were computed for each corporation the percentages of earnings upon capitalization both with and without the inclusion of the tax-exempt items. The rank correlation between the two series was perfect: +1.0. For 32 other corporations of the same group but with total net incomes of from $2,000 to $100,000 each, the rank correlation coefficient was again perfect. The second group similarly analyzed, Radio manufacturing, yielded almost exactly the same results.[7] That the same thing is true of most other individual industrial groups is not, of course, established by these experiments, but they afford presumptive evidence that probably no serious error is made upon this score in comparing distributions of the two types of net income for large groups of corporations. In other words, we are justified in saying in this, as in many other connections, that the presence of individually inadequate items of data, taken *en masse,* often may not interfere with fairly accurate final results—not because the errors happily cancel one another, but because the individual anomalies constitute too small a part of the aggregate to cause any great general distortion.

With these preliminary observations in mind, we may now examine our several samples, *seriatim.*[8]

3. SAMPLES FOR THE MANUFACTURING DIVISION

a. Large Manufacturing Corporation Series

i. Fragmentary descriptions of this sample have been given in previous chapters, but we have now to describe it

[7] For 62 corporations with incomes of over $100,000 the coefficient was +.9907, while for 35 corporations with incomes of from $2,000 to $100,000 it was +.9995.

[8] All that has been said in this section concerning the definition of net income applies to the Trade, Finance and Mining samples discussed in later sections quite as much as to Manufacturing.

SAMPLING AND WEIGHTING

more precisely and to evaluate it in detailed terms. The sample consists of identical corporations numbering 2,046 in every year of the period 1919–28. Consequently all the corporations included are at least ten years old, and many, of course, have been engaged in business much longer. Containing identical corporations throughout the period, the sample in every year consists of some corporations with negative and some with positive incomes, although, as will appear shortly, the number of deficits in any one year other than 1921 is slight.

Similarly, the effect of industrial mergers is in no way eliminated. Any growth in the size of a given corporation because of combination with other corporations during the period is reflected in the absolute data for sales, investment and net income, either for the sample as a whole (that is, All Manufacturing) or for the major or minor group in which the corporation is classified. Although impairing somewhat the significance of the absolute figures *per se,* this factor does not at all invalidate either comparisons between the growth rates of the absolute data or the time comparison of the percentages of earnings upon investment, as the effect of a merger is to increase the sales and income as well as the capital investment of a company.

As regards industrial classification, each corporation has been kept in exactly the same minor group throughout the period; the reason for this, and the bearing of mergers upon it, are discussed in Ch. 46.

The large corporations series contains only a small proportion of the entire universe of 70,000 to 90,000 manufacturing corporations—from 2.1 to 3.0 per cent in different years. But the total net income of the sample runs from 57 to 66 per cent of that for all manufacturing corporations of the country between 1922 and 1928.[9] In terms of volume of business, sales for the large corporations sample amount to from 42 to 46 per cent in different years of the same period. In terms of investment, the sample contains from 43 to 47 per cent of that for all manufacturing corporations in the country during the years 1926–28.[10] All in all, our large corporations series therefore constitutes a very large proportion of the activities of all manufacturing corporations in the country.

But so far as profitableness is concerned, the sample is somewhat biased in an upward direction. The fact that it is composed exclusively of corporations that have been in business for ten years or more exercises a kind of commercial or financial natural selection—the great numbers of corporations that constantly go in and out of business, each lasting but a few years, are not even touched. This qualification is not so important in manufacturing as in trading, where the length of business life, particularly for the smaller enterprises, is proverbially short; nevertheless it must be said that both are better samples of successful large corporations than of unsuccessful.

This is not to say that 'large corporations earn more than small ones', for whether this is so depends upon one's definition of 'large' and 'small'. The analysis of earnings rates by size of corporation *within* the large corporations sample, as presented in Chapter 5, showed that corporations with capitals of over $500,000 earn profits at lower rates than

[9] Comparable data between sample and universe prior to 1922 are not available.

[10] The investment figures for all manufacturing corporations in the country are estimates, subject, however, to rather small margins of error, as explained in Appendix A. Closely comparable data for other years on investment for all manufacturing corporations in the country are not available, but the ratios in question are doubtless not very different; we are justified in inferring this because of the figures for sales just cited for a longer period.

do those of smaller size. That analysis was not in terms of minor groups, but probably in nearly every specific industry there is an optimum beyond which it does not pay most enterprises to expand—at least, so far as the *rates* at which their capitals earn profits are concerned. But the entire group of all manufacturing corporations in the country (including those which fail to earn net incomes as well as those which do so) undoubtedly contains numerous enterprises of such small size that they enjoy the economies of large-scale production, relatively speaking, hardly at all, while our large corporations sample may include many companies operating at or near the peak of efficiency as well as those which have passed it. Then, too, many of the very small corporations [11] —often they are 'close corporations' owned and operated by members of a family—deduct charges for officers' salaries which are much larger relative to the income before such deductions than is the case with the generally larger concerns. Frequently these deductions, combined with other factors, may cause nominal deficits to be shown by such very small corporations. The proportion of deficits among all manufacturing corporations in the country is, of course, far higher than in our large corporations sample. For all manufacturing corporations of the country no data are available that divide the universe into any groups according to size of capital, or into any size groups in relation to the profitableness of operations upon any basis of assets or net worth; but we can obtain some general inkling as to the size of the corporations which showed net incomes as compared with those which reported deficits by computing the average sales per enterprise for each class of corporation. In 1928 this figure for all manufacturing corporations in the

---

[11] The expression 'very small corporations' is used here so as to avoid any identification with our 'small corporations' sample (which includes corporations with net incomes only) discussed in the following section.

country with net incomes was almost exactly one million dollars, whereas for all corporations reporting deficits it was only $258,000.

Indeed, in our large corporations series the proportion of enterprises with deficits is in most years very low. It runs less than 4 per cent of the companies in all years except 1920 and 1921, when it is 6 and 21 per cent respectively. As a result, our large corporations series as a whole (the corporations with deficits combined with those with net incomes) between 1924 and 1928 earns the following rates of net income to capitalization:

1924	1925	1926	1927	1928
10%	12%	12%	10%	11%

whereas *all* of the manufacturing corporations in the country for which we have estimated data for those same years show:

1924	1925	1926	1927	1928
8%	9%	9%	7%	9%

As a sample of *all* manufacturing corporations in the country, therefore, the large corporations series must be accepted with this clear qualification: the arithmetic mean rate of return is too high. There is, however, no evidence to indicate that *fluctuations* in the data of the large corporations series over the period 1919–28 do not satisfactorily reflect the relative *changes* that take place in the data for all manufacturing corporations in the country, in the aggregate. Whether fluctuations in the data of the large corporations series sample *when subdivided into minor groups* are representative of changes for other than such large corporations is, however, a matter which we shall not discuss until later in this chapter when other samples are compared with the one in question.

ii. But as representative of all of the manufacturing

corporations in the country *with net incomes,* the large corporations series, so far as we can tell, seems indeed to be an excellent sample, at least in terms of the calculation of arithmetic mean ratios for manufacture as a whole. If we exclude the corporations with deficits from both sets of figures, our large corporations sample, in respect of number, again constitutes a small proportion of all the manufacturing corporations in the country; the representation in the various years of the period is only 3.6 to 4.4 per cent, although in terms of the amount of net income received, the large corporations sample accounts for from 49 to 56 per cent of that received by all the 'with net' manufacturing corporations in the country between 1922 and 1928. Although containing only a 4 per cent representation by number the generally representative character of the sample's 'with net' corporations is evidenced by the closeness with which the earnings rates shown by it correspond with those for all such corporations in the country, in the three years of the period for which the latter data are available. The percentages of net income to capitalization shown by the sample in 1926, 1927 and 1928 are:

$$13.0 \qquad 10.9 \qquad 12.2$$

while those for all manufacturing corporations in the country are:

$$12.3 \qquad 10.9 \qquad 12.0$$

iii. All that has been said thus far, however, relates to the degree of validity attaching to the large corporations sample for purposes of arithmetic mean results. We may now go somewhat beyond this and inquire into its representativeness with respect to certain frequency distributions. The two inquiries are in a mathematical sense, of course, related, but it is quite conceivable that a sample might yield fairly good arithmetic mean data and yet not be typical in terms of the distribution of its component items. Accordingly we may compare the composition of our sample as best we can with that of the particular segment of all manufacturing corporations from which it is drawn and which it most nearly typifies.

It will be recalled that earlier in this chapter it was stated that a frequency distribution by size of net income is available for all of the country's corporations. This net income figure does not, however, include the tax-exempt items contained in the income of our samples. It will further be recalled that, for purposes of comparison with our samples, the manufacturing corporations of the country earning net incomes can be broadly classed into three groups: less than $2,000; $2,000 to $50,000; and over $50,000. Our large corporations sample is predominantly of incomes of $50,000 or over; in all years except 1921 approximately 90 per cent of the corporations of the sample have incomes of over this amount; and even in 1921 about 80 per cent have such incomes. We may thus regard it as belonging to the 'over $50,000' category. Both by number and by income received, the 'with net' corporations of the sample constitute a substantial proportion of this 'over $50,000 universe'. In no year does the number of corporations constitute less than a 23 per cent representation, while in several years it runs over 25 per cent. In terms of the amount of income the sample contains from 55 to 68 per cent of the total income received by all of the country's manufacturing corporations with over $50,000 incomes.

But 'the incomes above $50,000' includes a broad range; and we may now ask exactly how their relative distributions in our sample correspond with that for all manufacturing corporations in the country with such incomes, in the years 1920–28.[12]

For this purpose we set up six class intervals for size of income (it is to be noted that they are uneven) : $50,000–$100,000; $100,000–$250,000; $250,000–$500,000; $500,000 to $1,000,000; $1,000,000 to $5,000,000; and $5,000,000 and over. In all of these classes combined there are in most years approximately 8,000 corporations in the 'all manufacturing corporations of the country' distribution and approximately 1,800 corporations in each year in the distribution for the large corporations sample.[13]

The two distributions, for 1928, are given in Tables 90 and 91. But in all years the general results are much the

TABLE 90

FREQUENCY DISTRIBUTIONS OF NET INCOMES FOR ALL MANUFACTURING CORPORATIONS IN THE UNITED STATES WITH INCOMES OF OVER $50,000 IN 1928

SIZE OF INCOME	NUMBER OF CORPORATIONS	PERCENTAGE OF TOTAL
$50,000– 100,000	3,284	40.0
100,000– 250,000	2,647	32.3
250,000– 500,000	1,049	12.8
500,000–1,000,000	627	7.6
1,000,000–5,000,000	499	6.1
5,000,000 and over	101	1.2
Total	8,207	100.0

same. In the case of all manufacturing corporations of the country approximately 40 per cent of the total frequencies

[12] Data are not available to make comparisons for 1919.

[13] The number of corporations is not exactly the same in each year for the sample, first, because deficits in successive years are not, of course, necessarily repeated by the identical corporations; second, because the few incomes of under $50,000 are in each year omitted from the calculations. (They belong, of course, to no one of the brackets above $50,000. The extent to which their exclusion affects the results may be seen by examining Table 100.)

TABLE 91

FREQUENCY DISTRIBUTIONS OF TOTAL NET INCOMES FOR COMPANIES WITH INCOMES OF OVER $50,000, IN THE LARGE MANUFACTURING CORPORATIONS SAMPLE, 1928

SIZE OF INCOME	NUMBER OF CORPORATIONS	PERCENTAGE OF TOTAL
$50,000– 100,000	290	17.0
100,000– 250,000	500	29.3
250,000– 500,000	354	20.8
500,000–1,000,000	256	15.0
1,000,000–5,000,000	222	13.0
5,000,000 and over	84	4.9
Total	1,706	100.0

are found in the $50,000–$100,000 class interval; but in the case of the large corporations sample, in most years only about 16 or 17 per cent of the frequencies are found in this class.

The next class, the $100,000–$250,000 interval, contains approximately 32 per cent of the total frequencies in both cases.

The third class, the $250,000–$500,000 interval, contains about 13 per cent of the frequencies in the case of all manufacturing corporations in the country, but about 20 per cent of them in the case of the sample.

The next bracket, the $500,000–$1,000,000 class, contains about 7 per cent of the frequencies for all corporations in the country, but about 15 per cent for the sample; and the next class, the $1,000,000–$5,000,000 group, contains about 5 per cent of the frequencies for all corporations of the country, but about 12 per cent for the sample. The highest class, the $5,000,000 and over bracket, contains about 1 per cent of the frequencies for all corporations of the country, but about 4 per cent for the sample.

The correspondence between the two distributions is therefore far from close. Each set of distributions in itself shows a high degree of consistency from year to year. In nearly all years, however, the proportion of frequencies in the $50,000 to $100,000 interval is more than twice as great for all corporations of the country as for the large corporations series; while the proportion of frequencies in all of the brackets above $250,000 is substantially less for all manufacturing corporations in the country than for the sample. This may be partly explained by the difference in the definition of 'net income'. The inclusion of tax-exempt income in the sample figures undoubtedly results in some 'pushing-up' effect: it may take frequencies that would otherwise be in the lowest class and place them in the next higher one, and so on successively up through the brackets. The highest class interval, the open-end category of $5 million and over, includes relatively four or five times as many in the sample as in all manufacturing corporations. It is quite probable that the very largest corporations receive relatively the highest amounts of tax-exempt income, particularly in the form of intercorporate dividends. But with all due respect to this factor it still remains true that our large corporations sample possesses a substantial measure of bias in the direction of 'bigness'. As of 1928 the arithmetic mean capital per corporation for the sample (companies with net incomes) is $12 million, whereas that for all manufacturing corporations with net incomes (no figure is available for just those with incomes of over $50,000) is only $800,000.

In Tables 92 and 93 are given the quartiles for both the size of capital per corporation and the amount of income per corporation, for the 2,046 companies of the sample, in all years.

iv. We may now, with somewhat less elaboration, indicate the character of the large corporations sample when it is divided into major manufacturing groups.

TABLE 92

QUARTILES FOR SIZE OF CAPITAL[1] PER CORPORATION IN LARGE MANUFACTURING CORPORATIONS SAMPLE, 1919–28

	1919	1920	1921	1922	1923
Q1	$435,585	$555,000	$632,699	$617,411	$756,799
Q2	951,389	1,196,121	1,313,953	1,299,257	1,487,762
Q3	2,672,297	3,286,232	3,457,692	3,488,095	3,995,536

	1924	1925	1926	1927	1928
Q1	$799,665	$846,201	$871,114	$902,624	$925,578
Q2	1,600,575	1,714,660	1,793,814	1,880,435	1,972,222
Q3	4,335,366	4,618,750	4,695,946	4,914,474	5,322,967

[1] For 1924–28, this item includes bonded debt.

TABLE 93

QUARTILES FOR SIZE OF NET INCOME[1] PER CORPORATION IN LARGE MANUFACTURING CORPORATIONS SAMPLE, 1919–28

	1919	1920	1921	1922	1923
Q1	$138,753	$104,985	$14,250	$93,101	$116,406
Q2	245,613	218,316	87,833	219,847	242,599
Q3	660,088	495,013	240,245	495,937	625,000

	1924	1925	1926	1927	1928
Q1	$89,134	$101,696	$91,508	$83,422	$76,855
Q2	210,513	235,130	226,444	215,470	217,900
Q3	495,474	588,102	591,236	538,174	572,977

[1] In all years, this item includes non-taxable income.

It has been stated that by number the large corporations sample constitutes only a 2.1 to 3.0 per cent representation of all manufacturing corporations in the country. Divided into its 11 major groups and each of these then related to the figures for all manufacturing corporations in the country in each group, the ratios prevailing in the several groups in different years range from about 1 to about 7 per cent. In the Food group the range is from 1.4 to 1.7 per cent; in Metals from 3.0 to 4.9 per cent; in Paper from 5.5 to 7.3 per cent.

The sales of the corporations of the sample, however,

in 1928 amounted to from 18 to 69 per cent of the total business done by all the country's corporations in each major group; and the net income received in the same year constituted from 34 to 88 per cent. The data are given in Tables 94 and 95.

If only companies with net incomes in both the sample and for all manufacturing corporations of the country be

TABLE 94

SALES OF THE LARGE MANUFACTURING CORPORATIONS SAMPLE COMPARED WITH THE SALES OF ALL CORPORATIONS IN THE UNITED STATES, BY MAJOR GROUPS, 1928

(in millions of dollars)

	ALL UNITED STATES	SAMPLE	PERCENTAGE OF SAMPLE TO ALL UNITED STATES
Major group			
1 Foods	$13,955	$7,026	50
2 Textiles	7,675	1,389	18
3 Leather	1,686	380	23
4 Rubber	1,350	935	69
5 Lumber	2,731	541	20
6 Paper	1,665	501	30
7 Printing and publishing	2,455	623	25
8 Chemicals	8,634	4,469	52
9 Clay, stone and glass	1,605	550	34
10 Metals	20,266	11,266	56
11 Special manufacturing industries	2,340	539	23
Total, all manufacture	$64,361	$28,219	44

taken, the representation by number for the several major groups in the various years of the period ranges from somewhat over 1 per cent to about 10 per cent. In Foods the range is from 2.2 to 2.6 per cent; in Metals from 5.0 to 7.9 per cent; in Paper from 7.9 to 10.3 per cent. Although data are not available with which to segregate the figures for the corporations of the sample with net incomes only,

TABLE 95

NET INCOME OF THE LARGE MANUFACTURING CORPORATIONS SAMPLE COMPARED WITH THE NET INCOME OF ALL CORPORATIONS IN THE UNITED STATES, BY MAJOR GROUPS, 1928

(in millions of dollars)

Major group	ALL UNITED STATES	SAMPLE	PERCENTAGE OF SAMPLE TO ALL UNITED STATES
1 Foods	$598	$307	51
2 Textiles	216	80	37
3 Leather	53	29	55
4 Rubber	8	7	88
5 Lumber	82	44	54
6 Paper	121	41	34
7 Printing and publishing	242	98	40
8 Chemicals	1,081	780	72
9 Clay, stone and glass	147	89	61
10 Metals	1,768	1,175	66
11 Special manufacturing industries	164	85	52
Total, all manufacture	$4,480	$2,735	61

by major groups, the representation in such terms of course runs much larger.

v. It has been noted, however, that the large manufacturing corporations series is predominently a sample of corporations with net incomes of over $50,000, in most years, the corporations included in it constituting by number approximately 25 per cent of all manufacturing corporations in the country with such incomes. Among major groups the range of such representation in different years is from 12 to 38 per cent.[14] In the Food group it is from 20

---

[14] Except for the Special Manufacturing Industries group, which shows 10 per cent in one year. The ranges given above are for the several groups in the various years from 1920 to 1928, but exclude the figures for 1921, which are in most groups by far the highest percentages of all years, running to about 50 per cent in several groups. They are, of course, so high because in 1921 the number of corporations in the country with net incomes of over $50,000 showed a more substantial decline than did the

SAMPLING AND WEIGHTING [473]

to 27 per cent; in Metals from 25 to 40 per cent; in Paper from 23 to 40 per cent.

vi. Just as we compared the frequency distributions of the sample and of all corporations in the country for All Manufacturing, so may we also compare (Tables 96 and 97) similar distributions (again for companies with net incomes of over $50,000) by major groups for 1928. The group numbers correspond, of course, with those used in Book II.

The ratios are much the same as in the distribution for All Manufacturing. In every group the relative number of frequencies in the $50,000–$100,000 class is far lower for the sample than for all corporations in the country, in some instances only one-half or one-third as great. In the next interval, the $100,000–$250,000 class, the relative numbers are about the same; while in the upper brackets the proportions of frequencies in the samples in the various groups are considerably higher than those for all manufacturing corporations in the country.

In part these discrepancies are explicable upon the grounds already set forth in connection with those noted above for All Manufacturing; but again the samples in nearly all of our major groups are somewhat biased in the direction of 'bigness'.[15]

number in the sample, thus making the sample relatively a much larger one; and it seems fairer to omit this exceptional year in characterizing the samples' representativeness for the period 1920–28 in general. As stated previously, data for 1919 are not available.

[15] The reasoning of this and preceding passages does not imply the existence of any exact correlation between the amount of a corporation's income and the size of its capital. Probably no close correlation exists— and to assume one would beg the whole question of differences in earnings rates between corporations and industries. But this is not to say that very *broad* differences in the size of incomes, by and large, cannot serve to point differences in the size of capital which take the same direction. It is not necessarily true that a corporation with an income of $500,000 will have any larger capital than one with an income of $400,000; but it *is* generally

Table 96
NET INCOMES FOR ALL MANUFACTURING CORPORATIONS WITH INCOMES OF OVER $50,000 IN THE UNITED STATES, 1928

SIZE OF INCOME	MAJOR GROUP 1 NUMBER OF CORPORATIONS	PERCENTAGE OF TOTAL	MAJOR GROUP 2 NUMBER OF CORPORATIONS	PERCENTAGE OF TOTAL	MAJOR GROUP 3 NUMBER OF CORPORATIONS	PERCENTAGE OF TOTAL	MAJOR GROUP 4 NUMBER OF CORPORATIONS	PERCENTAGE OF TOTAL
$50,000– 100,000	432	41.1	452	42.5	77	40.2	22	28.2
100,000– 250,000	350	33.4	351	33.0	66	34.2	23	29.5
250,000– 500,000	110	10.5	145	13.6	26	13.5	14	17.9
500,000–1,000,000	71	6.8	79	7.4	18	9.4	12	15.4
1,000,000–5,000,000	67	6.4	35	3.3	5	2.6	6	7.7
5,000,000 and over	19	1.8	2	0.2	1	0.1	1	1.3
Total	1,049	100.0	1,064	100.0	193	100.0	78	100.0

	MAJOR GROUP 5		MAJOR GROUP 6		MAJOR GROUP 7		MAJOR GROUP 8	
$50,000– 100,000	278	48.5	119	36.8	290	45.2	306	36.3
100,000– 250,000	205	35.8	101	31.2	209	32.6	235	27.9
250,000– 500,000	51	8.9	52	16.0	70	10.9	128	15.2
500,000–1,000,000	27	4.7	31	9.5	41	6.4	75	8.9
1,000,000–5,000,000	12	2.1	21	6.5	31	4.8	76	9.0
5,000,000 and over	0	0.0	0	0.0	3	0.1	23	2.7
Total	573	100.0	324	100.0	644	100.0	843	100.0

	MAJOR GROUP 9		MAJOR GROUP 10		MAJOR GROUP 11			
$50,000– 100,000	174	43.5	908	36.0	226	44.0		
100,000– 250,000	126	31.5	817	32.3	164	31.9		
250,000– 500,000	39	9.8	350	13.9	64	12.5		
500,000–1,000,000	25	6.3	218	8.6	30	5.8		
1,000,000–5,000,000	31	7.8	187	7.4	28	5.4		
5,000,000 and over	4	1.0	46	1.8	2	0.4		
Total	399	100.0	2,526	100.0	514	100.0		

Table 97

TOTAL NET INCOMES FOR COMPANIES WITH INCOMES OF OVER $50,000 IN THE LARGE MANUFACTURING CORPORATIONS SAMPLE, 1928

SIZE OF INCOME	MAJOR GROUP 1 NUMBER OF CORPORATIONS	PERCENTAGE OF TOTAL	MAJOR GROUP 2 NUMBER OF CORPORATIONS	PERCENTAGE OF TOTAL	MAJOR GROUP 3 NUMBER OF CORPORATIONS	PERCENTAGE OF TOTAL	MAJOR GROUP 4 NUMBER OF CORPORATIONS	PERCENTAGE OF TOTAL
$50,000– 100,000	25	13.4	46	21.7	6	15.0	2	11.1
100,000– 250,000	61	32.8	65	30.6	15	37.5	4	22.3
250,000– 500,000	28	15.1	47	22.2	12	30.0	8	44.5
500,000–1,000,000	30	16.1	39	18.4	5	12.5	1	5.5
1,000,000–5,000,000	28	15.1	15	7.1	1	2.5	2	11.1
5,000,000 and over	14	7.5	0	0.0	1	2.5	1	5.5
Total	186	100.0	212	100.0	40	100.0	18	100.0

SIZE OF INCOME	MAJOR GROUP 5 NUMBER OF CORPORATIONS	PERCENTAGE OF TOTAL	MAJOR GROUP 6 NUMBER OF CORPORATIONS	PERCENTAGE OF TOTAL	MAJOR GROUP 7 NUMBER OF CORPORATIONS	PERCENTAGE OF TOTAL	MAJOR GROUP 8 NUMBER OF CORPORATIONS	PERCENTAGE OF TOTAL
$50,000– 100,000	50	33.5	18	19.6	18	20.3	18	9.8
100,000– 250,000	54	36.3	31	33.7	33	37.1	43	23.5
250,000– 500,000	28	18.8	21	22.8	15	16.8	44	24.0
500,000–1,000,000	11	7.4	14	15.2	10	11.2	27	14.8
1,000,000–5,000,000	6	4.0	8	8.7	10	11.2	31	17.0
5,000,000 and over	0	0.0	0	0.0	3	3.4	20	10.9
Total	149	100.0	92	100.0	89	100.0	183	100.0

SIZE OF INCOME	MAJOR GROUP 9 NUMBER OF CORPORATIONS	PERCENTAGE OF TOTAL	MAJOR GROUP 10 NUMBER OF CORPORATIONS	PERCENTAGE OF TOTAL	MAJOR GROUP 11 NUMBER OF CORPORATIONS	PERCENTAGE OF TOTAL
$50,000– 100,000	24	25.0	71	12.7	12	15.0
100,000– 250,000	20	20.8	153	27.3	21	26.2
250,000– 500,000	14	14.6	117	20.8	20	25.0
500,000–1,000,000	15	15.6	89	15.9	15	18.8
1,000,000–5,000,000	19	19.8	92	16.4	10	12.5
5,000,000 and over	4	4.2	39	6.9	2	2.5
Total	96	100.0	561	100.0	80	100.0

b. Small Manufacturing Corporations Series

i. This is a sample which contributed data for manufacturing as a whole, for all of the major groups, and for some of the minor groups discussed in Book III. It consists of non-identical corporations for the ten-year period, from 1,421 to 1,665 in each year. All have positive incomes, the majority between $2,000 and $50,000 per corporation. Just as in the large corporations sample it was stated that only about 10 per cent of the companies had incomes below $50,000, so here it may be said that of the small corporations in the present sample only 11 or 12 per cent in any year (other than 1921) have incomes that exceed $50,000; and none have incomes below $2,000. The small manufacturing corporations sample is therefore predominently representative of that segment of the universe containing corporations with incomes ranging from $2,000 to $50,000, and may be so regarded for purposes of comparison and appraisal.

By number the sample contains from 5 to 6 per cent of the manufacturing corporations in the country with such net incomes. In terms of income received, however, the proportion in various years runs from 8 to 10 per cent. As representative of all of the country's manufacturing corporations with net income, in terms of arithmetic mean earnings rates, the small manufacturing corporations sample comes almost as close to perfect correspondence as did the large corporations series. Again data are available to make this comparison in three years. The percentages of income to capitalization shown by the small corporations sample in 1926, 1927 and 1928 are:

true that companies which in most years have incomes of $5,000,000 will have larger capitals than those with incomes of $500,000. Upon this basis, therefore, it must be said that the data which have been reviewed at least suggest that our large corporations sample is biased in an upward direction with respect to the size of the corporations that compose it. The exact extent of this bias, is not, of course, susceptible of measurement.

SAMPLING AND WEIGHTING [477]

|11.7|11.6|11.5|

while those for all manufacturing corporations in the country are:

|12.3|10.9|12.0|

ii. We may next compare the small corporations sample with its 'specific universe' (that is, with that segment of the universe containing corporations with net incomes of from $2,000 to $50,000) by examining the frequency distributions for the size of net incomes. These incomes can be classed for both the sample and the corporations of the country. For this purpose it is possible to obtain comparable distributions containing only three class intervals: incomes of $2,000–$5,000; those of $5,000–$10,000; and those of $10,000–$50,000.

Here, in nearly all years, a very close correspondence indeed is apparent between the two distributions for the sample and the universe. In nearly all years, both for the sample and for all manufacturing corporations in the country, between about 30 and 35 per cent of the total frequencies are found in the lowest class interval. In all years approximately 23 per cent of the frequencies, in both, are found in the middle interval. And in all years, between about 40 and 45 per cent of the frequencies, for both the sample and all manufacturing corporations in the country, appear in the highest class interval.[16] The distributions appear in Tables 98 and 99.

iii. The small corporations sample may now be divided into major groups for characterization with respect to representativeness.

[16] As in the similar analyses undertaken for the large corporations sample, the distribution of incomes for the sample excludes the relatively few corporations with incomes not falling within any of the class limits designated.

Table 98

FREQUENCY DISTRIBUTIONS OF NET INCOMES FOR ALL MANUFACTURING CORPORATIONS IN THE UNITED STATES WITH INCOMES FROM $2,000 TO $50,000 IN 1928

SIZE OF INCOME	NUMBER OF CORPORATIONS	PERCENTAGE OF TOTAL
$2,000– 5,000	11,781	39.9
5,000–10,000	6,282	21.2
10,000–50,000	11,492	38.9
Total	29,555	100.0

Table 99

FREQUENCY DISTRIBUTIONS OF TOTAL NET INCOMES FOR COMPANIES WITH INCOMES FROM $2,000 TO $50,000 IN THE SMALL MANUFACTURING CORPORATIONS SAMPLE, 1928

SIZE OF INCOME	NUMBER OF CORPORATIONS	PERCENTAGE OF TOTAL
$2,000– 5,000	440	34.8
5,000–10,000	291	23.0
10,000–50,000	533	42.2
Total	1,264	100.0

For the Manufacturing division it has been said that the corporations of the sample afford a 5 to 6 per cent representation by number in nearly all years. For the several major groups this representation ranges from about 4 to 11 per cent.[17] The sample in the Food group contains from 4.5 per cent to 8.5 per cent of all manufacturing corporations in the country with net incomes of from $2,000–$50,000; in the Metals group from 5.3 to 9.5 per cent; in the Paper group from 5.2 to 9.3 per cent. In terms of amount of net income received, the samples of the major groups show representations ranging in 1928 from 5.2 to 9.9 per cent.

[17] Excluding figures of 2 and 3 per cent in several years for the Special Manufacturing Industries group.

The frequency distributions of net incomes for the several major groups of the sample in 1928 correspond rather closely with those for all manufacturing corporations in the country with incomes of from $2,000–$50,000. Where discrepancies are to be found, they are seldom excessive, and in large measure may probably be explained on grounds of the sort discussed in previous sections. A fairly typical group is Metals, in which the lowest interval of the sample shows 32 per cent of the frequencies as against 36 per cent in the universe; the middle bracket 22 per cent in both cases; and the highest interval, 46 per cent as against 42 per cent. The distributions for all groups, in 1928, are given in Tables 100 and 101.

c. Small Manufacturing Corporations Sample with Net Incomes under $2,000

This is a sample of non-identical corporations with positive net incomes, most of which are less than $2,000. Data are available in this sample for the five years 1924–28 only. The proportion of companies with incomes of $2,000 or over amounts to no more than 5 per cent of the companies in the sample, in any year except 1928, when about one-fifth have higher incomes. Virtually all of these larger incomes are, however, less than $5,000. The number of corporations in the series varies in the five years as follows: 1924, 570; 1925, 406; 1926, 1,008, 1927, 703; 1928, 1,-118. Most of the corporations included are small, the arithmetic mean capitalization ranging from $56,000 to $89,000 in different years. In no year do more than 2 per cent of the corporations included have capitals of over $500,000; and in all years at least 89 per cent have capitals under $250,000.

By number the corporations of this sample constitute a 2.3 to 6.5 per cent representation of all manufacturing cor-

Table 100

FREQUENCY DISTRIBUTIONS OF NET INCOMES FOR ALL MANUFACTURING CORPORATIONS IN THE UNITED STATES WITH INCOMES FROM $2,000 TO $50,000, BY MAJOR GROUPS, 1928

SIZE OF INCOME	MAJOR GROUP 1 NUMBER OF CORPORATIONS	PERCENTAGE OF TOTAL	MAJOR GROUP 2 NUMBER OF CORPORATIONS	PERCENTAGE OF TOTAL	MAJOR GROUP 3 NUMBER OF CORPORATIONS	PERCENTAGE OF TOTAL	MAJOR GROUP 4 NUMBER OF CORPORATIONS	PERCENTAGE OF TOTAL
$2,000– 5,000	2,024	41.5	1,797	43.1	292	38.0	63	39.9
5,000–10,000	1,032	21.1	843	20.3	153	19.9	37	23.4
10,000–50,000	1,833	37.4	1,528	36.6	324	42.1	58	36.7
Total	4,889	100.0	4,168	100.0	769	100.0	158	100.0

SIZE OF INCOME	MAJOR GROUP 5 NUMBER OF CORPORATIONS	PERCENTAGE OF TOTAL	MAJOR GROUP 6 NUMBER OF CORPORATIONS	PERCENTAGE OF TOTAL	MAJOR GROUP 7 NUMBER OF CORPORATIONS	PERCENTAGE OF TOTAL	MAJOR GROUP 8 NUMBER OF CORPORATIONS	PERCENTAGE OF TOTAL
$2,000– 5,000	937	36.3	233	31.1	1,698	45.5	714	34.9
5,000–10,000	570	22.1	151	20.2	838	22.4	439	21.4
10,000–50,000	1,074	41.6	365	48.7	1,194	32.1	895	43.7
Total	2,581	100.0	749	100.0	3,730	100.0	2,048	100.0

SIZE OF INCOME	MAJOR GROUP 9 NUMBER OF CORPORATIONS	PERCENTAGE OF TOTAL	MAJOR GROUP 10 NUMBER OF CORPORATIONS	PERCENTAGE OF TOTAL	MAJOR GROUP 11 NUMBER OF CORPORATIONS	PERCENTAGE OF TOTAL
$2,000– 5,000	597	41.0	2,445	36.1	981	43.6
5,000–10,000	307	21.1	1,460	21.6	452	20.1
10,000–50,000	552	37.9	2,853	42.3	816	36.3
Total	1,456	100.0	6,758	100.0	2,249	100.0

TABLE 101

FREQUENCY DISTRIBUTIONS OF TOTAL NET INCOMES FOR COMPANIES IN THE SMALL MANUFACTURING CORPORATIONS SAMPLE WITH INCOMES FROM $2,000 TO $50,000, BY MAJOR GROUPS, 1928

SIZE OF INCOME	MAJOR GROUP 1 NUMBER OF CORPORATIONS	PERCENTAGE OF TOTAL	MAJOR GROUP 2 NUMBER OF CORPORATIONS	PERCENTAGE OF TOTAL	MAJOR GROUP 3 NUMBER OF CORPORATIONS	PERCENTAGE OF TOTAL	MAJOR GROUP 4 NUMBER OF CORPORATIONS	PERCENTAGE OF TOTAL
$2,000– 5,000	71	35.7	63	37.1	12	32.4	4	40.0
5,000–10,000	47	23.6	39	22.9	10	27.0	2	20.0
10,000–50,000	81	40.7	68	40.0	15	40.6	4	40.0
Total	199	100.0	170	100.0	37	100.0	10	100.0

SIZE OF INCOME	MAJOR GROUP 5 NUMBER OF CORPORATIONS	PERCENTAGE OF TOTAL	MAJOR GROUP 6 NUMBER OF CORPORATIONS	PERCENTAGE OF TOTAL	MAJOR GROUP 7 NUMBER OF CORPORATIONS	PERCENTAGE OF TOTAL	MAJOR GROUP 8 NUMBER OF CORPORATIONS	PERCENTAGE OF TOTAL
$2,000– 5,000	45	34.6	11	28.9	56	39.1	29	30.5
5,000–10,000	29	22.3	9	23.7	36	25.2	21	22.1
10,000–50,000	56	43.1	18	47.4	51	35.7	45	47.4
Total	130	100.0	38	100.0	143	100.0	95	100.0

SIZE OF INCOME	MAJOR GROUP 9 NUMBER OF CORPORATIONS	PERCENTAGE OF TOTAL	MAJOR GROUP 10 NUMBER OF CORPORATIONS	PERCENTAGE OF TOTAL	MAJOR GROUP 11 NUMBER OF CORPORATIONS	PERCENTAGE OF TOTAL
$2,000– 5,000	24	40.7	104	32.4	21	33.8
5,000–10,000	12	20.3	71	22.1	15	24.2
10,000–50,000	23	39.0	146	45.5	26	42.0
Total	59	100.0	321	100.0	62	100.0

porations in the country with net incomes under $2,000. They account, however, for between 4.0 to 11.3 per cent of the total net income.

They are corporations not only of small absolute incomes, but also of low average earnings rates. In no year does any of the ten major groups into which the sample may be divided [18] earn more than 4 per cent upon its capitalization, while most of the figures run about 2 per cent. A few of the 20 minor groups into which the sample may be divided [19] show earnings rates of over 5 per cent in one year or another, but most earn only 2 or 3 per cent.

The percentages of net income to capitalization shown by the entire sample (all major groups combined) are as follows: 1924, 1.5; 1925, 2.0; 1926, 1.9; 1927, 1.4; 1928, 2.6. To be sure, these are but arithmetic mean figures, and the frequency distribution of the earnings rates of individual corporations indicates that many companies of the sample earned far higher rates of return. The distribution for 1928, for example, is given in Chart 66. The corporation standing at the upper quartile earns 10.2 per cent, and the median corporation earns 5.0 per cent. These returns on investment are, however, much lower than the corresponding data for the two other manufacturing corporations series already discussed.

It is not possible to undertake many of the tests of representativeness in connection with this sample which have been essayed in previous sections for other samples. We know, of course, that the profitableness of the corporations

---

[18] The Leather and Rubber groups are combined, but the classification of the nine other major groups is the same as in previous samples.

[19] The minor groups do not 'add up' to make major groups because many corporations belonging to various minor groups which were shown separately in other samples could not be so shown here. There is nevertheless included in the major groups some representation of all or most of the 73 minor groups found in other samples, but it is not possible to show each separately.

CHART 66
FREQUENCY DISTRIBUTION OF EARNINGS RATES OF INDIVIDUAL CORPORATIONS FOR 1928
SMALL MANUFACTURING CORPORATIONS WITH NET INCOMES UNDER $2000

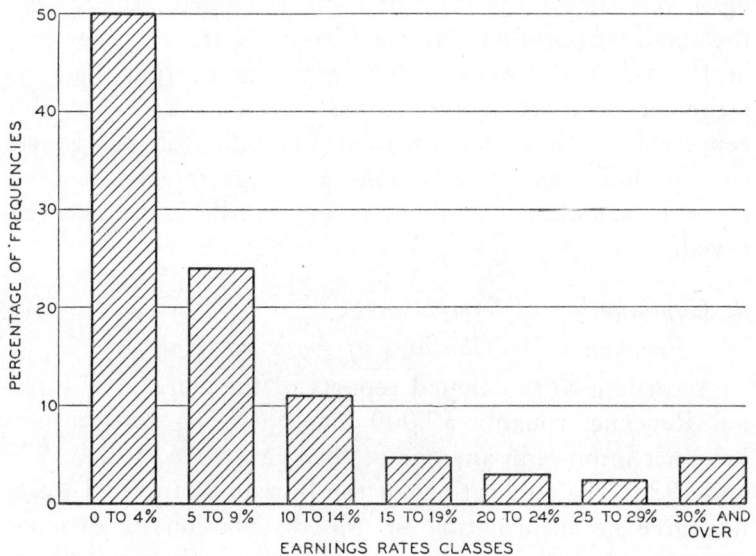

of this sample is much lower than that for all manufacturing corporations in the country taken *en masse,* but we are not able to compare this average figure with that for all of the manufacturing corporations of the country with incomes between $1 and $2,000. Nor is there available any distribution of incomes for all manufacturing corporations in the country with absolute incomes of this amount, with which to compare the income distributions of the corporations in this sample. Because of the absence of any assurance in these matters we have made but slight use of this sample throughout the volume, the only instance of its employment being the preparation of the frequency distributions of the earnings of individual corporations with positive net incomes as presented in Chapter 2. This utilization of the sample is discussed in the following section.

Although we have no information on the comparative distribution of incomes, in most years the sample contains much the same proportion of its 'specific universe' as does the small corporations sample (from about 4 to 6 per cent in 1926–28) and a somewhat larger proportion than the large corporations sample. Primarily upon the basis of this representation in each year, the combination of its frequencies for individual corporations' earnings rates with those of other samples, now about to be described, has been essayed.

d. *Combination of Samples—*
  Frequency Distributions of Earnings Rates

According to the annual reports of the Bureau of Internal Revenue, roughly 50,000 manufacturing corporations have net incomes in any one of the years 1925, 1926, 1927 and 1928. The publications of the Bureau of Internal Revenue give no information on the distribution of earnings rates or of capitals among these individual corporations, but, as has already been noted, they do give frequency distributions for the absolute size of the incomes alone. By first using these distributions in conjunction with our several samples and then expanding the latter, we are able to approximate a complete distribution of earnings rates for all of the country's corporations.

For this purpose, we employ three sets of data: (1) our 'large corporations' series already described both in this chapter and in Book II; (2) the 'small corporations' series described in this chapter and in Book III; (3) the 'small corporations with positive incomes of less than $2,000' series mentioned in the immediately preceding section of this chapter. Our problem is now to define as carefully as

SAMPLING AND WEIGHTING   [485]

possible—without being so meticulous as to give a specious impression of the accuracy of our results—the ratios existing between the sizes of these three samples and their respective universes; then by appropriate weighting, to combine and expand the three samples so as to obtain a fairly good picture of the entire universe of manufacturing corporations with net incomes. The procedure will assume a certain degree of 'representativeness' within each sample; and the extent to which this assumption is justified is something concerning which the reader who has considered the preceding sections of this chapter may himself judge.

The data for 1928 will afford an illustration. In 1928 the tabulations of the Bureau of Internal Revenue indicate that of the 55,007 manufacturing corporations in the country with net incomes:

17,245 earned under $2,000;
29,555 earned from $2,000 to $49,999;
8,207 earned $50,000 or more.

Taking first the sample for 'small corporations with positive incomes under $2,000', the 1,118 corporations of our sample are seen to amount to 6.5 per cent of the total number in the country having such incomes. There are thus actually about 16 times as many manufacturing corporations in the country with net incomes of from $1 to $1,999 as in our sample. Upon the assumption that the sample is fairly representative (an assumption probably not so well founded in the case of this sample as in that of the two others), we may therefore say that the proper frequency for any class interval of the distribution of earnings rates for *all* corporations in the country (with incomes of from $1 to $1,999 in 1928) is 16 times the number shown by the corresponding class interval in our sample (that is, 100 per cent, divided by 6.5 per cent, equals roughly 16). The

561 corporations which, in the sample, were found to have earned under 5 per cent upon their capitals are thus multiplied by 16 and appear as 8,976 corporations, in the 'Under five per cent' class interval, in the work-sheets which we now use to build up the new estimated distribution for the entire country.

Similarly, our 'small corporations' sample consists mainly of corporations with incomes between $2,000 and $49,999. It contains 1,421 corporations, or 4.8 per cent of the total number reported by the Bureau of Internal Revenue for those income classes. The frequencies for each class interval of the sample here are each multiplied by 20.

In the same manner our large corporations series, with 1,970 corporations in 1928, the incomes of which are mainly over $50,000, are seen to constitute a 24 per cent representation of all manufacturing enterprises in the country with incomes of over that amount in 1928. Frequencies in all class intervals of the sample distribution here are thus multiplied by four, in order to give an approximately correct picture of the actual numbers of large corporations in each class, in the entire universe—again upon the assumption that the sample is fairly representative.

Finally, the three new sets of (expanded) frequencies for each class interval are added together to give the completed estimated distribution for all sizes of corporations combined. The resulting totals are thus weighted by the relative numbers of small and large corporations belonging to each earnings rates class, and the bias that would attach to any simple combination of the original frequencies for the three samples—were the distributions of earnings rates different as between the three samples—is thus eliminated.

In other years different weights are used, but the method is the same. Table 102 gives the basic data for all years,

TABLE 102

BASIC DATA UNDERLYING THE DETERMINATION OF WEIGHTS EMPLOYED IN PREPARATION OF ESTIMATED FREQUENCY DISTRIBUTIONS OF EARNINGS OF INDIVIDUAL MANUFACTURING CORPORATIONS IN THE UNITED STATES, 1925-1928[1]

Three Samples

SIZE OF NET INCOME	NUMBER OF MANUFACTURING CORPORATIONS IN THE COUNTRY	SMALL CORPORATIONS WITH INCOMES OF LESS THAN $2,000 SERIES			SMALL CORPORATIONS SERIES			LARGE CORPORATIONS SERIES		
		NO. OF CORPORATIONS	PERCENT OF ALL CORPORATIONS IN THE COUNTRY	WEIGHT	NO. OF CORPORATIONS	PERCENT OF ALL CORPORATIONS IN THE COUNTRY	WEIGHT	NO. OF CORPORATIONS	PERCENT OF ALL CORPORATIONS IN THE COUNTRY	WEIGHT
1925										
Under $2,000	17,756	406	2.3	43						
2,000 to 49,999	27,986				1,461	5.2	19			
50,000 and over	8,395							2,016	24.0	4
Total	54,137									
1926										
Under $2,000	19,460	1,008	5.2	18						
2,000 to 49,999	27,548				1,468	5.3	19			
50,000 and over	8,086							1,996	24.7	4
Total	55,094									
1927										
Under $2,000	19,435	703	3.6	25						
2,000 to 49,999	26,470				1,665	6.3	16			
50,000 and over	7,715							1,984	25.7	4
Total	53,620									

TABLE 102 (continued)

BASIC DATA UNDERLYING EARNINGS OF CORPORATIONS

Three Samples

SIZE OF NET INCOME	NUMBER OF MANU-FACTURING CORPORATIONS IN THE COUNTRY	SMALL CORPORATIONS WITH INCOMES OF LESS THAN $2,000 SERIES			SMALL CORPORATIONS SERIES			LARGE CORPORATIONS SERIES		
		NO. OF CORPO-RATIONS	PERCENT OF ALL CORPORATIONS IN THE COUNTRY	WEIGHT	NO. OF CORPO-RATIONS	PERCENT OF ALL CORPORATIONS IN THE COUNTRY	WEIGHT	NO. OF CORPO-RATIONS	PERCENT OF ALL CORPORATIONS IN THE COUNTRY	WEIGHT
1928										
Under $2,000	17,245	1,118	6.5	16						
2,000 to 49,999	29,555				1,421	4.8	20			
50,000 and over	8,207							1,970	24.0	4
Total	55,007									

[1] See text for explanation. The final estimated frequency distributions themselves are given in Chapter 2.

together with the multiples or weights employed. The final distributions themselves appeared in Chapter 2.

4. SAMPLES FOR THE TRADING DIVISION

a. Large Trading Corporations Series

The number of corporations engaged in Trading in different years of the period 1919–28 range from 70,000 to 130,000. By number, our large corporations sample for Trade, which consists of 664 corporations in every year of the period, comprises in all years less than a 1 per cent representation, the figure varying from 0.5 per cent to 0.9 per cent. In terms of income, however, the 664 corporations of the sample in most years account for about 30 per cent of the total net income received by all trading corporations in the country.

As in the Manufacturing sample, however, the large corporations series for Trade contains relatively few companies with deficits, 2 per cent or less in most years.[20] In the entire country the number of Trading corporations with net incomes in 1928 was about 80,000 as compared with the total of 130,000. The number with net incomes in the sample in the various years comprises 0.8 per cent to 1.3 per cent of the universe of Trading corporations with net incomes. In terms of incomes received, the 'with net' corporations of the sample, however, in 1928 account for about 25 per cent of that for all Trading corporations in the country with such incomes.

Although not nearly so markedly as in Manufacturing, the large corporations series for Trading is principally a sample of enterprises with net incomes of over $50,000.[21]

---

[20] In 1920 and 1921, however, the figures were 7 and 17 per cent respectively.

[21] In most years the number of companies with incomes of under $50,000 is 20 per cent or less; but in 1928 the figure is 28 per cent, and in 1921,

[490] INDUSTRIAL PROFITS

In 1928 it contained 14 per cent of all such Trading corporations in the country.

As was done previously, we may compare the distribution of size of incomes for the sample and for all corporations in the country in the 'over $50,000' class. Tables 103 and 104 give results for 1928. The figures for that year, which are typical, exhibit essentially the same characteristics as did those for the large corporations series in Manufacturing: a much smaller preponderance of incomes in the

TABLE 103

FREQUENCY DISTRIBUTIONS OF NET INCOMES FOR ALL TRADING CORPORATIONS IN THE UNITED STATES WITH INCOMES OVER $50,000 IN 1928

SIZE OF INCOME	NUMBER OF CORPORATIONS	PERCENTAGE OF TOTAL
$50,000– 100,000	1,857	53.5
100,000– 250,000	1,071	30.9
250,000– 500,000	312	9.0
500,000–1,000,000	132	3.8
1,000,000–5,000,000	85	2.4
5,000,000 and over	14	0.4
Total	3,471	100.0

TABLE 104

FREQUENCY DISTRIBUTIONS OF TOTAL NET INCOMES FOR COMPANIES WITH INCOMES OF OVER $50,000 IN THE LARGE TRADING CORPORATIONS SAMPLE, 1928

SIZE OF INCOME	NUMBER OF CORPORATIONS	PERCENTAGE OF TOTAL
$50,000– 100,000	130	27.1
100,000– 250,000	192	40.1
250,000– 500,000	78	16.3
500,000–1,000,000	36	7.5
1,000,000–5,000,000	34	7.1
5,000,000 and over	9	1.9
Total	479	100.0

43 per cent. The latter figure, however, includes the corporations with deficits.

lowest bracket in the sample than for all the corporations of the country, and relatively larger frequencies in the higher brackets. The reason is in part undoubtedly the same as in the case of Manufacturing—the inclusion of tax-exempt income in the sample figures—and in part because the sample is biased in an upward direction with respect to the size of corporations.

b. *Small Trading Corporations Series*

This sample, like the small corporations series for Manufacturing, consists of non-identical corporations with positive net incomes most of which are between $2,000 and $50,000. It may be compared, therefore, with that segment of the universe of Trading corporations for the two years 1924 and 1928.

Of the 35,000 Trading corporations in the country with such net incomes ($2,000–$50,000) in 1924, the 1,350 corporations of the sample constituted only a 4 per cent representation. In 1928 the 1,337 corporations of the sample comprised a 3 per cent representation. In terms of net income received, however, the sample accounted for 5.5 per cent of the total in 1924 and 4.4 per cent in 1928.

Frequency distributions of the absolute net income amounts for the sample in these two years are not available.

5. SAMPLES FOR THE MINING DIVISION

a. *Large Mining Corporations Series*

Between 13,000 and 19,000 corporations were engaged in Mining in various years of the period 1919–28. The 88 corporations of our large corporations series constitute only about one-half of one per cent of these in every year. In terms of net income, however, they account for a widely varying proportion of the total.[22] In terms of all Mining corporations of the country with net incomes, the sample constitutes about a one to one and one-half per cent representation by number in most years. In terms of net income the corresponding ratio is not available.[23]

As in the cases of the two preceding industrial divisions, however, the large corporations sample for Mining is primarily one of corporations with net incomes of over $50,000. The corporations of the sample having such incomes constitute about 85 per cent of the total number in the sample in most years. We may accordingly compare the distributions of incomes for the sample and for all such corporations in the country.

The 1928 distributions are presented in Tables 105 and

TABLE 105

FREQUENCY DISTRIBUTIONS OF NET INCOMES FOR ALL MINING CORPORATIONS IN THE UNITED STATES WITH INCOMES OF OVER $50,000 IN 1928

SIZE OF INCOME	NUMBER OF CORPORATIONS	PERCENTAGE OF TOTAL
$50,000– 100,000	252	40.1
100,000– 250,000	206	32.8
250,000– 500,000	79	12.6
500,000–1,000,000	40	6.4
1,000,000–5,000,000	43	6.8
5,000,000 and over	8	1.3
Total	628	100.0

106. As in the other industrial divisions, the lower brackets show a smaller relative frequency in the sample than for all corporations in the country, while the four upper brackets all show the reverse. The reasons are doubtless the same

---

[22] For example, 19 per cent in 1923, and 85 per cent in 1927. In 1924 the figure exceeds 100 per cent.
[23] The *Source-Book* does not show separately the aggregate deficit for the Mining corporations with losses.

TABLE 106

FREQUENCY DISTRIBUTIONS OF TOTAL NET INCOMES FOR COMPANIES WITH INCOMES OF OVER $50,000 IN THE LARGE MINING CORPORATIONS SAMPLE, 1928

SIZE OF INCOME	NUMBER OF CORPORATIONS	PERCENTAGE OF TOTAL
$50,000– 100,000	11	14.9
100,000– 250,000	17	23.0
250,000– 500,000	14	18.9
500,000–1,000,000	12	16.2
1,000,000–5,000,000	15	20.3
5,000,000 and over	5	6.7
Total	74	100.0

as in the cases of the large corporations series for Manufacturing and Trading.

6. SAMPLES FOR THE FINANCE DIVISION

a. *Large Corporations Series*

The total number of financial corporations in the country ranges from about 70,000 in 1919 to 130,000 in 1928. By number, our 346 identical large corporations constitute less than a 1 per cent representation of those totals in all years. In terms of net income the sample accounts for 12 to 21 per cent of the total during different years of the period 1922–28.[24]

The number of financial corporations with net incomes ranges from about 50,000 to 80,000. Of this segment of the universe our sample constitutes again less than a 1 per cent representation by number, but in terms of net income it accounts for a much larger proportion, the 1928 figure being 11.1 per cent of the total.

Like the large corporations sample in the other indus-

[24] As remarked elsewhere, our Finance sample excludes all life insurance companies.

[494]   INDUSTRIAL PROFITS

trial divisions, however, that in Finance constitutes principally corporations with net incomes of over $50,000.[25] The distributions of net incomes for the sample and for all financial enterprises in the country with incomes in the 'over $50,000' group in 1928 are given in Tables 107 and 108. They disclose the tendency that has been previously remarked in the large corporations series: a smaller relative number of frequencies in the $50,000–$100,000 in-

TABLE 107

FREQUENCY DISTRIBUTIONS OF NET INCOME FOR ALL FINANCIAL CORPORATIONS IN THE UNITED STATES WITH INCOMES OF OVER $50,000 IN 1928

SIZE OF INCOME	NUMBER OF CORPORATIONS	PERCENTAGE OF TOTAL
$50,000– 100,000	2,110	45.7
100,000– 250,000	1,458	31.6
250,000– 500,000	512	11.1
500,000–1,000,000	274	6.0
1,000,000–5,000,000	222	4.8
5,000,000 and over	37	0.8
Total	4,613	100.0

TABLE 108

FREQUENCY DISTRIBUTIONS OF TOTAL NET INCOMES FOR COMPANIES WITH INCOMES OF OVER $50,000 IN THE LARGE FINANCIAL CORPORATIONS SAMPLE,[1] 1928

SIZE OF INCOME	NUMBER OF CORPORATIONS	PERCENTAGE OF TOTAL
$50,000– 100,000	32	9.6
100,000– 250,000	115	34.5
250,000– 500,000	79	23.7
500,000–1,000,000	45	13.4
1,000,000–5,000,000	49	14.6
5,000,000 and over	14	4.2
Total	334	100.0

[1] The finance sample excludes life insurance companies.

[25] In all years, the corporations with net incomes of over $50,000 comprise 94 per cent or more of the large corporations Finance sample.

come bracket than for all corporations in the country. The $100,000–$250,000 bracket again shows for the sample a much smaller relative frequency; while in all of the higher brackets the proportion of frequencies is far higher for the sample than for all corporations in the country. The explanation in terms of the inclusion of tax-exempt interest in the incomes of the sample is perhaps even more cogent in this group than in the other industrial divisions. To what extent the discrepancy is due mainly to this and to what extent to upward bias of the sample itself in respect of the size of corporations, we cannot say.

Chapter 44

COMPARISON OF MINOR GROUP SAMPLES

1. DESIRABILITY OF TESTING MINOR GROUP SAMPLES

ALL of the characterization and appraisal of our several samples undertaken in the preceding chapter was in terms of their representativeness either for industrial divisions as a whole or as major groups. We did not discuss their presumptive validity for minor groups. But it will be recalled that in the use of the large corporations series we subdivided Manufacturing into 73 minor groups, Trade into 22 groups, Mining into 6 groups, and Finance into 5 groups. The small corporations samples were not susceptible of division into so many separate categories, but still a substantial breakdown into minor industrial groups was made.

It might, of course, be assumed that if a sample is good for purposes of major groups, it is also satisfactory for the analysis of minor groups, since the major groups are made up of minor group classifications. This conclusion, however, follows only if the distribution of corporations by each minor group is as relatively uniform and representative as for the major group. The fact that, both by industrial divisions and by major groups, our samples have met certain tests of typicalness fairly well affords a *presumption* in favor of believing that many of the minor group samples that comprise it are probably also representative of their own specific universes; but it affords no certitude that this is so. We ought, therefore, to spare no effort to verify or disprove, to the fullest extent possible, the accuracy of this presumption.

The only decisive way to check the validity of these minor group samples would be to compare the results obtained from their use with similar data relating to their several universes.[1] Obviously, this is an impossible procedure, for were data for all of these universes available there would be no need to take samples. We are, however, fortunate in possessing certain more comprehensive samples for many groups than those which were made use of in some of our analyses, and in the case of a few groups we do possess virtually complete universes for all corporations with net incomes in such industries. Analysis of these data may now throw valuable light upon the general question of the probable validity of the data in our more restricted samples. For this purpose we have two sets of test data available for manufacturing. The first set enables us to check the accuracy of certain minor group samples in the large Manufacturing corporations series, while the second set makes possible the testing of certain samples in the small Manufacturing corporations series.

2. A TEST OF SAMPLES: LARGE MANUFACTURING CORPORATIONS

It will be recalled that our large corporations sample constitutes by number approximately a 4 per cent representation of the total number of manufacturing corpora-

[1] 'Universe' here is used, of course, in the sense of the complete minor group from which the sample is drawn: e.g., in the minor group, Bakery Products, comparison of the results in each of our samples would have to be made with the results for *all* corporations engaged in the manufacture of Bakery Products in the United States, similarly, with Package Foods, Castings and Forgings, etc., etc.

tions in the country with net incomes. For seven of the manufacturing minor groups we have available what amount to virtually complete universes of all the corporations in the country with net incomes in these groups. In some of these 'universes' the proportion of the total number of corporations in the country included runs as high as 95 per cent. The omissions are even slighter in terms of proportion of total investment and income represented than by number of corporations. Thus for practical purposes we may dismiss these deficiencies as negligible and may regard the 85 or 95 per cent representations that are available as constituting the whole of each of these seven industries.[2] The seven groups in question, together with the number of corporations in each for the sample and for the universe, are given below.[3]

	Number of corporations	
Minor group	In sample	In universe*
Tobacco	23	150
Cotton Spinning	12	141
Book and Music Publishing	17	180
Toilet Preparations	9	104
Textile Machinery	18	112
Engines and Parts	11	103
Railway Equipment	25	142

* Average yearly number

[2] The sets of data which we shall here term 'universes' are described in the *Source-Book* (p. 102) as "Data for corporations in selected subgroups ... samples which vary in the proportion in which they represent their respective universes, but ... (referring to the samples we are now terming as universes) which range from 80 per centum to 95 per centum in this respect". Data for the minor groups to which the part of the supplementary caption here quoted pertains, appear on pp. 134 ff. of the *Source-Book*. The term 'subgroup' is not entirely synonymous with the term minor group throughout the tables of the *Source-Book* (see p. 6) but for the seven industries here discussed, the two terms are identical, i.e., the seven subgroups in question correspond with the seven minor groups that are being tested.

[3] The number of corporations in the sample is the same in each year, the large corporations series, the reader will recall, being one of identical corporations. That for the universe is not the same in each year; the number shown above is an annual average.

MINOR GROUP SAMPLES [499]

We may now undertake three comparisons of the two sets of data for the seven groups: (a) the absolute levels of profitableness in the sample and in the universe as measured by the percentage of net income to capitalization in each; (b) relative fluctuations in profitableness over a time period; (c) relative profitableness in terms of the standing of each group relative to the others.

a. Absolute Profitableness of Samples and Universes

If we examine the earnings rates on investment received by the corporations of the sample and those of the universe in each group,[4] we find little or no discrepancy in most years of the period 1919–28 in some groups and fairly substantial discrepancies in others. To illustrate, the Tobacco group shows almost identical data in every year for the two series of figures. In the five years 1924–28, for example, the large corporations sample of 23 companies in this group showed the following rates of return:

    13.5   15.0   14.7   16.0   15.6;

while the figures for the universe were:

    15.0   15.5   14.7   16.0   15.6.

On the other hand, in Toilet Preparations, which shows the greatest discrepancies, the returns for the nine corporations of the sample were:

    37.6   32.4   28.8   28.1   25.4;

while for the universes the figures were:

    25.1   24.0   23.5   18.5   19.7.

However, while the discrepancies are large the rate of return is consistently high in both the universe and the sample

[4] It need not, of course, be said that the figures for the universes include the figures for the respective samples in all cases.

as compared with that in most other manufacturing minor groups. This point will be touched upon again later.

Between these two extremes of a virtually perfect sample in the Tobacco group and a much less perfect one in Toilet Preparations, the other five of these seven groups are ranged. The two series of figures for the ten years for each group are given in Table 109. The critical reader should now ask: how serious are the several discrepancies, individually and *en masse*?

Perfect correspondence throughout, of course, was not to be expected, both because of the general law of probabilities and because the large corporations sample differs in several known respects from the universe from which it is drawn.[5] Too great differences, however, if characteristic of most groups, would invalidate the sample for purposes of minor group analysis. But what is meant by 'too great'? What general criteria of the permissible limits of tolerance might be set up?

In passing judgment on the satisfactoriness of the sample, the specific purposes of the inquiry must govern any standards that are adopted (*cf.* Ch. 1). For purposes of ascertaining whether the return on investment in a given industry much exceeds, or falls short of, the interest rate on free capital or long-time loanable funds, one standard of accuracy might be adopted. For ascertaining whether the

[5] As we have elsewhere pointed out it contains: (1) corporations of greater than average size; (2) only corporations that remained in business for at least a ten-year period; and (3) in each year a small proportion of companies with deficits instead of positive net incomes. For the third reason, it is, of course, a somewhat better sample of all manufacturing in the country than it would otherwise be, but is a less typical sample of all the corporations in the country with net incomes. However, this third qualification is not very important in the years other than 1921, since the proportion of companies with deficits, as discussed in Ch. 8, is but slight, and essentially the sample may be regarded as one of corporations with net incomes; indeed, mainly as one of corporations with net incomes of over $50,000, as discussed in Ch. 43.

MINOR GROUP SAMPLES [501]

TABLE 109

EARNINGS RATES UPON INVESTMENT FOR SEVEN GROUPS, SAMPLE AND UNIVERSE, 1919–28

(samples from large corporations series)[1]

GROUP	1919	1920	1921	1922	1923	1924	1925	1926	1927	1928
Tobacco										
Sample	14.0	11.7	13.1	14.2	13.4	13.5	15.0	14.7	16.0	15.6
Universe	13.3	11.4	12.8	14.6	12.5	15.0	15.5	14.7	16.0	15.6
Cotton spinning										
Sample	47.0	37.4	10.4	16.0	13.8	7.6	12.3	10.1	10.4	9.5
Universe	32.3	25.8	9.5	12.3	12.4	8.2	9.4	7.9	9.5	9.6
Book and music publishing										
Sample	17.6	13.8	13.5	20.4	18.3	18.9	16.9	14.9	11.4	12.1
Universe	14.5	14.7	12.2	23.2	15.6	15.2	15.7	13.0	13.9	14.4
Toilet preparations										
Sample	39.3	19.6	29.2	53.2	35.5	37.6	32.4	28.8	28.1	25.4
Universe	20.5	15.7	18.4	25.7	20.3	25.1	24.0	23.5	18.5	19.7
Textile machinery										
Sample	27.4	17.2	22.6	22.3	18.3	10.6	14.8	14.4	15.9	14.6
Universe	25.2	21.3	19.0	17.4	18.1	13.7	16.2	15.8	14.3	13.0
Engines										
Sample	28.0	19.2	9.4	10.6	14.6	28.0	9.2	14.1	11.1	6.9
Universe	26.6	13.0	10.8	11.9	10.2	10.0	13.7	12.7	21.0	13.5
Railway equipment										
Sample	17.0	10.6	4.3	7.2	13.5	8.4	5.3	7.6	5.6	3.4
Universe	16.1	10.6	7.4	10.5	14.1	9.7	10.5	11.6	9.2	7.5

[1] See text for explanation.

tendency towards an equality of profit rates in different industries over a period is realized, another standard might be adopted. For ascertaining such fluctuations in profits and profit rates as are significant in endeavoring to throw light upon the cyclical movements in the several industries, still other standards might serve; and so on.

But no one absolute arithmetical measure of difference between the sample datum and the universe datum for the rate of earnings will serve even a specific purpose. We could not, for example, say that in these percentages of income to capitalization figures a difference of two points (2 'per cent') would indicate that the sample was either satisfactory or unsatisfactory. In an industry that showed a 4 per cent return for the sample, but a 6 per cent return for the universe, a two-point discrepancy might be regarded as more than negligible; for not only is the 6 per cent return one-half again as great as the 4 per cent, but also is equal to a so-called normal interest rate for capital employed in manufacturing industries, while the 4 per cent return is not. On the other hand, in an industry for which the sample data show a return of 22 per cent, whereas that for the universe is 20 per cent, the two-point discrepancy amounts to a difference of only one-tenth, instead of one-half, in profitableness and makes no real difference at all with respect to the economic and financial problems of the industry.

But if no absolute arithmetical measure of difference will serve, neither will a straight proportional or logarithmic formula suffice. One might, for example, be tempted to say that no discrepancy that approached anything like a 33 per cent difference in the datum of the sample and that of the universe should be permitted; yet again qualification is necessary. As between two such rates of return as 2 and 3 per cent upon investment, there is no significant difference; both are unsatisfactory returns; either datum shows that

MINOR GROUP SAMPLES [503]

the industry is unprofitable, stands relatively low in the scale, and does not earn as much as an ordinary interest rate on either working or permanent capital. But in the case of two such figures as 10 and 15 per cent, the one datum shows a very different situation than the other, even though their relation is exactly the same as that between 2 and 3 per cent. The industry earning 10 per cent, as we have seen in previous chapters, may be below the general average return, whether arithmetic mean or median be taken, for either the major group or industrial division to which it belongs; whereas the one earning 15 per cent may stand in most years in the forefront of the various industrial groups with which it is classed. Thus there is little to choose between an absolute measure or a straight proportional measure of the differences we are seeking to evaluate.

We therefore leave this question without an attempt at definite answer. We could set up an arbitrary scale of differences (an irregular, non-proportional sliding scale), apply it to the several samples, and thus summarize the situation quantitatively. This procedure has indeed been followed experimentally, on several bases. But the arithmetical results achieved depended mainly upon the assumptions made in drawing up such scales. The summarizing of the differences shown in Table 109, and the drawing of conclusions as to their significance, are therefore left to the reader.[6]

b. Time Fluctuations in Samples and Universes

But whether substantial absolute differences between the earnings rates of any particular sample and those of the

[6] The significance of the samples might, of course, be more elaborately tested by an application of the calculus of probabilities to our data. No effort is made to apply such mathematical technique in these chapters; however, basic data that would make possible a partial analysis of samples and universes appear in Appendix B.

universe are present, we may inquire concerning the comparative trends of the two sets of figures during the period 1919–28.

In general the earnings rates of the sample show the same trend as those for the universe in nearly all groups. The only conspicuous exception is Engines and Parts, where a correspondence between the two series prevails for the first three years of the period, but none is evident between 1922 and 1927.

No extended comment is called for in connection with the conclusion that these samples are fairly satisfactory indicators of *fluctuations* in the earnings rates of the industries which they represent. This generalization holds somewhat less well for the Toilet Preparations and for the Book and Music Publishing groups during parts of the period than for the others; but the several curves of Chart 67 indicate that on the whole, in most of these seven groups, the sample data follow the same general direction as those for the universe.

c. Relative Profitableness of Samples and Universes

Having discussed the 'absolute profitableness' of each industry, as well as the trends of each series of figures, we may now ask how good or bad these seven samples are with respect to the relative profitableness of one minor group compared with the others. For it will be recalled that much of the analysis in the earlier chapters of this volume was concerned not with absolute profit rates, but with the standing of particular minor groups, in any one year and over a period, relative to other groups and to average figures for an industrial division as a whole.

First, as to the standing of the sample datum and the universe datum for each group in any one year, relative to the other groups. If we take an arithmetic average of the

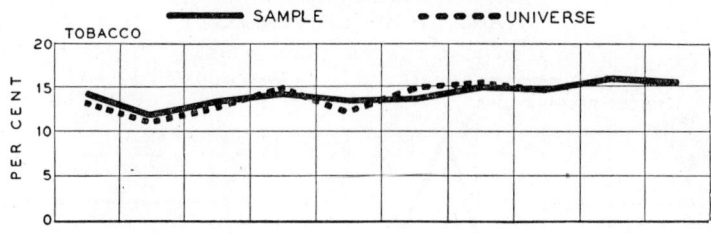

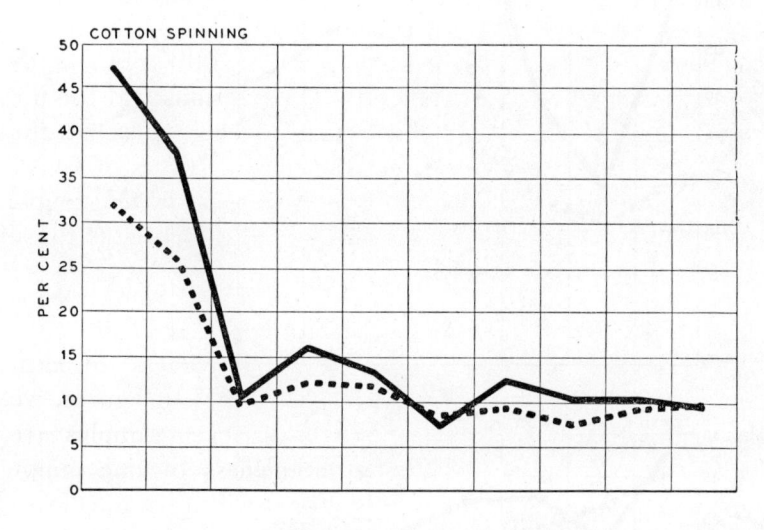

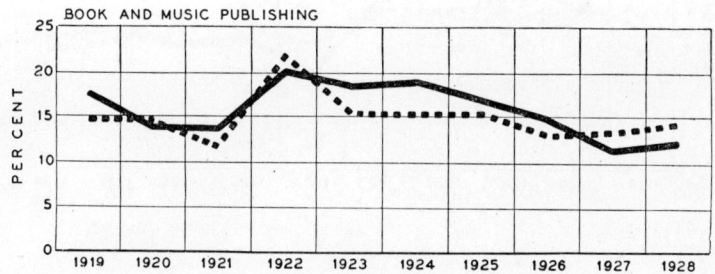

CHART 67
EARNINGS RATES OF SEVEN MINOR GROUP SAMPLES AND THEIR UNIVERSES
IDENTICAL CORPORATIONS SERIES
—— SAMPLE　　● ● ● ● ● UNIVERSE

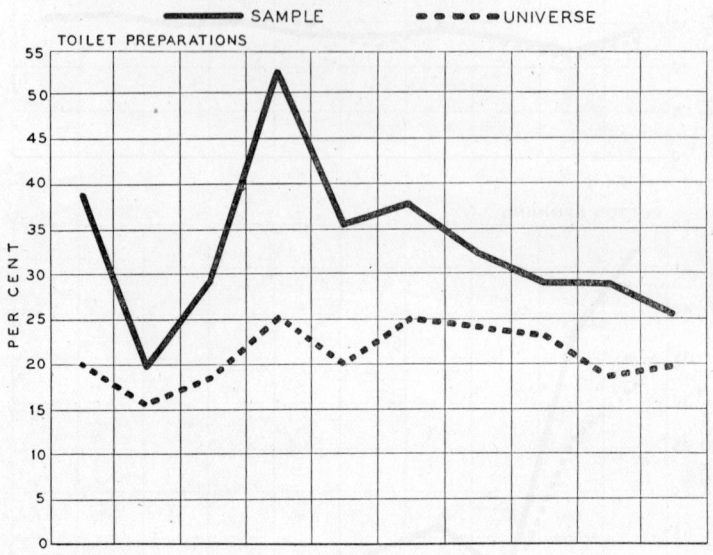

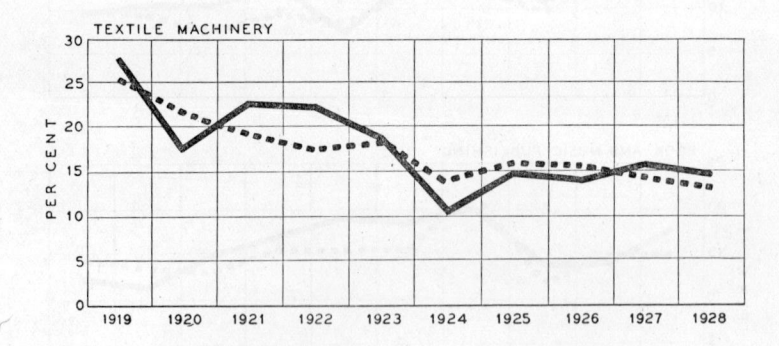

CHART 67 (CONT.)
EARNINGS RATES OF SEVEN MINOR GROUP SAMPLES
AND THEIR UNIVERSES
IDENTICAL CORPORATIONS SERIES
——— SAMPLE   • • • • UNIVERSE

CHART 67 (CONT.)
EARNINGS RATES OF SEVEN MINOR GROUP SAMPLES AND THEIR UNIVERSES
IDENTICAL CORPORATIONS SERIES
SAMPLE ——— UNIVERSE -----

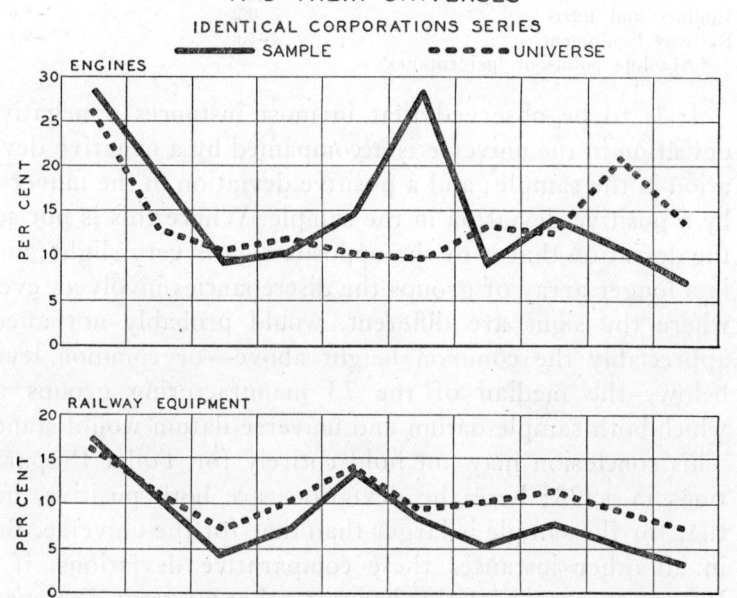

mean rates of return for each of our seven minor groups in, for example, 1928, we find that the average earnings rate upon investment for the seven universes is 13.3 per cent. We then compute the deviations of the individual figures for the seven universes from this average. Similarly, the average figure in the same year for the seven samples is 12.5 per cent; and we compute the deviations of the several samples from it. The results are given below.

Group	Deviations* Universe	Sample
Tobacco	2.3	3.1
Cotton Spinning	−3.7	−3.0
Book and Music Publishing	1.1	−0.4

	Deviations*	
Group	Universe	Sample
Toilet Preparations	6.4	12.9
Textile Machinery	−0.3	2.1
Engines and Parts	0.2	−5.6
Railway Equipment	−5.8	−9.1

* Absolute points or 'percentages'

It is to be observed that in most instances a negative deviation in the universe is accompanied by a negative deviation in the sample; and a positive deviation in the universe by a positive deviation in the sample. Where this is not so, the deviation that is of the opposite sign is very slight; and in a longer array of groups the discrepancies involved, even where the signs are different, would probably not affect appreciably the common height above—or common level below—the median of the 73 manufacturing groups at which both sample datum and universe datum would stand. This conclusion may not hold entirely for Toilet Preparations in 1928; here the deviations are both positive, but that for the sample is larger than that for the universe. But in all other instances these comparative deviations, if a larger array were involved, suggest that no great discrepancies in the relative standing of the groups would take place as between the use of complete universe data (were they available) and the use of the sample data for the large corporations series, when cast into minor groups. The same general conclusion applies to the observations of most other years of the period, the deviations for which are given in Table 110.

But even greater interest attaches to summary figures for the period as a whole, in these same terms; for our inquiry in Chapter 3 concerned the equality or non-equality of profit rates in different industries over a time period. With this in mind, we may compare the deviation of the *average of the ten annual earnings rates* for each sample group from the

TABLE 110

DEVIATIONS FROM MEAN EARNINGS RATE UPON INVESTMENT, 1919–28, AND FROM TEN-YEAR AGGREGATE RATE, SEVEN MINOR GROUPS

(samples from large corporations series)[1]

GROUP	1919	1920	1921	1922	1923	1924	1925	1926	1927	1928	1919–28[2]
						MEAN RATES					
All seven groups											
Samples	27.2	18.5	14.6	20.6	18.2	17.8	15.1	14.9	14.1	12.5	17.4
Universes	21.2	16.1	12.9	16.5	14.7	13.8	15.0	14.2	14.6	13.3	15.2
					DEVIATIONS FROM MEAN RATES						
Tobacco											
Sample	−13.2	−6.8	−1.5	−6.4	−4.8	−4.3	−0.1	−0.2	1.9	3.1	−3.3
Universe	−7.9	−4.7	−0.1	−1.9	−2.2	1.2	0.5	0.5	1.4	2.3	−1.1
Cotton spinning											
Sample	19.8	18.9	−4.2	−4.6	−4.4	−10.2	−2.8	−4.8	−3.7	−3.0	0.1
Universe	11.1	9.7	−3.4	−4.2	−2.3	−5.6	−5.6	−6.3	−5.1	−3.7	−1.5
Book and music publishing											
Sample	−9.6	−4.7	−1.1	−0.2	0.1	1.1	1.8	0.0	−2.7	−0.4	−1.6
Universe	−6.7	−1.4	−0.7	6.7	0.9	1.4	0.7	−1.2	−0.7	1.1	0.0
Toilet preparations											
Sample	12.1	1.1	14.6	32.6	17.3	19.8	17.3	13.9	14.0	12.9	15.5
Universe	−0.7	−0.4	5.5	9.2	5.6	11.3	9.0	9.3	3.9	6.4	5.9
Textile machinery											
Sample	0.2	−1.3	8.0	1.7	0.1	−7.2	−0.3	−0.5	1.8	2.1	0.4
Universe	4.0	5.2	6.1	0.9	3.4	−0.1	1.2	1.6	−0.3	−0.3	2.2

TABLE 110 (*continued*)

DEVIATIONS FROM MEAN EARNINGS RATE UPON INVESTMENT, 1919–28, AND FROM TEN-YEAR AGGREGATE RATE, SEVEN MINOR GROUPS

(*samples from large corporations series*)[1]

DEVIATIONS FROM MEAN RATES

GROUP	1919	1920	1921	1922	1923	1924	1925	1926	1927	1928	1919–28[2]
Engines											
Sample	0.8	0.7	−5.2	−10.3	−3.6	10.2	−5.9	−0.8	−3.0	−5.6	−2.3
Universe	5.4	−3.1	−2.1	−4.6	−4.5	−3.8	−1.3	−1.5	6.4	0.2	−0.9
Railway equipment											
Sample	−10.2	−7.9	−10.3	−13.4	−4.7	−9.4	−9.8	−7.3	−8.5	−9.1	−9.1
Universe	−5.1	−5.5	−5.5	−6.0	−0.6	−4.1	−4.5	−2.6	−5.4	−5.8	−4.5

[1] Ten-year aggregate.
[2] See text.

ten-year rates for each universe with a similar average of all seven universe groups.[7] These deviations, from the ten-year average earnings rates of 15.2 per cent and 17.4 per cent for the seven universes and samples respectively, are:

	Deviations of ten-year averages	
Group	Universe	Sample
Tobacco	−1.1	−3.3
Cotton Spinning	−1.5	0.1
Book and Music Publishing	0.0	−1.6
Toilet Preparations	5.9	15.5
Textile Machinery	2.2	0.4
Engines and Parts	−0.9	−2.3
Railway Equipment	−4.5	−9.1

Much the same things are to be said of this comparison as of that for the single year 1928 which was undertaken above. Even the broad discrepancy in Toilet Preparations exercises but little effect upon its relative standing: in any array either of samples or of universes it would stand as one of the most profitable minor groups. We cannot, of course, present such an array for the universes of our 73 manufacturing groups in contrast with that for our samples; but study of the deviations—'median difference coefficients' —discussed in Chapter 3, in conjunction with the data of the present section, confirms the conclusion just set forth.

As of restricted interest in this connection, we may finally rank the seven minor groups under discussion in terms of the earnings rates of the samples and universes respectively. The earnings rates themselves for the ten-year period are given in Table 110, but these are the ranks:

[7] These are not strictly 'ten-year aggregates' of the sort employed in previous chapters in the measurement of earnings rates for the period, as they are averages of the annual percentages of return on investment and not derived from a ten-year accumulation of the original investment and original income data. It seems wiser here to avoid the weighting that would result from the latter procedure, since in no group would the universe consist of the same number of corporations in successive years in the period. The differences that result, however, probably will not be large in any case.

INDUSTRIAL PROFITS

	Rank among all seven groups, the most profitable being first	
Group	Universe	Sample
Toilet Preparations	1	1
Textile Machinery	2	2
Book and Music Publishing	3	4
Engines and Parts	4	5
Tobacco	5	6
Cotton Spinning	6	3
Railway Equipment	7	7

It is obviously unnecessary to compute a coefficient of rank correlation between these two series of ranks when ordinary inspection indicates the high positive character of the correspondence; but were arrays of this character available for all 73 manufacturing groups, the coefficient would be high indeed if the same general relationships prevailed. Our assumption that such is the case is, of course, based only upon our knowledge of these seven groups. But it may be pointed out that the groups are selected quite at random; they merely happen to be ones in which universe data are available and which, with respect to the industrial classification of corporations within each group, chance to correspond with specific minor groups of the large corporations series sample.

3. A TEST OF THE SMALL MANUFACTURING CORPORATIONS SERIES

We may now proceed to test in the general manner of the preceding section several of the minor group samples in the small non-identical corporations series for Manufacturing. The number of minor groups for which 'universes' are available here chances again to be seven. But we must point out at the beginning that these seven universes are not of the same virtually complete character as those with which we compared the large corporations samples in the

MINOR GROUP SAMPLES [513]

preceding section. As a matter of fact, they are simply greatly enlarged samples, to which we may impute a higher degree of stability and representativeness than to the samples of our small corporations series. This calls for some further explanation.

In originally compiling the small corporations sample for the *Source-Book,* it was sought first to isolate the manufacturing corporations with net incomes of more than approximately $50,000;[8] then, for each year of the period studied, to assemble about a 5 per cent representation of the manufacturing corporations in the country with net incomes of from $2,000 to $50,000. The manufacturing sample thus drawn was then divided into 73 minor groups. In originally drawing this 5 per cent sample, however, it was anticipated that because of the varying sizes of the specific universes in the several minor groups, the minor group samples would be less good for some groups than for others. To illustrate, there are fewer corporations engaged in the manufacture of Railway Equipment or Textile Machinery than in the manufacture of Men's Clothing or Hardware and Plumbers' Supplies. A 5 per cent sample in the case of minor groups in which the absolute number of corporations in the universe was as low as 150 or 200 corporations, and in which the concentration of industry was marked, might yield a very much less reliable result than one in which the absolute number of corporations was 1,500 or 2,000. For this reason, the general 5 per cent sample of All Manufacturing corporations in the country (with incomes of between $2,000 and $50,000) was supplemented by larger samples of from about 50 to 100 corporations each in 24 specific manufacturing industries. Of these 24 specific manufacturing industries for which such larger samples were drawn (such industries being termed subgroups in the *Source-*

[8] This group was represented by the large corporations series.

Book), 17 represented—in terms of the industrial classification of activities included—less comprehensive divisions than the minor groups into which these activities were classified when the small corporations sample was later divided into 73 minor groups. The remaining seven, however, correspond exactly in this respect with certain minor groups of the small corporations sample; and we may accordingly subject them to the same processes of analysis that were employed in the preceding section.

Furthermore, these seven larger samples were actually employed in the minor group analyses of the earnings rates of small manufacturing corporations as presented in Book III, simply because they are presumably somewhat better samples than the smaller ones. Smaller samples were employed in Book III for minor groups for which such larger samples were not available—presumably in industries in which not the same need existed for bigger samples because of a larger number of corporations in the original universe or for other reasons such as a greater homogeneity of types of enterprise and activity within the minor group. It is, therefore, apparent that the comparison of these seven larger samples about to be undertaken is *with samples that were not used* in our analysis because they rest upon *a more slender* basis of probable accuracy than in the case of the several smaller samples (the 5 per cent representations) that were used, and that it was to safeguard against the probable defects in these seven samples that larger bodies of data were drawn for the same minor groups. We may thus feel quite certain that whatever the extent to which these small samples that were *not* used turn out to be representative of the larger bodies of data which they represent, this degree of excellence of 'fit' will be exceeded (or poorness of 'fit' will be lessened) in the smaller samples actually employed.

MINOR GROUP SAMPLES [515]

Our procedure now is to add together the original data for the corporations in the sample and in the larger sample in each of these seven groups, and for convenience to call the combination of these two sets of figures the 'universe' for the minor group in question. Actually it is in some instances not so large a proportion of the original total number of corporations in the industry as it was of the universes discussed in the preceding section; but comparison with those other data will be facilitated by adopting the same terminology. We then compare the data of the small samples with these 'universe' data.

The seven groups thus about to be discussed, together with the number of corporations in each for the sample and for the universe, are given below.

| | Number of corporations* | |
Minor group	In sample	In universe
Bakery Products	25	114
Flour	32	122
Dairying	47	135
Knit Goods	24	113
Lumber	49	137
Paints	20	66
Castings and Forgings	46	140

* Average yearly number

a. Absolute Profitableness of Samples and Universes

Comparing the rates of return upon investment earned by the corporations of the samples and of the universes in the years between 1919 and 1928, we find that in some minor groups scarcely any differences are perceptible, whereas in others the absolute discrepancies in some years are substantial. As an example of nearly perfect correspondence, we may take the minor group Dairying, in which the earnings rates of the sample in the five years 1924–28 are:

15.6   14.6   16.2   13.5   13.2;

while the figures for the universe are:

  15.4   14.6   14.7   13.0   12.0.

On the other hand, about the poorest case of correspondence is Bakery Products, where for the sample the figures are:

  12.9   22.3   17.1   10.1   17.1;

while in the case of the universe they are:

  12.8   14.5   13.8   12.7   14.8.

It is to be observed that the figures given second in Bakery Products in both series (the 1925 figures) are far apart indeed, although the discrepancies are not so serious in the other four years. The correspondence of the two sets of figures for this minor group is somewhat better for the first five years of the period 1919–23, the figures for which, together with those for all other groups, are given in Table 111.

b. Time Fluctuations in Samples and Universes

But examining not merely the absolute levels of earnings rates in the small manufacturing corporations samples and the universes, we may observe the two sets of curves over the ten-year period and we may ask how well the trends in the one set correspond with those in the other (Chart 68).

In four of the seven minor groups the correspondence is quite close: in Flour, Dairying, Castings and Forgings, and Lumber. In a fifth group, Bakery Products, the correspondence in the direction taken by the curves is fairly close in all but two or three years. In the two remaining groups, Knit Goods and Paints, correspondence for most of the period is absent; but in Paints it happens that for the period as a whole—that is, from 1919 to the end of 1928—

TABLE 111
EARNINGS RATES UPON INVESTMENT FOR SEVEN GROUPS, SAMPLE AND UNIVERSE, 1919-28
(samples from small corporations series)[1]

GROUP	1919	1920	1921	1922	1923	1924	1925	1926	1927	1928
Bakery products										
Sample	26.5	10.0	12.6	9.0	15.4	12.9	22.3	17.1	10.1	17.1
Universe	16.6	14.6	11.6	11.4	15.4	12.8	14.5	13.8	12.7	14.8
Flour										
Sample	20.2	6.3	8.6	9.8	11.5	8.1	8.9	9.7	8.7	10.8
Universe	21.0	8.5	9.0	10.5	9.9	9.7	9.5	9.1	8.8	10.3
Dairying										
Sample	18.0	16.8	18.8	17.3	11.2	15.6	14.6	16.2	13.5	13.2
Universe	17.9	14.7	16.4	16.0	13.0	15.4	14.6	14.7	13.0	12.0
Knit goods										
Sample	15.1	11.0	15.7	15.4	15.0	13.2	12.4	10.2	9.8	8.7
Universe	15.0	11.0	13.6	14.4	12.0	10.8	12.1	12.6	10.4	12.7
Lumber										
Sample	11.7	13.0	6.9	9.0	14.9	6.8	5.4	7.4	11.7	19.6
Universe	13.5	12.7	6.1	7.1	12.9	8.8	6.7	8.0	10.5	11.3
Paints										
Sample	27.1	23.3	10.8	11.9	11.8	16.1	17.8	12.1	13.8	12.1
Universe	24.5	16.7	10.9	16.8	13.9	12.8	12.7	12.2	13.2	12.0
Castings and forgings										
Sample	16.7	13.8	8.2	13.1	14.7	8.5	8.1	14.3	12.8	14.5
Universe	16.2	12.8	8.5	15.3	12.7	9.6	11.5	14.5	12.5	12.2

[1] See text for explanation.

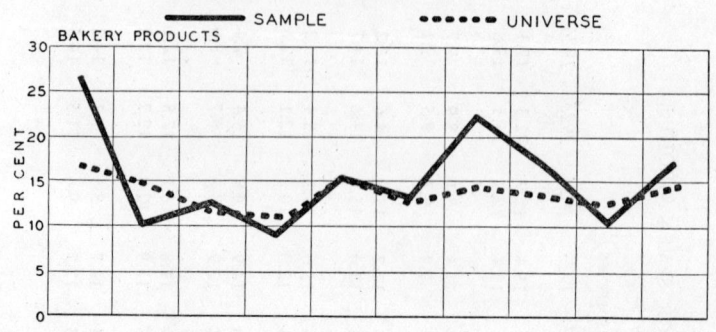

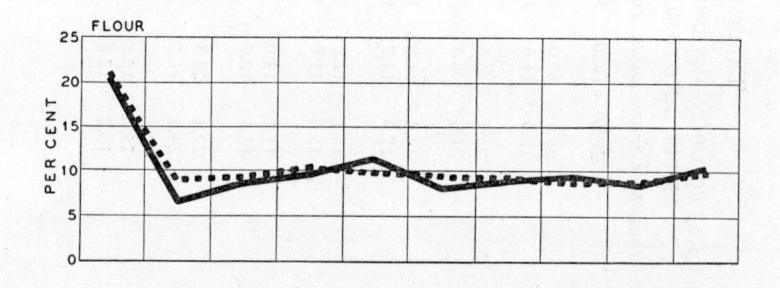

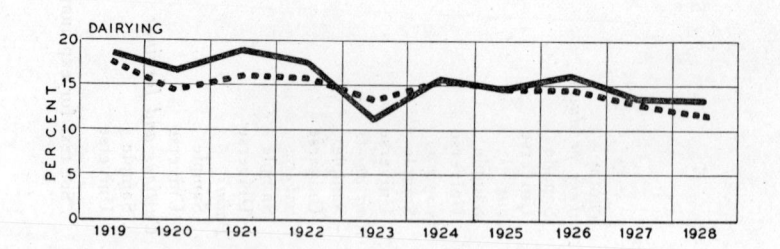

CHART 68
EARNINGS RATES OF SEVEN MINOR GROUP SAMPLES AND THEIR UNIVERSES
NON-IDENTICAL CORPORATIONS SERIES

MINOR GROUP SAMPLES [519]

CHART 68 (CONT.)
EARNINGS RATES OF SEVEN MINOR GROUP SAMPLES AND THEIR UNIVERSES

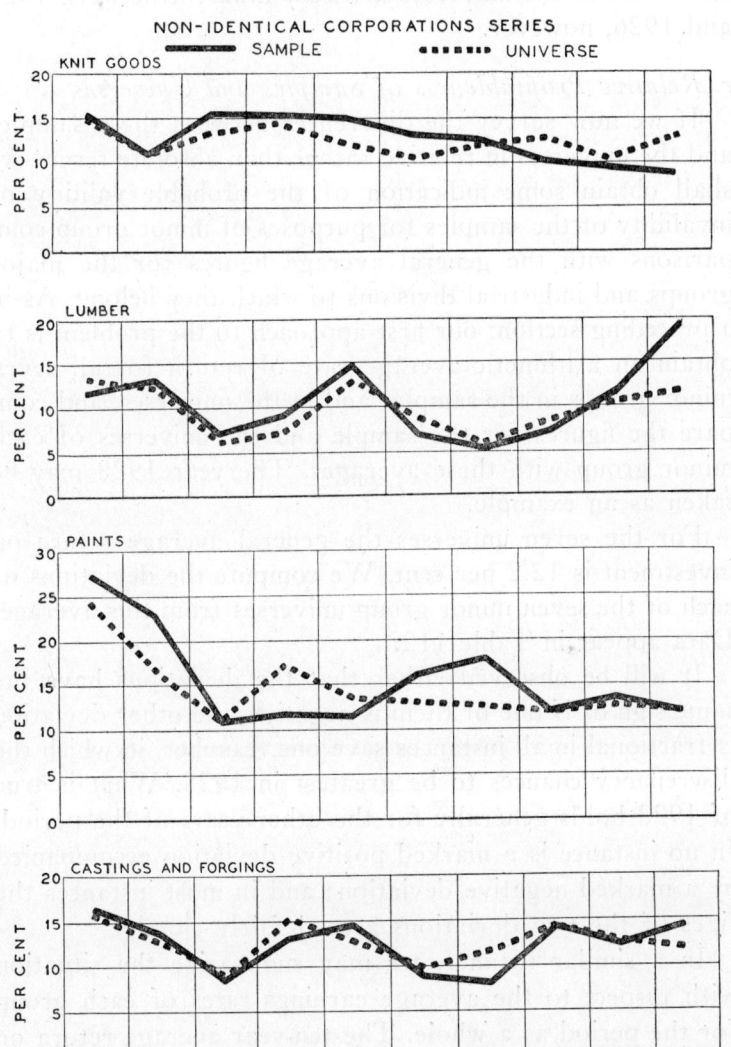

NON-IDENTICAL CORPORATIONS SERIES
——— SAMPLE ••••••• UNIVERSE

the two curves record roughly the same general decline in the rate of earnings. The interim courses of the sample curve and of the universes are very different between 1921 and 1926, however.

c. Relative Profitableness of Samples and Universes

If we now survey the differences between these samples and the universes in relative rather than absolute terms, we shall obtain some indication of the probable validity or invalidity of the samples for purposes of minor group comparisons with the general average figures for the major groups and industrial divisions to which they belong. As in a preceding section, our first approach to the problem is to obtain an arithmetic average rate of return for all seven minor groups in the samples and in the universes, and compare the figures for the sample and the universes of each minor group with these averages. The year 1928 may be taken as an example.

For the seven universes the general average return on investment is 12.2 per cent. We compute the deviations of each of the seven minor group universes from this average. Data appear in Table 112.

It will be observed either that the deviations have the same sign or if one of them is negative, the other deviation is fractional in all instances save one, Lumber, in which the discrepancy chances to be greatest in 1928. What is true of 1928 holds generally for the other years of the period. In no instance is a marked positive deviation accompanied by a marked negative deviation; and in most instances the sizes of the two deviations accord fairly closely.

In a similar manner, we may summarize the situation with respect to the average earnings rates of each group for the period as a whole. The ten-year average return on investment for the seven universes is 12.7 per cent, while

TABLE 112

DEVIATIONS FROM MEAN EARNINGS RATE UPON INVESTMENT, 1919–28, AND FROM TEN-YEAR AGGREGATE RATE, SEVEN MINOR GROUPS

(samples from small corporations series)[1]

GROUP	1919	1920	1921	1922	1923	1924	1925	1926	1927	1928	1919–28[2]
						MEAN RATES					
All seven groups											
Samples	19.3	13.5	11.7	12.2	13.5	11.6	12.8	12.4	11.5	13.7	13.2
Universes	17.8	13.0	10.9	13.1	12.8	11.4	11.7	12.1	11.6	12.2	12.7
				DEVIATIONS FROM MEAN RATES							
Bakery products											
Sample	7.2	−3.5	0.9	−3.2	1.9	1.3	9.5	4.7	−1.4	3.4	2.1
Universe	−1.2	1.6	0.7	−1.7	2.6	1.4	2.8	1.7	1.1	2.6	1.1
Flour											
Sample	0.9	−7.2	−3.1	−2.4	−2.0	−3.5	−3.9	−2.7	−2.8	−2.9	−2.9
Universe	3.2	−4.5	−1.9	−2.6	−2.9	−1.7	−2.2	−3.0	−2.8	−1.9	−2.1
Dairying											
Sample	−1.3	3.3	7.1	5.1	−2.3	4.0	1.8	3.8	2.0	−0.5	2.3
Universe	0.1	1.7	5.5	2.9	0.2	4.0	2.9	2.6	1.4	−0.2	2.1
Knit goods											
Sample	−4.2	−2.5	4.0	3.2	1.5	1.6	−0.4	−2.2	−1.7	−5.0	−0.5
Universe	−2.8	−2.0	2.7	1.3	−0.8	−0.6	0.4	0.5	−1.2	0.5	−0.2
Lumber											
Sample	−7.6	−0.5	−4.8	−3.2	1.4	−4.8	−7.4	−5.0	0.2	5.9	−2.6
Universe	−4.3	−0.3	−4.8	−6.0	0.1	−2.6	−5.0	−4.1	−1.1	−0.9	−2.9

TABLE 112 (continued)

DEVIATIONS FROM MEAN EARNINGS RATE UPON INVESTMENT, 1919–28, AND FROM TEN-YEAR AGGREGATE RATE, SEVEN MINOR GROUPS

(samples from small corporations series)[1]

DEVIATIONS FROM MEAN RATES

GROUP	1919	1920	1921	1922	1923	1924	1925	1926	1927	1928	1919–28[2]
Paints											
Sample	7.8	9.8	−0.9	−0.3	−1.7	4.5	5.0	−0.3	2.3	−1.6	2.5
Universe	6.7	3.7	0.0	3.7	1.1	1.4	1.0	0.1	1.6	−0.2	1.9
Castings and forgings											
Sample	−2.6	0.3	−3.5	0.9	1.2	−3.1	−4.7	1.9	1.3	0.8	−0.7
Universe	−1.6	−0.2	−2.4	2.2	−0.1	−1.8	−0.2	2.4	0.9	0.0	−0.1

[1] Ten-year aggregate.
[2] See text.

that for the seven samples is 13.2 per cent. Ten-year rates for each minor group are computed and the results given below.

Minor group	Deviations of Ten-year Averages Universe	Sample
Bakery Products	1.1	2.1
Flour	−2.1	−2.9
Dairying	2.1	2.3
Knit Goods	−0.2	−0.5
Lumber	−2.9	−2.6
Paints	1.9	2.5
Castings and Forgings	−0.1	−0.7

Again a close correspondence in both the direction and the extent of the deviations between samples and universes may be pointed out. Unquestionably, as in large corporations samples tested, any one of these samples would occupy much the same relative position in an array of 73 manufacturing groups as would the corresponding minor group universe, were it possible to obtain such an extended list of universe groups.

The final test relates to the rank of these seven group samples and universes respectively, among themselves. The arrangement by rank is given below.

Minor group	Rank among all seven groups, the most profitable being first Universe	Sample
Dairying	1	2
Paints	2	1
Bakery Products	3	3
Castings and Forgings	4	5
Knit Goods	5	4
Flour	6	7
Lumber	7	6

It may be reaffirmed that were series for 73 manufacturing groups available, the coefficient of rank correlation would be very high, if the rank relationships in the larger array were generally of the same sort as between these seven groups.

CHAPTER 45

THE VALUATION OF ASSETS: CAPITALIZATION PROBLEMS

1. THE NATURE OF THE PROBLEM

IN ALL of the analysis of earnings rates contained in this volume we have used as our base either the capitalization or total capital figures shown by the balance sheets of the corporations in the various samples. But the problems of accounting are complex, and the technique of keeping corporate books and preparing corporate statements is flexible, if not frequently capricious. To be sure, the data of nearly all of our samples comprise Government figures; and we may properly assume that most industrial data reported to the Government are in the main subject to fewer vagaries of accounting procedure than is the case with many figures compiled merely for the information of stockholders or the general public. Nevertheless, considerable variation of practice between individual corporations is possible; and it becomes necessary for us to ascertain the extent to which caprices of accounting procedure may influence our figures.

In all of this discussion, however, *let it be clearly understood that our interest is in the individual corporation only in so far as its figures contribute to, or exercise any significant influence upon, the value of a general group average or the structure of a frequency distribution in which the cor-*

poration is included. We fully recognize that in any individual case, no correspondence whatever between actual investment in terms of the capital contributed by security holders (both originally and through the reinvestment of earnings) and the reported balance sheet figures may obtain. But we are interested in such individual cases of gross understatement or overstatement of capital only for the light which estimates of their extent and prevalence may throw upon the probable defectiveness of our data for each industrial division, major group, and minor group, these several groups each being considered both in absolute terms and relative to one another.

Variations of accounting practice affect both our balance sheet and income account figures. Those affecting balance sheet items are of greater importance in our present problem than those which influence the income account; the operation of the income tax law has brought about a greater degree of standardization (although it is still far from exact) in general corporate accounting for income than for balance sheet items. We shall be concerned with both matters in this chapter, but shall approach the several problems involved from the point of view of the balance sheet and comment upon related charges to income as it becomes necessary to do so.

For our purposes, there are two principal sources of possible error (or if not of error, at least of the possession by our samples of heterogeneous accounting data blended in unknown proportions). Arbitrary policies of valuation make it possible for any company to carry either intangible items, such as patents and goodwill, or tangible capital assets, such as plant and equipment, upon either an ultra-conservative or an extravagant basis. And, in the case of any individual corporation, it may be repeated that the widest variations of policy are possible in this respect. As George O. May has strikingly expressed it:

> "Capital assets may be stated on the basis of cost or on the basis of a valuation. It may be a pre-war or a post-war basis. The cost may be a cost in cash or a cost in securities. If the latter, it may be a legal cost measured by a par value of a grossly inflated stock issue if the corporation was formed early in the century, or it may be greatly understated if the assets were acquired by a recent issue of stock without common [par] value."[1]

We may examine in turn these questions of patents and goodwill and plant and equipment valuations, as they affect our data.

2. VALUATION AND ABSOLUTE EARNINGS RATES: PATENTS AND GOODWILL

One simple and well-known way to inflate or water the stock issue of a corporation, happily somewhat less frequently practiced by large companies today than in the past, is to offset a capital liability by a substantial and often largely fictitious patent or goodwill account. These two items are not of exactly the same character from either an economic or an accounting point of view. Many economists would not admit goodwill as an item of capital, although they would grant that it constitutes an item of 'individual capital' to the owner of the business if it results in an accretion of income. Most accountants doubtless would recognize either item if it had been purchased, although, if not purchased, goodwill might be looked upon with a somewhat more suspicious eye by the conservative accountant than would patents developed at substantial and specifically

---

[1] *American Statistical Association Journal* (December 1929), p. 444.

ascertainable cost by the corporation itself. Frequently, of course, the development of new patented devices results in a decidedly higher rate of physical productiveness on the part of the enterprises that either perfect or eventually utilize them. A patent account in such cases is, of course, justified upon economic grounds whether the patent has been developed by the corporation in question or purchased by it from another company or persons. The *extent* to which patents may thus legitimately be capitalized is, of course, a moot question: no rule of valuation exists and, as the history of donated treasury stock witnesses, the courts will approve almost any value placed upon such an asset by vote of a board of directors, unless fraud can be established. Nevertheless, the presence of large patent and goodwill accounts—that is, large relative to the total of other assets —in industries in which the production process is not peculiarly one that makes large use of patented machinery, or of copyright materials, may be viewed with suspicion. No absolute proportion can be stated as being proper for patents and goodwill to bear to the capitalization or to total capital of an industry or enterprise; but there would perhaps be agreement that if, for an industrial group in which the conditions which have just been indicated do *not* generally prevail, the proportion of such intangibles to capital were more than 20 or 25 per cent this would constitute presumptive evidence of overcapitalization.[2]

Conversely, it perhaps will be agreed that if in industries of this kind (where peculiar conditions involving the use of patented machinery or copyrights are absent) *less* than 10 or 15 per cent of either capitalization or total capital

[2] If a definition of 'overcapitalization' in this connection is necessary, let the term mean a capitalization figure substantially in excess of either the cost of the assets or, as the courts say, of the 'prudent investment' necessary for their acquisition.

is accounted for by the figures at which patents and goodwill are carried, then no substantial overcapitalization is present, upon the score of these two items. We may thus examine the data of our samples, both by industrial divisions and by major and minor groups, to check the situation in these terms. All data are for 1925, the latest year for which they are available.

The ratio used will be that of combined patents and goodwill to capitalization, the latter term, as defined in earlier chapters, constituting the total of the following balance sheet items: (i) preferred stock, (ii) common stock, (iii) surplus and undivided profits. Since in nearly all of our Manufacturing and Trading groups, capitalization is not very different from total capital (the latter defined as capitalization plus bonded debt), we may regard the one result as being substantially the same as that which would be obtained through the use of the other figure.

For our large corporations series (2,046 corporations in All Manufacture), total patents and goodwill amount to slightly over one billion dollars, while total capitalization is 21 billion dollars. The ratio of patents and goodwill to capitalization is thus 4.9 per cent.

Divided into 11 major groups, ratios of less than 5 per cent are found in Textiles, Leather, Lumber, Chemicals, Clay, Stone and Glass, and Metals. Ratios of from 5 to 10 per cent are found in Paper and Special Manufacturing Industries. The Food and Rubber groups show ratios of 11.1 and 12.0 per cent, respectively.

The only ratio above 12 per cent is found in the major group Printing, where the proportion of patents and goodwill to capitalization is 20.0 per cent. This figure is accounted for largely by the high ratio of 28.1 per cent which, as will appear when we discuss the several minor groups below, characterizes Newspaper and Magazine Pub-

VALUATION PROBLEMS [529]

lishing; and doubtless is to be justified in large part upon the basis of copyrights which give to such assets as plates and electrotypes a value (on the basis of either cost or market) that substantially exceeds the expense of setting up type or casting plates.

In order to ascertain the maximum possible effect that patents and goodwill items carried on the balance sheets of these corporations could have upon our final figures, let us, however, make an extreme assumption which is obviously not justified: namely, that *none* of the patents and goodwill shown by any major group represents an actual investment. If this were so, to what degree would the complete exclusion of patents and goodwill affect our computed earnings rates for each major group?

Obviously, to no very great extent. Take, for example, the Metals group in which the proportion of patents and goodwill to capitalization is 4 per cent. The rate of net income to investment in the Metals group for the year in question was 12.1 per cent. If we subtract the nearly 400 million dollars shown as patents and goodwill for this group from its nine billion of capitalization and then recompute the percentages of net income to this capitalization the new earnings rate is changed only to 12.5 per cent. Similarly, in Food Products where the proportion of patents and goodwill to capitalization is 11 per cent, the new earnings rate computed on the reduced capitalization becomes 11.4 instead of 10.1 per cent. Even in Printing, where the high 20 per cent ratio of patents and goodwill to capitalization obtains, the original earnings rate of 17.2 per cent is changed only to 21.5 per cent.

How different, if at all, is the case with the 73 minor manufacturing groups? Sixteen groups show proportions of patents and goodwill to capitalization of 10 per cent or over. The presence of this amount of patents and goodwill, however, makes no marked difference in the rates of return. But eight other groups show patents and goodwill items that are 20 per cent or more of capitalization—the highest ratio being 42 per cent. One of these groups, as has been previously remarked, is Newspaper and Magazine Publishing, while three others are Proprietary Preparations, Toilet Preparations and Printing Machinery. In them all, copyrights, secret formulae or patented special devices could readily justify at least a part of the patent and goodwill account carried on the books. But again assuming that none of the amount so carried is justified, and recomputing, we obtain the ratios given below.

Minor group	Original earnings rate (including intangibles)	New earnings rate (excluding intangibles)
Confectionery	18.4	22.9
Tobacco	15.0	20.3
Men's Clothing	12.0	15.7
Stationery	6.1	8.8
Newspaper Publishing	18.2	25.3
Proprietary Preparations	21.0	28.0
Toilet Preparations	32.4	54.0
Printing Machinery	9.1	12.1

It is clear that only in Toilet Preparations is this difference really significant. And even in this group it is to be remarked that the extreme assumption which we have made as to the utter worthlessness of patents and goodwill as a valid investment item is not in the least justified, and that were one-half to two-thirds of their stated values allowed and retained in the capitalization base, the resulting earnings rate would then not differ so very significantly from that originally computed. Our conclusion, therefore, in the case of our manufacturing corporations samples, is that patents and goodwill items in the balance sheet do not in any significant way invalidate our results.

With respect to the large series of trading corporations

the results are so similar that they need not here be reviewed in detail. For All Trade the proportion of patents and goodwill to capitalization is 8 per cent; for Retail Trade it is 10.2 per cent; for Wholesale Trade, 2.7 per cent; for Wholesale and Retail Trade, 7.1 per cent. Most minor groups show very small ratios indeed, and in only two do they run as high as 15 per cent.

The small Manufacturing corporations series samples show much the same results as the large corporations. The aggregate patents and goodwill figure for all manufacturing groups combined, however, is slightly higher: 6.1 against 4.9 per cent.

For the small corporations series in Trade, aggregate figures are not available, but of 18 Trading groups, only three showed proportions of patents and goodwill to capitalization that exceeded 10 per cent, the highest of these three being 20 per cent. Clearly, our general conclusion for Manufacturing likewise applies here.

3. VALUATION AND ABSOLUTE EARNINGS RATES: CAPITAL ASSETS

The second possible major source of invalidity in our balance sheet figures is the plant and property account. If assets are in some cases stated upon a cost (or cost less normal physical depreciation) basis, and in other cases on the basis of appraisals, then to this extent our data are of a hybrid character; and if those appraisals which are conservative do not exactly offset those which are extravagant, we have no assurance that our computed earnings rates reflect the actual returns upon the investment that really accrue to the security holders. We are unable to check this point in quantitative terms as definitely as we could check the items of goodwill and patents; but certain general observations may enable us to form an opinion with respect to the broad limits of such probable discrepancies.

Again, if we take only one company, we find that the amount at which the plant account is carried may bear no relation to the investment made. We do not undertake to say that it may bear no relation to the 'value' of the plant. What the value of any industrial plant is as of any given date (unless value is defined simply as cost and adequate records are available to disclose it) is something which cannot be determined with precision by anyone. The market value of a plant obviously depends upon its earnings but what these earnings will be for the future years of the plant's life and, even assuming a fair stability and permanence of earnings, what should be the 'number of years purchase' used in calculating the valuation are controversial economic, accounting and legal matters on which we do not here propose to enter. For present purposes, in appraising the effect of variations in accounting policy upon our data, it will be sufficient to regard original cost less depreciation as a norm, and to inquire concerning the possible discrepancy between the sum of the positive deviations above this norm and the sum of those below it, in the data for any industrial group.

Some very large companies are conservative with respect to depreciation charges and their plant accounts. One of the best-known instances is the General Electric Company, which as of the end of 1928 carried plants that cost $205 million at $47.5 million.[3] This company not only makes an adequate annual charge for physical depreciation, but in addition charges a further generous portion of the value of its plant to an account called 'general plant reserve'. The two accounts, 'general plant reserve' and 'depreciation', are

[3] *Annual Report for 1928*, p. 6.

VALUATION PROBLEMS [533]

not separated in the published balance sheet; nor are charges to them shown separately in the published income statement. From various published figures that are given, however, it may be seen that the charge to this general plant reserve account can scarcely constitute any very great proportion of either net income or the amount that annual net income would be were this charge not made. The combined charge to the two accounts, in 1928 for example, was but $7.5 million, whereas the net profit figure in 1928 was $57 million.[4]

Our immediate interest is in seeing what influence such charges to 'plant reserves' have upon the stated earnings and asset figures of such corporations as the General Electric Company, in terms of specific problems of profits and profit rates discussed in this volume.

Charges to plant and equipment beyond what are regarded as normal depreciation rates proper may, of course, often be quite justified from both the economic and accounting points of view; certainly from the standpoint of business policy an excellent case can be made for the practice.[5] But

[4] Before interest payments on funded debt. The net income figure after such charges was 54 million. The two terms 'profit' and 'income' are used in this chapter as in the other parts of the volume (i.e., not as used in the General Electric or any other particular corporation's statement), but both concepts are frequently had in mind in connection with the valuation problems under discussion.

[5] In its 1926 report (from which paragraphs later published in the 1928 report are taken) the General Electric Company argues with cogency:

"Normal depreciation on buildings and equipment is based upon the estimated average effective life of each unit. It does not take into consideration the rapid obsolescence of plants and machinery in a rapidly developing industry like ours. The value of a plant, therefore, cannot safely be determined by first cost or by appraisal on the basis of reproduction cost less normal depreciation.

"It is for these reasons that your Company has followed the policy of providing a general plant reserve in excess of normal depreciation rates, so as to enable it to take promptly out of service buildings or equipment which, although not worn out physically, are inefficient and uneconomical. Failure to provide such a reserve would make the management much slower to abandon inefficient buildings and machinery, and would make the

fairly or otherwise, the General Electric Company is regarded not only by the electrical machinery industry but also by the business and accounting world generally as constituting an extreme case of conservatism in accounting procedure. If, therefore, we are able to estimate within rather close limits what the maximum possible effect of the General Electric Company's exceptional practice—from the point of view of business policy, let it be repeated, perhaps the sound one—can have upon the consistency of its figures with the data for other corporations in the Electrical Machinery minor group of our sample, we may be able to form some

Company less able to meet new conditions and, therefore, less effective in economical production and in competition.

"An illustration of this necessity is provided by the experience of your Company during the past four years, during which time fifteen factory properties have been sold, having a first cost of $3,727,749 against which normal depreciation reserves of $1,005,930 had been set aside, leaving a book value of $2,721,819. These properties were finally sold for $2,410,028, or a loss from first cost of $1,317,721, and a book loss of $311,791 which was charged against the general plant reserve. This illustration does not include machinery and equipment, on which further loss was sustained."

Such reserve strength with which to meet unforeseen losses of this character might, of course, be built up without specific charges to a general plant reserve before the calculation of net income, if a larger proportion of net income were simply retained in the business as a part of general surplus account. This would, however, imply that they were a part of profits rather than expense. But were such charges to expense not specifically made, and the net income figure thus appeared as a larger amount, stockholders would regard the business as being more prosperous and might demand larger dividends. The General Electric Company feels that such larger dividends are not justified, and even if not paid, the 'income' in question should not even appear on the balance sheet as a profit surplus—the accounting philosophy involved being that the final determination of what actually has been earned as net income in any one year cannot be made with precision until the experience of other years shows what has really been the rate of plant and equipment obsolescence in the earlier year. This is quite consistent, of course, with the statement that the value of the plant cannot be determined either by first cost or by appraisal less normal (physical) depreciation.

I am indebted to Mr. J. W. Lewis of the General Electric Company for information concerning the company's accounting policy in several respects.

general conclusion concerning the significance of our figures in that, as well as other, minor groups.

As regards the possible effect on net profit figures, it is first to be observed that theoretically a very liberal policy of provision for depreciation and obsolescence *might* have no great effect upon the income statement. This would be true only if new plant construction each year approximately equalled in cost the value of the old plant and equipment retired from service during that year; and if the rate at which new construction were written off were kept the same from year to year. This situation seldom, if ever, prevails, although in an old established enterprise in which the demand for the product has become entirely stabilized, an approach to it might result. This, however, is by no means the case with most companies, and it is not true of General Electric. Nor does the General Electric Company, as is sometimes alleged, in any sense ever charge off all, one-half or one-third of the entire cost of a new plant's construction —or anything approaching these amounts—against the earnings of the particular year in which the plant is built.[6]

Taking the 1928 figure as an example, we find that the charge to 'general plant reserve *and* depreciation' as before stated was seven and one-half million dollars, while the net profit for that year, reckoned after this charge, was 57 million. Let us assume that half of this charge had not been made. Net profit would then have been shown as about 61 million dollars instead of 57 million. Running similar calculations back to 1923, the results, in round numbers, are:

[6] The fact that in a particular year it may sometimes be observed that the Company's charge against general plant reserve and depreciation has amounted to either approximately the cost of new plant construction or to almost exactly half the cost is only a coincidence.

Year	One-half plant reserve and depreciation charge	Net profit	Net profit plus one-half plant reserve and depreciation charge
1928	4	57	61
1927	5	52	57
1926	6	50	56
1925	5	43	48
1924	5	45	50
1923	4	37	41

Next we may see what effect such charges have upon a company's invested capital figures as shown by the balance sheet. Net figures shown for capital assets are, of course, lower because of these accumulated charges than would otherwise be the case. The capitalization figures that appear on the liability side of the balance sheet (or, alternatively, a net worth figure computed by the subtraction of liabilities to other than stockholders from the total assets figure) may or may not be materially reduced because of the lower valuation at which fixed plant and equipment are carried. If a company were habitually to pay out *all* of its reported earnings in dividends, then an exceptionally large charge against plant account would merely result in the retention in the business of revenues (we do not undertake to call them net) that would otherwise have appeared as profits and would have been disbursed to shareholders. Total assets would be larger, by the amount of the excess depreciation charge, than if the charge had not been made and the sum had been paid out as dividends. To be sure, the figure representing the amount thus retained in the business is not earmarked and has no separate entity as a specific asset. It may be that the cash or United States Government securities account is larger in consequence, or it may be that inventories or other assets are greater—but in any event the figure is there. Unless a large truly secret reserve is created by charging new construction against the operations

VALUATION PROBLEMS [537]

of the year and not showing the asset upon the books at all, or unless the value of existing assets is written down more rapidly than they are being exhausted and an outstanding no-par stock issue is devaluated or capital surplus written down in consequence, no concealment of total assets —or of stockholders' equity or invested capital—would take place. This is, of course, true whether the method of recording depreciation on a balance sheet is by showing the original cost of the plant account, with the accumulated reserves against it entered as a subtraction and the net valuation extended, all on the asset side of the statement, or by showing the gross fixed investment figure as an asset and the reserve against it as a liability.[7]

The case is different, however, when, as is customary, a company regularly carries a part of its earnings to surplus. Here an excess charge against the plant account may result in appreciably smaller capitalization figures on the balance sheet and may fail to reflect assets retained in the business as reserves. In the General Electric Company, for example, we recall that the charge to plant reserve and depreciation in 1928 was $7.5 million. If only, say, $3.5 million had been charged and if out of the net profit figure (thus increased from $57 to $61 million) the same dividends were paid, then instead of approximately $8 million being carried to surplus, about $12 million would have been added.

[7] Under the second procedure, the depreciation reserve is shown as a liability item (as in published statements of the General Motors Corporation, for example), but presumably not in the 'Capital' or 'Net Worth' section of the liabilities side of the balance sheet (*cf.* R. B. Kester, *Accounting Theory and Practice* (1928), II, 188). If the valuations are at all sound from the point of view of the fairly correct appraisal of future earnings and the necessity for replacing depreciated and obsolete equipment, the reserve against plant has, of course, no proper place as a 'surplus' or 'profit' reserve and constitutes no part of capitalization. It does, however, increase the amount of total assets shown by the balance sheet. (To this extent, total assets would be a less reliable investment base than the capitalization or total capital figures employed in the present volume.)

But the total capital or capitalization figure would be far higher than that actually shown because the same procedure would have been followed in preceding years—in other words, these annual charges to plant reserve which for purposes of the present argument we regard as 'excess' charges would have accumulated over a period. As of the end of 1928, the General Electric accumulated general plant and depreciation reserve was 158 million dollars. What proportion of this represents a normal or customary depreciation reserve and what part conservative excess cannot be told from the published figures, but the annual 'excess' charge, in recent years at least, has been something less than the depreciation rate proper.[8] Let us, however, again make an assumption more extreme than the known figures warrant, and arbitrarily say that half of this accumulated depreciation reserve belongs to the surplus account—that is, should be put there in order to construct a capitalization figure that reflects a more conventional (albeit quite possibly less correct) valuation figure for plant and equipment. Upon this basis, the total capital of the company as of 1928 becomes 437 million instead of 358 million—the hypothetical figure thus being 22 per cent larger than that shown by the published statement. This is a substantial difference. Let us, in the same way, run the calculations back to 1923.

Year	Capital[1] as per books	Capital plus one-half plant and depreciation reserve[2]
1928	358	437
1927	340	415
1926	330	401
1925	305	370
1924	298	358
1923	304	360

[1] Includes general reserves, but not depreciation and plant reserves.
[2] Accumulated reserve as of end of each year.

[8] This has been stated to the writer by an official of the Company.

VALUATION PROBLEMS [539]

We may now employ this set of calculations in connection with the set of income figures previously computed, in which we added to each year's published profit figure one-half of the depreciation and plant reserve charge for that year; and in this way we can ascertain the difference in earnings rates as calculated with the two sets of income and capitalization figures. The results are given below (our computed figures being termed 'hypothetical').

Year	Earnings rates on basis of	
	Book figures	Hypothetical figures
1928	15.9	14.0
1927	15.3	13.7
1926	15.2	14.0
1925	14.1	13.0
1924	15.1	14.0
1923	12.2	11.4

It thus becomes apparent that a conservative policy of valuation may result in a somewhat *higher* ratio of net earnings to capitalization. The differences, however, are not large.[9] To what extent may we reasonably expect differences of this, or even of twice as serious a nature, to influence our general figures for an entire industry?

Taking as an example the minor group Electrical Machinery, we find that our large corporations series contains

[9] Moreover, in the case of General Electric, we have not mentioned that its furniture and fixtures account (for furniture and appliances other than in its factories) is carried at $1, as is also its patent account. However, these additional evidences of conservatism may not need to be considered in addition to the adjustment we have already made of the plant account, in calculating our hypothetical figures. The office furniture and appliances account would be small in comparison with the general plant account; while the patent account is not susceptible of any estimation. The practice of carrying patents at nominal sums is, however, fairly widespread among large corporations. In any event, we may perhaps be permitted to guess that our extreme procedure in adding as much as one-half of the general plant reserve to the surplus account constitutes a sufficiently generous adjustment of the figures to put the company upon a parity with most other large corporations that are distinguished neither for especial conservatism nor for recklessness in their accounting policies.

54 companies in this group. In 1928 the aggregate capitalization of these 54 companies is shown as 848 million dollars, while the combined net income is 140 million. Let us assume that the General Electric Company is one of these 54 companies.[10] If so, its capitalization and income figures would exercise a considerable influence upon any totals or arithmetic averages derived from the data of the sample, for upon almost any basis of valuation that might be adopted its capitalization would account for from one-third to one-half of the total for the group. Suppose, therefore, that we recast the data of the sample by taking cognizance of an assumed undercapitalization for General Electric—that, in other words, we increase the group's capitalization by an amount equal to one-half of the General Electric Company's accumulated depreciation and plant reserve shown in its published report, and likewise increase the income of the group by one-half of the charge to that account made for 1928. If this is done, the total capital of the group becomes 980 instead of 901 million, and its total profit becomes 146 instead of 142 million. The percentage of profit to capital is decreased from 15.8 to 14.9 as a result of this revision. Had the amount by which the General Electric Company is regarded as being 'undercapitalized' been made twice as great in the calculations, the change in the final earnings rate for the group would still

[10] The *Source-Book* does not identify any of the corporations in the various samples, but the total capitalization—nearly a billion dollars—shown for this sample of large corporations in the electrical industry makes it fairly certain that none of the three or four leading corporations engaged in this field is omitted from the sample—just as the total of capitalization shown by the sample for the group Motor Vehicles (almost two billion dollars in 1928) makes it certain that both the General Motors Corporation and the Ford Motor Company are included in the figures for the Motor Vehicles group. Thus while no identification of corporations is possible, the reader who studies the figures for any minor group, and who is conversant with the general composition of the industry examined, can in most cases tell whether the very largest companies are included.

have been reduced merely from 15.8 to 14.2 per cent; and were the assumed figure made three times as great, the change would be from 15.8 to 13.6 per cent.

It thus appears that no significant change in the results is likely to take place, in consequence of even a substantial measure of undervaluation by any one company in the industry. This, of course, assumes that the dominant or leading company is the *only* company in the industry for which the valuation figures deviate markedly from the customary accounting practice. But assume, however, that several large companies 'undervalue' their assets. Even if the number and size of the companies that do so are sufficient to bring as much as one-half of the industry's capitalization into question, but if the average extent of the deficiency is not much greater than in the General Electric Company, the difference between the two earnings rates involved would still not be appreciable. The effect would be to increase total capitalization by as much as one-seventh or one-sixth and somewhat to increase income, but in a much lower proportion; thus the newly derived earnings rate would in no case be significantly different from the old.

Much the same reasoning holds good for instances of overcapitalization. Even if, in a small minor group sample, one-third of the reported capitalization of the group belonged to firms which on an average reported *double* the amount of capital actually invested, a correction based upon this assumption would reduce the capitalization for the group by only one-sixth. If the earnings rate upon the capitalization as originally shown had been 15 per cent, it would become 18 per cent upon the reduced base; if it had been 10 per cent previously, it would become 12 per cent.

We have, however, made extreme assumptions. It is unlikely that, in any industrial group for which we have data, as much as one-third or one-half of the capitalization is in error by as much as one-half of, or double, itself. Furthermore, it is even more unlikely that the deviations are all on one side—that is to say, it is just as improbable to assume that in a given industry all firms that do not carry their plants at actual investment less depreciation accumulated at the usual rate show them at *more* than this figure, as it is to assume that all corporations in the industry carry their plants at less than this amount. The very diversity of practice in this respect may let us feel sure that in nearly every industrial group some corporations do the one thing, some the other. This is not to assume that the two sets of discrepancies obligingly cancel each other. But it remains true that the influence of undervaluation by certain dominant firms in an industry upon the figures for the group as a whole is partially offset by whatever overvaluation is practiced by other firms in the group. To this extent, our limits of probable error are even narrower than the possible ones which were indicated above when the effects of over- and undervaluation were considered separately.

Undoubtedly, industries differ somewhat in the extent to which arbitrary accounting practices of one sort or another prevail. But there is no reason for assuming that the difference between industries in this respect is as marked as between different companies in any given industry. At least, there is no evidence whatever to show that, with respect to valuation policies, a conservative point of view, or the reverse, is the peculiar attribute of all or most of the executive personnel in one industry as compared with another. If anything, our assumption would be that the reverse is more true, that such conservatism, or its absence, constitutes an intellectual quality that varies with the temperament and personality of the individuals in every industry and that such differences as may chance to prevail generally, in one industry as compared with another in this respect, can be neither of a broad nor of a well-defined nature.

As between the companies in any one industry, it may be reiterated, we know that variations of practice prevail, although we are unable to measure with any precision their general extent. But in concluding this part of the discussion, certain general observations, to which doubtless many competent observers among students of finance and accounting would agree, may be made.[11]

The tendency towards overcapitalization on the part of large American corporations, so prevalent in the last decade of the nineteenth century and the first decade of the twentieth, has not only abated but in some instances reversed itself. Most of the old 'watered stock' corporations that have remained in business through the period to which our data pertain have 'grown up to' their capitalizations. If anything, the present tendency among large corporations is to undervalue rather than overvalue their capital assets. The General Electric Company, used for illustrative purposes in this chapter, although a conspicuous instance of conservatism in this respect, is only one of many.

Many smaller companies undoubtedly greatly overvalue their assets, especially their fixed property accounts. Partly this is because the smaller corporations in the main are those that make the least use of public accountants and outside

[11] Some keen critics would not. Dr. Oswald W. Knauth, who has read this chapter, holds that the age of an industry probably affects the general level of its plant and equipment valuations. He says: "I confess that I am not convinced by the argument . . . . I simply don't believe that these variations in earnings rates in different industries represent the facts. I suggest that some industries with apparent high rates of return are industries in which the capital has been all written off, and *vice versa*. I can't prove it, but I don't think this proves anything either."

To 'prove' very much here—if proof means to establish beyond any doubt—is, of course, difficult. But the author desires to present Dr. Knauth's statement to the reader, as representing a more skeptical view than the conclusions of this chapter.

auditors. Often the inflation of property account may be undertaken with the deliberate purpose of making a more favorable impression upon the commercial banks which, in appraising a balance sheet as the basis of loan extensions, allow a given margin for excessive valuations before deciding upon the loan. It is perhaps not too hazardous a generalization to affirm that today large firms are apt to undervalue their plant accounts and small firms to overvalue them.[12] But while the validity of comparisons between individual corporations is often seriously affected as the result of the non-comparability of such valuations, our general conclusion is that no significant invalidation of the figures for most *industries* probably takes place as the result of such heterogeneity of accounting data in the Manufacturing and Trading divisions.

As to our samples for Finance and Mining, we can be far less certain. In certain fields of finance, where holding company pyramided upon holding company often gives the legerdemain of accounting full play, much is possible. While one minor group in our sample, Savings Banks, is doubtless entirely free from any such influence, two minor groups, Investments and All Other Finance, may reflect such arbitrary bookkeeping figures very greatly. The three other minor groups of the Finance sample, Commercial Banks, National Banks and Trust Companies, stand in an intermediate position in this respect. Most of the corporations in them doubtless carry their assets at reasonable figures (in this case, of course, the assets are mainly securities rather than physical property owned directly); but the affiliated investment companies of many such institutions bring up questions of valuation that cannot well be resolved

---

[12] This conclusion relates primarily to the types of manufacturing and trading corporations for which data are discussed in this volume—not to holding companies in the financial and public utility fields.

in general terms from data of the sort that are contained in our samples of these groups. In the Mining division, problems of charges to depletion, as well as to depreciation and obsolescence, and in some Mining fields the question of discovery value (see Ch. 25), probably subject our samples to much larger limits of possible error than in the Manufacturing and Trading groups.

4. VALUATION AND RELATIVE EARNINGS RATES: TIME FLUCTUATIONS

We have in the preceding section attempted to indicate the degree to which arbitrary valuations of plant and equipment might affect the data of our samples. Our general conclusion was that neither the absolute earnings rate for any one industry nor the comparison of earnings rates between industries would be so greatly affected by this factor as to invalidate the comparison of different industries. The data of most of our samples, however, are for a ten-year period and while the comparison of earnings rates in different industries at any one time may not be at all significantly affected by discrepancies in valuation policies, there remains the possibility that any general shift in policies that took place over the period would affect the year-to-year comparison of the figures. To investigate this question, supplementary information has been obtained from 67 companies interviewed in the course of a field study.[13]

The companies interviewed are fairly large, but in most instances not dominant, corporations. Data were collected on capital assets for certain years of the period 1919–30;

---

[13] This study was made for the National Bureau of Economic Research by Henry S. Dennison, with the collaboration of E. R. Burton. The information collected on capital assets and valuation policies was obtained specifically with a view to checking upon the problems presented by the material of our samples as discussed in the present chapter.

and each corporation was asked whether any *change* of policy with respect to the valuation of such assets took place during the period in question. In some instances, changes in policy or plant appraisals made in 1931 were reported, so the answers really relate to the thirteen-year period, 1919–31.

Fifty companies reported that 'no change' in policy took place; while 17 reported reappraisals of plant or changes of policy.

Of these 17 concerns,

a. Three reported reappraisals and the adoption of a valuation policy of cost-less-depreciation, either upon all property owned or upon all subsequent construction;

b. Seven reported reappraisals, but gave no information on the new valuations;

c. Six either wrote off all goodwill and intangibles, or substantially reduced these accounts;

d. One reported a change in depreciation and obsolescence policy that resulted in larger annual current charges, but gave no information on the revaluation of the accumulated reserve and property account.

We have here only 67 companies, but the diversity of industry is rather pronounced. There are included food products, rubber goods, electrical machinery, cotton spinning, men's clothing, machine tools, magazine publishing, writing paper and automobile manufacturing concerns as well as a few chain store companies. There are, of course, only one or a few companies in each group, but all major manufacturing groups, and the retail trade group, are represented. In size, as measured by sales, most of the companies involved do an annual volume of business ranging from approximately 2 to 20 million dollars each, although a few are much larger, having sales of 50 or 100 million.

With 50 of these 67 companies reporting no change

whatever in their valuation policy during the decade 1919–28, it seems not unlikely that this situation is typical of large manufacturing corporations that are not giant concerns and that, so far as this type of enterprise is concerned, the year-to-year comparability of at least our large Manufacturing and Trading corporations samples is not impaired because of any general changes in valuation policy during the period in question. It is interesting to find that of the companies reporting changes, most of those that gave specific information *reduced* their valuations of assets, thus confirming our earlier observation that the present tendency in the policy of large manufacturing concerns is in the direction of conservatism rather than of exaggeration in this respect.

Chapter 46

PROBLEMS OF CLASSIFICATION

1. CLASSIFICATION ON THE BASIS OF INDUSTRIAL OPERATIONS

ALL the analyses made of the earnings of different corporations and industrial groups in preceding chapters have presupposed certain classification principles. The basis of classification may have been industrial activity, financial ownership, the character of the net income, or some other criterion. But no such classification can be perfect. In the very nature of the case, to classify a corporation in this or that respect involves making a decision as to whether it belongs here or there; and all borderline cases need arbitrarily to be disposed of in one manner or another. While the classification difficulties involved, either explicitly or implicitly, in the several studies for which we have presented results may not be serious in most instances, they nevertheless are sufficiently important to require discussion.

The first problem relates both to the industrial classification of corporations as undertaken by the Bureau of Internal Revenue, in its published reports, *Statistics of Income*, and that adopted by the present writer in the original preparation of the various tables for the several samples in the Department of Commerce *Source-Book* upon which the analyses of the foregoing chapters rest.[1] In this connection,

[1] Upon these problems, William L. Crum, *Corporate Earning Power*, Ch.

it will be convenient to utilize the work of J. Franklin Ebersole and his collaborators, originally published in the *Review of Economic Statistics*.[2] We should, however, state that our discussion in no way constitutes a review of that work. (That thoughtful study was concerned chiefly with the problem of forecasting income, which is not germane to our purposes.) We shall extract certain passages from Ebersole's study that relate to the classification of corporations. Although of major importance for us, some of the points treated were of minor importance in the Ebersole article (several even appeared in footnotes); and the reader is asked to bear in mind that our criticism is of these details of argument, and in no way of Professor Ebersole's contribution to the subject of income forecasting.

The Bureau of Internal Revenue's industrial classifications assign a corporation to a particular industrial division, such as Manufacturing or Mining, or to a major group, such as Foods or Textiles, upon the basis of the company's predominant activity. Thus the Standard Oil Company of New Jersey would be characterized as an oil refining enterprise and placed in the major group Chemicals, and if placed further under a minor group caption (in the terminology of this study) would go under Petroleum Refining— although much of its activity is not manufacturing but mining (that is, drilling for oil). Similarly, the General Motors Corporation would be regarded as a motor vehicle producer; its manufacture of both electric refrigerators and

II, Classification Difficulties, and J. Franklin Ebersole, Susan S. Burr and George M. Peterson, Income Forecasting by the Use of Statistics of Income Data, *Review of Economic Statistics,* November 1929, may both be consulted to advantage. Ebersole *et al.* are much more skeptical of the validity of the industrial classifications employed by the Bureau of Internal Revenue than is Crum. Much seems to the present writer to hinge upon one's purpose in utilizing such data; likewise, the relative frequency with which a given type of error occurs is all-important, as will shortly be suggested.

[2] *Op. cit.*

sporting goods would be ignored. Because of this practice Ebersole, Burr and Peterson have contended that the overlapping between the Bureau of Internal Revenue's industrial classifications "is so great that each group, instead of adequately representing a single industry, merely represents a poor sample of all industry."[3] This contention rests upon the fact that many income tax returns represent large corporations that either engage in several types of business or else, if they are combinations of one sort or another, may file *consolidated* returns, that is, make one tax return that includes all affiliated companies. Nor can it be assumed, declare the writers just quoted, that errors caused by this overlapping can cancel one another: "For instance, if an automobile manufacturer owns a railroad and includes its income in a single return which is tabulated in manufacturing, there is no assurance that this is offset by some . . . bus company . . . manufacturing automobiles and included in transportation . . . ." The writers even go so far as to say that: "Since 1918 the *Statistics of Income* tabulations show merely the number of returns routed to the Statistics Section [the statistical division of the Bureau of Internal Revenue], there *being no data whatever* as to the actual number of corporations."[4]

Concerning these devastating criticisms, several observations may be offered. Taking them up in reverse order, it would appear that the statement that the *Statistics of Income* tabulations contain "no data whatever" on the actual number of corporations rests upon a rather legalistic definition of the term 'corporation'. In much current industrial and financial analysis the word corporation is frequently used as synonymous with 'enterprise'; and in this sense such an integrated enterprise as the United States Steel Corpo-

[3] *Ibid.*, p. 173.
[4] *Ibid.*, p. 172n. The italics are mine.

CLASSIFICATION   [551]

ration is spoken of as one corporation by the 'Street' quite as much as by the Bureau of Internal Revenue. Merely because, legally, the United States Steel Corporation may not necessarily be responsible for the actions of the numerous companies that it controls, is not to imply that, for many purposes, it should not be regarded as 'one corporation' or as 'the leading corporation' in the steel industry. While not indicating the number of *legally chartered corporations* in the country, the *Statistics of Income* tabulations undoubtedly indicate with reasonable accuracy the number of corporate *enterprises,* even though some of the larger ones own or control subsidiary concerns for which they report income data in their own returns.

As to the instance of the automobile manufacturer owning a railroad, the frequency of this occurrence is rather slight if by 'railroad' is meant anything more than a few switch tracks or loading spurs. The only real railroad that has ever been owned by an automobile manufacturer is a rather small carrier as railroad properties go, and the inclusion of its data under the heading of manufacture exercises an altogether insignificant effect upon the figures for that division. Here again the difference between data for an individual corporation and for a large group of corporations, several times remarked in the preceding chapter, should be borne in mind. Any one company's figures may be influenced by this, that or the other factor; but the quantitative effect thus exerted upon the total figures for the group is automatically less than that upon the single company's figures.

More serious is the overlapping between the manufacturing and mining divisions because many manufacturing corporations operate their own metal mines or oil wells. Here Ebersole, Peterson and Burr offer a criticism that is valid in many ways. We have, however, already touched upon this matter in Chapter 8 and pointed out that while the satisfactoriness of the mining data as adequately representative of *mining* activity is thus impaired, the satisfactoriness of the data for manufacturing activity is in some respects thereby enhanced. No adequate picture of the United States Steel Corporation, for example, as an integrated iron and steel enterprise could be obtained without including in its accounts such mining and transportation activities as are undertaken almost entirely for, and conduce directly to, the production of iron and steel products upon a large scale by the corporation in question. Again, everything depends upon the purpose of the investigation.[5]

Concerning, in this connection, the third count in the indictment of the Bureau of Internal Revenue's figures——that because of the consolidated report, each industrial group constitutes not merely a single set of industrial activities but a poor sample of all industries—the charge again seems too broad. First, the most egregious cases of conglomerate activities are the exceptions and not the rule. Ebersole, Peterson and Burr ask: "What is the main business of a company that owns, controls and files one return for operations covering . . . oil wells, pipe lines, refining, filling stations, electric light and gas plants and some investment companies?"[6] Presumably the corporation here in mind is the Cities Service Company, industrially an exceptionally diversified institution. If, however, 'electric light and gas plants' had been omitted from the list, the description of activities might well fit any one of several large oil companies other than Cities Service; and, if so, the answer

[5] Our statement here assumes that the investigator's primary interest lies in the steel industry as a whole, not in the performance of the non-integrated iron and steel companies *per se*. An investigator might, of course, for some purposes be concerned with the non-integrated as distinguished from the integrated enterprises.

[6] *Op. cit.,* p. 173n.

would simply be: the production of petroleum products, the several phases of the productive process being highly integrated. To be sure, the income arising from any one part of the process cannot be segregated in the data as given; but there is no really good reason to desire such a separation for purposes either of general economic analysis or of investment banking. An investor in the Standard Oil Company of New Jersey or the Texas Corporation invests his capital in these *several* activities, all of which are essential to the processing of oil for the final consumer. And waving aside Cities Service as representing an unusually diversified combination of activities, it is proper to regard a combination of oil wells, pipe lines, refineries, tank cars, and filling stations as constituting the normally related activities of oil production when carried on upon a large scale; and viewed in this way, the operation of pipe lines is just as much a part of the productive[7] activity of a large oil company as the operation of refineries and of filling stations.

This leads us to point out, in the second place, that a diversity of processes and activities is normally characteristic of many business enterprises whether incorporated or not. To take a trading group as an example, one would not object to the retention of the corner pharmacy—whether incorporated or otherwise—in a retail drug group because the enterprise deals in such items of hardware as alarm clocks and razors, in such foodstuffs as ice cream and candy, and in such drygoods as handkerchiefs, bandages and gauze —not to mention numerous articles other than drugs that such a store may often carry—for this conglomerate assemblage of products, traditionally and in reality, *is* a 'drug store'. To say that a datum showing the rate of return earned by such enterprises as compared with grocery or hardware stores can have no significance because the figure

[7] The term is, of course, employed in the economic sense.

represents income derived from the sale of heterogeneous products would be absurd. Similarly, to say that the enterprises denominated as 'department stores' do not constitute a particular type of business, the practices and earnings of which cannot be examined in comparison with other types of enterprise, would likewise be futile. The list could be extended.

But Ebersole presents an entirely valid criticism of the use of the consolidated return and its tendency to vitiate computations derived from *Statistics of Income* figures in pointing out that a given corporation may be not be kept in the same industrial classification in successive years. If, for example, a mail order house were at one time or another to begin the operation of retail stores and if the number of stores operated grew from year to year, a time might come when a very slight change in the nature of the enterprise might cause a complete change in classification. For example, at the start of the ten-year period, a corporation might derive 95 per cent of its gross revenues from mail order operations and 5 per cent or less from its one or several stores. If the proportion of business done by the retail stores so increased that, as of a given time, 49 per cent of the year's total business came from the stores and 51 per cent from the mail order trade, the corporation would still be classified as a mail order house. If, now, the next year 51 per cent of the gross revenues came from its stores, the corporation would then be shifted from the mail order group to another category. Not only would the character of the company's business have altered in no significant manner as between two years, but a distortion of the figures in both of the minor groups—that from which the corporation was taken and that into which it was put—would be effected. Thus, in any elaborate analysis of minor groups of industry, changes in classification that are made mechanically upon the basis of *predominant* activity are apt to affect disastrously the year-to-year comparability of the results for small minor groups. Whether or not sufficient distortion of this sort takes place as between *major* groups so as occasionally to vitiate such figures as are published in *Statistics of Income* is uncertain.

Our small corporations samples are somewhat subject to this qualification. There is no assurance that the same company (in so far as the samples may contain some of the same companies in successive years) is classified in the same minor group from year to year. In respect of small corporations, however, the qualification necessary on this score is far less serious than of large companies, as the influence of any one or two companies upon the total figures for an industrial group is slight.

All of our large corporations samples, however, consist of identical corporations from year to year; and these corporations have been kept in *exactly the same groups* throughout the entire ten-year period.

But there were several important instances in which to have kept a particular corporation in a particular group for the entire ten years would have meant closing one's eyes to the obvious fact that the nature of the corporation's business *had* substantially changed; for example, a company manufacturing crude chemicals might have undertaken the manufacture of paints and its paint business have grown to such a volume that it surpassed, not slightly but very greatly, the volume of its other chemical products. In a few such instances the company was not put into either classification but in a miscellaneous category; that is, in the particular instance just given, the company would have been placed neither in the Paints nor the Crude Chemicals group but in Miscellaneous Chemicals and Chemical Products, for the entire ten years. For in many such instances, blindly to keep corporations in the same group from year to year might effect as gross a distortion of results as to follow the rule of predominance.

It is clear that no completely satisfactory basis of classification is possible—any basis adopted must be in many respects arbitrary. Doubtless our practice of putting into miscellaneous categories the doubtful cases of our large corporations series solves the problem for purposes of sample studies that cover only ten or fifteen years. Probably no rule that could be employed continuously by the Bureau of Internal Revenue in its compilations would satisfy all users of the material. Over a long period of years, if the nature of a corporation's business indeed markedly changes it *should* be shifted out of one category into another. Perhaps a satisfactory working basis—although still arbitrary —would be to throw the enterprise in question into a new group only when the proportion of gross revenues derived from such activities constituted as much as, say, 75 or 80 per cent of its total volume of operations. In any event, the *Statistics of Income* data that we have employed in this book have been only for industrial divisions and major— not minor—industrial groups; and we may assume that reservations are necessary upon the score of industrial classification in few instances.[8] Our own large corporations

[8] Professor Ebersole and his co-authors do well in the articles cited to call attention to the qualifications that ought to be borne in mind by anyone who uses the figures published by the Bureau of Internal Revenue. For some purposes doubtless certain of the imperfections of classification may invalidate the *Statistics of Income* data in question; but for many purposes of general economic analysis, we cannot believe that they seriously do so. The position taken in this chapter is substantially that of Professor Crum, who has made much use of *Statistics of Income* data—particularly those for the net return upon sales and gross revenues—by industrial divisions and major groups in much the way in which those and other data have been employed in the present volume. In his *Corporate Earning Power* (1929) Crum states:

"In spite of these imperfections in classification, it is believed that the

CLASSIFICATION [557]

samples, to repeat, are not subject to any such reservations.[9]

2. INTERCORPORATE INCOME AND INVESTMENT

Many large corporations, whether consolidated or not, own stock interests in other corporations on which they receive dividends. These dividends constitute a part of the income of the corporation that receives them, although they are not taxable. The income amounts contained in some tables of *Statistics of Income* may be taken with or without the inclusion of such dividends; and in nearly all of the tables of our samples, they may be reckoned either way. But we are not, in the balance sheet data of our samples, able to segregate the intercorporate investment on which such dividends are earned. Thus the capitalization data of our samples, taken as absolute amounts, involve a certain duplication: the capitalization of some corporations reflects

---

aggregate figures for the various divisions, groups, and subgroups are significant and valuable. One of the chief reasons for this confidence is that many of the errors in classification are such that they tend to offset one another, and to have therefore a relatively small aggregate effect on the group total. Moreover, we are accustomed to use statistical data for which similar classification difficulties exist. Indeed, most statistical classification in economics and business is likely to be hazy and imperfect, and we are in the habit of making reservations in our reasoning from such figures. Reservations of this sort should be made in the study of these income data. Such reservations need not be more stringent, however, than in other like problems in economic and business analysis, and they certainly do not seriously impair the usefulness of the figures for such analyses . . ." (p. 23).

[9] This chapter, in unrevised form, was submitted to Professor Ebersole, who was good enough to make several valuable criticisms of which cognizance has been taken in the revision. However, of a part of Section 1, Professor Ebersole says, "Have you not overlooked two facts . . . the bias of the figures during a period of consolidation whereby a larger area of business comes under the control of the corporation (single or consolidated) bearing the *same name,* and the mortality of old corporations and the birth of new corporations within the same classification?" Possibly these two matters should be treated in this chapter; see, however, Ch. 34, 35, 43.

the ownership not merely of its own assets but also a part of the assets of other corporations. For purposes of calculating the earnings rate of any corporation upon its invested capital, such dividends must be included in income; and it is thus proper to retain the investment (on which such dividends are received) in capitalization. But since some duplication is thus involved if either the income or investment figures be considered as absolute amounts, and since from the point of view of any given corporation the income thus received is in most instances to be classed as non-operating income, it is desirable to ascertain the extent to which such intercorporate holdings and revenues obtain. We have no data directly upon capital holdings, but the proportion of total income received upon such investments serves as a rough guide to the relative investments themselves.

It will be sufficient to analyze the data for the large manufacturing corporations series in 1928.[10] For All Manufacture, the total of intercorporate income received by the 2,046 companies of the sample amounted to 12.7 per cent of the aggregate net income before the segregation of dividends received. The two largest major groups, Metals and Foods, show figures of only about 4 per cent each. The Chemicals group, however, has a ratio of 30 per cent.[11] The large proportion of intercorporate dividends present in this group must be regarded as a substantial qualification upon the significance of the absolute income and capital figures involved. Data for all groups are presented in Table 113.

[10] The original data for other years are available in the *Source-Book*.

[11] This is the highest ratio of any major group except Rubber, in which the figure is anomalously 119 per cent because the net income derived from operations is a deficit that is converted into a positive figure when the intercorporate dividends are added to it. Dividends received in the Rubber group in 1928 amount to about $9 million, while the aggregate total net income of the group (including such dividends) is $7.5 million. The Rubber group, however, experienced an exceptionally poor year in 1928, so the illustration is not typical.

CLASSIFICATION [559]

TABLE 113
DIVIDENDS RECEIVED IN RELATION TO NET INCOME:
LARGE IDENTICAL MANUFACTURING CORPORATIONS
SERIES, 1928

MINOR GROUP		PERCENTAGE OF DIVIDENDS RECEIVED TO NET INCOME
1	Bakery products	0.3
2	Flour	0.4
3	Confectionery	4.3
4	Package foods	2.0
5	Dairying	0.1
6	Canned goods	3.9
7	Meat packing	9.4
9	Beverages	3.1
10	Tobacco	4.6
11–8	Miscellaneous food products	7.6
12	Cotton spinning	0.1
13	Cotton converting	1.2
14	Cotton weaving	8.8
15	Weaving woolens	1.8
16	Silk weaving	1.1
17	Carpets	1.9
18	Men's clothing	0.4
19	Knit goods	1.0
20	Miscellaneous clothing	1.2
21	Miscellaneous textiles	0.6
22	Boots and shoes	0.3
23	Miscellaneous leather products	9.9
24	Rubber products	118.8
25	Lumber manufacture	5.2
26	Planing mills	5.5
27	Millwork	0.3
28	Furniture (non-metal)	4.0
29	Miscellaneous lumber products	0.6
30	Blank paper	20.4
31	Cardboard boxes	0.9
32	Stationery	1.0
33	Miscellaneous paper products	9.1
34	Newspapers and periodicals	23.5
35	Book and music publishing	0.5
36	Job printing	4.3
37	Miscellaneous printing and publishing	0.8
38	Crude chemicals	3.5
39	Paints	7.8
40	Petroleum refining	31.2
41	Proprietary preparations	0.5
42	Toilet preparations	1.6

Table 113 *(continued)*
DIVIDENDS RECEIVED IN RELATION TO NET INCOME

MINOR GROUP		PERCENTAGE OF DIVIDENDS RECEIVED TO NET INCOME
43	Cleaning preparations	0.4
44	Miscellaneous chemicals	48.5
45	Ceramics	0.8
46	Glass	0.6
47	Portland cement	4.2
48	Miscellaneous stone and clay products	1.4
49	Castings and forgings	2.6
50	Sheet metal	6.1
51	Wire and nails	8.4
52	Heating machinery	7.1
53	Electrical machinery	6.1
54	Textile machinery	2.3
55	Printing machinery	0.1
56	Road machinery	1.3
57	Engines	3.0
58	Mining machinery	1.4
59	General factory machinery	3.2
60	Office machinery	2.0
61	Railway equipment	24.6
62	Motor vehicles	1.6
63	Firearms	2.5
64	Hardware	2.4
65	Tools	6.8
66	Bolts and nuts	2.9
67	Miscellaneous machinery	2.0
68	Non-ferrous metals	8.4
69	Jewelry	0.8
70	Miscellaneous metal products	1.5
71	Scientific instruments	35.8
72	Toys	1.1
73	Pianos	0.9
74	Miscellaneous special manufacturing	1.7

MAJOR GROUP		
1	Foods	4.4
2	Textiles	2.2
3	Leather	1.8
4	Rubber	118.8
5	Lumber	3.1
6	Paper	12.1
7	Printing and publishing	18.5
8	Chemicals	30.1

TABLE 113 *(continued)*
DIVIDENDS RECEIVED IN RELATION TO NET INCOME

MINOR GROUP		PERCENTAGE OF DIVIDENDS RECEIVED TO NET INCOME
9	Stone, clay and glass	2.0
10	Metals	3.8
11	Special manufacturing industries	20.7
	All manufacturing	**12.7**

Only a few minor groups show high ratios of dividends received to total net income. All but eight of the 73 manufacturing industries have ratios of less than 10 per cent. The five which (apart from the Rubber group commented upon above) have ratios of 25 per cent or more are: Miscellaneous Chemicals, 48.5; Scientific Instruments, 35.8; Petroleum Refining, 31.2; Railroad Equipment, 24.6. In most minor groups, therefore, the proportion of intercorporate income and investments is not sufficiently large to modify greatly the absolute figures; and the earnings rates derived therefrom may be regarded substantially as earnings from operations.[12] In a few groups, such as those just listed, qualifications must, however, be made with respect to the interpretation of the absolute capital and income figures.

3. CONSOLIDATED AND NON-CONSOLIDATED REPORTS

Frequent reference has been made in the two preceding sections to consolidated corporations in contrast to those which report individual income and investment figures, either to the Bureau of Internal Revenue or otherwise. For neither the data published in *Statistics of Income* nor for the corporations of our samples have we precise information concerning the extent to which consolidated corporation

---

[12] That is, from the point of view of each group as a whole, but not necessarily from that of a particular corporation within any group.

reports may effect a distortion in the figures as grouped by major or minor groups of industries. We are, however, able to ascertain the general extent to which consolidated corporations share in the business of the country from the published *Statistics of Income* figures; and for the data of our large corporations sample in Manufacturing and Trade, we may compare the rates of return received by the two types of enterprise. Both sets of comparisons are for 1928. First, as to all of the manufacturing corporations in the country, the consolidated corporations in manufacturing are shown by *Statistics of Income* as having sales of 33 billion dollars, or about one-half of the total of 64 billion for all corporations (consolidated and non-consolidated combined). The consolidated corporations account for 2,700 million out of a total net income [13] of about 4,500 million. In Trade the proportion of business done by the consolidated corporations is much smaller. The consolidated enterprises show sales of about 7.5 billion as compared with sales of 42 billion by all Trading corporations of the country (consolidated and non-consolidated combined). The total income of the consolidated Trading corporations is about 400 million as compared with slightly over one billion for all Trading corporations.

Our large manufacturing corporations sample contains 2,046 corporations of which 127 are consolidated and 1,919 are not.[14] The capitalization of the consolidated corporations equals about $10.5 billion, while that for the two classes combined is $25 billion. The income for the consoli-

[13] Called 'compiled net profits before deduction of tax-exempt items in order to arrive at statutory or taxable income'.

[14] The definition of consolidated corporation contained in the *Source-Book* is as follows: "*Consolidated corporation* means one which, in its accounting, merges the income account and balance sheet items of its subsidiaries with those of the parent company. Thus corporations 'not consolidated' may in some cases be affiliated with, may own or be owned by, other companies, but do not merge their financial data in their reports."

CLASSIFICATION   [563]

dated corporations is about one billion, while that of the two classes combined is about $2.75 billion.

Separating the two sets of figures, we may ask if the average rate of income received by the consolidated corporations as a group upon capitalization is larger than that for non-consolidated corporations. The difference is not significant: in the former group, 10.3 per cent; in the latter group 11.4 per cent.

This is for Manufacturing as a whole. The data may, however, be divided into several major groups. In some groups, the consolidated corporations doubtless earn more, in others less, than the non-consolidated. Just how significant these differences by major groups are cannot be said, as the absolute number of consolidated corporations is small in all groups except the large Metals group where the difference in the two figures is slight. The data are given for whatever they may be worth in Table 114. The data by minor indus-

TABLE 114

CLASSIFICATION OF 2,046 MANUFACTURING CORPORATIONS: CONSOLIDATED OR NOT CONSOLIDATED, 1928

	NUMBER OF CORPORATIONS	TOTAL NET INCOME	CAPITALIZATION	PERCENTAGE INCOME TO CAPITALIZATION
Major group 1				
Consolidated	23	$114,467,190	$1,376,535,540	8.3
Not consolidated	192	192,836,410	1,389,350,730	13.9
Total	215	307,303,600	2,765,886,270	11.1
Major group 2				
Consolidated	9	5,127,330	191,700,720	2.7
Not consolidated	280	75,144,500	1,021,134,010	7.4
Total	289	80,271,830	1,212,834,730	6.6
Major group 3				
Consolidated	6	19,660,470	117,293,920	16.8
Not consolidated	48	9,238,560	137,607,730	6.7
Total	54	28,899,030	254,901,650	11.4
Major group 5				
Consolidated	5	1,106,870	30,131,660	3.7
Not consolidated	185	43,146,360	495,598,570	8.7
Total	190	44,253,230	525,730,230	8.4

TABLE 114 *(continued)*

CLASSIFICATION OF 2,046 MANUFACTURING CORPORATIONS: CONSOLIDATED OR NOT CONSOLIDATED, 1928

	NUMBER OF CORPORATIONS	TOTAL NET INCOME	CAPITALIZATION	PERCENTAGE INCOME TO CAPITALIZATION
Major group 7				
Consolidated	5	23,899,520	52,617,120	45.4
Not consolidated	95	74,474,620	405,872,910	18.4
Total	100	98,374,140	458,490,030	21.5
Major group 8				
Consolidated	22	348,613,470	3,194,568,510	10.9
Not consolidated	188	431,289,550	3,548,596,880	12.2
Total	210	779,903,020	6,743,165,390	11.6
Major group 9				
Consolidated	8	15,890,130	150,791,350	10.6
Not consolidated	106	73,131,850	548,850,140	13.4
Total	114	89,021,980	699,641,490	12.8
Major group 10				
Consolidated	41	557,543,210	5,323,318,410	10.4
Not consolidated	607	617,513,790	5,313,580,140	11.6
Total	648	1,175,057,000	10,636,898,550	11.1
All manufacturing				
Consolidated	127	1,094,179,880	10,599,447,240	10.3
Not consolidated	1,919	1,642,649,750	14,379,550,490	11.4
Total	2,046	2,736,829,630	24,978,997,730	11.0

trial groups are not available; but it is fair to conclude that with most minor groups perhaps containing not more than one or two consolidated corporations, the effect of such differences in earning power as may prevail between consolidated and non-consolidated corporations in particular sets of related industrial classifications is not such as to distort the minor group figures in many instances.

In Trade, our large corporations sample contains 14 consolidated corporations and 650 non-consolidated corporations. The aggregate capitalization of the 14 consolidated corporations is 271 million while that of both classes combined is 2.5 billion. The income of the consolidated corporations is 48 million while that for the two classes combined

CLASSIFICATION [565]

is 307 million. Here a substantial difference in earnings rates for the two types of enterprise is found; the consolidated corporations earn 17.8 per cent upon capitalization, while the non-consolidated average 11.6 per cent. Data are not available by major groups. We may, however, conclude that if the consolidated corporations are at all widely distributed among the various Trading minor groups, the effect of overlapping industrial classifications is not at all significant, since the 14 consolidated corporations that earn this high return possess only about 10 per cent of the aggregate capitalization of the sample.

4. CALENDAR AND FISCAL YEAR RETURNS

The data of both *Statistics of Income* and of our samples contain, among the income accounts classified as belonging to any calendar year, certain corporations whose accounting period is a fiscal year ending in some month other than December. The proportion is not large. We have no figures showing the exact percentage they constitute in each industrial division or major group, but in the *Statistics of Income* data the percentage for all divisions combined runs from 4 to 11 at the most.[15] In 1928 about 55,000 corporations filed tax returns for fiscal years ending not earlier than July 1, 1928 or later than June 31, 1929, out of a total of 496,000 corporations.

The fact that as many as ten per cent—or in some major or minor groups even a greater proportion—of the corporations for which data are classified as belonging to any one year do report income that is earned partly in months of the following calendar year undoubtedly has an effect upon the time fluctuations of our data. But again this influence

[15] Data available for the years 1925–28 yield the following percentages: 4.6, 5.1, 4.2, 11.1.

would not seem to be large. Of the 55,000 corporations that filed returns for fiscal years ending between the middle of 1928 and the middle of 1929, roughly as many have fiscal years ending in one month as in another, except January and June which were more popular as terminal points. The distribution as given in *Statistics of Income* is as follows:

Fiscal year ending	Number of returns	Fiscal year ending	Number of returns
July 1928	3,719	January 1929	6,538
August 1928	3,624	February 1929	3,851
September 1928	3,967	March 1929	5,230
October 1928	3,689	April 1929	4,779
November 1928	3,630	May 1929	5,132
		June 1929	10,661
	Total	54,820	

Many of the returns filed for fiscal years ending 'not later than June 30, 1929' thus report income of which a substantial proportion was actually earned in 1928. Probably no less than 80 or 85 per cent of the corporations in any major or minor group report calendar year data, and a portion of the fiscal year returns data belongs to the calendar year with which they are classified; therefore no very grave fear need be entertained that the inclusion of the fiscal year figures invalidates our time comparisons.[16]

---

[16] Crum, who in the work already cited analyzes the fiscal year situation carefully for 1926, concludes with respect to the data of *Statistics of Income:* ". . . the really significant difficulty is that changing business conditions may have an apparent effect upon the current fortunes of corporations which report for fiscal years ending considerably before December, different from that for corporations reporting for fiscal years ending considerably after December. Furthermore, if it should turn out that the bulk of the early dates tend to apply to enterprises in a particular type of industry, and the bulk of the later dates tend to apply to enterprises in some other lines of business, there may be, on this ground also, a tendency towards bias. Under the actual circumstances, however, with the calendar year returns exceeding 94 per cent of the total (in 1926) it seems probable that these disparities even at the worst cannot damage seriously the year-to-year comparisons based on the tabulated figures." (Ch. II, Classification Difficulties, p. 25; see also Crum's discussion in Appendix A, *op. cit.*, pp. 317–8.)

Akin to this problem of the fiscal year for the income account is that of the date at which balance sheet figures are taken for corporations that do report calendar year data. In obtaining the capital figures for any given year the ideal practice would be to take an average of daily, weekly, or monthly figures for the amount of capital invested; but needless to say no such data are available. All that the statistical investigator can ordinarily obtain is a balance sheet figure as of either the beginning or the end of the year. Taking either the beginning or the end of the year figure biases the resulting earnings rate in the one direction or the other. An alternative would be to average the two capital figures, when samples made this feasible—in our large identical manufacturing corporations series, for example. But had we done this in our several analyses, our general arithmetic average earnings rates would not have been exactly comparable with the earnings rates of our frequency distributions of individual corporations in the various major groups, as the latter are available only upon single, and not average, bases.

Although an average base represents a theoretically better practice, the difference in result is not large in the case of our several data. If, for example, in any major or minor group the invested capital as of the beginning of the year were 100 and the net profit were 11, the rate of return computed upon the beginning of the year base would be 11 per cent; if at the end of the year the capital were 105, the rate of return based upon that figure would be 10.5 per cent, or rounded off, 11.0 per cent. It is thus apparent that even if the invested capital of a group were 10 or 15 per cent larger (instead of only 5 per cent as assumed in the illustration) during the year, the difference between the earnings rates as computed on an end-of-the-year basis and an average basis would not be serious. In our several samples the balance sheet data were taken (by necessity) as of January 1 in the years 1919–22; as of either January 1 or December 31 in 1923; and as of December 31 in the years 1924–28. All income account data are for the entire year ended December 31, except in the relatively few instances of corporations with fiscal years that run otherwise.

5. CLASSIFICATION OF CORPORATIONS WITH AND WITHOUT NET INCOME

The most frequent characterization of 'successful' and 'unsuccessful' corporations made upon the basis of the published *Statistics of Income* figures is to contrast the number of corporations reporting net incomes with the number reporting no net incomes. The result shows that nearly as many corporations annually fail to return an income as to report one. Such comparison, while striking, does not tell the whole story for at least two reasons. In the first place, as Crum has pointed out, while nearly half of the corporate enterprises report to the Bureau of Internal Revenue that they earn no net income, most corporations of this kind are very small; and nothing like one-half of the total corporate business of the country is carried on without a profit. Instead, only about 20 per cent of all corporate business is done at a loss, 80 per cent of the aggregate volume showing a net income even for income tax purposes.

In the second place, many of the corporations that show no net income for income tax purposes may have net incomes and may, as Ebersole, Peterson and Burr have stated, remain permanently in business. In certain instances the income is largely of the tax-exempt nature; in other instances, or occasionally even in the same case, a close corporation may well pay out substantial salaries to its officers, "and

CLASSIFICATION [569]

thus have no taxable income remainder after deducting enough for depreciation to keep its capital intact."[17]

For these two reasons the *Statistics of Income* data—although strictly correct in light of the definitions of terms underlying them—are to be interpreted with caution. Nevertheless, they point to the undoubtedly large proportion of corporate enterprises that annually receive no great income upon their invested capital; and a somewhat closer scrutiny of our several samples from this point of view is therefore needed.

Our several large corporations series, of course, each year contain corporations reporting deficits. These deficits are not deficits for purposes of income tax return as above discussed, but are true net deficits after counting in the two tax-exempt items of dividends received and interest upon Government securities. We are not able to segregate the sales of the corporations with deficits in our samples and ascertain what proportion of total business volume was done at a profit; but we are able to segregate the capitalization of the enterprises with true net losses ('true' in that tax-exempt income is not waved aside) and to ascertain what proportion of all of the capitalization in the sample earned a profit. Taking our 2,046 large manufacturing corporations series as representative of *large-scale* manufacturing, we find in 1928 that a net income was earned on 94 per cent of the investment. In 1927 the figure is 90 per cent, while in 1926 it is 96 per cent. In a year of depression such as 1921 it is 70 per cent.

While our large corporations samples contain enterprises with deficits, our several small corporations series do not. The earnings rates computed for them enable us to ascertain what returns upon investment are received by small corporations that *do* earn net incomes; but no light is thus

[17] Ebersole *et al., op. cit.,* p. 171.

thrown upon the extent of the losses suffered by small corporations that *fail* to return such incomes. We have available (Table 115), however, a small sample of such corporations in Manufacture. Since the data relate only to the two years 1926 and 1928 and are susceptible of division into less than a score of minor groups, they were not introduced earlier.

This series we may call a sample of 'non-identical small manufacturing corporations with negative net incomes'. It contains 487 corporations in 1926, and 376 corporations in 1928. The incomes are 'net' in the same inclusive sense in which the term has been used in connection with our other samples. They include tax-exempt items such as corporate dividends received and interest on non-taxable securities. But they are not, of course, adjusted to take cognizance of such partly questionable deductions from income as relatively large officers' salaries, etc. that may be involved.[18] Our immediate interest is in seeing what part of the capitalization of these companies the annual net loss thus computed represents.

For All Manufacturing, the negative earnings rate upon capitalization for this sample is 8.1 per cent in 1926 and 6.5 per cent in 1928. In the ten major groups into which the data may be divided (the Leather and Rubber groups are combined) the figures run as high as 22 per cent in 1926, but in no case exceed 12 per cent in 1928. The Paper group in both years, and the Leather and Rubber group in 1928, should be disregarded as the numbers of corporations in the samples are clearly too small to be of significance.

The division of the data into minor groups shows that

[18] Colonel M. C. Rorty observes that since the payment of salaries large in proportion to profits occurs mainly, although not exclusively, in small corporations, and is far from universal there, the proportion of aggregate corporate profits thus misclassified as payment for services must be a very small fraction of the whole.

CLASSIFICATION　　　　　　　　　　　　　　　　　　[571]

in neither year did the net loss sustained by any group amount to more than about 13 per cent of the capitalization. In most instances the figure runs between 5 and 10 per cent. It is, however, to be observed that in many of these minor group samples the number of corporations is very small. While the distorting elements that would be occasioned in such small samples, were any very large corporations included, are here entirely absent, it is nevertheless to be remarked that possibly the only very valid figures of Table 115 are those for All Manufacturing—the 8.1 per cent and 6.5 per cent losses for 1926 and 1928 respectively —and for the several major groups that contain more than a few corporations each.

TABLE 115

PERCENTAGE OF NET LOSS TO CAPITALIZATION: SMALL NON-IDENTICAL MANUFACTURING CORPORATIONS WITH NEGATIVE INCOMES IN 1926 AND 1928

MINOR GROUP		NUMBER OF CORPORATIONS 1926	1928	PERCENTAGE OF LOSS TO CAPITALIZATION 1926	1928
1	Bakery products	9	11	9.6	9.5
2	Flour	25	17	7.4	4.9
5	Dairying	10	10	6.3	7.0
11	Miscellaneous food products	21	13	10.8	6.9
18	Men's clothing	11	8	7.0	11.0
19	Knit goods	7	..	4.9	..
20	Miscellaneous clothing	22	41	9.7	11.3
21	Miscellaneous textiles	8	26	0.5	7.2
25	Lumber manufacture	29	..	5.8	..
34	Newspapers	9	..	3.8	..
37	Miscellaneous printing and publishing	6	9	6.5	11.0
48	Miscellaneous stone and clay products	12	7	5.6	4.7
49	Castings and forgings	17	11	8.4	7.1
53	Electrical machinery	9	6	4.2	4.6
67	Miscellaneous machinery	8	7	13.4	11.6

TABLE 115 *(continued)*

PERCENTAGE OF NET LOSS TO CAPITALIZATION

		NUMBER OF CORPORATIONS 1926	1928	PERCENTAGE OF LOSS TO CAPITALIZATION 1926	1928
MINOR GROUP					
70	Miscellaneous metal products	11	6	9.9	5.0
74	Miscellaneous special manufacturing	23	18	12.2	8.4
MAJOR GROUP					
1	Foods	98	74	8.3	5.4
2	Textiles	71	97	3.2	8.6
3–4	Leather and rubber	25	8	22.0	4.7
5	Lumber	71	27	7.7	7.7
6	Paper	7	7	10.8	7.2
7	Printing	33	25	4.9	12.1
8	Chemicals	34	37	19.1	4.4
9	Clay, stone and glass	17	11	6.5	3.7
10	Metals	99	67	5.7	7.9
11	Special manufacturing industries	32	23	11.2	8.3
	All manufacturing	487	376	8.1	6.5

6. DEFICITS IN CAPITAL ACCOUNT

One problem of the classification of corporations for purposes of earnings rates analysis, which is present in the case of corporations both with and without net income, is the treatment of accumulated deficits in capitalization. If a corporation has sustained marked losses for several years, it is possible that not only will it fail to show a surplus but also that its original capitalization will have become to some extent impaired, perhaps substantially so. Among the small corporations this situation is far more common than is ordinarily realized, although to the public accountant it is a fairly familiar phenomenon.

So long as the amount of the deficit (in this section we use the term 'deficit' in reference to capital account) is relatively small, it may be subtracted from the original capitalization and the net figure regarded as the amount of capital investment actually in the business. But when the amount of the accumulated deficit becomes large, such treatment is unsatisfactory and occasionally leads to grotesque results. A small corporation, for example, might begin business with an original capitalization of $250,000, and over a period of years undergo successive losses so that at the end of the period in question its accumulated deficit amounted to $240,000. The net capitalization or stockholders' equity remaining would thus amount to $10,000. Such a corporation might, however, in the next year earn a positive net income of $2,000. Reckoned upon a capitalization base of $10,000, such an income would give an earnings rate of 20 per cent. Or, as a more extreme illustration, a good year might bring the corporation's income to $10,000 or more; in this event the earnings rate would appear to be 100 per cent or over—an absurd result. For while the stockholders' equity in the corporation is indeed only $10,000, there is far more than that amount of capital invested in the business; its ownership has merely been shifted from the stockholders to the creditors, who, should the enterprise be liquidated, would receive the bulk of the proceeds from the sale of the fixed and other assets liquidated. The figures of the illustration are hypothetical, but the proportions involved represent approximately the situation found in several actual cases. It is therefore of interest to ascertain the extent to which such deficits in capital account prevail, as well as necessary to explain the treatment accorded them in the data of our samples.

In each of the years 1925–28 the original data from which our small manufacturing corporations series (with positive incomes of from $2,000 to $50,000) was drawn consisted of approximately 1,650 corporations. Of these

1,650 corporations, in every year about 100 companies showed accumulated deficits. Thus *at least* 6 per cent of the small manufacturing corporations of the country (the sample is biased in that it contains only corporations with positive incomes) show an impairment of the original capital invested.

The range of these deficits is wide. The distribution in 1928, for example, discloses that 8 out of 107 corporations had accumulated deficits of over 100 per cent of their original capitalization; 26 had deficits of over 50 per cent; while 46 had deficits of over 20 per cent. There are thus roughly as many of these companies with deficits of over as of under 20 per cent. Upon this arbitrary basis—and because a subtraction of 20 per cent of the original capital in reckoning the remaining stockholders' equity provides a base that does not significantly distort the resulting earnings rate—the corporations having accumulated capital deficits of less than 20 per cent were retained in the sample, the amount of the deficit being subtracted from the total capital stock. All companies with deficits of 20 per cent or more were excluded from the sample.

The exclusion of such corporations is perhaps open to the objection that it puts aside certain enterprises that may merely for a time have lost money through the abandonment of processes or equipment that have not proved successful. Such corporations may, however, be engaged in activities of another sort which later prove to be profitable, and may therefore remain permanently in business.[19] In this and perhaps in other ways, our small corporations sample therefore excludes certain types of corporation that undoubtedly constitute a part of nearly every industry. But since the corporations with deficits constituted only about 6 per

[19] I am indebted to Professor Roy B. Kester of Columbia University for several suggestions in connection with the present discussion.

cent of the original number of companies analyzed in the preparation of the samples, and since only about half of this number was excluded, less than 3 per cent of the corporations have been put aside for this reason.

As remarked earlier, the same phenomenon presents itself with corporations that show net losses in each year as well as with those that show positive incomes. Our two other small manufacturing corporations samples, that for 'small corporations with incomes of over $2,000' and that for 'small corporations with negative net incomes', were treated similarly. Figures upon the prevalence of capital deficits for these two samples separately are not available; but for the two samples combined the frequency of such capital deficits is considerably higher than for the 'small corporations with net incomes of over $2,000' discussed above. The percentage of companies excluded as the result of capital deficits of over 20 per cent in each of the four years 1925–28 is as follows: 1925, 11.4; 1926, 14.1; 1927, 20.6; 1928, 7.4.

7. REGIONAL CLASSIFICATION DIFFICULTIES

The classification of corporations upon the basis of their geographical location as undertaken in Chapter 5 requires further comment here. As was pointed out in the discussion of that chapter, the only regional classification that it was possible to make consisted of the assignment of corporations to this or that geographical region upon the basis of the location of their head offices. This is far from perfect procedure in any case, and with some corporations may result in an altogether meaningless allocation of capital and income to any particular geographical region. To some extent, of course, refuge may be taken in the view that a partial offsetting occurs. Some New England companies, may, for example, own plants in Pennsylvania, while certain Pennsylvania companies may own plants located in New England. But while this may tend somewhat to balance the discrepancies in the amount of capital assigned to the several regions, there is no assurance that it effects any proper balance in earnings rates, and indeed to the extent that it takes place, really begs the question as to what the real differences in the earnings rates of different regions may be.

Less difficulty on this score is probably to be found in the Trading division where, except for chain stores, the several enterprises that may be owned by a given corporation are apt to be located either in the same state or at least within the same geographical region. But on the whole we should regard this classification by geographical regions as one of the least satisfactory in the entire volume; and any significance that the results may possess lies simply in the demarcation of corporations according to the locality of their 'organization headquarters', or, as Willard L. Thorp has expressed it, of their 'central office' managements [20]—not in differences of the regional profitableness of Manufacturing or Trading activities *per se*.[21]

[20] *The Integration of Industrial Operation* (Census Monograph III, 1924).
[21] Here the writer is unable to agree with Crum that the geographically ramified activities of individual enterprises probably do not distort significantly the use of corporation data classified by regions. To be sure, the data that Crum has thus employed (classified by the several states of the union) are broad data for the entire universe of corporations and not for samples of the sort we are using; and undoubtedly the difficulties encountered with data for the entire universe are less serious than for samples. Nevertheless the argument that discrepancies tend to offset one another seems to the writer not so well proved in this particular instance as in other instances of classification discussed by Crum in the illuminating chapter, Classification Difficulties, of the book to which we have referred previously.

Chapter 47

PROFITS AND THE REGULATION OF PRODUCTION

1. DIVERSITY AND UNIFORMITY

THE various statistical analyses of the preceding chapters have established certain facts which have a bearing upon economic theory and economic policy alike. To these broader implications of our data we have thus far paid but scant attention, preferring to let the several findings stand by themselves, quite apart from whatever economic and social conclusions might follow from them. But in this concluding chapter we may draw together the main threads that have been spun at rather full length throughout the preceding pages and see in what direction they seem to lead.

In this resumé, attention is first to be called to the striking corroboration that the investigation affords of the presence of uniformities amid the wide diversities of economic phenomena. This tendency has been remarked by other investigators, notably by Mills in his *The Behavior of Prices*. Our data clearly confirm the view that, while the variations in economic data are so great as to preclude the quasi-mechanical treatment or prediction of individual events, out of the observation of a sufficient number of diversities, definite and significant uniformities emerge. To the superficial observer, economic phenomena either entirely defy analysis: that is, seem to be characterized only by diversity; or else, present a specious uniformity: that is, when biased samples are viewed, fail to disclose the wide variations that exist. But neither of these simple conclusions is in most instances valid; certainly neither is in the present instance. The two significant facts remarked by Mills in his conclusion with respect to the system of prices stand out clearly with respect to the behavior of profit rates; on the one hand, the presence of the widest diversities; and, on the other hand, the prevalence of "just those uniformities for which the scientist searches in attempting to reduce masses of facts to understandable terms".

We need not here review our findings in formal summary;[1] one or two illustrations of the presence of diversity and uniformity alike in the realm of business profits will suffice. It will be recalled that during the ten years 1919–28, the average earnings rates upon investment of our 2,046 large manufacturing corporations series varied between 2.9 and 18.3 per cent; and that in all these years a wide diversity was present in the individual earnings rates of the 2,046 companies. Yet despite these broad diversities, in every one of these ten years at least 45 per cent of the corporations earned over 10 per cent. In each of the five years 1924–28, the median corporation earned either 12 or 13 per cent (in one year, 13.6 per cent). And for the same five-year period, the earnings rate of the corporation at the upper quartile was in every year 18, 20, or 22 per cent. Similarly, in all years some large corporations earned profits at low rates and some at high rates; and in all years the smaller enterprises show a similar diversity in earning capacity. Yet consistently, year after year, the larger enterprises *as a class* show lower earnings rates than the smaller ones as a class.

[1] A concise summary has appeared in Ch. 1, sec. 4.

In the parallel presence of uniformities and diversities such as these lie both our hope of understanding and our difficulties in controlling the economic system. To some of these difficulties we shall revert later in this chapter.

2. THE REWARD OF CAPITAL AND THE REGULATION OF PRODUCTION

It was indicated in Chapter 1 that from the point of view of economic principles, one of the most valuable contributions a comprehensive study of earnings and investment data could make to the understanding of profits is to determine whether 'in the long run' the rates of return upon capital approach an equality among different industries. Our findings (Ch. 3) are that whatever might happen under certain assumed conditions, actual profit rates in different industries manifest little tendency to become equal. There are, to be sure, uniformities in the distribution patterns from year to year (see the diagrams in Appendix D); but nothing like even a roughly uniform rate of return among different industries results over a period. How good are the data on which this very definite conclusion rests, and is the period considered a 'long run'?

As to the first question, the reader who has not read Chapters 43–46 must do so if he wishes to form a complete conclusion for himself. Most readers who have already done so will doubtless agree that our 2,046 large manufacturing corporations series is for the present purpose a rather representative sample of corporate activity. The fact that it is a sample of identical corporations gives it greater stability, that is, makes it less subject to erratic time fluctuations, than would otherwise be the case, and in some ways ought to aid rather than handicap an effort to disclose whatever 'tendency towards uniformity' exists in the actual world of business. The ten-year data of these 2,046 corporations (amounting in all to 20,460 'corporation-year cases'), it is to be remembered, were tabulated according to the Marshallian precept: "from the aggregate profits of the successful [must be subtracted] the aggregate losses of those who . . . . failed."[2] Marshall included producers who have "perhaps disappeared from the trade", that is, withdrawn from business entirely, and the data for these corporations in each industry we could not obtain. But the scale and character of industry have changed materially since Marshall wrote. Today few very large enterprises that fail to earn profits for several years really go out of business entirely; they merge, reorganize or continue an independent existence but alter the character of their production, that is, shift to new products and activities (Ch. 3). All losses incurred by any of our 2,046 going concerns—and in time of depression, the amount of such losses was substantial—were subtracted from the net gains of the companies earning profits, and the resulting net income figure was then related to the combined aggregate capital of the several corporations. When so treated, the earnings rates for the 73 manufacturing industries, as represented by our samples, show no equality whatever for the ten-year period as a whole.

As to the question, is a ten-year period long enough, something has already been said in Chapter 3. It may be pointed out that the period 1919–28 includes several cycles. But an even longer period is available in the data of our 71 manufacturing companies. These cover a thirteen-year stretch, 1919–31. This series, it will be recalled, is a tested set of data closely representative of the larger series during the first ten of these 13 years (Ch. 6). We are unable to

[2] *Principles of Economics,* 1st ed., p. 658.

divide it into minor industrial groups, but we may be certain that if it could be so divided the discrepancies between minor groups would be even more marked than those between major groups; for our experience with averages in general and profit rate figures in particular indicates that the more purely homogeneous each group of items becomes, the greater becomes the average deviation of the several sets of items from the mean or median value of all the items taken together.

And among major groups, this thirteen-year series evidences no uniformity of earnings rates. A thirteen-year period, however, affords much opportunity for the exhaustion and withdrawal of fixed capital,[3] and for the investment of new funds in this, that or the other direction. If it be contended that more than a ten- or thirteen-year period is essential for the tendency of profits towards an equality to work itself out in practice, then the 'long run' becomes, to say the least, a somewhat unrealistic concept as applied to the problems of modern industry. Economic theory is fast losing its character as a study of 'economic statics'; but it can scarcely afford to limit its consideration of 'dynamics' to phenomena that take place only over twenty-, thirty- or

[3] See, in this connection, the report on depreciation rates, *Depreciation Studies,* published by the Bureau of Internal Revenue (January 1931), in which normal depreciation rates on various types of new industrial equipment are shown to run in many instances as high as 10 per cent annually, thus providing for the replacement of the equipment in ten years' time. There are, of course, many variations from this figure, some types of equipment carrying rates of only 5.0, 6.6 or 8.0 per cent, others carrying rates of 12.5, 16.6 or even 33.3 per cent; but in most industries much machinery and equipment require replacement in ten years' time or less. Furthermore it may be noted that not all of the capital of the industries of our samples (either the larger ten-year series or the smaller 13-year one) was *new* in 1919; and that much of their capital, therefore, could have been withdrawn (i.e., not replaced as it wore out) in far less than ten years following 1919. Replacing many units of equipment, in other words, becomes (at the time of replacement) a variable, not a fixed, expense as of the year in which the replacement is contemplated.

fifty-year periods. This is not to say that it would not be desirable to have a twenty-year series of profit rates in different industries. But none seems necessary to justify our present conclusions, which, as we have remarked elsewhere, are in some respects the more firmly established just because they are for a more limited period.[4] The reader who seriously questions these general statements should, if he has not done so, read footnote 3 just preceding, and also examine the discussion in Chapter 3.

If we accept the conclusion that no equalization of profit rates between industries takes place, what does this then signify with respect to the functioning of the industrial system? Inevitably, it means that competition, as a regulator of the flow of productive resources, is a less efficient instrument than we have traditionally believed. It means that the mechanism of price and profit, which is supposed spontaneously and automatically to increase production here and decrease it there, works haltingly; that is, that long 'lags' and many 'maladjustments' occur. These lags and maladjustments are apparently present even in prosperous years. Then, however, they are not so remarked because they are less striking than in periods of severe depression.

Thus the goods which society wants, it gets, in normal years of prosperity, at least after a fashion; but competition between industries in no sense brings the rewards of the groups of producers who supply these different commodities to anything like a common level. These diverse earnings rates of different industries cannot be regarded as differentials due to the 'rent' of superior business abilities, or we should have to assume either that all the producers in some industries possessed greater managerial skill than all the producers in others; or, that the average degree of business

[4] *Cf.* Ch. 3 and 46, on the difficulties of classification that would attend the analysis and use of any such extended series.

ability is markedly greater in the industries of higher earnings rates. The first assumption we know to be unfounded because of diversities in the earning power of different enterprises, and the second assumption seems very unlikely.[5] Nor can the element of difference in either 'risks' or 'uncertainties' in various industries account for the persistent differentials in earnings rates; but this matter we have discussed sufficiently in Chapter 3.

3. FAILURE OF INVESTMENT TO FOLLOW MARKET DEMAND

Just as profit rates fail to approximate equality over periods of ten or thirteen years, so do they often fail to shut off the investment of new capital in fields already overcrowded. In more than one-sixth of the 73 manufacturing industries in which we analyzed the absolute course of sales, investment and income over the period 1922–28, it will be recalled, capital investment increased faster than did the volume of sales, in spite of the concurrent decline in profit rates in these industries.

[5] We need not here discuss the changed character and definition of the entrepreneur as a productive factor in modern large-scale industry; but it is clear that Francis A. Walker's concept of the rent of individual talents has slight applicability to the problem of the profit rates earned upon the present invested capital of industries that include such enterprises as the United States Steel Corporation or the General Electric Company, not to mention hosts of smaller but still almost entirely publicly-owned concerns. The common stockholders, numbering hundreds of thousands in some industries, supply the bulk of the capital used; and no question of direct personal talents exercised by 'owner-managers' enters, except where the *tantiéme* (or bonus system) for the payment of the *bulk* of an executive's remuneration is employed. In this country, even in the cases of General Motors and Bethlehem Steel, bonuses of this sort constitute but a very small fraction of corporate net income. To speak, on the other hand, of the mass of common stockholders as exercising 'managerial judgment' in 'delegating' the direction of their capitals to others is a mere sophism, or at best, a legal explanation of the corporate phenomenon. Whoever has disposed of a proxy, whether he has returned it to the corporation or thrown it in the wastebasket, is aware of the correctness of this statement.

Several explanations of this condition present themselves. First, undoubtedly the decline in the general rate of return was not known to the entrepreneurs in every industry where it was taking place. Second, in several industries even the lowered rates of profit prevailing at the end of the period were far above the cost of new capital, either in the sense of borrowed capital or of an imputed interest rate upon the capital reinvested out of earnings. Of course, these fields of investment still seemed not to be overcrowded according to current standards of profitableness.

Two observations on this situation, however, are to be made. That the rate of earnings *declined* in several industries in which the investment of capital took place too rapidly ('too rapidly' in that it greatly outran the growth of sales volume) indicates that some competitive mechanism did automatically function. That is to say, a certain amount of 'unconscious control', in F. M. Taylor's phrase, was exercised upon *profit rates*. This, however, by no means arrested the investment of new funds which, in many instances at least, were not at all needed in these industries. But neither the actual cost of new capital (both long-term and increased short-term borrowings) nor the imputed interest rate upon the funds 'ploughed back' into these industries, when deducted from the declining profit rates in question, *left as large a yield* upon the shareholders' equities in these several industries *as could have been received upon the reinvested funds had they been diverted to other industries in which the profit rates were either actually higher or increasing*. In this sense, it must be repeated, the flow of investment funds by no means followed the competitive channels indicated by economic speculations about what would happen if business men knew the conditions prevailing in every trade, if investment encountered no obstacles and if capital could be withdrawn readily from relatively unprofitable trades.

A third reason for the failure of these declining profit rates to check the flow of capital into the industries in question is found in the diversity of the earnings rates of individual enterprises. Even where some entrepreneurs do know that the trends of *general* sales and *general* profit rates are tapering off, or are actually declining, the willingness to make new commitments exists just because it is also well known that in any given industry individual fortunes vary widely. Any particular corporation may see that the sales curve is tapering off, yet, confident that *it* can not only maintain but actually increase its proportion of the total business done, it erects new plants or extends old ones. Thus what would be a desirable policy of expansion from the social point of view (assuming that no markedly improved or unique product that could not be manufactured by other producers results) is ignored; social and individual objectives here part company. Whether an expansion policy thus decided upon is desirable even from the individual point of view, of course, becomes clear only later. It may prove desirable or not; but because there is a possibility that it may, the uncertainty is chanced. The several sales and investment figures of the various industries presented in Chapter 7 and in the various chapters of Book II afford ample evidence of reckless policies of plant expansion on the part of many corporations in a number of industries.

To return to the relation between our findings and the traditional doctrine of the tendency of profits towards an equality: no doubt investors prefer a higher rate of return upon their capital to a lower rate, 'other things being equal'. In this very general sense there exists a 'tendency' towards an equalization of profit rates—not only among the different enterprises belonging to an industry but also among all the business enterprises in which investors might place their capital. But this 'tendency' cannot equalize profit rates in practice unless investors know what earnings their capital would realize in the near future if put into different enterprises. No economic theorist supposes that investors possess such knowledge in definite form. Hence no theorist supposes that profit rates are really equalized in fact. The serious matter is that no theorist can say how much or how little investors know about differences in profit rates. Hence no theorist knows how effective is the 'tendency' towards the equalization of these rates. On that important issue no one can say anything definite until he resorts to empirical investigation.[6] What the present study of American corpo-

[6] Note, for example, how cautiously John Stuart Mill states the 'tendency' in question: "On an average (whatever may be the occasional fluctuations) the various employments of capital are on such a footing as to hold out, not equal profits, but equal expectations of profit, to persons of average abilities and advantages." *Principles of Political Economy,* Book II, Ch. XV, p. 412 of Ashley's edition.

Needless to say, we can get no statistics of "expectations of profit". Nor can we segregate among investors "persons of average abilities and advantages". Presumably Mill's statements are valid under the conditions which he had in mind. But the fact remains that, under actual conditions, wide differences in the average rates of profits received by enterprises engaged in different branches of trade maintain themselves with little change for periods covering a decade or more.

The present findings do not conflict with those of Professor Horace Secrist's recent book, *The Triumph of Mediocrity in Business* (Ann Arbor, 1933). Using data for individual enterprises, Secrist arrays their profit rates on the basis of average size in initial periods of two or three years, follows the average rates for groups at given positions in his arrays through successively widening spans of years, compares these average ratios with those for the entire frequency distributions in successive periods, and finds (1) that the ratios which were initially low or high relatively to the mean tend to remain low or high relatively to the later means, but (2) that the ratios tend to diverge from the means by relatively smaller margins as longer and longer periods are brought under observation. Could the data underlying the present investigation be subjected to an elaborate analysis of Secrist's type, they might well show a tendency towards 'regression' in his sense. But that finding would not diminish the significance attaching to the demonstration offered above that the dispersion of the average profit rates in different industries maintains itself with slight change over periods

ration earnings data contributes is a series of measurements showing how wide and how enduring are the discrepancies among the profit rates actually realized over a decade or more by thousands of business enterprises engaged in a wide variety of money-making ventures. On the basis of this showing, the 'tendency' towards equalization of profit rates is not sufficiently strong to prevent differences exceeding 100 per cent between the *average* profit rates earned by considerable groups of corporations from appearing and maintaining themselves over a full decade.

4. 'BUSINESS PLANNING' AS A STATISTICAL PROBLEM[7]

What has been said concerning diversity and uniformity, together with what has been remarked concerning the fundamental weakness of competition as a regulator of production and productive capacity, indicates both the need for and the manifold difficulties of attempts deliberately to control the apportionment of capital and the rate of profit in competitive industry. *It cannot be too strongly emphasized that the problem of control is not one of 'industry' but of 'industries'.* Any agency that attempted to supplement the existing defective, lagging mechanism of unconscious competitive regulation with a completely conscious scheme of control would have to deal with at least one or two hundred separate industries. Our data for Manufacturing, Trade, Mining and Finance were divided into 106 fields;

as long as the available data cover. It is important practically and interesting theoretically to know that the profit rates both of fortunate and unfortunate enterprises drift towards mean rates in the long run rather than away from them. It is even more important practically and quite as interesting theoretically to know that despite this 'triumph of mediocrity in business', wide differences in actual profit rates remain substantially stable year after year.

[7] This section was written before the passage of the National Industrial Recovery Act in June 1933, but the writer sees no occasion to alter the text.

and the wide diversities between them were noted. Doubtless many of these 106 fields—for purposes of this kind—would need to be subdivided still further; and as before remarked, all of our analyses have indicated that after the subdivision of larger groups into smaller groups, the ranges of variation never diminish but always increase. Even assuming that adequate data were available in time to be of use during a cyclical upswing in general business, the problem of deciding in which industries the expansion was going too far, and what the repercussions of a damper applied to some industries would be on each of the various other industries involved, would be extraordinarily difficult.[8] Even in any *one* industry, the diversities of earning capacity, productive capacity and productive activities between different enterprises would present problems of accounting, cost accounting and production control of a varied and difficult character. Yet if competition alone does not regulate the economic machine as adequately even in normal years as we have been accustomed to believe—and it seems clear that it does not—then some attack upon these problems may be undertaken in the not distant future.

But one of the most important results of our findings is to suggest, let it be reiterated, that in any such attack no general average figures will suffice. The many diversities and uniformities alike must be marshalled and measured, both recognized as related and essential parts of any true industrial picture. If, for example, the comparative growths of sales and investment in *all* 73 manufacturing groups combined are examined, no appreciable discrepancy between

[8] This is not to say that no attempts at central planning or control should be made. The writer, in fact, has elsewhere urged that partial experiments in this direction be undertaken. The purpose here is not, however, to undertake any full discussion of business planning, but merely to indicate how complex is the situation that any comprehensive *national* efforts at such planning would have to face.

them appears. One might say that "supply of capital and demand for products over the period 1923–28 approximately kept pace"; or, that "no undue expansion of manufacturing facilities is discernible".[9] But entrepreneurs do not invest capital in manufacturing as a whole, nor are laborers employed by, or unemployed in, 'industry in general'. Business decisions are made, commitments are undertaken, poor adjustments occur between specific industrial groups, enterprises and commodities. General averages at best give only a notion of 'general drift', and the 'general drift' of all industries averaged together may in some respects be not the drift of the most important industries at all—important, that is, in their potential power to contribute to an upsetting of the economic equilibrium. Whether the question of industrial stabilization is approached from the point of view of the control of credit or of the allocation of physical production facilities, the need for more than merely average figures is exactly the same.[10]

[9] The increase in the 1928 figure for sales in our 2,046 large manufacturing corporations over the 1923 figure is 25.2 per cent, and that in investment is 25.9 per cent.

[10] Recent discussions of monetary and business cycle theory are beginning to stress this point of view. Cf. Hayek, who aptly remarks: "If monetary theory . . . still attempts to establish causal relations between aggregates or general averages, this means that monetary theory lags behind the development of economics in general . . . I would even go so far as to assert that, from the very nature of economic theory, averages can never form a link in its reasoning" (*Prices and Production*, pp. 4–5; London 1931). The latter statement may be too sweeping, but the first sentence is significant without question. Diversities of the sort that the present investigation has sought to measure, as well as of the kind that Hayek emphasizes, have been also stressed by Wesley C. Mitchell, in both the original edition of *Business Cycles* (1913) and in his later writings; likewise, F. W. Taussig, J. M. Clark, W. L. Crum and Horace Secrist, as well as other scholars, have called attention to the matter, while F. C. Mills, in his work on prices, has reviewed in that connection the entire question. The expression 'general drift' as applied to the utility of index numbers is employed by Taussig.

5. THE PUBLICITY OF CORPORATE ACCOUNTS

Whatever the prospects for an improved control of industrial activities, it is at least clear that a primary essential is currently available information about the sales, investments and earnings of our various industries. The business world does not have adequate information of this kind now. And unless the Government should annually assemble and release, either through the Department of Commerce or the Treasury, sets of data at least as elaborate as those on which the present investigation is based (preferably more so), or unless all businesses suddenly become willing periodically to divulge in detail the results of their operations, we shall not have any such information during the next cyclical upswing.

The person who has not worked in the field of corporate earnings does not realize the paucity of published financial data. In hardly an industry are complete data released upon production, earnings, investment and the like by more than a very few companies. Even some of the leading corporations do not publish sales figures. Relatively few give with frankness their annual charges to both depreciation and obsolescence accounts. And probably not more than a dozen have released regularly, since 1919, their figures upon *all* of the items just enumerated.[11] These statements, of course, have no reference to the railroad and public utility fields, in

[11] The writer, in a study carried out for him by Miss Lillian Epstein at the National Bureau of Economic Research, endeavored to check various results of his Government study by smaller samples of the same industrial groups taken from published corporation reports. Fifty leading companies, in various manufacturing and trading industries, were studied. For only 15 out of these 50 corporations could continuous series for sales and capitalization figures be had over the period 1919–28, while the number furnishing depreciation charges and related data together with sales figures was even smaller.

which state or Federal authority compels the full publicity of accounts.

Why such publicity should not be forthcoming it is difficult to see. It would cost the corporations nothing, nor would it injure them. The advent of the modern trade association has done much to free the business world from the fear that trade secrets will be obtained by competitors. Several trade associations now collect confidential data from their members. As to why this practice could not be extended, and the data made available not only to all members of the associations but to the members of all other industries and to the general public as well, it is again difficult to give any convincing answer. Our concept of what constitutes an industry 'affected with a public interest', is constantly widening, and it would surely be a small price for the competitive system of private unregulated enterprise to pay for the privilege of continuing its existence were the country to require of it a full publicity of industrial accounts, rendered either in semi-standardized manner or with such completeness of detail as to enable adjustments that would permit one set of data to be assembled or compared with others.

For it is to be noted, in conclusion, that a competitive system of corporate enterprise would not be so wasteful as is often assumed, were it possible to keep industry operating approximately at capacity. While the mortality in certain fields, notably retail trading, is high, the loss of social capital occasioned by business ineptitude is doubtless not nearly so great as the misleading statement that "half the corporations lose money" would imply. To begin with, a money loss to the individual business unit may not always mean an economic loss to society; but even assuming that it does, there is no reason to believe that a large fraction of corporate enterprises really earn either no profits or profits at such low rates that they can scarcely manage to get along. Many close corporations, as we have earlier indicated, are really partnerships in all but a legal sense; and their owners often earn good livings out of them and efficiently produce goods and services upon a small scale, even though they report no net income for income tax purposes.[12] The larger corporations, on the other hand, carry on the great bulk of their activities at a profit—in most years, 90 per cent or more of their invested capital earns a net income. To be sure, the receipt of a profit is not always synonymous with efficient production; but in the absence of purely predatory activities, it may be assumed that the ability to market goods without loss indicates that the producer is at least successfully satisfying the demand of some portion of the community.

In other words, the "great numbers of enterprises which are dragging along with a very low rate of return on their property", as Crum has put it,[13] by no means constitute the bulk of manufacturing or trading companies, especially if allowance is made for variation between the accounting practices of the close corporations and those not closely owned. It is only fair to note that Crum was thinking of averages derived from the total data published in the Treasury Department's volumes, *Statistics of Income,* which contain no frequency distributions of the earnings rates of individual corporations. And these averages, like so many others, prove to be misleading. Our distributions of individual earnings rates indicate that most fairly large corporations in both manufacture and trade, far from dragging along, in normal years earn over 10 per cent upon their

---

[12] See Ch. 1 and 43.
[13] *Op. cit.,* p. 193. *Cf.* the writer's earlier discussion of this point in the *Quarterly Journal of Economics,* February 1930, Statistical Light on Profits, pp. 330–3.

investments; and even in years of depression such as 1921, some 70 per cent of such companies earn the equivalent of an interest rate upon free capital. For the enterprises that succeed in remaining in business, Adam Smith's 'double interest' as a customary or satisfactory rate of profit is not at all exceptional. Concerning the earnings rates of the smaller and the 'close' corporations, we have, as has already been indicated, no good figures that are really comparable with those for the larger corporations; but it may perhaps be doubted if *most* of those *which remain in business* really earn less than normal interest upon their capital. It has never been supposed that all corporations *would* earn 'satisfactory' rates of return; for it is through their losses that inefficient enterprises are eliminated from a competitive economic system.

But even from the point of view of a competitive economy, losses of capital that are due mainly to inefficiency of management are one thing, and those caused by lack of correct information are another. Could current data concerning earnings rates, sales, investments and other operating results be made available to all entrepreneurs, whether in one industry or another, whether contemplating new ventures in different fields or the extension of already established ventures in old, many losses might be avoided. To be sure, such information would help only those not too blind to take heed or too confident of their own competitive survival. But fuller publicity of accounts would be a partial step towards better individual business planning at least; and it is one which could be taken by industry itself, were a sentiment for it sufficiently developed. Should the more difficult task of supplanting the competitive system with any type of centrally controlled economy ever be attempted— the many complexities which all such proposals involve, whether their sponsors are aware of them or not, have been indicated—complete statistical information of the kind mentioned, while not ensuring success, would be the first prerequisite.

GLOSSARY

THE principal technical terms employed in this volume are briefly defined below. The list is not complete, but will be helpful to readers who do not examine carefully the first few chapters of Books I, II and III. Ch. 1 and 47 employ several of the terms in their general economic and accounting senses; but the other chapters use them in their technical senses chiefly. For further definitions the reader is referred both to the several chapters of this volume and to pages 2–3 of the *Source-Book for the Study of Industrial Profits,* by R. C. Epstein in collaboration with F. M. Clark (Washington, Department of Commerce, 1932).

INCOME ACCOUNT ITEMS

Income, net income or total net income. The net earnings of a corporation after the payment of all business expenses and fixed charges including interest on funded debt, but unless otherwise specified, before the payment of Federal income taxes. If the amount of funded debt is small, as is the case with most of the corporations and industries treated, then *net income* is not very different from *profit* or *total profit* as defined immediately below.

Profit or *total profit. Net income* plus interest payments on funded debt, estimated as explained in Appendix A. In Chapter 1 *net income* and *profit* are used synonymously, since in all instances there the two figures virtually coincide.

Earnings. A general term used to signify either *net income* or *total profits,* when the two terms are practically the same in amount.

BALANCE SHEET ITEMS

Capitalization. The invested capital of a corporation as measured by the sum of its preferred stock, common stock, surplus and undivided profits. Special reserves are in most instances excluded. For qualifications as to the time of the year for which the figure is taken, and for other discussion, see Ch. 45 and 46.

Total capital. *Capitalization* plus *funded debt.*

Investment or *invested capital.* A general term used to signify either *total capital* or *capitalization* when the two terms are virtually the same in amount.

RATIOS

Earnings rate. The percentage of *net income* to *capitalization;* or, where the two ratios are not very different, either that percentage or the percentage of *total profit* to *total capital.* When a distinction between the two is necessary, the context makes clear which meaning is intended.

Earnings rate, or return, on sales. The percentage of *net income* for the year to the dollar volume of output or merchandise stock disposed of during the year. The figure for dollar volume of business is after sales returns and allowances, but before the deduction of cost of goods sold or of any other element of business expense.

Capital turnover. The item of *sales* divided by *total capital;* or, when *total capital* and *capitalization* are not very different in amount, by *capitalization.*

STATISTICAL EXPRESSIONS

Series. A succession of figures for the same item, relating to different years, corporations or industries; e.g., a set of *income* data for 71 manufacturing corporations for each of the thirteen years, 1919 through 1931.

Sample. A set of data representing some field, say, Food Products manufacture, but comprising only a *part* of the entire field; e.g., the income and capitalization data for 215 food manufacturing companies, which amount to only a part of the total income and capitalization of all food manufacturing enterprises in the United States.

Universe. The complete field which *sample* data only represent, i.e., in the illustration just given, the aggregate income and capitalization of *all* food manufacturing companies.

Array. A series of data arranged in order of magnitude; e.g., a list

GLOSSARY [597]

of 215 food companies ranked according to the size of their capitalizations, from the smallest to the largest.

Median. The central or middle figure of an array; e.g., in the illustration above, the 108th food company counting from either the top or bottom of the list.

Upper or lower quartile. The figure standing, not in the center or middle of an array, but exactly *one-fourth* of the distance from the top or the bottom.

APPENDICES

Appendix A

EXPLANATIONS OF METHODS USED IN PREPARING CERTAIN CHARTS AND TABLES

TABLES 1, 3, 5, 6, CHAPTER 2

Estimate of Long-Time Interest

INTEREST payments on long- and short-term debt are not segregated in the reports of the Bureau of Internal Revenue. In order to determine the rate of returns on total capital (capital stock equity plus funded debt) it was necessary to estimate the amount of interest paid on the funded debt. A rate of 5½ per cent was adopted as an average interest rate, and in each year interest, computed as 5½ per cent of the funded debt, was added to income to determine the profit earned on total capital. See note, *The Item of Interest on Funded Debt in the Several Samples.*

'Stepping Up' Investment Data, Tables 1, 3, 5, 6

Each year the number of corporations submitting income statements to the Bureau of Internal Revenue is somewhat larger than the number submitting balance sheets. To obtain a more accurate figure for the return on capital, both 'capitalization' and 'total capital' have been estimated for those corporations submitting only income statements and added to the investment amounts reported by the corporations submitting balance sheets. These estimated or 'stepped up' capital and capitalization figures have been computed as follows. In 1928, for example, 81,748 manufacturing corporations submitted balance sheets, showing a total capitalization of $38,537,804,973, while 86,803 (106.2 per cent of this number) submitted income statements. This involves the assumption that the average capitalization per company of the companies that filed balance sheets is no larger or smaller than of those that did not. We may *estimate* the capitalization of the 86,803 corporations to be $40,927,148,881 (106.2 per cent of $38,537,804,973). But since it is probably true that most of the 5,055 corporations that failed to file balance sheets are relatively small, the rate of return computed on the 'stepped up' capitalization figures to this extent understates the actual rate of return, just as that computed on the simple 'not stepped up' figures overstates the actual situation. For this reason, means between the ratios of income or profit to the 'stepped up' and 'not stepped up' capitalization or total capital figures are used as the most accurate available measurement of the aggregate return on capital for all corporations in the country, in the Manufacturing, Trading, Mining and Financial divisions.

TABLE 2, CHAPTER 2

The ten-year series of data for the 3,144 identical corporations were in their original form compiled by separate industrial divisions: i.e., Manufacturing, Trade, Finance, Mining. In obtaining composite figures comparable with the total amounts reported for all manufacturing, trade, finance and mining corporations in the United States, it is necessary that each of these four industrial groups be given the same relative importance in the sample of 3,144 corporations as in the actual data for the country as a whole, otherwise, the composite figures might be quite inaccurate because of the undue preponderance of one industrial division in the sample. For example, the Mining division shows a much lower mean return than the other divisions. It happens that Mining contains a tenth or less of the total capitalization of the four divisions (for all corporations in the country), but if the Mining division did constitute any very large proportion of the total capitalization of the sample, then the composite return for the sample could not well be compared, in its unweighted form, with the return for the United States as a whole. Upon theoretical grounds, weighting of the investment and income data is therefore indicated.

As a matter of technique, in making this adjustment—or in weighting the four divisions of our sample—it is more feasible to adjust the income figures than the investment data. (For purposes of further analysis and comparison it is desirable to keep the capitalization and total capital figures as actually reported for the 3,144 corporations.) To obtain the desired weighting in the final computed ratios through

APPENDICES   [603]

adjustment of the income data, the following procedure is employed. The total capital (or capitalization) for the 3,144 corporations in each year is redistributed among the four industrial groups in the same proportion in which the data for the country as a whole are distributed among such industrial groups in that year.[1] The ratio of the *actual* amount of capitalization reported by each division of the sample to the amount it would have had if the distribution of capital in the sample had been 'correct' is then determined; and this ratio is applied to the income as actually reported for each industrial division of the sample. Thus the ratio of the sum of the computed amounts of income to the actual total capitalization is accurately comparable with the rate of return computed for all corporations in the four industrial groups in the country as a whole. The following example will show more clearly the several steps involved in computing this ratio.

In 1928 the total capitalization for manufacturing, trade, finance and mining corporations of the country reported in *Statistics of Income* was distributed among the industrial groups as follows: manufacturing corporations, 49.3 per cent of the total; trade, 13.4 per cent; finance, 29.6 per cent; mining, 7.7 per cent. If the total capitalization for the 3,144 corporations of our sample ($32,031,200,000) had been distributed in those same proportions in that year, each industrial division in our sample would have reported the capitalization listed in column (b) below instead of the actual data for each division recorded in column (a).

	(a) Actual capitalization	(b) Computed capitalization	(c) Ratio of computed to actual capitalization
Manufacturing	$24,925,000,000	$15,791,381,600	0.63
Trade	2,502,500,000	4,292,180,800	1.72
Finance	2,931,700,000	9,481,235,200	3.23
Mining	1,672,000,000	2,466,402,400	1.48
Total	$32,031,200,000	$32,031,200,000	

[1] This is done in each of the years 1924–28. For the years 1919–23, however, data for the entire United States are not available. The relationships prevailing in 1926 are applied, in the manner set forth below, to the capitalization data of the sample in each of these years. The year 1926 is chosen because the data in *Statistics of Income* are probably somewhat more suited to the purpose at hand than those of 1924, as in 1924 the capital stock tax returns, instead of income tax returns, were utilized as the basis for the published balance sheet figures.

The ratio of the computed to the actual capitalization is given in column (c). Thus, if the total capitalization reported for the 3,144 corporations were distributed among the four industrial groups in the same proportion as the total capitalization for these same groups in the country as a whole is distributed in that year, the Manufacturing corporations of the sample would have reported only 63 per cent of their actual capitalization figure. Similarly, (assuming such a smaller sample to have been as representative as the larger one) they would have reported 63 per cent of the actual income amount. Applying this ratio of computed to actual capitalization to the actual income as given in column (d) below, the computed income figure listed in column (e) is obtained:

	(d) Actual income	(e) Computed income
Manufacture	$2,736,450,000	$1,723,963,500
Trade	306,900,000	527,868,000
Finance	303,600,000	980,628,000
Mining	132,400,000	195,952,000
Total	$3,479,350,000	$3,428,411,500

The properly weighted rate of return on the capitalization of the 3,144 corporations, which gives to each industrial group the same relative importance that it has in the data for the entire United States, is, then, the ratio between the total computed income ($3,428,-411,500) and the actual total capitalization ($32,031,200,000), or 10.7 per cent. There are shorter methods of obtaining the same result, but the redistribution of the absolute figures effected above seems most clearly to illustrate the logic of the weighting process.

TABLE 7, CHAPTER 2

Data are not available in the annual reports of the Bureau of Internal Revenue for the computation of the rate of return on the capitalization of all manufacturing corporations with net incomes of over $2,000 for the entire ten-year period 1919–28. Assuming, however, that our sample of 'small corporations' with incomes of $2,000 to $50,000, and our sample of 'large corporations' with incomes of $50,000 or more are fairly representative, we may, by proper weighting, expand these data so as to give a picture of the entire universe.[2]

[2] For comment upon the character of these two samples, see Ch. 43.

APPENDICES [605]

In this process of weighting, three steps are involved. The first is to determine the ratio between the size of each of the samples and the number of corporations with the same sizes of net income [3] for the country as a whole. The second, to determine from this ratio the appropriate weighting. The third, to weight the actual data and combine them.

For example, in 1928 the Bureau of Internal Revenue reported 29,555 manufacturing corporations in the entire country with net incomes of $2,000 to $50,000, and 8,207 with net incomes of $50,000 or more. In the same year in our small corporations sample there were 1,421 corporations, or 4.8 per cent of the total number in the country with net incomes of $2,000–$50,000; and in our large corporations sample there were 1,970 corporations, or 24.0 per cent of the total number in the country with net incomes of $50,000 or over. Thus, in that year, there were actually in the United States, with incomes of $2,000 to $50,000, just about 20 times the number of corporations in the one sample and just about 4 times the number with incomes of $50,000 or more as in the other sample. Applying these weights of 20 and 4 respectively to the data of the two samples and combining them, we obtain a total net income for manufacturing corporations with incomes of over $2,000 in 1928 amounting to $11,973,800,000 and a total capitalization of $98,448,000,000. These estimates possess no validity as absolute figures; because the average size of the corporations in our large corporations sample is greater than that of most typical corporations with incomes in the 'over $50,000' grouping, these weighted absolute figures are far larger than those which actually prevail. But although they are even absolutely higher than the actual data obtained from *Statistics of Income* for that year and presented in Table 6 (for all manufacturing corporations in the country with net incomes, including those under $2,000), the rate of return computed for the estimated data of Table 7 is only slightly different from that for the actual data of Table 6: 12.2 per cent as against 12.0 per cent.

As in the case of Table 2, a shorter method to attain the same results could be employed by directly adjusting the ratios themselves and in this instance avoiding the use of the 'fictitious' absolute figures; but the logic of the adjustment is perhaps seen better by weighting the absolute data.

[3] For qualifications concerning definition, again see Ch. 43.

ESTIMATED EARNINGS RATES FOR ALL MANUFACTURING IN THE COUNTRY, 1921 AND 1931, GIVEN IN CHAPTER 1

The earnings rates for the 71 companies series described in Ch. 6 were compared with the figures for all manufacturing corporations in the country, for the five years 1924-28. It was found that the latter rates averaged 63.0 per cent of the former. This ratio was then applied to the earnings figures of the 71 companies for 1921 and 1931, and the resulting figures, 2.4 and 2.3 per cent respectively were called rough estimates for all manufacturing corporations in the country in those years. No decimal points are made use of in the text, as the margin of possible error is very large. The figures should be regarded as the broadest of estimates, since the assumption that underlies them is, of course, that the earnings rates of these 71 companies bore the same relation to those for all manufacturing corporations in the country in 1921 and 1931 as they did on an average in the years 1924-28.

The five annual ratios in 1924-28, for which the mean ratio is 63.0 per cent, are as follows: 62.6; 58.5; 56.4; 64.6; 73.1.

71 COMPANIES SERIES DATA FOR 1931, GIVEN IN CHAPTER 6

The Lumber figure for 1931 is preliminary, the earnings rate of one corporation in the group being estimated; but the possible error involved is very slight. Upon the total figures for all groups the trifling amount of possible error in the data for this company, which is a relatively small concern, can have no effect whatever. The total estimated capitalization of the Stone and Lumber groups (the two are combined, as explained earlier) in 1931 is 233 million dollars, while that for all 71 companies is just over six billion. The capitalization of the one corporation in question in 1930 was less than 20 million; so that even if an error of as much as 50 per cent were involved in estimating its 1931 figure, the difference in the 233 million figure could not be over 5 per cent either way, and in the 6 billion figure would be only one-third of 1 per cent.

APPENDICES [607]

THE ITEM OF INTEREST ON FUNDED DEBT IN THE SEVERAL SAMPLES

The distinction between *net income* and *total profit* as drawn throughout this volume lies in the inclusion of interest charges upon funded debt in the latter. As elsewhere remarked, however, these interest amounts are estimated. The statement of the *Source-Book* (p. 3) is as follows: "*Estimated interest upon bonded debt* is, in the case of the corporations for which data are presented in Parts I and VI, the equivalent of five per centum of the amount of all funded or long-time obligations, while for the corporations in other parts of the book it is the equivalent of six per centum of such funded obligations." By the corporations in Parts 1 and VI are meant the several large identical corporations series discussed in the present volume. Upon the funded debts of the corporations of all other samples discussed in the present volume the rate of 6 per cent has been applied.

The basis on which 5 and 6 per cent were selected as the respective interest rates for 'large' and 'small' corporations in the original calculations of the data published in the *Source-Book* may be stated briefly. For large corporations there seemed to be little question that 5 per cent represented a very close approximation: the Standard Statistics Company's index of the average yield of fifteen high-grade industrial bonds between 1922 and 1928 (annual averages of monthly figures) ranged only between 4.8 and 5.3 per cent. (In 1920 and 1921 the figure was 6.0 per cent.)

For small corporations no general indexes are published by the Standard Statistics Company or other agencies for the period in question. The writer, however, investigated conditions in four banking centers: New York City, Buffalo, Cleveland and San Francisco. In New York City the consensus among the persons interviewed seemed to be that while the rate of interest paid by small industrials (corporations too small for public financing) varied greatly, it ran higher in most instances than for the larger companies; and 7 or 8 per cent was thought to be a more usual figure. In Buffalo, of ten small industrial enterprises with bond issues, nine paid 6 per cent and one paid 5.5 per cent. In Cleveland it was stated by a banker that "such financing . . . has been carried on . . . during the past ten years at rates that were almost never below six per cent, and which in almost every case carried in addition a bank charge that would amount roughly to an additional one-half per cent. In other words this kind of financing has cost the smaller companies about 6½ per cent per year as a minimum, and more frequently 7 per cent or 7½ per cent. Nevertheless, while these are the general facts, it is also true that each business of financing has been an individual deal, both in our institution and in other banks, with various collateral considerations involved . . . [and] . . . the banks do not compile massed records or make index numbers of such transactions." In San Francisco no adequate information on which to generalize was obtained except for the savings bank rate applied to real estate mortgages which a banker there states "has been, during the period 1919–1928, uniformly 6 per cent. However, in the case of small industrials . . . in need of working capital . . . [where] the value of their property did not justify a savings bank loan at the above-mentioned rate and other assets had to be pledged to enable brokers to float a small bond issue, the rate would, of course, have been much higher because of the heavy costs that such bond issue would have inevitably to undergo."

There is not space here to discuss the sale of bonds at a discount and the collateral considerations affecting the real cost of financing these small industrials through long-term borrowed capital. But disregarding the undoubtedly great variations in individual instances, it is probably fair to conclude that most of these small companies *pay out* 6 per cent or more annually as interest upon their funded debt, and that this rate represents a sufficiently satisfactory figure for our purposes, namely, to ascertain the rate of net return upon total capital before the payment of fixed charges, as well as that upon capitalization after their deduction.

EARNINGS RATES BEFORE AND AFTER TAXES

It was pointed out in Chapter 1 that for all years after 1921 the difference between earnings rates before and after payment of Federal income taxes is only slight. The statement related to arithmetic mean averages, but is also true of the frequency distributions for the earnings rates of individual corporations, as shown by experiments conducted for two industrial groups, Bakery Products and Radios and Parts. The individual corporations in each group were arrayed according to their rates of earnings before and after taxes, and the correlation is either perfect or almost perfect. Data from p. 201 of

APPENDICES [609]

the *Source-Book* are as follows. (Four cases are presented, large corporations and small corporations being treated separately in both groups.)

Subgroup	No. of corps.	Description of sample: corporations with total net incomes which, before taxes, range approximately from:	Coefficients of rank correlation (all positive)	Arithmetic mean	Median	Upper quartile	Lower quartile
Bakery Products	32	$2,000–$100,000	.9989	12.2	14.0	30.0	6.7
" "	18	All over $100,000	1.0000	16.6	15.0	22.5	9.2
Radios and Parts	35	$2,000–$100,000	.9969	14.4	12.3	23.7	6.5
" " "	62	All over $100,000	.9997	12.2	15.0	24.7	8.0

(Data for percentage of net income to capitalization, before taxes)

Appendix B.

Absolute Data Underlying Certain Charts and Tables

Appendix Table 1
ABSOLUTE DATA UNDERLYING TEXT TABLE 1[1]

	1924	1925	1926	1927	1928
Net income					
before tax	$5,082,498,150	$7,265,056,676	$7,108,391,872	$6,383,238,998	$8,168,188,016
after tax	4,394,363,215	6,337,968,093	6,165,838,961	5,520,872,122	7,246,929,777
Capitalization[2]					
not stepped up	80,899,555,431	89,207,935,711	87,853,383,955	93,962,040,536	101,476,040,078
stepped up	91,096,068,588	98,758,296,316	106,629,953,741	103,115,303,552	114,610,810,975
Total profit					
before tax					
not stepped up	5,679,677,273	7,889,556,411	7,695,321,957	7,076,795,179	9,024,475,226
stepped up	5,766,909,170	7,968,172,064	7,845,796,552	7,156,544,369	9,153,806,934
after tax					
not stepped up	4,991,542,338	6,962,467,828	6,752,769,046	6,214,428,303	8,103,216,987
stepped up	5,078,774,235	7,041,083,481	6,903,243,641	6,294,177,493	8,232,548,695
Total capital[2]					
not stepped up	91,757,357,665	100,562,476,342	98,524,840,054	106,572,152,910	117,044,898,444
stepped up	103,539,905,320	111,542,212,473	120,037,311,558	117,175,401,214	132,531,154,932

[1] Compiled from *Statistics of Income*.
[2] In all text discussions involving the capitalization, total capital, or profit figures of this table, the means between the 'not stepped up' and the 'stepped up' figures are used. See Appendix A for an explanation of the method of 'stepping up'. The 'stepped up' capitalization and 'stepped up' total capital figures in this table were obtained by the addition of the corresponding items for each of the four industrial divisions shown in Table 3. The results obtained by this addition are slightly different from those which would be obtained by applying the stepping up process to the capitalization or total capital shown above. This difference (ranging from about 200 million to about one and one-half billion, on capitalization amounts of 100 billion) is due to the fact that the four industrial divisions, which have, of

APPENDICES [613]

APPENDIX TABLE 2
ABSOLUTE DATA UNDERLYING TEXT TABLE 2 [1]

	1919	1920	1921	1922	1923
Net income					
[2] before tax	$2,907,255,700	$2,415,264,800	$973,331,700	$2,358,788,300	$2,724,273,800
[2] after tax	2,186,662,400	1,935,849,700	752,597,100	2,129,658,000	2,451,657,800
Capitalization	17,030,700,000	20,793,100,000	22,161,800,000	22,186,000,000	25,012,300,000
	1924	1925	1926	1927	1928
Net income					
[2] before tax	2,450,994,000	3,027,897,400	3,252,057,700	2,954,223,000	3,428,411,500
[2] after tax	2,193,499,300	2,691,838,000	2,884,804,500	2,616,828,200	3,085,838,800
Capitalization	25,584,800,000	26,830,600,000	28,227,200,000	30,155,800,000	32,031,200,000
	1924	1925	1926	1927	1928
Total profit					
[2] before tax	2,602,430,575	3,182,169,585	3,406,583,425	3,155,973,230	3,613,090,970
[2] after tax	2,349,365,805	2,847,392,685	3,040,203,525	2,815,511,030	3,271,696,470
Total Capital	28,290,910,000	29,784,240,000	31,190,450,000	33,440,020,000	35,495,780,000

course, different capitalization amounts, do not have the same proportionate numbers of incomplete items, i.e., numbers of corporations not reporting balance sheets. It is also to be noted that all balance sheet data for 1924 and 1925 rest upon capital stock tax returns and not income tax returns.

[1] Compiled from *Source-Book* figures.
[2] Income and profit figures weighted as explained in Appendix A.

Appendix Table 3
ABSOLUTE DATA UNDERLYING TEXT TABLE 5 [1]

	1926	1927	1928
Net income			
before tax	$8,623,311,960	$8,065,343,000	$9,801,827,651
after tax	7,680,759,049	7,203,652,492	8,880,569,412
[2] Capitalization			
not stepped up	69,535,775,729	72,066,881,010	82,077,763,229
stepped up	77,469,634,805	78,863,460,747	90,720,375,480
[2] Profit			
before tax			
not stepped up	9,033,643,685	8,491,148,440	10,354,999,658
stepped up	9,090,382,882	8,539,663,595	10,421,994,787
after tax			
not stepped up	8,091,090,774	7,629,457,932	9,433,741,419
stepped up	8,147,829,971	7,677,973,087	9,500,736,548
[2] Total capital			
not stepped up	76,996,352,542	79,808,798,100	92,135,436,089
stepped up	85,961,833,393	87,487,471,547	101,996,141,514

[1] Compiled from *Statistics of Income*.

[2] In all text discussions involving the capitalization, total capital or profit figures of this table, the means between the 'not stepped up' and the 'stepped up' figures are used. See Appendix A for an explanation of the method of 'stepping up'. The 'stepped up' capitalization and 'stepped up' total capital figures were obtained by the addition of the corresponding items for each of the four industrial divisions shown in Table 6. See Appendix Table 1, note 2 for an explanation of the slight differences between these totals and the results obtained by applying the 'stepping up' method to the capitalization or total capital shown above.

APPENDICES [615]

APPENDIX TABLE 4
ABSOLUTE DATA UNDERLYING TEXT TABLE 7[1]

	1919	1920	1921	1922	1923
Net income[2]	$10,640,440,000	$8,851,960,000	$3,069,630,000	$7,921,760,000	$9,571,760,000
Capitalization[2]	55,820,000,000	64,081,000,000	39,315,000,000	69,413,000,000	78,701,000,000

	1924	1925	1926	1927	1928
Net income[2]	8,826,360,000	10,860,560,000	11,652,040,000	9,779,680,000	11,973,800,000
Capitalization[2]	82,324,000,000	86,947,000,000	90,518,000,000	89,796,000,000	98,448,000,000

[1] Compiled from *Source-Book*.
[2] Income and capitalization figures weighted as explained in Appendix A.

APPENDIX TABLE 5
DATA FOR CHARTS 35 TO 38[1]

(A) PERCENTAGE TOTAL NET INCOME AFTER TAX TO CAPITALIZATION

Group	1919	1920	1921	1922	1923	1924	1925	1926	1927	1928	1929	1930	1931
1 Foods	-.2	4.5	4.9	8.3	8.3	7.9	8.3	9.8	8.4	9.2	10.5	11.6	9.5
2 Textiles	18.0	5.0	7.4	11.7	12.2	5.7	7.4	7.0	7.6	5.7	7.2	-.7	-2.3
3 Chemicals	14.0	8.3	2.4	9.3	5.4	8.5	11.7	12.2	7.5	12.2	11.6	7.5	3.1
4 Metals	22.3	12.3	7.0	18.4	14.4	13.7	16.2	16.2	11.2	11.1	16.8	10.4	3.2
5 Paper and printing	10.5	14.7	6.4	17.0	15.4	19.9	20.9	21.0	23.6	29.0	26.7	22.3	13.7
6 Stone and lumber	12.7	14.3	6.7	12.5	17.3	12.4	11.3	10.9	8.4	9.1	11.5	3.7	-.5
7 Leather and rubber	13.4	2.7	-7.4	5.7	4.6	6.7	12.2	10.2	6.1	2.3	4.5	-3.7	-3.4
8 Special manufacturing industries	17.2	9.2	5.3	18.4	19.3	17.0	16.4	17.8	18.5	16.5	11.9	8.2	4.3
All manufacturing	13.4	8.4	3.8	12.1	10.3	10.7	13.0	13.3	9.6	10.4	13.2	8.3	3.6

[1] Data for 1919–28 rest on Tables 49 and 51 of the *Source-Book*; for 1929–30, on Tables 50 and 52 of the *Source-Book*; for 1931, on Errata and Addenda Sheet to *Source-Book*. See Ch. 6 of present volume for explanation.

(B) ABSOLUTE NET INCOME AND CAPITALIZATION

APPENDIX TABLE 5 (continued)

(in millions of dollars)

Group	1919 Total net income after tax	1919 Capitalization	1920 Total net income after tax	1920 Capitalization	1921 Total net income after tax	1921 Capitalization	1922 Total net income after tax	1922 Capitalization
1 Foods	-1.16	611.75	30.42	673.15	34.42	703.11	55.62	670.02
2 Textiles	25.03	138.99	9.32	187.91	12.64	169.85	21.78	185.69
3 Chemicals	90.88	649.06	65.31	788.42	25.89	1,069.99	89.48	965.04
4 Metals	189.61	850.76	134.06	1,086.19	77.87	1,110.44	216.43	1,173.28
5 Paper and printing	8.41	80.11	12.74	86.41	6.08	94.95	15.41	90.71
6 Stone and lumber	15.75	124.34	19.85	139.25	10.47	155.93	19.41	155.25
7 Leather and rubber	46.33	345.43	11.06	411.14	-28.82	388.62	20.59	361.13
8 Special manufacturing industries	8.29	48.19	5.84	63.24	3.79	71.95	13.23	71.95
All manufacturing	383.14	2,848.63	288.60	3,435.71	142.34	3,764.84	451.95	3,673.07

Group	1923 Total net income after tax	1923 Capitalization	1924 Total net income after tax	1924 Capitalization	1925 Total net income after tax	1925 Capitalization	1926 Total net income after tax	1926 Capitalization
1 Foods	63.00	757.61	58.60	738.15	62.15	748.54	79.40	812.80
2 Textiles	26.50	216.58	12.51	220.54	15.86	213.87	14.07	200.66
3 Chemicals	56.18	1,059.05	90.71	1,063.92	126.47	1,082.13	143.78	1,179.39
4 Metals	239.39	1,666.25	229.19	1,672.46	291.76	1,797.53	340.52	2,096.03
5 Paper and printing	14.23	92.31	18.35	92.06	19.46	93.33	20.11	95.59
6 Stone and lumber	32.84	189.72	24.15	194.49	24.59	217.96	24.41	223.31
7 Leather and rubber	17.52	379.14	25.59	384.02	48.13	395.85	40.79	400.03
8 Special manufacturing industries	16.11	83.60	16.21	95.44	15.07	91.63	18.03	101.32
All manufacturing	465.77	4,444.26	475.31	4,461.08	603.49	4,640.84	681.11	5,109.13

APPENDICES

Group	1927 Total net income after tax	1927 Capitalization	1928 Total net income after tax	1928 Capitalization	1929 Total net income after tax	1929 Capitalization	1930 Total net income after tax	1930 Capitalization	1931 Total net income after tax	1931 Capitalization
1 Foods	65.11	778.67	73.58	802.85	84.69	807.26	97.84	840.89	81.30	855.65
2 Textiles	16.83	221.22	12.13	214.36	18.37	256.38	−1.64	238.69	−5.00	217.72
3 Chemicals	96.30	1,291.50	179.14	1,469.05	201.29	1,736.16	135.66	1,800.52	52.24	1,691.93
4 Metals	243.88	2,182.47	246.28	2,215.47	444.16	2,649.57	281.42	2,718.64	81.95	2,577.67
5 Paper and printing	23.97	101.38	26.39	90.89	30.63	114.61	25.73	115.61	15.21	111.37
6 Stone and lumber	18.73	223.12	20.91	229.46	29.04	253.36	9.25	248.51	−1.20	233.34
7 Leather and rubber	25.33	415.76	9.13	404.29	20.55	452.49	−15.52	420.13	−10.91	324.70
8 Special manufacturing industries	21.75	101.80	20.18	122.42	15.83	133.06	9.17	111.35	3.40	79.46
All manufacturing	511.90	5,315.92	587.74	5,648.79	844.56	6,402.89	541.91	6,494.34	216.99	6,091.84

APPENDIX TABLE 6

ABSOLUTE DATA UNDERLYING TABLES IN BOOK II[1]

(Key to group numbers shown in Text Table 12)

(A) SALES, 1919–28, 2,046 MANUFACTURING CORPORATIONS   *(in millions of dollars)*

Minor group	Number of corporations	1919	1920	1921	1922	1923	1924	1925	1926	1927	1928
1	17	233	304	236	228	260	271	284	315	323	320
2	32	256	292	200	181	185	208	231	228	235	228
3	21	150	144	98	98	116	118	123	127	115	114
4	19	229	204	129	136	159	182	200	201	201	212
5	26	330	345	293	282	329	339	368	382	403	435

APPENDIX TABLE 6 (continued)

Minor group	Number of corporations	1919	1920	1921	1922	1923	1924	1925	1926	1927	1928
6	16	151	125	105	124	121	131	139	148	147	169
7	23	3302	3170	2097	2014	2210	3349	3860	3550	3802	3991
8											
9	11	19	22	23	15	18	19	23	24	24	25
10	23	637	824	792	758	799	840	878	922	972	979
11–8	27	707	819	407	451	512	500	498	503	553	553
12	12	13	17	7	11	14	13	16	14	13	15
13	18	66	81	54	62	76	61	64	62	63	62
14	49	319	358	220	248	289	267	303	278	284	271
15	31	226	211	184	209	237	204	212	204	187	168
16	17	130	113	98	103	123	114	138	136	129	128
17	18	62	81	61	88	99	85	93	90	87	76
18	25	178	225	165	162	190	174	176	180	183	184
19	42	108	140	103	130	146	137	148	163	165	159
20	23	69	91	64	68	80	75	83	89	89	92
21	54	212	249	158	196	239	225	253	241	235	234
22	25	199	213	182	206	227	217	248	231	243	236
23	29	237	182	107	128	138	130	136	138	149	144
24	26	770	1079	580	678	763	727	1030	1035	948	935
25	64	137	158	93	128	159	144	148	154	131	152
26	26	122	34	22	30	37	34	37	34	32	31
27	17	31	42	25	34	41	37	36	34	32	34
28	55	67	81	60	72	84	84	92	95	93	91
29	28	99	126	86	126	185	193	218	220	180	233
30	35	159	251	153	161	187	180	210	204	227	276
31	33	50	81	37	46	60	58	64	65	63	65
32	20	62	100	53	60	66	64	65	68	68	67
33	23	87	120	76	89	106	106	100	96	89	93

[618] INDUSTRIAL PROFITS

APPENDICES [619]

34	20	105	144	134	147	179	198	222	275	302	436
35	17	32	38	36	38	42	45	46	45	47	47
36	46	81	118	91	90	98	103	108	115	118	182
37	17	11	18	13	14	14	15	16	17	18	18
38	9	82	101	58	75	85	79	87	95	91	100
39	42	133	152	103	125	139	138	154	157	151	152
40	52	2041	2895	2150	2154	2244	2383	2752	3201	3608	3197
41	56	160	176	140	156	177	186	201	212	216	214
42	9	9	13	14	14	16	16	17	18	19	20
43	16	233	181	180	189	202	234	261	271	288	272
44	26	474	460	299	344	413	436	480	524	512	514
45	48	61	90	63	81	103	99	108	113	105	103
46	18	119	176	113	134	175	157	170	166	149	153
47	21	55	80	72	87	111	115	125	123	122	119
48	27	109	144	82	106	136	136	157	168	167	175
49	99	2683	3405	1681	1997	3278	2801	3087	3472	2881	3044
50	20	51	61	27	42	60	58	64	65	63	66
51	20	94	117	55	72	98	83	87	91	78	83
52	42	125	161	103	125	167	165	165	181	176	187
53	54	632	789	592	552	726	787	799	916	860	899
54	18	52	71	61	50	54	44	51	49	52	49
55	12	23	28	21	24	29	29	33	33	31	31
56	22	90	103	81	75	104	109	122	139	139	147
57	11	16	18	12	12	18	20	20	26	28	34
58	12	137	153	92	121	142	112	127	160	135	141
59	23	107	121	84	72	87	76	89	95	91	101
60	13	73	90	69	75	91	92	104	106	110	126
61	25	507	486	283	316	609	397	333	385	323	251
62	32	1477	1864	1178	1612	2343	2143	2631	3145	3058	3639
63	11	34	49	29	36	43	45	46	47	46	51
64	40	243	316	192	254	333	326	355	374	344	347

Appendix Table 6 (continued)

Minor group	Number of corporations	1919	1920	1921	1922	1923	1924	1925	1926	1927	1928
65	30	99	105	39	58	76	69	78	85	78	90
66	15	24	30	11	20	27	23	28	28	27	32
67	32	112	125	75	82	105	102	121	132	130	138
68	48	780	911	495	658	824	830	1001	940	908	1066
69	24	50	51	31	36	41	38	40	42	43	45
70	45	541	634	280	328	413	407	507	554	557	699
71	23	134	136	107	122	144	146	153	161	164	172
72	12	16	21	15	18	23	25	27	28	28	31
73	11	38	48	35	42	51	48	53	54	47	43
74	43	206	264	214	228	263	249	237	270	282	293

Major group	Number of corporations	1919	1920	1921	1922	1923	1924	1925	1926	1927	1928
1 Foods	215	6014	6249	4380	4287	4709	5957	6604	6400	6775	7026
2 Textiles	289	1383	1566	1114	1277	1493	1355	1486	1457	1435	1389
3 Leather	54	436	395	289	334	365	347	384	369	392	380
4 Rubber	26	770	1079	580	678	763	727	1030	1035	948	935
5 Lumber	190	456	441	286	390	506	492	531	537	468	541
6 Paper	111	358	5552	319	356	419	408	439	433	447	501
7 Printing and publishing	100	229	318	274	289	333	361	392	452	485	623
8 Chemicals	210	3132	3978	2944	3057	3276	3472	3952	4478	4885	4469
9 Stone, clay and glass	114	344	490	330	408	525	507	560	570	543	550
10 Metals	648	7950	9688	5491	6617	9668	8756	9888	11065	10158	11266
11 Special manufacturing industries	89	394	469	371	410	481	468	470	513	521	539
All manufacturing	2046	21466	25225	16378	18103	22538	22850	25736	27309	27057	28219

APPENDICES [621]

(B) TOTAL NET INCOME, 1919–28, 2,046 MANUFACTURING CORPORATIONS.

(in millions of dollars)

Minor group	Number of corporations	1919	1920	1921	1922	1923	1924	1925	1926	1927	1928
1	17	19.78	18.45	24.17	27.92	29.22	33.75	33.67	40.58	43.54	41.22
2	32	12.41	1.98	5.15	4.58	6.03	10.68	6.41	6.62	7.94	7.78
3	21	28.06	11.45	5.60	13.47	15.90	18.62	18.58	18.81	17.66	16.51
4	19	10.90	2.42[2]	9.66	13.86	11.89	15.33	12.48	17.40	16.14	15.85
5	26	13.63	5.22	7.28	14.03	15.64	12.71	17.38	18.41	18.72	19.46
6	16	18.99	7.05	7.04	15.79	12.67	15.17	12.80	12.53	11.36	14.51
7	23	17.98[2]	1.64	40.65[2]	10.23	25.11	30.23	21.87	44.00	15.37	31.81
8											
9	11	.88[2]	.05	.44	1.45	2.62	1.29	3.00	3.14	2.31	3.95
10	23	63.89	64.88	77.08	83.31	87.13	84.27	95.42	102.92	109.60	109.52
11–8	27	72.65	33.49	21.96[2]	33.39	43.32	42.01	30.02	40.82	33.47	46.64
12	12	2.35	2.62	.83	1.12	1.24	.61	1.23	1.01	1.04	.95
13	18	9.15	1.40	4.42	7.24	7.54	3.09	4.72	2.81	5.14	4.29
14	49	62.03	27.23	20.64	26.98	30.25	3.38	11.42	8.31	28.22	12.46
15	31	36.07	.67	21.65	30.25	24.88	4.30	8.64	2.83	7.90	2.95
16	17	24.55	1.15	6.81	10.98	11.74	6.37	13.45	7.85	4.65	4.90
17	18	12.97	7.43	10.64	22.86	20.87	10.02	9.50	7.28	8.41	5.54
18	25	23.23	11.93	7.96	13.12	17.71	11.25	14.62	14.03	16.45	14.40
19	42	17.13	7.32	9.59	16.47	12.07	9.13	15.62	16.08	12.73	12.78
20	23	8.67	2.60	1.51	6.08	6.77	4.46	6.33	7.25	7.45	6.55
21	54	37.05	15.05	15.95	26.41	30.52	20.58	21.37	12.55	18.28	15.42
22	25	23.53	16.38	11.03	21.84	20.70	22.51	21.69	21.18	26.90	24.42
23	29	29.01	7.70[2]	6.44[2]	8.84	3.97	6.72	7.35	5.74	10.41	4.47
24	26	93.14	12.09	76.51[2]	19.59	32.63	40.63	114.91	53.79	45.40	7.50
25	64	25.39	34.54	5.30	21.80	35.96	20.10	20.77	21.00	13.90	15.91
26	26	3.47	5.75	1.89	5.22	6.07	5.02	4.76	3.45	2.60	2.29

APPENDIX TABLE 6 (continued)

Minor group	Number of corporations	1919	1920	1921	1922	1923	1924	1925	1926	1927	1928
27	17	4.84	4.96	.60	4.46	6.13	3.05	2.51	2.77	2.85	3.14
28	55	11.48	11.47	4.53	10.78	11.90	9.87	11.41	10.99	8.53	7.66
29	28	11.49	7.94	5.76	13.54	16.89	22.31	22.44	19.97	8.49	15.23
30	35	19.67	48.64	3.78	12.16	22.17	23.83	19.30	19.27	19.30	19.80
31	33	7.08	12.17	.31	4.23	6.12	4.72	5.63	5.49	7.69	6.52
32	20	5.90	10.88	1.53[2]	3.51	2.35	2.85	3.68	3.96	5.73	5.79
33	23	12.12	17.19	3.53	7.29	8.10	9.10	9.08	9.64	7.01	8.60
34	20	20.33	27.06	23.01	38.10	36.73	43.20	36.37	56.40	63.66	74.59
35	17	4.04	4.00	4.05	6.33	6.78	7.54	7.25	6.69	5.91	6.55
36	46	11.51	17.79	10.33	13.16	13.89	13.80	13.96	14.66	13.13	15.16
37	17	1.87	3.65	2.20	2.35	1.88	1.77	2.14	2.10	1.99	2.05
38	9	12.28	10.96	6.11	17.05	10.43	9.42	11.97	11.41	12.64	15.90
39	42	17.15	13.03	4.20	16.22	17.24	14.92	17.21	17.47	14.84	17.96
40	52	301.39	417.30	40.13	254.72	155.67	256.87	420.52	470.03	235.97	515.58
41	56	30.46	22.93	16.15	35.48	34.66	36.03	41.28	46.24	49.19	50.69
42	9	1.57	.98	1.75	3.19	2.84	3.38	3.24	3.45	3.65	4.07
43	16	11.57	7.07[2]	10.34	19.18	18.03	22.01	23.37	29.08	28.51	27.77
44	26	65.37	37.59	30.73	49.30	68.00	84.39	90.75	122.90	121.73	147.91
45	48	12.07	15.32	7.19	13.23	19.89	16.01	17.44	18.39	15.43	13.58
46	18	17.83	23.46	8.26	15.06	27.64	19.68	19.25	17.15	12.20	15.87
47	21	8.02	9.65	9.01	16.91	29.47	27.25	30.67	30.84	26.55	27.81
48	27	15.51	15.81	1.54	13.38	22.21	20.72	27.32	29.13	27.16	31.77
49	99	311.37	331.85	11.76[2]	65.24	239.22	164.24	201.53	255.20	171.09	236.25
50	20	4.99	4.68	4.95[2]	2.75	5.54	4.59	5.07	5.91	4.44	6.25
51	20	11.98	11.56	.34[2]	8.77	13.50	9.21	9.27	9.73	8.02	11.76
52	42	21.69	15.81	6.66	18.20	30.52	25.75	24.72	26.06	18.21	17.55
53	54	108.35	77.51	42.45	80.34	121.76	120.10	127.30	143.06	114.68	139.82
54	18	13.14	10.86	14.02	14.70	11.00	8.35	11.81	11.34	13.18	12.09

APPENDICES

	Number of corporations	1919	1920	1921	1922	1923	1924	1925	1926	1927	1928
55	12	5.86	5.17	3.47	5.18	6.05	4.51	3.99	5.46	4.97	5.92
56	22	15.31	16.96	6.85	11.06	17.84	17.93	18.74	19.25	17.87	21.92
57	11	3.36	2.88	1.60	1.81	3.07	7.00	3.42	5.35	6.09	4.48
58	12	20.67	19.34	3.17	11.99	15.91	6.16	11.61	18.26	13.65	13.13
59	23	23.84	16.79	6.77	13.54	21.02	14.36	22.94	23.10	19.94	25.25
60	13	13.29	11.22	4.78	7.20	9.67	10.23	15.23	15.13	19.47	21.42
61	25	68.31	51.50	21.00	31.29	70.74	41.09	24.62	39.62	29.43	17.42
62	32	274.22	172.54	78.19	258.77	270.89	246.19	366.80	372.39	299.53	314.57
63	11	4.09	3.68	.78	4.09	5.59	4.79	5.11	6.13	6.07	10.17
64	40	42.64	43.02	4.45	32.71	55.74	42.28	45.51	40.91	32.40	36.19
65	30	25.06	19.73	3.24[2]	8.15	12.55	7.94	11.77	14.06	10.48	17.07
66	15	3.73	4.58	.37[2]	3.50	4.47	2.54	4.06	4.48	3.62	5.51
67	32	20.59	13.17	2.84[2]	10.04	15.11	11.80	15.77	19.37	14.47	17.83
68	48	78.21	44.00	12.57	65.73	81.45	81.80	116.49	99.85	96.99	130.50
69	24	6.98	4.04	.57	3.41	4.25	3.24	2.98	3.50	4.10	4.37
70	45	88.48	56.93	17.61[2]	17.15	55.41	46.79	79.45	91.83	85.21	105.41
71	23	35.11	27.41	17.62	43.36	45.14	26.40	46.80	48.16	43.67	47.71
72	12	2.63	2.71	1.68	2.23	3.14	3.14	3.40	3.37	3.72	4.35
73	11	5.16	5.29	.95	5.02	6.99	5.63	6.61	6.56	4.21	3.35
74	43	29.31	25.05	16.68	31.00	31.90	22.08	13.84	32.01	28.66	30.08

Major group	Number of corporations	1919	1920	1921	1922	1923	1924	1925	1926	1927	1928
1 Foods	215	221.45	141.79	73.81	218.03	249.53	264.06	251.63	305.23	276.11	307.25
2 Textiles	289	233.20	77.40	100.00	161.51	163.59	73.19	106.90	80.00	110.27	80.24
3 Leather	54	52.54	8.68	4.59	30.68	24.67	29.23	29.04	26.92	37.31	28.89
4 Rubber	26	93.14	12.09	76.51[2]	19.59	32.63	40.63	114.91	53.79	45.40	7.50
5 Lumber	190	56.67	64.66	18.08	55.80	76.95	60.35	61.89	58.18	36.37	44.23
6 Paper	111	44.77	88.88	6.09	27.19	38.74	40.50	37.69	38.36	39.73	40.71
7 Printing and publishing	100	37.75	52.50	39.59	59.94	59.28	66.31	59.72	79.85	84.69	98.35

APPENDIX TABLE 6 (continued)

Major group	Number of corporations	1919	1920	1921	1922	1923	1924	1925	1926	1927	1928
8 Chemicals	210	439.79	495.72	109.41	395.14	306.87	427.02	608.34	700.58	466.53	779.88
9 Stone, clay and glass	114	53.43	64.24	26.00	58.58	99.21	83.66	94.68	95.51	81.34	89.03
10 Metals	648	1,166.16	937.82	166.22	675.62	1,071.30	880.89	1,128.19	1,229.99	993.91	1,174.88
11 Special manufacturing industries	89	71.21	60.46	36.93	81.61	87.17	57.25	70.65	90.10	80.26	85.49
All manufacturing	2,046	2,471.11	2,004.24	504.21	1,783.69	2,209.94	2,023.09	2,563.64	2,758.51	2,251.92	2,736.45

(c) CAPITALIZATION, 1919–28, 2,046 MANUFACTURING CORPORATIONS

(in millions of dollars)

Minor group	Number of corporations	1919	1920	1921	1922	1923	1924	1925	1926	1927	1928
1	17	130	153	161	155	195	181	208	216	229	236
2	32	49	61	58	51	64	66	65	67	67	65
3	21	67	87	85	79	89	97	101	108	104	109
4	19	55	70	65	67	71	74	78	86	90	90
5	26	66	78	88	90	76	105	134	139	146	200
6	16	65	81	77	77	95	103	103	103	112	114
7	23	505	554	581	542	656	694	675	693	681	699
8											
9	11	47	46	47	45	43	43	45	48	51	46
10	23	457	556	588	588	648	625	637	701	684	704
11–8	27	418	483	409	433	464	434	441	449	469	498
12	12	5	7	8	7	9	8	10	10	10	10
13	18	33	39	37	49	45	46	48	48	51	52
14	49	191	225	219	236	275	264	264	258	278	263

15	31	160	173	190	199	215	205	209	184	207	197
16	17	64	97	82	77	89	79	94	95	97	105
17	18	49	61	67	63	85	82	83	82	84	83
18	25	92	127	118	116	125	124	122	120	124	126
19	42	45	58	58	64	76	83	93	98	109	114
20	23	25	34	35	33	41	41	46	48	51	53
21	54	108	136	131	134	165	168	189	182	210	201
22	25	71	90	97	107	128	137	135	139	153	165
23	29	83	114	97	91	92	91	93	83	90	87
24	26	489	589	607	538	546	560	607	629	660	583
25	64	159	195	210	214	227	224	237	224	234	233
26	26	13	16	19	19	25	27	28	28	27	27
27	17	26	32	34	34	39	39	39	39	39	38
28	55	37	47	54	53	65	66	69	72	73	73
29	28	62	70	72	74	98	116	129	140	139	151
30	35	149	178	199	185	227	227	281	291	341	389
31	33	23	32	37	35	38	40	42	42	43	51
32	20	32	56	62	65	61	58	60	61	51	55
33	23	46	56	66	62	80	83	85	92	91	96
34	20	77	90	107	106	137	177	200	190	270	282
35	17	23	29	30	31	37	40	43	45	52	54
36	46	58	68	79	79	89	89	94	101	103	109
37	17	6	8	9	9	10	10	10	11	11	12
38	9	82	92	92	93	107	109	114	119	123	134
39	42	63	79	85	81	100	101	108	113	114	121
40	52	1641	2112	2769	3230	3384	3496	3812	4561	4896	5257
41	56	110	134	142	136	180	184	197	208	218	233
42	9	4	5	6	6	8	9	10	12	13	16
43	16	83	118	124	141	115	119	120	119	126	143
44	26	464	464	576	606	684	671	642	681	715	833
45	48	98	105	112	123	131	135	144	151	155	160
46	18	61	73	87	86	116	114	124	126	122	134

APPENDIX TABLE 6 (continued)

Minor group	Number of corporations	1919	1920	1921	1922	1923	1924	1925	1926	1927	1928
47	21	86	99	111	112	142	160	179	203	214	217
48	27	75	92	102	94	116	127	139	149	170	186
49	99	2698	3149	3216	3043	3544	3511	3572	3297	3762	3964
50	20	31	37	40	38	42	44	43	45	50	53
51	20	67	74	77	71	84	81	81	83	81	85
52	42	106	124	130	121	140	149	160	153	192	191
53	54	496	642	665	600	737	719	756	800	809	848
54	18	48	63	62	66	60	79	80	79	83	83
55	12	33	39	41	40	44	44	44	50	52	48
56	22	57	77	79	79	93	95	103	110	114	129
57	11	12	15	17	17	21	25	37	38	55	65
58	12	57	77	93	86	105	100	104	114	118	129
59	23	151	177	176	175	186	176	177	174	178	189
60	13	59	71	75	80	75	89	88	96	102	121
61	25	401	487	493	435	523	488	466	519	527	520
62	32	707	937	927	1023	1302	1425	1545	1801	1859	1948
63	11	35	39	37	36	45	46	49	50	51	52
64	40	147	198	236	209	267	280	287	300	311	329
65	30	84	101	104	96	101	100	102	96	109	112
66	15	19	21	21	20	24	24	24	26	27	29
67	32	85	103	111	101	112	108	118	125	126	132
68	48	628	748	656	761	732	835	823	794	862	882
69	24	19	26	27	27	31	32	33	34	35	36
70	45	521	596	610	566	618	580	614	624	642	674
71	23	106	124	135	141	158	157	162	163	173	175
72	12	10	11	15	17	20	20	22	24	25	27
73	11	30	38	42	42	49	48	50	55	56	57
74	43	112	139	157	153	179	187	183	204	217	243

APPENDICES

Major group	Number of corporations 1919	1920	1921	1922	1923	1924	1925	1926	1927	1928
1 Foods	215	1859	2169	2159	2127	2401	2422	2487	2610	2633	2761
2 Textiles	289	772	957	945	978	1125	1100	1158	1125	1221	1204
3 Leather	54	154	204	194	198	220	228	228	222	243	252
4 Rubber	26	489	589	607	538	546	560	607	629	660	583
5 Lumber	190	297	360	389	394	454	472	502	503	512	522
6 Paper	111	270	322	364	347	406	408	468	486	526	591
7 Printing and publishing	100	164	195	225	225	273	316	347	347	436	457
8 Chemicals	210	2447	3004	3794	4293	4578	4689	5003	5813	6205	6737
9 Stone, clay and glass	114	320	369	412	415	505	536	586	629	661	697
10 Metals	648	6461	7801	7893	7690	8886	9030	9306	9408	10145	10619
11 Special manufacturing industries	89	258	312	349	353	406	412	417	446	471	502
All manufacturing	2046	13491	16282	17331	17558	19800	20173	21109	22218	23713	24925

[627]

Appendix Table 6 *(continued)*

(D) BONDED DEBT, 1924–28, 2,046 MANUFACTURING CORPORATIONS

(in millions of dollars)

Minor group	Number of corporations	1924	1925	1926	1927	1928
1	17	11.16	10.48	7.06	6.46	6.62
2	32	.06	..	1.50	1.40	1.30
3	21	3.67	4.06	3.52	3.32	3.21
4	19	3.16	2.93	3.05	6.04	6.04
5	26	5.22	12.63	4.09	5.85	9.58
6	16	.69	.64	.71	.68	.65
7	23	253.88	313.96	223.63	273.39	258.88
8						
9	11	.08	.43	.40	.42	.42
10	23	59.81	61.66	37.57	71.79	70.58
11–8	27	39.99	46.19	49.23	52.44	54.27
12	12	.02	..	..	..	..
13	18	2.46	2.27	.10	2.16	2.22
14	49	.03	4.07	25.63	23.95	4.48
15	31	2.65	2.57	2.53	2.55	3.59
16	17	6.20	.69	4.53	7.68	13.15
17	18	.31	.38	.37	.33	.33
18	25	2.53	2.57	1.86	1.28	1.22
19	42	2.31	8.22	7.31	7.14	7.13
20	23	1.20	1.18	1.07	1.22	1.20
21	54	8.62	7.52	5.96	4.89	6.09
22	25	2.22	2.27	2.61	2.89	1.92
23	29	5.64	5.25	2.25	4.62	7.93
24	26	149.79	180.12	224.07	231.85	223.69
25	64	14.18	15.47	3.26	16.96	17.12
26	26	.20	.04	.49	.46	.33
27	17	.01	2.82	1.53	.78	1.03
28	55	.82	.69	3.77	7.55	7.75
29	28	6.78	9.41	7.82	5.74	12.02
30	35	33.12	70.70	105.38	114.48	60.11
31	33	1.71	1.49	.07	1.14	1.00
32	20	10.84	10.56	11.41	7.04	6.66
33	23	7.75	10.49	8.19	10.35	7.24
34	20	31.46	48.04	59.47	97.45	102.63
35	17	.36	1.09	1.07	1.01	..
36	46	3.19	4.04	4.01	12.35	8.99
37	17	..	.11	..	.19	.29
38	9	.05	.09	.08	.07	.05
39	42	4.30	3.75	1.09	.85	1.02
40	52	223.43	236.06	377.52	453.80	460.75
41	56	7.04	7.83	5.07	6.22	4.38
42	9	.02	..	..	..	..

Appendix Table 6 *(continued)*

Minor group	Number of corporations	1924	1925	1926	1927	1928
43	16	.70	.75	.55	.55	.13
44	26	39.03	7.79	17.13	15.23	28.66
45	48	2.49	1.75	3.28	7.11	5.88
46	18	3.93	2.20	1.37	2.00	1.20
47	21	10.29	8.77	8.85	10.99	29.29
48	27	.61	.53	.40	.47	5.03
49	99	951.59	928.03	931.30	898.06	914.11
50	20	5.02	5.46	6.33	2.67	8.90
51	20	.43	.39	.33	.42	1.19
52	42	5.67	4.98	3.90	16.30	15.33
53	54	55.98	41.47	42.52	52.49	52.53
54	18	..	5.56	1.56	6.06	6.07
55	12	6.18	6.08	6.03	6.31	11.68
56	22	.13	.08	.08	3.95	5.07
57	11	.53	.44	.48	1.01	.75
58	12	2.29	.26	1.87	..	..
59	23	5.08	3.88	3.20	2.75	2.36
60	13	1.29	1.24	1.13	.94	.93
61	25	21.67	37.24	34.36	23.95	22.63
62	32	34.93	39.14	31.09	36.22	34.45
63	11	.17	.13	.01	.10	.13
64	40	5.97	16.47	15.55	17.06	15.14
65	30	2.17	1.88	1.04	3.87	3.53
66	15	..	..	..	..	..
67	32	1.36	1.32	3.89	10.56	14.53
68	48	79.65	66.08	68.07	70.32	94.42
69	24	.37	.52	.21	.51	.60
70	45	37.65	40.63	29.34	36.98	40.99
71	23	.56	.25	.10	.04	3.76
72	12	..	..	.07	1.32	1.32
73	11	2.10	2.19	.26	2.48	2.18
74	43	8.47	7.38	3.10	.02	2.45

Major group	Number of corporations	1924	1925	1926	1927	1928
1 Foods	215	377.72	452.98	330.76	421.79	411.55
2 Textiles	289	26.33	29.47	49.36	51.20	39.41
3 Leather	54	7.86	7.52	4.86	7.51	9.85
4 Rubber	26	149.79	180.12	224.07	231.85	223.69
5 Lumber	190	21.99	28.43	16.87	31.49	38.25
6 Paper	111	53.42	93.24	125.05	133.01	75.01

APPENDIX TABLE 6 *(continued)*

Major group	Number of corporations	1924	1925	1926	1927	1928
7 Printing and publishing	100	35.01	53.28	64.55	111.00	111.91
8 Chemicals	210	274.57	256.27	401.44	476.72	494.99
9 Stone, clay and glass	114	17.32	13.25	13.90	20.57	41.40
10 Metals	648	1218.13	1201.28	1182.29	1190.53	1245.34
11 Special manufacturing industries	89	11.13	9.82	3.53	3.86	9.71
All manufacturing	2046	2193.27	2325.66	2416.68	2679.53	2701.11

APPENDICES [631]

APPENDIX TABLE 6 (continued)

(E) FEDERAL INCOME TAX, 1919–28 (INCLUDING EXCESS PROFITS TAX, 1919–21), 2,046 MANUFACTURING CORPORATIONS

(in millions of dollars)

Minor group	Number of corporations	1919	1920	1921	1922	1923	1924	1925	1926	1927	1928
1	17	4.09	3.93	5.80	3.34	3.52	4.09	4.26	5.32	5.77	4.89
2	32	3.51	.39	.93	.92	.72	1.31	.84	.82	1.09	.85
3	21	9.78	2.51	2.49	1.55	1.82	2.18	2.28	2.42	2.27	1.88
4	19	2.40	.59	2.38	1.63	1.44	1.86	1.55	2.24	2.05	1.80
5	26	3.11	1.44	1.57	1.70	1.92	1.56	2.22	2.42	2.39	2.29
6	16	3.71	1.24	1.18	1.91	1.55	1.87	1.60	1.60	1.35	1.66
7	23	2.59	.80	1.71	2.68	2.88	3.37	2.36	5.01	2.06	3.09
8											
9	11	.36	.58	.44	.23	.23	.25	.35	.32	.33	.38
10	23	11.05	10.22	15.64	9.75	10.02	9.98	11.82	13.15	14.00	12.46
11–8	27	14.42	6.10	1.75	2.91	3.88	4.54	3.76	4.94	4.05	5.16
12	12	.73	.84	.10	.13	.15	.07	.15	.13	.13	.11
13	18	2.61	.35	1.09	.91	.84	.35	.59	.35	.66	.49
14	49	17.96	8.10	3.52	3.14	3.37	1.09	1.39	1.41	3.06	1.41
15	31	8.34	1.35	4.39	3.57	2.96	1.33	1.02	.95	.92	.56
16	17	7.86	.81	1.71	1.11	1.41	.77	1.72	1.09	.86	.63
17	18	3.46	4.23	2.48	2.52	2.48	1.20	1.18	.92	1.08	.64
18	25	6.99	3.89	1.73	1.55	2.12	1.45	1.85	1.83	2.16	1.66
19	42	5.60	1.59	2.89	2.03	1.45	1.19	1.97	2.12	1.68	1.39
20	23	2.58	.97	.63	.65	.73	.58	.77	.87	.98	.76
21	54	11.98	4.25	3.70	2.97	3.60	2.39	2.69	2.20	2.22	1.96
22	25	7.51	4.14	1.93	2.58	2.52	2.76	2.79	2.83	3.63	3.00
23	29	8.58	.65	.53	1.06	.71	.74	.90	.91	1.35	.74
24	26	22.25	1.82	.53	1.13	1.11	3.78	12.00	2.61	5.82	2.70
25	64	5.20	8.79	.75	2.54	4.33	2.43	2.57	2.59	1.83	1.82

APPENDIX TABLE 6 (continued)

Minor group	Number of corporations	1919	1920	1921	1922	1923	1924	1925	1926	1927	1928
26	26	.94	1.85	.30	.62	.68	.58	.57	.41	.32	.25
27	17	1.09	1.03	.14	.49	.67	.38	.36	.33	.38	.37
28	55	3.46	3.20	1.05	1.26	1.41	1.19	1.45	1.44	1.10	.89
29	28	2.79	2.25	1.78	1.89	2.01	2.76	2.88	2.72	1.35	1.75
30	35	3.55	13.49	1.60	2.13	2.47	2.45	2.49	2.49	2.33	1.90
31	33	1.73	4.01	.28	.43	.64	.55	.71	.72	1.01	.75
32	20	1.40	2.98	.48	.42	.55	.49	.59	.63	.71	.66
33	23	3.32	5.05	.54	.85	.94	1.07	1.13	1.13	.82	1.06
34	20	6.10	8.36	5.84	4.67	4.38	4.14	4.32	5.45	6.19	6.73
35	17	.83	.85	.76	.77	.83	.92	.91	.87	.76	.73
36	46	2.79	5.08	2.29	1.51	1.57	1.66	1.69	1.83	1.63	1.67
37	17	.52	1.22	.63	.27	.22	.21	.26	.27	.25	.23
38	9	2.44	2.15	.88	1.31	1.14	1.05	1.41	1.42	1.59	1.80
39	42	4.82	2.95	.85	1.79	2.05	1.79	2.16	2.25	2.01	1.90
40	52	63.42	83.14	6.37	21.22	14.35	27.26	40.07	46.13	18.30	40.88
41	56	8.84	5.85	4.04	3.49	4.10	4.35	5.16	5.81	6.34	5.93
42	9	.46	.29	.52	.35	.34	.41	.40	.44	.47	.47
43	16	2.16	1.41	2.58	2.29	2.21	2.69	3.01	3.87	3.65	3.32
44	26	7.92	4.52	2.64	4.11	5.09	5.36	7.03	9.62	9.21	9.07
45	48	2.02	3.27	1.29	1.54	2.41	1.94	2.19	2.39	1.98	1.58
46	18	4.79	7.24	1.34	1.76	3.40	2.35	2.38	2.17	1.54	1.86
47	21	1.04	1.29	1.20	2.04	3.57	3.33	3.90	4.03	3.43	3.11
48	27	3.46	3.22	.98	1.26	2.45	2.49	3.45	3.82	3.52	3.78
49	99	52.95	59.19	1.35	5.47	26.71	18.97	24.81	31.94	21.25	26.80
50	20	1.86	1.02	.32	.36	.41	.39	.59	.70	.52	.70
51	20	2.33	2.14	.25	.66	1.44	.95	1.07	1.17	.92	1.24
52	42	6.52	2.91	1.16	2.05	3.59	3.10	3.08	3.29	2.20	2.33
53	54	125.21	12.49	5.25	8.97	13.30	13.84	15.37	18.16	14.07	15.60

APPENDICES [633]

	1919	1920	1921	1922	1923	1924	1925	1926	1927	1928
54	3.31	2.52	3.32	1.69	1.31	1.07	1.52	1.57	1.74	1.45
55	1.72	1.06	.62	.63	.70	.55	.62	.69	.70	.74
56	3.82	4.43	1.36	1.13	2.07	2.14	2.34	2.50	2.26	2.49
57	1.01	.69	.26	.20	.36	.42	.41	.50	.50	.50
58	5.61	5.02	.38	1.34	1.89	.75	1.48	2.43	1.80	1.64
59	4.84	2.95	1.41	1.69	2.15	1.86	2.31	2.76	2.56	2.76
60	3.52	2.46	.89	.80	1.19	1.26	1.97	2.02	2.58	2.40
61	15.30	7.76	2.70	3.04	7.92	4.37	2.68	4.80	3.40	1.87
62	90.24	43.81	40.90	25.61	32.01	29.85	45.30	49.29	44.86	45.13
63	.64	.58	.19	.41	.67	.56	.62	.76	.77	1.18
64	11.61	10.88	1.25	3.74	6.43	5.08	5.66	5.30	4.02	4.22
65	7.09	4.97	.23	.93	1.13	.91	1.46	1.82	1.31	1.88
66	.84	1.11	.04	.32	.56	.29	.49	.56	.48	.62
67	5.50	2.30	.33	.82	1.50	1.41	2.09	2.37	1.85	2.03
68	13.93	7.00	2.98	7.15	8.78	9.76	14.15	12.39	10.38	13.98
69	2.16	.90	.32	.27	.47	.39	.37	.46	.54	.50
70	28.09	8.81	2.77	2.11	3.39	5.14	9.96	12.03	11.33	12.72
71	9.67	5.98	3.27	3.33	3.51	3.24	3.83	4.11	4.06	3.61
72	.65	.66	.27	.27	.38	.38	.43	.44	.49	.51
73	.99	1.07	.27	.52	.79	.69	.85	.82	.55	.40
74	7.60	6.30	4.00	3.17	3.84	2.68	2.46	3.41	3.75	3.50

Major group	Number of corporations	1919	1920	1921	1922	1923	1924	1925	1926	1927	1928
1 Foods	215	55.02	27.80	33.89	26.62	27.98	31.01	31.04	38.24	35.36	34.46
2 Textiles	289	68.11	26.38	22.24	18.58	19.11	10.42	13.33	11.87	13.75	9.61
3 Leather	54	16.09	4.79	2.46	3.64	3.23	3.50	3.69	3.74	4.98	3.74
4 Rubber	26	22.25	1.82	.53	1.13	1.11	3.78	12.00	2.61	5.82	2.70
5 Lumber	190	13.48	17.12	4.02	6.80	9.10	7.34	7.83	7.49	4.98	5.08
6 Paper	111	10.00	25.53	2.90	3.83	4.60	4.56	4.92	4.97	4.87	4.37
7 Printing and publishing	100	10.24	15.51	9.52	7.22	7.00	6.93	7.18	8.42	8.83	9.36

APPENDIX TABLE 6 (*continued*)

Major group	Number of corporations	1919	1920	1921	1922	1923	1924	1925	1926	1927	1928
8 Chemicals	210	90.06	100.31	17.88	34.56	29.28	42.91	59.24	69.54	41.57	63.37
9 Stone, clay and glass	114	11.31	15.02	4.81	6.60	11.83	10.11	11.92	12.41	10.47	10.33
10 Metals	648	388.10	185.00	68.28	69.39	117.98	103.06	138.35	157.51	130.04	142.78
11 Special manufacturing industries	89	18.91	14.01	7.81	7.29	8.52	6.99	7.57	8.78	8.85	8.02
All manufacturing	2046	703.57	433.29	174.34	185.66	239.74	230.61	297.07	325.58	269.52	293.82

(F) SALES, 1919–28, 664 TRADING CORPORATIONS

(*in millions of dollars*)

Minor group	Number of corporations	1919	1920	1921	1922	1923	1924	1925	1926	1927	1928
75	15	48	57	50	63	83	86	113	114	110	107
76	17	49	54	48	51	57	58	61	60	59	58
77	93	880	1037	946	931	1062	1056	1123	1179	1188	1190
78	27	105	119	106	111	117	118	127	131	154	141
79	12	15	20	19	14	26	28	25	30	30	30
80	14	332	438	387	490	592	648	790	1022	1253	1530
81	11	14	13	9	10	11	11	12	13	13	14
82	27	27	38	24	27	33	31	32	34	34	33
83	15	23	29	18	18	20	19	21	21	21	21
84	52	725	808	688	747	855	962	1091	1185	1273	1438
85											
86	25	64	78	64	63	71	71	75	79	80	75
87	29	120	140	97	108	121	108	111	108	106	102
88	59	377	413	288	289	326	334	340	339	330	334
89	43	185	215	143	158	189	179	184	182	179	176

APPENDICES [635]

Minor group	Number of corporations	1919	1920	1921	1922	1923	1924	1925	1926	1927	1928
90	23	84	111	123	122	142	125	143	120	129	112
91	13	32	42	25	37	50	46	46	45	41	41
92	18	140	202	141	148	160	156	157	147	152	151
93–85	82	566	582	435	435	538	517	531	560	545	529
94											
95											
96	10	39	50	42	42	60	52	46	52	44	39
97	16	35	40	27	30	36	36	37	38	37	36
98	11	11	20	14	17	20	16	16	16	16	15
99–95	52	250	312	240	232	259	227	225	218	216	214

Major group	Number of corporations	1919	1920	1921	1922	1923	1924	1925	1926	1927	1928
12 Retail trade	283	2218	2613	2295	2462	2856	3017	3395	3789	4135	4562
13 Wholesale trade	292	1568	1783	1316	1360	1597	1536	1587	1580	1562	1520
14 Retail and wholesale trade	89	335	422	323	321	375	331	324	324	313	304
All trade	664	4121	4818	3934	4143	4828	4884	5306	5693	6010	6386

(G) TOTAL NET INCOME, 1919–28, 664 TRADING CORPORATIONS

(in millions of dollars)

Minor group	Number of corporations	1919	1920	1921	1922	1923	1924	1925	1926	1927	1928
75	15	3.6	2.8	.9	2.6	3.8	3.7	5.5	4.3	3.4	3.6
76	17	6.3	2.0	1.8	3.9	4.4	4.2	4.9	3.6	4.0	4.3
77	93	94.3	44.6	47.6	67.7	78.5	62.1	66.1	66.4	64.5	54.9
78	27	11.1	7.2	5.6	7.9	7.7	6.3	7.7	7.9	8.0	8.4
79	12	1.1	2.3	1.2	2.2	2.4	2.1	1.4	1.3	1.7	1.8
80	14	11.6	8.6	15.9	19.9	23.4	27.9	28.9	35.2	39.5	47.7

APPENDIX TABLE 6 (continued)

Minor group	Number of corporations	1919	1920	1921	1922	1923	1924	1925	1926	1927	1928
81	11	2.8	1.2	.4	.9	.9	.7	1.1	1.6	1.3	1.9
82	27	1.5	3.6	1.2	2.3	2.7	2.4	2.6	2.5	2.1	2.3
83	15	2.4	3.3	.6	1.6	1.3	1.4	1.7	1.5	1.7	1.9
84	52	58.5	17.2	5.8	61.3	65.5	76.8	99.0	98.4	109.0	114.3
85											
86	25	2.9	3.9	1.7	2.3	3.2	3.0	3.1	3.0	2.8	3.2
87	29	12.2	2.2	2.2	4.6	5.4	3.2	4.0	3.0	4.0	3.7
88	59	14.6	3.7	2.1	9.3	9.5	9.1	8.1	6.8	7.0	6.7
89	43	14.0	13.6	1.2[a]	7.1	11.5	6.2	8.0	7.1	7.1	8.0
90	23	6.0	3.4	2.7	4.9	5.5	4.6	2.9	3.0	4.5	5.3
91	13	1.6	2.6	.5	2.0	1.7	1.4	1.3	1.3	.9	.8
92	18	4.9	9.2	.1[a]	3.4	4.8	3.8	4.0	3.2	3.2	4.1
93–85	82	32.8	24.7	3.5	17.6	29.4	20.4	20.2	23.3	17.6	16.8
94											
95											
96	10	1.2	1.8	.9	1.9	3.0	2.7	2.7	3.3	2.4	2.4
97	16	2.8	2.6	.3	1.3	1.8	1.3	1.8	1.7	1.4	1.4
98	11	.4	1.8	.6	1.4	1.7	1.2	.9	.8	.8	.6
99–95	52	19.6	17.3	12.7	16.7	19.4	15.9	14.0	16.0	14.0	12.8

Major group	Number of corporations	1919	1920	1921	1922	1923	1924	1925	1926	1927	1928
12 Retail trade	283	193.2	92.8	81.0	170.3	190.6	187.6	218.9	222.7	235.2	241.1
13 Wholesale trade	292	89.0	63.3	11.4	51.2	71.0	51.7	51.6	50.7	47.1	48.6
14 Retail and wholesale trade	89	24.0	23.5	14.5	21.3	25.9	21.1	19.4	21.8	18.6	17.2
All trade	664	306.2	179.6	106.9	242.8	287.5	260.4	289.9	295.2	300.9	306.9

APPENDICES [637]

(H) CAPITALIZATION, 1919–28, 664 TRADING CORPORATIONS

(in millions of dollars)

Minor group	Number of corporations	1919	1920	1921	1922	1923	1924	1925	1926	1927	1928
75	15	4.4	8.2	8.1	8.9	13.9	14.6	16.5	18.6	19.4	19.8
76	17	13.3	19.3	19.8	20.0	26.3	30.3	33.6	32.9	35.1	34.2
77	93	277.4	371.1	378.1	389.4	471.6	491.8	522.2	546.3	550.7	581.7
78	27	29.2	45.5	47.7	49.1	57.9	56.7	59.7	62.1	65.7	70.4
79	12	8.4	10.0	11.7	11.5	14.6	14.6	17.7	17.4	19.0	18.4
80	14	39.2	53.4	60.9	72.8	105.8	118.6	137.3	162.3	179.5	221.3
81	11	6.4	9.4	8.6	9.0	10.1	10.6	10.9	11.3	11.6	12.6
82	27	11.3	15.6	17.6	16.9	19.8	22.4	22.4	25.0	25.6	27.3
83	15	9.0	13.7	14.4	13.5	14.3	14.5	14.9	14.8	15.9	18.0
84	52	359.7	429.9	408.7	431.0	440.6	470.0	520.9	561.0	629.6	753.8
85											
86	25	16.1	19.8	22.3	22.6	24.3	25.4	27.0	27.2	28.2	30.8
87	29	32.8	40.5	36.3	39.5	43.0	43.2	44.0	42.9	43.8	44.0
88	59	67.4	79.1	81.6	80.6	86.5	84.2	86.7	88.2	89.8	91.0
89	43	66.4	81.1	80.6	77.2	89.2	91.0	92.9	92.0	92.5	93.2
90	23	24.1	27.8	29.3	30.0	40.7	41.6	44.7	44.4	46.5	49.5
91	13	5.7	18.3	19.7	18.1	20.1	20.8	20.9	19.5	18.6	17.6
92	18	27.0	32.4	37.0	34.5	36.2	35.9	38.1	38.1	38.2	40.3
93–85	82	147.9	159.2	171.8	155.1	176.8	177.1	181.0	181.3	190.1	193.5
94											
95											
96	10	10.3	11.0	12.9	12.7	16.9	18.3	19.7	21.3	22.4	22.3
97	16	12.4	14.8	15.3	14.9	15.8	16.2	17.5	17.8	18.3	18.5
98	11	6.0	7.1	8.2	8.1	9.7	10.5	10.9	11.2	11.7	11.8
99–95	52	92.4	105.7	118.4	113.3	131.5	130.9	135.4	139.3	137.8	132.5

APPENDIX TABLE 6 (continued)

Major group	Number of corporations	1919	1920	1921	1922	1923	1924	1925	1926	1927	1928
12 Retail trade	283	758.3	976.1	975.6	1022.1	1174.9	1244.1	1356.1	1451.7	1552.1	1757.5
13 Wholesale trade	292	387.4	458.2	478.6	457.6	516.8	519.2	535.3	533.6	547.7	559.9
14 Retail and wholesale trade	89	121.1	138.6	154.8	149.0	173.9	175.9	183.5	189.6	190.2	185.1
All trade	664	1266.8	1572.9	1609.0	1628.7	1865.6	1939.2	2074.9	2174.9	2290.0	2502.5

Appendix Table 6 *(continued)*

(1) BONDED DEBT, 1924–28, 664 TRADING CORPORATIONS

(in millions of dollars)

Minor group	Number of corporations	1924	1925	1926	1927	1928
75	15	.87	3.96	3.81	3.37	4.77
76	17	..	.05	..	..	..
77	93	54.98	77.64	61.17	97.03	105.83
78	27	15.93	16.27	17.06	12.87	16.96
79	12	.04	.04	.34	..	.67
80	14	.08	.19	.23	2.67	3.57
81	11	1.12	1.02	1.29	1.17	1.13
82	27	.16	.15	.14	.23	.44
83	15	..	..	..	..	.01
84	52	16.05	19.80	24.23	26.57	37.54
85						
86	25	.47	.45	.42	.43	.50
87	29	.31	.30	.26	.25	.33
88	59	.55	.88	.36	.81	.83
89	43	4.19	4.22	4.31	3.54	3.35
90	23	3.84	4.99	4.65	4.38	4.28
91	13	.05	.60	.05	.44	.43
92	18	2.34	.90	1.45	1.54	1.44
93–85	82	2.05	2.17	3.51	4.02	10.89
94						
95						
96	10	.20	.08	.10	.10	.14
97	16	.08	..	.07	.07	.07
98	11	.11	.09	.12	.12	.25
99–95	52	8.79	9.55	8.54	7.99	6.07

Major group	Number of corporations	1924	1925	1926	1927	1928
12 Retail trade	283	89.23	119.12	108.27	143.91	170.92
13 Wholesale trade	292	13.80	14.51	15.01	15.41	22.05
14 Retail and wholesale trade	89	9.18	9.72	8.83	8.28	6.53
All trade	664	112.21	143.35	132.11	167.60	199.50

Appendix Table 6 (continued)

(J) FEDERAL INCOME TAX, 1919–28 (INCLUDING EXCESS PROFITS TAX, 1919–21), 664 TRADING CORPORATIONS

(in millions of dollars)

Minor group	Number of corporations	1919	1920	1921	1922	1923	1924	1925	1926	1927	1928
75	15	1.38	.91	.21	.34	.46	.45	.71	.56	.46	.42
76	17	2.23	.36	.31	.47	.53	.51	.62	.46	.52	.49
77	93	28.55	9.32	8.23	8.27	9.18	7.57	8.40	8.69	8.43	6.71
78	27	3.57	1.57	1.01	.96	.94	.79	.99	1.05	1.06	1.00
79	12	.56	.62	.21	.24	.29	.26	.18	.17	.23	.22
80	14	3.67	1.77	4.30	2.43	2.88	3.44	3.71	4.71	5.20	5.65
81	11	.89	.24	.06	.11	.11	.10	.15	.21	.18	.23
82	27	1.02	.96	.19	.28	.33	.29	.33	.32	.27	.26
83	15	.98	.64	.11	.18	.16	.17	.22	.20	.22	.22
84	52	12.72	5.86	6.26	5.53	6.57	9.55	12.68	12.95	14.53	12.02
85											
86	25	.79	.90	.28	.27	.38	.37	.40	.40	.38	.39
87	29	3.60	.46	.34	.52	.66	.39	.52	.39	.50	.43
88	59	3.63	.94	.73	.96	1.04	1.12	1.02	.89	.90	.77
89	43	4.13	2.89	.42	.74	1.10	.71	.99	.93	.93	.93
90	23	1.98	.79	.63	.54	.62	.55	.33	.35	.57	.59
91	13	.52	.80	.16	.20	.20	.17	.16	.16	.11	.09
92	18	1.43	2.66	.18	.31	.43	.39	.45	.36	.33	.42
93–85	82	9.88	6.77	2.15	1.89	3.21	2.42	2.50	2.96	2.25	1.92
94											
95											
96	10	.30	.81	.15	.24	.36	.33	.34	.41	.30	.27
97	16	.82	.61	.09	.13	.17	.16	.23	.22	.20	.16
98	11	.29	.50	.10	.16	.21	.15	.11	.10	.11	.07
99–95	52	6.22	3.91	2.12	1.78	2.11	1.57	1.58	1.59	1.47	1.15

APPENDICES

Major group	Number of corporations	1919	1920	1921	1922	1923	1924	1925	1926	1927	1928
12 Retail trade	283	55.57	22.25	20.89	18.81	21.45	23.13	27.99	29.32	31.10	27.22
13 Wholesale trade	292	25.96	16.21	4.89	5.43	7.64	6.12	6.37	6.44	5.97	5.54
14 Retail and wholesale trade	89	7.63	5.83	2.46	2.31	2.85	2.21	2.26	2.32	2.08	1.65
All trade	664	89.16	44.29	28.24	26.55	31.94	31.46	36.62	38.08	39.15	34.41

(K) SALES, 88 MINING CORPORATIONS, 1919–28

(in millions of dollars)

Minor group	Number of corporations	1919	1920	1921	1922	1923	1924	1925	1926	1927	1928
100	33	91	136	104	79	108	82	85	106	97	85
101[3]	11[3]	2	5	4	4	5	6	7	10	11	11
102	9	16	23	17	18	22	22	25	29	34	34
103	9	7	10	9	10	14	13	15	18	17	19
104	15	252	303	149	307	398	390	463	508	457	566
105	11	69	89	83	70	93	89	78	88	82	79
All mining	88	435	561	362	484	635	596	666	749	687	783

[641]

APPENDIX TABLE 6 (continued)

(L) TOTAL NET INCOME, 88 MINING CORPORATIONS, 1919–28
(in millions of dollars)

Minor group	Number of corporations	1919	1920	1921	1922	1923	1924	1925	1926	1927	1928
100	33	13.5	34.6	15.1	14.2	16.7	6.7	9.7	14.2	10.5	8.7
101	11	4.1	9.7	1.1	1.0[2]	1.9[2]	1.8	2.6	4.5	3.6	7.7
102	9	2.9	3.6	1.7	3.4	4.5	4.4	5.8	6.3	7.4	5.4
103	9	1.4	2.0	1.7	3.1	3.3	3.2	4.9	5.7	5.6	5.0
104	15	10.3	12.5	22.6[2]	5.8	30.7	26.9	51.9	53.1	41.2	94.4
105	11	15.01	17.9	15.6	13.0	21.2	14.6	11.3	18.1	12.8	11.2
All mining	88	47.3	80.3	12.6	38.5	74.5	57.6	86.2	101.9	81.1	132.4

[2] Net loss.

(M) CAPITALIZATION, 88 MINING CORPORATIONS, 1919–28
(in millions of dollars)

Minor group	Number of corporations	1919	1920	1921	1922	1923	1924	1925	1926	1927	1928
100	33	128	147	167	176	185	186	186	185	195	195
101	11	82	89	104	91	104	142	129	115	120	133
102	9	22	28	29	31	34	36	40	44	47	50
103	9	15	20	21	22	25	27	29	31	31	40
104	15	717	949	976	956	1003	1083	1105	1081	1070	1112
105	11	90	106	120	74	102	103	104	124	127	142
All mining	88	1054	1339	1417	1350	1453	1577	1593	1580	1590	1672

Appendix Table 6 *(continued)*

(N) BONDED DEBT, 1924–28 *(in millions of dollars);* AND DEPLETION,[3] 1924, 1926, 1928 *(in dollars),* 88 MINING CORPORATIONS

Bonded debt

Minor group	Number of corporations	1924	1925	1926	1927	1928
100	33	29.1	25.4	11.3	10.3	22.7
101	11	1.2	8.8	7.7	6.5	9.2
102	9	2.8	2.3	4.9	7.5	9.9
103	9	.9	.6	.5	1.2	4.2
104	15	215.9	233.7	255.0	254.8	203.1
105	11	40.9	35.0	28.5	32.1	27.9
All mining	88	290.8	305.8	307.9	312.4	277.0

Depletion

Minor group	Number of corporations	1924	1926	1928
100	33	1756540	1321427	910419
101[3]	11[3]	1636121	1714201	1099695
102	9	249154	275771	294922
103	9	458585	185139	317959
104	15	33020075	37289664	45632181
105	11	3030608	1946750	2051535

APPENDIX TABLE 6 (*continued*)

(o) FEDERAL INCOME TAX (INCLUDING EXCESS PROFITS TAX, 1919–21), 88 MINING CORPORATIONS, 1919–28
(*in millions of dollars*)

Minor group	Number of corporations	1919	1920	1921	1922	1923	1924	1925	1926	1927	1928
100	33	2.20	9.37	2.33	1.60	1.96	.88	1.21	1.73	1.48	1.02
101	11	.60	1.99	.16	.07	.03	.11	.17	.49	.48	.66
102	9	.41	.72	.22	.41	.55	.54	.74	.84	.99	.64
103	9	.22	.36	.27	.38	.40	.39	.63	.74	.73	.58
104	15	1.39	2.24	.08	1.09	2.22	3.29	5.41	6.02	4.86	8.77
105	11	2.59	3.29	2.50	1.42	2.22	1.66	1.31	2.12	1.66	1.07
All mining	88	7.41	17.97	5.56	4.97	7.38	6.87	9.47	11.94	10.20	12.74

(p) TOTAL GROSS INCOME, 1919–28, 346 FINANCIAL CORPORATIONS
(*in millions of dollars*)

Minor group	Number of corporations	1919	1920	1921	1922	1923	1924	1925	1926	1927	1928
106	18	12.5	18.0	20.1	23.0	26.6	29.0	32.1	34.0	35.5	35.1
107	30	33.6	49.2	51.5	48.8	53.9	60.2	63.8	78.9	100.9	109.8
108	105	215.3	268.6	258.4	211.5	217.0	222.8	249.0	277.8	302.7	337.0
109	56	87.6	107.6	112.5	94.7	94.2	102.4	110.4	123.2	134.4	149.5
110 111–110	137	230.7	280.7	261.2	282.9	310.7	334.5	386.6	407.4	401.4	429.3
All finance	346	579.7	724.1	703.7	660.9	702.4	748.9	841.9	921.3	974.9	1060.7

APPENDICES [645]

(Q) TOTAL NET INCOME, 1919–28, 346 FINANCIAL CORPORATIONS

(in millions of dollars)

Minor group	Number of corporations	1919	1920	1921	1922	1923	1924	1925	1926	1927	1928
106	18	3.7	4.9	4.6	7.4	7.1	6.9	8.6	9.0	7.4	9.0
107	30	11.8	13.1	11.9	15.0	17.5	15.8	16.6	15.6	29.5	30.9
108	105	86.0	99.7	62.0	78.6	74.6	67.7	72.0	85.1	86.6	101.3
109	56	23.3	30.5	18.7	24.3	20.5	27.5	32.1	31.4	40.0	46.3
110											
111–110	137	57.8	52.6	42.9	75.2	66.6	74.9	91.7	92.4	98.5	116.1
All finance	346	182.6	200.8	140.1	200.5	186.3	192.8	221.0	233.5	262.0	303.6

(R) CAPITALIZATION, 1919–28, 346 FINANCIAL CORPORATIONS

(in millions of dollars)

Minor group	Number of corporations	1919	1920	1921	1922	1923	1924	1925	1926	1927	1928
106	18	31.0	35.0	40.3	45.5	53.2	57.7	64.3	67.7	75.3	80.2
107	30	60.4	85.9	102.5	111.0	124.7	140.6	143.2	197.9	297.4	380.6
108	105	487.2	596.4	691.6	650.6	750.5	738.6	789.0	879.8	956.7	1072.1
109	56	145.6	220.6	258.3	260.3	270.4	279.4	302.7	312.9	335.3	425.3
110											
111–110	137	494.7	661.3	712.1	581.9	694.9	679.3	754.5	796.0	898.1	973.5
All finance	346	1218.9	1599.2	1804.8	1649.3	1893.7	1895.6	2053.7	2254.3	2562.8	2931.7

Appendix Table 6 *(continued)*

(s) BONDED DEBT, 1924–28, 346 FINANCIAL CORPORATIONS

(in millions of dollars)

Minor group	Number of corporations	1924	1925	1926	1927	1928
106	18	.09	..	.82	..	..
107	30	2.50	2.81	3.42	3.23	2.50
108	105	..	.66	4.32	..	.47
109	56	3.13	4.92	4.69	.41	.25
110 111–110	137	104.11	170.44	93.31	121.05	283.75
All finance	346	109.83	178.83	106.56	124.69	286.97

APPENDICES

APPENDIX TABLE 6 (continued)

(T) FEDERAL INCOME TAX, 1919–28, 346 FINANCIAL CORPORATIONS

(in millions of dollars)

Minor group	Number of corporations	1919	1920	1921	1922	1923	1924	1925	1926	1927	1928
106	18	.30	.56	.50	.49	.60	.56	.73	.70	.74	.56
107	30	1.60	1.73	1.05	.82	.79	.85	.94	1.11	2.38	1.62
108	105	11.27	14.38	5.89	4.53	3.27	3.39	4.79	5.51	6.23	6.69
109	56	1.89	4.02	1.42	1.69	1.39	1.70	2.64	2.63	3.91	4.02
110											
111–110	137	6.82	5.62	5.42	7.08	6.88	7.58	10.30	10.26	10.91	11.70
All finance	346	21.88	26.31	14.28	14.61	12.93	14.08	19.40	20.21	24.17	24.59

[1] Absolute data for Book III appear in the *Source-Book*.
[2] Net loss.
[3] Figures for minor group 101 include only 8 of the 11 corporations belonging to this group, because of lack of data for the other three corporations.

[647]

Appendix C

SUPPLEMENTARY FREQUENCY DISTRIBUTIONS

Appendix Table 7

FREQUENCY DISTRIBUTIONS OF INDIVIDUAL TOTAL CAPITALS, LARGE IDENTICAL MANUFACTURING CORPORATIONS SERIES

Size of capital (thousands of dollars)	1924	1928
Zero to 249	37	31
250 to 499	193	156
500 to 749	237	203
750 to 999	224	173
1,000 to 1,499	297	290
1,500 to 1,999	174	180
2,000 to 2,499	125	137
2,500 to 2,999	104	105
3,000 to 3,499	59	99
3,500 to 3,999	57	61
4,000 to 4,499	41	43
4,500 to 4,999	49	43
5,000 to 9,999	179	209
10,000 to 14,999	71	89
15,000 to 19,999	43	46
20,000 to 24,999	22	32
25,000 to 49,999	68	67
50,000 and over	66	82
Total frequencies	2,046	2,046

Appendix Table 8

FREQUENCY DISTRIBUTIONS OF PERCENTAGE OF NET INCOME TO CAPITALIZATION, INDIVIDUAL COMPANIES OF LARGE IDENTICAL CORPORATIONS SERIES, COMPARED WITH DISTRIBUTION OF PERCENTAGE PROFIT TO TOTAL CAPITAL, 1928

CLASS INTERVAL (PER CENT)	Major group 1 PERCENTAGE NET INCOME TO CAPITAL-IZATION	Major group 1 PERCENT-AGE PROFIT TO TOTAL CAPITAL	Major group 2 PERCENTAGE NET INCOME TO CAPITAL-IZATION	Major group 2 PERCENT-AGE PROFIT TO TOTAL CAPITAL	Major group 3 PERCENTAGE NET INCOME TO CAPITAL-IZATION	Major group 3 PERCENT-AGE PROFIT TO TOTAL CAPITAL	Major group 4 PERCENTAGE NET INCOME TO CAPITAL-IZATION	Major group 4 PERCENT-AGE PROFIT TO TOTAL CAPITAL
Under zero	4	4	16	16	5	5	6	6
Zero to 4	22	23	70	71	6	6	4	4
5 to 9	53	54	83	82	15	15	5	5
10 to 14	53	56	60	62	16	16	6	7
15 to 19	38	36	33	32	10	10	2	2
20 to 24	24	22	9	10	2	2	.	.
25 to 29	9	8	12	11	.	.	1	1
30 to 34	4	4	2	2	.	.	1	1
35 to 39	2	2	2	2	.	.	.	.
40 to 44	1	1	.	.	.	.	.	.
45 to 49	1	1	2	1	.	.	.	.
50 to 54	.	.	.	.	.	.	.	.
55 to 59	2	2	.	.	.	.	.	.
60 to 64	.	.	.	.	.	.	.	.
65 to 69	.	.	.	.	.	.	.	.
70 to 74	.	.	.	.	.	.	.	.
75 to 79	.	.	.	.	.	.	.	.
80 to 84	.	.	.	.	.	.	.	.
85 to 89	.	.	.	.	.	.	.	.
90 to 94	1	1	.	.	.	.	.	.
95 to 99	.	.	.	.	.	.	.	.

APPENDICES [651]

	Major group 5	Major group 6	Major group 7	Major group 8
100 to 199	. .	. .	. .	. .
200 to 499	1	. .	. .	. .
500 and over	. .	. .	. .	. .
Total frequencies	215	289	54	26

	Major group 5	Major group 6	Major group 7	Major group 8
Under zero	2	2	.	7
Zero to 4	36	14	6	26
5 to 9	53	37	18	38
10 to 14	47	28	30	47
15 to 19	24	11	21	24
20 to 24	17	9	6	27
25 to 29	6	5	8	9
30 to 34	2	2	8	9
35 to 39	2	3	4	6
40 to 44	. .	. .	3	2
45 to 49	. .	. .	1	3
50 to 54	. .	. .	1	3
55 to 59	. .	. .	1	1
60 to 64	1	. .	. .	. .
65 to 69	. .	. .	. .	. .
70 to 74	. .	. .	1	2
75 to 79	. .	. .	. .	. .
80 to 84	. .	. .	. .	. .
85 to 89	. .	. .	. .	. .
90 to 94	. .	. .	. .	1
95 to 99	. .	. .	. .	1
100 to 199	. .	. .	. .	2
200 to 499	. .	. .	. .	3
500 and over	. .	. .	. .	. .
Total frequencies	190	111	100	210

APPENDIX TABLE 8 (continued)

CLASS INTERVAL (PER CENT)	Major group 9 PERCENTAGE NET INCOME TO CAPITALIZATION	Major group 9 PERCENTAGE PROFIT TO TOTAL CAPITAL	Major group 10 PERCENTAGE NET INCOME TO CAPITALIZATION	Major group 10 PERCENTAGE PROFITS TO TOTAL CAPITAL	Major group 11 PERCENTAGE NET INCOME TO CAPITALIZATION	Major group 11 PERCENTAGE PROFIT TO TOTAL CAPITAL
Under zero	3	3	29	29	2	2
Zero to 4	14	13	57	57	10	10
5 to 9	30	33	156	163	20	20
10 to 14	24	23	133	129	25	26
15 to 19	15	15	110	114	8	8
20 to 24	9	10	67	64	15	14
25 to 29	6	6	33	33	6	6
30 to 34	9	8	22	21	2	2
35 to 39	1	1	15	12	..	..
40 to 44	2	1	12	12	1	1
45 to 49	..	..	2	2	..	..
50 to 54	1	1	5	5	..	..
55 to 59	..	..	3	3	..	..
60 to 64	..	..	1	1	..	..
65 to 69	..	..	..	..	..	..
70 to 74	..	..	1	1	..	..
75 to 79	..	..	..	..	..	..
80 to 84	..	..	1	1	..	..
85 to 89	..	..	..	..	..	..
90 to 94	..	..	..	..	..	..
95 to 99	..	..	1	1	..	..
100 to 199	..	..	..	..	..	..
200 to 499	..	..	..	..	..	..
Total frequencies	114	114	648	648	89	89

Appendix D
BLOCK DIAGRAMS OF EARNINGS RATES

APPENDIX CHART 1
FREQUENCY DISTRIBUTIONS OF PERCENTAGE NET INCOME TO CAPITALIZATION, 73 MANUFACTURING GROUPS

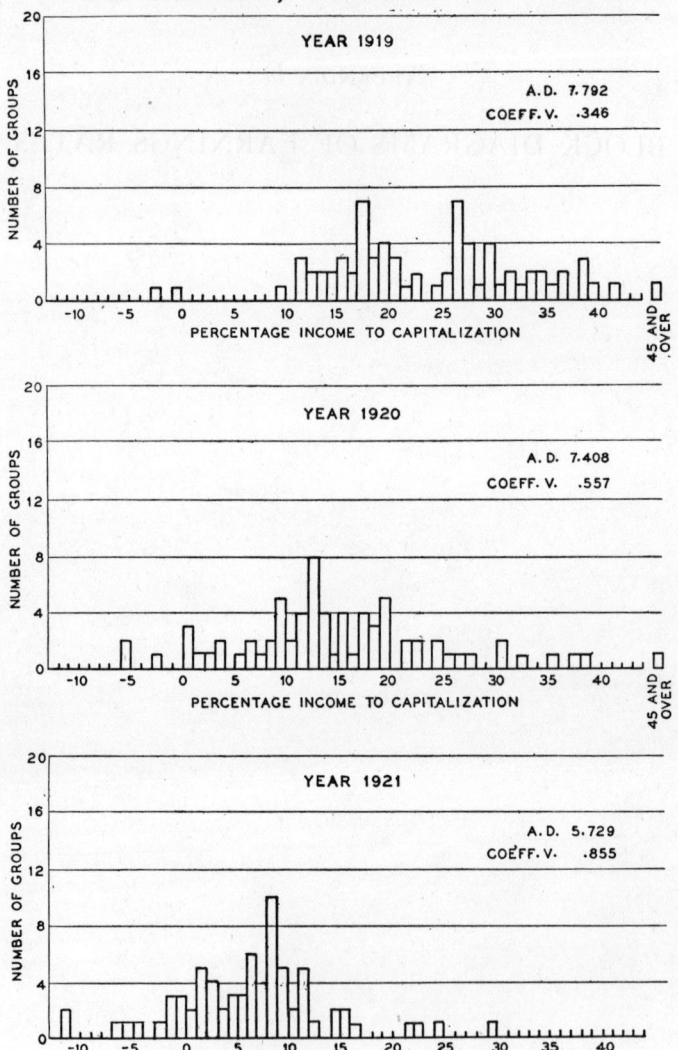

APPENDICES [655]

APPENDIX CHART 1 (CONT.)
FREQUENCY DISTRIBUTIONS OF PERCENTAGE NET INCOME TO CAPITALIZATION, 73 MANUFACTURING GROUPS

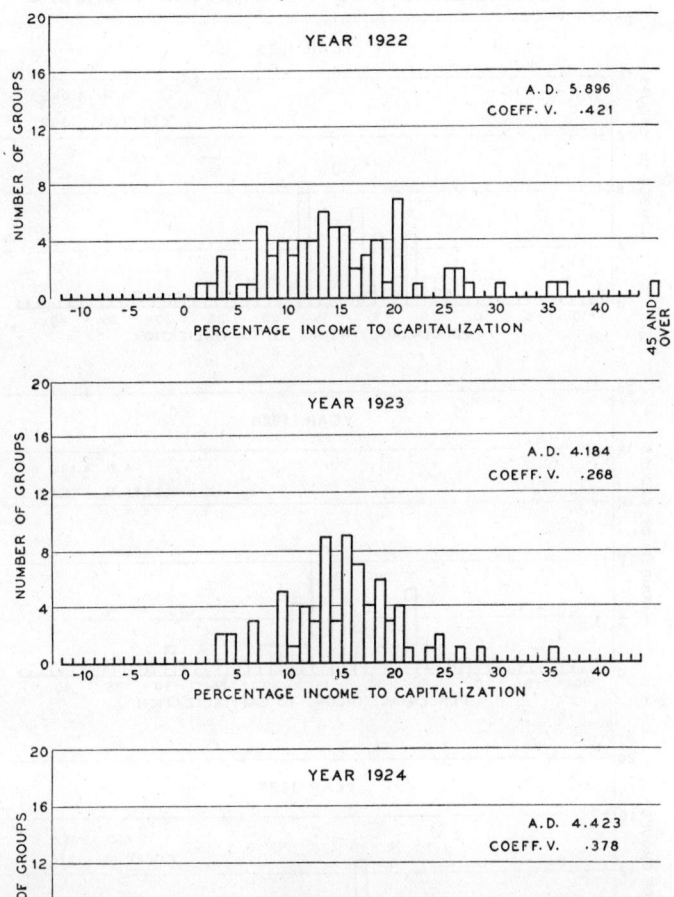

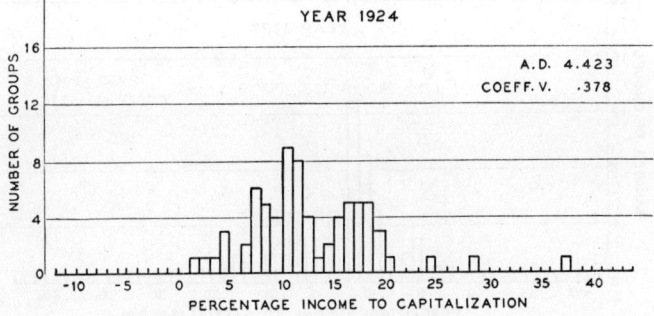

YEAR 1922
A.D. 5.896
COEFF. V. .421

YEAR 1923
A.D. 4.184
COEFF. V. .268

YEAR 1924
A.D. 4.423
COEFF. V. .378

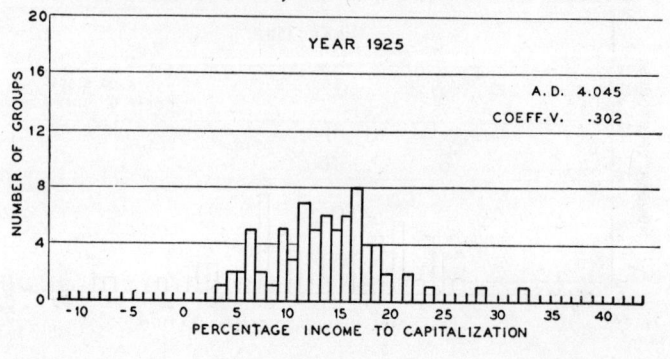

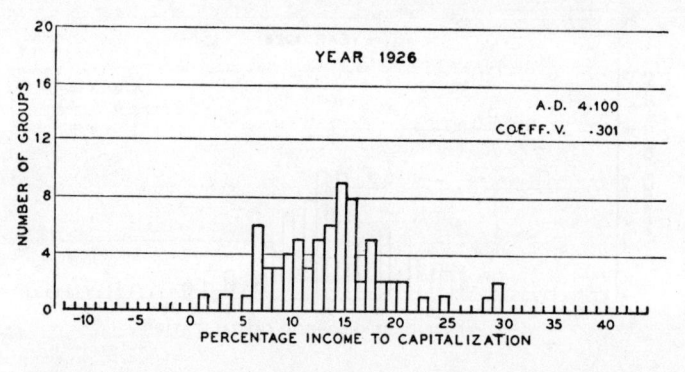

APPENDIX CHART 1 (CONT.)
FREQUENCY DISTRIBUTIONS OF PERCENTAGE NET INCOME TO CAPITALIZATION, 73 MANUFACTURING GROUPS

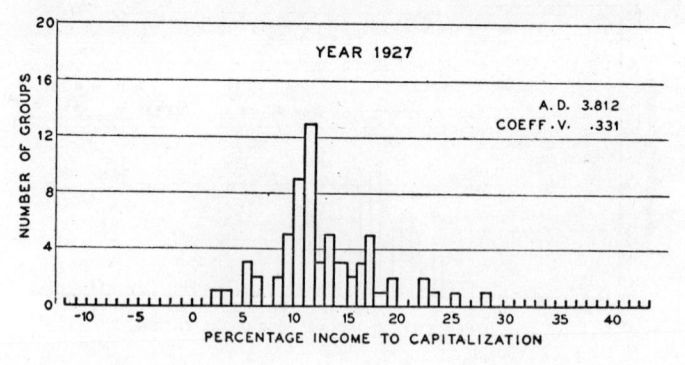

APPENDICES

APPENDIX CHART 1 (CONT.)
FREQUENCY DISTRIBUTIONS OF PERCENTAGE NET INCOME TO CAPITALIZATION, 73 MANUFACTURING GROUPS

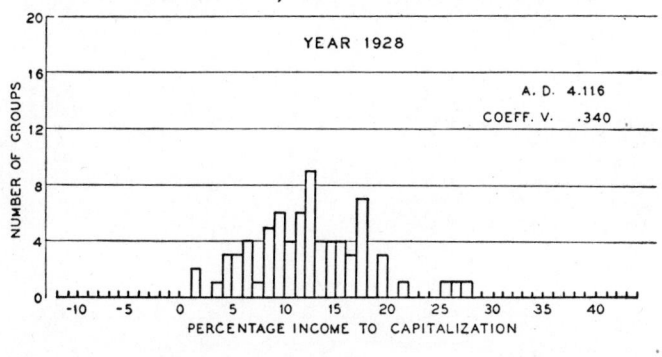

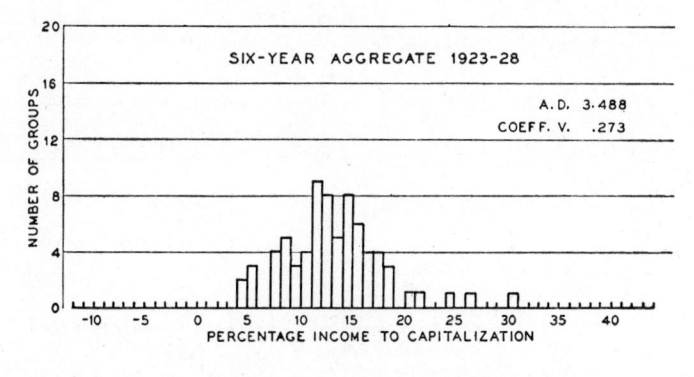

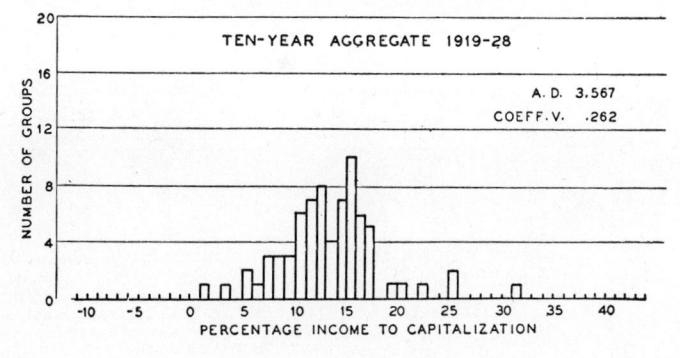

YEAR 1928
A.D. 4.116
COEFF. V. .340

SIX-YEAR AGGREGATE 1923-28
A.D. 3.488
COEFF. V. .273

TEN-YEAR AGGREGATE 1919-28
A.D. 3.567
COEFF. V. .262

TABLES

BOOK I

1 Estimated Earnings Rates, All Corporations in Manufacturing, Trade, Finance and Mining, 1924–28   50
2 Earnings Rates, 3,144 Corporations in Manufacturing, Trade, Finance and Mining, 1919–28 and 1924–28   53
3 Estimated Earnings Rates, All Corporations by Industrial Divisions, 1924–28   54
4 Earnings Rates, 3,144 Corporations by Industrial Divisions, 1919–28 and 1924–28   56
5 Estimated Earnings Rates, All Corporations with Net Incomes in Manufacturing, Trade, Finance and Mining, 1926–28   58
6 Estimated Earnings Rates, All Corporations with Net Incomes in Manufacturing, Trade, Finance and Mining, by Industrial Divisions, 1926–28   58
7 Earnings Rates, Manufacturing Corporations with Net Incomes of over $2,000, 1919–28   60
8 Frequency Distributions of Earnings Rates, Manufacturing Corporations with Net Incomes, 1925–28   63
9 Frequency Distributions of Earnings Rates, Trading Corporations with Net Incomes of over $2,000, 1925–28   64
10 Frequency Distributions of Earnings Rates, Manufacturing Corporations with Net Incomes of over $2,000, 1925–28   65
11 Percentages of Manufacturing Corporations Earning Less than Given Rates of Profit upon Capital, 1925–28   67
12 Minor Group Classification, 3,144 Corporations, Showing Size of Samples   72
13 Earnings Rates, 106 Minor Groups in 1921 and 1928,

	Ranged in Order of Profitableness from the Lowest to the Highest Figures	75
14	Median Difference Coefficients for Relatively Profitable Industries	92
15	Median Difference Coefficients for Relatively Unprofitable Industries	95
16	Average Deviations and Coefficients of Variation for Percentages of Net Income to Capitalization, 27 *Highest* Minor Groups	99
17	Average Earnings Rate, 27 Highest Minor Groups in Each Year 1919–28, Traced through Successive Years and Run Back through 1919	102
18	Average Deviations and Coefficients of Variation for Percentages of Net Income to Capitalization, 27 *Highest* Minor Groups	104
19	Average Deviations and Coefficients of Variation for Percentages of Net Income to Capitalization, 27 *Lowest* Minor Groups	106
20	Average Deviations and Coefficients of Variation for Percentages of Net Income to Capitalization, 10 *Highest* Minor Groups	108
21	Average Deviations and Coefficients of Variation for Percentages of Net Income to Capitalization, 10 *Lowest* Minor Groups	109
22	73 Manufacturing Groups, Return on Sales and Rate of Capital Turnover, 1928	118
23	73 Manufacturing Groups Ranked by Earnings Rates	122
24	22 Trading Groups, Return on Sales and Rate of Capital Turnover, 1928	125
25	22 Trading Groups Ranked by Earnings Rates	126
26	Earnings Rates, 2,046 Manufacturing Corporations by Capital Classes, 1924 and 1928	133
27	Earnings Rates in Foods, Chemicals and Metals, by Broad Capital Classes	136
28	Earnings Rates in Foods, Chemicals and Metals, by Detailed Capital Classes	138
29	Code for Geographical Regions	141
30	Earnings Rates, 2,046 Manufacturing Corporations Classified by Geographical Regions, 1924 and 1928	142

TABLES

31	Earnings Rates, 664 Trading Corporations Classified by Geographical Regions, 1924 and 1928	143
32	Earnings Rates, 71 Companies by Major Groups, 1919–31	156
33	71 Companies Series, Percentage Income to Capitalization after Tax, by Major Groups	157
34	Ranges in Percentages of Net Income to Capitalization, for 15 Industries Showing Increasing Earnings Rates, 1922–28	166
35	Ranges in Percentages of Net Income to Capitalization, for 28 Industries Showing Declining Earnings Rates, 1922–28	168
36	Condensed Composite Balance Sheets of 71 Companies in All Major Manufacturing Groups as of December 31, 1927–30	187
37	Rank of 73 Manufacturing Groups in Sales Decline Compared with Rank in Income Decline, 1920–21	195
38	Rank of 73 Manufacturing Groups in Sales Increase Compared with Rank in Income Increase, 1921–22	198
39	Rank of 73 Manufacturing Groups in Sales Decline, 1920–21, Compared with Rank in Sales Increase, 1921–22	200
40	Rank of 73 Manufacturing Groups in Income Decline, 1920–21, Compared with Rank in Income Increase, 1921–22	202
41	Average Income and Sales Declines, 1920–21, Ranged by Sales Decline Classes, 67 Manufacturing Industries	205

BOOK II

Manufacturing—Large Identical Corporations Series:

42	Manufacturing and Its Major Groups	241
43	Foods Groups	247
44	Textile Groups	252
45	Leather and Leather Products	258
46	Rubber and Rubber Products	262
47	Lumber Groups	266
48	Paper Groups	270
49	Printing and Publishing Groups	274
50	Chemical Groups	279

51	Stone, Clay and Glass Groups	283
52	Metals Groups	289
53	Special Manufacturing Industries Groups	296

Trading—Large Identical Corporations Series:

54	Trade and Its Major Groups	309
55	Retail Trade Groups	314
56	Wholesale Trade Groups	318
57	Wholesale and Retail Trade Groups	323
58	Mining Groups, Large Identical Corporations Series	332
59	Finance Groups, Large Identical Corporations Series	342

BOOK III

60	Manufacturing and Its Major Groups, Small Non-identical Corporations Series	364
61	Manufacturing and Its Major Groups, Large Identical Corporations Series	369
62	Foods Groups, Small Non-identical Manufacturing Corporations Series	372
63	Distributions of Earnings Rates, Foods, Large Identical Manufacturing Corporations Series	376
64	Textile Groups, Small Non-identical Manufacturing Corporations Series	379
65	Distributions of Earnings Rates, Textiles, Large Identical Manufacturing Corporations Series	382
66	Leather and Leather Products, Small Non-identical Manufacturing Corporations Series	385
67	Distributions of Earnings Rates, Leather, Large Identical Manufacturing Corporations Series	388
68	Rubber and Rubber Products, Small Non-identical Manufacturing Corporations Series	391
69	Distributions of Earnings Rates, Rubber, Large Identical Manufacturing Corporations Series	393
70	Lumber Groups, Small Non-identical Manufacturing Corporations Series	395
71	Distributions of Earnings Rates, Lumber, Large Identical Manufacturing Corporations Series	398
72	Paper Groups, Small Non-identical Manufacturing Corporations Series	401

TABLES [663]

73 Distributions of Earnings Rates, Paper, Large Identical Manufacturing Corporations Series ... 404
74 Printing and Publishing Groups, Small Non-identical Manufacturing Corporations Series ... 407
75 Distributions of Earnings Rates, Printing and Publishing, Large Identical Manufacturing Corporations Series ... 410
76 Chemical Groups, Small Non-identical Manufacturing Corporations Series ... 413
77 Distributions of Earnings Rates, Chemicals, Large Identical Manufacturing Corporations Series ... 416
78 Stone, Clay and Glass Groups, Small Non-identical Manufacturing Corporations Series ... 419
79 Distributions of Earnings Rates, Stone, Clay and Glass, Large Indentical Manufacturing Corporations Series ... 422
80 Metals Groups, Small Non-identical Manufacturing Corporations Series ... 425
81 Distributions of Earnings Rates, Metals, Large Identical Manufacturing Corporations Series ... 429
82 Special Manufacturing Industries Groups, Small Non-identical Corporations Series ... 431
83 Distributions of Earnings Rates, Special Manufacturing Industries Groups, Large Identical Corporations Series ... 434
84 Trade and Its Major Groups, Small Non-identical Corporations Series ... 439
85 Frequency Distributions of Percentages of Total Profit to Total Capital, Individual Corporations, 1925–28. All Trade ... 441
86 Retail Trade Groups, Small Non-identical Corporations Series ... 443
87 Frequency Distributions of Percentages of Total Profit to Total Capital, Individual Corporations, 1925–28. Major Group 12: Retail Trade ... 446
88 Wholesale Trade Groups, Small Non-identical Corporations Series ... 448
89 Frequency Distributions of Percentages of Total Profit to Total Capital, Individual Corporations, 1925–28. Major Group 13: Wholesale Trade ... 451

BOOK IV

90	Frequency Distributions of Net Incomes for All Manufacturing Corporations in the United States with Incomes of over $50,000 in 1928	467
91	Frequency Distributions of Total Net Incomes for Companies with Incomes of over $50,000, in the Large Manufacturing Corporations Sample, 1928	468
92	Quartiles for Size of Capital per Corporation in Large Manufacturing Corporations Sample, 1919–28	470
93	Quartiles for Size of Net Income per Corporation in Large Manufacturing Corporations Sample, 1919–28	470
94	Sales of the Large Manufacturing Corporations Sample Compared with the Sales of All Corporations in the United States, by Major Groups, 1928	471
95	Net Income of the Large Manufacturing Corporations Sample Compared with the Net Income of All Corporations in the United States, by Major Groups, 1928	472
96	Net Incomes for All Manufacturing Corporations with Incomes of over $50,000 in the United States, 1928	474
97	Total Net Incomes for Companies with Incomes of over $50,000 in the Large Manufacturing Corporations Sample, 1928	475
98	Frequency Distributions of Net Incomes for all Manufacturing Corporations in the United States with Incomes from $2,000 to $50,000 in 1928	478
99	Frequency Distributions of Total Net Incomes for Companies with Incomes from $2,000 to $50,000 in the Small Manufacturing Corporations Sample, 1928	478
100	Frequency Distributions of Net Incomes for all Manufacturing Corporations in the United States with Incomes from $2,000 to $50,000, by Major Groups, 1928	480
101	Frequency Distributions of Total Net Incomes for Companies in the Small Manufacturing Corporations Sample with Incomes from $2,000 to $50,000, by Major Groups, 1928	481
102	Basic Data Underlying the Determination of Weights Employed in Preparation of Estimated Frequency Distributions of Earnings of Individual Manufacturing Corporations in the United States, 1925–1928	487

TABLES [665]

103 Frequency Distributions of Net Incomes for All Trading Corporations in the United States with Incomes over $50,000 in 1928   490
104 Frequency Distributions of Total Net Incomes for Companies with Incomes of over $50,000 in the Large Trading Corporations Sample, 1928   490
105 Frequency Distributions of Net Incomes for All Mining Corporations in the United States with Incomes over $50,000 in 1928   492
106 Frequency Distributions of Total Net Incomes for Companies with Incomes of over $50,000 in the large Mining Corporations Sample, 1928   493
107 Frequency Distributions of Net Income for All Financial Corporations in the United States with Incomes of over $50,000 in 1928   494
108 Frequency Distributions of Total Net Incomes for Companies with Incomes of over $50,000 in the Large Financial Corporations Sample, 1928   494
109 Earnings Rates upon Investment for Seven Groups, Sample and Universe, 1919–28   501
110 Deviations from Mean Earnings Rate upon Investment, 1919–28, and from Ten-year Aggregate Rate, Seven Minor Groups   509
111 Earnings Rates upon Investment for Seven Groups, Sample and Universe, 1919–28   517
112 Deviations from Mean Earnings Rate upon Investment, 1919–28, and from Ten-year Aggregate Rate, Seven Minor Groups   521
113 Dividends Received in Relation to Net Income: Large Identical Manufacturing Corporations Series, 1928   559
114 Classification of 2,046 Manufacturing Corporations: Consolidated or Not Consolidated, 1928   563
115 Percentage of Net Loss to Capitalization: Small Nonidentical Manufacturing Corporations with Negative Incomes in 1926 and 1928   571

Appendix Tables
1 Absolute Data Underlying Text Table 1   612
2 Absolute Data Underlying Text Table 2   613
3 Absolute Data Underlying Text Table 5   614
4 Absolute Data Underlying Text Table 7   615

5	Data for Charts 35 to 38	615
6	Absolute Data Underlying Tables in Book II	617
7	Frequency Distributions of Individual Total Capitals, Large Identical Manufacturing Corporations Series	649
8	Frequency Distributions of Percentage of Net Income to Capitalization, Individual Companies of Large Identical Corporations Series, Compared with Distribution of Percentage Profit to Total Capital, 1928	650

CHARTS

BOOK I

1 Percentage of Net Income to Capitalization, 3,144 Corporations by Industrial Divisions, 1919–28   55
2 Frequency Distributions of Earning Rates, All Manufacturing Corporations with Net Incomes, 1925–28   62
3 Frequency Distributions of Percentage of Income to Capitalization, 106 Minor Groups   80
4 Interquartile Range, Percentage Income to Capitalization, 106 Minor Groups   85
5 Coefficients of Variation of 27 Highest Minor Groups in each year, 1919–24, followed through Successive Years   98
6 Earnings Rates, 2,046 Manufacturing Corporations   117
7 Percentage of Net Income to Sales and Percentage of Total Profit to Total Capital, 664 Trading Corporations   124
8 Percentage of Net Income to Capitalization, 2,046 Corporations, All Manufacturing Groups, 1919–28   145
9 Percentages of Net Income to Capitalization, as Relatives on 1927 Base, 2,046 Corporations, All Manufacturing Groups, 1919–28   147
10 Frequency Distribution of Individual Percentages of Total Profit to Total Capital, 2,046 Manufacturing Corporations, 1926 and 1928   148
11 Volume of Sales, Capitalization and Net Income, 2,046 Corporations, All Manufacturing Groups, 1919–28   148
12 Total Profit, Total Sales and Total Disbursements to Security-Holders, All Manufacturing Groups, 1924–28   150
13 Total Profit as a Percentage of Sales, All Manufacturing Groups, 1924–28   151
14 Percentage of Net Income to Capitalization, after Tax,

	1919–28, 2,046 Manufacturing Corporations and a Sample of 71 Companies	153
15	Percentage of Net Income to Capitalization, after Tax, 71 Manufacturing Companies, 1919–31	154
16	Relatives for Earnings Rates for 71 Manufacturing Companies and for *Annalist* and A. T. and T. Indexes of Business Activity, 1919–31	158
17	Percentage of Net Income to Capitalization, 15 Industries Showing Increasing Earnings Rates, 1922–28	165
18	Sales and Capitalization, 15 Industries Showing Increasing Earnings Rates, 1922–28	166
19	Percentage of Net Income to Capitalization, 28 Industries Showing Declining Earnings Rates, 1922–28	169
20	Sales and Capitalization, 28 Industries Showing Declining Earnings Rates, 1922–28	170
21	Percentage of Net Income to Capitalization, 30 Industries Showing No Trend in Earnings Rates, 1922–28	171
22	Sales and Capitalization, 30 Industries Showing No Trend in Earnings Rates, 1922–28	171
23	Percentage of Net Income to Capitalization, 13 Industries in which Capitalization Grew Faster than Sales, 1922–28	173
24	Sales and Capitalization, 13 Industries in which Capitalization Grew Faster than Sales, 1922–28	174
25	Percentage of Net Income to Capitalization in Two Minor Groups, 1922–28	176
26	Sales and Capitalization in Two Minor Groups, 1922–28	177
27	Percentage of Net Income to Capitalization in Two Minor Groups, 1922–28	178
28	Sales and Capitalization in Two Minor Groups, 1922–28	179
29	Percentage of Net Income to Capitalization, Producers' Goods and Consumers' Goods Industries, 1922–28	181
30	Sales and Capitalization, Consumers' Goods Industries, 1922–28	182
31	Sales and Capitalization, Producers' Goods Industries, 1922–28	182
32	Sales in 'Quick', 'Intermediate' and 'Durable' Consumption Goods Industries, 1922–28	184
33	Capitalization in "Quick," 'Intermediate" and "Durable" Consumption Goods Industries, 1922–28	185

CHARTS [669]

34 Percentage of Net Income to Capitalization in "Quick," "Intermediate" and "Durable" Consumption Goods Industries, 1922–28   185
35 Dispersion of Percentage Declines in Sales and Income in 73 Manufacturing Industries, 1921 Compared with 1920 (or 1919)   190
36 Dispersion of Percentage Declines or Increases in Sales and Income in 73 Manufacturing Industries, 1924 Compared with 1923   192
37 Dispersion of Percentage Declines or Increases in Sales and Income in 73 Manufacturing Industries, 1927 Compared with 1926   194
38 Ratio of Income Declines to Sales Declines, Ranged by Sales Decline Classes, 1921 Compared with 1920   205

BOOK II

Identical Corporations Series, 1919–28:
39 All Manufacture   218
40 Major Group 1: Foods   220
41 Major Group 2: Textiles   222
42 Major Group 3: Leather   223
43 Major Group 4: Rubber   225
44 Major Group 5: Lumber   227
45 Major Group 6: Paper   229
46 Major Group 7: Printing and Publishing   230
47 Major Group 8: Chemicals   231
48 Major Group 9: Stone, Clay and Glass   233
49 Major Group 10: Metals   235
50 Major Group 11: Special Manufacturing Industries   237

51 Frequency Distribution of Earnings Rates, Individual Companies (identical corporations series), All Manufacture   240

Identical Corporations Series, 1919–28:
52 All Trading Corporations   301
53 Major Group 12: Retail Trade   303
54 Major Group 13: Wholesale Trade   305
55 Major Group 14: Wholesale and Retail Trade   306

56	Frequency Distribution of Earnings Rates, Individual Companies (identical corporations series), All Trade	308
57	Identical Corporations Series, 1919–28, Major Group 15: Mining	329
58	Frequency Distribution of Earnings Rates, Individual Companies (identical corporations series), Major Group 15: All Mining	331
59	Identical Corporations Series, 1919–28, Major Group 16: Finance	339
60	Frequency Distribution of Earnings Rates, Individual Companies (identical corporations series), Major Group 16: All Finance	341

BOOK III

61	Percentage Net Income to Sales, All Manufacture	354
62	Arithmetic Mean Percentage Net Income to Capitalization, All Manufacture	357
63	Median Earnings Rates, All Manufacture	358
64	Frequency Distribution of Earnings Rates, Individual Companies, All Manufacture	362
65	Frequency Distribution of Earnings Rates, Individual Companies, All Trade	438

BOOK IV

66	Frequency Distribution of Earnings Rates of Individual Corporations for 1928: Small Manufacturing Corporations with Net Income under $2,000	483
67	Earnings Rates of Seven Minor Group Samples and Their Universes: Identical Corporations Series	505
68	Earnings Rates of Seven Minor Group Samples and Their Universes: Non-identical Corporations Series	518

Appendix Chart

1	Frequency Distributions of Percentage Net Income to Capitalization, 73 Manufacturing Groups	654

INDEX

American Telephone and Telegraph Company, 157n, 158, 192–3
Annalist, 157n, 158, 192
Assets, capital, 186–8, 531–45
Automobiles
  accessories, 443–6
  trade, 73, 77, 78, 90, 91, 92, 125, 126, 313–7, 443–6, 633, 634, 636, 638, 639
Average deviation, 96, 104, 106, 108–9
Averages
  inadequacy of, 588–9
  value of, 577–8
BAGWELL, LUCILE, 35n
Bakery products, 72, 78, 118, 122, 197, 199, 201, 203, 247–51, 371–7, 515, 516, 517, 518, 521, 523, 559, 571, 616, 620, 623, 627, 630
Banks (*see also* Trust companies)
  commercial, 73, 76, 77, 342–5, 643, 644, 645, 646
  national, 73, 76, 77, 342–5, 643, 644, 645, 646
  savings, 73, 76, 77, 342–5, 544, 643, 644, 645, 646
Beverages, 43, 72, 75, 76, 93, 95, 118, 122, 165, 166, 195, 198, 201, 203, 247–51, 559, 617, 620, 623, 627, 630
BLISS, J. H., 35n, 114n
Bolts and nuts, 72, 75, 78, 120, 123, 195, 198, 200, 202, 287–94, 560, 619, 622, 625, 628, 632
Boots and shoes
  manufacture, 43, 72, 77, 92, 118, 122, 197, 199, 201, 203, 258–61, 559, 617, 620, 624, 627, 630
  trade, 443–6

BOWMAN, RAYMOND T., 35n
Boxes, cardboard, 72, 75, 77, 119, 122, 195, 198, 200, 202, 270–3, 400–5, 559, 617, 621, 624, 627, 631
Building material, 73, 75, 76, 125, 126, 313–7, 318–22, 633, 634, 635, 636, 638, 639 (*see also* Lumber)
Bureau of Internal Revenue (*see* Internal Revenue)
BURR, SUSAN S., 549n, 550, 551, 552, 568
BURTON, E. R., 545n
Business planning (*see* Planning)

Canned goods, 72, 77, 118, 122, 167, 168, 196, 198–200, 203, 247–51, 559, 617, 620, 623, 627, 630
Capital, 611–4 (*see also* Definitions of terms)
  concentration of, 137–40
  mobility of, 107, 111–2, 581
  return on, 40, 579–83
Capitalization, 50–113, 595–6, 602–3, 611–4, 623–6, 636–7, 641, 644 (*see also* Definitions of terms)
Carpets, 72, 75, 78, 118, 122, 167, 168, 197, 198, 201, 203, 252–7, 559, 617, 620, 624, 627, 630
Castings and forgings, 43, 72, 75, 84, 93, 95, 119, 123, 165, 166, 196, 198, 200, 202, 287–94, 424–9, 515, 516, 517, 519, 522, 523, 560, 571, 618, 621, 625, 628, 631
Cement, Portland, 72, 77, 119, 120–1, 123, 167, 168, 173, 175, 178–9, 197, 198, 201, 203, 283–6, 560, 618, 621, 625, 628, 631
Ceramics, 72, 76, 119, 123, 167, 168,

[671]

INDEX

196, 198, 201, 203, 283–6, 418–23, 560, 618, 621, 625, 628, 631
Chemicals
  all, 135–7, 138, 139–40, 152n, 154n, 156, 157, 159–60, 186, 228, 231–2, 241–5, 278–82, 356, 360, 364–9, 412–7, 471–5, 480–1, 528, 558, 560, 564, 572, 614–6, 619, 623, 626, 629, 632
  Crude, 72, 76, 77, 119, 122, 165, 166, 196, 198, 200, 203, 278–82, 559, 618, 621, 624, 627, 631
  miscellaneous, 72, 76, 78, 117, 119, 123, 165, 166, 196, 199, 200, 203, 278–82, 560, 618, 621, 625, 628, 631
CLARK, FLORENCE M., 16, 35n, 595
CLARK, J. M., 3, 589n
Classification, problems of, 548–76
Clay (*see also* Stone, Glass)
  all manufacture, 232–3, 241–5, 283–6, 356, 360–1, 364–9, 418–23, 471–5, 480–1, 528, 561, 564, 572, 619, 623, 626, 629, 633
  mining, 73, 75, 77, 330–6, 640, 641, 642, 643
    miscellaneous products, manufacture of, 72, 76, 78, 119, 123, 196, 198, 200, 202, 283–6, 418–23, 560, 571, 618, 621, 625, 628, 631
Cleaning preparations, 72, 77, 78, 119, 123, 165, 166, 197, 199, 201, 202, 278–82, 560, 618, 621, 625, 628, 631
Clothing
  men's manufacture of, 72, 76, 77, 118, 122, 183, 196, 198, 201, 202, 252–7, 378–83, 530, 559, 571, 617, 620, 624, 627, 630;
    trade of, 73, 77, 125, 126, 313–7, 443–6, 633, 634, 636, 638, 639
  miscellaneous, 72, 76, 77, 118, 122, 196, 199, 200, 202, 252–7, 378–83, 559, 571, 617, 620, 624, 627, 630

Coal (*see also* Fuel, Lumber, Wood).
  bituminous mining, 73, 75, 77, 330–6, 640, 641, 642, 643
  trade, 73, 76, 125, 126, 127, 323–6, 633, 634, 635, 636, 638, 639
Coefficient of variation, 96–100, 104, 106, 108–9
Commission dealers, 73
Committee on Recent Economic Changes, 3, 4
Competition, 111–2
Confectionery, 43, 72, 76, 77, 118, 122, 196, 199, 200, 202, 247–51, 371–7, 530, 559, 616, 620, 623, 627, 630
Consolidated corporations, 550, 552–5, 561–5
Consumers' goods industries, 47–8, 180–6
Control of production, 33–4, 178, 587–9
COPELAND, MELVIN T., 13n
Cotton
  converting, 72, 76, 77, 118, 122, 167, 168, 196, 199, 200, 202, 252–7, 559, 617, 620, 623, 627, 630
  spinning, 72, 76, 77, 118, 122, 195, 198, 200, 202, 252–7, 498, 501, 505, 507, 509, 511, 512, 559, 617, 620, 623, 627, 630
  weaving, 72, 75, 77, 118, 122, 196, 199, 200, 202, 252–7, 559, 617, 620, 623, 627, 630
CRUM, WILLIAM L., 35n, 86n, 115n, 128n, 548n, 556n, 566n, 568, 576n, 589n, 592
Cycles in profits, 144–205

Dairying, 72, 76, 77, 118, 120–1, 122, 167, 168, 173, 197, 198, 201, 203, 247–51, 371–7, 515, 516, 517, 518, 521, 523, 559, 571, 616, 620, 623, 627, 630
Deficits, 462–4, 569–75
Definitions of terms, 40–1, 50, 91, 163–4, 170, 210–1, 595–7
Demand (*see* Supply and demand)

INDEX [673]

DENNISON, HENRY S., 545*n*
Depletion, 545
Depreciation, 532–44, 581*n*
Diversity of economic data, 577–8
Dividends, 236, 304–6
DORIOT, GEORGES F., 13*n*
Drugs, 73, 76, 77, 125, 126, 313–7, 318–22, 443–6, 447–51, 633, 635, 636, 638, 639
Drygoods, 73, 76, 77, 95, 125, 126, 313–7, 318–22, 443–6, 447–51, 633, 635, 636, 638, 639

Earnings rates, 39–60, 595, 611–4
  (*see also* Definitions of terms)
  by geographical regions, 140–3, 575–6
  by size of corporations, 131–7
  distribution of, 60–8, 79–86
  permanence of differences in, 88–113
  range of, 41–3
  uniformity of, 577–9
  variation in, 44–7, 70–8
EBERSOLE, J. FRANKLIN, 549, 550, 551, 552, 554, 556*n*, 557*n*, 568, 569*n*
ELLIS, HAVELOCK, 37*n*
Engines, 72, 75, 77, 119, 123, 167, 168, 173, 196, 198, 200, 203, 287–94, 498, 501, 504, 507, 508, 510, 511, 512, 560, 618, 621, 625, 628, 632
EPSTEIN, LILLIAN, 590*n*
EPSTEIN, RALPH C., 16, 19*n*, 35*n*, 86*n*, 128*n*, 595
Equality of earnings rates, 33–4, 112
  as affected by risk, 86–8
  conclusions concerning, 101–11, 579–82
  J. S. Mill's statement of, 586*n*
  over ten-year period, 84–6
Equilibrium (*see* Supply and demand)
Exporters (*see* Importers and exporters)

FABRICANT, SOLOMON, 8*n*

Federal Trade Commission, 5*n*, 13*n*
Finance, 52–9, 66, 73, 76, 77, 213–5, 337–45, 544, 643, 644, 645, 646
Firearms, 72, 76, 78, 119, 123, 165, 167, 196, 198, 200, 202, 287–94, 560, 618, 622, 625, 628, 632
Flour, 72, 77, 118, 120–1, 122, 196, 199, 200, 202, 247–51, 371–7, 515, 516, 517, 518, 521, 523, 559, 571, 616, 620, 623, 627, 630
Foods
  all, 134–6, 138, 139–40, 152*n*, 154*n*, 156, 157, 160, 183, 219–21, 241–5, 247–51, 355, 359, 364–9, 371–7, 471–5, 480–1, 528, 529, 558, 560, 563, 572, 614–6, 619, 622, 626, 628, 632
  miscellaneous products, 43, 72, 75, 76, 95, 118, 122, 195, 199, 200, 202, 247–51, 371–7, 559, 571, 617, 620, 623, 627, 630
Forgings (*see* Castings and forgings)
FRASER, CECILE E., 13*n*
Frequency distributions
  and trade, 62–7
  of earnings rates in manufacture, 61–3, 65–6
  of earnings in 106 industries, 80–6
  of earnings in 73 industries, 652–5
FRIDAY, DAVID, 35*n*
Fuel, 73, 76, 125, 127, 323–6, 633, 634, 635, 636, 638, 639 (*see also* Coal, Wood)
Furniture
  manufacture, 72, 76, 77, 92, 119, 122, 167, 168, 183, 196, 198, 201, 203, 266–9, 394–9, 559, 617, 621, 624, 627, 631
  trade, 73, 76, 77, 125, 126, 313–7, 443–6, 447–51, 633, 635, 636, 638, 639

Gas and oil wells, 73, 75, 93, 95, 330–6, 640, 641, 642, 643
General Electric Company, 532–40
General Motors Corporation, 537*n*, 540*n*
Glass, 72, 77, 92, 119, 123, 167, 168,

173, 196, 198, 200, 202, 232–3, 241–5, 283–6, 356, 360–1, 364–9, 418–23, 471–5, 480–1, 528, 560, 561, 564, 572, 618, 619, 621, 623, 625, 626, 628, 629, 631, 633
Goodwill, 526–31
Gravel, 73, 77, 330–6, 640, 641, 642, 643
Groceries, 73, 75, 76, 78, 91, 92, 95, 125, 126, 313–7, 318–22, 443–6, 447–51, 633, 635, 636, 638, 639
Gross income (*see* Income, gross)

Haberdashery, 443–6
Hardware
  manufacture, 72, 76, 119, 123, 167, 168, 196, 198, 200, 202, 287–94, 560, 618, 622, 625, 628, 632
  trade, 73, 75, 76, 95, 125, 126, 127, 313–7, 318–22, 323–6, 443–6, 447–51, 633, 634, 635, 636, 638, 639
HAYEK, F. A., 589*n*
HAYES, GORDON, 159*n*

Importers and exporters, 73, 76, 77, 125, 126, 318–22, 634, 635, 636, 638, 639
Income
  gross, 337–45, 643
  intercorporate, 557–61
  net, 50–113, 191–205, 568–72, 595, 604, 611–4, 620–3, 634–5, 641, 644
Index numbers, 589*n*
Instruments, scientific, 43, 73, 78, 84, 90, 92, 120–1, 123, 197, 199, 201, 203, 295–9, 560, 619, 622, 625, 628, 632
Interest, 49–69, 601, 607–8 (*see also* Definitions of terms, Methods, explanation of)
Internal Revenue, Bureau of, 8, 16, 19, 32, 45*n*, 581*n*
Investment, 46, 47, 114–27, 172–80, 186–8, 583–7, 595, 601–2 (*see also* Definitions of terms, Capital, mobility of)

Jewelry
  manufacture, 73, 76, 77, 120, 123, 183, 196, 199, 200, 202, 287–94, 560, 619, 622, 625, 628, 632
  trade, 73, 76, 77, 125, 126, 313–7, 443–6, 447–51, 633, 635, 636, 638, 639

KESTER, R. B., 537*n*, 574*n*
KNAUTH, OSWALD W., 543*n*
KNIGHT, FRANK H., 87*n*
Knit goods, 72, 76, 78, 118, 122, 167, 168, 173, 196, 198, 201, 203, 252–7, 378–83, 515, 516, 517, 519, 521, 523, 559, 571, 617, 620, 624, 627, 630
KUZNETS, SIMON, 8*n*

LAIDLER, HARRY W., 128*n*
Leather
  all, 152*n*, 154*n*, 156, 157, 223–4, 241–5, 258–61, 355, 359, 364–9, 384–9, 471–5, 480–1, 528, 560, 563, 570, 572, 614–6, 619, 622, 626, 628, 632
  miscellaneous products, 43, 72, 75, 118, 120–1, 122, 195, 198, 200, 202, 258–61, 384–9, 559, 617, 620, 624, 627, 630
LEWIS, J. W., 534*n*
LIVERMORE, SHAW, 128*n*
Lumber (*see also* Building material)
  manufacture, 72, 75, 76, 118, 122, 152*n*, 154*n*, 156, 157, 167, 168, 196, 198, 200, 202, 225–7, 241–5, 266–9, 355, 360, 364–9, 394–9, 471–5, 480–1, 515, 516, 517, 519, 520, 521, 523, 528, 559, 560, 563, 571, 572, 614–6, 617, 619, 620, 622, 624, 626, 627, 628, 630, 632
  trade, 73, 75, 76, 125, 126, 127, 313–7, 318–22, 323–6, 633, 634, 635, 636, 638, 639

Machinery (*see also* Engines)
  electrical, 72, 76, 77, 119, 123, 165, 166, 197, 198, 201, 203, 287–94, 540, 560, 571, 618, 621, 625, 628, 631

INDEX [675]

factory, 72, 76, 77, 115, 119, 120–1, 123, 165, 166, 196, 198, 201, 202, 287–94, 560, 618, 622, 625, 628, 632
heating, 72, 76, 119, 123, 167, 168, 196, 198, 200, 202, 287–94, 424–9, 560, 618, 621, 625, 628, 631
mining, 72, 76, 119, 123, 196, 198, 200, 202, 287–94, 560, 618, 622, 625, 628, 632
miscellaneous, 72, 75, 77, 120, 123, 165, 167, 196, 199, 200, 202, 287–94, 424–9, 560, 571, 619, 622, 625, 628, 632
office, 72, 76, 78, 119, 123, 197, 199, 201, 203, 287–94, 560, 618, 622, 625, 628, 632
printing, 72, 77, 119, 123, 197, 199, 201, 203, 287–94, 560, 618, 621, 625, 628, 631
textile, 72, 77, 78, 92, 119, 120–1, 123, 167, 168, 173, 197, 199, 201, 203, 287–94, 498, 501, 506, 508, 509, 511, 512, 513, 560, 618, 621, 625, 628, 631

Manufacture
all, dividends, 236; earnings, 52–60, 131–4, 217–9, 238–45, 353–69; investment, 116–23, 216–9, 356–61; sales, 116–23, 216–8, 353–6
special industries, 73, 77, 92, 120, 123, 152n, 154n, 156, 157, 167, 168, 197, 199, 201, 203, 234, 236, 237, 241–5, 295–9, 356, 361, 364–9, 430–5, 471–5, 480–1, 528, 560, 561, 572, 614–6, 619, 622, 623, 625, 626, 628, 629, 632, 633

MARSHALL, ALFRED, 33, 34n, 88n, 580
MAY, GEORGE O., 5n, 14, 526
MEANS, GARDINER C., 128n, 137
Meat packing, 43, 72, 75, 84, 93, 95, 114, 117, 118, 120–1, 122, 165, 166, 196, 199, 200, 202, 247–51, 371–7, 559, 617, 620, 623, 627, 630
Median difference coefficient, 91–2, 95
Metal, sheet, 72, 75, 77, 119, 123, 172, 195, 198, 200, 202, 287–94, 424–9, 560, 618, 621, 625, 628, 631
Metals
all, 93, 136, 137, 138, 139–40, 152n, 154n, 156, 157, 159–60, 186, 234–5, 241–5, 287–94, 356, 361, 364–9, 424–9, 471–5, 480–1, 528, 529, 558, 561, 564, 572, 614–6, 619, 623, 626, 629, 633.
miscellaneous products, 73, 77, 120, 123, 165, 167, 195, 199, 200, 202, 287–94, 424–9, 560, 572, 619, 622, 625, 628, 632
non-ferrous, 72, 76, 77, 120, 123, 165, 167, 196, 198, 200, 202, 287–94, 560, 619, 622, 625, 628, 632

Methods, explanation of, 484–8, 601–9
MILL, JOHN STUART, 34n, 88n, 586n
MILLS, F. C., 3, 19n, 37n, 88n, 577, 578, 589n
Mills, planing, 43, 72, 76, 77, 119, 122, 167, 195, 198, 200, 203, 266–9, 559, 617, 621, 624, 627, 631
Millwork, 72, 76, 119, 122, 167, 168, 196, 200, 202, 266–9, 559, 617, 621, 624, 627, 631
Mining
all, 52–9, 66, 73, 213–5, 327–36, 545, 640, 641, 642, 643
metal, 73, 76, 95, 330–6, 640, 641, 642, 643
miscellaneous, 73, 76, 77, 330–6, 640, 641, 642, 643
MITCHELL, WESLEY C., 163n, 589n
Mobility of capital (see Capital, Investment)
Monopoly, 128–9
Motor vehicles, 43, 72, 77, 92, 119, 123, 172, 176–7, 183, 196, 198, 200, 202, 287–94, 424–9, 560, 618, 622, 625, 628, 632 (see also Automobiles)
MÜLLER, HERBERT, 13n
MÜLLER, J. P., 35n

INDEX

Nails (*see* Wire and nails)
National Industrial Recovery Act, 587*n*
National Industrial Administration (*see* National Industrial Recovery Act)
NERLOVE, S. H., 35*n*
Net income (*see* Income, net)
Newspapers and periodicals, 43, 72, 78, 84, 91, 92, 119, 122, 197, 199, 201, 203, 274–7, 406–11, 528, 530, 559, 571, 617, 621, 624, 627, 631
Nuts (*see* Bolts and nuts)

Oil wells (*see* Gas and oil wells)

Package foods, 72, 78, 118, 122, 196, 199, 200, 202, 247–51, 559, 616, 620, 623, 627, 630
Paints, 72, 76, 77, 92, 119, 122, 167, 168, 196, 198, 200, 202, 278–82, 412–7, 515, 516, 517, 519, 522, 523, 559, 618, 621, 624, 627, 631
Paper (*see also* Printing and publishing)
  all manufacture, 152*n*, 154*n*, 156, 157, 159, 227–9, 241–5, 270–3, 356, 360, 364–9, 400–5, 471–5, 480–1, 528, 560, 572, 614–6, 619, 623, 626, 628, 632
  blank, manufacture of, 43, 72, 75, 76, 95, 119, 122, 167, 168, 169, 196, 199, 200, 202, 270–3, 400–5, 559, 617, 621, 624, 627, 631
  miscellaneous products, manufacture of, 72, 76, 119, 122, 167, 168, 173, 196, 199, 201, 202, 270–3, 559, 617, 621, 624, 627, 631
  trade, 73, 75, 76, 95, 125, 126, 318–22, 634, 635, 636, 638, 639
Patents, 526–31
Periodicals (*see* Newspapers and periodicals)
PETERSON, GEORGE M., 549*n*, 550, 551, 552, 568
Petroleum refining, 72, 76, 78, 119, 122, 172, 196, 199, 201, 202, 278–82, 412–7, 559, 618, 621, 624, 627, 631

Pianos, 73, 75, 76, 120, 123, 167, 168, 173, 183, 196, 198, 201, 202, 295–9, 560, 619, 622, 625, 628, 632
Planning, business
  difficulties of, 587–8
  individual, 593
  lack of, 33
  national, 588
  need for statistical data in, 593
POWLISON, KEITH, 13*n*
Printing and publishing
  all, 152*n*, 154*n*, 156, 157, 159, 228, 230, 241–5, 274–7, 356, 360, 364–9, 406–11, 471–5, 480–1, 528, 529, 560, 564, 572, 614–6, 619, 623, 626, 629, 632
  job, 72, 77, 78, 92, 119, 122, 197, 199, 201, 203, 274–7, 406–11, 559, 617, 621, 624, 627, 631
  miscellaneous, 43, 72, 77, 78, 90, 91, 92, 119, 122, 196, 199, 201, 203, 274–7, 406–11, 559, 571, 617, 621, 624, 627, 631
Producers' goods industries, 180–6
Production (*see* Supply and demand, Control of production)
Profits (*see* Earnings rates)
Proprietary preparations, 43, 72, 77, 78, 92, 119, 120–1, 122, 183, 197, 199, 201, 203, 278–82, 530, 559, 618, 621, 624, 627, 631
Publicity of corporate accounts, 590–4
Publishing, book and music, 72, 77, 78, 119, 122, 167, 168, 173, 175–7, 197, 199, 201, 203, 274–7, 498, 501, 504, 505, 507, 509, 511, 512, 559, 617, 621, 624, 627, 631 (*see also* Printing and publishing)

Quarrying, stone, 73, 76, 330–6, 640, 641, 642, 643

Railway equipment, 43, 72, 75, 76, 94, 95, 119, 123, 167, 168, 169, 173, 175, 178–9, 196, 199, 200, 202, 287–94, 498, 501, 507, 508, 510, 511, 512, 513, 560, 618, 622, 625, 628, 632

INDEX [677]

Regulation of industries, 587–94
Relativity in statistical data, 37–9
Reorganization, 110–1
Risk, 86–8
ROBINSON, LELAND REX, 35*n*
RORTY, M. C., 9*n*, 12*n*, 19*n*, 23*n*, 570*n*
Rubber products, 43, 72, 75, 84, 94, 95, 118, 120–1, 122, 152*n*, 154*n*, 156, 157, 172, 196, 199, 200, 202, 224–6, 241–5, 263–5, 355, 359–60, 364–9, 390–3, 471–5, 480–1, 528, 558*n*, 559, 560, 570, 572, 614–6, 617, 619, 620, 622, 624, 626, 627, 628, 630, 632

Sales, 46, 114–27, 172–80, 191–205, 616–9, 633–4, 640
Sampling
  finance, 493–5
  major groups, 469–79
  manufacture, 460–89, 497–523
  mining, 491–3
  minor groups, 496–523
  trade, 489–91
Sand, 73, 77, 330–6, 640, 641, 642, 643
SECRIST, HORACE, 12*n*, 35*n*, 586*n*, 589*n*
SELTZER, LAURENCE H., 13*n*
Shoes (*see* Boots and shoes)
Silk weaving, 72, 75, 77, 118, 122, 167, 168, 169, 196, 199, 201, 202, 252–7, 559, 617, 620, 624, 627, 630
Size of corporation, 128–31
SLOAN, LAWRENCE H., 35*n*
SMITH, ADAM, 33, 34*n*, 88*n*, 593
Standard Statistics Company, 607
Stationery, 43, 72, 75, 76, 119, 122, 165, 166, 196, 199, 200, 202, 270–3, 400–5, 530, 559, 617, 621, 624, 627, 631
Statistics of Income, 15*n*, 17, 19, 20, 50*n*, 68*n*, 214*n*, 457*n*, 548, 611*n*, 613*n*
STERRETT, J. E., 12, 24, 35*n*
Stone (*see also* Clay)
  all, 152*n*, 154*n*, 156, 157, 232–3, 241–5, 283–6, 356, 360–1, 364–9, 418–23, 471–5, 480–1, 528, 561,
  564, 572, 614–6, 619, 623, 626, 629, 633
  miscellaneous products, 72, 76, 78, 119, 123, 196, 198, 200, 202, 283–6, 418–23, 560, 571, 618, 621, 625, 628, 631
Stores, department, 73, 76, 77, 125, 126, 313–7, 443–6, 633, 635, 636, 638, 639
SUMMERS, H. B., 128*n*, 133, 134*n*
SUMNER, Mrs. JOHN D., 100*n*
Supply and demand, 33, 107, 174–5, 178, 584, 589

TAUSSIG, F. W., 589*n*
Taxes
  corporate income, 6, 630–3, 639–40, 643, 646
  excess profits, 13–4
TAYLOR, F. M., 584
Terminology (*see* Definitions of terms)
Textiles
  all, 152*n*, 154*n*, 156, 157, 221–2, 241–5, 252–7, 355, 359, 364–9, 378–83, 471–5, 480–1, 528, 560, 563, 572, 614–6, 619, 622, 626, 628, 632
  miscellaneous, 72, 76, 77, 118, 122, 167, 168, 173, 196, 198, 200, 202, 252–7, 378–83, 559, 571, 617, 620, 624, 627, 630
THORP, WILLARD L., 576
TIPPETTS, CHARLES S., 128*n*
Tobacco, 72, 77, 118, 122, 197, 199, 201, 203, 247–51, 498, 500, 501, 505, 507, 509, 511, 512, 530, 559, 617, 620, 623, 627, 630
Toilet preparations, 43, 44, 72, 78, 84, 90–2, 119, 122, 167, 168, 173, 175–7, 183, 197, 199, 201, 203, 278–82, 498, 500, 501, 504, 506, 508, 509, 511, 512, 530, 559, 618, 621, 624, 627, 631
Tools, 72, 75, 77, 119, 123, 165, 167, 195, 198, 200, 202, 287–94, 424–9, 560, 619, 622, 625, 628, 632
Toys, 73, 77, 92, 118, 120, 123, 183,

196, 198, 201, 203, 295–9, 560, 619, 622, 625, 628, 632

Trade
 all, dividends, 304–6; earnings, 52–9, 300–2, 307–12, 436–41; investment, 300–2, 436–7; sales, 123–7, 300–2
 retail, all, 73, 302–6, 307–12, 313–7, 323–6, 439–41, 442–6, 531, 634, 635, 637, 638, 640; miscellaneous, 73, 75, 77, 125, 126, 313–7, 323–6, 443–6, 633, 634, 635, 636, 638, 639
 wholesale, all, 73, 304–6, 307–12, 318–22, 323–6, 439–41, 447–51, 531, 634, 635, 637, 638, 640; miscellaneous, 73, 76, 125, 126, 318–22, 323–6, 447–51, 634, 635, 636, 638, 639

Treasury Department (*see* Internal Revenue, *Statistics of Income*)

Trust companies, 73, 76, 342–5, 643, 644, 645, 646 (*see also* Banks)

TUGWELL, R. G., 37*n*

Uniformity in economic data, 577–8

VAIHINGER, HANS, 37*n*
Valuation, 524–47
Value of product, 149–51
Variation (*see* Coefficient of variation, Diversity)

WALKER, FRANCIS A., 583*n*
Weighting, 455–95
Wire and nails, 72, 75, 77, 119, 123, 195, 198, 200, 202, 287–94, 560, 618, 621, 625, 628, 631
Wood, 73, 76, 125, 127, 323–6, 633, 634, 635, 636, 638, 639 (*see also* Coal, Fuel)
Woolens, weaving, 43, 72, 75, 77, 118, 122, 167, 168, 169, 197, 199, 201, 202, 252–7, 559, 617, 620, 624, 627, 630

PUBLICATIONS OF THE
NATIONAL BUREAU OF ECONOMIC RESEARCH

*1. INCOME IN THE UNITED STATES
By WESLEY C. MITCHELL, WILLFORD I. KING, FREDERICK R. MACAULAY AND OSWALD W. KNAUTH
Volume I (1921) Summary 152 pp.
2. Volume II (1922) Details 440 pp.
3. DISTRIBUTION OF INCOME BY STATES IN 1919 (1922)
By OSWALD W. KNAUTH 30 pp., $1.30
*4. BUSINESS CYCLES AND UNEMPLOYMENT (1923)
By the NATIONAL BUREAU STAFF and 16 COLLABORATORS 405 pp., $4.10
*5. EMPLOYMENT, HOURS AND EARNINGS IN PROSPERITY AND DEPRESSION, UNITED STATES, 1920–22 (1923)
By WILLFORD I. KING 147 pp.
6. THE GROWTH OF AMERICAN TRADE UNIONS, 1880–1923 (1924)
By LEO WOLMAN 170 pp., $2.50
7. INCOME IN THE VARIOUS STATES: ITS SOURCES AND DISTRIBUTION, 1919, 1920 AND 1921 (1925)
By MAURICE LEVEN 306 pp., $3.50
8. BUSINESS ANNALS (1926)
By WILLARD L. THORP, with an introductory chapter, Business Cycles as Revealed by Business Annals, by WESLEY C. MITCHELL
380 pp., $2.50
9. MIGRATION AND BUSINESS CYCLES (1926)
By HARRY JEROME 256 pp., $2.50
10. BUSINESS CYCLES: THE PROBLEM AND ITS SETTING (1927)
By WESLEY C. MITCHELL 489 pp., $5.00
*11. THE BEHAVIOR OF PRICES (1927)
By FREDERICK C. MILLS 598 pp.
12. TRENDS IN PHILANTHROPY (1928)
By WILLFORD I. KING 78 pp., $1.00
13. RECENT ECONOMIC CHANGES (1929)
By the NATIONAL BUREAU STAFF and 15 COLLABORATORS
2 vol., 950 pp., per set, $7.50
14. INTERNATIONAL MIGRATIONS
Volume I, Statistics (1929), compiled by IMRE FERENCZI of the International Labour Office, and edited by WALTER F. WILLCOX
1,112 pp., $7.00
18. Volume II, Interpretations (1931), edited by WALTER F. WILLCOX
715 pp., $5.00
*15. THE NATIONAL INCOME AND ITS PURCHASING POWER (1930)
By WILLFORD I. KING 394 pp.

* *Out of print.*

16. CORPORATION CONTRIBUTIONS TO ORGANIZED COMMUNITY WELFARE SERVICES (1930)
    By Pierce Williams and Frederick E. Croxton   347 pp., $2.00
17. PLANNING AND CONTROL OF PUBLIC WORKS (1930)
    By Leo Wolman   260 pp., $2.50
19. THE SMOOTHING OF TIME SERIES (1931)
    By Frederick R. Macaulay   172 pp., $2.00
20. THE PURCHASE OF MEDICAL CARE THROUGH FIXED PERIODIC PAYMENT (1932)
    By Pierce Williams   308 pp., $3.00
21. ECONOMIC TENDENCIES IN THE UNITED STATES: ASPECTS OF PRE-WAR AND POST-WAR CHANGES (1932)
    By Frederick C. Mills   639 pp., $5.00
22. SEASONAL VARIATIONS IN INDUSTRY AND TRADE (1933)
    By Simon Kuznets   455 pp., $4.00
23. PRODUCTION TRENDS IN THE UNITED STATES SINCE 1870 (1934)
    By Arthur F. Burns   363 pp., $3.50
24. STRATEGIC FACTORS IN BUSINESS CYCLES (1934)
    By John Maurice Clark   238 pp., $1.50
25. GERMAN BUSINESS CYCLES, 1924–1933 (1934)
    By Carl T. Schmidt   288 pp., $2.50
26. INDUSTRIAL PROFITS IN THE UNITED STATES (1934)
    By Ralph C. Epstein   672 pp., $5.00
27. MECHANIZATION IN INDUSTRY (1934)
    By Harry Jerome   400 pp., $3.50

THE BULLETIN

Subscriptions to the National Bureau *Bulletin* (5 issues, $1) may begin with any of the following numbers:

48. ASPECTS OF RECENT PRICE MOVEMENTS, F. C. Mills (Oct. 31, 1933)
49. NATIONAL INCOME, 1929–32, Simon Kuznets (rev. ed., June 7, 1934)
50. RECENT CORPORATE PROFITS, Solomon Fabricant (April 18, 1934)
51. RECENT CHANGES IN PRODUCTION, C. A. Bliss (June 28, 1934)
52. GROSS CAPITAL FORMATION, 1919–33, Simon Kuznets (Nov. 15, 1934)